Azure for Developers

Third Edition

The definitive guide to creating secure, scalable Azure apps
with GenAI, serverless, and DevOps pipelines

Kamil Mrzygłód

‹packt›

Azure for Developers

Third Edition

Portfolio Director: Kartikey Pandey
Relationship Lead: Preet Ahuja
Project Manager: Sonam Pandey
Content Engineer: Apramit Bhattacharya
Technical Editor: Simran Ali
Copy Editor: Safis Editing
Proofreader: Apramit Bhattacharya
Indexer: Manju Arasan
Production Designer: Prashant Ghare
Growth Lead: Amit Ramadas

First published: November 2018
Second edition: August 2022
Third edition: July 2025
Production reference: 1040725

Published by Packt Publishing Ltd.
Grosvenor House
11 St Paul's Square
Birmingham
B3 1RB, UK

ISBN 978-1-83620-351-3

www.packtpub.com

Foreword

I have had the privilege of following Kamil Mrzygłód's career for several years, and in that time, he has consistently stood out as a thought leader and hands-on expert in the Microsoft Azure community. With a solid foundation in software engineering and cloud architecture, Kamil brings a rare blend of technical depth and pragmatic clarity to everything he does. This book is a testament to that combination.

In Azure for Developers, Kamil distills more than a decade of hands-on experience into a clear and actionable guide for developers looking to design, build, and optimize applications on Azure. Whether you're new to the platform or already familiar with its services, this book will meet you where you are and take you deeper. Each topic — be it Azure Functions, Storage, Container Instances, DevOps, or Durable Functions — is addressed with just the right level of detail to spark real understanding.

Kamil doesn't just teach concepts; he demonstrates them. Through practical use cases, simple but effective visuals, and Azure CLI scripts that Dev and DevOps engineers will immediately put to work, readers gain knowledge they can immediately apply. The paragraphs on securing services and managing identity across Azure services reflect Kamil's sharp awareness of how critical cloud security and access control are today — and how frequently they're underexplained elsewhere in the context of Azure Development.

Another strength of this book lies in its flow and design. There's no bouncing between linked resources or overwhelming the reader with fluff. Instead, each section is concise, self-contained, and perfectly aligned with real-world development patterns. Kamil's inclusion of GitHub Actions to support CI/CD processes is an especially nice touch, helping readers streamline deployments as part of a modern DevOps lifecycle.

This isn't just another Azure book — it's a companion for every serious cloud developer, even if you already know some topics well. What sets it apart is not only its accuracy and utility, but the author's ability to make even the most abstract cloud concepts feel approachable. Kamil writes in a clear, straightforward voice, making this book accessible to readers across the globe, no matter their fluency in English or familiarity with Azure.

Whether you're diving into Azure Storage patterns, which are, by the way, very well explained, building durable cloud services, or automating your workflows, Kamil's guidance will not just illuminate what's possible; it will show you how to make it happen.

I have benefited from this one a lot, and I believe you're in good hands.

Michal "Furman" Furmankiewicz

Principal Program Manager, Microsoft

Contributors

About the author

Kamil Mrzygłód is a technical lead at the Polish company Jit Team. He has worked with various Microsoft technologies for the last 15 years. He's a former Microsoft Azure MVP who focuses on developer-oriented services and methodologies. In his daily work, Kamil helps companies from various industries – including digital banking, procurement, and FMCG – with the proper use of the cloud, cost reduction, and improvements for the CI/CD process.

I want to thank the team working on this book for their dedication and hard work. You made it much better than it initially was.

About the reviewers

Jean-Benoit Paux has more than 15 years of experience in the IT industry, particularly in the areas of support engineering, Microsoft infrastructure consulting, and cloud architecture. He assists various clients in defining their Azure cloud strategy, building their cloud foundations, and implementing security controls. Over the last few years, he has also succeeded in applying his expertise by building hybrid architectures using Azure and Azure Stack portfolio products. As a Microsoft Certified Trainer, Jean-Benoit enjoys sharing his knowledge on different IT matters, including teaching Azure and Microsoft 365 courses.

I'd like to thank this book's author and Packt Publishing for the opportunity to review this book. It led to many valuable discussions and brought great enthusiasm to the process of making this book worthwhile. I would also like to thank the Microsoft Azure Stack support engineers and PM I had the opportunity to work with who taught me a lot about the internals, and who sometimes spent days and nights with us troubleshooting this wonderful product.

Alaa Barqawi is a senior technical support engineer specializing in Microsoft Azure and **Azure Kubernetes Service** (**AKS**). With over 19 years of experience in the tech industry, he has built deep expertise in DevOps, Linux systems, and cloud-native technologies. Alaa's technical toolkit includes Kubernetes, AKS, Docker, and a range of development languages such as Python, Bash, and JavaScript.

In his current role, Alaa supports complex Azure environments, helping customers troubleshoot and optimize their cloud infrastructure. With a strong foundation in automation, container orchestration, and CI/CD pipelines, Alaa is passionate about delivering scalable solutions and sharing knowledge across teams.

Table of Contents

Part 2: Web Applications and Workflows in Microsoft Azure

3

4

Developing Static Web Applications   69

5

Going Serverless with Azure Functions   97

8

Building Workflows Using Durable Functions   179

Part 3: Containers in Microsoft Azure

9

Learning About Azure Container Registry   205

12

Hosting Containers with Azure App Service   285

Part 4: Storage, Messaging, and Monitoring

13

Storing Data with Azure Storage   311

16

Adding Monitoring to Your Application   405

Part 5: AI, ML, and DevOps

17

Integrating an Application with Azure OpenAI Service   433

18

Leveraging Azure Machine Learning to Automate Machine Learning Tasks   463

19

Using GitHub Actions to Build and Deploy Applications to Azure   491

20

Developing, Testing, and Deploying Azure Logic Apps   521

Preface

Microsoft Azure is a robust cloud platform that is able to address hundreds of different business scenarios. It comes with a variety of application-oriented services, which can be used to implement messaging, store data, and monitor the system as a whole. With the rapid adoption of AI technologies such as generative AI (and especially LLMs), Azure has become one of the best building and hosting platforms for modernizing your application. Keeping up to date in such a dynamic environment is a challenge though. This is why this book was created. It will guide you through various services and concepts and explain how Azure components can be used to achieve the best results. With the addition of new topics (such as Azure OpenAI Service and GitHub Actions), it will help you gain confidence when working with the cloud when building a new application or modernizing an existing one.

Who this book is for

The book is for developers, QA engineers, and solutions architects who want to understand how application-oriented Azure services work and can be used to implement new or modernize existing applications and systems for scalability, reliability, and maintainability on the Azure platform. This includes personas such as the following:

- Software developers building Azure-based applications or looking for a way to modernize existing legacy applications
- Solutions architects looking at simplifying infrastructure management for their systems
- QA engineers who need to understand how to build automation for Azure-based services by gaining knowledge about the development of such services

What this book covers

Chapter 1, Getting Started with an Azure Account and Selecting an IDE, provides an introduction to Azure as a platform and instructions on how to set up a local environment.

Chapter 2, Choosing Between Azure CLI and Azure PowerShell, introduces you to the two most important command-line interface tools and the ways to configure them.

Chapter 3, Hosting Applications with Azure App Service, explains how to use Azure App Service as your main service for hosting web applications.

Chapter 4, Developing Static Web Applications, explores different options for hosting static web applications without the need to set up infrastructure.

Chapter 5, Going Serverless with Azure Functions, introduces serverless components and function-as-a-service using Azure Functions as the baseline for your application.

Chapter 6, Managing Secrets and Configuration in Azure, shows how to implement best practices for storing and managing secrets and configuration using Azure Key Vault and Azure App Configuration.

Chapter 7, Integrating Services with Azure Logic Apps, explains how to leverage a low-code solution to build workflows using Azure Logic Apps.

Chapter 8, Building Workflows Using Durable Functions, follows up on the workflow-based processes implemented in Azure and introduces Durable Functions as a low-level tool for implementing advanced application scenarios.

Chapter 9, Learning About Azure Container Registry, introduces a managed container registry in Azure.

Chapter 10, Building Ad Hoc Workloads Using Azure Container Instances, guides you through using Azure Container Instances as a simple platform for running containerized workloads with minimal configuration.

Chapter 11, Developing Microservices with Azure Container Apps, provides an extensive guide on how to implement microservices architecture using Azure Container Apps and compares it with other Azure services such as Azure Kubernetes Service.

Chapter 12, Hosting Containers with Azure App Service, follows up on the previous chapters and elaborates on the use of containers in the context of Azure App Service and web applications.

Chapter 13, Storing Data with Azure Storage, introduces the capabilities of Azure Storage with the main focus on Table Storage and Blob Storage, their use cases, and their limitations.

Chapter 14, Using Queues in Microsoft Azure, provides a detailed introduction to implementing queue-based services and compares messaging solutions such as Queue Storage, Azure Event Hub, and Azure Service Bus.

Chapter 15, Using Relational Databases in Microsoft Azure, explains how relational databases can be used in Azure, the differences between databases hosted on-premises and in the cloud, and what types of relational databases are supported in Azure as managed services.

Chapter 16, Adding Monitoring to Your Application, introduces Azure Monitor, Application Insights, and Log Analytics as the main building blocks for the logging and monitoring of cloud-based services.

Chapter 17, Integrating an Application with Azure OpenAI Service, provides an extensive introduction to managed OpenAI models served by Azure and the ways of integrating them with your application.

Chapter 18, Leveraging Azure Machine Learning to Automate Machine Learning Tasks, guides you through use cases of Azure Machine Learning and automation concepts for training machine learning models for applications.

Chapter 19, Using GitHub Actions to Build and Deploy Applications to Azure, explains how to automate deployments of applications using GitHub Actions as your platform for CI/CD pipelines.

Chapter 20, Developing, Testing, and Deploying Azure Logic Apps, elaborates on the concepts presented in *Chapter 7* and provides additional details on building a workflow that is testable.

To get the most out of this book

To get the most from this book, you need to understand the basics of at least one programming language such as C#, Java, Python, or JavaScript. You should also understand the basics of Azure (ideally, have the AZ-900 certification) and be proficient with the IDE of your choice and running commands in the system terminal.

Software/hardware covered in the book	Operating system requirements
Azure CLI	Windows, macOS, or Linux
Azure PowerShell	Windows, macOS, or Linux
Azurite	Windows, macOS, or Linux
Azure Storage Explorer	Windows, macOS, or Linux
Visual Studio Code	Windows, macOS, or Linux

If you are using the digital version of this book, we advise you to type the code yourself or access the code from the book's GitHub repository (a link is available in the next section). Doing so will help you avoid any potential errors related to the copying and pasting of code.

Download the example code files

You can download the example code files for this book from GitHub at `https://github.com/PacktPublishing/Azure-for-Developers-Third-Edition/`. If there's an update to the code, it will be updated in the GitHub repository.

We also have other code bundles from our rich catalog of books and videos available at `https://github.com/PacktPublishing/`. Check them out!

Conventions used

There are a number of text conventions used throughout this book.

`Code in text`: Indicates code words in text, database table names, folder names, filenames, file extensions, pathnames, dummy URLs, user input, and X/Twitter handles. Here is an example: "Let's perform a quick check using `curl`."

A block of code is set as follows:

```
param parLogicAppName string = 'logicapp'

resource la 'Microsoft.Logic/workflows@2019-05-01' = {
  name: parLogicAppName
  location: resourceGroup().location
  properties: {
    state: <Enabled>
  }
}
```

Any command-line input or output is written as follows:

```
az keyvault secret set-attributes \
--name <secret-name> \
--vault-name <key-vault-name> \
    --expires Y-m-d'T'H:M:S'Z'
    --not-before Y-m-d'T'H:M:S'Z'
    --enabled true
```

Bold: Indicates a new term, an important word, or words that you see onscreen. For instance, words in menus or dialog boxes appear in **bold**. Here is an example: "You can install it by opening Visual Studio Code, going to the **Extensions** menu on the left."

> **Tips or important notes**
> Appear like this.

Get in touch

Feedback from our readers is always welcome.

General feedback: If you have questions about any aspect of this book, email us at customercare@ packtpub.com and mention the book title in the subject of your message.

Errata: Although we have taken every care to ensure the accuracy of our content, mistakes do happen. If you have found a mistake in this book, we would be grateful if you would report this to us. Please visit www.packtpub.com/support/errata and fill in the form.

Piracy: If you come across any illegal copies of our works in any form on the internet, we would be grateful if you would provide us with the location address or website name. Please contact us at copyright@packtpub.com with a link to the material.

If you are interested in becoming an author: If there is a topic that you have expertise in and you are interested in either writing or contributing to a book, please visit `authors.packtpub.com`.

Share Your Thoughts

Once you've read *Azure for Developers, Third Edition*, we'd love to hear your thoughts! Scan the QR code below to go straight to the Amazon review page for this book and share your feedback.

`https://packt.link/r/1-836-20351-9`

Your review is important to us and the tech community and will help us make sure we're delivering excellent quality content.

Stay Sharp in Cloud and DevOps – Join 44,000+ Subscribers of CloudPro

CloudPro is a weekly newsletter for cloud professionals who want to stay current on the fast-evolving world of cloud computing, DevOps, and infrastructure engineering.

Every issue delivers focused, high-signal content on topics like:

- AWS, GCP & multi-cloud architecture

- Containers, Kubernetes & orchestration

- **Infrastructure as Code** (IaC) with Terraform, Pulumi, etc.

- Platform engineering & automation workflows

- Observability, performance tuning, and reliability best practices

Whether you're a cloud engineer, SRE, DevOps practitioner, or platform lead, CloudPro helps you stay on top of what matters, without the noise.

Scan the QR code to join for free and get weekly insights straight to your inbox:

https://packt.link/cloudpro

Download a free PDF copy of this book

Thanks for purchasing this book!

Do you like to read on the go but are unable to carry your print books everywhere?

Is your eBook purchase not compatible with the device of your choice?

Don't worry, now with every Packt book you get a DRM-free PDF version of that book at no cost.

Read anywhere, any place, on any device. Search, copy, and paste code from your favorite technical books directly into your application.

The perks don't stop there, you can get exclusive access to discounts, newsletters, and great free content in your inbox daily

Follow these simple steps to get the benefits:

1. Scan the QR code or visit the link below

https://packt.link/free-ebook/978-1-83620-351-3

2. Submit your proof of purchase
3. That's it! We'll send your free PDF and other benefits to your email directly

Part 1:
Setting Up Your Environment

Before diving into building and managing resources in Azure, it's essential to set up a solid foundation. This part introduces you to the core concepts of identity, authentication, and authorized access in Azure. You'll learn how to create and manage an Azure account, understand access controls, and configure your local environment to suit your development workflow. Whether you're a developer, system administrator, or DevOps professional, you'll find practical guidance on choosing the right tools and interfaces for interacting with Azure efficiently.

This part has the following chapters:

- *Chapter 1, Getting Started with an Azure Account and Selecting an IDE*
- *Chapter 2, Choosing Between Azure CLI and Azure PowerShell*

Getting Started with an Azure Account and Selecting an IDE

Welcome to the third edition of *Azure for Developers*, where your journey to mastering cloud development begins with setting up your account and choosing the right tools to bring your ideas to life.

For many developers, the most difficult step when starting with Microsoft Azure is obtaining a cloud account and configuring the local environment. While this topic may sound trivial, it really isn't. Azure offers you multiple ways to start working with cloud infrastructure, and choosing the right option is crucial so you can focus on learning rather than fixing cloud account access.

We will start by explaining how to create an Azure account and what the basic operations are for working with that cloud platform, so you have a good understanding of the baseline for Azure and the overall cloud setup. Then, we will talk about setting up your local environment, which will make it easier for you to work through the exercises included in the book.

In this chapter, we're going to cover the following main topics:

- Creating an Azure account
- Installing the Azure CLI and Azure PowerShell
- Learning basic operations
- Using service principals and managed identities
- Choosing the right IDE for working with Azure
- Integrating your IDE with Azure
- Learning about plugins and additional workloads
- Using Azure emulators

Technical requirements

For exercises in this chapter, you'll need the **Azure CLI**. The process of installing and configuring it will be explained later in this chapter.

Creating an Azure account

To start building your applications using Azure, you'll need an account. An account in Azure is in fact a subscription, which acts as a high-level building block, allowing charges for Azure services to be linked with your payment method. There are several ways to create an account – we'll try to find the one that suits you the best.

Note that most of the accounts for Azure aren't free of charge. However, as you may not always be able to access an account provided by your company, we'll also try to find a way to be able to learn without spending a penny.

Types of Azure accounts

In general, accounts in Azure can be put in one of two categories:

- Work or school accounts
- Personal accounts

The names of these accounts describe exactly what they are – if you're an employee, you may be given access to a work account. Such a work account may have access to Microsoft Azure, so you don't need to set up the environment on your own. Personal accounts, however, are your private accounts – they're not linked with your employer (or your own company, if you have one).

The benefit of work/school accounts is being able to work with Azure without paying for cloud services. Charges are covered by the owner of an account, so you can be fully focused on development.

> **Note**
> Remember that even if you're using a work/school account, you may be accountable for unexpected charges. This is why it's extremely important to understand the implications of your actions when working with platforms such as Microsoft Azure – what you'll hopefully learn in this book.

For this book, I strongly recommend obtaining your own personal account. This is not only important from the learning perspective – work/school accounts may have additional policies and restrictions applied, making it impossible to complete some of the exercises.

Let's see how to use an Azure account.

How to use an Azure account

Depending on the type of account, you'll follow a slightly different path to create and use it. We'll start with work/school accounts, as they're the easiest to use.

Using a work/school account

To use any Azure account, you need to go to the Azure portal. To do that, open your browser and enter the following URL: `https://portal.azure.com/`. It'll direct you to a login screen where you need to enter your email address. If you enter your work email address, you'll be redirected to your company's login page, where you'll be asked to provide all the necessary details.

> **Note**
>
> Your company may require additional authentication methods to confirm your identity. This may include things such as SMS codes, mobile authentication, or even hardware tokens. Those are beyond the scope of this book. If you're having difficulty authenticating using your work/school account, contact your IT department.

The downside of using a work/school account is being limited to the policies and permissions applied by Azure account administrators in your company. This is why we'll consider using a personal account, so you can be your own boss in the Azure world.

Using a personal account

To use a personal account in Azure, you'll need to obtain a subscription. There are multiple ways of doing so – you could contact a local reseller, find a Microsoft partner, or even sign an agreement with Microsoft. These are, however, more *business-oriented* ways of working with Azure. For the sake of learning (or even building your own software), there are simpler ways to get started. Let's consider the following options:

- Azure free account
- Pay-as-you-go account

Those two possibilities will give you the same capabilities, but if you never worked with Azure before, I advise you to create a free account (`https://azure.microsoft.com/en-us/free/`). It has the following benefits:

- $200 Azure credit for the first 30 days
- A subset of Azure resources available for 12 months for free

This free account is then converted to a standard pay-as-you-go account. It's up to you to decide which option to choose.

> **Note**
>
> When using a free account, remember that certain resources are free for 12 months only *up to* a certain spending limit. For instance, you can run virtual machines for 750 hours for free each month. However, if you choose a machine tier that isn't included (for example, E-series) or cross that limit (by deploying additional machines and keeping them running), you'll be still charged extra.

In this book, I'll be reminding you to remove resources when they're not needed anymore. When learning about Azure, it's also a good practice to perform cleanup activities for your cloud infrastructure from time to time. It allows you to keep charges at bay and use free tiers efficiently.

Once you have set up your Azure account, you can start using it by installing the Azure CLI or Azure PowerShell, which we will explain in the next section.

Installing the Azure CLI and Azure PowerShell

As we're going to discuss both the Azure CLI and Azure PowerShell, we need to install them first. The installation process is pretty straightforward for both of these tools; however, before we proceed, we need to quickly explain both of these tools. If you don't want to install the tools locally or use your local machine, you can use Cloud Shell, which is a dedicated environment available to all Azure accounts. You can read more about it at `https://azure.microsoft.com/en-us/get-started/azure-portal/cloud-shell`.

Understanding the importance of the CLI

While your main work environment may be an IDE and a specific programming framework, when working with Azure, you'll realize that there are additional areas of work that need to be covered. You may create and configure resources in Azure using the Azure portal, but that way of working is rarely advisable and, if possible, should be avoided. In many cases, you could also benefit from using an Infrastructure-as-Code approach, but this approach requires a lot of skill and is beneficial only if you're aiming at full infrastructure automation and a declarative approach.

A CLI (whether it's the Azure CLI or Azure PowerShell) should become one of your default tools for Azure as it grants you the following benefits:

- Speeds up your work by allowing you to keep your working environment on your machine

- Allows you to migrate your work from a local machine to CI/CD pipelines without changes

- Teaches you best practices (avoiding manual work and describing operations using commands rather than one-time actions in the Azure portal)

- Even if you don't consider a CLI a must, consider spending some time learning how to use one as you may benefit from it in future projects in your career

Difference between Azure CLI and Azure PowerShell

In general, both the Azure CLI and Azure PowerShell have the same set of capabilities. They can be used to deploy, manage, and validate Azure resources in multiple environments. In most scenarios, the choice between those tools depends solely on your preferences – some people tend to gravitate towards one of them and rarely switch between them.

When making a decision, you need to take the following factors into account:

- It's better if everybody in your team uses the same tool; don't mix them between team members.

- Make sure your CI/CD runners will be able to run the selected tool if you plan to introduce automation (and believe me – sooner or later you'll need to do so because of the increasing number of tasks needed to deploy applications to Azure).

- The Azure CLI may be preferred by people working on Linux/macOS, while Azure PowerShell may be more comfortable for Windows users. Still, nothing prevents you from using the Azure CLI on Windows (especially with Windows Subsystem for Linux), and Azure PowerShell can be used successfully on Unix-based systems (thanks to PowerShell Core).

Installing the Azure CLI

Installing the Azure CLI is a straightforward process that follows dedicated steps depending on the operating system you're using. Currently, you can install the Azure CLI in the following environments:

- Windows (`https://learn.microsoft.com/en-us/cli/azure/install-azure-cli-windows`)

- macOS (`https://learn.microsoft.com/en-us/cli/azure/install-azure-cli-macos`)

- Multiple Linux distributions:

  - RHEL / CentOS (`https://learn.microsoft.com/en-us/cli/azure/install-azure-cli-linux?pivots=dnf`)

  - SLES / OpenSUSE (`https://learn.microsoft.com/en-us/cli/azure/install-azure-cli-linux?pivots=zypper`)

- Ubuntu/Debian (`https://learn.microsoft.com/en-us/cli/azure/install-azure-cli-linux?pivots=apt`)

- Azure Linux (`https://learn.microsoft.com/en-us/cli/azure/install-azure-cli-linux?pivots=tdnf`)

- Inside a Docker container (`https://learn.microsoft.com/en-us/cli/azure/run-azure-cli-docker`)
- **Windows Subsystem for Linux** (**WSL**) (`https://learn.microsoft.com/en-us/windows/wsl/install`)

If you're using a different Linux distribution than the listed ones, you can try to install the Azure CLI directly from a script (`https://learn.microsoft.com/en-us/cli/azure/install-azure-cli-linux?pivots=script`). It's a manual process that requires you to run a dedicated script that takes care of the installation process, but it will definitely be helpful when you want to have more control over it.

> **Tip**
> Remember that after installation, you may need to close your terminal so that it reloads all the globally available applications.

After successful installation of the Azure CLI, run the following command:

```
az --version
```

If everything is correct, you should see output similar to this:

```
thecloudtheory@DESKTOP-NEC1MEQ:~$ az --version
azure-cli                         2.60.0 *

core                              2.60.0 *
telemetry                          1.1.0

Dependencies:
msal                               1.28.0
azure-mgmt-resource              23.1.0b2

Python location '/opt/az/bin/python3'
Extensions directory '/home/thecloudtheory/.azure/cliextensions'

Python (Linux) 3.11.8 (main, Apr 24 2024, 04:14:09) [GCC 11.4.0]
```

If instead you see an error indicating that the `az` command isn't available, go through this checklist:

- Ensure that you have restarted your terminal. If this doesn't work, try to reboot your computer.
- Confirm that the Azure CLI is available in your `PATH` environment variable:

  - For Windows run `SET`

- For Linux / macOS run `env`
- Alternatively, you could just try to print the variable using `echo $PATH`

Let's try now to install Azure PowerShell as an alternative to the Azure CLI.

Installing Azure PowerShell

Installing Azure PowerShell is similar to installing the Azure CLI – it can also be installed on various operating systems:

- Windows (`https://learn.microsoft.com/en-us/powershell/azure/install-azps-windows`)
- Linux (`https://learn.microsoft.com/en-us/powershell/azure/install-azps-linux`)
- macOS (`https://learn.microsoft.com/en-us/powershell/azure/install-azps-macos`)
- Docker container (`https://learn.microsoft.com/en-us/powershell/azure/azureps-in-docker`)

Connecting to Azure

Both tools we're discussing can connect to Azure using a single command. For the Azure CLI, you need to run this command:

```
az login
```

For Azure PowerShell, you need to run this command:

```
Connect-AzAccount
```

The authentication process will be the same no matter which tool you're using. In fact, most of the operations work in the same way for both the Azure CLI and Azure PowerShell. There may be some differences (as different versions of those tools may use different API versions for Azure resource providers), but most likely you won't be able to tell the difference.

Let's see how to perform basic operations in Azure.

Learning basic operations

To start working with Azure, you'll need to understand how to perform certain operations, such as signing in, switching accounts, and even switching tenants. We'll get to that shortly, but before we start, let's discuss briefly how Azure is structured.

Basic Azure structure

In Azure, there are several building blocks, which you'll be using when developing applications and infrastructure. The main building block is called the **tenant**. A tenant is the most important component as it links Azure subscriptions with user accounts. When you create an Azure account, it's automatically linked to a new tenant (unless your account is a work/school account, which is created inside an existing tenant).

If you went through the Azure account creation process, you created three separate components:

- Azure tenant
- Azure subscription
- User account in Azure tenant (global/account administrator)

To help you understand these components better, take a look at *Figure 1.1*, which provides a high-level overview.

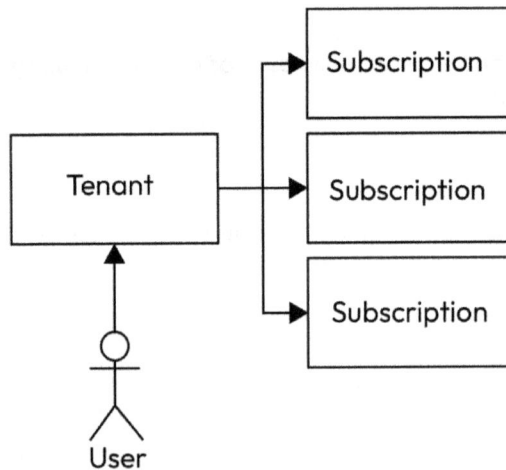

Figure 1.1 – High-level overview of the created components

If you use work/school accounts, all those steps (creating and configuring a tenant and signing up for a subscription) are performed by your company's IT department.

To be able to use any of these components, we need to sign in to Azure. Let's do that.

Signing in to Azure

I have already mentioned that one of the ways to sign in to Azure is to use the Azure portal (see the *Using a work/school account* section earlier in the chapter). However, that's not the intended way of using Azure (and also not the best way to learn about it). This is why, for the major part of this book, we'll focus on managing and configuring cloud services using either the CLI or infrastructure templates.

To simplify the learning path, in this chapter, we'll focus on the CLI. Open a terminal application on your computer (it can be any kind of terminal – whether it's the standard Command Prompt on Windows or Shell on UNIX-based systems) and execute the following command:

```
az login
```

This command should open a browser on your local machine, where you'll be directed to a login screen. If that's the case, just continue with the selected credentials (remember to make a choice between your work and personal credentials).

> **Tip**
>
> If you're using a Windows machine with WSL, a browser window may not open automatically. In this case, just click on the link displayed in your terminal.

Sometimes, a plain login command may not be enough. This might be the case when you have multiple tenants to select from and your browser remembers the default one. In this scenario, you may not be able to change the currently selected account. To fix that, you'll need to use a dedicated parameter.

> **Signing in to a specific tenant**
>
> If you need to select an Azure tenant when signing in, use the following command:
>
> ```
> az login --tenant <tenant-id|tenant-name>
> ```
>
> You can obtain a value for the –tenant parameter from your IT department. Remember that, in general, you shouldn't need to use it – save it for special occasions.

Switching subscriptions in Azure CLI

In many companies, you may have access to more than a single environment in Azure. For example, you're developing an application and were given access to a development and test environment. Even though permissions may be different for you in those environments, you're still allowed to perform a certain set of operations against them. When signing in to Azure with CLI, a context is set to the default subscription. You can check it with the following command:

```
az account show
```

It'll display basic information, including the current user you're using for interacting with Azure and the subscription name:

```
{
  (… additional data)
  "name": "My Subscription",
  "state": "Enabled",
  "tenantId": "c2d4fe14-0652-4dac-b415-5a65748fd6c9",
  "user": {
    "name": "kamil@mycompany.com",
    "type": "user"
  }
}
```

In this example, my subscription name is My Subscription. Now, if I want to learn whether I have access to more subscriptions, I can use the following command:

```
az account list -o table
```

If you can see more than a single item on the list, it means that you're allowed to switch the context:

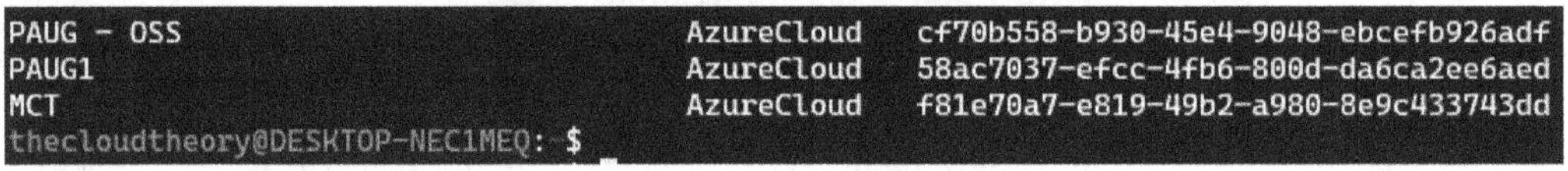

```
PAUG - OSS                       AzureCloud   cf70b558-b930-45e4-9048-ebcefb926adf
PAUG1                            AzureCloud   58ac7037-efcc-4fb6-800d-da6ca2ee6aed
MCT                              AzureCloud   f81e70a7-e819-49b2-a980-8e9c433743dd
thecloudtheory@DESKTOP-NEC1MEQ: $
```

Figure 1.2 – Subset of subscriptions my account has access to

If you want to change the subscription you're working with (which impacts the context of the operations you're performing), execute the following command:

```
az account set -s <subscription-name|subscription-id>
```

For instance, I could use that command to switch the context from the default subscription (which is MCT) to PAUG1:

```
az account set -s PAUG1
```

Switching between subscriptions is important when working with tools such as a CLI. Lots of commands work in a certain context, and if you don't switch it, you may accidentally perform an operation on an invalid environment.

> **Tip**
> When working with a CLI, it's always a good practice to check the context after signing in or returning to work after a long period.

Until now, we've been talking about performing operations in Azure using your user account. However, for the majority of scenarios, you won't be performing those operations manually. When developing applications, you need to integrate some services or authorize communication, so you can, for example, upload a file. This is where service principals and managed identities will come in handy. Let's discuss them.

Using service principals and managed identities

To understand service principals and managed identities, let's consider the following scenario: you're developing an application that allows users to upload photos from a user and store them in Azure. If you want to use a managed cloud service such as Azure Storage, you'll need to find a way to authorize upload operations. In Azure, there are two options:

- Use an access key
- Use an access token

Using an access key, which can be quickly developed and deployed, is the simplest option. It's also the least desirable from the security point of view as it requires your application to store and manage access keys. A much better option (in terms of management and design) is to allow your application to obtain an access token. In this scenario, you'd control access to Azure services by giving your application a certain set of permissions.

If you want to leverage that option, you'll have to choose between two possibilities:

- Service principal
- Managed identities

Let's discuss them briefly.

What are service principals?

Service principals in Azure are special objects in your Azure tenant that are not users but can act like they are. A service principal is a part of app registration that is used when you implement authentication flows for your applications in Entra ID or Azure B2C.

Signing in as a service principal

We discussed how to sign in to your Azure account using the Azure CLI and the `az login` command. The same command can be used to sign in as a service principal or managed identity, though the set of parameters used in the authentication flow will differ.

> **Note**
>
> If you want to create a service principal, take a look at the following tutorial in the Azure documentation: `https://learn.microsoft.com/en-us/cli/azure/azure-cli-sp-tutorial-1`.

To sign to Azure using your service principal credentials, you could use the following command:

```
az login -u <service-principal-name> -p <password> --tenant <tenant-
id|tenant-name>
```

There's also an alternative way of authenticating by using a certificate:

```
az login -u <service-principal-name> -p <path-to-certificate> --tenant
<tenant-id|tenant-name>
```

Keep in mind that when authenticating as a service principal, you always need to provide a tenant via a parameter.

What are managed identities?

Managed identities in Azure are a dedicated way of integrating your cloud services with an Entra ID tenant. They simplify management by automating some operational aspects of service principals and app registrations (e.g., secret rotation). Currently, they're the default way of implementing the right authorization flow for Azure services.

Azure supports two kinds of managed identities:

- System-assigned
- User-assigned

The basic difference between them is the provisioning process. System-assigned identities are uniquely created for a given resource instance, and each instance can have only one of them. User-assigned identities, on the other hand, may be assigned to more than a single resource instance.

> **Note**
>
> We'll talk more about managed identities in the upcoming chapters, when we'll be implementing various features for applications.

Keep in mind that not all Azure services support managed identities. To learn more about managed identities, visit `https://learn.microsoft.com/en-us/entra/identity/managed-identities-azure-resources/managed-identities-status`.

Signing in as a managed identities

To authenticate in Azure with a managed identity, we'll follow the same principles as previously – the only difference is the syntax. For instance, if you want to authenticate using a system-assigned identity, you can use this simple syntax:

```
az login --identity
```

However, for user-assigned identity, as a single resource instance may have more than one assigned to it, you need to specify the identifier of the identity:

```
az login --identity -u <managed-identity-id>
```

We'll be learning how to create and assign identities in the next chapters. For now, we need to discuss one thing—what's the use case for authentication with managed identity credentials? That's a very good question, because managed Identities are a feature of the Azure platform. This means that you're unable to use them on your local machine. If we're unable to use them locally, what's the point of the Azure CLI or other CLI tools allowing us to use those credentials? They become helpful in scenarios such as running your application on a virtual machine or inside a container. In such cases, a managed identity may be enabled for a resource while we still have the technical capability to access that resource (e.g., using SSH or an RDP session). If we're able to connect to a resource, we can run the CLI inside it and use managed identity credentials manually to test or debug our workloads.

Let's switch our focus now to a slightly different topic – choosing an IDE to work with Azure and integrating it using plugins and extensions.

Choosing the right IDE for working with Azure

Azure is one of the most popular platforms for building applications with a cloud infrastructure. To develop those applications, we need to be able to integrate our local workstation with Azure's capabilities. Being a developer means that your main working environment is an IDE. The choice of a suitable IDE relies on the technology stack you're using. If you're .NET developer, you may work with applications such as Visual Studio or Rider. Java developers might be using IntelliJ or Eclipse. Python developers may use PyCharm. There are many choices, so it's important to understand the implications of our decisions, especially when thinking about development in Azure.

> **Note**
>
> In this book, we're going to focus on the most popular technology stacks that are closely related to Azure. This means that we're not going to talk about languages such as C, C++, or Rust, as they're rarely used with Azure directly.

To understand which IDE you should choose, we need to discuss the most important traits of that software from the developer's point of view.

Understanding your profile

When choosing an IDE, you need to understand your technical profile and what kind of operations you're going to perform using Azure. In general, we can find the following profiles:

- **Dev + Ops**: People who develop applications but also are familiar with certain parts of cloud infrastructure or are expected to work with the infrastructure.

- **Dev only**: People who work with the application's code only and either don't have access to the underlying infrastructure or are not expected to work with it directly.

- **Dev + data**: people who work with application code and don't work with infrastructure but need access to the data plane of their application (e.g., files in storage and databases).

Now, depending on your profile, you may expect different capabilities from your IDE. If you work only with code, most probably you won't need advanced IDE integrations, and the only thing you need is templates for a subset of services (such as Azure Functions or Azure Container Apps). In this case, any popular IDE will probably suffice.

For developers working with the data plane, their IDE will also need to support certain plugins for connecting to storage or databases. That requirement may be mitigated if you choose to use a separate software for managing a database (such as Azure Data Studio) or a generic storage solution.

For advanced users who work on both development and infrastructure, their IDE must allow them to directly integrate with Azure resources. This will involve not only access to the data plane but also to the control plane of Azure services. In such cases, you'll need to ensure that the chosen IDE covers those requirements.

Implications of choosing an operating system

In many development teams, developers tend to use different operating systems even if they're working on the same application. While a diverse setup such as this has certain disadvantages when compared to a uniform configuration, some companies allow developers to choose their preferred way of working. In such scenarios, it's important to ensure that the development tools selected inside the team can run across different systems.

One example of a problematic setup could be the use of an Azure Cosmos DB emulator. While it works perfectly fine when run in-process on a Windows machine and it can also run in a container, setting it up to run on both Windows and non-Windows machines can be challenging. This also applies to language-specific extensions for IDEs, which could offer different sets of functionalities of varying quality, depending on the software and operating system they work on.

Implications of choosing hardware

Another important factor when building and configuring your local ecosystem is the chosen hardware. While a couple of years ago this problem was almost non-existent (as support for 64-bit CPU architecture became standard, so running both 32-bit and 64-bit applications was not a problem), the current CPU market is a little bit more diverse. This especially affects developers working on MacBooks because ARM architecture for M2 and M3 chips causes some problems with the common toolset (for instance, some Docker images published by Microsoft don't support ARM processors by default, so you need to use alternative ones).

If you're about to choose your workstation, make sure that your selected ecosystem can run on it. If you're responsible for designing the working environment for your developers, take those factors into account and validate that the selected toolset is a viable choice.

Using Visual Studio Code

Visual Studio Code is a free-to-use IDE for developers that gives you the freedom to install any workload you need, depending on your technology stack. It has also a wide variety of plugins and extensions for Azure, making it a great choice for development. The downside, however, is the fact that Visual Studio Code isn't dedicated to any specific workloads, meaning some integration methods or plugins may not give you the desired results.

For the purpose of this book (and so we can keep all the exercises as generic as possible), my assumption will be that you can install and use Visual Studio Code on your machine. This will ensure that even if you can't afford the IDE of your choice, you're able to proceed with the examples and commands we'll be executing.

It's also important to remember that Visual Studio Code supports every programming language. It doesn't matter if you're using Java, C#, Python, Go, or PHP – they all can be used with Visual Studio Code, and you can benefit from the Azure integrations Visual Studio Code offers as well.

Let's dive deeper into the topic by seeing how to integrate your IDE with Azure.

Integrating your IDE with Azure

In order to integrate your IDE with Azure, you need to check whether plugins and workloads are available for it. To help you with that, I have prepared a quick summary with links, which will help you set up your local environment.

JetBrains IntelliJ

IntelliJ (`https://learn.microsoft.com/en-us/azure/developer/java/toolkit-for-intellij/install-toolkit`) provides quite an advanced extension for working with Azure that enables you to work with the following Azure services:

- Azure Web App
- Azure Functions
- Azure Container Apps
- Azure Storage
- Azure Virtual Machine
- Azure Redis Cache
- Azure OpenAI

It's a great choice for all web developers who want to encapsulate all their work within the same tool without needing to use additional tools.

Eclipse

Eclipse (`https://learn.microsoft.com/en-us/azure/developer/java/toolkit-for-eclipse/installation`) is another IDE that allows you to work with Azure, though the integration isn't as advanced as the one for IntelliJ. However, it can help you manage resources such as Azure Redis Cache, Azure Storage, and even Azure Virtual Machine. What's more, it can be used to develop web applications with Azure Web Apps and even work with Spark jobs running on Azure.

Visual Studio

It shouldn't be a surprise that the best support for developers working in Azure comes from a Microsoft product. Visual Studio (`https://learn.microsoft.com/en-us/visualstudio/azure/overview?view=vs-2022`) provides a wide range of workloads and plugins that simplify the management and development of applications when using Azure. It integrates with services such as the following:

- Azure Application Insights
- Azure Redis Cache
- Azure Cosmos DB
- Azure Key Vault

- Azure SignalR
- Azure SQL Database
- Azure Storage
- Azure App Configuration

If you're using this IDE, you'll most likely be able to develop your application and run it on Azure without any other software needed.

Visual Studio Code

Visual Studio Code (`https://learn.microsoft.com/en-us/dotnet/azure/configure-vs-code`), an alternative to Visual Studio, provides almost unlimited integration options with Azure. There are plugins for tens of Azure services that allow you to access their control plane and data plane. The downside of this IDE is the fact that some integrations and options either require manual configuration or are not as intuitive as in Visual Studio. However, for me, Visual Studio Code is the IDE of choice, and I use it for both small and big projects.

JetBrains PyCharm

PyCharm (`https://www.jetbrains.com/help/pycharm/big-data-tools-azure.html`) provides limited support for Azure services and concentrates on a big data toolset rather than typical software development scenarios. If you're going to develop data pipelines with Python, you may benefit from PyCharm. For web-oriented development, a better option could be Visual Studio Code with Python and Azure plugins.

Once you have selected your IDE and installed the necessary plugins and extensions, we will discuss additional plugins and workloads that may be helpful in day-to-day tasks. Note that Azure, as a platform, evolves very quickly. To make sure your development environment is compatible with the recent additions, always make sure your IDE, plugins, and extensions are up to date.

Learning about plugins and additional workloads

No matter which IDE you choose, it's important to be aware of additional tools that could be useful when developing an application. Let's start with WSL, which could help to provide a uniform local setup for all developers inside a team.

WSL

WSL (`https://learn.microsoft.com/en-us/windows/wsl/install`) is one of the best features for developers using mixed operating systems (Windows/Linux/macOS). It can also be helpful if you want to get the most out of tools that target UNIX-based systems at first (which is often true for software meant for the development of containerized applications). WSL gives you the ability to work on your Windows machine as if it were running a Linux-based operating system, making development much easier in a number of ways (for instance, it allows you to develop, run, and test shell scripts on Ubuntu, which is very often used as a default operating system for CI/CD pipelines runners).

Another benefit of WSL is the ability to run an application on the same operating system (or at least in the same operating system family) as in Azure. For instance, you can develop an application to run on a Linux-based machine or host (for virtual machines or Azure Web Apps).

Azure Storage Explorer

Azure Storage Explorer (`https://azure.microsoft.com/en-us/products/storage/storage-explorer/`) is a free tool for interacting with the data plane of Azure Storage. It allows you to browse and manage data stored within Azure Storage without needing to develop your own toolset or install additional plugins for IDEs. It provides seamless integration with Azure local storage emulators and can be considered one of the most useful tools up an Azure developer's sleeve.

Service Bus Explorer

Service Bus Explorer (`https://github.com/paolosalvatori/ServiceBusExplorer`) is an OSS solution for working with Azure Service Bus. It's almost a must-have for developers working with that Azure service because it allows them to manage and test topics, queues, and subscriptions with ease. It also works with Azure Event Hub and Azure Notification Hub, making it an excellent choice for developing messages-based applications. While the Azure portal has a similar tool, its capabilities are rather limited compared to its OSS counterpart.

The only downside of Service Bus Explorer is its rather limited usefulness for Linux/macOS users (as it only runs on Windows, you'd need a local virtual machine to use it).

Azure Data Studio

If you want a tool that enables you to work with storage solutions in Azure, you must consider Azure Data Studio (`https://learn.microsoft.com/en-us/azure-data-studio/download-azure-data-studio`). It's another free tool that integrates with services such as Azure SQL, MySQL, PostgreSQL, and Azure Cosmos DB. It's a full-blown data-oriented and developer-oriented solution with additional features such as IntelliSense, code snippets, and source code integration. It can be also extended by installing additional plugins, putting it at a similar level of extensibility as Visual Studio Code.

AzCopy

AzCopy (`https://learn.microsoft.com/en-us/azure/storage/common/storage-use-azcopy-v10?tabs=dnf`) is a useful utility for copying, downloading, importing, and moving blobs and files between Azure Storage accounts. It can be used not only for development purposes but also as part of your data pipelines. As it's a basic command-line application, it can be easily integrated with various tools and pipelines.

For the last topic of this chapter, let's discuss Azure emulators, which may become a key ingredient in development scenarios requiring a high level of isolation from existing Azure resources.

Using Azure emulators

When developing an application, you often need to decide how local development is performed. While running an application locally is quite a simple task, running its dependencies may be challenging. Let's discuss how to decouple real Azure services from local workstations so that every developer can host their own environment that is secure from outages and unwanted changes.

Benefits of emulators

Consider the following scenario: you're developing an application that requires an SQL database. If that application is hosted on Azure, it may be tempting to deploy a dedicated Azure SQL instance for development only. This, however, has serious implications:

- Developers are going to share the same instance of a database.
- If Azure SQL isn't available, local development is affected.
- It's difficult to test changes in isolation.

To overcome those problems, you'll need to consider the following options:

- Deploy a dedicated SQL database for each developer.
- Emulate the database service.
- Run a database inside a container.
- Require all developers to install a database engine locally.

All these options are viable from a technical point of view. The amount of value they provide will vary depending on your use case. While the purest solution would be to grant each developer their own cloud environment (aka sandbox), this solution is also the most expensive one. The options regarding emulation, containerization, and standalone installation will be simpler and cheaper, but at the expense of possible bugs (emulation), additional technical requirements or licensing (containerization), or complex software management (standalone installation). Let's dive deeper into this topic.

Emulation, containerization, and standalone installation

Even if you're a fan of emulation, containerization, or standalone installation, you need to consider additional factors before implementing any of those patterns in the context of development for Azure. Emulation may look tempting in many scenarios, but the downside of that approach is error-prone emulation (because emulators, well… emulate, so cannot be considered a 100% viable replacement). More importantly, Azure doesn't support the emulation of all services. In fact, it is only possible to emulate a limited number of Azure components (and they are mainly storage-based solutions). When working with compute in Azure (such as Azure Web App and Container Apps), you won't be able to provide a viable emulation mechanism.

Emulators may share some traits with containerization as most emulators can run in a container. This is helpful when planning a uniform way of running dependencies – you can use tools such as Docker Compose to give your developers or yourself a simple mechanism to build and destroy your local environment. Emulators may also complete a containers-based setup if certain services are available only via an emulator rather than a dedicated container image.

Standalone installations will be useful in less dynamic environments that don't require frequent updates and are stable enough not to need frequent updates. The downside of this approach is the challenges that arise when performing the build and destroy (mainly for testing and validating changes). While emulators and containers can be easily started from scratch, if you need to manage, for example, a database locally, additional scripts will be needed to make it a performant solution.

Emulators in Azure

As mentioned, Azure provides a limited number of viable emulators for local development. There are, however, certain solutions that you may find beneficial in your development scenarios.

Azurite

Azurite (`https://learn.microsoft.com/en-us/azure/storage/common/storage-use-azurite`) is an OSS emulator for Azure Storage that provides almost the same set of capabilities as its Azure counterpart. It can be used to develop applications using Table, Blob, and Queue Storage (File Service isn't available because of the quite different set of protocols used for it). It can be also integrated with Visual Studio Code, so you can easily decide when and how it's supposed to run. Azurite is the best emulator in Azure; it works without problems in many scenarios and local setups.

Azure Storage Explorer integrates seamlessly with Azurite by giving you a dedicated connection configuration based on the emulator's default parameters.

Azure Cosmos DB emulator

If your application is going to use Azure Cosmos DB, you may find emulating that service a viable and useful option. As Cosmos DB is quite an expensive service, being able to run it locally will be an extensive help, especially in the early phase of a project.

The Azure Cosmos DB emulator (`https://learn.microsoft.com/en-us/azure/cosmos-db/how-to-develop-emulator`) unfortunately isn't as easy to use as Azurite. By default, it works only on Windows machines. If you want to run it on another operating system, you need to use Docker or a similar container engine. Containerized environments don't work well in some scenarios, so you may find this emulator frustrating from time to time. Still, it is an option that is always worth considering.

Azure Service Bus emulation

Azure Service Bus (or, in general, all messaging services in Azure) is one of the most important components for many applications. Unfortunately, there isn't a dedicated emulator for this service, meaning that you need to find your own way of decoupling local development from a running service. There are at least two options worth considering:

- Azure Service Bus Emulator: `https://github.com/piotr-rojek/devopsifyme-sbemulator`

- RabbitMQ in Docker: `https://hub.docker.com/_/rabbitmq`

The first project is an OSS emulator, which will require careful validation on your end as it hasn't been widely adopted yet. The second option uses RabbitMQ, which uses the same protocol as Azure Service Bus, but has different features available. If your application doesn't use features that are unique to Azure Service Bus (such as sessions or transactions), RabbitMQ will most likely do the trick.

> Tip
> Using RabbitMQ as a local emulator for Azure Service Bus will require a layer of abstraction built into your application. In this case, it may be worth considering a library such as MassTransit, which will greatly simplify your setup. You can find more information on the official web page of the project: `https://masstransit.io/`.

Instead of emulating you could consider two additional options:

- Deploying Azure Service Bus for each developer

- Structuring topics and queues in Azure Service Bus instance in a way, which allows developers to have dedicated ones for their workflow

While those solutions may be more complex and more expensive in some cases (especially if you deploy an instance of Azure Service Bus for each developer), they will also address more issues and make development less prone to compatibility issues.

Azure SQL Database emulator

If you don't want to run a standalone installation of SQL Server, you can use the Azure SQL Database emulator (`https://learn.microsoft.com/en-us/azure/azure-sql/database/local-dev-experience-sql-database-emulator`), which is in fact a very thin layer on top of the Azure SQL Edge container image. It's a viable choice for every application using Azure SQL Database in their design. It simplifies management overhead and can be easily integrated with Visual Studio Code.

Azure Data Explorer Kusto emulator

In the next chapters of this book, you will learn about the Kusto language, which is a dedicated language for making queries against traces, metrics, and logs gathered from your applications in Azure Log Analytics workspaces. As writing those queries may be cumbersome, especially if you don't have the necessary data (or don't have access to it), running this emulator (`https://learn.microsoft.com/en-us/azure/data-explorer/kusto-emulator-overview`) could be an interesting alternative to speed up your development.

As you can see, Azure provides quite a limited set of emulators, which can be used locally. To get the most from that cloud platform, you'll often need to combine multiple methods and patterns so that development can be as smooth as possible. Throughout this book, we'll be discussing various ways to improve the development process, so you can focus on creating new functionalities rather than fighting configuration or infrastructure.

Let's summarize the findings from this chapter and learn more about the next steps.

Summary

In this chapter, you learned about the basic structure and operations of Azure. We discussed how you can obtain access to the Azure environment and explored the differences between work/school and personal accounts. You also learned how to sign in to your account, switch the working context, and change the Azure tenant if needed.

We also talked about service principals and managed identities, which will become some of the most important components in the next chapters. In the last part of this chapter, we covered IDEs and additional plugins and emulators that may help you when developing applications in Azure. This knowledge will become important in the next chapters, as we'll start building simple applications to showcase certain features of Azure services.

In the next chapter, we'll cover the differences between the Azure CLI and Azure PowerShell. Going through this topic will help you build your own scripts and integrate them with CI/CD pipelines, which are often developed along with many applications.

2

Choosing between Azure CLI and Azure PowerShell

As a developer working with Microsoft Azure, you'll need to execute commands, implement scripts, and even build automation using one of many tools offered by Microsoft. While some tasks may be performed using dedicated SDKs, using CLI will be a preferred way to work in many scenarios, as it offers a much more robust way to completing a task, especially if you're targeting simpler solutions. This is why we're going to discuss the differences between Azure CLI and Azure PowerShell, as this will allow you to select your tool of choice.

Note that to simplify the learning process and address the majority of use cases, through the course of this book, we'll mostly focus on using Azure CLI. This doesn't mean, however, that you should skip learning about Azure PowerShell. There are cases where Azure PowerShell offers much better capabilities or will be the only way to perform an operation.

In this chapter, we're going to cover the following main topics:

- Enabling plugins and extensions
- Working with Azure CLI and Azure PowerShell in CI/CD

Technical requirements

In this chapter, you'll need a terminal or command prompt of your choice (for instance, ConEmu, Windows Terminal, or similar). You will also need Azure CLI and Azure PowerShell installed (see the *Installing Azure CLI and Azure PowerShell* section in *Chapter 1* for instructions).

Enabling plugins and extensions

Azure CLI and Azure PowerShell come with a predefined set of features and capabilities. They're enough to perform most of the needed actions but may not be enough if you're looking for a very specific operation. For instance, there's a dedicated extension for Azure CLI, which allows you to connect to virtual machines through Azure Bastion. Such an operation is possible to perform manually but requires a certain set of steps to execute. With such extension, the connection is made with a single command.

Installing extensions in Azure CLI

An extension can be installed in Azure CLI with the following command:

```
az extension add --name <extension-name>
```

Once installed, you can update it in a similar way:

```
az extension update --name <extension-name>
```

Note that Azure CLI supports the automatic installation of extensions. When you run a command in Azure, which is an extension not available on your machine, Azure CLI can detect it and install it automatically. To enable that feature, use the following command:

```
az config set extension.use_dynamic_install=yes_prompt
```

In Azure CLI, extensions, even the ones that are built-in, can be accessed via aliases. This is especially helpful for commands, which are shared between resources (such as `list`). For instance, let's assume that you'd like to write `ls` instead of `list` for all commands in Azure CLI. This will simplify your scripting process in the following way:

```
az group list -> az group ls
az vm list -> az vm ls
```

Such an alias can be created with the following command:

```
az alias create --name ls --command list
```

If you liked the topic and want to learn more about it, take a look at the documentation for Azure CLI:

https://learn.microsoft.com/en-us/cli/azure/azure-cli-extension-alias

Installing extensions in Azure PowerShell

Extensions in Azure PowerShell are additional PowerShell modules and can be installed in the same way. To find a list of such modules, take a look at the list published on a GitHub page:

```
https://github.com/Azure/azure-powershell/blob/main/documentation/
azure-powershell-modules.md
```

In general, a module for Azure PowerShell will be installed using the following command:

```
Install-Module -Name Az.{{service}}
```

Note that it's better to avoid installing too many modules at once. As such extensions are meant for more advanced tasks, it's always better to find a use case first and only then install a module. This allows you to keep your working environment clean and simplifies version (upgrade) management.

> **Note**
>
> Remember that if any extension used by you locally becomes part of your CI/CD pipelines, it must be available on the CI/CD agent.

Let's now cover the last topic of this chapter, which is integrating Azure CLI and Azure PowerShell with CI/CD pipelines.

Working with Azure CLI and Azure PowerShell in CI/CD

Most applications built and deployed to Azure require some kind of CI/CD pipelines to perform all the required tasks. They involve tasks such as compilation, test runs, configuration adjustments, and artifact deployments. In the last part of this chapter, we'll discuss what is needed to use Azure CLI and Azure PowerShell effectively in such environments.

> **Prerequisites**
>
> If you decide to use Azure CLI or Azure PowerShell in your CI/CD pipelines, they automatically become a prerequisite. This means that they must be available to CI/CD runners in order to be executed. In some products (such as Azure DevOps and GitHub), both Azure CLI and PowerShell are part of the OS images used in managed runners. Other (self-hosted agents, Jenkins, and Bamboo) will require additional steps before you can run scripts.
>
> If you need to install Azure CLI or Azure PowerShell, consult the *Installing extensions in Azure CLI* and *Installing extensions in Azure PowerShell* sections from the beginning of this chapter. The process for installing those tools for CI/CD agents isn't different from the installation process, which you can perform when working locally.

Upgrading Azure CLI and Azure PowerShell

When working with Azure CLI or Azure PowerShell while building CI/CD pipelines, you need to carefully consider when and how those tools are supposed to be updated. Again, if you use CI/CD agents, which already contain them, you won't need to perform that operation manually. For self-hosted agents, you'll need to come with an update strategy.

> **Note**
>
> In many organizations, the responsibility for managing CI/CD self-hosted agents is on dedicated teams (such as infrastructure or platform teams). However, in the face of DevOps methodology, you may find it beneficial to understand how this process works.

Managing Azure CLI and Azure PowerShell doesn't differ from managing other shared tools, which you may use in your CI/CD pipelines (such as package managers, test runners, or other CLI build tools). The important thing here is how tightly coupled your pipelines are with a specific version of a tool. At some point, a subset of commands offered by Azure CLI or Azure PowerShell may become obsolete or deprecated. When this happens, you need to come up with a mitigation plan:

1. Discover all the pipelines that depend on such commands.

2. Inform owners that their pipeline will need an update.

3. Propose a deadline for performing a migration or mitigating risk, and mention that a pipeline will become broken after Azure CLI or Azure PowerShell upgrade.

Once everybody is on the same page, you may proceed with an upgrade. If you manage your CI/CD infrastructure using a dedicated tool such as *Chef*, *Puppet*, or *Ansible*, the process of upgrading CLI tool will be pretty straightforward – all you need is to upgrade your configuration and either perform the upgrade in-place (meaning you don't need to install everything from scratch) or reprovision CI/CD agent. You can find instructions for upgrades here:

- Azure CLI: `https://learn.microsoft.com/en-us/cli/azure/update-azure-cli`

- Azure PowerShell: `https://learn.microsoft.com/en-us/powershell/azure/install-azps-windows?view=azps-12.0.0&tabs=powershell&pivots=windows-psgallery#update-the-az-powershell-module`

> **Note**
>
> The decision of whether you perform the upgrade in-place or reprovision the whole CI/CD agent depends on the impact of such operation on your or other teams. For instance, if your CI/CD process relies on a caching mechanism, which is linked to a machine running CI/CD runner, you may need to mitigate temporal lack of cache (in case you decide to reprovision a machine running it).

In the end, it's important to understand that Azure CLI or Azure PowerShell in the CI/CD process may become a shared dependency. If that's the case, you cannot install or upgrade it on your own.

Authenticating in CI/CD with Azure CLI or Azure PowerShell

Regardless of whether you use Azure CLI or Azure PowerShell locally or with your CI/CD pipelines, the general method for authentication is the same. The only difference is that the CI/CD process won't be able to access credentials interactively. This means that you need to find a method to authenticate without user interaction. In fact, we'll have a limited number of options here:

- **Using service principal with password**: This is a method that will use a user-agnostic account with a provided password.

- **Using service principal with a certificate**: This is a similar method to the previous one, but this time using a public and private key pair for authentication instead of a password.

- **Using Managed Identity**: This is a dedicated overlay for service principals, which automates management and governance.

- **Using Workload Identity**: This is one of the recent methods for authentication. It allows you to use an identity assigned to a workload to connect to Azure. The benefit of this approach is decoupling the authentication process from the used infrastructure or a framework (for instance, you can integrate with it with Kubernetes and reuse it across different cloud providers).

If you run your CI/CD agent on Azure (for instance, as an Azure Virtual Machine), you'll be able to use all those methods. For on-premises or other providers, the only possibility to authenticate will be using service principal credentials.

> **Note**
> Theoretically, it's possible to use personal credentials to authenticate in Azure CLI and Azure PowerShell. However, such a method won't work in all scenarios (due to additional security policies like enforcement of multi-factor authentication) and is a rather bad practice.

Some CI/CD tools (such as Azure DevOps) offer an integrated way to authenticate to Azure using a feature called service connection. It allows you to define credentials and authentication methods in centralized storage, so you don't need to configure them for each pipeline. You can read more about those at `https://learn.microsoft.com/en-us/azure/devops/pipelines/library/service-endpoints`.

Another example is Azure Login action for GitHub actions. It can be simply used in your workflow as follows:

```
permissions:
  id-token: write
  contents: read
jobs:
  build-and-deploy:
    runs-on: ubuntu-latest
    steps:
      - name: Azure login
        uses: azure/login@v2
        with:
          client-id: ${{ secrets.AZURE_CLIENT_ID }}
          tenant-id: ${{ secrets.AZURE_TENANT_ID }}
          subscription-id: ${{ secrets.AZURE_SUBSCRIPTION_ID }}
```

As you can see, it requires providing specific values as configuration in order to select proper authentication flow. Once such action runs successfully, you'll be able to run Azure CLI and Azure PowerShell commands without re-authenticating. You can find all details about that action at `https://github.com/marketplace/actions/azure-login`.

That's all for this chapter! Let's summarize all the findings and topics we covered.

Summary

In this chapter, we talked about Azure CLI and Azure PowerShell tools, which will be helpful when interacting with Microsoft Azure. While you can work with the whole platform using Azure Portal, knowledge of those tools will be beneficial for^ in the long run, as they give you the possibility to become much more productive with Azure and can be easily integrated with CI/CD pipelines. Those are often used when deploying applications to cloud. We learned this in this chapter.

In the next chapter, we'll start working with our first Azure service – Azure App Service. It's one of the most important services for hosting web applications and the information presented there will be crucial for understanding a significant number of chapters presented later in the book.

Part 2:
Web Applications and
Workflows in Microsoft Azure

This part explores how to develop, deploy, and manage modern web applications in Azure. You will learn about the core services that power scalable web solutions, including how to host both dynamic and static websites and implement serverless functions. Additionally, this part covers tools and techniques for securing application secrets, automating business processes, and orchestrating long-running workflows using Azure's low-code and serverless platforms.

Whether you are building customer-facing apps or internal tools, this part will help you design flexible cloud-native architectures that streamline operations and improve maintainability.

This part has the following chapters:

- *Chapter 3, Hosting Applications with Azure App Service*
- *Chapter 4, Developing Static Web Applications*
- *Chapter 5, Going Serverless with Azure Functions*
- *Chapter 6, Managing Secrets and Configuration in Azure*
- *Chapter 7, Integrating Services with Azure Logic Apps*
- *Chapter 8, Building Workflows Using Durable Functions*

3
Hosting Applications with Azure App Service

Many applications that are hosted in Microsoft Azure are web applications serving various purposes. Those may be e-commerce apps, CRMs, landing pages, or even complex, customized solutions created specifically for your client's needs. Microsoft Azure is a platform that will give you multiple options for hosting such applications depending on the desired scale, performance goals, and technology stack. In this chapter, we're starting the second part of the book, which is focused on hosting web applications and workflows using Microsoft Azure as a hosting platform.

In this chapter, we're going to cover the following main topics:

- Deploying and configuring Azure App Service
- Managing application configuration
- Understanding the scalability of Azure App Service
- Using managed identities to integrate with other services
- Learning about use cases

Technical requirements

To perform the exercises in this chapter, you'll need the following software:

- IDE (preferably VS Code)
- Azure CLI

Deploying and configuring Azure App Service

The most popular service in Microsoft Azure, which allows you to host web applications, is called Azure App Service. It consists of two main components:

- Compute (Azure App Service plan)

- Code and configuration (Azure Web App / Function App)

The fact that there are two separate elements (i.e., there's no 1:1 relation between compute and code) gives you flexibility when planning your app capacity. It also means that you can have a single computer component that links to several web applications with their own configuration. You can think about such a setup as something that was very often done when hosting applications on-premises – you had a single web server, which ran 10s of different web services. The only difference here between cloud and on-premises is the placement of a physical server – when using Microsoft Azure, it's installed in the selected cloud region, while you get access to a subset of its functionalities.

To better understand the relation between deployed code and infrastructure in Azure App Service, see the following diagram (*Figure 3.1*). It presents multiple instances of web applications (Azure Web Apps) linked to the same server (Azure App Service plan). Those web applications could host the same code or separate services. It's up to you to decide how you want to structure your deployment.

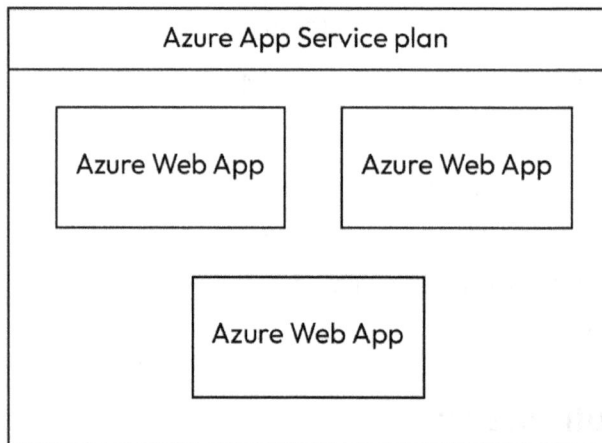

Figure 3.1 – High-level diagram explaining the connection between
Azure Web App and an Azure App Service plan

Let's start learning about Azure App Service by deploying the compute (web server) part.

Deploying an Azure App Service plan

An Azure App Service plan can be easily deployed using various methods, including CLI or infrastructure as code. If you're a fan of CLI, you could use Azure CLI and deploy it using the following command:

```
az appservice plan create \
-g <resource-group> \
-n <plan-name>
```

This is the simplest command possible when deploying the Azure App Service plan, which will deploy the default configuration for the service. Let's add some more parameters to have more control over it:

```
az appservice plan create \
-g <resource-group> \
-n <plan-name> \
    --sku F1 \
    --location <location>
```

This command will also instruct Azure to deploy the Azure App Service plan using the `F1` **Stock Keeping Unit** (**SKU**) (you can refer to it as a *tier* in Azure) value (*F1* in that case is roughly translated to *Free*) and in the selected region (implied by the `--location` parameter).

> **Tip**
> You can find all possible locations of Azure's regions by running the `az account list-locations` command in your terminal. Remember, though, that best practice recommends that all resources be stored in the same location as their resource group.

Besides location, SKU, and plan name, Azure expects you to also pass a resource group name where a plan will be created. Resource groups in Azure are logical containers, which group resources serving similar purposes. Because having a resource group is a prerequisite, let's create one in your subscription:

```
az group create \
    -n <resource-group-name> \
    -l <location>
```

You could also use resource groups that you created previously or were given to you as your place for testing and learning.

> **Note**
> If you're using an account that is your work or school account, you may not have the necessary permissions to create resource groups. If that's the case, contact your subscription administrator or use a personal account.

The last thing is the **Operating System (OS)** used to host your application. Currently, Azure supports either Windows or Linux machines to host web applications. If you want to select which OS will be used, use the —is-linux switch as follows:

```
az appservice plan create \
    -g <resource-group-name> \
    -n <plan-name> \
    --is-linux
```

Once you're satisfied with all the values, run the commands and wait for them to complete. Creating an Azure App Service plan isn't a complicated task so it shouldn't take long. Because we're using the F1 tier, such a plan can be safely provisioned in your subscription without a risk, which you'll be charged for. Remember, though, that other SKUs, especially those described as Premium or Isolated, are meant for commercial scenarios. This means that they offer much more useful features but are quite expensive options and provide little value over Free / Basic tiers when learning.

By now, your Azure App Service plan should be created and available. Let's now create Azure Web App, which will be our container for the code and configuration of our application.

Deploying Azure Web App

As mentioned previously, Azure App Service consists of two separate components. One, which is responsible for providing compute for your web application, we deployed in the previous section. Now, we'll focus on the second part, which is responsible for hosting your code and configuration.

> **Note**
>
> In this chapter, we're focused on Azure Web App but bear in mind that that's not the only service that integrates with Azure App Service plans. In the next chapters, we're going to deploy Function Apps, which are very closely related to Azure Web Apps, and also use Azure App Service plans for accessing provisioned compute components.

To deploy Azure Web App, we can use the following Azure CLI command:

```
az webapp create \
    -g <resource-group-name>
    -p <app-service-plan-name>
    -n <webapp-name>
```

Note that deployment of Azure Web App requires two values, which we used previously:

- The name of a resource group
- The name of the Azure App Service plan

The reason why you need to provide both of them is quite simple to explain. Azure App Service plans are resources that must be unique only in the context of a resource group. In Azure, it's perfectly fine to have multiple plans with the same name as long as they're provisioned inside separate resource groups. I don't recommend such an approach though – it makes governance of resources quite tricky as you'll always need a resource group name to distinguish different plans.

The example command that was used to deploy the Azure Web App will use default values and is rarely useful. A much more interesting command will require the use of an additional parameter:

```
az webapp create \
    -g <resource-group-name>
    -p <app-service-plan-name>
    -n <webapp-name>
    --runtime <runtime-identifier>
```

Depending on your technology stack, you may want to deploy different applications. Azure Web App doesn't make any assumptions when it comes to the selected runtime – you can as easily deploy .NET application as the one written in Java or server-side JavaScript. To learn about supported runtimes, run the following command:

```
az webapp list-runtimes
```

The returned list will contain runtimes grouped by OS (Windows/Linux) with the following syntax:

```
<stack>:<version>

DOTNETCORE:8.0
PYTHON:3.12
PHP:8.3
NODE:20-lts
JAVA:21-java21
```

It's important to select the correct runtime when deploying Azure Web App as it implies which web server is supposed to be used in order to host your application.

> **Note**
>
> When preparing infrastructure for your application, note which OS you're going to host it. For instance, if you need PHP runtime, Azure Web Apps don't support running it on Windows machines. On the other hand, if you need to host an ASP.NET application, the only supported OS will be Windows.

Once your Azure Web App instance is created, it will automatically be provisioned with a public URL and **Secure Sockets Layer** (**SSL**) certificate created. You can find the URL by running the following command:

```
az webapp show \
    -n <webapp-name> \
    -g <resource-group-name> \
    --query defaultHostName
```

Note that we're using the `--query` parameter to instruct Azure CLI that we want to extract specific information from the whole Azure Web App configuration. If you omit that parameter, you'll still be able to find the URL – it'll be much more difficult though as the returned configuration will contain 10s of different values.

The URL returned by Azure CLI will allow you to access your application in your browser. By default, Azure Web App is accessible with both HTTP and HTTPS protocols, so it doesn't matter which is used. For instance, assuming I named my application `afd01`, both URLs presented here will be fully functional:

```
http://afd01.azurewebsites.net/
https://afd01.azurewebsites.net/
```

Such behavior is fine for development and testing but is rarely used in production scenarios, where you want your application to have a dedicated and secure domain. In such cases, Azure Web App can be configured to redirect all HTTP requests to reach the HTTPS endpoint instead. We'll be talking more about such features in the next part of this chapter.

Deploying application

For now, you should have both the Azure App Service plan and Azure Web App deployed, meaning we have our infrastructure in place and ready to host our application. The deployment process of any web application will be different, but we'll try to discuss all the possibilities and see what steps are needed to complete it.

Generally speaking, no matter if you want to deploy an application manually or use a CI/CD tool, the process will look similar. We can divide it into the following parts:

- Building an application.
- Packaging application as build artifact.
- Deploying application.

In our case, the deployment step will require satisfying certain prerequisites for Azure Web Apps. This implies using one of the available deployment methods:

- **ZIP/WAR package**
- **File Transfer Protocol (FTP)**
- **Running from package**
- **Configuring continuous deployment**

Depending on your use case, you may find one option to be more useful than another. Let's quickly characterize all of those to understand their pros and cons.

ZIP/WAR package

When a ZIP/WAR package is selected, Azure Web App expects that you archive your application as a ZIP, WAR, JAR, or EAR package. Once deployed, Azure automatically unpacks your archive and puts all the files inside the default directory for the application. The default path varies depending on the OS selected for the Azure App Service plan:

- `D:\home\site\wwwroot`: Windows
- `/home/site/wwwroot`: Linux

Deployment using the ZIP/WAR package can be performed by either using the UI in Kudu or an automated deployment method including Azure CLI, Azure PowerShell, Kudu PI, or an **Azure Resource Manager** (**ARM**) / Bicep template.

> **Note**
>
> **Kudu** is an advanced part of Azure Web App and is rarely used as a deployment method. However, as it gives you access to a number of debugging and validation tools, we're going to cover it in the next part of this chapter.

Assuming we'd like to use Azure CLI for deployment, and you already archived all the files required for your application, you could use the following command to deploy it:

```
az webapp deploy \
--resource-group <resource-group-name> \
--name <webapp-name> \
--src-path <zip-package-path>

az webapp deploy \
--resource-group <resource-group-name> \
--name <webapp-name> \
--src-path ./<package-name>.war
```

Note that it doesn't matter which archive type you're using – the command for deployment stays the same and the only difference is the file extension used for the archive. When the preceding commands are used, Azure CLI uses Kudu API to perform all the deployment operations under the hood. If you're interested, you can check that API reference here – `https://learn.microsoft.com/en-us/azure/app-service/deploy-zip?tabs=cli#kudu-publish-api-reference`.

The same Azure CLI command can be used to deploy individual files. Such a scenario may look quite strange, but there are cases when you need to fix a deployment or replace a single file without reloading all the application's executables. This involves hotfixes or configuration-related changes, which are stored within static files. To perform such an operation, you could use the following command:

```
az webapp deploy \
--resource-group <resource-group-name> \
--name <webapp-name> \
--src-path <file-path> \
--type=<startup|lib|static>
```

For a full reference of the command, you could take a look at the following page: `https://learn.microsoft.com/en-us/cli/azure/webapp?view=azure-cli-latest#az-webapp-deploy`.

As you can see, the command used for deployment changes slightly when you want to deploy individual files. In such a case, you're supposed to use the `--type` parameter, which indicates the kind of file.

> **Tip**
>
> When the ZIP/WAR deployment option is used, Azure will replace existing files only if their timestamps don't match the ones that come from the new package. This means that you can easily replace static files containing configuration or seed data without impacting other applications' files or the need to remove those files manually.

There's also a special case for deployment when your application is not accessible publicly. This involves scenarios with a private endpoint or deploying Azure Web App on an Isolated tier. Another possibility is blocking access to Kudu as a security rule, which is one of the common scenarios in the enterprise world. If that's the case, you won't be able to push a deployment package directly. Instead, you should put it on a publicly available type of storage, for instance using Blob Storage:

```
az webapp deploy \
--resource-group <group-name> \
--name <app-name> \
--src-url "https://<account-name>.blob.core.windows.net/<container>/
myapp.zip \
--type zip
```

As you can see, to perform such a deployment, we're using `--src-url` instead of `--src-path`. This allows Azure Web App to pull the package instead of accepting incoming requests. Note that Azure Web App must be able to access the selected storage location – this may involve making appropriate changes to the network configuration.

Let's now discuss the next deployment method, which is FTP.

FTP

As of today, FTP is much less popular than 10 or 20 years ago. This doesn't mean that this deployment method is no longer used. If you need to use FTP to deploy an application, I have good news – it's still supported in Azure. What's more, Azure supports both FTP and **File Transfer Protocol Secure** (**FTPS**) endpoints in case you need to use the one that is more secure (which I strongly advise you to do).

To deploy an application using FTP, you'll need to generate deployment credentials. There are two types of such credentials available:

- **User-level credentials**: They stay the same for the whole Azure account. This means that you can have single credentials for all Azure Web Apps.

- **App-level credentials**: They allow for granular access and are scoped to a single Azure Web App only.

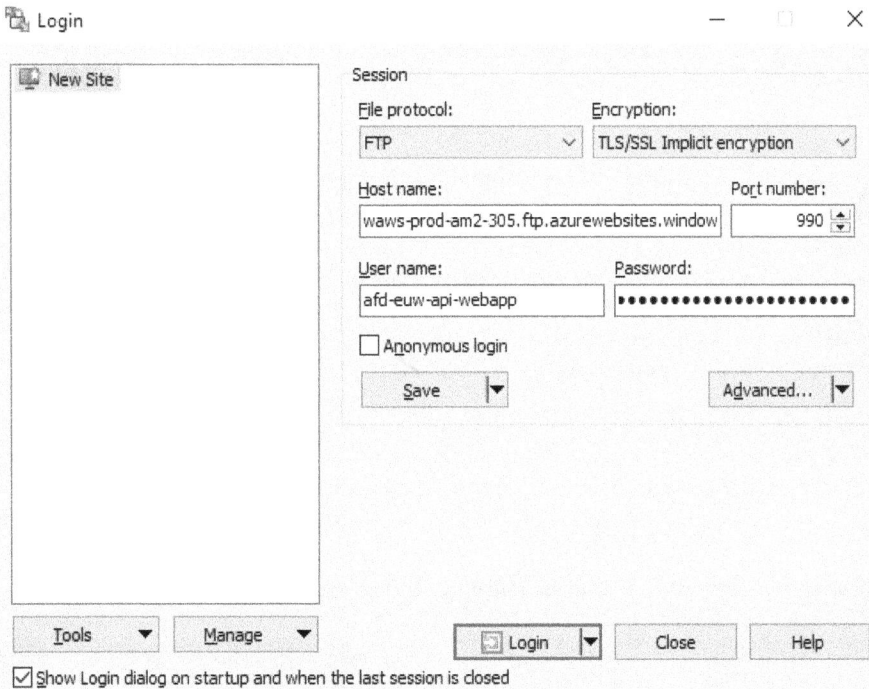

Figure 3.2 – Connecting with Azure Web App using FTPS and configured app-level credentials

You need to choose which credential type is needed for your scenario. The general recommendation is to use app-level credentials, especially in production environments, as they cannot be used for cross-application deployments. Setting the credentials is quite a simple operation; for example, for user-level credentials, you'll need to run the following command:

```
az webapp deployment user set \
--user-name <username> \
--password <password>
```

For application-level credentials, you have two options, which depend on the desired deployment method. You can select either deployment using a publishing profile or local Git deployment. The reason why local Git deployment is an option is because Azure Web App supports continuous deployment using Git. In short, you could treat the Azure Web App instance as a repository and automatically deploy changes upon the Git push operation. To obtain credentials for a publish profile, use the following command:

```
az webapp deployment list-publishing-profiles \
--resource-group <resource-group-name> \
--name <webapp-name>
```

For local Git deployment, the command will be slightly different:

```
az webapp deployment list-publishing-credentials \
--resource-group <resource-group-name> \
--name <webapp-name> \
--query scmUri
```

If you use the command for local Git deployment, the result will be Git remote URI, which could be used for deployment. The only thing needed will be appending /<webapp-name>.git at the end as the URI returned by the command doesn't contain it. You can read more about local Git deployment here: https://learn.microsoft.com/en-us/azure/app-service/deploy-local-git?tabs=cli.

Let's discuss now how one can deploy an application directly from a ZIP package.

Running from package

We already mentioned that Azure Web App allows you to deploy an application using the ZIP/WAR package. Remember that this deployment method takes a package you provide and unpacks it to the specific directory. Such a method works most of the time and provides a simple deployment pipeline without many unexpected steps. However, it also introduces the following overhead:

- During deployment, you may face file locks between the deployed package and the runtime.
- Web application may start even though deployment is not completed yet.

- In some scenarios, the deployment performance may be degraded due to the unpacking operation not being able to complete within the expected time limit.

- Using packaged sources tends to introduce cold starts as files often need to be unpacked and replaced before being mounted on a server.

If you want to avoid those problems, you could consider deploying an application using the "run from package" method. The difference between this method and ZIP/WAR deployment is the fact that the "run from package" method doesn't unpack the package. Instead, Azure mounts the package as the read-only `wwwroot` directory. Technically, it doesn't change anything from your point of view – you still deploy a ZIP package. This allows you to keep most of the CI/CD pipelines intact. The only difference will be the actual deployment step. As Azure Web App doesn't support running from package natively, you'll need to perform an extra step before deployment. That step is to enable running from the package on your Azure Web App:

```
az webapp config appsettings set \
--resource-group <resource-group-name> \
--name <webapp-name> \
--settings WEBSITE_RUN_FROM_PACKAGE="1"
```

This will add a new setting to your Azure Web App configuration, so it knows you want to use the "run from package" deployment method.

> **Tip**
>
> Because the `az webapp config appsettings set` command adds a new setting in the configuration, you could achieve the same effect when using the infrastructure-as-code approach. Consider going down that path rather than deploying the whole infrastructure declaratively instead of imperatively.

Once the configuration is set, you can use the same deployment command as we used previously:

```
az webapp deploy \
--resource-group <resource-group-name> \
--name <webapp-name> \
--src-path <filename>.zip
```

What's interesting is that Azure allows you to run your web application as a package even if it's stored in external storage (such as Blob Storage). If you want to use that feature, you need to add one more entry to the web application's configuration:

```
az webapp config appsettings set \
--name <webapp-name> \
--resource-group <resource-group-name> \
--settings WEBSITE_RUN_FROM_PACKAGE="<path-to-zip>.zip"
```

In such a scenario, you no longer need to deploy the package as a separate step. The only thing that you need to remember is the fact that replacing the package (without changing its name) will require you to restart your instance of Azure Web App (because there's no push mechanism that would notify Azure Web App about the change).

Let's now talk about one more deployment mechanism, which is continuous deployment.

Continuous deployment

Azure Web App offers a special feature that allows you to deploy your application continuously. This includes not only source integration but also leverage the Azure App Service build server. As of today, the following runtimes are supported:

- ASP.NET
- ASP.NET Core
- PHP
- Ruby
- Node.js
- Python
- HTML
- Azure WebJobs
- Azure Functions

If you want to use the automatic build feature, you'll also need to make sure that your repository contains the required files. You can find the list of those files here: `https://learn.microsoft.com/en-us/azure/app-service/deploy-continuous-deployment?tabs=github%2Cgithubactions#prepare-your-repository`.

Natively, Azure Web App supports GitHub, Bitbucket, Azure Repos, and local Git as the sources. Unfortunately, the configuration of continuous deployment cannot be done via Azure CLI or other interfaces. If you want to configure it, you need to go to the Azure portal, find your Azure Web App instance, and click on **Deployment Center**:

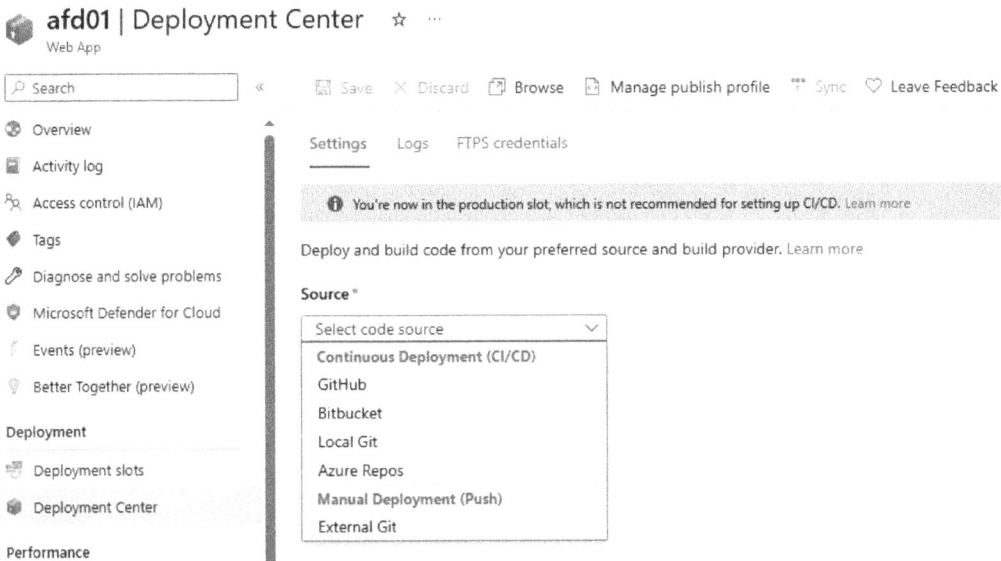

Figure 3.3 – Deployment Center in the Azure portal

From that point, you'll need to provide all the connection details needed for a particular source. You can find all the needed details in the documentation for Azure Web Apps: `https://learn.microsoft.com/en-us/azure/app-service/deploy-continuous-deployment?tabs=github%2Cgithubactions#configure-the-deployment-source`.

We talked a lot about possible deployment methods for your Azure Web Apps. Let's switch our focus now to the configuration of that service in relation to web applications hosted there.

Managing the application's configuration

Almost every web application contains a configuration of some sort. Such configuration may be provided via static files (it could be XML, JSON, YAML, or another similar format), key-value storage, or another customized source. The choice of a particular method depends on the technology stack you're using – the source that works for Java may not be a viable option for PHP or Node.js applications. Fortunately, Microsoft Azure is able to support all the popular use cases and offers various possibilities to manage the application's configuration.

App settings

The most common way to manage the configuration of a web application in Microsoft Azure is by using a feature called App Settings. You can consider it a simple key-value storage, which is natively supported by every Azure Web App instance. Under the hood, each key is translated to an environment variable, which then is available in runtime for your application. Then, if you want to access it, you need to use a method of accessing values of environment variables provided by the language or framework used for the hosted application.

Let's use a couple of examples to better understand the concept. Let's say you're going to host an ASP. NET Core application in Azure. You selected Azure Web App as your hosting platform and configured a key named DatabaseName in App Settings. In your code, you'd load the value of that key using the IConfiguration interface like so:

```
using Microsoft.Extensions.Configuration;

namespace Foo
{
    public class Bar
    {
        private IConfiguration _configuration;

        public Bar(IConfiguration configuration)
        {
            _configuration = configuration;
        }

        public SomeMethod()
        {
            var databaseName = _configuration["DatabaseName"];
        }
    }
}
```

As you can see, the value of the key can be loaded in the same way as you'd do when loading it from the appsettings.json file shipped with your application. The only thing needed here is to make sure that you configure your application to load configuration values from environment variables as well.

> **Note**
>
> Remember that ASP.NET Core applications hosted in Azure Web App using the Azure App Service plan on Linux require you to access hierarchical configuration data using double underscore.

Let's use another technology stack for comparison with ASP.NET Core. For instance, if your application is written in Node.js, to access the same key as for ASP.NET Core, you'd use the following method:

```
process.env.DatabaseName
```

For PHP, you'd use the following approach:

```
getenv("DatabaseName")
```

As you can see, the configuration provided by App Settings in Azure Web App is completely transparent for your application and it doesn't require introducing changes to the code base. This is a very important feature of Azure Web App – it allows you to migrate your application to Azure without impacting the code base itself. It's also useful when switching between environments (for instance – development and production).

Let's see now how App Settings can be configured.

Configuring App Settings

The most important thing about App Settings (besides the fact that they're mapped to environment values) is that they are standard Azure resources. This allows you to treat them as a native component for every Azure Web App and manage it in the same way as you'd treat the rest of your infrastructure. For instance, if you want to configure them using Azure CLI, you can use the following command:

```
az webapp config appsettings set \
--name <webapp-name> \
--resource-group <resource-group-name> \
--settings <setting-name>="<value>"
```

You can also edit them in bulk using slightly different syntax:

```
az webapp config appsettings set \
--resource-group <resource-group-name> \
--name <webapp-name> \
--settings "@file.json"
```

When editing settings in bulk, you need to provide the full path to a file containing the values (note that we're using @file.json, which would indicate that file.json is available in the same directory as the working directory in your terminal; it's also important to prefix the path with @ to allow Azure CLI to load the content of the file rather than pointing to the file itself). The schema for the settings file looks like the following:

```
[
  {
    "name": "foo",
    "slotSetting": false,
```

```
      "value": "foo"
  },
  {
    "name": "bar",
    "value": "bar"
  }
]
```

Note that settings in the file are JSON array consisting of objects, for which there are two required fields:

- `name`
- `value`

The third field, named `slotSetting`, indicates whether this particular setting is swapped when changing Azure Web App slots or not. We'll talk more about slots later in the chapter.

Remember that you could also manage your App Settings using Azure Bicep code. Such a method is the safest one as it keeps all the changes in code and allows you to version them:

```
resource webapp 'Microsoft.Web/sites@2023-12-01' = {
  name: 'webapp'
  location: 'West US'

  properties: {
    siteConfig: {
      appSettings: [
        {
          name: 'key1'
          value: 'value1'
        }
        {
          name: 'key2'
          value: 'value2'
        }
      ]
    }
  }
}
```

Azure Web Apps allow you to also configure connection strings as a special case for application settings. The difference is mostly noted for ASP.NET and ASP.NET Core applications, which have a dedicated section named `<connectionStrings>` in their XML config. In general, for other language stacks, you should stick with App Settings to store connection strings.

The reason for that is a feature of Azure, which prefixes keys stored as connection string with a dedicated string:

- `SQLCONNSTR_`: For SQL Server
- `MYSQLCONNSTR_`: For MySQL
- `SQLAZURECONNSTR_`: For Azure SQL Database

There are also additional prefixes added for the rest of the connection types (such as PostgreSQL, Notification Hub, Service Bus, Event Hub, or Redis Cache). You can find the complete list here: `https://learn.microsoft.com/en-us/azure/app-service/configure-common?tabs=cli#configure-connection-strings`.

Connection strings have also a dedicated Azure CLI command to use:

```
az webapp config connection-string set \
--resource-group <resource-group-name> \
--name <webapp-name> \
--settings "@settings.json"
```

Besides slightly different command names, the rest of the parameters stay the same. Let's talk now about one more kind of setting, which is not related to your application, but rather Azure Web App instance itself.

Security concerns when using App Settings

As you can see, App Settings allow you to store any custom value and inject it into your application as an environment variable. While the functionality itself is secure enough for most applications, we need to carefully consider whether App Settings is a valid place for storing any secrets. As App Settings doesn't support any additional security mechanism for preventing secrets from being accessed by unauthorized users or services, storing secrets isn't the best idea. This is why we should consider an alternative to that.

> **Note**
>
> App Settings is encrypted-at-rest so anyone accessing the physical drive storing it wouldn't be able to decrypt unless the decryption key is also compromised. However, we need to not only consider physical access (which is rarely the case in cloud scenarios) but also accessing App Settings via the Azure portal, CLI, or REST API. For those cases, encryption-at-rest won't be enough and the only thing preventing users or services from reading secrets is the lack of necessary permissions. Still, permissions granted for Azure Web Apps using the **Role-based Access Control** (**RBAC**) model may not be enough, hence there's a need to find a better approach.

In Azure, there's a dedicated service, which is meant for storing and managing secrets. It's called **Azure Key Vault** and offers native integration with Azure Web App via a feature called Azure Key Vault references. A **reference** is a special value provided for your App Settings key instead of an actual secret. There are two types of references available:

```
@Microsoft.KeyVault(SecretUri=https://myvault.vault.azure.net/secrets/
mysecret/)
@Microsoft.KeyVault(VaultName=myvault;SecretName=mysecret)
```

Both references return the same value and can be used interchangeably. The only difference is if you want to point to a specific version of a secret stored in Azure Key Vault. In such a case, the only valid syntax would be the first one:

```
@Microsoft.KeyVault(SecretUri=https://myvault.vault.azure.net/secrets/
mysecret/8sd78asdjhdas7854asd)
```

Technically, this feature is pretty simple:

1. You add your secrets as secrets in Azure Key Vault.

2. Instead of providing the values of those secrets as plain text, you put a reference to a secret stored in Azure Key Vault.

3. Upon startup, Azure Web App resolves the reference and injects the value of a secret as an environment variable.

For instance, if you add a key named MY_SECRET in the App Settings of your Azure Web App instance and provide Azure Key Vault reference as its value, the whole process will be transparent for your application as you'd use standard plain text value. However, from the Azure Web App configuration point of view, the value of a secret is never visible – you need to obtain access to Azure Key Vault, which is a much more difficult process as Azure Key Vault is secured by an additional layer of security, which can be managed independently from Azure Web App configuration.

> **Note**
>
> Because Azure Key Vault has its own layer of security for its data plane, Azure Web App needs to obtain access to it in order to resolve references. This is done via managed identities. We'll discuss that later in the chapter.

There's also an alternative approach when using Azure Key Vault to obtain secrets. If you don't want to use Azure Key Vault references, you may use Azure Key Vault **Software Development Kit (SDK)** and fetch secrets directly in your application's code base. Here's an example for .NET (the Azure. Security.KeyVault.Secrets package):

```
var client = new SecretClient(vaultUri: new Uri(vaultUrl), credential:
new DefaultAzureCredential());
var secret = client.GetSecret("mysecret");
```

The same can be done for instance for Java (the `azure-security-keyvault-secrets` library):

```
SecretClient secretClient = new SecretClientBuilder()
    .vaultUrl("<your-key-vault-url>")
    .credential(new DefaultAzureCredentialBuilder().build())
    .buildClient();
KeyVaultSecret secret = secretClient.getSecret("mysecret");
```

With this approach, you'll be able to retrieve secrets without interacting with Azure Web App configuration. There's a downside to that approach though – it couples your code base with infrastructure (as opposed to using Azure Key Vault references, where all configurations can be managed as part of your infrastructure). This is why you need to consider carefully if such an approach is valid in your scenario, and if you can accept the consequences.

Before we dive into the scalability of Azure Web Apps, let's talk for a moment about Azure App Configuration, which is an alternative approach for storing and managing configuration.

General settings

Azure Web Apps offer a number of customizations, which allow you to configure the web application according to your needs. We talked about configuring app-related parameters using App Settings, and now it's time to discuss how Azure Web App can be configured as a service. You may wonder what you could configure on the Azure Web App level in order to address your requirements. This may involve enabling things such as HTTP 2.0, the Always On feature, Web Sockets, or even remote debugging. All of those settings can be configured using a single command:

```
az webapp config set \
--resource-group <group-name> \
--name <app-name> \
--use-32bit-worker-process [true|false] \
--web-sockets-enabled [true|false] \
--always-on [true|false] \
--http20-enabled \
--auto-heal-enabled [true|false] \
--remote-debugging-enabled [true|false] \
--number-of-workers
```

Those settings are special cases if your application needs to handle either a legacy scenario (32-bit process support), needs to be online all the time to avoid cold starts (Always On), should allow connectivity over HTTP 2.0, should allow remote debugging or has a specific number of jobs (workers), which should run in the background. You can find the complete list of available settings here: `https://learn.microsoft.com/en-us/cli/azure/webapp/config?view=azure-cli-latest#az-webapp-config-set`.

There's also one important topic to discuss before we move forward, which is using Azure App Configuration for managing web application configuration.

Using Azure App Configuration

Azure App Configuration is a dedicated Azure service designed to handle app configuration scenarios. It's a centrally managed store for all the settings and feature flags, which offers native integration with other Azure services. It's especially helpful when integrated with Azure Web App, as it allows you to share configuration across different instances or environments of your application. It also integrates with Azure Key Vault, so you can secure all the secrets in the same way as you'd do with Azure Web App + Azure Key Vault scenario.

Let's see how we can use and integrate Azure App Configuration with a simple step.

Deploying Azure App Configuration

The first step is to deploy Azure App Configuration if there's no instance that we could use. It can be done with the following command:

```
az appconfig create \
--location <location> \
--name <store-name> \
--resource-group <resource-group-name>
```

This command creates an Azure App Configuration instance (called `store`) in the selected location and resource group. Once it's created, you can proceed to the next step.

Adding a new key-value pair

In the created store, you can add new key-value pairs in a similar way as you did for App Settings. In fact, Azure App Configuration is a service that works similarly to App Settings, while adding additional layers, which help you manage your configuration in more advanced scenarios. To add a new key-value pair, you can use the following command:

```
az appconfig kv set \
--name <store-name> \
--key <key-name> \
--value <value>
```

The Azure App Configuration store supports both flat and hierarchical keys. In other words, both of the following options will work:

- `Key`
- `Key:Key2:Key3`

This allows you to support standard cases for web applications, where configuration is often grouped into logical blocks for easier management. Once the key-value pair is added to your store, you can proceed and integrate Azure App Configuration with Azure Web App. Here's an example of how such a configuration could look like:

- `Key: Environment; Value: Development`
- `Key: FeatureToggles:AnonymousLoginEnabled; Value: True`

    Such a configuration could be mapped to the following JSON configuration file:

```
{
    "Environment": "Development",
    "FeatureToggled": {
        "AnonymousLoginEnabled": true
    }
}
```

Let's see now how we could integrate Azure App Configuration with our web application.

Integrating with Azure Web App

Azure Web App integration for Azure App Configuration is similar to Azure Key Vault references:

```
@Microsoft.AppConfiguration(Endpoint=https://<store-name>.azconfig.io;
Key=myAppConfigKey)
```

There's also an alternative version, which allows you to pass a label (use it if your key is labeled by you or somebody else):

```
@Microsoft.AppConfiguration(Endpoint=https://<store-name>.azconfig.io;
Key=myAppConfigKey; Label=myKeysLabel)
```

Note that passing the Azure App Configuration reference is not enough to access the configuration stored in your store. Once again, similar to Azure Key Vault, you'll need to use managed identities in order to give your Azure Web App instance a way to authenticate and authorize access. We'll talk more about that scenario later in the chapter.

Integrating with your code base

Azure App Configuration can also be integrated directly with your application using a dedicated SDK for your language stack. For instance, you could inject all the configuration in .NET using the following code snippet (`Microsoft.Extensions.Configuration.AzureAppConfiguration` package):

```
var builder = new ConfigurationBuilder();
builder.AddAzureAppConfiguration(
    Environment.GetEnvironmentVariable(
```

```
        "AzureAppConfigurationConnectionString")
);
```

The same is also available for Python:

```
from azure.appconfiguration.provider import (
    load,
    SettingSelector
)
import os

connection_string =
    os.environ.get("AzureAppConfigurationConnectionString ")
config = load(connection_string=connection_string)
```

Azure App Configuration SDK supports also Java and Node.js. Take a look here for more details: `https://learn.microsoft.com/en-us/azure/azure-app-configuration/overview`.

As we talked a lot about the configuration of Azure Web App, let's now discuss some advanced concepts related to scalability. It's important to understand what Azure Web Apps offers to handle increasing user load and how you can configure them to be a reliable service.

Understanding the scalability of Azure App Service

In this chapter, we're going to discuss how scalable Azure App Service is and what can be done to improve its performance. When developing a web application, you'll often face situations when your application needs to handle a higher load than originally anticipated. In on-premises scenarios, such a situation was difficult to handle because it required us to have reserved hardware in place. In cloud scenarios, it's much easier to handle unexpected traffic spikes as we can provision our infrastructure dynamically. Let's start with an introduction to scalability concepts, which are present in Microsoft Azure.

Scaling up and out

The most basic concept when it comes to scalability is scaling up/out. This can be referred to as vertical (up) or horizontal (out) scalability as well. Let's characterize those concepts:

- **Scale up (vertical scaling)**: This changes how much CPU, GPU, memory, disk space, or additional features your instance will have.

- **Scale out (horizontal scaling)**: This increases the number of instances on which your application works.

Of course, both those operations could be reversed. In that case, the reversed operations are defined as follows:

- **Scale down (vertical scaling)**: This decreases the size of a virtual machine used for your web application.

- **Scale in (horizontal scaling)**: This decreases the number of instances of your application.

It's important to understand the difference between those two concepts, as they impact how your application handles load and may imply changes to the system architecture. The most notable difference between those two scalability concepts is the fact that horizontal scaling requires the use of a load balancer, while vertical scaling may not be efficient enough if your application cannot leverage additional compute power.

Azure App Service supports both kinds of scaling, but introduces the following limitations:

- Scaling up is available within available App Service plan tiers; however, you cannot customize the hardware.

- Azure uses its own load balancer to handle scale-out scenarios.

- If you scale out, the overall price for Azure App Service will be multiplied by the number of instances currently operating.

- Certain features of Azure App Service may be blocked for lower tiers.

- Automated scale-up/scale-out is not available for the Free, Shared, and Basic tier.

Let's now see how we can perform scale-up/scale-out operations.

Performing scale-up/scale-out operations

To scale up your Azure App Service, you need to either perform a manual update to the Azure App Service plan or configure an automated scale-out. It's worth mentioning that all the scaling operations are performed on the Azure App Service plan level, not on the web application itself. It means that if you attach more than a single web application to the same Azure App Service plan, they will all benefit from increased compute power (or will all be affected by decreased capacity in case of a scale-down/scale-in operation). Let's start with the manual operation and see how it impacts our Azure Web App.

Scaling up/out manually

Manually scaling up and out of Azure App Service is pretty easy as it can be done using Azure Portal, CLI, or REST API. If you're using infrastructure as code, it can be also performed as part of your infrastructure configuration. For the sake of this exercise, we'll use Azure CLI. Let's run the following command:

```
az appservice plan update \
--name <plan-name> \
--resource-group <resource-group-name> \
--sku B1
```

As you probably remember, we originally created our Azure App Service plan using the F1 tier, which stands for Free. Now, we're changing the tier to B1, which is Basic, offering dedicated hardware and much more stable performance. We scaled it up to a more powerful machine, so our application should be much more stable now. The tier we chose is also no longer free, so if you want to save your credits, just scale down to F1:

```
az appservice plan update \
--name <plan-name> \
--resource-group <resource-group-name> \
--sku F1
```

When performing those operations, remember that your application will be restarted, which may potentially impact your customers. Unless it's a critical situation, I advise against scaling up during the daily peak of your customers.

> **Note**
>
> Technically, the Basic tier doesn't provide dedicated hardware. You should rather think of it as a dedicated virtual machine with a dedicated web server (this is not the case for Free and Shared tires, where there's no clear physical and logical separation between customers). For dedicated hardware, you'd need to deploy Azure **App Service Environment** (**ASE**), which offers Isolated tiers and superb performance when compared to the rest of the available tiers. However, the deployment of ASE and private web applications is beyond the scope of this book. If you want to read more about it, take a look at the following documentation: https://learn.microsoft.com/en-us/azure/app-service/environment/overview.

Updating the tier of your application can be considered a scale-up operation because it impacts the overall performance and changes the number of CPU cores, memory, and available disk space. If we want to scale out now, we need to change the number of workers that are assigned for that particular plan:

```
az appservice plan update \
--name <plan-name> \
--resource-group <resource-group-name> \
--number-of-workers <number-of-workers>
```

Let's try now to set the number to two (remember that you need to have at least a B1 plan in order for that operation to succeed):

```
az appservice plan update \
--name <plan-name> \
--resource-group <resource-group-name> \
--number-of-workers 2
```

Once the command completes, the App Service plan you're using will be scaled out to two instances, so the load can be distributed between them. The number of workers available for the plan depends on the selected tier – it's 3 instances for the Basic tier, 10 instances for Standard, 30 instances for Premium, and up to 100 instances for the Isolated one.

We successfully scaled up and out our application. This is, however, a manual approach, which isn't as useful and productive as an automated one. Let's now try to configure automated scaling to simplify operations.

Using automated scaling

As we discussed, you may use manual scaling anytime, but it's not as productive and simple as using automated scaling. For production workloads, when incoming traffic will be much more dynamic in most scenarios, constantly monitoring your application for performance issues and doing scale-up or out on your own will be difficult to perform. This is why Azure App Service introduces two other options for improving the performance of your application:

- Scaling out automatically
- Scaling out automatically with rules

Both options do exactly the same thing (which is performing scale-out operation automatically) but slightly differ in terms of execution and use cases. In short, scaling out automatically without rules is basically scaling out automatically with a single rule, which is HTTP traffic. There is, however, one more thing that makes scaling out automatically without rules interesting – it allows you to use prewarmed instances, so even if you're scaling out, you still have a ready-to-go instance to serve all the incoming requests.

Using automated scaling out

To enable that feature, you can use the following Azure CLI command:

```
az appservice plan update \
--name <plan-name> \
--resource-group <resource-group-name> \
--elastic-scale true \
--max-elastic-worker-count <max-burst>
```

The value of the <max-burst> parameter is the same value we discussed when talking about manual scaling out in the previous section of this chapter. There's also an app-level setting, which you can use to inform Azure how many always-ready instances you want to have:

```
az webapp update \
--resource-group <resource-group-name> \
--name <webapp-name> \
--minimum-elastic-instance-count <always-ready-count>
```

Remember, though, that this command will set the minimum number of such always-ready instances. It doesn't necessarily imply the maximum burst for those instances and it's up to Azure to decide how many such instances are needed.

Under the hood, automated scaling out works as follows:

1. Azure constantly monitors the performance of your application via health checks.

2. If an increased load is detected, health checks become more and more frequent.

3. If Azure detects that health checks are deteriorating, it requests additional instances for your application to create.

4. After the load stabilizes or goes down, Azure will initiate a scale-in operation to return to the default configuration.

The overall performance of the whole operation depends on your programming stack and the startup time of your application. Generally speaking, the "heavier" your application is, the slower the scale-out operation will be.

Let's now talk about scaling out automatically with rules, which gives you more control over the process.

Using rules for scaling out automatically

Enabling automated scaling out on your Azure App Service plan is a simple and quick way to handle the dynamic load and improve the reliability of your application. Unfortunately, it doesn't give you enough control over the metrics used for making the decision if scaling out is needed. This is why there's an additional option for implementing autoscale for Azure Web App – rules. Rule-based autoscale is based on Azure Monitor, which allows you to collect and choose metrics needed to make the decision about scaling out your application.

To implement autoscale based on rules for your web application, you'll need to create a couple of additional resources. The first one is creating autoscale settings:

```
az monitor autoscale create \
--count <number-of-instance> \
--max-count <max-number-of-instance> \
--min-count <min-number-of-instance> \
--name <settings-name> \
--resource <plan-name> \
--resource-group <resource-group-name> \
--resource-type Microsoft.Web/serverFarms
```

> **Note**
>
> Remember that the `--resource` parameter defines the target resource and needs to be aligned with the `--resource-type` parameter. As we're defining scaling of Azure App Service, we need to point out to the Azure App Service plan as it's where scaling is being done.

Once the instance of settings is created, let's proceed with creating scale-out and scale-in rules:

```
az monitor autoscale rule create \
--resource-group <resource-group-name> \
--autoscale-name <settings-name> \
--scale out <scale-out-value> \
--condition "CpuPercentage > 75 avg 5m"

az monitor autoscale rule create \
--resource-group <resource-group-name> \
--autoscale-name <settings-name> \
--scale in <scale-in-value> \
--condition "CpuPercentage< 25 avg 5m"
```

Let's describe those rules for a better understanding:

- If CPU utilization reaches 75% on average over the last 5 minutes, additional instances will be added to your plan based on the `<scale-out-value>` value.

- If CPU utilization drops below 25% on average over the last 5 minutes, your plan will be scaled in based on the value of the `<scale-in-value>` parameter.

Once rules are created, your Azure App Service plan will be automatically scaled out and in if the selected metric reaches a certain threshold. If you want to learn more about available metrics, use the following Azure CLI command to get a full list:

```
az monitor metrics list-definitions \
--resource <resource-id>
```

Great; now, you should be aware of the basics of how to configure scale-up and out operations for your web application! It's time to discuss managed identities – one of the key features for integrating Azure Web Apps with other services and also a key component for completing the setup of Azure Key Vault and Azure App Configuration references.

Using managed identities to integrate with other services

In the previous sections of this chapter, we discussed how Azure Web Apps can be integrated with Azure Key Vault and Azure App Configuration to extend their functionality and make them more secure and manageable. In order to complete such integrations, we need to grant our web applications a persona – a principal they can use in order to authenticate and authorize. Such a persona is called a managed identity – a feature that can be used in many Azure services to simplify integration and improve security. Let's find out how managed identities can be used in Azure Web App.

System and user-assigned identities

Simply put, a managed identity is an artificial user or a principal that can be assigned with single or multiple instances of Azure services. Originally, similar functionality could be achieved using service principals, which are part of the Microsoft Entra ID directory. However, using service principles has certain downsides:

- They're not typical Azure resources, hence, cannot be managed via Azure Resource Manager.

- Creating and managing service principals requires assigning permissions on the Microsoft Entra ID level, which complicates development and makes management more difficult.

- They require secrets or certificates to be generated and maintained, so an additional process needs to be in place in order to avoid downtime.

Fortunately, the managed identities feature was introduced to challenge those problems and simplify development. While the whole feature is quite popular now, still not all Azure services support it. You can find the complete list here: `https://learn.microsoft.com/en-us/entra/identity/managed-identities-azure-resources/overview#what-azure-services-support-the-feature`.

In order to start using managed identities, you need to understand their basic concepts. Let's start with the system and user-assigned identities. Each managed identity can be a system or user-assigned identity. The difference between them is quite simple:

- System-assigned identity is a unique identity created for a specific instance of Azure service. It cannot be shared and will always be named after the resource for which it was created. They also cannot be created and follow the life cycle of a resource they're connected to – instead, they're automatically generated if such managed identities are enabled.

- User-assigned identities are created separately from Azure services and have separate life cycles. Each user-assigned identity can be assigned to multiple Azure services, so they can have a uniform access model. User-assigned identity can be created using Azure Portal, CLI, and infrastructure as code.

Besides the differences explained earlier, both system and user-assigned identities work the same. Let's talk now about authorization when managed identities are used.

Managed identities and RBAC

Because enabling or assigning managed identities gives an instance of Azure service an identity, it means that it can go through an authentication process and be challenged against authorization rules. When your application is hosted on a service leveraging managed identities, Azure takes care of obtaining an authentication token (which will be retrieved from Microsoft Entra ID). Once the application has the token, it can be used for performing authorization. Authorization of managed identities works in the same way as authorization of any other user authenticated in Azure. For instance, if you want to give a managed identity read access to all resources inside a subscription, you'll need to give it a role that grants read permission and assign it to that subscription level.

Because authorization doesn't change when managed identities are used, you can implement a transparent security mechanism for your application, no matter if you run it locally or host it in the cloud. The only thing to remember is to grant your account the same level of access as intended for the application. You need to do that because running the application locally (with the assumption that you connect to other Azure services) will also require an access token. This can be done via a dedicated package:

- **Azure.Identity (.NET)**: `https://www.nuget.org/packages/Azure.Identity`
- **Azure Identity library (Java)**: `https://learn.microsoft.com/en-us/azure/developer/java/sdk/identity`

- **Azure Identity client library (Python)**: `https://learn.microsoft.com/en-us/python/api/overview/azure/identity-readme?view=azure-python`

- **Azure/identity (Node.js)**: `https://www.npmjs.com/package/@azure/identity`

All those packages allow you to authenticate against Microsoft Azure using different kinds of credentials. Because there's a chain of methods to obtain credentials (you can use the interactive method, Azure CLI, Azure PowerShell, client credentials, and managed identity credentials), you'll be able to implement a seamless process for authentication, no matter which environment your application is going to work.

All Azure Identity packages expose a dedicated object called `DefaultAzureCredential`. It has specific functionality, which is useful if you want the authentication process to work without any changes to the code base or configuration. It goes through all available credential types to find the one method which is available in the current working environment. This is why the whole process is so helpful – the same method can be used for locally hosted applications (because it'll fetch credentials from Azure CLI or Azure PowerShell) and for Azure-based services (where, for instance, managed identities can be available).

> **Tip**
> The `DefaultAzureCredential` object is the quickest way to implement authentication in your application. However, it may also be a little slow in some scenarios (as it goes through the whole chain of credentials). If you want the whole process to be more specific, you can use `ChainedTokenCredential`, where you're allowed to specify the order of execution for all credentials and also provide only the ones that are valid for your application.

We've talked about theory – let's go to practice now. First, let's enable managed identities for our Azure Web App.

Implementing managed identities for Azure Web App

If we want to enable managed identities for Azure Web App, we need to decide whether we need to implement a specific type of identity (system or user-assigned) or enable both. Enabling both is a valid scenario in some cases – for example, you'd use system-assigned identity to give your resource a wider set of permissions (because such identity is scoped to a single instance only), while keeping user-assigned identity for performing common tasks that were already validated for a number of other services (for instance, reading data from Azure Storage, which isn't directly related with your application, yet such access level is reused with other services, which need to do the same).

To enable system-assigned identity, we need to run the following command:

```
az webapp identity assign \
    --resource-group <resource-group-name> \
    --name <webapp-name>
```

This command would enable system-assigned identity to the Azure Web App instance you provided without performing any other operation. As a result, you'll need to grant the required access using a separate command. For example, if you'd like to grant Reader access to a resource, you'd need to use the following command:

```
az role assignment create \
--assignee <principal-name> \
--role Reader \
--scope <resource-id>
```

The problem here is that we don't know the name of the principal and we also don't know its object ID (so we cannot use the --assignee-object-id parameter instead). However, if you run the first command, you should get a response like this:

```
{
    "principalId": "e33bac5c-...-d640a73f38d8",
    "tenantId": "c2d4fe14-...-5a65748fd6c9",
    "type": "SystemAssigned",
    "userAssignedIdentities": null
}
```

Such a response includes the principalId field, which is exactly what we'd need to provide to grant our principal a Reader role:

```
az role assignment create \
--assignee-object-id "e33bac5c-...-d640a73f38d8" \
--role Reader \
--scope <resource-id>
```

As an alternative, you could use additional parameters to enable managed identities and create a role assigned in a single command:

```
az webapp identity assign \
--resource-group <resource-group-name> \
--name <webapp-name> \
--role Reader \
--scope <resource-id>
```

The result of both commands will be the same – it's up to you which is more helpful in your scenario. What we did was enable system-assigned identity for our Azure Web App. This means that from now on, our web application can use that identity and authorize based on the granted permissions. If we want to use a user-assigned identity, we'll need to create it as the first step:

```
az identity create \
--name <identity-name> \
--resource-group <resource-group-name>
```

Once the identity is created, we can assign it to our Azure Web App:

```
az webapp identity assign \
--name <webapp-name> \
--resource-group <resource-group-name> \
--identities [system] <user-assigned-identity-id>
```

Note that we're providing two separate values for the `--identities` parameter – one is a hardcoded value, `[system]`, second one is the resource ID of our user-assigned identity resource. We're doing that because we want to keep both identities assigned to our Azure Web App instance. If you omit `[system]` in that command, Azure will disable system-assigned identity, which may impact current working functionalities.

> **Note**
>
> Disabling the system-assigned identity or removing the user-assigned identity from the Azure Web App doesn't remove RBAC assignments. Once the operation is complete, your application won't be able to use this particular managed identity access, but you'll need to perform cleanup on your own.

Remember that adding a new identity to your application requires you to pass all the currently assigned identities. If you happen to forget about one of them, such an assignment will be deleted. You can use that fact for management operations for managed identity assignments (such as deleting obsolete ones).

We talked about managed identities and how to connect them with Azure Web Apps. Let's complete that exercise by completing integration with Azure Key Vault and Azure App Configuration.

Connecting to Azure Key Vault and Azure App Configuration

In order to give your application access to Azure Key Vault or Azure App Configuration, you need to allow it to access its data planes. The operation will be slightly different for those services, hence we'll split the explanation into two separate parts.

Connecting to Azure Key Vault

Azure Key Vault has two different access models:

- Access policies
- RBAC

If access policies are used, you'll need to create a policy that is linked to the identity of your web application:

```
az keyvault set-policy \
--name <keyvault-name> \
--secret-permissions get list \
--object-id <managed-identity-object-id>
```

The preceding command will grant get and list permissions for the provided identity. As Azure Key Vault may contain also keys and secrets, you may need to provide additional parameters if you want to extend access:

- `--key-permissions`
- `--certificate-permissions`

However, for most scenarios (which are integrating Azure Web App with Azure Key Vault via references), the provided permissions for secrets will be enough.

> **Tip**
> If you want to learn what permissions are available, run the `az keyvault set-policy -h` command.

On the other hand, there may be Azure Key Vaults that are not secured via access policies but rather RBAC assignments. In such cases, you need to use the following command:

```
az role assignment create \
--assignee-object-id <managed-identity-object-id> \
--role "Key Vault Secrets User" \
--scope <keyvault-resource-id>
```

With that command, you'll grant your application the same set of permissions as it would have when granting get and list permissions for secrets when using access policies.

Connecting to Azure App Configuration

To integrate Azure Web App with Azure App Configuration, we'll follow the same pattern as we did for Azure Key Vault. As Azure App Configuration doesn't support access policies (instead, you could use an access key, but it provides no value for integration with Azure Web App), we'll need to assign an appropriate role in order to give the managed identity access.

To do that, let's run the following command:

```
az role assignment create \
--assignee-object-id <managed-identity-object-id> \
--role "App Configuration Data Reader" \
--scope <app-configuration-resource-id>
```

With this single operation, you're granting access to your instance of Azure App Configuration for Azure Web App. From now on, it'll be able to resolve references for the configuration store and load values stored there.

> **Note**
>
> Even if you don't use Azure App Configuration references, role assignments will be needed to grant your application access to the store. In other words, you'd perform exactly the same steps, regardless of whether you keep the integration on Azure Web App or the code base level.

This is everything for now about managed identities. Will come back to that topic later in the book when talking about other Azure services. Let's finish this chapter with the last subject, which is use cases and reference architectures.

Learning about use cases

Azure Web Apps are, as the name suggests, the main solution for hosting web applications in Azure. They provide an integrated environment, which simplifies the deployment, management, and operations of such applications. However, before you decide to use that service to host your application, you need to consider all the pros and cons. Let's dive deeper into the topic.

Scalability and Azure Web Apps

Azure Web Apps offer quite a robust environment for hosting web applications. We discussed how the scale is based on manual or automated patterns, but still haven't got a chance to talk about their capability to scale. The limitations to scale up and scale out your application when using Azure Web App depend on the selected tier. Because tiers impact offered capabilities and pricing, you need to carefully consider which one is needed to cover your application's requirements.

When using Azure Web Apps, you need to remember that they don't offer an option to manage your applications as a whole. Yes, they may be linked to the same Azure App Service plan, but from the scalability point of view, they will be managed individually. This means that there's no native way to scale them beyond already discussed options (auto-scale and rules). What's more, you may find Azure Web App a little bit too "heavy" for some services, which prevents you from a better utilization of offered compute power.

Microservices architecture

As just discussed, Azure Web Apps are offered with a fixed size, meaning there's no way to optimize utilization. Sure, you can base your deployments on provided metrics, so they are deployed to underutilized Azure App Service plans, but you cannot easily manage how much CPU and memory is assigned to each instance. For such cases, it may be better to use other services (e.g., Azure Container Apps, Azure Kubernetes Service). Still, for microservices architecture, Azure Web Apps can be a good choice; however, you need to understand how they will interact with your deployment and hosting model. If you seek a platform that is easy to maintain, robust, web-oriented, and provides everything that's important for hosting web applications without unnecessary overhead, Azure Web Apps will be definitely an option to consider.

Background jobs

Azure Web Apps offer an additional feature called **Azure WebJobs**. **WebJobs** are worker services working in the background and executing code apart from the main application. This is a great choice for asynchronous operations such as processing a queue, generating reports, sending emails, and similar activities, which take lots of time and are tightly coupled with the lifetime of your application. While the capabilities of Azure WebJobs are quite limited (they are extended by Azure Functions), I find them an excellent addition to many web applications hosted in Azure.

Multi-tenant and single-tenant applications

Because Azure Web Apps can be easily scaled up and offer good performance, especially when using the Isolated tier, they can be a great choice for multi-tenant applications, which often require a significant amount of compute power to handle the increasing load. For single-tenant applications though, you may find Azure Web Apps difficult to manage. This is caused by the fact that each instance of such an application will be a separate resource in Azure. Resources in Azure may have quotas and they need to be deployed, managed, and secured. In high-scale scenarios, such an approach may introduce unnecessary overhead for your IT operations. If that is the case, it may be better to consider Azure Container Apps or Azure Kubernetes Service to host the workloads.

Landing pages and static web apps

Some web applications are built as landing pages or static web apps. While both those kinds of applications can be easily hosted using Azure Web Apps, they may not be able to leverage all the useful features. Because Azure Web Apps is not a free service, you will want to utilize your instances the best you can to optimize spending. This is why, for landing pages, it'll be better to use static website hosting in Azure Storage. This solution offers basic features needed for web applications and simplified deployment models and charges you almost nothing for your application.

For web applications, such as **Single Page Application** (**SPAs**), it may be better to use Azure Static Web Apps. It's a dedicated service for applications that act as a frontend for backend applications or are applications running in a browser. Azure Static Web Apps offer two tiers (*free* and *paid*), can leverage co-hosted API to extend your application, and offer many more features that are important in advanced scenarios when compared with static websites in Azure Storage.

That's all in *Chapter 3* for now! Let's summarize our findings and learn what awaits us in *Chapter 4*.

Summary

In this chapter, we discussed the basic concepts of hosting and managing web applications in Microsoft Azure using Azure Web Apps. We talked about deployment modes, configuration management, and integrations with other Azure services, such as Azure Key Vault and Azure App Configuration. We also talked about the scalability of web applications in Azure and how Azure Web Apps can address hosting applications in production.

In the next chapter, you'll extend your knowledge about hosting applications in Azure by learning about development methods for static services using Microsoft Azure as the platform.

Join the CloudPro Newsletter with 44000+ Subscribers

Want to know what's happening in cloud computing, DevOps, IT administration, networking, and more? Scan the QR code to subscribe to **CloudPro**, our weekly newsletter for 44,000+ tech professionals who want to stay informed and ahead of the curve.

https://packt.link/cloudpro

4

Developing Static Web Applications

In the previous chapter, we discussed how you can host and develop web applications using Azure Web Apps and Azure App Service plans. Those services are core components for every dynamic application, which requires the underlying server to host the backend that's handling incoming requests. While Azure Web Apps will work great for both dynamic and static web applications, sometimes, it's better to choose a dedicated service to simplify development and lower the cost of the infrastructure.

When building static websites in Azure, we'll need to learn about hosting options and the capabilities of two separate Azure services. This will help us better understand their use cases and integration options.

In this chapter, we're going to cover the following main topics:

- Using and configuring an Azure Storage static website
- Deploying a static website to Azure Storage
- Using Azure Static Web Apps to host your application
- Integrating Azure Static Web Apps with Azure App Service
- Learning about use cases

Technical requirements

To complete the exercises in this chapter, you'll need the following software:

- An IDE (preferably Visual Studio Code)
- The Azure CLI
- A **command-line interface (CLI)**
- Node.js with NPM
- Azure Functions Core Tools

The source code for this chapter can be found here: `https://github.com/PacktPublishing/`
`Azure-for-Developers-Third-Edition/tree/main/ch04`

Using and configuring an Azure Storage static website

Before we start learning about different services that allow you to host static web applications in Azure, let's quickly define what a static web application is. In many scenarios, an application requires a web server, which can handle incoming HTTP requests. Depending on the technology stack, such a server will offer a different set of capabilities, but the important thing here is the architecture of your application. If both the frontend and the backend of that application are hosted by a web server, Azure Web Apps will be a valid choice. However, if you wish to build a **single-page application** (**SPA**), Azure Web Apps may be overkill. This is because the SPA requires a different set of features and doesn't require much compute power (because it's hosted in a browser, which runs on the computer of the application's client). If you don't want to use another service in Azure, you'll be just fine when using Azure Web Apps and hosting applications written in React, Svelte, AngularJS, or any other JavaScript-based framework. However, if you want to simplify development and hosting and also lower the cost of the chosen infrastructure, there are better choices. Let's start with one of them, which is a static website on **Azure Storage**.

Configuring Azure Storage to host a static website

We're starting with the simplest possible service, which allows you to host a static web application. Azure Storage, which is mostly used for storing blobs, serves as a file share or key-value storage and has a very interesting feature called a **static website**. In short, it leverages the existing storage capabilities of Azure Storage to host the static files of your website and exposes it via one of its endpoints. To get started, we'll need to prepare a simple HTML page, which we'll then upload and host in Azure. Let's proceed with a very simple example:

```
<!DOCTYPE html>
<html lang="en">
  <head>
    <meta charset="UTF-8">
    <meta name="viewport"
          content="width=device-width, initial-scale=1.0">
    <title>Azure Storage Static Website</title>
  </head>
  <body>
    <h1>Welcome to Azure Storage Static Website</h1>
    <p>This is a simple static website hosted on Azure Storage.</p>
    <p>
      For more information, visit
      <a href="https://docs.microsoft.com/en-us/azure/storage/blobs/
      storage-blob-static-website">
```

```
        Static website hosting in Azure Storage</a>.</p>
   </body>
</html>
```

Save the preceding HTML as `index.html` on your computer and proceed to your CLI. To upload the static website, we'll need to use the Azure CLI and copy the file from our working directory to a container in Azure Storage. However, before we're able to do that, we need to enable a static website by running the following commands:

```
az storage account create \
--name <storage-account-name> \
--resource-group <resource-group-name> \
--location <location>

az storage blob service-properties update \
--account-name <storage-account-name> \
--static-website \
--404-document <error-document-name> \
--index-document <index-document-name>
```

The first command is used to create a storage account. Then, the second command requires us to provide two additional parameters in addition to the account's name:

- **404 document**: This will be displayed when a route doesn't match when somebody accesses your static website.

- **Index document**: The main page of your application that's accessed by default.

For now, let's use the following values for those documents:

- **Index document**: `index.html`

- **404 document**: `error.html`

> **Not**
>
> Enabling static website hosting for Azure Storage is an operation that can be performed on a data plane of that service. This means that you're unable to enable it using **Azure Resource Manager** (**ARM**) (ARM templates or Azure Bicep). Note that Terraform works differently as you can switch the static website on without having to perform additional steps.

Now that you've configured your Azure Storage instance, let's proceed with uploading the website.

Deploying the static website to Azure Storage

Once your storage account has been updated with both index and 404 document names, we can work on uploading them so that they can be used in our application. Let's get started:

1. Because we've already instructed Azure Storage to enable static website capability, it'll automatically create a place where those HTML files can be uploaded. We can find them by running the following command:

    ```
    az storage container list \
    --account-name <storage-account-name> \
    -o table
    ```

2. As a result, we should get a single entry describing a dedicated static web application container (we can consider it a dedicated directory for the application files). This result should look as follows:

    ```
    Name      Lease Status      Last Modified
    ------    --------------    -------------------------
    $web                        2024-07-01T10:46:42+00:00
    ```

3. As we can see, there's a dedicated container named $web, which we'll use for uploading our static website. To do that, we need to upload the index.html file we created previously in this chapter. Once we have this file, we can use the following command to upload it:

    ```
    az storage blob upload \
    --account-name <storage-account-name> \
    --container-name "$web" \
    --file index.html \
    --name index.html
    ```

4. Once the file has been uploaded, we can access our website based on the provided URL. There are multiple ways to obtain the endpoint, but in our case, we'll stick with the Azure CLI. To get it, use the following command:

    ```
    az storage account show \
    --name <storage-account-name> \
    --query primaryEndpoints.web
    ```

    Your endpoint will be named differently, but it's supposed to look similar to mine. In my case, the preceding command returned the following result:

    ```
    "https://afd04.z6.web.core.windows.net/"
    ```

> **Note**
>
> If you don't want to use the Azure CLI to perform data plane operations in Azure Storage, feel free to use Azure Storage Explorer, which provides a graphical interface for interacting with blobs, file shares, queues, and tables: `https://azure.microsoft.com/en-us/products/storage/storage-explorer`.

Now, we're able to check the website. When we paste the obtained URL into our browser's address bar, we should be able to see our static website:

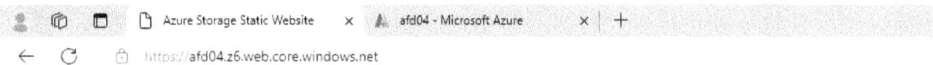

Welcome to Azure Storage Static Website

This is a simple static website hosted on Azure Storage.

For more information, visit <u>Static website hosting in Azure Storage</u>.

Figure 4.1 – Static website accessed with a browser

1. We need to do the same for the 404 (Not Found) document so that it correctly returns an error if there's no page based on the provided URL:

```
az storage blob upload \
--account-name <storage-account-name> \
--container-name "$web" \
--file error.html \
--name error.html
```

2. For that error page, I used the following HTML document:

```
<!DOCTYPE html>
<html lang="en">

<head>
    <meta charset="UTF-8">
    <meta name="viewport"
        content="width=device-width, initial-scale=1.0">
    <title>Azure Storage Static Website</title>
</head>

<body>
    <h1>Error!</h1>
    <h2>Given page doesn't exist.</h2>
```

```
    </body>
  </html>
```

3. Now, try to access your website by appending an additional value to the URL. Instead of the default error page, you should see the customized document you uploaded:

Figure 4.2 – Error page returned by the static website

Congratulations – you just created your first static website using Azure Storage! Unfortunately, our web page is a little bit too static – it's just plain HTML with no dynamic elements. Let's see whether static websites in Azure Storage allow us to add interactive elements via JavaScript files.

Uploading JavaScript scripts

Most static websites integrate with JavaScript to either interact with the UI or introduce a comprehensive framework for managing business logic (which is the case for most SPAs). However, in this section, we aren't going to build an application from scratch. Instead, we'll focus on checking whether anything additional needs to be configured so that our application can support JavaScript. Let's begin:

1. To get started, let's change our `index.html` file so that it looks like this:

```html
<!DOCTYPE html>
<html lang="en">

<head>
  <meta charset="UTF-8">
  <meta name="viewport"
        content="width=device-width, initial-scale=1.0">
  <title>Azure Storage Static Website</title>
</head>

<body>
  <h1>Welcome to Azure Storage Static Website</h1>
    <p>
      This is a simple static website hosted on Azure
      Storage.
    </p>
```

```
<p>
   For more information, visit
   <a href="https://docs.microsoft.com/en-us/azure/storage/
   blobs/storage-blob-static-website">
      Static website hosting in Azure Storage
   </a>.
</p>
<script src="./script.js"></script>
</body>
</html>
```

As you can see, we're adding a `<script>` tag, which will point to the root directory of our application.

2. Our script will be a single `console.log()` command, which will print text to the console in the browser:

```
console.log('Hey, I am a JavaScript file!');
```

3. Now, let's upload our file:

```
az storage blob upload \
--account-name <storage-account-name> \
--container-name "$web" \
--file index.html \
--name index.html
   --overwrite

az storage blob upload \
--account-name <storage-account-name> \
--container-name "$web" \
--file script.html \
--name script.html
```

Note that we're using the `--overwrite` parameter in the first command. It instructs the Azure CLI to change the content of the file if it already exists.

4.   Once the upload commands have finished running, reload your static website in your browser. If you access its console (*F12* in most browsers), you'll be able to see the text we're printing using JavaScript:

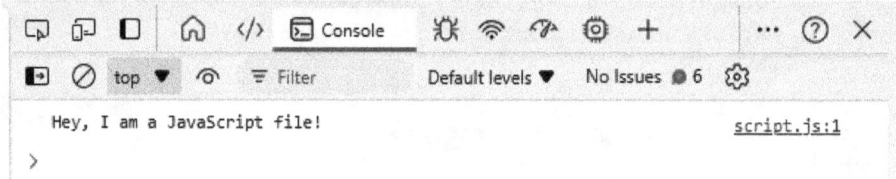

Figure 4.3 – Simple text generated by the JavaScript script loaded in the static website

As you can see, there's nothing that prevents you from incorporating full frameworks (such as React, Angular, or Vue) into your static website and hosting it in Azure using Azure Storage. No additional configuration is needed, which makes the whole setup extremely simple.

> **Note**
>
> You might be wondering what will happen if you start implementing routing in your static website. Because you can't override the default rewrite rules so that they always point to your base URL in Azure Storage, you may find that the UX of your application struggles as users will always need to access the main document of the website. One of the mitigations for this is implementing the redirect in the 404 document or using the same logic in both places so that the 404 (Not Found) document can still properly render your web application.

There's one additional topic that's important to cover regarding static websites, but unfortunately, it's outside the scope of this book. If you want to learn more about integrating static websites with CDN, take a look at this documentation: `https://learn.microsoft.com/en-us/azure/cdn/cdn-create-a-storage-account-with-cdn`.

As you can see, static websites in Azure Storage are great in simpler scenarios, when you don't need advanced features such as authentication, configuration management, or backends. In the next section, we're going to discuss Azure Static Web Apps, which offers those capabilities and is designed to handle more advanced scenarios.

Using Azure Static Web Apps to host your application

At the beginning of this chapter, we started discussing Azure's capabilities for hosting static web applications by introducing static websites in Azure Storage. If you went through that part, you should already be aware that this solution, while simple and quick to implement, is missing some key components needed for a more advanced application. The next few sections are going to cover Azure Static Web Apps – a service that's specifically designed to host static web applications and provide the necessary integrations.

Introduction to Azure Static Web Apps

Azure Static Web Apps is a managed service available in Microsoft Azure that you can leverage to host an application that doesn't require a *traditional* backend. This means that it runs in your customer's browser (hence you'll be limited to using technologies such as HTML, CSS, and JavaScript). It offers a useful set of features that come in handy in various scenarios:

- Seamless authentication provider integration (including Microsoft Entra ID and GitHub)
- GitHub/Azure DevOps integration
- Integrated API support (for handling additional use cases, such as proxies or secrets)
- Support for configuration values (application settings) – we discussed them in *Chapter 3*
- A globally distributed application source for improved performance

Azure Static Web Apps is an ideal solution for cases such as SPAs, common static websites (which could be generated with tools such as Hugo), or typical web applications written in JavaScript.

To understand this service better, let's discuss all the capabilities and features that it offers, starting with hosting plans.

Hosting plans

Azure Static Web Apps offers the following hosting plans:

- **Free**
- **Standard**
- **Dedicated**

Each hosting plan offers a slightly different set of features and quotas. The great thing about them is that you're free to change your plan when needed. In other words, you could start with a Free hosting plan and then switch to the Standard one.

> **Note**
>
> The Premium hosting plan for Azure Static Web Apps was in preview when this chapter was written. It comes with similar capabilities to the Standard plan but guarantees data residency. It may come in handy in regulated areas such as banking or finance, but the downside is that it doesn't provide global distribution for your website's content.

When working with Azure Static Web Apps, you need to consider the following elements:

- How many staging environments do you need for your application
- The maximum application size

- How many custom domains you'd like to have

- Whether you need integration with Azure Functions as your backend (so that you can host a dedicated API for your static web application)

- Whether you need custom registrations for authentication

- Whether your application must be hosted privately and accessed via Private Endpoint

If you want to learn about the exact values of each hosting plan, feel free to go to `https://learn.microsoft.com/en-us/azure/static-web-apps/plans`.

> **Note**
> Remember that the Free hosting plan doesn't offer any SLAs, meaning it's not suited for production scenarios.

Now, let's talk about the configuration capabilities of Azure Static Web Apps.

Configuration concepts

Conceptually, Azure Static Web Apps offers several different methods for configuring your application:

- Application configuration

- Build configuration

- Application settings

As these concepts may be a little bit unclear at the moment, let's try to explain them in detail. Application configuration is a static configuration defined in a dedicated file named `staticwebapp.config.json`. It can be used for several different capabilities, such as routing, networking, authorization, or even HTTP response overrides. This is one of the most crucial components in the whole setup as it covers everything that was missing from static websites when we were using Azure Storage. As this file may become quite big, let's split the examples into a separate section (you can find a reference to all the configuration values in the documentation: `https://learn.microsoft.com/en-us/azure/static-web-apps/configuration`).

We'll start with routes in our application. A route is part of the URL a user accesses when they want to interact with your application. In static web applications, URLs are often handled by the appropriate router, which is provided by a frontend framework (such as Angular or React). Since some routes may require special treatment, we may need to configure them in Azure Static Web Apps.

This is how you'd define possible routes, along with their controls:

```
{
  "trailingSlash": "auto",
  "routes": [
    {
      "route": "/profile*",
      "allowedRoles": ["authenticated"]
    },
    {
      "route": "/images/*",
      "headers": {
        "cache-control": "must-revalidate, max-age=15770000"
      }
    },
    {
      "route": "/api/*",
      "methods": ["PUT", "POST", "PATCH", "DELETE"],
      "allowedRoles": ["administrator"]
    },
    {
      "route": "/login",
      "rewrite": "/.auth/login/github"
    },
    {
      "route": "/logout",
      "redirect": "/.auth/logout"
    }
  ]
}
```

As you can see, we're allowed to configure several different aspects when it comes to routing:

- `allowedRoles`: This may help you limit access to a specific role.
- `rewrite`: This will help you rewrite a request to another endpoint.
- `methods`: This will limit which HTTP methods are allowed.

It's a quite powerful feature that can significantly enhance security and help you avoid workarounds in your code.

> **Note**
> Remember that roles will only work for HTTP requests. This means that if your web application is using client-side routing, Azure Static Web Apps won't be able to control access as no HTTP request will ever be sent to the backend.

The next thing that can be configured in the file is the navigation fallback:

```
"navigationFallback": {
    "rewrite": "/",
    "exclude": ["/images/*.{png,jpg,gif}", "/css/*", "/static/*"]
}
```

As per this example, navigation fallback will be helpful if you need to instruct your website not to rewrite requests if they link to static resources. This is a common scenario for SPAs – most frameworks use client-side routing, and if a user refreshes a page in their browser, they should stay on the same page. This can be done by rewriting all the requests to the base URL or file but leaving static content with no rewrite so that the paths to the static files stay the same.

Another section we could use in the configuration is for response overrides:

```
"responseOverrides": {
    "400": {
        "rewrite": "/bad-request"
    },
    "401": {
        "redirect": "/login",
        "statusCode": 302
    },
    "403": {
        "rewrite": "/forbidden"
    },
    "404": {
        "rewrite": "/not-found"
    }
}
```

At the time of writing, Azure Static Web Apps supports the 400, 401, 403, and 404 HTTP status codes. As you can see, you're allowed to use either `redirect` or `rewrite` for the response. The choice depends on the functionality you're implementing (`redirect` if you want to restart the flow and `rewrite` if you want to keep the existing response and just change the resulting URL).

Azure Static Web Apps also allows you to configure MIME types if your application uses custom files. Note that these aren't the default types that are supported by this service:

```
"mimeTypes": {
    ".json": "text/json"
}
```

Configuring this section allows you to tell the service and the browser what type of file it should expect when it loads static content.

> **Note**
>
> Remember that the application configuration we're discussing here applies to servers only. When a browser accesses your web application, the server will respond with the content of the application (static files such as HTML, CSS, or JavaScript), and, based on the configuration, additional headers or MIME types. If your application leverages client-side routing, you may still need to implement several of those features on your own as the requests will never reach the server.

If you want to learn about all the possible configuration values, take a look at the official documentation: `https://learn.microsoft.com/en-us/azure/static-web-apps/configuration`. Next, we're going to cover the build configuration.

Build configuration

Azure Static Web Apps can be automatically built using one of the supported CI/CD tools (Azure DevOps or GitHub Actions). The build configuration allows you to define the important steps and parameters for the build pipeline:

- The source code of the application
- The source code for the API (backend)
- The output location for the application's artifacts
- The build command for both the application and API
- The build command's timeout

The build configuration's filename and location depend on the CI/CD system in use:

- `.github/workflows/azure-static-web-apps-<RANDOM_VALUE>.yml` for GitHub Actions
- `azure-pipelines.yml` for Azure DevOps

The process of building the application is performed by the native task:

- `Azure/static-web-apps-deploy`: GitHub Actions
- `AzureStaticWebApp`: Azure DevOps

Technically, these tasks are defined like so. Let's start with GitHub Actions:

```
- name: Build And Deploy
      uses: Azure/static-web-apps-deploy@v1
      with:
        azure_static_web_apps_api_token: ${{ secrets.AZURE_STATIC_
        WEB_APPS_API_TOKEN }}
        action: "upload"
        app_location: "src"
        api_location: "api"
        output_location: "out"
```

Here's the configuration when using Azure DevOps:

```
- task: AzureStaticWebApp@0
    inputs:
      app_location: 'src'
      api_location: 'api'
      output_location: out
      azure_static_web_apps_api_token: $(deployment_token)
```

As you can see, both tasks are similar in structure – in fact, the only difference is the overall syntax, which is unique to the tool in use. There's also one important parameter that we need to discuss: `azure_static_web_apps_api_token`. When an application is deployed to Azure Static Web Apps, you need to authorize the operation. You can do this using **deployment tokens**. They're generated per application and are considered secrets, so you can't include them in the source code of your pipeline. For both Azure DevOps and GitHub Actions, you should store your deployment token securely to prevent unauthorized access.

> **Note**
>
> From a security point of view, leaking a deployment token will be considered a severe issue. Anyone who obtains the token will be able to upload malicious code to Azure Static Web Apps that can be used for phishing attacks.

During the build phase, you may also need to configure environment variables. This is important if the process relies on additional values that are considered dynamic (for example, they change per environment) or are considered secrets and can't be mounted directly into the script. Here's an example regarding Azure DevOps:

```
inputs:
  app_location: 'src'
  api_location: 'api'
  output_location: 'public'
  azure_static_web_apps_api_token: $(deployment_token)
env:
  MY_SECRET: $(SECRET_VALUE)
  ENVIRONMENT: 'test'
```

Once the variables have been mounted, they will be accessible to your builder via standard Node.js methods (for instance, using `process.env`).

Now, let's discuss the last configuration component: application settings.

Application settings

We discussed the application settings in Azure Web Apps in *Chapter 3*. The concept is similar for Azure Static Web Apps. However, since we're talking about applications that aren't dynamic, once downloaded by the end user, they won't be able to leverage the application settings defined at the service level. This is why this feature isn't meant for the application itself, but rather its backend (API). In this section, we'll focus on using and configuring them in a way that helps your static website provide an enhanced experience.

Application settings can easily be configured using the Azure CLI or ARM templates/Bicep. For the Azure CLI, you can use the following command:

```
az staticwebapp appsettings set \
--name <static-webapp-id> \
--setting-names "foo=bar"
```

We'll cover that in the next part of this chapter, so please be patient. Once Azure Static Web Apps' settings have been configured, you can access them in the same way as environment variables defined for the build configuration:

```
const connectionString = process.env.DB_CONN_STRING;
```

As you can see, from an implementation point of view, using application settings doesn't change a thing. You're still allowed to work with the same methods and functions as with typical JavaScript applications. The only difference is the source of the data, which, in this case, would be the Azure Static Web Apps service.

Now that we've covered some of the basics of working with Azure Static Web Apps, let's switch our focus to building and deploying an example application.

Working with Azure Static Web Apps locally

Azure Static Web Apps comes with a dedicated CLI tool that you can use to integrate the local environment with the service in the cloud. This CLI comes with a set of useful features to help you in development:

- A local server for running the application
- An authentication/authorization server mock
- Proxies for the frontend development server and API endpoints (backend)

To get started with the CLI, we need to perform a set of predefined steps. They're described in detail here:

1. To get started, you'll need to install the tool locally. You can do this using the following command:

   ```
   npm install -g @azure/static-web-apps-cli
   ```

2. Once it's been installed, you need to prepare your local environment. Note that swa in the following command stands for Static Web Apps:

   ```
   mkdir swa-app
   cd swa-app
   swa init
   ```

3. Then, let the CLI detect the configuration of your application. Once you're satisfied with it, just hit *Enter* to complete the process.

> **Tip**
> The command we're using for installation will install the CLI globally. Note that you may need to use sudo to have it installed in the shared directory on your computer.

4. Now, let's try to run the server:

   ```
   swa start
   Welcome to Azure Static Web Apps CLI (1.1.10)
   (node:228624) [DEP0040] DeprecationWarning: The `punycode`
   module is deprecated. Please use a userland alternative instead.
   (Use `node --trace-deprecation ...` to show where the warning
   was created)
   Using configuration "swa-app" from file:
      /home/thecloudtheory/azure-for-developers/ch04/swa-app/
   swa-cli.config.json
   ```

```
[swa] (node:228642) [DEP0040] DeprecationWarning: The `punycode`
module is deprecated. Please use a userland alternative instead.
[swa] (Use `node --trace-deprecation ...` to show where the
warning was created)
[swa]
[swa] Serving static content:
[swa]    /home/thecloudtheory/azure-for-developers/ch04/swa-app
[swa]
[swa] Azure Static Web Apps emulator started at http://
localhost:4280. Press CTRL+C to exit.
[swa]
```

As you can see, the server (emulator) is now available locally under a specific port (4280).
When you access the website in your browser, you should see the following page:

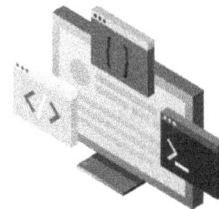

Figure 4.4 – 404 page returned by the SWA server

5. The reason why we see the 404 error page is that we haven't set any content for our application
    yet. Let's change that – create a file named index.html and save it in the swa-app directory
    we created for this exercise:

```html
<!DOCTYPE html>
<html lang="en">
<head>
    <meta charset="UTF-8">
    <meta name="viewport"
          content="width=device-width, initial-scale=1.0">
    <title>Azure Static Web App</title>
</head>
<body>
    <h1>Welcome to Azure Static Web App</h1>
```

```
      </body>
      </html>
```

Now, when you refresh the page in your browser, you should see our index page instead of the 404 error page:

←   C   ⓘ   localhost:4280

Welcome to Azure Static Web App

Figure 4.5 – Index page server created by the SWA server

From now on, you can develop your application based on your expectations. You can add additional frameworks, content, and configuration. Your local environment will be emulating the behavior of the website as it was hosted in Azure.

Next, let's see how we can mock authentication and authorization with our local server hosted by the SWA CLI.

Enabling authorization and authentication

As mentioned previously, Azure Static Web Apps has native integration for Microsoft Entra ID and GitHub as identity providers. The SWA CLI enables you to emulate those providers, so you can test your application locally without interacting with the actual service. Let's see how to do that:

1. To begin the test, let's add two links to our index.html file:

    ```
    <body>
      <h1>Welcome to Azure Static Web App</h1>
      <h2>Login</h2>
      <p>
        <a href="/.auth/login/aad">Login with Entra ID</a><br>
        <a href="/.auth/login/github">Login with GitHub</a>
      </p>
    </body>
    ```

2. Once you add those, refresh the page in your browser and click on the first one. You should see the following page:

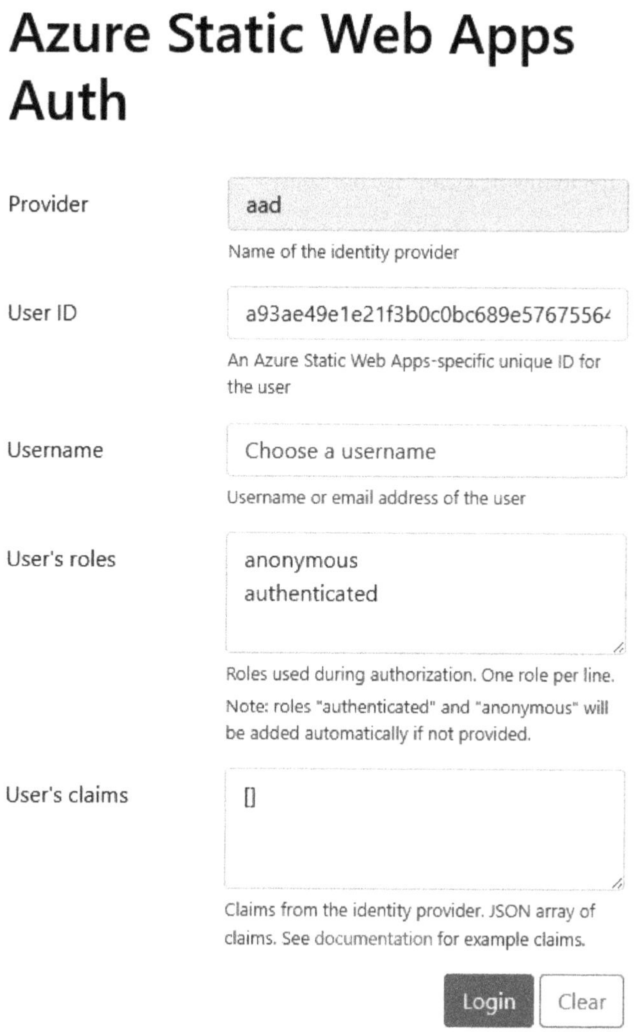

Azure Static Web Apps Auth

Provider

aad

Name of the identity provider

User ID

a93ae49e1e21f3b0c0bc689e5767556∠

An Azure Static Web Apps-specific unique ID for the user

Username

Choose a username

Username or email address of the user

User's roles

anonymous
authenticated

Roles used during authorization. One role per line.

Note: roles "authenticated" and "anonymous" will be added automatically if not provided.

User's claims

[]

Claims from the identity provider. JSON array of claims. See documentation for example claims.

Login   Clear

Figure 4.6 – The authentication/authorization screen provided by the SWA CLI

As you can see, the request to the `/.auth/login` page is intercepted by the emulator and allows you to provide details of a user, who will now be considered authenticated. Based on the roles and claims, you could build an authorization mechanism for securing certain areas of your application or limit the visibility of some concepts. You can consider claims to be permissions that have been assigned for a particular access token. They can be used to control the flow of your application or limit access to a page or a section for a user.

> **Note**
> While Azure Static Web Apps may provide authentication and authorization mechanisms, how you implement the logic based on those components is your responsibility.

3.   Let's try to define the following claims for our user:

```
[{
"name":"User"
}]
```

4.   Then, click the **Login** button. You'll be redirected to the `index` page of our application. However, this time, the user is already signed in.

5.   Let's try to load the data by making some changes. First, add the following block to your `index.html` file:

```html
<div id="user-info-block" style="display: none;">
  <h2>User Info</h2>
  <p id="user-info">
    <strong>User ID:</strong> <span id="user-id"></span><br>
    <strong>User Name:</strong> <span id="user-name"></span><br>
    <strong>User Email:</strong> <span id="user-email">
      </span><br>
    <strong>User Roles:</strong> <span id="user-roles"></span>
  </p>
  </div>
```

6.   Next, create a file named `script.js` and include the following script there:

```javascript
async function getUserInfo() {
    const response = await fetch('/.auth/me');
    const payload = await response.json();
    const { clientPrincipal } = payload;
    return clientPrincipal;
}

(async () => {
    const user = await getUserInfo();

    if (user) {
        document.getElementById('user-id').innerText =
            user.userId;
        document.getElementById('user-name').innerText =
            user.claims[0].name;
        document.getElementById('user-email').innerText =
```

```
      user.userDetails;
    document.getElementById('user-roles').innerText =
      user.userRoles;
    document.getElementById('user-info-block').style.display =
      'block';
  } else {
    document.getElementById('user-info-block').style.display =
      'none';
  }
})();
```

7. Finally, let's include the script using the `<script>` block:

```
<script src="./script.js"></script>
```

8. As a result, once you refresh your browser, you should see the following web page:

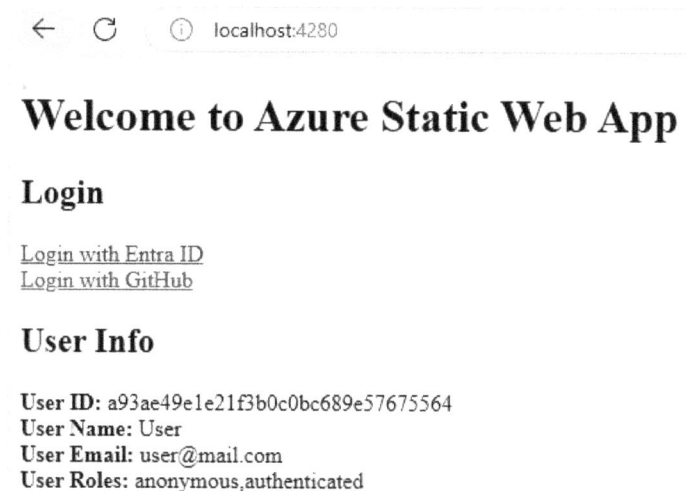

Figure 4.7 – Authenticated user information presented on the web page

As you can see, everything is handled by the SWA CLI server. The mocked authentication and authorization provider is especially helpful in scenarios where you need to quickly change user details such as roles or claims. Without the mock, you'd need to constantly make changes to the user's object within your provider's directory. This is a cumbersome and difficult-to-automate process. With the local server, you can modify the user's attributes within seconds simply by re-authenticating.

As the next step, we'll discuss the API backends that are available for Azure Static Web Apps.

Integrating Azure Static Web Apps with Azure App Service

Azure Static Web Apps allows you to host additional components called API backends. They have several use cases, but generally speaking, they're useful if you need to implement functionality that needs to be hosted as a sidecar for your application. This includes the following scenarios:

- Building a proxy for the actual backend of your application
- Interacting with stateful resources such as databases
- Handling secrets

When it comes to integration, Azure Static Web Apps supports the following services as backends for your APIs:

- Azure Functions
- Azure API Management
- Azure App Service
- Azure Container Apps

The important thing here is that all these services can host a fully customizable backend (which is then considered a **bring-your-own** (**BYO**) backend). Azure Functions can be hosted as either a managed service (which is natively integrated with Azure Static Web Apps) or as a standalone application.

For this chapter, we'll focus on Azure Functions and Azure App Services as our main hosts.

Using Azure Functions as a backend

In this exercise, we'll learn how to use Azure Functions as a backend:

1. To get started with Azure Functions as a backend for our static website, we'll need to create a function app locally. Run the following command to do that (make sure you're in the swa-app directory you created in the previous exercise):

    ```
    mkdir api
    cd api
    func init swa-app-api --worker-runtime javascript --model V4
    func new templates
    ```

2. When asked, select HTTP trigger as your function template. The generator should create a file named httpTrigger.js in the api/src/functions directory. This function is named message and can be called using either the GET or POST HTTP call. It will load the value of the name key from a query string and include it in the response string. The function should look like this:

```
const { app } = require('@azure/functions');

app.http('message', {
    methods: ['GET', 'POST'],
    authLevel: 'anonymous',
    handler: async (request, context) => {
        context.log(
            `Http function processed request for url "${request.
            url}"`);
        const name =
            request.query.get('name') ||
            await request.text() ||
            'world';
        return { body: `Hello, ${name}!` };
    }
});
```

3. Now, let's run our application by using the following command:

```
swa start --api-location api
```

4. Upon initialization, the SWA CLI will compile our backend for the frontend application. To complete the setup, we also need to make a call from the static website to the backend. Let's implement this.

Tip

Azure Functions Core Tools only supports certain versions of Node.js. If you need to work with multiple versions of that runtime, you need to install a valid version individually (Windows) or use a tool such as n, which can be installed using the sudo npm install -g n command.

The call to our API backend will be a simple HTTP request. Let's add the following lines to our index.html file:

```
<div id="message-block">
  <h2>Message</h2>
  <p id="message"></p>
</div>
```

```
<script src="./script.js"></script>
<script>
  (async function() {
    const response = await fetch(`/api/message`);
    const message = await response.text();
    document.querySelector('#message').textContent = message;
  }());
</script>
```

As you can see, we're using the `fetch()` method to get a response from our API. Then, we're just using the response value as the input for our HTML. Note that we don't need to provide additional details to discover the API endpoint – the SWA CLI takes care of that as part of the emulation.

Now, let's learn how we can use Azure App Service as our backend.

Using Azure App Service as a backend

There are multiple benefits of using Azure App Service over Azure Functions when it comes to hosting a backend. However, remember that those solutions aren't supposed to exclude each other – the usage depends on the use case. While Azure Functions is perfect for hosting simple and robust APIs, which can serve your application individually, Azure App Service can be considered a generic backend that's shared across multiple applications. As the concept of linking an Azure App Service backend is slightly different compared to integrated Azure Functions, we need to discuss the details of this integration.

Deploying Azure Static Web Apps

To link backends with Azure Static Web Apps, we need to deploy it using the Standard plan. Remember that such a plan is no longer free – if you want to save money, remove it (or downgrade it) immediately after completing this exercise. We'll start with the following Azure CLI command:

```
az staticwebapp create \
 --name <static-webapp-name> \
 --resource-group <resource-group-name> \
 --sku Standard
```

Once the resource has been created in Azure, we can try to link the backend.

Linking Azure App Service backend

To instruct Azure Static Web Apps to use Azure App Service as a backend, we need to update the configuration of our instance:

1. To link the backend, we can use one more Azure CLI command:

```
az staticwebapp backends link \
--name <static-webapp-name> \
--resource-group <resource-group-name> \
--backend-resource-id <resource-id>
```

2. As you can see, to complete the link operation, we need to find the resource ID of our backend. To do that, we need to select an existing Azure Web App instance or create a new one. For this integration, any web application that can return HTTP responses will suffice. For instance, I used the following command to create a .NET Web API application with the existing template:

```
mkdir backend
dotnet new webapi -n backend -o ./
```

Such an application consists of a single endpoint that returns a hardcoded weather forecast. In your case, you can use any programming stack as you wish – as mentioned previously, the API backend functionality for Azure Static Web Apps is technology-agnostic. This means that so long as you can host your application in Azure App Service, you'll be able to integrate the backend with your static website.

3. To deploy the API application, we need to create an Azure Web App. Please refer to *Chapter 3*, where we discussed multiple deployment methods if you need assistance. Once the application has been deployed, you can fetch its resource ID by using the following command:

```
az webapp show \
--name <webapp-name> \
-g <resource-group-name> \
--query id
```

4. Once you have the resource ID, you can run the az staticwebapp backend link command.

> **Note**
>
> When linking the backend to your Azure Static Web Apps instance, make sure that the Azure Web App instance runs on Azure App Service plan B1 or higher. What's more, if your backend is in a different region than the static website, use the --backend-region parameter to indicate in which region the backend has been deployed.

You should receive an output similar to mine:

```
{
    "backendResourceId": "/subscriptions/…/resourceGroups/afd-rg/
providers/Microsoft.Web/sites/…",
    "createdOn": "2024-07-07T13:17:44.451843+00:00",
    "id": "/subscriptions/…/resourceGroups/afd-rg/providers/
Microsoft.Web/staticSites/…/builds/default/linkedBackends/…",
    "kind": null,
    "location": "Central US",
    "name": "afd04",
    "provisioningState": "Succeeded",
    "region": "westeurope",
    "resourceGroup": "afd-rg",
    "type": "Microsoft.Web/staticSites/builds/linkedBackends"
}
```

Once all commands have been completed successfully, your Azure Static Web Apps instance will be able to connect with the backend since it was part of your application. Let's test the connection.

Deploying Azure Static Web Apps

In the previous exercises, we created a simple static website that used an API backend written in Azure Functions. Now that we're going to be using the BYO backend, we need to introduce a couple of changes:

1. First, let's change the endpoint we're calling (in my case, it'll be /weatherforecast):

    ```
    <script>
      (async function() {
        const response = await fetch(`/api/weatherforeacst`);
        const message = await response.json();
        document.querySelector('#message').textContent = message;
      }());
    </script>
    ```

2. Next, we must instruct the service to use the linked backend by providing a configuration in the workflow configuration file. Introduce the following change if you're deploying the application using Azure DevOps or GitHub Actions (here's an example for the former):

    ```
    inputs:
    app_location: 'src'
    api_location: ''
    output_location: 'public'
    skip_api_build: true
    azure_static_web_apps_api_token: $(deployment_token)
    ```

Note that we're providing an empty string as the value of the `api_location` parameter and also skipping the API build (as it's not part of our application). Once the application has been deployed, you can access the endpoint provided by the API backend – you should see that your service fetches the data without any issues and that the data is returned as expected.

Finally, let's talk about use cases for Azure Static Web Apps.

Learning about use cases

In this chapter, you had a chance to compare the capabilities of Azure Static Web Apps with the ones offered by Azure Storage. As you've seen, Azure Static Web Apps is designed to be a fully managed environment that you can use for static website development. The fact that it offers a native emulator for the web server and identity provider is especially helpful in dynamic and complex setups. Thanks to this feature, you should be able to easily start working on your application and allow development to take place in isolation from the live components.

If we compare the hosting options for static websites, you'll see that Azure offers several different environments:

- Azure Storage Static Website
- Azure Static Web Apps
- Azure App Service
- Azure Container Apps
- Azure Kubernetes Service

All these services can be used to host your static website. The difference here is the actual effort needed to get started, deploy, and maintain an application. We could characterize those services as follows:

- If you want the simplest possible option for hosting small static websites such as landing pages, blogs, or portfolios, Azure Storage is the best option.
- If you want to simplify development and operations and give your developers a place where they can easily develop the application without interacting with the existing infrastructure, Azure Static Web Apps is the best choice.
- If you want to have a generic service for hosting web applications, which is a well-known cloud component with lots of use cases, great support, and simple configuration, you should go for Azure App Service.
- If you need to containerize your application but don't want to manage the underlying infrastructure plus have flexible pricing based on usage, Azure Container Apps is something you should consider.
- For enterprise scenarios, where you aim for high availability, compliance, low-level control, and flexibility, choose Azure Kubernetes Service.

When making a choice, you also need to consider how your application will be deployed. When we were talking about Azure Storage and Azure Static Web Apps, we discussed that those services offer slightly different deployment models – this will become important when you wish to work in a team and develop an operating model for the application:

- Containers give you flexibility and portability, so using Azure Container Apps, Azure App Services, or Azure Kubernetes Service as your hosting platform for static websites will be beneficial in such cases.

- Azure Static Web Apps can natively integrate with version control systems, which allows you to quickly link repositories with the hosting environment.

- If you want to use a plain old FTP-like deployment model with files, Azure Storage supports such needs.

As you can see, depending on your needs, you can achieve the same results with different services. The only thing that isn't supported by static websites hosted using Azure Storage is integration with backends (such as APIs or databases). To have such functionality implemented using that service, you'll need to host a backend or proxy to a backend using one of the other services.

That's all for *Chapter 4*! Let's summarize our findings and see what awaits in the next chapter.

Summary

In this chapter, we completed various exercises to help us understand the capabilities of Azure when it comes to hosting static websites. We talked about Azure Storage and Azure Static Web Apps as the two main components you can use to deploy and host static applications. Then, we compared their features to understand whether there are any trade-offs when using one of those services. We also discussed how other Azure services may help when it comes to hosting static websites.

In the next chapter, we're going to talk about Azure Functions. We briefly mentioned it in this chapter as one of the services we can use as an API backend in Azure Static Web Apps. There, we'll talk more about the **Function-as-a-Service (FaaS)** approach, serverless, and building managed APIs.

5

Going Serverless with Azure Functions

In the previous chapters, we focused on developing web applications using traditional services, which allow us to host both our application's code and its framework. Those services give you lots of flexibility and options but also require additional effort to configure the underlying infrastructure (even if it's minimized when compared to hosting options based on an on-premises model). If you want to purely focus on app development, it's possible to leverage serverless platforms and the **Function-as-a-Service** (**FaaS**) model, where you deploy only the parts of your application that bring actual value. One of Azure's services allowing you to do so is Azure Functions.

In this chapter, we will delve into new topics, as we're going to introduce the first serverless service. Through the course of the chapter, you'll see that services such as Azure Functions aren't very different when compared to Azure App Service. It gives you a way to bootstrap your services without obsolete boilerplate code, which is important in certain scenarios such as cutting down time to market for your application.

In this chapter, we're going to cover the following main topics:

- Understanding the differences between Azure App Service and Azure Functions
- Developing applications using Azure Functions
- Using input and output bindings
- Designing an application using Azure Functions
- Building a deployment pipeline
- Learning about use cases

Technical requirements

To perform exercises from this chapter, you'll need the following software:

- IDE of your choice (for example, Visual Studio Code)

- Azure CLI

- Azure Functions Core Tools

- Azurite

The source code for this chapter can be found here: `https://github.com/PacktPublishing/Azure-for-Developers-Third-Edition/tree/main/ch05`

Understanding the differences between Azure App Service and Azure Functions

When it comes to developing web applications, you always need to provide the components:

- Web server (such as IIS, Nginx, or Apache)

- Web framework (ASP.NET, Spring, Express.js, or similar)

- The application's code

Most cloud services that allow you to host such applications provide a very specific web server or framework option, or require you to select the appropriate combination for both. In Azure, when using Azure App Service, you need to select an **Operating System** (**OS**) and a programming language stack with a required version, as well as pack the web framework as part of your application. This approach has several benefits:

- Greater flexibility and control over the code base

- Ability to provide custom middleware

- Easier integration with external components

As with every solution, it also has some disadvantages:

- Longer time to market due to a greater number of prerequisites to meet

- Handling boilerplate code, which provides little value to the overall solution but is required to get started with an application

- More difficult setup and deployment as you need to track and manage your web server and code base

To cope with those challenges, cloud providers started to offer a dedicated platform called serverless. Serverless, contrary to the name, doesn't mean that there are no servers. It's rather a different hosting model that allows you to leverage a much more flexible pricing model (based on usage) and also simplifies management via greater abstraction over cloud infrastructure. In serverless services, there are no more concepts such as servers, CPU, memory, or storage – instead, you're given a set of dedicated metrics, which are based on the general usage of a service. Those metrics may be different for each serverless service but have one common trait – they can be adjusted with ease and scale dynamically with your application.

One of those serverless services in Azure is Azure Functions. It is also considered a FaaS platform (as opposed to Azure App Service, which is **Platform-as-a-Service (PaaS)**. FaaS is a unique hosting model, which gives you the following benefits:

- Simplifies development thanks to a dedicated framework integrated with the platform
- Flexible pricing model, which enables you to pay only for usage (in some scenarios, it allows you to cut down the cost of infrastructure almost to nothing)
- Native bindings, which allow you to integrate with other Azure services with ease and with minimal config
- Event-based architecture thanks to triggers, which can listen to changes in other services and decouple your application from infrastructure

Besides those high-level features of Azure Functions, there's also one more important concept, which is related to hosting and computing allocated for your application. In Azure App Service, we needed to deploy the Azure App Service plan as our underlying infrastructure providing CPU, memory, and storage for our application. In Azure Functions, the Azure App Service plan is still valid – but it's only one of all available hosting models for that service.

To better understand the difference between Azure App Service and Azure Functions, we could characterize the main features of those services:

- **Azure App Service**: Hosting web applications and APIs; scalability based on Azure App Service plan; fixed cost; predictable performance
- **Azure Functions**: Event-driven; you can select a fixed and predictable hosting model or pay-per-consumption; ideal for lightweight APIs, jobs, and background tasks

Let's now describe the available hosting models for Azure Functions in detail.

Hosting model – Azure App Service plan

The Azure App Service plan is the traditional hosting model for both Azure Web Apps and Azure Functions. As Azure Functions is conceptually based on Azure App Service, it offers the same capabilities and is limited to the same things as Azure Web Apps when the Azure App Service plan is used as a hosting model. When you want to use Azure Functions and integrate it with an Azure App Service plan, you'll be given the following capabilities:

- All your functions can run indefinitely, making it a great option for long-running jobs.
- You have a fixed monthly price – sudden spikes in web traffic won't affect your monthly bill.
- You have stable performance, which can be scaled up/in when needed.
- You have control over scale-up/out/in operations.
- If **Always On** is enabled, your application won't be affected by cold starts (unless your deployment method requires a restart).

However, the Azure App Service plan makes Azure Functions *less serverless*. As you cannot benefit from a flexible pricing and scalability model, the only benefit here will be the provided web framework. Still, this hosting option is a viable choice in many scenarios that require predictability and a stable hosting environment.

Hosting model – Consumption plan

When you want to go truly serverless, a **Consumption plan** is what you need for Azure Functions. When hosting your functions with that plan, you don't control the underlying infrastructure and let the platform do its job. This means that your instance of Azure Functions will be priced based on usage. Scale-out/in operations will also be managed via the platform, so the operating model of that hosting model is greatly simplified.

> **Note**
> When the Consumption plan is used, a scale-up operation isn't possible as there's no specific compute tier provided.

With a consumption plan, you can achieve a setup in which you will pay almost nothing for your application. As the pricing in that model is based on CPU and memory used (this metric is called *GB-s*, which stands as an artificial metric based on used CPU time and memory utilization per second), you can model your application to make the most of it. This gives you lots of flexibility and allows for aggressive cost optimizations, especially if the application you're building isn't supposed to run all the time.

Some great use cases for consumption plans are as follows:

- Schedule-based jobs that don't require lots of time to complete

- One-time business operations that scale with the number of your customers (such as user activation, sending welcome emails, or registering a webhook)

- Orchestrations, which can be divided into logical steps (this is achievable using Durable Functions, which we'll discuss later in the book)

When using a consumption plan, always remember its limitations:

- You cannot fully control its scaling capabilities.

- You shouldn't try to keep your functions "hot" as it reduces the benefit of a serverless hosting plan.

- Functions based on a consumption plan cannot be integrated with virtual networks.

- The max timeout for executing a function using a consumption plan is 10 minutes.

- You can have a maximum of 1,200 outbound connections per instance of the Azure Functions service.

If you feel that those limitations are too much, let's discuss another hosting option, which is called the **Premium plan**.

Hosting model – Premium plan

If you want to combine the flexibility of a consumption plan with more predictable performance and network integration, as well as longer runtime durations, you should consider the Premium plan for your functions. If this is your choice, you need to remember that the Premium plan offers slightly different pricing when compared to the consumption plan or App Service plan:

- You pay for the core seconds used by your functions.

- Additionally, you pay for memory allocated for functions.

Initially, this pricing seems similar to that offered by the Consumption plan. However, the consumption plan charges you for the number of executions and resource consumption (per second). Additionally, you cannot scale the Premium plan down to zero instances – you always need to have at least one active instance.

To cope with cold starts, the Premium plan offers you two different modes:

- **Always ready instances**
- **Prewarmed instances**

The difference between those modes is the cost allocation. As long as a prewarmed instance isn't utilized, you're not charged for it. Once your application starts to scale out, the prewarmed instance can be activated and as it becomes an active instance, it'll start to incur costs.

> **Note**
>
> Active and prewarmed instances need to be adjusted depending on your application's performance characteristics. There's no single pattern that could be applied to all workloads.

The Premium plan is also a good alternative if the maximum timeout (10 minutes) for the consumption plan isn't enough. With the Premium plan, you can run your functions for up to 30 minutes before they start to return timeouts.

Before we start the development of our first function, let's discuss one more hosting model – the **Flex Consumption** plan.

Hosting model – Flex Consumption plan

To address some limitations of the standard consumption plan, Azure started to offer one more hosting plan for Azure Functions, which is the Flex Consumption plan. This plan follows the same philosophy as the standard one but gives you more flexibility and allows for more customizations. It's also much better suited for production scenarios. There are some key elements that make a real difference here:

- The Flex Consumption plan supports virtual networks.
- It allows for configuring always ready instances.
- Additionally, it provides a better quota for a maximum of scale-out instances (200 in the consumption plan, 1,000 in the Flex Consumption plan).

When it comes to pricing, the Flex Consumption plan follows the same pattern as the consumption plan. The main difference is the presence of active instances. If you decide to have those, you can ensure that the Azure platform will have the necessary compute waiting to handle the incoming load.

> **Note**
>
> By the time this chapter was written (July 2024), the Flex Consumption plan was in public preview.

With this introduction, let's now switch to something more practical. We'll start with building and deploying our first Azure Functions instance to see how this service works.

Developing services using Azure Functions

As you will see, the development of applications and services using Azure Functions will be slightly different than "traditional" ones. The main difference is a dedicated programming model, which consists of both an SDK and runtime.

As Azure Functions comes with a dedicated development toolset, let's learn how you can use it to get started and create your first function:

1. In order to start developing with Azure Functions, you'll need to install **Azure Functions Core Tools** (you can find it at `https://learn.microsoft.com/en-us/azure/azure-functions/functions-run-local`) on your machine. This tool is needed to do the following:

    *   Install the Azure Functions CLI locally for function management.

    *   Install the required toolset for development.

    *   Integrate with plugins and extensions used in various IDEs (such as Visual Studio Code).

2. Once the toolset is installed, run the following command in your terminal:

    ```
    func -v
    ```

    As a result, you should see a version returned, such as the following:

    ```
    4.0.5907
    ```

    Note that Azure Functions offers multiple versions of its runtime. If you start developing your application, it's always worth starting with the most recent one. The version of the runtime affects the capabilities of your functions; hence, you will need to consult the documentation if you decide to deviate from the newest version available.

3. Let's initialize our project:

    ```
    mkdir <new-directory>
    cd <new-directory>
    func init
    ```

    As a result, Azure Functions Core Tools will ask you what worker runtime should be selected:

    ```
    Select a number for worker runtime:
    1. dotnet (isolated worker model)
    2. dotnet (in-process model)
    3. node
    4. python
    5. powershell
    6. custom
    ```

4. Depending on your choice, you need to select a different number and confirm it by pressing *Enter*. To get started, I'll choose `Node.js` as my runtime. Then, I'll choose `JavaScript` for the language and wait for the CLI to complete initialization.

> **Note**
>
> Choices available when using the CLI may differ depending on the selected runtime. Remember that some runtimes need to install certain dependencies before the boilerplate code is created – in that case, be patient as the operation may take several minutes.

5. As a result, on your computer, you should see an empty Azure Functions project created with no functions yet. To add your first function, let's use the following command:

```
func function new -name HTTPTriggerFunction
```

This time, you'll be given a set of several options available to select from:

```
Select a number for template:
1. Azure Blob Storage trigger
2. Azure Cosmos DB trigger
3. Durable Functions entity
4. Durable Functions orchestrator
5. Azure Blob Storage trigger (using Event Grid)
6. Azure Event Grid trigger
7. Azure Event Hub trigger
8. HTTP trigger
9. Azure Queue Storage trigger
10. Azure Service Bus Queue trigger
11. Azure Service Bus Topic trigger
12. Timer trigger
13. Dapr Publish Output Binding
14. Dapr Service Invocation Trigger
15. Dapr Topic Trigger
```

6. As we want to start with the most basic function (and we already called it `HTTPTriggerFunction`), let's select `HTTP trigger` from the list and press *Enter*. Now, when you go to your project directory, you will find `/src/functions/HTTPTriggerFunction.js` created with some boilerplate code:

```
const { app } = require('@azure/functions');

app.http('HTTPTriggerFunction', {
  methods: ['GET', 'POST'],
  authLevel: 'anonymous',
  handler: async (request, context) => {
```

```
        context.log(`Http function processed request for url
          "${request.url}"`);
        const name =
          request.query.get('name') ||
          await request.text() ||
          'world';
        return { body: `Hello, ${name}!` };
    }
});
```

7. Now, go to the main directory of your Azure Functions project in your terminal and run the following command:

    func host start

    This will start the Azure Functions runtime installed locally, which will be listening to incoming triggers. As we already defined a single trigger (HTTP request), we'll also see that there's a single endpoint available:

    ```
    Functions:
            HTTPTriggerFunction: [GET,POST] http://localhost:7071/
    api/HTTPTriggerFunction
    ```

8. Copy the URL presented in your terminal and use your browser to access it. You should see the same result as I did:

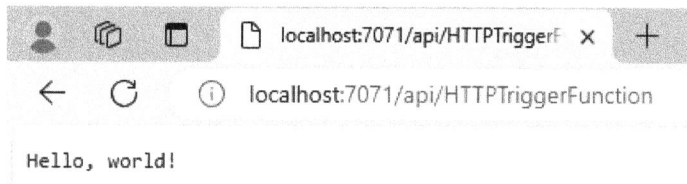

Figure 5.1 – Result of running a function triggered by an HTTP request

    In your terminal, you'll also see that the host running on your computer processed the request:

    ```
    [2024-07-17T12:46:09.328Z] Executing 'Functions.
    HTTPTriggerFunction' (Reason='This function was programmatically
    called via the host APIs.', Id=095f14cf-0c07-4871-b768-
    29e689caf0c2)
    [2024-07-17T12:46:09.422Z] Http function processed request for
    url "http://localhost:7071/api/HTTPTriggerFunction"
    [2024-07-17T12:46:09.499Z] Executed 'Functions.
    HTTPTriggerFunction' (Succeeded, Id=095f14cf-0c07-4871-b768-
    29e689caf0c2, Duration=196ms)
    ```

Congratulations, you just created and used your very first function! Let's try to use other triggers to see how they differ from each other.

Using the Timer trigger

The Timer trigger is a unique trigger. It allows you to define a schedule, based on which your functions will run. It's useful if you want to perform some operations periodically (scanning, performing clean-ups, or orchestrating a process). As this type of trigger requires storage configured for your function, make sure you have installed Azurite to be able to run the function locally. For detailed instructions for installation and an overall guide, look at the following documentation page:

https://learn.microsoft.com/en-us/azure/storage/common/storage-use-azurite

Once Azurite is available on your machine, make sure you have the following entry in your local.settings.json file:

```
{
  "IsEncrypted": false,
  "Values": {
    ...other values...
    "AzureWebJobsStorage": "UseDevelopmentStorage=true"
  }
}
```

We're using UseDevelopmentStorage=true to indicate that we want to use a local emulator for storage for our functions.

It can be created in the same way as you did for HTTP trigger – the only difference is that we are selecting the Timer trigger as the valid option for our scenario. As a result, the CLI will create the following function:

```
const { app } = require('@azure/functions');

app.timer('TimerTriggerFunction', {
    schedule: '0 */5 * * * *',
    handler: (myTimer, context) => {
        context.log('Timer function processed request.');
    }
});
```

This function will run every five minutes and display a text in the console attached to the host. Try to run your host to see what happens:

```
[2024-07-17T12:52:53.239Z] Worker process started and initialized.
[2024-07-17T12:52:53.368Z] The listener for function 'Functions.
TimerTriggerFunction' was unable to start.
```

```
[2024-07-17T12:52:53.369Z] The listener for function 'Functions.
TimerTriggerFunction' was unable to start. Microsoft.Azure.WebJobs.
Extensions.Timers.Storage: Could not create BlobContainerClient for
ScheduleMonitor.
```

As you can see, the host is unable to start because it's unable to create the `BlobContainerClient` object. The `Timer` trigger, to work correctly, requires integration with Azure Storage. To do so, you need to provide credentials for that service. There are two possibilities here:

- We can use a real Azure Storage account and either use access keys or your individual credentials. This can be cumbersome for typical local development.

- We can use an emulator – Azurite.

If Azurite is already available on your machine, you can run it using the following command:

```
azurite \
--silent \
--location <local-path-to-store-data> \
--debug <custom-path-for-debug-log>
```

Then, find the `local.settings.json` file in your Azure Functions project directory and set the `AzureWebJobsStorage` key value to the following:

```
{
  "IsEncrypted": false,
  "Values": {
    "FUNCTIONS_WORKER_RUNTIME": "node",
    "AzureWebJobsFeatureFlags": "EnableWorkerIndexing",
    "AzureWebJobsStorage": "UseDevelopmentStorage=true"
  }
}
```

Once all steps are completed, running your host locally should succeed. Now, we can wait five minutes and check whether the host console contains the text we expect:

```
[2024-07-17T13:02:02.413Z] Host lock lease acquired by instance ID '00
0000000000000000000000609398C'.
[2024-07-17T13:05:00.055Z] Executing 'Functions.TimerTriggerFunction'
(Reason='Timer fired at 2024-07-17T15:05:00.0177403+02:00',
Id=1fc3f4b4-5298-4012-83b7-14a62cd32f04)
[2024-07-17T13:05:00.125Z] Timer function processed request.
[2024-07-17T13:05:00.148Z] Executed 'Functions.TimerTriggerFunction'
(Succeeded, Id=1fc3f4b4-5298-4012-83b7-14a62cd32f04, Duration=119ms)
```

Azure Functions uses the NCRONTAB expression (https://github.com/atifaziz/ NCrontab) to configure the schedule for your functions triggered by a timer. To understand it better, let's consider a few examples:

- 0 */5 * * * *: Function runs every five minutes.

- 0 */1 * * * *: Function runs every minute.

- 0 0 10 * * *: Function runs every day at 10 AM.

- 0 0 10 * * 1-3: Function runs at 10 AM from Monday to Wednesday.

Depending on your needs, you should configure a different schedule. It's also important to make sure that a function completes before it's triggered once again. This is a common scenario if you're aiming for short intervals and, for some reason, a function is unable to be completed within the expected timeframe. In such a scenario, your functions will start to overlap. This doesn't need to be anything critical. However, if you're managing a stateful process via Azure Functions, the fact that the process overlaps may cause bugs. Unfortunately, Azure Functions doesn't offer any kind of semaphore, which would prevent it from running multiple functions in parallel – if you need such functionality, you'll need to implement it on your own (for instance, by using a single field in a database, which tells whether there's an ongoing function running or not).

We covered some basics related to the development of applications using Azure Functions. Let's extend that knowledge by discussing input and output bindings.

Using input and output bindings

As we have discussed, Azure Functions uses triggers to start the execution of the logic implemented by you. They're event-based services and should be used as such. Triggers are one of three main elements when it comes to building blocks for your functions:

- **Triggers** are used to define which event starts the execution of a function. You can have only one trigger per function.

- **Input bindings** allow you to inject additional data into your function each time it's triggered. You can have multiple input bindings in each function.

- **Output bindings** enable you to easily integrate the result of running your function with an external service and inject it into a database, queue, or blob storage.

The aim of bindings is to simplify integrations with other Azure services (or even third-party components), so you can focus on providing correct business logic via your code. They abstract away lots of low-level concepts such as authentication, authorization, listeners, or connection pools. As they seamlessly integrate with Azure Functions and are often delivered as a single package, it's possible to greatly simplify development and decouple your code base from infrastructure-related concepts.

> **Note**
>
> It's possible to write your own triggers and bindings. The best way to do this is to read how existing bindings are developed – you can find them on GitHub, for instance, at `https://github.com/Azure/azure-functions-dotnet-worker`.

Let's discuss how bindings are structured and how they can be configured for your functions.

Understanding triggers, input bindings, and output bindings

As mentioned previously, bindings in Azure Functions can be divided into three categories: triggers, inputs, and outputs. We already used triggers in this chapter by creating two functions. One was triggered by an HTTP request, the second by a timer. Triggers are mandatory for each function (as opposed to input/output bindings). What's more, you can have only one trigger per function. Their responsibility is to listen to incoming events and start the execution of the code provided as the body of a function. To understand them better, we need to explain how triggers are structured, and one type of trigger is available.

Triggers in Azure Functions

Azure Functions supports a variety of different triggers – they allow you to start the execution of your function when receiving an HTTP request, when a new file is created, when there's new data in Azure SQL, or even when there's a new message in a queue. A full list of official triggers can be found at `https://learn.microsoft.com/en-us/azure/azure-functions/functions-triggers-bindings?tabs=isolated-process%2Cpython-v2&pivots=programming-language-csharp#supported-bindings`.

Let's use an example of `HTTP trigger` to understand the structure of triggers in Azure Functions. Here's how they are defined for multiple languages – starting with .NET:

```
[Function("HttpFunction")]
public IActionResult Run(
    [HttpTrigger(AuthorizationLevel.Anonymous, "get")]
    HttpRequest req)
{
    // Your code...
}
```

This is how it's used in Java:

```
@FunctionName("TriggerStringGet")
public HttpResponseMessage run(
        @HttpTrigger(name = "req",
            methods = {HttpMethod.GET},
            authLevel = AuthorizationLevel.ANONYMOUS)
```

```
        HttpRequestMessage<Optional<String>> request,
        final ExecutionContext context)
{
    // Your code...
}
```

As the third example, let's see how `HTTP trigger` works in JavaScript:

```
const { app } = require('@azure/functions');

app.http('httpTrigger', {
    methods: ['GET', 'POST'],
    authLevel: 'anonymous',
    handler: async (request, context) =>
    {
    // Your code...
    },
});
```

As you can see, even if we're using different language stacks, the structure of a trigger looks similar:

- We need to define HTTP methods, which should trigger your function.
- We define the authorization mode implying how a user using your function needs to authorize (some triggers support function keys as an authorization method – this is exactly what's being used for `HTTP trigger`).
- We get access to the request object, which we can use to obtain more information about a request (for instance, payload).

Each trigger defines a different set of parameters that can be used. While `HTTP trigger` allows you to define HTTP methods and the authorization mode, the Queue Storage trigger asks you about a queue name and provides access to the message object instead of an HTTP request:

```
[Function("QueueTrigger")]
public string[] Run([QueueTrigger("<queue-name>")] Album myQueueItem,
FunctionContext context)
{
    // Your code...
}
```

Also, all triggers connecting to other services (for instance, Queue Storage and Blob Storage) expect you to provide credentials allowing them to access a service. This depends on the implementation of a trigger – some require you to provide access keys, and some may expect a username and password, while the rest may integrate with Managed Identity for a seamless experience.

> **Tip**
>
> You should aim for Managed Identity whenever you can. This allows you to simplify operations related to secrets' management and rotation, hardens your architecture, and prevents accidental leakage of credentials.

Let's now discuss the difference between triggers and input bindings.

Input bindings in Azure Functions

Input bindings, as opposed to triggers, don't start the execution of your function. Instead, they allow you to inject additional data, which may be useful for a function to execute its code. Each function can have multiple input bindings defined if needed. Here's an example where we're defining both a trigger and input binding:

```
[Function("BlobTrigger")]
public static string BlobTriggerFunction(
    [BlobTrigger("input-files/{name}")] string inputFile,
    [BlobInput("file-processing-rules/rule.xml")] string ruleFile,
    FunctionContext context)
{
    // Your code…
}
```

This function, when triggered, will perform the following actions:

- It will load the `file-processing-rules/rule.xml` file from the attached Blob Storage and inject the content into your function.

- It will execute everything that's defined in the body of the function.

Naturally, the function will trigger a new file to be created in the linked Azure Storage account. The trigger is responsible for listening for changes, while input is used to link to a static file and fetch its content.

> **Note**
>
> BlobTrigger has an in-built listener object, which is responsible for listening to new files being uploaded into Blob Storage. It works by pulling information from the Blob Storage service, which means that it may not be reliable if you need to check for files frequently or if you rarely upload new files. If you want to invert the mechanism by introducing a pub/sub pattern, it may be better to use the Event Grid trigger.

When using input bindings, remember that they rarely allow you to define parameters for a binding dynamically. Most of the time, they expect you to define static values, which cannot easily be modified. If you need to load data based on a dynamic set of parameters, it's better to either implement your own binding or just implement that logic on your own as a part of a function.

Let's now discuss the second kind of binding, which is output binding.

Output bindings in Azure Functions

As the name suggests, output bindings allow you to link the output of your function with a selected service. They are used to simplify integrations in the same way as input bindings do. The difference here is the code needed to implement and use output bindings. Here's an example:

```
[BlobOutput("file-processing-output/{name}-output.txt")]
public static string BlobTriggerFunction (
    [BlobTrigger("input-files/{name}")] string inputFile,
    [BlobInput("file-processing-rules/rule.xml")] string ruleFile,
    FunctionContext context)
{
    // Your code…
    return "Output";
}
```

We slightly modified the piece of code we used as an example for input bindings and added output bindings via the `BlobOutput` attribute. Now, we have a function that does the following:

- Triggered by blobs stored in Blob Storage
- Provides the contents of `file-processing-rules/rule.xml` each time a function is triggered
- Stores a file named `file-processing-output/{name}-output.txt` as a result of running a function

As you can see, when bindings are used, you don't need to define or create objects dedicated to handling a connection. Everything is done in the background by the bindings, so you can focus on providing business logic instead of boilerplate code.

The fact that you can define bindings via attributes works for C# and Java. The same function written in JavaScript would look like this:

```
const { app, input, output } = require('@azure/functions');

const blobInput = input.storageBlob({
    path: 'file-processing-rules/rule.xml',
    connection: 'StorageConnectionString',
```

```
});

const blobOutput = output.storageBlob({
    path: 'file-processing-output/{name}-output.txt',
    connection: 'StorageConnectionString',
});

app.storageBlob('blobTriggerFunction', {
    path: 'file-processing-input/{name}',
    connection: 'StorageConnectionString',
    extraInputs: [blobInput],
    return: blobOutput,
    handler: (inputFile, context) => {
        // Your code...
        return "Output"
    },
});
```

It really doesn't matter which language stack you're going to use in your functions. All native triggers and bindings support similar capabilities (unless they're not supported by the runtime itself) and follow the same development patterns for writing the functions.

As we have covered lots of technical details about Azure Functions and its features, let's talk for a moment about ways to design your functions and their architecture.

Designing an application using Azure Functions

When we started talking about Azure Functions, we discussed how the serverless/FaaS model impacts your architecture and use cases that are valid for that approach. In this part of the chapter, I'd like to cover the pros and cons of Azure Functions, its integration methods, and overall capabilities, which may impact your design decisions.

Let's start by learning about valid scenarios to use Azure Functions as a foundation for your services.

Valid scenarios for Azure Functions

In Azure Functions, use cases are heavily dependent on the selected hosting model. Use cases that are applicable for the consumption plan are not the same use cases when the App Service plan is used. To find the best choice, we need to understand the functional requirements that need to be satisfied. Here are some use cases that could be valid for Azure Functions:

- Providing metadata for other services and applications
- Prototyping web APIs

- Implementing web jobs

- Acting as a proxy

Now, all those use cases could be covered by Azure Web Apps. However, there are certain benefits of using Azure Functions for each of them. Consider Azure Functions if the following is true:

- It's difficult to define a pattern for applications that want to request metadata from your service. If it is done at irregular intervals, sometimes in bursts, it may not make much sense to implement an auto-scale feature (yet you still need to be able to handle those bursts). As Azure Functions can be auto-scaled automatically when the consumption plan is used, you may find it useful as an alternative to standard web applications, for which you need to have a pre-defined infrastructure deployed and capacity reserved.

- From time to time, you may need to prototype a service or an API. If you need to provision not only what provides business value but also a bunch of boilerplate code, such a prototype will quickly become a service of its own. With Azure Functions and the consumption plan, you can both simplify your code base and save money for your infrastructure.

- Web jobs are a common pattern for asynchronous processing of data integrated with web applications. While Azure App Service supports Web Jobs as part of its infrastructure, you'll quickly realize that Azure Functions offers the same functionality with additional features and a better SDK. However, for web jobs running in Azure Functions, you need to consider which hosting plan will be the best. For short-running jobs, consumption plans (including the Flex consumption plan) will work just fine. For long-running operations (hours or days), the App Service plan for Azure Functions will be the only valid option.

- Azure Functions with flexible hosting options can also act as a proxy for other services or APIs. They can also be implemented as an overlay for a legacy system (for instance, to integrate with Microsoft Entra ID authentication). Their pay-as-you-go nature can be helpful in cutting down and optimizing infrastructure and development costs.

Based on the preceding examples, you could say that most cases for Azure Functions are based on the consumption plan. While such a statement is not 100% accurate, it actually reflects the general design principles when Azure Functions is considered:

- You want to cut down on the cost of infrastructure, which is idle most of the time.

- You're looking for a simple and cheap way to provide an additional layer atop a legacy system because it is easier and faster to implement one more component instead of changing the old code base.

- You want to test your idea without provisioning complex infrastructure and using tons of boilerplate code.

- You're looking for a lightweight infrastructure component that can return certain data.

- Your application is event-based and Azure Functions, with its native integrations with other services, is a natural choice.

However, all those considerations are not the only ones that you should take into account when designing an application that is based on Azure Functions. It's worth remembering that code hosted in Azure Functions is treated as functions or methods (as opposed to Azure App Service, where you host a full web application, often including its UI). There are also specific design patterns, which will be discussed shortly as the next step.

Design patterns for Azure Functions

Like all services, Azure Functions follows some dedicated design patterns to provide the best experience. Depending on your expectations, you can treat that service as a base, an extension, or a sidecar for your application, which gets deployed next to your main application and provides additional functionalities. You also need to remember that some features in Azure Functions are heavily dependent on the selected hosting model. They're also based on Azure App Service, so some options (such as deployment modes, availability, and monitoring) will be the same in both those services.

Let's talk about the overall design and architecture for Azure Functions. Serverless services are built around abstract concepts, which focus more on the available capacity for a service, rather than existing hardware. This is why you stop thinking about how many machines or databases you need and try to figure out how many users, requests, or messages your application will need to handle. Azure Functions help you to handle a constantly increasing load without making changes to your application. You can leverage that by using a proper pattern and developing your application accordingly. Let's consider the simplest scenario – you have a single queue and consumer, which processes messages:

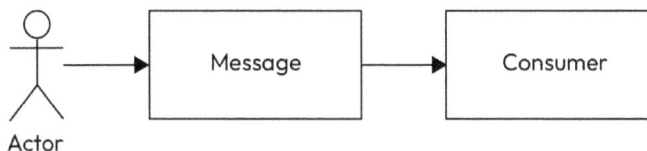

Figure 5.2 – Simple message with a consumer

Now, if you decide to scale out your application, you need to do that on your own by either scaling out instances of a consumer or consumers within a single instance:

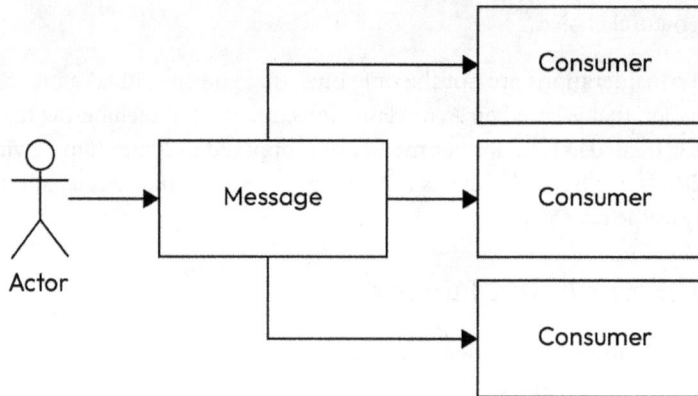

Figure 5.3 – Multiple consumers running on multiple instances

The concept of having multiple instances representing multiple consumers is easy to implement if your provisioning mechanism gives enough abstraction to cover all the technical details of the process (for instance, deployment on a Kubernetes cluster). Of course, you could achieve similar results by keeping a single instance only:

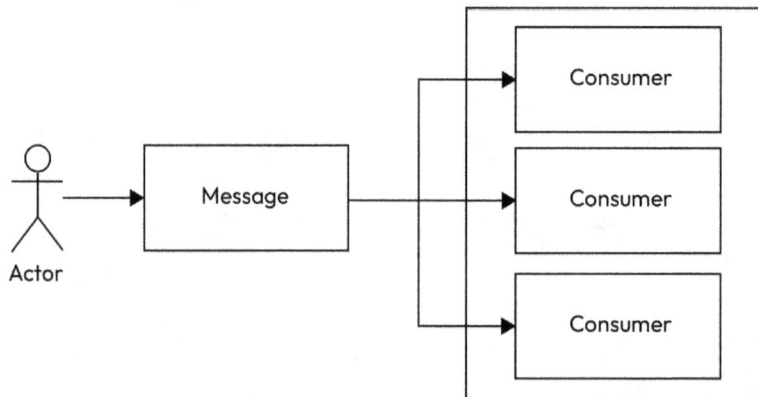

Figure 5.4 – Multiple consumers within a single instance

Azure Functions implements the necessary mechanism depending on the use case. Remember that there are two factors to take into consideration:

- The listener for the incoming events
- The functions host itself

The scale-out operation will happen independently and be performed by the scale manager implemented by Azure. Thanks to that, you don't need to worry about how you'd implement one of those patterns – you only need to understand it to see whether you need to introduce additional elements to complete the implementation.

One of the most common patterns for integration is calling other HTTP endpoints. The high-level implementation will look like this:

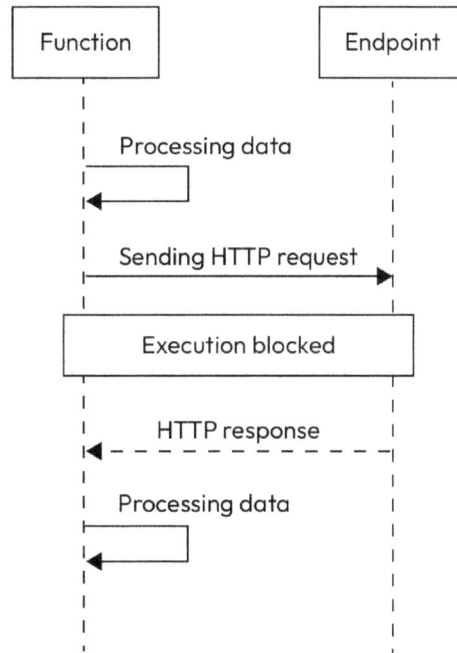

Figure 5.5 – Sending an HTTP request from Azure Functions

The common thing about HTTP requests is the fact that they're blocking operations. It means that until an HTTP response has been sent, the execution of your function will be blocked. This is important from a cost perspective – with a consumption plan, you're paying for your function being idle. Fortunately, this can be changed with Durable Functions, which we'll be discussing in *Chapter 7*.

Designing for security with Azure Functions

As Azure Functions is based on the same framework as Azure Web Apps, it can leverage the same features and functionalities as standard web applications. This includes two major aspects that need to be addressed with each application:

- Managing configuration
- Securing the application

The first assumption you always need to make is not to store sensitive values using **App Settings** in Azure or via static configuration files in your application. Azure Functions can integrate with both **Azure Key Vault** and **Azure App Configuration** for better and easier management of configuration values. It also supports Azure Key Vault references, so you can manage mapping between secrets and configuration values using an infrastructure-as-code approach.

When it comes to security, there are multiple layers that we need to consider:

- Authentication
- Authorization
- Network-level security

Fortunately, Azure Functions is a service that still allows you to host code that is written by yourself. This means that it can integrate with any identity provider that supports standard protocols and security frameworks, as long as you're able to provide the necessary configuration and implement the integration.

> **Note**
>
> Azure Functions integrates natively with Microsoft Entra ID for authentication. While this simplifies configuration, I personally rarely use that feature. The reason for that is simple – very often, I need to be compliant with security controls and other directions given by risk and compliance teams, which means that I need to control all critical aspects of the application. In simpler or less critical workloads though, you can find the native configuration quite handy.

When implementing authentication and authorization, remember that Azure Functions was never designed to act as a typical web hosting platform. Its scalability and overall development framework indicate that it's meant as a managed solution for implementing even-driven processes, rather than typical APIs.

If you need to consider network-level security, remember that Azure Functions may not be able to integrate with virtual networks in Azure if you're using the consumption plan. This is a blocker in many companies, which require such workloads to be accessed privately. If you need to support private connectivity, you need to use other hosting plans (which obviously impact monthly charges and the set of available features).

Let's talk now about building a deployment pipeline for our functions.

Building a deployment pipeline

In order to build a deployment pipeline for Azure Functions, we need to create our application and prepare the infrastructure for it. In this section, we'll create all the prerequisites and then build CICD pipelines in both Azure DevOps and GitHub Actions.

Deploying infrastructure

To get started with deployment, let's create the infrastructure needed for Azure Functions:

```
az group create \
-l <location> \
-n <resource-group-name>

az storage account create \
-g <resource-group-name> \
-l <location> \
-n <storage-account-name>

Az functionapp create \
--consumption-plan-location <location> \
--name <function-app-name> \
--os-type <os-type> \
--resource-group <resource-group-name> \
--runtime <runtime> \
--storage-account <storage-account-name>
```

In my case, I used `linux` for the OS type and `dotnet` for the runtime – you can use any other combination of OS and runtime available for Azure Functions (for instance, Windows as OS and PowerShell as the runtime). If you're not sure about a runtime, use the following command to see all the supported values:

```
az functionapp list-runtimes
```

Once your infrastructure is ready, we can continue with creating a function app locally and then a pipeline for deploying it.

Creating functions locally

To create functions locally, we need to use the Azure Functions CLI as we did in the previous sections. Let's create a brand-new project with a single function:

```
func init --worker-runtime <runtime>
func new --name HTTPTriggerFunction
```

When a list with available templates is presented, select `HttpTrigger` as our value. After a moment, the CLI should create boilerplate code for our function. In my case (C# language, dotnet runtime), the function will look like this:

```
[FunctionName("HTTPTriggerFunction")]
public static async Task<IActionResult> Run(
```

```csharp
    [HttpTrigger(AuthorizationLevel.Function, "get", "post",
        Route = null)]
    HttpRequest req,
    ILogger log)
{

    log.LogInformation("C# HTTP trigger function processed a
    request.");

    string name = req.Query["name"];

    string requestBody = await new StreamReader(req.Body).
        ReadToEndAsync();
    dynamic data = JsonConvert.DeserializeObject(requestBody);
    name = name ?? data?.name;

    string responseMessage = string.IsNullOrEmpty(name)
        ? "This HTTP triggered function executed successfully. Pass
            a name in the query string or in the request body for a
            personalized response."
        : $"Hello, {name}. This HTTP triggered function executed
            successfully.";

    return new OkObjectResult(responseMessage);
}
```

Of course, selecting another language or runtime will generate different code for your function. It won't matter from a deployment perspective as long as those values are compatible with the selected runtime for the Azure Functions service instance. Once the code is generated, let's start building our CICD pipeline.

Building a CICD pipeline in Azure DevOps

We will build our first pipeline in Azure DevOps with the following steps:

1. The first thing you'll need is a repository, where you will put the code of your functions. You can find detailed instructions for creating a repository at https://learn.microsoft.com/en-us/azure/devops/repos/git/create-new-repo?view=azure-devops.

2. Once the repository is created, use the following command to update the remote locally:

    ```
    git remote add origin <git-repository-location>
    ```

3. With the repository initialized, you can push the local code base to the Azure DevOps instance:

    ```
    git push --set-upstream origin master
    ```

4. We can now start building our pipeline. To do so, go to **Pipelines** on the left (*Figure 5.6*) and click on the **Create Pipeline** button (*Figure 5.7*):

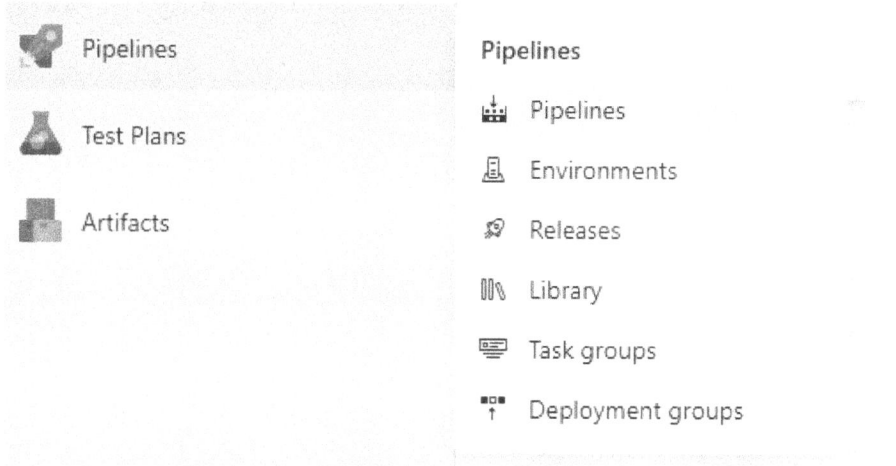

Pipelines

Test Plans

Artifacts

Pipelines

Pipelines

Environments

Releases

Library

Task groups

Deployment groups

Figure 5.6 – Accessing Pipelines from the main menu of Azure DevOps

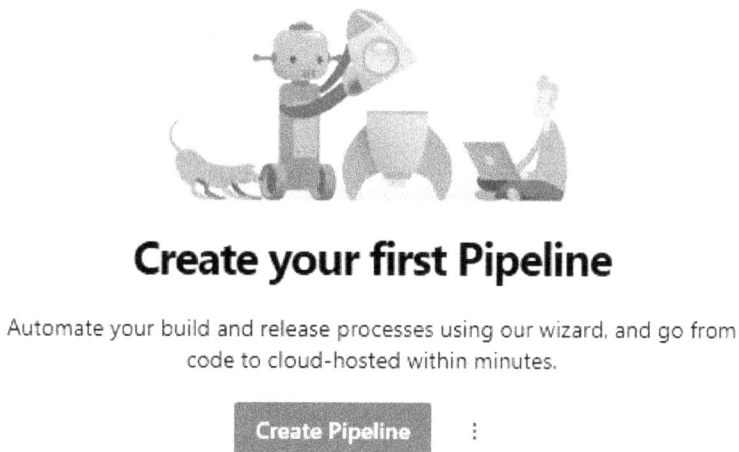

Create your first Pipeline

Automate your build and release processes using our wizard, and go from code to cloud-hosted within minutes.

Create Pipeline

Figure 5.7 – First step of creating a pipeline

5. Then, select the **Azure Repos Git** option to see available repositories in your project. Find the repository where you pushed your code and then select **Starter pipeline**. You'll see a starter pipeline generated, which we need to modify. Here is the full pipeline code needed for deployment of Azure Functions:

```
trigger:
- master

pool:
  vmImage: ubuntu-latest

steps:
- task: AzureFunctionApp@2
  inputs:
    connectedServiceNameARM: '<service-connection-name>'
    appType: 'functionAppLinux'
    appName: '<function-app-name>'
    package: '$(System.DefaultWorkingDirectory)/**/*.zip'
    runtimeStack: '<runtime>'
    deploymentMethod: 'auto'
```

As our parameters may be different depending on the selected language and runtime, I put some placeholders so as not to confuse you. In my case, I needed to use the following values:

- `<function-app-name>` - `afd05`

- `<runtime>` - `DOTNET|6.0`

There's one more parameter needed to make it work. It's named `connectedServiceNameARM`. This parameter is responsible for defining a service connection used for your deployment. Service connections in Azure DevOps are out of the scope of this book, but we can quickly define them for clarity. As you're already aware, Azure expects anybody interacting with control and data planes to be authenticated and authorized. When we want to deploy code to Azure Functions, we need to somehow pass credentials, which will allow the pipeline to authenticate. As passing on your personal credentials is never a good idea, we can use service principals or Managed Identity instead. Service connections are just another abstraction layer for the connection mechanism, so you don't need to configure and manage integrations each time you work on a pipeline. You can read more about them at `https://learn.microsoft.com/en-us/azure/devops/pipelines/library/service-endpoints?view=azure-devops`.

> **Note**
>
> Remember that some runtimes may require you to compile and pack the application before you deploy it. The provided example only presents the deployment step and isn't sufficient for some of the available runtimes (for example, .NET).

Once your deployment step is configured properly, you can start the pipeline anytime and wait for the deployment to complete. Your function will be handled by Azure from now on and can be integrated with other services running in the cloud or on-premises.

Let's compare the deployment of a Function App using Azure DevOps with GitHub Actions.

Building a CICD pipeline in GitHub Actions

GitHub Actions follows a similar philosophy when it comes to building and configuring pipelines as Azure DevOps. The difference here is the syntax and authentication mechanism to interact with resources in Azure. Follow these steps to build a CI/CD pipeline in GitHub Actions:

1. To get started, once again, we need to create a repository. You can find detailed instructions at `https://docs.github.com/en/repositories/creating-and-managing-repositories/creating-a-new-repository`.

2. Once you have the repository, go to it and select **Actions**:

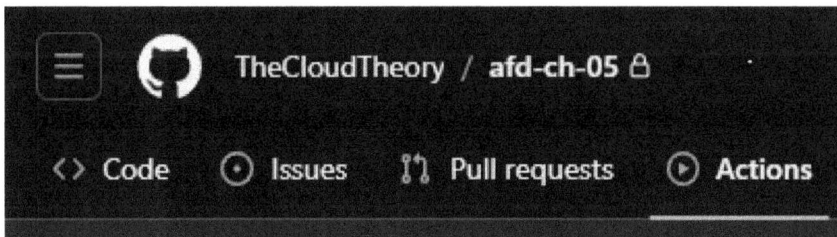

Figure 5.8 – Actions section in GitHub

3. Next, in the **Search workflows** search box, enter `functions` and press *Enter* on your keyboard. You'll see a number of templates which can be used to start building your pipeline:

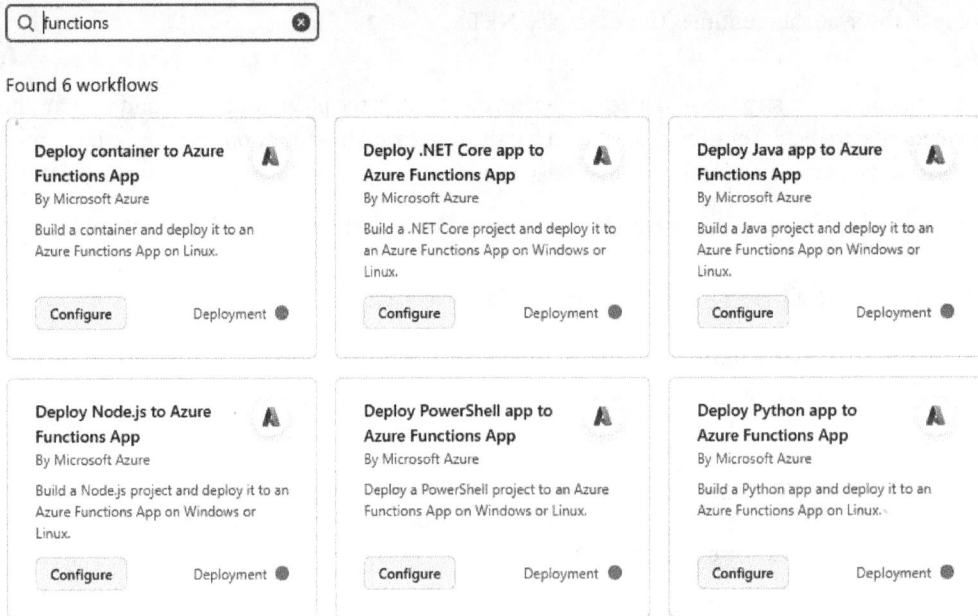

Figure 5.9 – Workflow templates for Azure Functions

In my case, I selected a template for deploying the .NET Core app as a function app. The template looks like this:

```
name: Deploy DotNet project to Azure Function App

on:
  push:
    branches: ["main"]

env:
  AZURE_FUNCTIONAPP_NAME: 'your-app-name'
  AZURE_FUNCTIONAPP_PACKAGE_PATH: '.'
  DOTNET_VERSION: '6.0.x'

jobs:
  build-and-deploy:
    runs-on: linux-latest
    environment: dev
    steps:
```

```
- name: 'Checkout GitHub Action'
  uses: actions/checkout@v4
- name: 'Run Azure Functions Action'
  uses: Azure/functions-action@v1
  id: fa
  with:
    app-name: ${{ env.AZURE_FUNCTIONAPP_NAME }}
    package: '${{ env.AZURE_FUNCTIONAPP_PACKAGE_PATH }}/
    output'
    publish-profile: ${{ secrets.AZURE_FUNCTIONAPP_PUBLISH_
    PROFILE }}
```

I removed some steps from the template as they refer to the process of building a .NET application (which is not relevant if you're using a different runtime), but the main step will be the same for all the runtimes. As you can see, we need to use similar parameters as we used for deploying Azure Functions in Azure DevOps. This time, however, we're using a publish profile to provide credentials.

4. It's possible to use Azure RBAC, but in order to do that, we need to change our pipeline:

```
- name: 'Login via Azure CLI'
  uses: azure/login@v1
  with:
    creds: ${{ secrets.AZURE_RBAC_CREDENTIALS }}
- name: 'Run Azure Functions Action'
  uses: Azure/functions-action@v1
  id: fa
  with:
    app-name: ${{ env.AZURE_FUNCTIONAPP_NAME }}
    package: '${{ env.AZURE_FUNCTIONAPP_PACKAGE_PATH }}/output'
```

5. To make it work, you'll need to configure the AZURE_RBAC_CREDENTIALS secret variable in GitHub. You can find all the necessary details needed to configure it at https://github. com/Azure/functions-action#using-azure-service-principal-for- rbac-as-deployment-credential.

Conceptually, both Azure DevOps and GitHub Actions follow the same patterns when it comes to developing pipelines. Both will require you to provide the necessary credentials and authorize the principal to run the pipeline. Feature-wise, they also provide the same functionality, so you can safely choose either of them to build your CICD platform.

As the last step in this chapter, let's talk about use cases for Azure Functions.

Learning about use cases

Azure Functions offers a nice addition to the standard development model as it provides an event-driven and robust development framework for prototyping, web jobs, and integrations. We can divide use cases for those services into the following groups:

- Validating concepts (prototypes, interim solutions that should be easy to develop and host, and proofs of concept)

- Proxies (API gateways, transparent proxies, forward proxies, and reverse proxies)

- Web APIs

- Web Jobs

- Compute nodes for integration with other services

As Azure Functions is quite a robust service, it's difficult to find a single purpose for it. The serverless nature helps in development and has the potential to cut down on the cost, but you need to remember that it also makes testing much more difficult. Azure Functions is also mostly based on its ability to integrate with other services. This means that local development and testing will be challenging, as you need to either provide sandbox environments for development or base your work on emulators.

Azure Functions is definitely much better suited for handling web jobs than Azure Web Apps. The SDK and the platform offered by this service allow for much better control over the order of execution, listeners, and error handling. Azure Functions natively integrates with Azure Application Insights for monitoring and alerting, so you can easily follow the same technology stack that is selected for other Azure services.

In my career, I have used Azure Functions for several different projects to implement features, such as the following:

- A schedule-based workflow responsible for fetching cost data from various cloud vendors, processing it, and storing it in a relational database; this workflow runs several times a day and also performs validation of data stored and presented to the end user

- A lightweight proxy for external devices and software to communicate with Azure Event Hubs

- An API for scheduling provisioning of dedicated clusters of virtual machines

In the next part of the book, we will talk about Durable Functions, which extends the capabilities of Azure Functions and offers a much better development framework for long-running operations and orchestrations. This doesn't mean that you cannot build such workloads using Azure Functions. However, it doesn't offer an orchestration mechanism natively, making it difficult to build reliable workflows, which require external signals or need to persist a state between executions.

Let's summarize our learnings from this chapter and see what awaits in the next one.

Summary

In this chapter, we discussed Azure Functions – a serverless platform for building event-driven applications. You learned about various hosting options for this service and bindings, which allow us to trigger functions and inject or output values. The next major topic was building your own function locally and then integrating it with CICD pipelines. Even though we used Azure DevOps and GitHub Actions, the same concepts can be used for other software such as Bamboo or Jenkins. We also learned that the deployment of Azure functions is a cross-platform concept, meaning that you can deploy them from any environment, as long as you're able to authenticate to Azure.

In the next chapter, we're going to discuss Azure Key Vault and Azure App Configuration in detail to better understand security concepts for storing secrets, configuration management, and integration options with web applications.

6

Managing Secrets and Configuration in Azure

In the previous chapters, we discussed the importance of handling secrets and configuration properly. We completed a few exercises, where we integrated our application with Azure Key Vault and Azure App Configuration to see how native services in Azure can help us implement an easy-to-manage, reliable, and robust setup. As there are various use cases worth discussing and additional topics to talk about, I've prepared a dedicated chapter that covers them.

This chapter aims to give you more details on how Azure Key Vault and Azure App Configuration can be integrated with your application. We're also going to talk about how those services can be integrated and how to structure access and values for ease of management.

In this chapter, we're going to cover the following main topics:

- Using Azure Key Vault to store secrets
- Integrating an application with Azure Key Vault
- Using Azure App Configuration to store configuration details
- Understanding integration options for Azure App Configuration
- Learning about use cases

Technical requirements

To complete the exercises in this chapter, you'll need the following software:

- The Azure CLI
- An IDE of your choice (for instance, Visual Studio Code)
- (Optional) `curl`

Using Azure Key Vault to store secrets

Let's start our discussion with secrets and the overall approach to storing and managing them. Almost every application operates using secrets. They are used to access databases, connect to external services, or perform certain operations. Secrets, as the name implies, mustn't be accessed or viewed by unauthorized parties. This means that your company may require additional means of security when an application handles them. There are dedicated services (often called **vaults**) that excel at providing secure access and storage layers for secrets – for Azure, it's Azure Key Vault, which we're going to discuss in a moment.

> **Note**
>
> Azure Key Vault isn't the only service meant for storing secrets. There are other products available, such as **HashiCorp Vault** (`https://www.hashicorp.com/products/vault`), **AWS Secrets Manager** (`https://docs.aws.amazon.com/secretsmanager/latest/userguide/intro.html`), and **GCP Secret Manager** (`https://cloud.google.com/security/products/secret-manager`). They all serve the same purpose, but because they are managed services, each of them has a different interface and capabilities.

To visualize the need for proper secrets management, let's complete the following exercise, where we will create a simple application and try to use a secret in it:

1. We'll start by deploying a new instance of Azure Web Apps and adding a single secret there:

    ```
    az group create \
    -n <resource-group-name> \
    -l <location>

    az appservice plan create \
    -n <plan-name> \
    -g <resource-group-name> \
    --is-linux \
    --sku Free

    az webapp create \
    -g <resource-group-name> \
    -p <plan-name> \
    -n <webapp-name> \
    -i nginx
    ```

2. Upon executing these commands, you should have a single Azure Web Apps instance that's been deployed with `nginx` as an example application. Let's perform a quick check using `curl`:

```
curl https://<webapp-name>.azurewebsites.net
<!DOCTYPE html>
<html>
  <head>
    <title>Welcome to nginx!</title>
    <style>
      html { color-scheme: light dark; }
      body {
        width: 35em;
        margin: 0 auto;
        font-family: Tahoma, Verdana, Arial,
          sans-serif;
      }
    </style>
  </head>
  <body>
    <h1>Welcome to nginx!</h1>
    <p>If you see this page, the nginx web server is
      successfully installed and working. Further
      configuration is required.</p>

    <p>For online documentation and support please
      refer to
      <a href="http://nginx.org/">nginx.org</a>.<br/>
      Commercial support is available at
      <a href="http://nginx.com/">nginx.com</a>.
    </p>

    <p><em>Thank you for using nginx.</em></p>
  </body>
</html>
```

3. Great – we have an application up and running! Now, it's time to add a secret to it:

```
Az webapp config appsettings set \
-g <resource-group-name> \
-n <webapp-name> \
--settings MY_SECRET=SecretValue
```

This command sets the value of `MY_SECRET` in the **App settings** area of our Azure Web Apps instance to `SecretValue`. Once our application starts, `MY_SECRET` will be available as an environment variable and its value will be available to our code. However, by continuing with such an implementation, we're exposing our secret to anyone or anything, which has access to the **App settings** area of the given instance of Azure Web Apps. Of course, we can address that by disallowing a principal from reading them, but unfortunately, that's easier said than done.

4. To prevent a principal from reading the configuration value of your web application, you could give it `read` permissions only. You can use any role that doesn't grant `write/*` permissions on your instance of Azure Web Apps (for instance, the standard `Reader` role). When applied, a principal will see the following information in the Azure portal (or an error in the CLI):

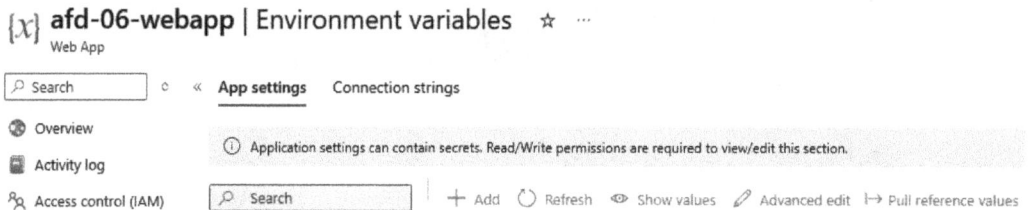

Figure 6.1 – A lack of write permissions blocking access to App settings

However, as you can see, this approach has some serious flaws:

- It prevents a principal from reading all the values.
- It blocks a principal from doing everything else that's not directly related to **App settings.**

To address this issue, you could introduce a custom role, which would block anything related to **App settings** only. As an example, adding the following statement to your role definition would do the trick:

```
"notActions": [
    "microsoft.web/sites/config/web/appsettings/*"
]
```

To help you understand this better, let's take a look at one of the inbuilt role definitions (the `Contributor` role):

```
{
    "Name": "Contributor",
    "Id": "b24988ac-6180-42a0-ab88-20f7382dd24c",
    "IsCustom": false,
    "Description": "Lets you manage everything except access
        to resources.",
    "Actions": [
```

```
      "*"
    ],
    "NotActions": [
      "Microsoft.Authorization/*/Delete",
      "Microsoft.Authorization/*/Write",
      "Microsoft.Authorization/elevateAccess/Action",
      "Microsoft.Blueprint/blueprintAssignments/write",
      "Microsoft.Blueprint/blueprintAssignments/delete"
    ],
    "DataActions": [],
    "NotDataActions": [],
    "AssignableScopes": [
      "/"
    ]
  }
```

As you can see, it consists of the name of a role, as well as its ID, description, and an indicator of whether it's a custom or inbuilt role, plus a few sections defining what is allowed and disallowed by the role (`Actions`, `NotActions`, `DataActions`, `NotDataActions`). Each definition must also provide an assignable scope. The most important thing to remember here is the difference between an action and a data action. Actions refer to control plane operations such as creating a resource, updating it, or reading its configuration. Data actions are related to data plane operations such as reading tables from a database or interacting with secrets in Azure Key Vault. In Azure, role definitions require you to grant permissions for a principal explicitly. If, for example, you want to allow somebody with read permissions to read all Azure App Service services inside a resource group, you need to add a proper statement to the `Actions` section and create a role assignment at the resource group level. If you want to exclude more specific permission from a role, you need to use a `NotActions` or `NotDataActions` section.

This is why we added the `microsoft.web/sites/config/web/appsettings/*` permission in our example. However, this still means that any principal with higher permissions will be able to access the values of secrets (unless you have a customized process for preparing and managing the role definition and maintaining it carefully). As secrets require proper management and segregated access, we need to find a better way to work with them. This is where Azure Key Vault comes in handy.

Now, let's talk about the different kinds of objects that can be stored there.

Storing keys, secrets, and certificates

Azure Key Vault allows you to store various secrets – not only typical strings such as passwords or API keys. There are three different kinds of secrets that you can store using this service:

- Generic secrets (strings)
- Keys
- Certificates

In this section, we'll focus on their use cases and differences when storing, generating, and using them. Let's start with generic secrets, which we've already discussed multiple times.

Secrets in Azure Key Vault

A typical secret in development could be a connection string to a database, a user password, or an API key that authorizes your application when it's connected to a third-party service. Those are the most common use cases for storing sensitive information using Azure Key Vault and are the most popular kind of secrets you can store using a dedicated secret store. However, as Azure Key Vault is a managed service dedicated to storing such sensitive values, it provides additional capabilities for them, some of which you may find useful.

The important thing about secrets in Azure Key Vault is their additional attributes, which decorate each secret that's stored within the service:

- Exp – *expiration date* (default: forever): This is a metadata attribute that informs a user that a secret has been deprecated and shouldn't be used.
- Nbf – *not before* (default: now): This provides the reverse logic of the exp attribute and informs a user that a secret can't be used before a certain date.
- Enabled (default: true): In connection with the exp and nbf attributes, this can be used to further limit access to a secret.

The exp, nbf, and enabled attributes are mutable, which means that you're allowed to set and modify them. Azure Key Vault provides two additional attributes for secrets, but they're read-only:

- Created: Indicates when a secret was created.
- Updated: Indicates when a secret was updated.

All these attributes are helpful in various scenarios, such as auditing, performing operational tasks, and sunsetting old values.

> **Note**
>
> The `exp`, `nbf`, `created`, and `updated` attributes are stored as `IntDate` values (integer values representing dates). However, when interacting with the Azure Key Vault data plane, the API allows you to provide UTC datetime instead for easier interaction.

These attributes can be set using tools such as the Azure CLI:

```
az keyvault secret set-attributes \
--name <secret-name> \
--vault-name <key-vault-name> \
    --expires Y-m-d'T'H:M:S'Z'
    --not-before Y-m-d'T'H:M:S'Z'
    --enabled true
```

By replacing `Y-m-d'T'H:M:S'Z'` with a correct value, you can set both the `expires` and `not-before` dates with a single command.

Now, let's talk about keys in Azure Key Vault.

Keys in Azure Key Vault

Keys stored in Azure Key Vault are used for cryptographic operations (such as performing encryption) and can be divided into two types:

- **Software-protected**
- **HSM-protected**

> **Note**
>
> **HSM** stands for **Hardware Security Module**. As the name implies, they are physical devices that are responsible for digital keys that are used in various operations, such as generating digital signatures or strong authentication methods. They are specialized hardware components, which makes them quite expensive, so they may not be suitable for the applications you're working on. If you want to read more about them, take a look at `https://en.wikipedia.org/wiki/Hardware_security_module`.

When working with Azure Key Vault, you need to remember that two types of services are available:

- **Vaults**
- **Managed HSMs**

While vaults provide a simple and cost-effective solution for managing keys, some applications (requiring strict security, compliance, and undergoing detailed regulatory reviews) may need a managed HSM. However, for simplicity, we're not going to use HSMs in our examples.

Azure Key Vault provides multiple protection methods for keys, depending on their type. For instance, software-protected RSA keys are available in vaults only (Standard SKU), while RSA-HSM keys are supported by both vaults (Premium SKU) and managed HSMs (a Premium SKU in Azure Key Vault offers such possibilities thanks to the fact that it's a multi-tenant HSM solution under the hood. This grants less control over the infrastructure and provides less isolation but is a less expensive solution).

Often, you'll be using keys from Azure Key Vault to enable customer-managed encryption on various services, such as Azure Storage or Azure SQL. One of the most common scenarios for using Azure Key Vault development scenarios is for encrypting/decrypting data instead of performing compute-heavy operations inside an application.

There's one more type of secret that we can use in Azure Key Vault: certificates. Let's discuss them before we go back to using Azure Key Vault in applications.

Certificates in Azure Key Vault

Certificates are very common secrets in web development and service-oriented architectures as they are used in multiple scenarios:

- You can obtain a certificate so that your customers can connect with your application securely using HTTPS.

- They can be used to validate the communication channel between your application and third-party services.

- They are useful in keeping internal communication secure if you're implementing a mechanism for generating and validating the certificate chain for applications.

While the use cases for certificates should be quite clear, let's discuss the operational problem they generate. If your applications use certificates, you need a way to store them securely. What's more, certificates could expire – it'd be best if we had a mechanism that could monitor their expiration dates and either regenerate a certificate automatically or notify us that there's a need to regenerate them. Fortunately, Azure Key Vault can serve both purposes.

Technically, when a certificate is created in Azure Key Vault, it consists of three separate components:

- Metadata

- Key

- Secret

All of these components are stored in Azure Key Vault and, depending on the certificate policy, may or may not be exportable (this only applies to keys since HSM-backed keys cannot be exported). Certificates in Azure Key Vault support the same attributes as secrets, though the `nbf` and `exp` fields are no longer mutable.

The important thing to remember is the fact that Azure Key Vault allows you to generate certificates for a limited set of certificate providers:

- **DigiCert**
- **GlobalSign**

If your company requires you to obtain certificates from other providers, you won't be able to use a subset of functionalities available in Azure Key Vault. Still, this service can be used to store and access them securely via a dedicated access policy or RBAC permissions.

Let's see what we need to connect to Azure Key Vault and the available possibilities, depending on the method we use.

Integrating an application with Azure Key Vault

Depending on your use case, the approach for integrating Azure Key Vault with your application will be different. Generally speaking, we can divide the allowed methods into two groups:

- Azure-managed
- Application-managed

In this section, we'll use this separation to discuss the pros and cons of both methods. To start, let's talk about Azure-managed integrations.

Using Azure-based integrations for Azure Key Vault

Azure-based integrations are integrations that are managed by the platform (Azure) and are application-agnostic. In other words, those integrations are supposed to work for all platforms and technology stacks while providing a similar set of capabilities. We discussed one such integration when we talked about Azure App Service and Azure Web Apps. In this case, you can integrate your application with Azure Key Vault using Azure Key Vault references:

```
@Microsoft.KeyVault(SecretUri=https://myvault.vault.azure.net/secrets/
mysecret/)
```

Each reference is a special string that's put as the value of your app setting in Azure Web Apps. References are resolved automatically when your application starts and can be provided to it by mapping the secrets as environment variables. The benefit of this approach is a simplified setup – all you need to do is give your application permissions to access Azure Key Vault (using either access policies or RBAC permissions). The rest is done by the platform, and your application can obtain secrets without knowing how they're injected.

> **Note**
> Remember that Azure Web Apps needs an identity to be able to communicate with Azure Key Vault. This can be done using Managed Identity for both system-assigned and user-assigned identities.

Azure Key Vault can also integrate with Azure Kubernetes Service using a dedicated provider called Secrets Store CSI Driver. It allows you to mount not only secrets but also keys and certificates and can be used for secrets synchronization and autorotation. If you're not familiar with Kubernetes or Azure Kubernetes Service in general, feel free to skip this section. For a better understanding of the concepts mentioned here, take a look at the following documentation:

- `https://secrets-store-csi-driver.sigs.k8s.io/`
- `https://github.com/Azure/secrets-store-csi-driver-provider-azure`

If you want to use that driver in your cluster, there are two options. First, you can enable it when a cluster is being deployed:

```
az aks create \
--name <cluster-name> \
--resource-group <resource-group-name> \
--enable-addons azure-keyvault-secrets-provider \
--generate-ssh-keys
```

For already existing clusters, you can just upgrade them by providing a specific add-on:

```
az aks enable-addons \
--addons azure-keyvault-secrets-provider \
--name <cluster-name> \
--resource-group <resource-group-name>
```

Once enabled, you can start configuring your cluster so that it connects to specific Azure Key Vault instances and start mounting secrets where you need them. As those operations are quite detailed and we haven't discussed Azure Kubernetes Service yet, so we won't explain them in this chapter. However, if you're interested, you can read about them in the Azure documentation: `https://learn.microsoft.com/en-us/azure/aks/csi-secrets-store-driver`.

For Azure Container Apps, when you want to leverage integration with Azure Key Vault, you can follow the same pattern as for Azure Web Apps. For this service, you can still use Azure Key Vault references to integrate quickly and cleanly. This has one more benefit – as the configuration for the integration will stay the same (Azure Container Apps also needs you to provide an identity, which will be used to make the connection), you can easily move from Azure Web Apps to Azure Container Apps if you need better control over compute or need to modernize your application.

All Azure-based integrations have the following things in common:

- You need to configure Managed Identity at the service layer.
- You need to take care of access policies or RBAC permissions for the identity that's been integrated with your service.
- Each integration has an individual setup method but once initialized, they provide the secrets in the same way.
- Your applications are unaware of the secret store storing the sensitive data, which makes multi-cloud/multi-vendor/multi-platform design easier.
- The platform takes care of providing, refreshing, and caching secrets (note that you may need to restart your application in some cases so that it fetches new values).

However, there are some disadvantages when using Azure-based integrations:

- They are not fully vendor-agnostic – if you need to decouple your application from a secret store, Azure Key Vault references may be useful, but Secrets Store CSI Driver for Azure Key Vault may be a risky decision if you need to go multi-cloud.
- Even if your application isn't aware of the secret store being used, the effort needed to set up Azure Key Vault and the access layer may be significant. In that case, it may be better to use one of the vendor-agnostic solutions for storing secrets (such as HashiCorp Vault).

Now, let's see how challenging it is to use Azure Key Vault integration directly within your application's code.

Integrating applications with Azure Key Vault directly

Each application can be integrated with Azure Key Vault directly using one of the following methods:

- REST API
- SDK

Both provide a similar set of functionalities – the SDK is just a thin layer for the REST API, which encapsulates several common operations (authentication, error handling, and logging) and simplifies development. Still, if you think that the SDK isn't suited to your needs, you're free to integrate with the API directly.

> **Note**
>
> We're going to use the SDK in our examples for simplicity.

When integrating your application with Azure Key Vault, you'll need to create a dedicated set of objects, depending on your language stack. For instance, for .NET, if you want to interact with keys, you'd need to create a `KeyClient` object:

```
var keyVaultName =
    Environment.GetEnvironmentVariable("KEY_VAULT_NAME");
var kvUri = $"https://{keyVaultName}.vault.azure.net";
var client = new KeyClient(new Uri(kvUri),
    new DefaultAzureCredential());
```

A similar operation can be achieved using Python:

```
import os
from azure.keyvault.keys import KeyClient
from azure.identity import DefaultAzureCredential

keyVaultName = os.environ["KEY_VAULT_NAME"]
KVUri = "https://" + keyVaultName + ".vault.azure.net"

credential = DefaultAzureCredential()
client = KeyClient(vault_url=KVUri, credential=credential)
```

It's also possible to interact with Azure Key Vault using JavaScript:

```
const { KeyClient } = require("@azure/keyvault-keys");
const { DefaultAzureCredential } =
    require("@azure/identity");

const credential = new DefaultAzureCredential();
const keyVaultUrl = process.env["KEY_VAULT_URL"];
const client = new KeyClient(keyVaultUrl, credential);
```

All these examples have the following things in common:

- They create an instance of `KeyClient` to interact with keys in Azure Key Vault.
- They use an instance of the `DefaultAzureCredential` class to authenticate.
- They have the same interface for the objects, so I didn't need to change anything beyond the syntax.

> **Note**
>
> Each example also assumes that the name of the Azure Key Vault instance is provided in an environment variable. Of course, this is not mandatory – you can inject it using any other method and they will still work correctly.

What's important about these methods and implementations is the mechanism behind each of the performed operations. To obtain credentials, we can use the `DefaultAzureCredential` object, which is part of the identity package available for each supported language stack. This object is responsible for fetching credentials based on the implemented sequence, which tries to get credentials from multiple sources (the Azure CLI, Azure PowerShell, environment variables, Managed Identity etc.). Thanks to that object, we can have a working application for both local and cloud environments. The only difference is the credentials – while locally, *Azure CLI and Azure PowerShell credentials* are likely to be the most popular sources, for deployed applications, those credentials will no longer be available. In that case, `DefaultAzureCredential` will try to get them from other valid sources (*Managed Identity, Client Secret, or Client Certificate credentials*).

While the identity package takes care of authentication, Azure Key Vault is still responsible for authorization. This means that any principle defined in your credentials has to have access to the Azure Key Vault data plane (for secrets, keys, certificates, or all of them). Since we're integrating our application with Azure Key Vault directly, this means that we need to start catching all kinds of errors that may be returned from the data plane of Azure Key Vault. This couples your application with Azure, which may be useful in several scenarios.

Let's consider the following situation – you want your application to be hosted on different platforms (Azure being one of them). It becomes obvious that you cannot rely on platform-based integrations – they are only available to Azure and won't work in other places. To solve that problem, you could integrate your application directly with Azure Key Vault. This is possible, but still, you need to remember that not all credentials will work. Since an application may work on other platforms besides Azure, you cannot use Managed Identity – the only multi-platform credentials are those that are based on a service principal (Client Secret or Client Certificate). Another possibility would be using a platform-specific solution and just synchronizing all the objects between all the vaults/secret stores. It's also possible to use a generic solution such as HashiCorp Vault and have the same interface everywhere.

> **Tip**
>
> It's also possible to change the configuration of your application, depending on the platform where it's hosted. In that case, you could use Managed Identity for Azure and a service principal for other platforms.

As you can see, interaction with Azure Key Vault is possible whether you're using Azure-based integration or want to integrate your application directly. As with each solution, there are some considerations worth discussing before you make a choice:

- Application-based integration may help you in multi-platform deployments if you don't need to make a full switch (something that may happen during DR scenarios).

- Application-based integration still requires you to provide the necessary credentials and configure access, similar to what you'd do for Azure-based integration.

- If you integrate your application with Azure Key Vault directly, you gain the flexibility of choosing when secrets are fetched, cached, and refreshed.

- In multi-platform scenarios, it may be better to stick to platform-based integrations as they often work similarly. Delegating secret store integration to a platform may be an easier solution.

- If you leverage a managed authentication mechanism, all the secrets will be available to all the processes attached to your host. Using application-based authentication methods will only limit access to the secrets of the application.

Now, let's learn how to use Azure Key Vault for one more important operation that's used in various applications – encrypting and decrypting a string.

Using Azure Key Vault and encrypting and decrypting a string

The process of encrypting and decrypting a string involves using an encryption key and Azure Key Vault to perform encryption. Conceptually, it is implemented as follows:

1. You create an encryption key and store it in Azure Key Vault.

2. You load the key into your application.

3. You use the key to encrypt or decrypt your string.

All these operations are performed using the Azure Key Vault SDK for all supported programming languages. For instance, you could use the following code snippet written in C# to encrypt a string:

```
var rsaKeyName = $"rsa-key-{Guid.NewGuid()}";
var rsaKey = new CreateRsaKeyOptions(
    rsaKeyName,
    hardwareProtected: false
)
{
    KeySize = 2048,
};

var kvKey = keyClient.CreateRsaKey(rsaKey);
```

```
var cryptoClient = new CryptographyClient(
    kvKey.Id,
    new DefaultAzureCredential()
);

var text = Encoding.UTF8.GetBytes("data to be encrypted");
var result = cryptoClient.Encrypt(
    EncryptionAlgorithm.RsaOaep256,
    Text
);
```

Here, we are creating an RSA key that gets uploaded into Azure Key Vault. Then, we use the same SDK to get the key metadata, define the data to be encrypted, and finally encrypt it. A similar technique could be used for another programming language, such as JavaScript:

```
const credential = new DefaultAzureCredential();
const serviceClient = new KeyClient(
    `https://${process.env.AZURE_KEYVAULT_NAME}
        .vault.azure.net`,
    credential
);

const keyVaultKey = await serviceClient.getKey('myRsaKey');
const encryptClient = new CryptographyClient(
    keyVaultKey,
    credential
);
const text = 'text to encrypt';
const algorithm = KnownEncryptionAlgorithms.RSAOaep256;
const encryptParams = {
    algorithm,
    plaintext: Buffer.from(text)
};
const result = await encryptClient.encrypt(encryptParams);
```

If you look closely, you will see that for both programming languages, the concept of encrypting a string is the same. In the GitHub repository for this chapter, you will find full examples of how to perform the encrypt and decrypt operation using the supported programming languages and the Azure Key Vault SDK.

> **Note**
> It's also possible to use symmetric keys to perform the operations discussed here, but that feature requires using a Managed HSM version of Azure Key Vault. From an implementation perspective, the approach is the same.

You should employ the following good practices when you're using Azure Key Vault to encrypt and decrypt strings:

- Make sure you control how an encrypt/decrypt operation can be performed by using a proper set of permissions (whether you use access control or Azure RBAC).

- Proper monitoring of Azure Key Vault will help you understand who, what, and how uses the keys.

- Keys should be rotated regularly – it's up to the application to decide, but having that process implemented improves the overall security of a solution.

- Encrypted data can't be read without a decryption key, but it should still be kept in a safe place.

- Keys may have different versions – when you use them for encryption, make sure you store the version number so that you know which version is supposed to be used to decrypt a string.

In this section, we discussed several important technical details related to Azure Key Vault and its capabilities for building applications hosted in Azure. Now, let's learn how Azure Key Vault integrates with Azure App Configuration and how both services can help you modernize your application's stack.

Using Azure App Configuration to store configuration details

When building an application, most of the time, you'll need to store its configuration. There are multiple options available – some are better suited for desktop applications; some work better with web applications or console applications. Here are a few options you can utilize:

- INI files
- XML files
- Databases
- APIs

Each option has its use cases, as well as pros and cons. In this section, however, we're going to discuss an alternative to all those methods for storing and managing configuration. Azure offers a native service that can help you manage your application's configuration properly: Azure App Configuration. What's even more interesting is that it integrates with Azure Key Vault seamlessly, so you can benefit from both services and set up a flexible and cost-effective solution for managing the types of configuration values your application may need.

Let's start by discussing how Azure App Configuration is structured and how you can reference the values it stores.

Understanding the main features of Azure App Configuration

Azure App Configuration is a service that offers several useful features:

- Configuration management
- Feature management
- Configuration snapshots
- Soft delete for configuration values

It's a dedicated store for any kind of value you'd like to integrate with your application. It works with various language stacks (.NET, Java, Python, JavaScript) and services (e.g., Azure Kubernetes Service, Azure Functions, or traditional web applications). It has the following main use cases:

- Implementing feature flags for your application so that you can manage them in real time
- Changing the configuration values of your application without the need to redeploy it
- Centralized management across applications and environments

Technically, Azure App Configuration is just a form of key-value storage with a dedicated layer for interacting with services. This makes the whole setup quite simple and allows you to focus on implementing business logic rather than spending time configuring integration with infrastructure components.

> **Note**
>
> Multiple architectures work with Azure App Configuration. Even though it allows you to centralize the configuration and management aspects, this doesn't mean that you need to follow that design. You can create Azure App Configuration per application or even per application and per environment. It's up to you how you want to approach the integration and separate configuration values. However, remember that Azure App Configuration is charged per store per day. This means that for non-production environments, it may quickly become quite an expensive solution.

To understand all its features better, let's deploy an instance of Azure App Configuration and play around with its functionalities.

Deploying Azure App Configuration

To deploy Azure App Configuration, you can use the Azure portal, ARM templates, Bicep, Terraform, and CLI tools. For the exercises in this section, we'll use the Azure CLI for simplicity. Let's start by running the following commands:

```
az group create \
--name <resource-group-name> \
--location <location>

az appconfig create \
--location <location> \
--name <store-name> \
--resource-group <resource-group-name>
```

These commands will create a resource group and an Azure App Configuration store. Since we're using the default value, the configuration store that we're creating with our command will be created using Standard SKU. This means that your store will charge you each day. If you want to create a free version, use the following command instead:

```
az appconfig create \
--location <location> \
--name <store-name> \
--resource-group <resource-group-name> \
    --sku Free
```

Remember that the free version of Azure App Configuration comes with several limitations and quotas, which may make development and working with the service difficult. A good approach is to get started with the free version and change the SKU once you cannot utilize it anymore.

> **Note**
>
> You're only allowed to create one configuration store per subscription using the Free SKU. If you want, you can reuse the existing instance if it's available or just remove the paid version immediately once you've finished working with it.

Once an instance of the service has been created, we can try to create our first key-value element in it.

Creating configuration

To create a key-value element as part of your configuration, run the following command:

```
az appconfig kv set \
--name <store-name> \
--key <key> \
--value <value>
```

For instance, if you want to create a single configuration value named `Logging:LogLevel` with a value of `Debug`, run the following command:

```
az appconfig kv set \
--name <store-name> \
--key "Logging:LogLevel" \
--value "Debug"
```

Providing keys with the `<key1>:<key2>` syntax allows you to create a hierarchical structure so that you can reference whole levels if needed instead of individual values. Of course, you can provide more than two keys if needed. If your configuration is a multi-level object, the following references are valid:

- `<key1>`
- `<key1>:<key2>`
- `<key1>:<key2>:<key3>`

It's up to you and your application to define how complex the configuration becomes and the best way to reference it. With a value in the configuration created, let's discuss one additional thing that integrates with it: labels.

Using labels

Let's say that your application has been deployed to three separate environments:

- Test
- PreProd
- Production

All these environments may have a different value for the configuration used by it. If we use Azure App Configuration, we'll quickly realize that it's impossible to define the same key multiple times but with different values. To overcome that limitation (so that each environment can have its own values), we can use labels. Conceptually, our configuration will look like this:

- Key: `Logging:LogLevel` | Value: `Debug` | Label: `Test`

- Key: `Logging:LogLevel` | Value: `Information` | Label: `PreProd`

- Key: `Logging:LogLevel` | Value: `Error` | Label: `Production`

To reflect this setup in Azure App Configuration, we need to run the same command three times:

```
az appconfig kv set \
--name <store-name> \
--key "Logging:LogLevel" \
--value "Debug" \
--label Test

az appconfig kv set \
--name <store-name> \
--key "Logging:LogLevel" \
--value "Information" \
--label PreProd

az appconfig kv set \
--name <store-name> \
--key "Logging:LogLevel" \
--value "Error" \
--label Production
```

Once added, our configuration key will look like it was defined only once but has three different values.

> **Note**
>
> Since we used the same key for the configuration that we used in the previous example, `Logging:LogLevel` will have four different values since one was created without a label.

If we want to query the values, we can use the following command:

```
az appconfig kv list \
    --key "Logging:LogLevel"
    --name <store-name>
```

Your result should look similar to mine:

```
{
    "contentType": "",
    "etag": "zj9FXs6EbEswTqVPrCvcK8igM85OQIPDW7eo6vJUr8c",
    "key": "Logging:LogLevel",
    "label": null,
    "lastModified": "2024-08-11T12:30:30+00:00",
    "locked": false,
    "tags": {},
    "value": "Debug"
},
// You should see 3 more results returned
```

If you only want to fetch values for a given label, use the same command but with an additional parameter:

```
az appconfig kv list \
    --key "Logging:LogLevel"
    --name <store-name> \
    --label <label-name>
```

Thanks to labels, you can easily switch between different sets of configuration values, depending on the current environment. This allows you to keep immutable keys while changing only their values (your application logic is untouched).

Now, let's learn how to implement and use feature flags using Azure App Configuration.

Implementing feature flags using Azure App Configuration

Feature flags are a useful feature in medium to large-sized applications as they allow you to perform A/B testing and validate ideas without the need to publish them to all your customers. Azure App Configuration has a dedicated capability that allows you to implement feature flags. This simplifies the overall setup and allows you to keep the same source for configuring both the application and its features.

To configure a new feature flag, run the following command:

```
az appconfig feature set \
--name <store-name> \
--feature <feature-name>
```

This will create a new feature flag that's disabled by default. To enable it, you must run a separate command:

```
az appconfig feature enable \
--name <store-name> \
--feature <feature-name>
```

The rest of the implementation is application-specific. Azure App Configuration comes with a set of SDKs that can be used for one of the supported language stacks. For instance, you could enable feature flags in ASP.NET Core with the following middleware:

```
builder.Configuration.AddAzureAppConfiguration(options =>
{
    options.Connect(connectionString)
        .Select("SomeLabel:*", LabelFilter.Null)
    options.UseFeatureFlags();
});
```

For Python, the configuration would be slightly different:

```
config = load(endpoint=endpoint,
    credential=InteractiveBrowserCredential(),
    feature_flag_enabled=True,
    feature_flag_refresh_enabled=True)


feature_manager = FeatureManager(config)
```

You can find detailed instructions on how to do this in the documentation for Azure App Configuration: https://learn.microsoft.com/en-us/azure/azure-app-configuration/manage-feature-flags?tabs=azure-portal#next-steps.

What's important about using feature flags with Azure App Configuration is that the service isn't responsible for enabling/disabling features. Sure, you can enable/disable feature flags at the store level or even implement feature filters that can link a feature with a time window, geographic location, or even a user's browser, but this only works at the configuration level. How changing a feature flag impacts your users depends solely on your implementation. In the following simple example, we're using a feature flag to display a developer console in our application:

```
if (await featureManager
    .IsEnabledAsync("IsDevelopmentModeActive"))
{
    DisplayDeveloperConsole();
}
```

Now, let's learn how Azure App Configuration integrates with our application and how we can connect it with Azure Key Vault so that we can store sensitive values in the configuration.

Understanding integration options for Azure App Configuration

Azure App Configuration supports several language stacks with dedicated SDKs, all of which simplify development and make the whole integration process a seamless experience. At the time of writing, Azure App Configuration supports the following:

- .NET (ASP.NET Core, .NET, .NET Framework)
- Java (Sprint)
- Python
- JavaScript

Conceptually, each SDK works in the same way. At the beginning of this chapter, we discussed how Azure Key Vault SDK works and how you can authenticate your application when connecting to the service. For Azure App Configuration, the concept is similar. The only difference is the availability of access keys, which can be used to interact with your instance of the service.

> **Note**
>
> Access keys are simple but rather primitive options for accessing services. They cannot be used for authorization as you need to decide whether you're using read-write or read-only keys – there's no other option. They are also difficult from an auditing perspective as you cannot be sure who (or what) is using them. I strongly recommend basing your implementation on Azure RBAC from the very beginning when starting a new project.

Let's look at some examples of accessing Azure App Configuration using different languages. We'll start with .NET. The following example connects with the service using Managed Identity credentials:

```
var builder = WebApplication.CreateBuilder(args);
builder.Configuration.AddAzureAppConfiguration(options =>
options.Connect(
    new Uri(
        https://<app-configuration-store-name>.azconfig.io
    ),
    new ManagedIdentityCredential()));
```

Note that to configure the connection, we only need the store's name. These credentials are obtained using an assigned Managed Identity and querying the metadata endpoint. It's perfectly fine to change the implementation and use the `DefaultAzureCredential` object instead – this will allow you to connect with Azure App Configuration using both local and remote credentials.

> **Tip**
> If you'd like to use a user-assigned identity, make sure you're passing the `clientId` value of the identity object to notify the identity package of which identity it should use.

If you'd like to use JavaScript, the implementation will be slightly different:

```
const {
    load
} = require("@azure/app-configuration-provider");
const connectionString =
    process.env.AZURE_APPCONFIG_CONNECTION_STRING;

async function run() {
    const settings = await load(connectionString);
    const message = settings.get("message");
    const greeting =  settings.get("app.greeting");
    const json = settings.get("app.json");

    console.log(`message: ${message}`);
    console.log(`greeting: ${greeting}`);
    console.log(`json: ${json}`);
}

run().catch(console.error);
```

As you can see, we're using the `azure/app-configuration-provider` package and connecting to Azure App Configuration using a connection string. The code will display three separate messages – one for each configuration value that's obtained from the configuration store. Note that we're using dot notation (`.`) to access the hierarchy of keys. This example assumes that we have the following hierarchy:

- `message`
- `app.greeting`
- `app.json`

What's also presented here is the ability to store JSON objects as configuration values (accessed using the `app.json` key).

For Python, the syntax will, once again, be slightly different:

```
from azure.appconfiguration.provider import (
    load
)
import os
```

```
connection_string =
    os.environ.get("AZURE_APPCONFIG_CONNECTION_STRING")

config = load(connection_string=connection_string)

print(config["message"])
print(config["json"]["key1"])
```

This Python application would write two separate values to stdout – the value of the message key and the value of the key1 field of a JSON object stored as a json key. As you can see, you can easily traverse a JSON tree when the results are coming from Azure App Configuration, especially in languages that aren't strongly typed.

Besides different language stacks, Azure App Configuration easily integrates with a subset of other Azure services. Let's discuss them before we summarize what we've learned in this chapter.

Integrating Azure App Configuration with other Azure services

Several services integrate with Azure App Configuration for better user experience and simplified integration. In this section, we're going to characterize them and explain how those integrations can help you.

Integrating with Azure Key Vault

We'll start this discussion by looking at how to integrate with Azure Key Vault. We've already discussed the value of Azure Key Vault references – they can help us reference sensitive values that are part of our application's configuration securely. If you wish to use Azure App Configuration, it's worth using those references as part of the configuration stored in Azure App Configuration.

> **Note**
> Azure Key Vault references for Azure App Configuration are only available for ASP.NET Core and Sprint Boot applications!

From an infrastructure perspective, to use Azure Key Vault references, you need to give your application permission to access Azure Key Vault. This can be done in the same way as you did for standard Azure Web Apps and Azure Key Vault integration. However, you need to remember that Azure App Configuration and Azure Key Vault don't communicate with each other. This means that the integration process happens at the SDK level, rather than the service level.

Due to this, you'll need to point to the Azure App Configuration SDK to resolve references using the credentials provided. Here's an example for an ASP.NET application:

```
builder.Configuration.AddAzureAppConfiguration(options =>
{
    options.Connect(connectionString);
    options.ConfigureKeyVault(keyVaultOptions =>
    {
        keyVaultOptions.SetCredential(
            new DefaultAzureCredential()
        );
    });
});
```

If you have a Java application, you'll find the following documentation page helpful for configuring it correctly: https://learn.microsoft.com/en-us/azure/azure-app-configuration/ use-key-vault-references-spring-boot?tabs=yaml.

Now, let's learn how to use Azure App Configuration in Azure Kubernetes Service.

Integrating with Azure Kubernetes Service

To integrate Azure App Configuration with Azure Kubernetes Service, you'll need a dedicated configuration provider – that is, **App Configuration Kubernetes Provider** (https://mcr. microsoft.com/product/azure-app-configuration/kubernetes-provider/ about). It'll take responsibility for creating ConfigMaps and Secrets based on your configuration. To enable your applications hosted on Kubernetes to fetch data from the provider, you'll need to deploy it and as many provider objects as needed. Here's some example YAML that you could use for deployment purposes:

```
apiVersion: azconfig.io/v1
kind: AzureAppConfigurationProvider
metadata:
  name: appconfigurationprovider-<prefix>
spec:
  endpoint: <your-app-configuration-store-endpoint>
  target:
    configMapName: <config-map-name>
    configMapData:
      type: json
      key: <filename>.json
  auth:
    workloadIdentity:
      managedIdentityClientId:
        <your-managed-identity-client-id>
```

Note that you'll also need to integrate your cluster with Azure using Managed Identity.

> **Tip**
>
> Remember that you can still keep the integration with Azure App Configuration at the application level and take care of connections in your code base.

Integrating with Azure App Service

Integrating Azure App Configuration with Azure App Service looks almost the same as integrating with Azure Key Vault. All you need to do is provide Azure App Configuration references as values for your configuration instead of actual values:

```
@Microsoft.AppConfiguration(
    Endpoint=https://<store-name>.azconfig.io;
    Key=<key>;
    Label=<label>
)
```

Of course, you still need to authenticate – to do that, you'll need to enable Managed Identity for your web application and add the necessary permissions for Azure App Configuration so that the principal can authorize correctly.

> **Note**
>
> This kind of integration works for both Azure Web Apps and Azure Functions without additional changes.

The last service that we're going to discuss is Azure Container Apps.

Integrating with Azure Container Apps

Since we haven't discussed Azure Container Apps yet, we won't discuss the technical details of the integration here. At the moment, we're deploying our own instance of that service and deploying an application there. However, to give you a better understanding of the capabilities of both services, I'll quickly explain how the integration works.

To allow your Azure Container App to connect with Azure App Configuration, you'll need a **Service Connector**. Service Connectors are managed connections that allow you to integrate your application with other services without additional configuration. Such a connection is available for Azure App Configuration – once enabled, your application can connect with Azure App Configuration using a dedicated environment variable containing the connection string for your configuration store. We'll cover that in detail in *Chapter 11*.

That's all this chapter. Let's summarize what we've learned by explaining use cases for Azure App Configuration and checking out what awaits in the next chapter.

Learning about use cases

Azure App Configuration has several use cases that we were able to identify and characterize throughout this chapter. The main scenarios where this service is useful are as follows:

- Configuration management centralization
- Feature flags
- Zero-downtime updates for configuration values

All these scenarios become important during the later stages of application development and when building production environments. While other solutions could provide similar functionalities, keeping everything within Azure may help you keep your integrations clean and simple as you can leverage the native capabilities of that cloud platform.

Besides those high-level scenarios, Azure App Configuration is also a solution for reliable configuration as it provides a restore and soft delete mechanism to keep your configuration untouched if someone deletes something by mistake. The SDKs provided by that service can be also used to refresh configuration values in place so that you don't need to restart your application to receive updated values.

Remember that you can extend your knowledge by reading the documentation for the service. I strongly recommend taking a look at the following link to get started and then choosing your own learning path: `https://learn.microsoft.com/en-us/azure/azure-app-configuration/overview`.

That's all for *Chapter 6*. Let's see what you'll learn in *Chapter 7*.

Summary

In this chapter, you learned about Azure App Configuration – a service that allows you to manage the configuration of your application. We discussed various capabilities of this service, including various integration options, interactions with Azure Key Vault, and how to structure your configuration store to reflect the architecture of your application. Since Azure App Configuration is one of the simpler services in Azure, it's a great place to start for everyone who wants to learn about managing and using Azure components in their applications.

In the next chapter, we'll step away from language stacks for a moment and take a look at a low-code solution for implementing workflows in Azure called **Azure Logic Apps**.

7

Integrating Services with Azure Logic Apps

In *Chapter 5*, you learned about your first serverless service in Azure – Azure Functions. When using these services as your building block, you need to use one of the supported programming languages and write some code on your own. As you're probably aware, there's another category of serverless services that are named **low-code** tools. They allow you to achieve similar results to Azure Functions but with almost no code needed.

One of the low-code solutions is Azure Logic Apps. This chapter is designed to explain that service to you, so you understand the building blocks, capabilities, and valid use cases, and know when and how to use it.

In this chapter, we're going to cover the following main topics:

- Understanding the building blocks of Azure Logic Apps
- Developing an application using Azure Logic Apps
- Considerations for choosing Azure Logic Apps
- Understanding use cases

Technical requirements

To perform the exercises in this chapter, you'll need the following:

- Visual Studio Code
- Azure CLI

Understanding the building blocks of Azure Logic Apps

Azure Logic Apps is a low-code service that allows you to create applications with no or a small amount of code. It doesn't require you to know a programming language. Instead, it focuses on its own building blocks and uses general knowledge such as protocols, APIs, and integrations to construct a working workflow executing defined steps.

Let's define the main building blocks for Azure Logic Apps for a better understanding of the concepts, which will be introduced later in the chapter.

Workflows in Azure Logic Apps

Each Azure Logic App is, in fact, a workflow containing any number of steps executing your logic. You can think about a workflow as a block diagram, which is built using conditions, loops, and actions. It's also important to remember that each workflow needs to be triggered by a trigger of some sort. Triggers in workflows are like triggers in Azure Functions – they can react to incoming HTTP requests, predefined schedules, or external events.

Workflow controls

We already mentioned that workflows look like block diagrams with dedicated steps controlling their flow. Workflows in Azure Logic Apps can be controlled by the following controls:

- Conditional statements
- Switch statements
- Branches
- Loops
- Scopes

All those concepts should be quite familiar to you as they exist in most programming languages. Logically, they are no different than controls, which you could use to write your application with C#, Java, or Python. However, as workflows are basically JSON documents, the development of low-code applications may look a little bit odd to you initially.

Variables

Some workflows require you to save an interim value or just persist it for the time the workflow is executed. To avoid a cumbersome method to store those values, Azure Logic Apps supports variables. They can be initialized and used whenever you need them.

One of the special use cases for variables is loops. We'll explain those in detail in the next part of the chapter.

Connectors

One of the most important building blocks for Azure Logic Apps is connectors. They enable you to integrate with other services using a dedicated and simplified configuration. Connectors are a game-changer if you want to quickly build a service that doesn't need a coded solution. With just a few clicks, you can connect with services such as Microsoft Exchange, SQL Server, SAP, or SFTP. Thanks to a simple interface, they allow you to focus on building an actual solution instead of challenging yourself with a custom code base.

There are three kinds of connectors available:

- Built-in
- Managed
- Custom

The difference between built-in and managed connectors is sometimes a little bit blurry. For instance, there are both built-in and managed connectors for **File Transfer Protocol** (**FTP**). The difference between them is that the built-in one allows you to connect only to FTP servers that are hosted in Azure. The managed one can connect with any FTP server that is publicly available.

The custom connectors require a little bit more description to fully understand them. Even though Azure Logic Apps offers tens of different in-built connectors, you still may find it difficult to build a proper integration with one of the less popular services or platforms. There are also cases when using the native connectors isn't considered compliant, so you need to build your very own integration. For such scenarios, Azure Logic Apps allows you to build custom connectors.

If you decide to build a custom connector, you will need to follow the guidelines provided by Microsoft and publish it for your Azure Logic Apps instance. The full tutorial is available in the Azure Logic Apps documentation at `https://learn.microsoft.com/en-us/azure/logic-apps/create-custom-built-in-connector-standard`.

> **Note**
> As of now, custom connectors can be written in .NET only.

As theory is never as interesting as practice, let's switch our focus to the next part of the chapter, where we start building an application using Azure Logic Apps.

Developing an application using Azure Logic Apps

The process of development and deployment for Azure Logic Apps is slightly different from that of Azure Web Apps or Azure Functions. The main difference is that there's no typical code available – instead, you either write the definition of your service using JSON or leverage the UI. Before we start developing our first application, let's first deploy the service.

Deploying Azure Logic Apps

To deploy Azure Logic Apps, we'll use the Azure CLI.

Use the following commands to create your own instance:

```
az storage account create \
-g <resource-group-name> \
-n <storage-account-name>

az logicapp create \
-g <resource-group-name> \
-n <logic-app-name>
-s <storage-account-name>
```

As you can see, you need a storage account with Azure Logic Apps to be able to use the service. Azure Logic Apps, similar to Azure Functions, uses Azure Storage to store a number of files and metadata required for the service to run. You'll also notice that the CLI returns the following message:

```
Created App Service Plan <logic-app-name>_app_service_plan in resource
group <resource-group-name>
Application Insights "<logic-app-name>" was created for this
Function App. You can visit https://portal.azure.com/#resource/
subscriptions/.../resourceGroups/<resource-group-name>/providers/
microsoft.insights/components/<logic-app-name>/overview to view your
Application Insights component
```

It turns out that Azure Logic Apps requires two additional components to work:

- Azure App Service plan
- Azure Application Insights

The App Service plan, however, is not a typical plan – it's created using the **WS1** SKU, which stands for **Workflow Standard**. This plan allows you to host your application using Azure Logic Apps with a fixed pricing and predictable performance. Azure Logic Apps, however, also offers a Consumption plan (similar to the one offered by Azure Functions). If you want to use it, you need to use another method of deployment, as the Azure CLI doesn't allow you to specify a Consumption plan as the hosting method.

To create an Azure Logic Apps instance for the Consumption plan, you need to use a separate command:

```
az logic workflow create \
--resource-group <resource-group-name> \
--name <logic-app-name>
```

> **Note**
>
> `az logic` is an extension module for the Azure CLI. If it's not already installed on your machine, you'll be asked to install it the first time you use the command.

As an alternative, you could use a Bicep file:

```
param parLogicAppName string = 'logicapp'

resource la 'Microsoft.Logic/workflows@2019-05-01' = {
  name: parLogicAppName
  location: resourceGroup().location
  properties: {
    state: <Enabled>
  }
}
```

You can deploy it using the following command:

```
az group deployment create \
--resource-group <resource-group-name> \
--template-file <template-file-path>
```

The interesting thing about Azure Logic Apps and different deployment models is the fact that you need to use completely different **Infrastructure as Code (IaC)** definitions depending on the model. As you can see in the previous code, we're using the `Microsoft.Logic/workflows@2019-05-01` resource definition to deploy Azure Logic Apps for the Consumption plan. If you want to use an Azure App Service plan, you need to deploy it using the `Microsoft.Web/sites` resource definition and provide `functionapp,workflowapp` as its kind.

> **Note**
>
> Check the GitHub repository for the full code snippet allowing you to deploy Azure Logic Apps with an Azure App Service plan using an ARM template.

Great, we have our instance deployed – it's time to start developing our first Azure Logic App.

Developing an Azure Logic App

We've already mentioned that Azure Logic Apps are JSON documents with a specific schema, which you can modify and mold to your needs. The very basic structure of each Azure Logic App looks like this:

```
{
    "contentVersion": "1.0.0.0",
    "parameters": {},
```

```
    "actions": {},
    "triggers": {},
    "outputs": {},
    "$schema": "https://schema.management.azure.com/providers/
    Microsoft.Logic/schemas/2016-06-01/workflowdefinition.json#"
}
```

You may find it similar to ARM templates as it also provides information about the schema, content version, parameters, and even outputs. The difference here is the presence of actions and triggers – we will discuss them shortly. Before we do that, let's use the available Visual Studio Code plugins to integrate with our Azure Logic App.

Using the Visual Studio Code plugin to work with Azure Logic Apps

Even though Azure Logic Apps can be developed using JSON definitions, it's rather a cumbersome approach. Generally speaking, it's much better to use the available UI editors to make changes. One of the available tools is an extension for Visual Studio Code. Let's see how to use it with Azure Logic Apps:

1. You can install it by opening Visual Studio Code, going to the **Extensions** menu on the left, and searching for `logic app`:

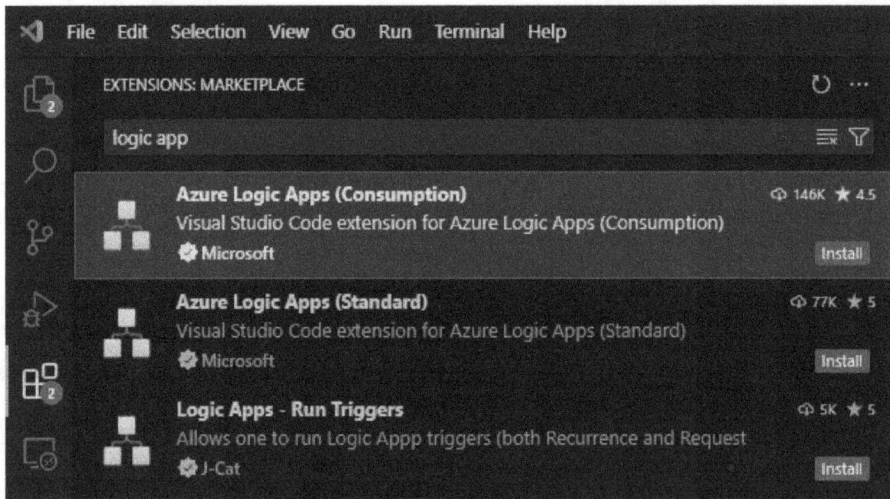

Figure 7.1 – Available extensions for Azure Logic Apps

There are two extensions available for Azure Logic Apps:

- **Azure Logic Apps (Consumption)**
- **Azure Logic Apps (Standard)**

Install the one that reflects the deployment model of your Azure Logic App (if you deployed it using the Azure CLI, you need the Standard version; for an ARM template/Bicep, it depends on which resource definition you used).

Note

For simpler scenarios, prototyping, and proofs of concept, you may use the Azure portal to develop your Azure Logic Apps. From the portability and maintenance point of view, it's not the best approach but serves well if you accept the trade-offs. In this book, however, we'll be focusing more on learning how Azure Logic Apps can be developed without the portal.

---

2. When the extension is installed (the process may take a while, so be patient), press *Ctrl + Shift + P* and find the `Azure: Sign In` command to authenticate to your Azure account. Follow the instructions provided by the extension to complete the process.

Tip

Remember to select the correct account when you're signing in.

---

3. Once you're authenticated, press *Ctrl + Shift + A* to open the **AZURE** tab and go to the **RESOURCES** section. You should be able to find your Azure Logic App as I did:

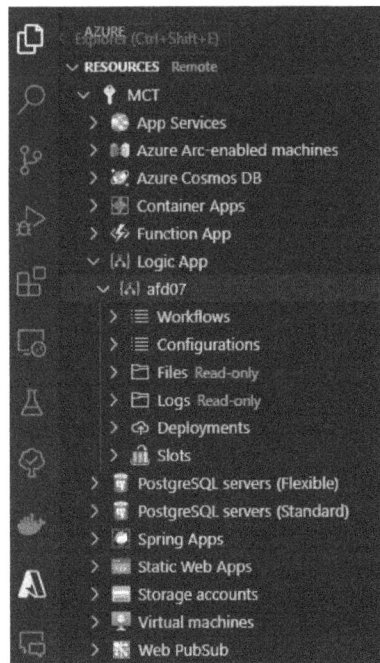

Figure 7.2 – The RESOURCES tab in Visual Studio Code with a single Azure Logic App

If you see your application, Visual Studio Code is ready to work.

Let's make our first changes.

Making changes in Azure Logic Apps

To make our first changes in Azure Logic Apps, we'll use Designer, which is available in the Azure portal. To access it, right-click on your Azure Logic App in Visual Studio Code and select **Open in Portal**:

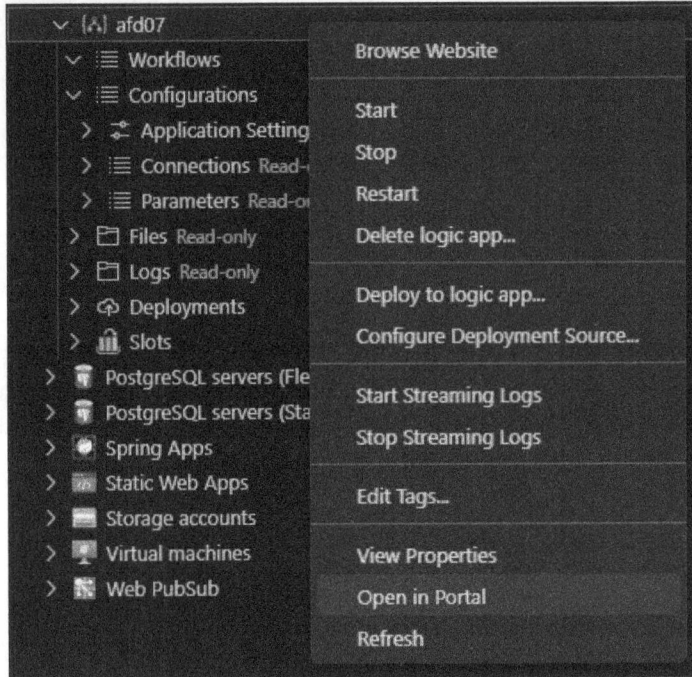

Figure 7.3 – Opening the Azure Logic App in the Azure portal

After a moment, your browser should open and show the Azure Logic App to you. Now, it's important to understand that the process of developing and managing Azure Logic Apps will be different depending on your hosting model. We'll describe them both for a better understanding of the differences.

Making changes in Azure Logic Apps – workflow model

To open the designer, we can just kick off by creating the workflow from scratch. To do that, open your Azure Logic App in the Azure portal and click the **Create workflow** button (as shown in *Figure 7.4*):

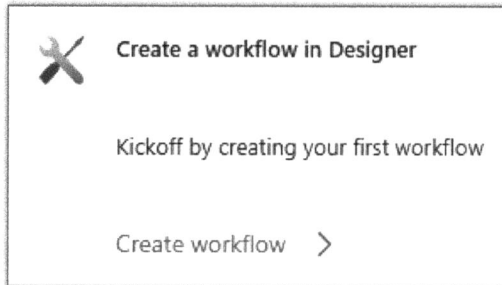

Figure 7.4 – Creating a workflow

You can now just click the **Add** button to get started with a new workflow. A new window will appear where you can provide the name of your workflow and define whether it's a stateful or a stateless one. For the sake of simplicity, let's select the **Stateless** option for now:

Figure 7.5 – Defining basic information about the workflow

The reason we're creating a workflow is because this hosting model of Azure Logic Apps allows you to have multiple workflows defined inside the same instance of Azure Logic Apps. This is a great concept if you have tens or even hundreds of flows defined – it gives you a simplified management model and helps in maintaining clean infrastructure.

Once your workflow is created, you can access it and start developing using Designer:

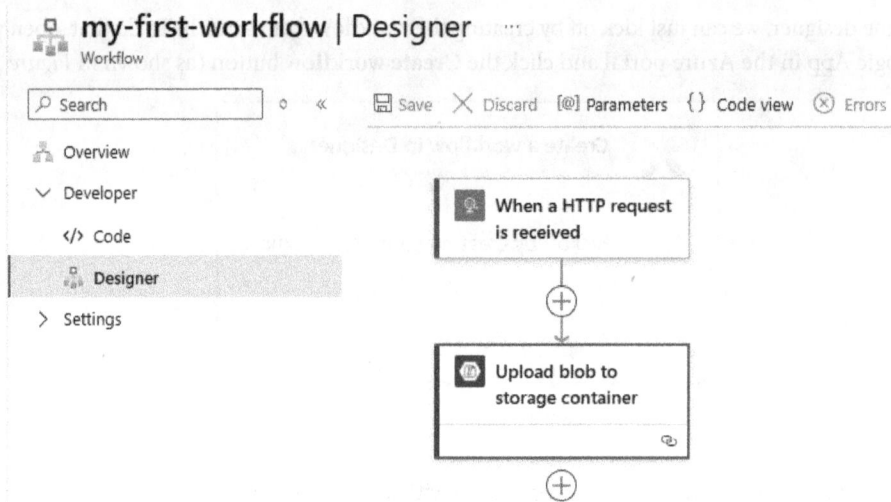

Figure 7.6 – Simple Azure Logic App triggered by an HTTP request

My Logic App has the following logic:

- It's triggered by an HTTP request.

- For each incoming request, it uploads a file to Azure Blob Storage.

When I click on the **When a HTTP request is received** trigger, I can see that the Azure portal allows me to define the configuration for it:

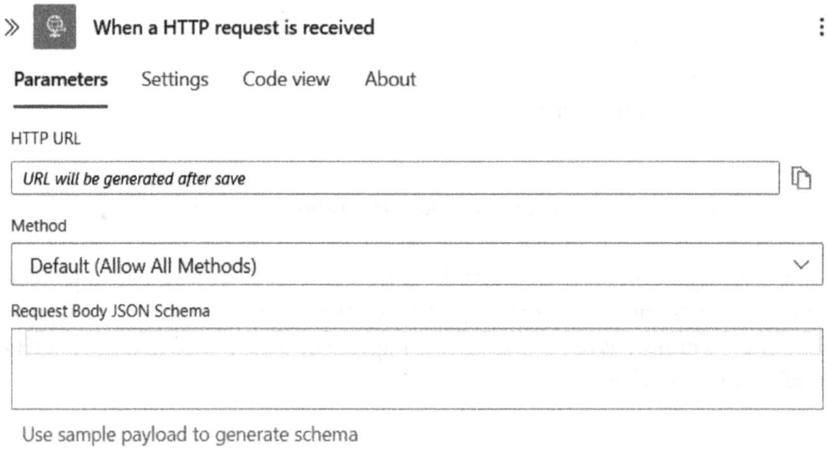

Figure 7.7 – Configuration of the HTTP trigger for a workflow

The portal presents the visual representation of the configuration stored as a JSON document. If I take a look at its definition, it has one action and one trigger. The action is defined as follows:

```json
"actions": {
    "Upload_blob_to_storage_container": {
        "type": "ServiceProvider",
        "inputs": {
            "parameters": {
                "containerName": "container",
                "blobName": "blob",
                "content": "foo"
            },
            "serviceProviderConfiguration": {
                "connectionName": "AzureBlob",
                "operationId": "uploadBlob",
                "serviceProviderId": "/serviceProviders/AzureBlob"
            }
        },
        "runAfter": {}
    }
}
```

The trigger looks like this:

```json
"triggers": {
    "When_a_HTTP_request_is_received": {
        "type": "Request",
        "kind": "Http",
        "inputs": {
            "method": "POST",
            "schema": {
                "type": "object",
                "properties": {
                    "foo": {
                        "type": "string"
                    }
                }
            }
        }
    }
}
```

As you can see, the definition is very verbose – it's difficult to tell what the purpose of the provided fields is and how we should interpret them. This is why Azure Logic App should be developed using Designer – the JSON definition is great because it allows us to version and store the applications in code, but it's a horrible syntax for developing business logic.

Let's check how we can work with Azure Logic Apps using the Consumption model and Visual Studio Code.

Making changes in Azure Logic Apps – Consumption model

An Azure Logic App deployed using the **Consumption model** works slightly differently from the one created for the workflow model. The main difference is the fact that workflow-based Azure Logic Apps allow you to create multiple workflows using a single instance of a service. For the Consumption plan, you need to create a separate instance for each workflow you want to develop. You can do that by performing the following steps:

1. To start developing Azure Logic Apps in Visual Studio code, press *Ctrl + Shift + A* and open the **LOGIC APPS (CONSUMPTION)** tab:

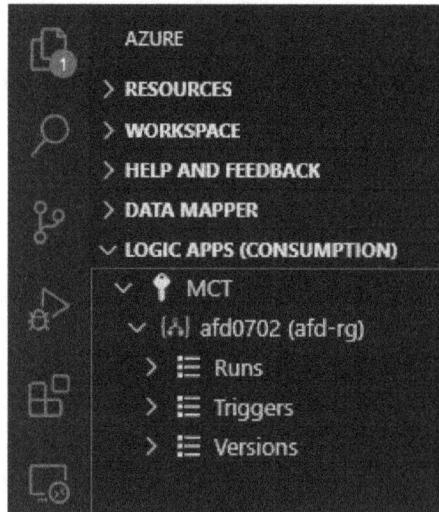

Figure 7.8 – View of Azure Logic Apps in the Consumption model in Visual Studio Code

2. You can then right-click on the name of your Azure Logic App and select **Open in Editor**. This will open a new tab in Visual Studio Code with the JSON schema of your application. You should see the following empty definition:

```
{
    "$schema": "https://schema.management.azure.com/providers/
    Microsoft.Logic/schemas/2016-06-01/workflowdefinition.
    json#",
    "contentVersion": "1.0.0.0",
    "parameters": {},
    "triggers": {},
    "actions": {},
    "outputs": {}
}
```

As you installed the extension, which integrates Visual Studio Code with Azure Logic Apps, you should be able to see syntax suggestions when you start typing.

3. Let's try to add a new trigger named `my-first-trigger`. Once you start working with the file, you will see that Visual Studio Code starts suggesting possible values:

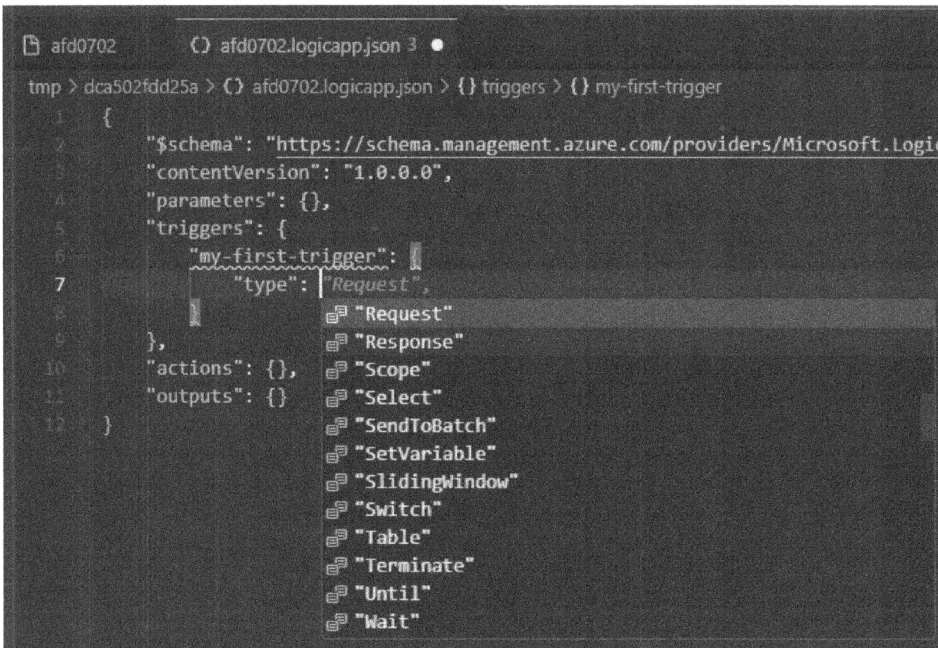

Figure 7.9 – Integration of Visual Studio Code with Azure Logic Apps schema

4.   Let's try to create the same trigger as we had for the workflow Azure Logic Apps instance:

• Type: `Request`

• Inputs: `schema object`

Your code should look similar to mine:

```
"triggers": {
    "my-first-trigger": {
        "type": "Request",
         "kind": "Http",
        "inputs": {
            "schema": {
                "type": "object",
                "properties": {
                    "name": {
                        "type": "string"
                    }
                }
            }
        }
    }
}
```

You can read it as follows – the Azure Logic App has a single trigger (HTTP request), which has a defined schema containing a single name field.

5.   Let's add an action to complete the setup:

```
"my-first-action": {
    "type": "Response",
    "inputs": {
        "statusCode": 200,
        "body": {
            "message": "@{triggerBody()?[<name>]}"
        }
    }
}
```

As you can see, we're adding an action named `my-first-action`, which is defined as a simple response message containing a specific field from the request's body. To access it, we're using the `triggerBody()` function and then the name of the field to use it.

> **Note**
> The JSON schema for building Azure Logic Apps is a detailed document with lots of various tricks and built-in features. The best way to understand it is to use the official reference: `https://learn.microsoft.com/en-us/azure/logic-apps/logic-apps-workflow-definition-language`.

6. To see our Azure Logic App in action, we need to submit it to Azure. The extension we're using can upload new definitions with each save of the modified JSON. However, in case it doesn't happen automatically, press *Ctrl* + *Shift* + *P* and run the `Azure Logic Apps (Consumption):` `Promote` command. After the upload, Designer should present the following blocks:

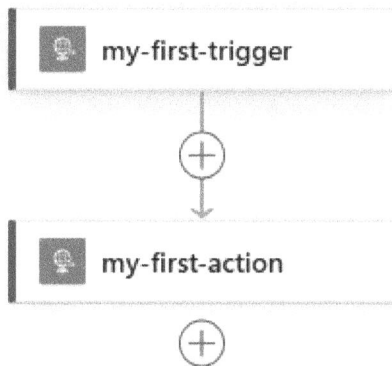

Figure 7.10 – Designer view for the deployed application

7. As our Azure Logic App is triggered via an HTTP request, we need to obtain its URL. In order to do that, the easiest way is to use the Azure portal as it removes a lot of unnecessary burden involved when obtaining the URL via other methods.

> **Tip**
> If you need to obtain the workflow URL programmatically, the best way to do that is to use the REST API: `https://learn.microsoft.com/en-us/rest/api/logic/workflows/list-callback-url?view=rest-logic-2016-06-01&tabs=HTTP`.

If you want to get the workflow URL from the portal, go to your Azure Logic App instance and copy the **Workflow URL** value:

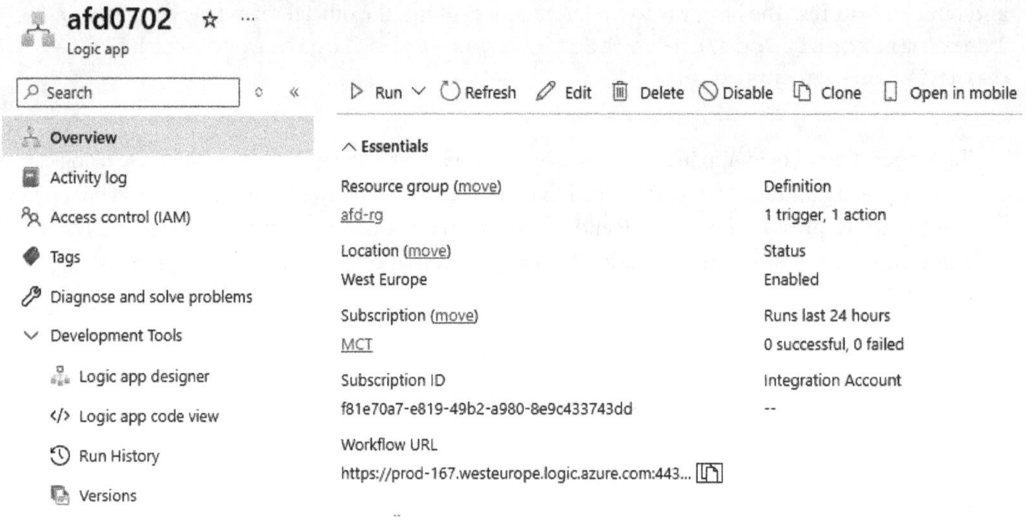

Figure 7.11 – Obtaining the workflow URL

8. Once you have the URL, you can try to trigger the workflow. If you did everything as I did, you could send the following cURL request to get the result:

```
curl --request POST \
  --url '<workflow-url>' \
  --header 'Content-Type: application/json' \
  --data '{
      "name": "Kamil"
}'
```

The result should contain the value of the name field:

```
{
      "message": "Kamil"
}
```

As you can see, we quickly coded a simple application without a single compilation or script. This is the basic concept of each low-code/no-code solution – to provide as many building blocks as possible that are also flexible enough to cover most of the use cases.

To understand the service even better, let's discuss all the considerations when you should and when you shouldn't select Azure Logic Apps.

Considerations for choosing Azure Logic Apps

Even though low-code/no-code solutions such as Azure Logic Apps are a great option for coding common things such as generic workflows, simple data processors, or proofs of concept, they can also be easily used in enterprise scenarios, which require integrating services such as SAP. Due to their serverless nature, they can scale with no human interaction and offer a great balance between the complexity of a solution and the actual effort to develop it.

Still, Azure Logic Apps are not meant to cover all the scenarios. Yes, they offer lots of flexibility, but you still need to develop them within a certain framework. You cannot easily move them between environments and their syntax will become difficult to understand after a while (similar to ARM templates).

When designing a solution, you need to ask yourself what kind of application you're going to build:

- Do you need to integrate your application with a test suite?

- Do you have people who are familiar with the nature of low-code/no-code services?

- Do you have strict requirements for data privacy and network isolation?

- Do you need to introduce additional middleware for your service so it starts processing data after a set of checks?

- What kind of authentication and authorization is required by your application?

- How often will your application be executed?

Depending on the answer, you may find Azure Logic Apps more or less useful. Let's try to discuss those points in detail.

Testing Azure Logic Apps

As Azure Logic Apps are basically a set of JSON documents, it's difficult to test them in isolation. This means that besides some common static checks, the testing of Azure Logic Apps is focused on **end-to-end (E2E)** testing. Test suites for Azure Logic Apps may become quite sophisticated, as you often need to coordinate everything between a number of external services. Another important factor is pricing, which depends on the hosting model. If you're using the workflow/App Service plan model, you don't need to worry about the price of your application – the pricing is fixed. For the Consumption plan, you need to consider how much impact your tests imply on the infrastructure.

Understanding low-code/no-code solutions

Low-code/no-code solutions are not ordinary programs that you may be used to developing on a daily basis. They are flexible frameworks with robust development environments but may become really cumbersome if you need to implement complex logic. Such solutions are great if you have preprocessed data or a simple business domain. Using Azure Logic Apps to handle difficult transformations or decisions (such as insurance calculations or data analysis) may render your application not only slow but also very expensive as you have a limited way to optimize your code.

Data privacy and network security

As with every cloud service, data privacy and network security are key elements of all enterprise platforms. Azure Logic Apps are no different here – you need to understand the capabilities of the service and design a solution that is compliant with your requirements. It's important to remember that in Azure Logic Apps, you have different levels of logs and access that need to be controlled. Depending on the workflow type (Consumption versus Standard), you will have different Azure **Role-Based Access Control** (**RBAC**) roles to use. You also have run history data, which means you need to either secure it via IP restrictions or by obfuscation. You can read more about this here: `https://learn.microsoft.com/en-us/azure/logic-apps/logic-apps-securing-a-logic-app?tabs=azure-portal#obfuscate`.

> **Note**
> Azure Logic Apps supports managed identity authentication. This allows for simplifying the management of workflows when using Azure connectors.

For integrating with virtual networks, you need to deploy your Azure Logic App using either a workflow or Azure App Service plan (App Service Environment V3) hosting model. This is required to provide connectivity to a private network as the Consumption plan (similar to Azure Functions) doesn't give you that possibility. Some time ago, that kind of design was developed using **Integration Service Environment** (**ISE**). As of now, though, ISE is considered retired and can no longer be used in new instances.

For more information about setting up private connectivity, take a look at the following document: `https://learn.microsoft.com/en-us/azure/logic-apps/secure-single-tenant-workflow-virtual-network-private-endpoint`.

Customizing Azure Logic Apps

By design, Azure Logic Apps cannot be extended – you're given a predefined set of connectors that you can configure and use. Still, they possess a certain level of extensibility, so you can decorate workflows with custom logic. One of the common patterns is delegating all the custom logic to an external (custom) API. Depending on your use case, there are multiple ways to achieve that – you can either use a standard request-response API, webhook, or pooling trigger.

More information about custom APIs can be found in the Azure Logic Apps documentation: `https://learn.microsoft.com/en-us/azure/logic-apps/logic-apps-create-api-app`.

It's also possible to develop a custom connector for Azure Logic Apps. This approach helps you encapsulate all the logic as a shared package, which you can ship and share even outside your organization.

To read more about custom connectors, take a look at the following documentation: `https://learn.microsoft.com/en-us/azure/logic-apps/custom-connector-overview`.

Authentication and authorization

We already mentioned that Azure Logic Apps supports managed identities for accessing other Azure resources. This approach allows you to avoid storing credentials and secrets within Azure Logic Apps and simplifies management. As this Azure service works similarly to Azure Functions, you need to consider which triggers you're going to use. For triggers that don't need human interaction, authentication is non-existent (as the user doesn't need to authenticate). For HTTP triggers (requests), the Azure Logic App is triggered via an authorized URL. As you don't have full control over that process, consider using publicly available Azure Logic Apps with HTTP endpoints as the last resort solution.

Scalability of Azure Logic Apps

Azure Logic Apps is a serverless service, meaning you don't really control its infrastructure. They will scale up and down automatically depending on the applied load. The scaling behavior of Azure Logic Apps depends on the hosting model – they scale differently for Consumption and Standard (single-tenant) or App Service plan models. If you need predictable performance, it's advised to use the latter models. They will give you a similar performance to Azure Web Apps and are a great choice for every application that needs to be reliable.

Pricing of Azure Logic Apps

As with all cloud services in Azure, understanding the pricing is one of the keys to successfully using a service. In this chapter, we discussed multiple hosting models for Azure Logic Apps. Depending on the selected model, the pricing for this service will be different, affecting the rationale behind selecting it over alternatives (such as Azure Functions).

On a high level, Azure Logic Apps can be deployed as either a single-tenant or multi-tenant solution. Single-tenant deployment, which is used for developing advanced and complex workflows, is charged based on vCPU and memory utilized. Multi-tenant deployments are priced based on usage – the price scale is linear with each execution. If you don't need to consider additional features such as virtual network integration, usage-based pricing will be easier to handle and often also cheaper. It will scale with the utilization of your application and is a great choice if you need to carefully plan your cloud spent.

The pricing of single-tenant deployments of Azure Logic Apps doesn't scale with usage – you pay a fixed price each month. Such an approach makes it much more difficult to scale costs with the utilization of your application. It doesn't really matter whether it was executed one time or one million times – the price stays the same. The benefit of fixed pricing, though, is its predictability – it's also immune to attacks leveraging the dynamic pricing of your services.

Separate pricing is reserved for connectors used in your instance of Azure Logic Apps. They are priced per call (which may be different from the number of executions of your workflow – this is true for calls that use pagination, for example). The pricing is different for Standard and Enterprise connectors. When planning your Azure Logic App and calculating cost, make sure you take that into account.

For a detailed overview of pricing, take a look at the following documentation page: `https://learn.microsoft.com/en-us/azure/logic-apps/logic-apps-pricing`.

> **Note**
>
> Remember that data retention in Azure Logic Apps is also charged separately from the rest of the metrics. If you make lots of calls or your application is triggered very often, the amount of data stored due to persisting execution history may start to be visible on your monthly invoice. When compared with the rest of the pricing, though, the cost of data retention is rarely impactful.

Now we have discussed the considerations for Azure Logic Apps, let's talk about possible use cases for this service.

Understanding use cases

Azure Logic App excels in handling workflows that require multiple connections to either Azure or typical enterprise services. The audience of that service is not just developers – you could introduce it to people in your IT department who don't know a programming language yet are skillful enough to develop processes with integrations on their own. This means you could use Azure Logic Apps as a solution for transferring a subset of engineering responsibilities off your development teams to the rest of the IT department. By design, development teams are skilled in delivering customized solutions that are difficult to develop using existing tools. Using their skills to develop an application with a *point-and-click* solution seems like a waste of your company's resources.

On the other hand, Azure Logic Apps can become a very useful tool for developing prototypes or proofs of concept. An easy-to-learn development model, simple configuration, and consumption-based pricing make this service a great asset, even for a typical developer. Azure Logic Apps can be also used as an extension of your application – thanks to tens of ready connectors, you could use it to replace your boilerplate code and integrate your application with Azure Logic Apps as a single entity.

That's all that we have for this chapter. Let's summarize all the lessons and see what awaits in the next chapter.

Summary

In this chapter, we focused on learning about Azure Logic Apps. This is another serverless service offered by Azure, but as you can see, it offers quite a different development model when compared to Azure Functions. We saw multiple hosting models for Azure Logic Apps, which require a slightly different approach to both local setup and deployment. You can also see that it's possible to develop your application using either a visual designer or JSON schema. Both allow you to achieve the goal of developing functionality and it's a matter of preference to select the approach that suits you the most.

In the next chapter, we'll go back to Azure Functions, but this time, we'll discuss the way of building durable workflows using Durable Functions.

Join the CloudPro Newsletter with 44000+ Subscribers

Want to know what's happening in cloud computing, DevOps, IT administration, networking, and more? Scan the QR code to subscribe to **CloudPro**, our weekly newsletter for 44,000+ tech professionals who want to stay informed and ahead of the curve.

https://packt.link/cloudpro

8

Building Workflows Using Durable Functions

In the previous chapter, we talked about Azure Logic Apps and general ideas for low-code/no-code solutions. We implemented a basic workflow that could be managed even by someone who is not a proficient developer. Azure Logic Apps provide an intuitive and robust development model for quickly creating both simple and advanced workflows. This chapter is going to present you with how to develop similar concepts with a low-level framework, Durable Functions.

As Durable Functions is meant for building workflows, you may not find it useful if you're mostly focused on CRUD or service-oriented applications. However, if you need to coordinate a distributed process in a reliable way, it's definitely something worth learning about.

In this chapter, we're going to cover the following main topics:

- Understanding the differences between Azure Logic Apps and Durable Functions
- Developing a workflow using Durable Functions
- Implementing advanced concepts for workflows
- Learning about use cases

Technical requirements

For the exercises in this chapter, you'll need the following:

- Visual Studio Code
- Azure Functions Core Tools

The source code for this chapter can be found here: https://github.com/PacktPublishing/Azure-for-Developers-Third-Edition/tree/main/ch08.

Understanding the differences between Azure Logic Apps and Durable Functions

Azure Logic Apps is a low-code solution for building workflows. Yes, you can use JSON to manage and develop these apps, but JSON is not a programming language. The schema for Azure Logic Apps provides a subset of functions and functionalities available to most of the general-purpose programming languages but cannot be used to develop advanced business logic because of its verbosity and general clumsiness. While Azure Logic Apps can be used for workflows, where complexity comes from the process itself (you need to integrate lots of different services), it will struggle when complexity is the product of business rules involved in the process. In such scenarios, you may find **Durable Functions** a better alternative.

To understand the differences, let's compare the major features of both services.

Integrating external services

The overall concept for Azure Logic Apps and Durable Functions is the same – you can use them to build workflows. However, they are fundamentally different when it comes to the development philosophy. Azure Logic Apps is focused on business processes and integrations. Durable Functions is focused on low-level details and orchestrating actions needed to complete a process.

> Note
>
> The interesting thing about the whole comparison is the interchangeability of both services we're discussing. You're free to integrate Azure Logic Apps with Durable Functions, and vice versa. If one service is unable to cover a specific requirement, you can try to make a *polyfill* using another one. This gives you lots of flexibility and enables you to separate different development methods suited for different stages of the process development.

The implication of a different philosophy is the lack of native integrations in Durable Functions. It acts more like a framework rather than a SaaS service, which is useful if you want to customize your solution. On the other hand, it makes each integration an individual effort – you need to develop them from scratch and understand all the interim steps. While it may be tempting to always develop something by yourself (because you have control over it), using Azure Logic Apps for the beginning or offloading some development to a low-code solution may be a quick win, especially if you're not familiar with the framework.

Developing workflows

With Azure Logic Apps, the process of developing a workflow is quite straightforward. We can use Designer or leverage the JSON schema to build a workflow using a compatible IDE. It's also possible to use the Azure portal as an alternative to local development. With Durable Functions, the whole process is very different – you need to prepare your local environment, install the appropriate extensions, and build your solution in a similar way to a typical application.

The concepts applicable to both solutions will also be different. In Azure Logic Apps, we had our workflow with actions being building blocks, whereas in Durable Functions, we focus on using orchestrations. Each orchestration consists of one or more actions (resembling actions from Azure Logic Apps) that you need to code by yourself. The benefit of Durable Functions is full extensibility and easier integration with other components such as logging, authentication, authorization, and test suites.

Durability of workflows

As the name suggests, Durable Functions is meant for durability. These functions are designed to withstand conflicts, transient errors, and unreliable network connections. One of the most important concepts of Durable Functions is the replay mechanism. In short, it allows you to run the same instance of your orchestration multiple times without affecting the interim results of the workflow. You could call workflows built with Durable Functions transactional – they allow you to build eventually consistent processes without thinking about how to achieve that.

While similar functionality could be achieved with Azure Logic Apps, it's not really meant for processes, which have strict reliability requirements. Sure, you can implement checks and replay mechanisms on your own, but the main use case for this service is to develop workflows that will connect multiple services without implementing lots of boilerplate code meant for handling unexpected scenarios. Durable Functions outshines Azure Logic Apps when you expect guarantees that your process can be completed without implementing tens of safeguards along the way.

Hosting Durable Functions and Azure Logic Apps

Both Durable Functions and Azure Logic Apps are considered serverless services. The difference here comes from the fact that Azure Logic Apps is a separate product with its own control plane. Durable Functions, however, is built on top of Azure Functions – they follow the same concepts as triggers and bindings and are basically logical continuations to function as a service. Note that both Durable Functions and Azure Logic Apps use the Azure App Service plan for their foundation. This introduces similar limitations to both of them (such as the maximum time for responding to HTTP-based requests).

The benefit of the serverless approach is the capability to pay only for usage. If you can accept the limitation of the Consumption hosting plan, you'll be able to build workflows where cost scales with their usage pattern.

To see how the Durable Functions service works in action, let's start with developing our first workflow.

Developing a workflow using Durable Functions

To fully understand Durable Functions, we'll need to complete a number of exercises presenting the main concepts of the framework. Before we get started, we need to discuss which languages are supported by these services.

At the time of writing, Durable Functions supports the following programming languages:

- .NET (C#, F#)
- JavaScript and TypeScript
- Python
- PowerShell
- Java

The support for different languages was added in different runtime versions (for instance, while C# was supported from version 1.0, support for Java was added in version 4.0). However, as we're going to work with the newest version of the framework, you shouldn't worry about the support as long as you're planning to use one of the supported languages.

To get started on our journey with Durable Functions, let's talk about patterns for which these functions are applicable.

Understanding application patterns

Durable Functions is a very specialized variance of Azure Functions as these functions are meant for stateful workloads, which need to be handled in a reliable manner. This means that they offer quite a different development framework to allow you to satisfy those requirements. In general, Durable Functions have a few generic use cases for which they're a perfect match.

Function chaining

One of the main use cases is **function chaining**. In short, this is a pattern that allows you to call different functions in a sequence. It's a common pattern that is used in data flows when you want to offload some part of your work to another service or when you need to call multiple services to update the same set of data.

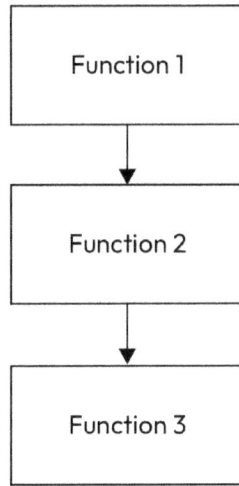

Figure 8.1 – Function chaining by sequentially calling three functions

Note that function chaining can be done in two ways:

- Sequentially
- In parallel

Chaining functions sequentially will have a limited use case for Durable Functions as you may not need control over other functions being called. A much better approach is to treat Durable Functions as an orchestrator responsible for calling functions in sequence and aggregating the results.

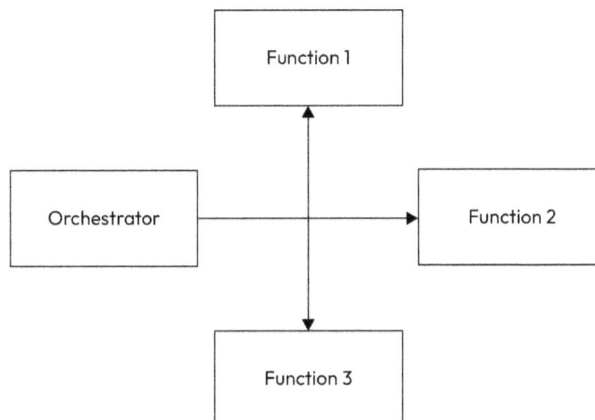

Figure 8.2 – Chaining functions with an orchestrator function

You may wonder what the benefit of using Durable Functions over Azure Functions is when chaining functions. You need to remember that we're talking about building workflows. If, hypothetically, you call *function 1* and then *function 2* and your workflow fails, you'll lose all the information from the called functions (unless you have some kind of persistence mechanism in your service). When you replay the workflow, you'll need to call the functions again, which can be difficult in stateful services (because you could have changed the state of an entity). Still, this could be mitigated by implementing a proper rollback mechanism, but such solutions are neither simple to implement nor easy to maintain. Durable Functions do the heavy lifting by persisting the state and reusing results.

Fan out/fan in

Another pattern worth discussing is the **fan out/fan in** pattern, which allows you to parallelize the processing of data. This pattern is useful if you can divide the data you're processing into chunks. If it's possible, then we could try to spin a number of additional processing units to speed up computations.

> **Note**
>
> Fan out/fan in is a common pattern used not only in applications but also in infrastructure. For instance, when you send data to Azure Event Hubs, it's partitioned and sent to several internal queues. When you attach a consumer to read that data, it'll basically *fan in* the partitions into a single data stream.

The reason that Durable Functions are useful in fan out/fan in scenarios is their ability to easily process data in parallel and store the results. This allows you to not only do everything much safer but also quicker (as any failure during data processing will not cause a full retry for all the chunks).

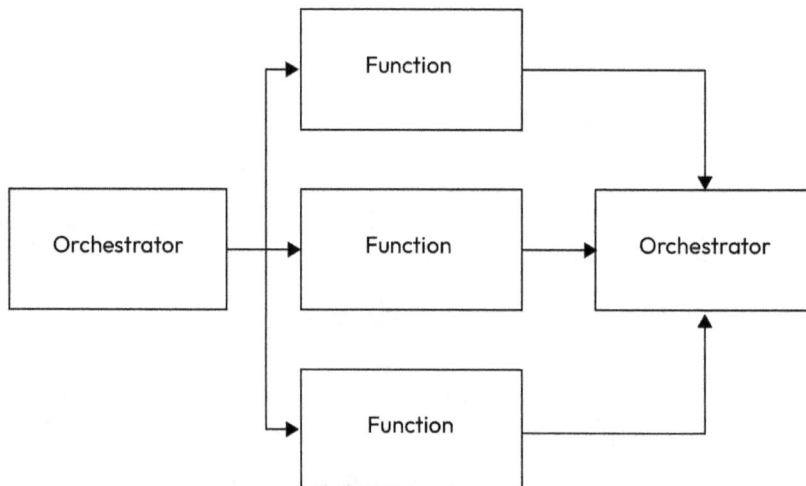

Figure 8.3 – Fan out/fan in scenario in Durable Functions

The capabilities of Durable Functions make them a great choice for any kind of data-oriented workflow/pipeline. They combine the scalability of Azure Functions with the durability of services meant for data processing, making it much easier to process big data volumes without conflicts and errors.

Asynchronous HTTP APIs

One of the most interesting use cases for Durable Functions is building asynchronous HTTP APIs. Let's consider the following scenario – a user initiates an operation that will generate a report. As report generation could be a lengthy process, we're providing additional endpoints that can be used by a user to get the status of the requested operation. I visualized it in *Figure 8.4*.

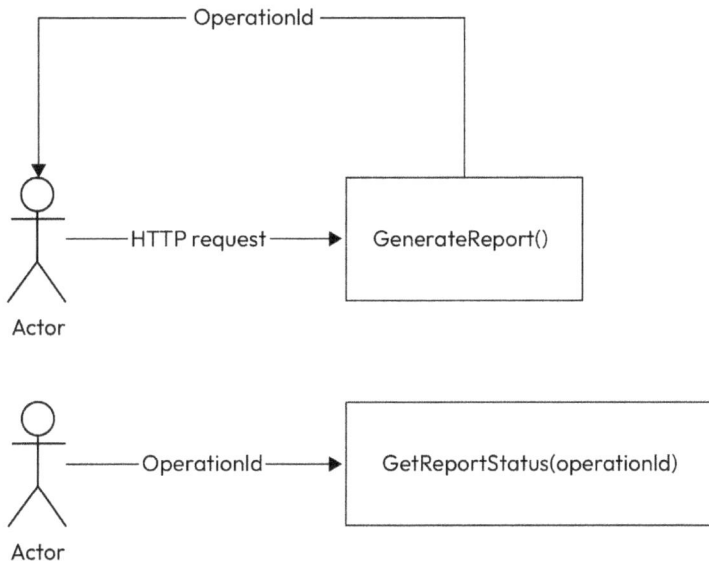

Figure 8.4 – Simple design diagram for the asynchronous HTTP API

The ability to request an update about the status of an operation is a valuable piece of the user experience of a system. It allows you not only to control the process but also extends the integration options (as you can implement pooling in other services, to make HTTP calls and wait for the process to complete). In Durable Functions, implementing such HTTP APIs is a piece of cake – each request is a separate orchestration with its own status, which means all you need is to return the unique identifier to a user. Then, the same identifier can be used to query orchestrations and verify their status.

> **Note**
>
> The whole concept of asynchronous HTTP APIs can be implemented in a number of different ways in Durable Functions. Using the identifier of an orchestration is only one of the possibilities.

Before we proceed to use Durable Functions in our code, let's cover the last common use case – human interaction.

Human interaction

In some workflows, human intervention is needed to verify the current status of the process and either acknowledge it or cancel the processing. This has various use cases, including automated document generation, supervised learning of ML models, and handling orders in an e-shop. All those cases have one thing in common – they need to be able to wait for an intervention indefinitely. Once again, this is possible to implement using services such as Azure Functions, but Durable Functions has a number of advantages:

- In the Consumption model, you don't pay when awaiting a response.
- The state is stored in the database, so the workflow knows from what place the process needs to be resumed.
- Durable Functions has a dedicated method for handling external events, making it much more intuitive when developing.

You can, of course, combine all the patterns in the same application if needed. Durable Functions is a very generic framework that doesn't make lots of assumptions. This makes it a really interesting asset if you expect lots of customization from your workflows.

Let's see now how we can implement a workflow using Durable Functions.

Developing a simple workflow

Let's create a simple workflow that we can run locally by performing the following steps:

1. To get started with Durable Functions, we need to create a function app locally. To do so, create a new directory on your computer and run the following command:

   ```
   func init
   ```

2. Select your worker runtime based on the list provided by the CLI (in my case, it was `dotnet`) and a language (in my case, it was C#). The CLI will create a new function app.

3. We can now use the new function app as the host for our orchestration. To create an orchestration, press *Ctrl* + *Shift* + *P*. On the window that appears, select **Azure Functions: Create function…**, and select **Durable Functions Orchestration** as the template. Take a look at *Figure 8.5* for reference.

Figure 8.5 – Context menu in Visual Studio Code

4. Follow the wizard default options for the rest of the steps and wait for your orchestration to be generated. Once the operation is complete, run the following command in your terminal:

`func host start`

After a moment, you should see output similar to mine:

```
[2024-09-08T12:54:43.891Z] Found /home/thecloudtheory/azure-
for-developers/ch08/ch08.csproj. Using for user secrets file
configuration.
[2024-09-08T12:54:47.844Z] Worker process started and
initialized.
Functions:
        MyFirstOrchestration_HttpStart: [GET,POST] http://
localhost:7071/api/MyFirstOrchestration_HttpStart
        MyFirstOrchestration: orchestrationTrigger
        SayHello: activityTrigger
```

5. Let's copy the host URL and test our orchestration by pasting it in the browser's address bar.

> **Note**
>
> If your function app isn't starting, make sure it can connect to Azure Storage (local or cloud instance).

When you send a request to the endpoint provided by your orchestration, you should see that it triggers the whole workflow and reports the results in the console (I removed some entries for clarity):

```
[2024-09-08T12:56:01.296Z] Executing 'Functions.
MyFirstOrchestration_HttpStart' (Reason='This function was
programmatically called via the host APIs.', Id=fa4af8cb-2ff1-
498c-9cc0-cc20f4aa38fa)
[2024-09-08T12:56:01.690Z] Scheduling new
MyFirstOrchestration orchestration with instance ID
'1fa99144c6df4caeae5980d6f9f22f20' and 0 bytes of input data.
[2024-09-08T12:56:01.983Z] Started orchestration with ID =
'1fa99144c6df4caeae5980d6f9f22f20'.
[2024-09-08T12:56:02.089Z] Executed 'Functions.
MyFirstOrchestration_HttpStart' (Succeeded, Id=fa4af8cb-2ff1-
498c-9cc0-cc20f4aa38fa, Duration=820ms)
[2024-09-08T12:56:02.148Z] Executing 'Functions.
MyFirstOrchestration' (Reason='(null)', Id=d9ca2052-b4f3-4a86-
8e38-a36bdce148ea)
[2024-09-08T12:56:02.203Z] Saying hello.)
[2024-09-08T12:56:02.341Z] Saying hello to Tokyo.
[2024-09-08T12:56:02.454Z] Saying hello to Seattle.
[2024-09-08T12:56:02.515Z] Saying hello to London.
[2024-09-08T12:56:02.515Z] Executed 'Functions.SayHello'
```

```
(Succeeded, Id=63c2081b-eea3-4d6e-ae4e-deef6a98c9a1,
Duration=2ms)
[2024-09-08T12:56:02.548Z] Executing 'Functions.
MyFirstOrchestration' (Reason='(null)', Id=d42bf244-92af-44af-
9fa3-f90a20d1d707)
[2024-09-08T12:56:02.556Z] Executed 'Functions.
MyFirstOrchestration' (Succeeded, Id=d42bf244-92af-44af-9fa3-
f90a20d1d707, Duration=8ms)
```

As you can see, our orchestration called a number of functions, each returning a different result. Let's discuss all the concepts presented here for a better understanding of how Durable Functions work.

Orchestrations in Durable Functions

Orchestration in Durable Functions is the main component, and is responsible for directing the execution of a workflow. Each orchestration is defined like this:

```
[Function(nameof(MyFirstOrchestration))]
public static async Task<List<string>> RunOrchestrator(
    [OrchestrationTrigger] TaskOrchestrationContext context)
{
    // Body of an orchestration
}
```

As Durable Functions is based on Azure Functions, you can find some similarities here:

- The [Function] attribute is used to indicate that a method is a function.

- The [OrchestrationTrigger] attribute indicates that a function is triggered as an orchestration.

Each orchestration gets a unique identifier that can be used to correlate different activities with each other. Note that orchestration is the only part of the workflow that can be called by a user (not including the human interaction endpoint).

Orchestration must be triggered by another function. In our case, we're using a trigger of the HttpTrigger type from another function that schedules a new orchestration with each HTTP call:

```
[Function("MyFirstOrchestration_HttpStart")]
public static async Task<HttpResponseData> HttpStart(
    [HttpTrigger(AuthorizationLevel.Anonymous, "get", "post")]
    HttpRequestData req,
    [DurableClient] DurableTaskClient client,
    FunctionContext executionContext)
{
    var instanceId =
        await client.ScheduleNewOrchestrationInstanceAsync(
```

```
        nameof(MyFirstOrchestration));

    return await client.CreateCheckStatusResponseAsync(req,
    instanceId);
}
```

When called, it'll return the following response:

```
{
    "id": "1fa99144c6df4caeae5980d6f9f22f20",
    "purgeHistoryDeleteUri": "http://localhost:7071/runtime/webhooks/
durabletask/instances/1fa99144c6df4caeae5980d6f9f22f20?code=4mT2
NufAOeOHM37BEm1HmTqOcOhtnESwun9MefzDex94AzFuB44Fjw==",
    "sendEventPostUri": "http://localhost:7071/runtime/webhooks/
durabletask/instances/1fa99144c6df4caeae5980d6f9f22f20/raiseEvent/
{eventName}?code=4mT2NufAOeOHM37BEm1HmTqOcOhtnESwun9MefzDex94
AzFuB44Fjw==",
    "statusQueryGetUri": "http://localhost:7071/runtime/webhooks/
durabletask/instances/1fa99144c6df4caeae5980d6f9f22f20?code=4mT2NufAOe
OHM37BEm1HmTqOcOhtnESwun9MefzDex94AzFuB44Fjw==",
    "terminatePostUri": "http://localhost:7071/runtime/webhooks/
durabletask/instances/1fa99144c6df4caeae5980d6f9f22f20/
terminate?reason={{text}}&code=4mT2NufAOeOHM37BEm1HmTqOcOhtnESwun9
MefzDex94AzFuB44Fjw=="
}
```

As you can see, it implements endpoints for four different activities:

- Purging the history of execution (`purgeHistoryDeleteUri`)
- Human interaction (`sendEventPostUri`)
- Getting the status (`statusQueryGetUri`)
- Terminating (`terminatePostUri`)

Each URL contains a `code` parameter that authorizes a user or a service calling the endpoint. Those endpoints are scoped to a single instance of orchestration, meaning you cannot use them to interact with other orchestrations.

When we call the endpoint for the status, we get the following response:

```
{
    "name": "MyFirstOrchestration",
    "instanceId": "1fa99144c6df4caeae5980d6f9f22f20",
    "runtimeStatus": "Completed",
    "input": null,
    "customStatus": null,
```

```
    "output": [
        "Hello Tokyo!",
        "Hello Seattle!",
        "Hello London!"
    ],
    "createdTime": "2024-09-08T12:56:01Z",
    "lastUpdatedTime": "2024-09-08T12:56:02Z"
}
```

The response contains all the valuable information for anyone interested in obtaining the status of the operation. You can find information there about the overall state of our process and also inputs and outputs. This shows how useful Durable Functions really are – they provide lots of useful features out of the box and allow you to focus on the important stuff.

Implementing activities

Activities are the building blocks of each orchestration. They are atomic and specialized operations that are meant to execute one particular task. In our example, there's a single activity defined that returns a simple "Hello, {name}!" string:

```
[Function(nameof(SayHello))]
public static string SayHello([ActivityTrigger] string name,
FunctionContext executionContext)
{
    return $"Hello {name}!";
}
```

It's important to remember that activities are meant to focus on simple and static tasks (idempotency). The reason for that is both the reliability and durability of workflows. Activities also have an *at least once* execution guarantee. If you build them to give different results for the same input, you may find it difficult to not only build a reliable process but also debug it.

> **Note**
> Remember that activities can be triggered only by orchestration. This ensures that the Durable Functions framework persists in its current state and preserves its capability to replay a workflow.

Each orchestration can have any number of activities called. You can also reuse activities across different orchestrations. However, it's good practice not to create orchestrations that are too complex. When building activities, try to find a sweet spot between complexity and atomicity.

Let's talk now about advanced concepts related to Durable Functions, so you can fully understand the provided capabilities.

Implementing advanced concepts for workflows

Orchestrations and activities already provide lots of necessary features needed to build reliable workflows using Durable Functions. However, the framework gives you many more features that are suited for a number of various tasks. In this section, we'll focus on using them and applying viable use cases.

Critical sections

Even though orchestrations are single-threaded (which means you don't need to worry about race conditions), there are cases where you need to be sure that only one orchestration can be active at a particular moment. This includes scenarios such as interactions with external systems or persisting data in non-transactional systems. You can also consider scenarios that would require the use of distributed transactions. For all those cases, Durable Functions introduce the concept of a critical section. It's implemented with the following syntax:

```
[Function("Critical")]
public static async Task Synchronize(
    [OrchestrationTrigger] IDurableOrchestrationContext context)
{
    var lockId = new EntityId("Foo", "Bar");
    using (await context.LockAsync(lockId))
    {
    }
}
```

Critical sections require you to provide an identifier as a reference to a durable entity (which we'll discuss in a moment). Then, we use the LockAsync method to open up a block, which will prevent other orchestrations from entering (you can consider it some kind of semaphore). This allows synchronizing the workflow across multiple orchestrations running at the same moment.

> **Note**
>
> Critical sections are available only in version 2.0 of Durable Functions. They are also available only for .NET.

Without using critical sections, you'll need to implement your own synchronization mechanism. This is doable using leases in Blob Storage and some extra code used by your orchestrations, for example.

Durable entities

Durable Functions allow you to define an entity that implements its own identity and internal state. You can ask an entity to perform an operation, and it will act as a separate service with its own logic. You can consider entities as a way to segment the domain when using orchestrations and activities. While you cannot call an entity from an activity, they offer an interesting concept to further extend the capabilities of your workflows.

A simple entity can look like this:

```
[Function("Store")]
public static Task DispatchAsync(
    [EntityTrigger] TaskEntityDispatcher dispatcher,
    StoreData data)
{
    return dispatcher.DispatchAsync(operation =>
    {
        switch (operation.Name.ToLowerInvariant())
        {
            case "add":
                operation.State.SetState(data);
                return new(data);
            case "reset":
                operation.State.SetState(new StoreData());
                break;
            case "get":
                return new(operation.State.GetState<StoreData>());
            case "delete":
                operation.State.SetState(null);
                break;
        }

        return default;
    });
}
```

This entity is responsible for handling multiple operations (add, reset, get, or delete) performed on a certain type (StoreData). Note that the type of state of an entity is selected by yourself – it can be both a primitive type (such as int or bool) and a complex type.

> **Note**
>
> The syntax for durable entities will depend on the programming language and runtime. The examples provided in this chapter present the concept using C# and a dotnet-isolated runtime.

Durable entities can be compared to the actor model, which allows you to concurrently process data by using stateful blocks with their own state. Such blocks (which can be called actors or entities) implement their own logic, which can not only perform data processing but also spawn new actors, pass messages, and make decisions. Because the model is meant to perform concurrent operations, you can use durable entities to process data in parallel – Durable Functions will take care of scaling out and coordinating the workflow.

You can call an entity from either a typical function or from an orchestration. What you do is use `DurableTaskClient` and interact with it via the `Entities` object. Take a look at the following example, where `client` is an instance of `DurableTaskClient`:

```
client.Entities.SignalEntityAsync(<entityId>, <operation>,
<additional-data>)
```

In our example, we could call the entity by executing the following code:

```
var data = new StoreData();
var entityId = new EntityInstanceId("Store", "myStore1");
client.Entities.SignalEntityAsync(entityId, "add", data)
```

When creating `entityId`, you need to provide the name of your entity (represented by the name of a function representing it) and a unique key to distinguish it from other entities.

Before we continue, let's discuss a real-world example for a better understanding. If you used Durable Functions to develop a process as part of an e-commerce application, you could utilize a durable entity to describe a basket/bag holding all the items about to be purchased by a customer. Such a basket would have its own representation with corresponding methods (add item, remove item, duplicate item, etc.). To represent an action when a customer puts a new item into the basket, we could use the following code:

```
var data = new ShopBasketItem("Shoes");
var entityId =
    new EntityInstanceId("Basket", Guid.NewGuid.ToString());
client.Entities.SignalEntityAsync(entityId, "add", data)
```

Such an approach would allow you to easily control a basket as a separate entity with its own state. It also makes business logic much easier to handle as you represent a business entity as an individual object instead of providing an abstraction via a database.

Sub-orchestrations

In Durable Functions, it's possible to define nested orchestrations called sub-orchestrations. Conceptually, they're meant to allow you to split your workflow into smaller pieces. This allows for a better organization of your code base and separate concerns of different modules in your code. Here's how you can call another orchestration:

```
[Function("OrchestrationExample")]
 [Function("OrchestrationExample")]
public static async Task ProvisionNewDevices(
    [OrchestrationTrigger] TaskOrchestrationContext context)
{
    await context.CallSubOrchestratorAsync("Suborchestration", new {
        userId = 1
    });
}


[Function("Suborchestration")]
public static async Task Suborchestration(
    [OrchestrationTrigger] TaskOrchestrationContext context)
{
    // Do something
}
```

What's interesting about sub-orchestrations is the ability to use them as both root-level orchestrations and a piece of another orchestration. This is valuable in a number of scenarios where you may have a process that can be performed either partially or end to end.

Eternal orchestrations

By definition, an orchestration ends once all the activities are completed. To run it again, you need to trigger it from scratch. To overcome that limitation, you could think about implementing an infinite loop, which will call activities infinitely. While this solves one problem, it'll generate another one. Orchestrations in Durable Functions keep track of their activities by persisting all the information in the history. If orchestration runs infinitely, you'll need infinite storage. This may hurt your application's performance and cause a number of issues when executing workflows. This is why Durable Functions introduced the concept of eternal orchestrations:

```
[FunctionName("EternalExample")]
public static async Task EternalExample(
    [OrchestrationTrigger] IDurableOrchestrationContext context)
{
    await context.CallActivityAsync("DoSomething", null);
```

```
    context.ContinueAsNew(null);
}
```

In order to continue execution as eternal orchestration, you could simply continue the execution by using the `ContinueAsNew` method. This starts a new orchestration with a new history, which can be easily validated and maintained. Eternal orchestrations are especially useful when used with timers (for schedule-based executions).

Singleton orchestrations

We talked previously about how Durable Functions allow you to use critical sections to limit how many orchestrations can proceed to a certain section in a moment. However, sometimes, you may want to allow only a single orchestration to run for the whole workflow. In order to do that, you need to implement part of the logic on your own. Let's start with the basics – when orchestration starts, it returns its identifier. We saw that previously when we ran our first orchestration. When we called it, it returned the following ID:

```
{
    "id": "1fa99144c6df4caeae5980d6f9f22f20",
    // Other endpoints...
}
```

This ID is generated automatically by the framework. If we want to pass it manually, we need to make it explicitly:

```
[Function("MyFirstOrchestration_HttpStart")]
public static async Task<HttpResponseData> HttpStart(
    [HttpTrigger(AuthorizationLevel.Anonymous, "get", "post",
        Route = "/orch/start/{instanceId}")]
    HttpRequestData req,
    [DurableClient] DurableTaskClient client,
    FunctionContext executionContext,
    string instanceId
    )
{
    await client.ScheduleNewOrchestrationInstanceAsync(
        nameof(MyFirstOrchestration),
        null,
        new StartOrchestrationOptions
        {
            InstanceId = instanceId,
        });
```

```
    return await client.CreateCheckStatusResponseAsync(req,
    instanceId);
}
```

The client will receive the instance ID, which can then be used to make sure there's no orchestration running with the same ID. However, this is the tricky part – if we want to make sure no other orchestration runs, we need to find them all or query for an existing one using its instance ID. For instance, we can run the following code to check for the existing orchestration:

```
var existingInstance = await client.GetInstanceAsync(instanceId);
```

If we want to check all the orchestrations, we need to use slightly different code:

```
await foreach (var orchestration in client.GetAllInstancesAsync())
{
    // Do something
}
```

We can limit the number of orchestrations returned by the GetAllInstancesAsync() method by applying a filter:

```
var existingInstance = await client.GetInstanceAsync(instanceId);
await foreach (var orchestration in client.GetAllInstancesAsync(new
OrchestrationQuery(
    DateTimeOffset.Now.AddMinutes(-5),
    DateTimeOffset.Now,
    [OrchestrationRuntimeStatus.Running],
    null)))
{
    // Do something
}
```

Then, we make sure that there's no orchestration running, but this approach is also problematic as it implies that there would be only a single type of orchestration defined within a function app. In most scenarios, this won't be the case, so we need to find a better solution. For that, we need to implement predefined identifiers for orchestrations and return them to the client. Here's how we can implement this. Instead of accepting any identifier of an orchestration, we define it inside an orchestration itself:

```
[Function("MyFirstOrchestration_HttpStart")]
public static async Task<HttpResponseData> HttpStart(
    [HttpTrigger(AuthorizationLevel.Anonymous, "get", "post",
        Route = "/orch/start/{instanceId}")]
    HttpRequestData req,
    [DurableClient] DurableTaskClient client,
    FunctionContext executionContext
```

```
    )
{
    const string instanceId = "SingletonOrchestration";
    await client.ScheduleNewOrchestrationInstanceAsync(
        nameof(MyFirstOrchestration),
        null,
        new StartOrchestrationOptions
    {
        InstanceId = instanceId,
    });

    return await client.CreateCheckStatusResponseAsync(req,
    instanceId);
}
```

Now, we want to make sure that if there's an active instance of SingletonOrchestration, we return an error:

```
if (existingInstance == null ||
    existingInstance.RuntimeStatus ==
        OrchestrationRuntimeStatus.Completed ||
    existingInstance.RuntimeStatus ==
        OrchestrationRuntimeStatus.Failed ||
    existingInstance.RuntimeStatus ==
        OrchestrationRuntimeStatus.Terminated)
{
    await client.ScheduleNewOrchestrationInstanceAsync(
        nameof(MyFirstOrchestration),
        null,
        new StartOrchestrationOptions
    {
        InstanceId = instanceId,
    });

    return await client.CreateCheckStatusResponseAsync(req,
    instanceId);
}
return req.CreateResponse(HttpStatusCode.Conflict);
```

This allows us to make sure only a single instance of an orchestration can run in the same moment. While this approach has its use cases (for instance, you need to interact with an external system in sequence), make sure you're not overusing it. Durable Functions are designed in a way that supports multiple instances of the same orchestration function running at the same moment. In fact, this is the intended way of using this framework. Artificially limiting execution to a single orchestration is an exception and should be used with care.

Versioning

The last concept we'll be discussing in this section is how we can version orchestrations. When designing a workflow based on Durable Functions, you need to consider that at some point in time, you'll want to update your code. As orchestrations can be long-running functions, we need to discuss what will happen if we decide to restart our function app to deploy updated code.

If you do deployment for a stateless service or short-living process, the impact of changes could be ignored. The process will be canceled, and we should be able to safely restart it. For Durable Functions (or stateful services in general), performing changes in the middle of the process may cause errors or conflicts. We talked about how Durable Functions replay the whole workflow by reusing the persisted state. If we decide that we want to change something in the code, it may impact how the logic is performed.

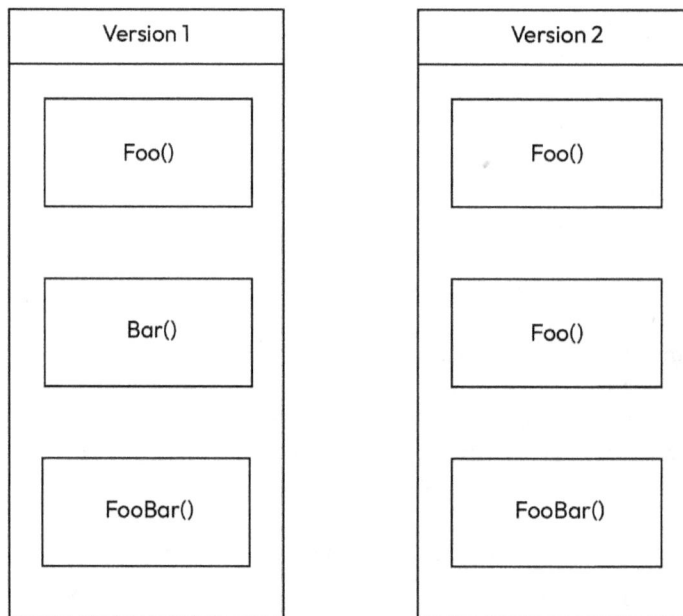

Figure 8.6 – Different logic in two separate versions of the same orchestration

Let's take a look at *Figure 8.6*. The diagram shows two separate versions of the same orchestration. As you can see, there's a breaking change in the process as in *Version 2*, we no longer call `activity Bar()`. Let's consider what happens if our orchestration is replayed after it called `Foo()` and `Bar()` and then gets canceled because we deployed *Version 2*. Once the orchestration resumes, it will no longer get the result for the `Bar()` activity. Instead, it will get the result for `Foo()` twice. If we do not introduce any safeguard mechanism for that, an orchestration that started for *Version 1* will provide invalid results as it had never assumed other logic. To overcome that problem, we have four separate strategies:

- Doing nothing
- Stopping orchestrations before deployment
- Side-by-side deployment
- Stopping new orchestrations

Each of those strategies will have its use cases. If you want to just *do nothing*, you won't need to introduce any changes to the way you proceed with deployment. You accept the risk and do not worry about invalid results. This is applicable mostly in development scenarios, where you want to quickly validate your changes, and invalid results have no impact on the business.

Stopping all orchestrations is a viable option for production workloads but only if you can afford not to complete the process. In that scenario, you need to query all orchestrations and stop them one by one. Once terminated, you can safely deploy the new version. This approach can be also safely performed if the new code has safeguards to support multiple versions of your workflow and you have a method to replay all the triggers for orchestrations.

Side-by-side deployment is a safe approach for making changes as it deploys a new instance of your function app, so you can safely process both old and new workflows. It will incur an additional cost, though, and may be a little bit complex if you need to split requests coming to your function apps (via a traffic manager, load balancer, or in-app logic).

Stopping new orchestrations could be considered something in between stopping all orchestrations and side-by-side deployment. This approach is implemented in the following way:

1. Stop the process that triggers new orchestrations.
2. Wait until all orchestrations finish.
3. Deploy the latest version.
4. Restart the process of triggering new orchestrations.

This is just a high-level plan, so we need to consider several additional considerations – for instance, how you will prevent new orchestrations from triggering depends on how you have implemented that process. If you have control over it, it should be simple as you can disable the service responsible for doing that or simply implement a flag, which will allow you to control the process. If you offloaded triggering new orchestrations to external services, you would need to make changes there.

> **Tip**
>
> It is a clever idea to always place a proxy service between a client and Durable Functions. This allows you to control incoming requests and make changes if needed. This pattern is called *decoupling* and is often used when your external actor can interact with your system.

Another thing to consider is how you wait for your orchestrations to finish. We talked about finding orchestrations that have finished or were terminated in the section covering singleton orchestrations. The same approach could be used here – you could simply deploy a separate function that queries the store of Durable Functions and returns information about the orchestrations in progress. You would then monitor them and wait for the moment you can trigger a new deployment. This must include a way to stop orchestrations if needed – if they take too long and you cannot wait anymore to deploy an updated version, you must have a way to terminate them gracefully.

I hope the level of detail in this section will allow you to handle versioning in Durable Functions proficiently. Let us proceed now to the last section of this chapter, where we will discuss use cases for stateful workflows and functions.

Learning about use cases

It is important to understand that Durable Functions is not meant for handling all workflows. There are some key indicators that can tell you whether using this framework will solve the challenges you are facing:

- You need to implement a stateful workflow that must be persisted and consists of several logical steps.

- You expect great flexibility from the framework, which allows you to implement even extraordinarily complex business processes.

- You have a team that is proficient in one of the programming languages supported by Durable Functions.

- The team working with Durable Functions understands how to build distributed systems, which require both parallelization and bottlenecking of the data process pipeline.

- You expect the built solution to be fully aligned with the development tools and standards you have in your project.

When compared with Azure Logic Apps, Durable Functions will provide similar functionalities and capabilities but will also require much greater effort to achieve comparable results (from the business point of view). This is why you need to justify the use of this framework and commit to it. Because this is a low-level framework that introduces a few new concepts and strict programming rules, it is always better to assess it before going for a production-ready solution.

When it comes to business use cases, you can use Durable Functions for the following scenarios:

- Implementing processes requiring human interaction
- Handling workflows that may run in an unstable environment
- Scaling out workers processing data in a way that ensures consistency and allows you to restart the process without losing already obtained results
- Chaining multiple services so you can easily control how data is processed and make necessary changes if needed

There are also other possible scenarios, which we will not be able to cover here as they may appear in the future. Whichever scenario you find for Durable Functions, always make sure you understand the pros and cons of this framework. This will prevent you from overcomplicating your setup and code base.

That is all for this chapter! Let us summarize all the lessons and see what you will learn in the next chapter.

Summary

In this chapter, we talked about Durable Functions, which is a framework based on Azure Functions for building stateful and durable workflows. Even though it shares some similarities with Azure Logic Apps, it is a different tool with different use cases. We not only discussed the basics of how you could implement an orchestration with activities but also checked advanced topics such as versioning, singleton orchestrations, and eternal orchestrations, which are important in real-world scenarios.

In the next chapter, we will start a completely new section of the book, which covers containers in Microsoft Azure. As a warmup, we will talk about Azure Container Registry, which is a private registry hosted in the cloud.

Further reading

If you found Durable Functions interesting, make sure you read more about it in the documentation at `https://learn.microsoft.com/en-us/azure/azure-functions/durable/durable-functions-overview`.

Part 3:
Containers in Microsoft Azure

This part introduces the fundamentals of containerized application development and deployment in the Azure ecosystem. You will explore how to build, manage, and run containers using Azure services designed for flexibility and scalability. From managing private container images to deploying microservices and running ad hoc workloads, this part provides a practical guide to working with containers in real-world scenarios.

By the end of this part, you will understand how to choose the right container platform for your use case and integrate containers into your application life cycle with ease.

This part has the following chapters:

- *Chapter 9, Learning About Azure Container Registry*
- *Chapter 10, Building Ad Hoc Workloads Using Azure Container Instances*
- *Chapter 11, Developing Microservices with Azure Container Apps*
- *Chapter 12, Hosting Containers with Azure App Service*

9

Learning About Azure Container Registry

When developing applications, you often need to consider how they will be built and hosted. To make the right call, you will need to consider things such as the hosting platform, development environment, and frameworks you're using. While some applications are perfectly fine when hosted in-process, some may require a more elaborate approach. To ensure you can host your applications anywhere, you need to leverage containerization. As containerized applications need to be shared, you'll need to build container images and use container registries to host them. One such registry is the **Azure Container Registry service**.

This chapter will allow you to start utilizing Azure Container Registry as your private catalog of container images. As this service natively integrates with a number of other Azure services, knowing how to use it properly will be crucial in further extending your knowledge about developing applications in Azure.

In this chapter, we're going to cover the following main topics:

- Publishing and pulling a container image using Azure Container Registry
- Structuring your registry
- Integrating Azure Container Registry with CI/CD pipelines
- Using cache and multi-arch images
- Learning about use cases

Technical requirements

To perform the exercises from this chapter, you'll need the following software installed:

- Azure CLI.

- IDE of your choice.

- Container runtime (Docker Engine, Colima, or similar) and the Docker CLI. Note that you could use a tool such as Podman to perform the exercises in this chapter, but you will need to translate its commands to the Docker CLI.

The source code for this chapter can be found here: `https://github.com/PacktPublishing/Azure-for-Developers-Third-Edition/tree/main/ch09`.

Publishing and pulling a container image using Azure Container Registry

Containers are one of the best ways to run and host your application in a platform-agnostic way. When an application is containerized, you can start it on any machine that supports running containers. It's also one of the prerequisites for running services running technologies such as Kubernetes. The common thing for all containerization technologies is a container registry. Let's quickly characterize it.

To create a container, you need a **container image**. A container image is a package that can be used to create an instance of an application and host it on a platform of choice. The difference between images and containers is crucial to understanding what we're going to cover in this chapter:

- Images define the layers of which your application consists. Each image is uniquely identified by its tag and can be hosted and shared using a container registry. Images are not hosted on platforms such as Kubernetes or by container engines – they encapsulate everything needed to run an application and act as a blueprint for an instance of your application.

- Containers are instances of your application based on the selected image. A container is a living organism – you may connect to it, place it inside a network, and interact based on the provided interface. You can create multiple containers based on the same image and control them individually, whether it's CPU/memory quotas, network segmentation, or authorization policies.

By using simple developer terms, you could think about images and containers as classes and objects. An image (class) defines the behavior and implementation; when you create a container (instance) you can utilize the interface defined by the former.

If you want to publish a container image, you need to decide which registries you're going to use. The most common separation of registries is separating them based on their network availability:

- **Public registries** – These are available to anyone without additional layers of network protection. They may require authentication and implement authorization or be available anonymously. An example of such a registry is **Docker Hub**.

- **Private registries** – These are not available over the public internet and provide additional layers of protection to secure your images from unauthorized access and exfiltration. Azure Container Registry is an example of a private registry. Other cloud providers also offer their own private registries. An example of a cloud-agnostic private registry is **Harbor** (`https://goharbor.io/`).

For most production workloads, you'll be rather interested in using private registries. Public registries are great for personal projects or publicly available images such as Linux distributions or frameworks.

Let's see now how we can push and pull images using Azure Container Registry. To get started, we'll need an instance of our registry deployed.

Deploying Azure Container Registry

Creating an instance of Azure Container Registry is one of the simplest operations you can do in Azure. All you need is a single Azure CLI command:

```
az acr create \
-n <registry-name> \
-g <resource-group-name> \
--sku Basic
```

The preceding command will create a container registry with the given name, in the selected resource group, and with the `Basic` tier. The reason we're selecting the `Basic` tier is both pricing (this is the cheapest option) and the lack of non-functional requirements, which would push us into selecting more advanced tiers. Don't worry, we'll cover them later in the chapter.

> **Note**
>
> Azure Container Registry has some strict naming requirements for the name of a registry. If you experience errors related to the selected name, make sure it contains alphanumerical characters only.

Once the container registry is created, the most important parameter for now is something called the login server. You can obtain it using the following command:

```
az acr show \
-n <registry-name> \
-g <resource-group-name> \
--query loginServer
```

In my case, the result of that command was `afd09cr.azurecr.io`. This value will be important when pushing and pulling images so make sure you note it somewhere so you can use it later.

Alternatively, we could deploy the same configuration using the following Bicep code:

```
resource acr 'Microsoft.ContainerRegistry/registries@2023-07-01' = {
  name: '<registry-name>'
  location: resourceGroup().location
  sku: {
    name: 'Basic'
  }
  properties: {}
}
```

To deploy such a template, use the following command:

```
az deployment group create \
--template-file <path-to-bicep-file> \
--resource-group <resource-group-name>
```

Once the command is executed, your container registry should be created in the selected resource group. Then, you can obtain the value of its login server in the same way as we did for deploying a registry using the Azure CLI.

Great, we have a registry we can work with. It's time to write a simple Dockerfile to test push and pull operations.

Preparing a Dockerfile

A Dockerfile is a text file used to describe layers building your container image. If you're not familiar with this concept, I strongly advise you to read its documentation and reference: `https://docs.docker.com/reference/dockerfile/`.

For our purpose, we'll try to prepare a generic image that we can easily run and modify later:

1. To keep things as simple as possible, let's use the following HTML file:

    ```html
    <html>
    <head>
        <title>Chapter 9</title>
    </head>
    <body>
        <h1>Hello!</h1>
    </body>
    </html>
    ```

2. Now, we'll prepare a Dockerfile that will host that file on an instance of the `nginx` server:

    ```
    FROM nginx:latest
    COPY index.html /usr/share/nginx/html/index.html
    ```

3. Let's build our image now using the following Docker CLI command:

    ```
    docker build -t azure-for-developers:ch09 .
    ```

4. For the image name and tag of my Docker image, I selected `azure-for-developers:ch09`. In your case, it can be any value you want. Once the image is built, let's test it locally using the following command:

    ```
    docker run -d -p 8080:80 azure-for-developers:ch09
    ```

5. This command should create a container based on our image and run it locally, forwarding port `8080` on the host machine (your computer) to port `80` on the container. Now, try to access `http://localhost:8080` on your computer. You should see a simple web page looking exactly as presented in *Figure 9.1*.

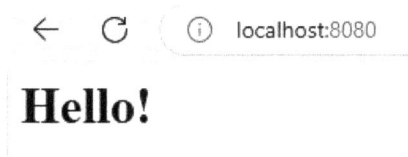

Figure 9.1 – Running container hosting HTML page using nginx

Great, we have everything we need to integrate our work with Azure Container Registry. Let's try to push our image to the registry created in the previous section.

Pushing an image to the container registry

To push an image to a container registry, we'll need to perform one additional operation. To understand why we need to do it, run the following command:

```
docker images
```

As a result, you should see a list of all the container images you have locally. Here's an excerpt from the output of the command when I run it on my computer:

```
REPOSITORY              TAG   IMAGE ID
azure-for-developers  ch09  5d91ec40bf95
```

The important thing for us is the first two columns. The first one is REPOSITORY, and the second one is TAG. Container registries use the concept of repositories to separate images that describe completely different services. Tags are used to version your images and separate the different stages of the development of an application (for instance, alpha, beta, release candidate, etc.). They can also indicate different flavors of your image (such as different Linux distributions). Now, if we want to push an image to a registry, we need to somehow point our image to it. As we cannot simply push an image using the docker push command (because it'd assume we're pushing to a public registry), we need to retag our image. To do so, let's use the following command:

```
docker tag azure-for-developers:ch09 <login-server>/azure-for-developers:ch09
```

As you can see, the change we're introducing is prepending the name of our image with the name of the login server we got previously. Now, let's try to push our image:

```
docker push afd09cr.azurecr.io/azure-for-developers:ch09
The push refers to repository [afd09cr.azurecr.io/azure-for-developers]
97182578e5ec: Waiting
34a52cbc3961: Waiting
d1875670ac8a: Waiting
58b3c2408a08: Waiting
af17adb1bdcc: Waiting
67b9310357e1: Waiting
302e3ee49805: Waiting
cd986b3703ae: Waiting
e386844d8966: Waiting
failed to authorize: failed to fetch anonymous token: unexpected
status from GET request to https://afd09cr.azurecr.io/oauth2/
token?scope=repository%3Aazure-for-developers%3Apull&scope=repository
%3Aazure-for-developers%3Apull%2Cpush&service=afd09cr.azurecr.io: 401
Unauthorized
```

It seems there's a problem with our push – we're getting 401 Unauthorized in response. This happens because we didn't authenticate before connecting with our container registry and we're unauthorized to perform the push operation against the data plane. In the next section, we'll discuss what our options are to fix that issue.

Connecting with Azure Container Registry

Azure Container Registry supports two authentication methods when making connections:

- Microsoft Entra ID

- Admin user (login)

As a rule of thumb, I'd suggest using Microsoft Entra ID as your default method of authentication and authorization. It allows you to easily integrate with other Azure services and keep configuration as simple as possible. Admin user is a viable option if you need to connect to Azure Container Registry outside of Azure. It's basically a login and password setup, which is quick to configure but doesn't allow you to control who is accessing your container registry.

We'll try now to configure Microsoft Entra ID authentication for Azure Container Registry and use it locally:

1. If you want to use Microsoft Entra ID to access Azure Container Registry, add the AcrPush role to the account accessing the registry. If it's you, you need to add that role to your account. There are multiple ways of adding a role assignment for an account in Azure – for this exercise, I suggest you try adding it using Bicep:

    ```
    resource acrpush 'Microsoft.Authorization/
    roleAssignments@2022-04-01' = {
      name: guid('acrpush', acr.id)
      scope: acr
      properties: {
        principalId: '<object-id>'
        roleDefinitionId: resourceId('Microsoft.Authorization/
        roleDefinitions', '8311e382-0749-4cb8-b61a-304f252e45ec')
      }
    }
    ```

    With the presented code snippet, you can easily assign the AcrPush role (represented by the GUID 8311e382-0749-4cb8-b61a-304f252e45ec) for any principal in your Microsoft Entra ID tenant – all you need is to replace the <object-id> placeholder with the object ID of a principal you want to use for interacting with Azure Container Registry. If you want to find the value of that identifier, you could use the az ad sp list command, which allows you to find a principal based on its name using the --spn parameter. This snippet will create an assignment on your registry level and will automatically fetch the role definition ID based on the parameters provided.

2. Now, let's sign in to our registry with the following command:

```
az acr login -n <registry-name>
```

3. Once the login operation succeeds, let's test the push command once again:

```
docker push <login-server>/azure-for-developers:ch09
The push refers to repository [afd09cr.azurecr.io/azure-for-
developers]
e386844d8966: Pushed
58b3c2408a08: Pushed
cd986b3703ae: Pushed
302e3ee49805: Pushed
34a52cbc3961: Pushed
97182578e5ec: Pushed
af17adb1bdcc: Pushed
d1875670ac8a: Pushed
67b9310357e1: Pushed
ch09: digest: sha256:5d91ec40bf954f5e5454fa8c1efcc1700
a619b51a12d744a51a5515dfd32bfe1 size: 856
```

Great, it seems everything works as intended. As you can see, using Microsoft Entra ID as an authentication method allows you to keep everything as part of your code base and quickly set up proper access to a registry.

4. There's an alternative way of connecting to Azure Container Registry, named admin user. In order to use it, we need to enable it. You can do this by running the following CLI command:

```
az acr update \
-n <registry-name> \
--admin-enabled true
```

5. If you want to keep everything in Bicep, you can also do it by updating the registry definition in your Bicep file:

```
resource acr 'Microsoft.ContainerRegistry/registries@2023-07-01'
= {
  name: '<registry-name>'
  location: resourceGroup().location
  sku: {
    name: 'Basic'
  }
  properties: {
    adminUserEnabled: true
  }
}
```

6. Once the deployment is complete, you should be able to fetch the credentials using the Azure CLI:

```
az acr credential show -n afd09cr
{
  "passwords": [
    {
      "name": "password",
      "value": "9IVq7eNAPzmR2Dsb3yN64j..."
    },
    {
      "name": "password2",
      "value": "zz/12mhMZ5UrGV6QGUfSCM..."
    }
  ],
  "username": "afd09cr"
}
```

Those credentials can be used to get access to your container registry instance. If you want to utilize them, simply use the `docker login` command instead of `acr login`.

> **Note**
>
> When using the Azure CLI to connect to your instance of Azure Container Registry, the CLI will obtain and cache proper credentials based on the internal logic. Note that if you have high permissions (such as Global Administrator) in your Azure environment, you may not need to assign `AcrPush` nor configure an admin user in order to access any container registry.

This way of obtaining access to a container registry is useful in scenarios where a client connecting to Azure Container Registry doesn't have an Azure account or isn't hosted in Azure. An example of such a scenario is implementing a CI/CD pipeline where your runners aren't hosted on Azure VMs.

So far, we've been able to create an image and push it to our instance of the container registry. Let's see what needs to be done to pull an image on a machine.

Pulling an image from Azure Container Registry

Pulling an image from an instance of a container registry follows the same principles as pushing it. We still need to obtain a full reference to our image (login server, repository, and tag) and be able to authorize our operation. If you secured access using the admin user, you won't need to do anything extra – that method gives full access to the data plane of Azure Container Registry, so you can push and pull images without limitations.

If you're using Microsoft Entra ID, though, you'll need to assign a new role to a principal. This role is named `AcrPull`:

```
resource acrpull 'Microsoft.Authorization/roleAssignments@2022-04-01'
= {
  name: guid('acrpull', acr.id)
  scope: acr
  properties: {
    principalId: '<object-id>'
    roleDefinitionId: resourceId('Microsoft.Authorization/
    roleDefinitions', '7f951dda-4ed3-4680-a7ca-43fe172d538d')
  }
}
```

In the preceding code snippet, the GUID we are using (`7f951dda-4ed3-4680-a7ca-43fe172d538d`) is the identifier of the `AcrPull` role and is the same for each Azure environment. Now, if you want to pull an image, you can simply use the following command:

```
docker pull afd09cr.azurecr.io/azure-for-developers:ch09
ch09: Pulling from azure-for-developers
Digest: sha256:5d91ec40bf954f5e5454fa8c1efcc1700a
619b51a12d744a51a5515dfd32bfe1
Status: Downloaded newer image for afd09cr.azurecr.io/
azure-for-developers:ch09
afd09cr.azurecr.io/azure-for-developers:ch09
```

Remember that you need to log in to Azure Container Registry first before pulling an image! You'll need to perform that operation each time a new machine is provisioned – a scenario common for CI/CD pipelines.

Let's learn more about Azure Container Registry by discussing more about the internal structure of this service and other available capabilities.

Structuring your registry

In the previous section, we mentioned that you can host multiple images inside the same registry. To separate different services, you should leverage a **repository**. In Azure Container Registry, repositories are created automatically each time you push a new image or artifact. The reason we're making such a separation now is that Azure Container Registry can not only host images but it's also designed to host any artifact that is compatible with **Open Container Initiative** (**OCI**) artifacts.

This standard allows you to package any content (such as files, audio, or even images) using the same specification as we're using for container images. In our case, one of the use cases for using OCI artifacts in Azure Container Registry would be storing Bicep modules. As we'll be treating Azure Container Registry as a generic registry for hosting artifacts, we need to discuss the proper structure and place it appropriately when architecting a solution.

Choosing the correct amount of registries

To get started, let's consider the following problem: we've deployed one container registry to satisfy the requirements given by one of our development teams. After several weeks, another team decided to containerize their application and is in desperate need of having a dedicated registry. While we could simply deploy another instance of Azure Container Registry, there could be better alternatives that we should consider.

The initial setup may look like the one presented in *Figure 9.2*. This diagram presents a simple design, where each team has its own registry deployed in Azure.

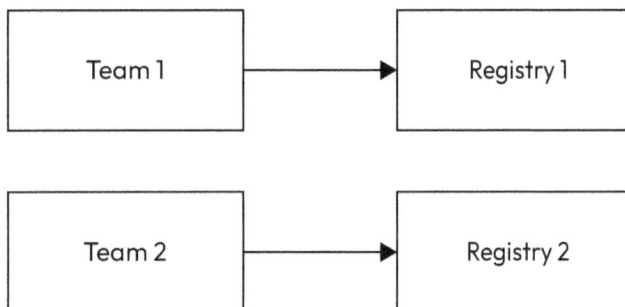

Figure 9.2 – A dedicated registry for each development team

While such a setup may look simple to deploy and manage, it may quickly become insufficient if we consider additional requirements such as environment separation. The evolution of that design is presented in *Figure 9.3*.

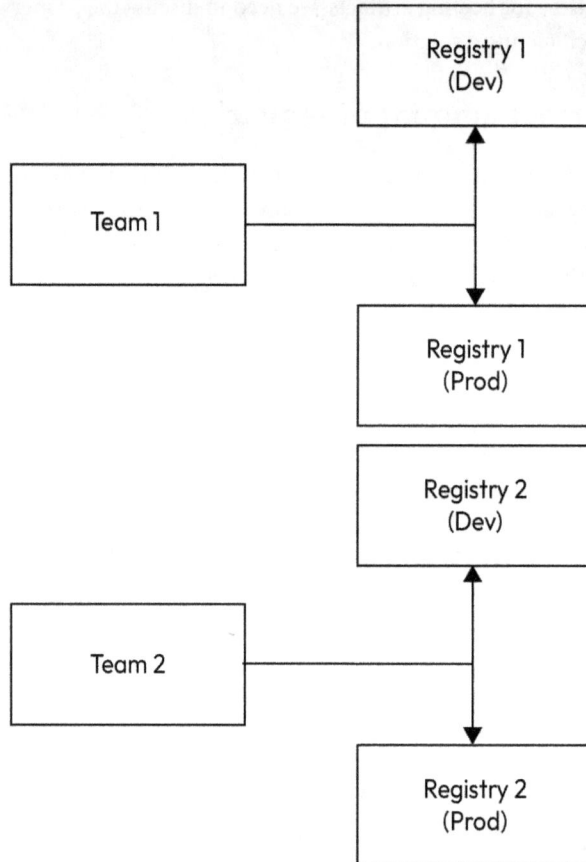

Figure 9.3 – A dedicated registry per team and environment

If we go for that option, each team will have a dedicated registry per environment. The advantage of such a setup is the ability to offload some operational work to dedicated engineers and decouple the architecture of the infrastructure from the architecture of different applications.

It may be also worth mentioning that having a dedicated registry per environment isn't the only viable case when developing an application. If you develop a system that is deployed globally and needs to be dynamically provisioned, you may find it beneficial to have a dedicated registry for each specific geographical location. We can visualize that with the following diagram (*Figure 9.4*):

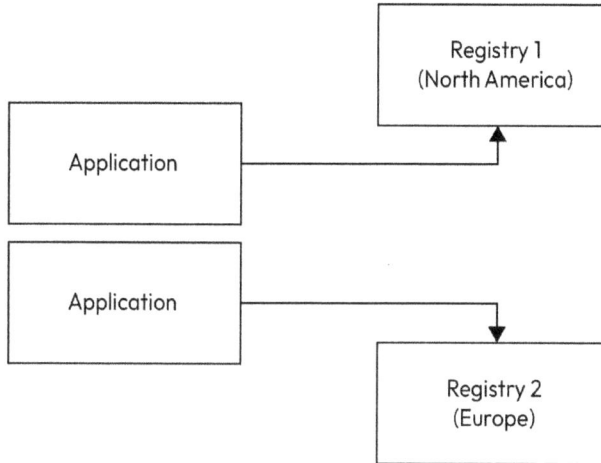

Figure 9.4 – Registries deployed per geographical location

Using multiple container registries for various locations is useful when you want to keep predictable performance (by avoiding network latency) or it is required to be compliant with regulations or network policies. Note that with Azure Container Registry, you have two methods of achieving that:

- The first idea is to deploy each registry individually to separate regions.

- The second idea is based on the geo-replication feature in Azure Container Registry, where you can manage a single instance of a registry and let Azure replicate all the objects stored within it.

In most cases, using geo-replication rather than deploying individual instances of Azure Container Registry will be the preferred way of making all the registry objects available in a separate region, unless you really need to isolate your infrastructure (for instance, you may need to integrate it with a different network).

> **Note**
> When considering geo-replication, remember that it's available only for the Premium SKU in Azure Container Registry. This could be a good point in discussing the differences between deploying separate registries versus using geo-replication and managing a single registry.

If you want to read more about geo-replication in Azure Container Registry, take a look at the following documentation: `https://learn.microsoft.com/en-us/azure/container-registry/container-registry-geo-replication`.

Coming back to the team we discussed, we need to remember that some teams may require a different number of environments. If we decide to control them centrally, it may be difficult to properly manage which images or artifacts are deployed to which environment. The centralized approach is presented in *Figure 9.5*.

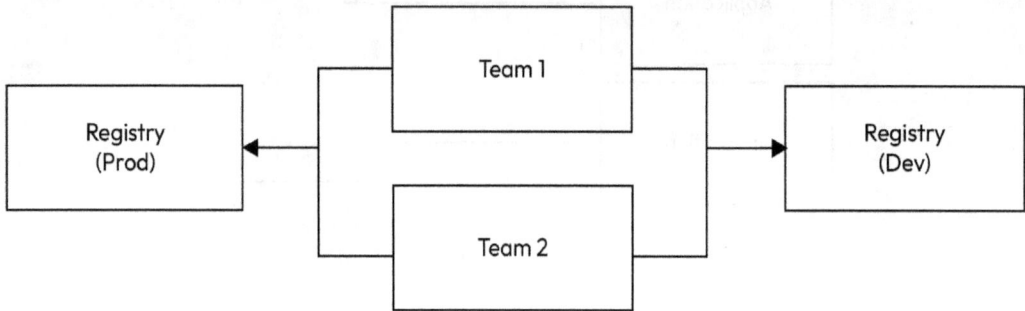

Figure 9.5 – Centralized approach for hosting registries

There's one issue when it comes to using the centralized approach – we're unable to control which applications access which artifact. If we want to change that, we'll need to use scope maps. Let's discuss them to get a better understanding of how they work.

Using scope maps

If, for some reason, we don't want to deploy multiple registries (for instance, cost savings), we could deploy only a few centralized instances of Azure Container Registry and allow multiple services to access them. Now, if we don't want to give each application full access to the contents of a registry, we need to somehow limit it. In order to do that in Azure Container Registry, we need to use **scope maps**. Each scope map is a simple mapping between repositories and provided credentials. It allows you to limit access for an account only to a subset of repositories created in Azure Container Registry and ensure that an application or a service is unable to access data they are not supposed to.

To create a scope map, we could use the following Azure CLI command:

```
az acr scope-map create \
-n <map-name> \
-r <registry-name> \
--repository azure-for-developers content/read
```

The preceding command will create a new scope map with the given name for a provided registry and will allow a principal to read the contents of a repository. For reference, I used the same repository as we created in the previous section.

Now, to see the scope map in action, we need to generate credentials using it. This can be achieved with one more command:

```
az acr token create \
--scope-map <map-name> \
-r <registry-name> \
-n <token-name>
```

The result of running that command is a set of credentials that will look like this:

```
"passwords": [
  {
    "creationTime": "2024-09-29T16:07:34.172290+00:00",
    "expiry": null,
    "name": "password1",
    "value": "k2EGSUkLy3ipiE1MySuwgN2OP3Zfygbz/..."
  },
  {
    "creationTime": "2024-09-29T16:07:34.172305+00:00",
    "expiry": null,
    "name": "password2",
    "value": "jhJB3FQCT2Le6b/ir+m+5+Q9uDffxvpfOBb/..."
  }
],
"username": "my-token"
```

As you can see, it's a similar value to the admin user credentials we discussed previously in the chapter. The obvious downside of using scope maps is the need to switch to the user and password authorization model. On the other hand, scope maps eliminate the main issue of using an admin user, which is the lack of proper control over who and how accesses an instance of the container registry.

Let's test our credentials now. To do that, we can leverage the Docker CLI and run the following command:

```
docker login \
-u "<token-name>" \
-p " <password-value> " \
 <login-server>
```

With credentials used, you shouldn't be able to push an image to our container registry as the set of permissions used for the token generation contains only read permissions. Here's the result of pushing an image on my computer:

```
docker push afd09cr.azurecr.io/azure-for-developers:ch09
The push refers to repository [afd09cr.azurecr.io/azure-for-
developers]
e386844d8966: Already exists
34a52cbc3961: Layer already exists
97182578e5ec: Layer already exists
cd986b3703ae: Layer already exists
58b3c2408a08: Layer already exists
af17adb1bdcc: Layer already exists
d1875670ac8a: Layer already exists
302e3ee49805: Layer already exists
67b9310357e1: Layer already exists
failed commit on ref "manifest-sha256:b20a51824e72a90a20f23507d02ab659
5f84dc63e8b306ae54ac43c5d3a76d61": server message: insufficient_scope:
authorization failed
```

As you can see, I got an `authorization failed` response from Azure Container Registry. This is the expected result as the CLI used scoped credentials, which don't provide permission to write anything to a registry. By using scope maps, you can easily limit access to segments of your registry to improve security. For centralized registries, it's a must for every platform to be considered production-ready.

> **Note**
>
> The downside of using scope maps as of the time of writing is their lack of Microsoft Entra ID support. They are still a viable option for properly managing security and access to your registry, but the fact that you're unable to link them with service principals or managed identities somehow limits their use cases.

Let's talk now about how we can structure our registry when using it for hosting both images and other artifacts.

Hosting images and generic artifacts

We talked about how Azure Container Registry can be used to host not only container images but also other artifacts that are compatible with OCI. One such artifact is the Bicep modules. Yes, you can use Azure Container Registry as a place where you push modules representing your infrastructure. However, this introduces a challenge when trying to keep things separated.

While it's perfectly fine to host both images and OCI artifacts in the same registry, it's often a better idea to perform a split. There are a number of benefits of such an approach:

- Consumers of container images are (most of the time) different from consumers of OCI artifacts.

- While you could use scope maps to limit access to different parts of the registry, you may not want to change the authentication method and use Azure RBAC as often as possible.

- The life cycle of OCI artifacts will be most likely different from container images and you don't always want to handle two separate scenarios using the same piece of infrastructure (the same registry).

Remember that in Azure Container Registry, there's no concept of a repository in a repository. This means that there's no way to keep all the OCI artifacts under the same umbrella repository and keep the rest separated. If you need to use the same registry for all types of artifacts, you'll need to introduce proper naming conventions and use wildcards when building scope maps to limit access.

Container images are used to host applications, whereas OCI artifacts (such as Bicep modules) are used for everything but hosting an application. This is the reason I always suggest having separate registries and separate things stored in Azure Container Registry logically. It's not only easier in the long term but also allows you to develop your system incrementally without cross-cutting responsibilities and concerns.

Let's talk now about integrating Azure Container Registry with CI/CD pipelines.

Integrating Azure Container Registry with CI/CD pipelines

Integrating your CI/CD pipeline with Azure Container Registry is one of the most common things you will be developing when building a containerized application. The good thing here is the simplicity of that operation – most of the time, all you need is to obtain proper credentials and use them in your pipeline. There are also other things we need to take into account (such as networking). We'll discuss them shortly in this section.

Designing a CI/CD pipeline for Azure Container Registry

Let's start by discussing how our pipeline should be structured to use Azure Container Registry. From the pipeline perspective, a connection with Azure Container Registry must be made to either pull or push an image (or artifact). The operation used depends on the purpose of the pipeline:

- If we're building an application, we'll most likely need to push an image as the artifact.

- If we're running a custom-build agent, we may need to pull an image of that agent and then run the rest of the pipelines after a container starts.

- We may need to pull an image to run a custom tool or a service while executing other pipeline steps. This includes scenarios such as running a mock, a database, or other required service (e.g., for testing).

The integration between the CI/CD pipeline and Azure Container Registry depends on the tool we're using. In this section, we'll cover GitHub Actions and Azure DevOps as examples.

Choosing the proper authentication method

When building a CI/CD pipeline and integrating it with Azure Container Registry, the most important aspect is authentication. Previously in this chapter, we discussed two separate methods of authentication:

- Microsoft Entra ID
- Admin user (or tokens with scope maps)

Your choice of method will depend on the capabilities of your CI/CD tool. Many tools offer so-called shared/managed agents, which are provisioned by the tool itself and are not managed by you. Those agents are not able to connect natively to Azure unless you explicitly provide credentials. If you recall, the Azure CLI allows you to authenticate to Azure using service principal credentials (username and password, or username and certificate). In such a case, it would be possible to use Microsoft Entra ID to connect to Azure Container Registry. For such agents, though, it's impossible to use a managed identity and avoid sharing credentials unless you use a federated identity for making the connection. Workload identity is a method of achieving a trust relationship between Azure DevOps and the selected service principal, so it can obtain Azure tokens without the need to deploy your infrastructure for CI/CD runners inside Azure. It can be extremely useful in scenarios where you have your agents provisioned within your on-premises network but want to avoid providing and maintaining credentials for service principals (as agents hosted on-premises cannot be integrated with a managed identity).

An alternative is to either use an admin user or generate scoped credentials using scope maps. The advantage of such an approach is simpler management and a lower security risk (because a leaked scoped credential for the container registry doesn't give an attacker access to Azure's control plane). It also simplifies the pipeline slightly as you don't need to store and pass Azure credentials and use them to authenticate to Azure.

Integrating Azure DevOps with Azure Container Registry

Azure DevOps offers a native integration method with Azure Container Registry using service connections. As Azure Container Registry is compatible with Docker Registry, you can use the same method to authenticate to a generic Docker registry and your instance of Azure Container Registry. The process of creating such a service connection is out of the scope of this book; however, there's a detailed tutorial explaining how you could implement it in Azure DevOps at `https://learn.microsoft.com/en-us/azure/devops/pipelines/ecosystems/containers/publish-to-acr?view=azure-devops&tabs=javascript%2Cportal%2Cmsi#create-a-docker-registry-service-connection`.

> **Note**
>
> Azure DevOps allows you to choose how you want to authenticate to Azure Container Registry by selecting between service principal authentication, managed identity, or workload identity. Using service principal authentication will require admin access to the Microsoft Entra ID tenant as Azure DevOps needs to leverage the Azure Resource Manager connection created as a prerequisite. If you're using self-hosted agents, though, I strongly recommend you use the managed identity authentication model, which greatly simplifies the whole process.

Once a service connection is created, you can utilize it in any pipeline like so:

```
trigger:
- master

pool:
  vmImage: ubuntu-latest

steps:
- task: Docker@2
  inputs:
    containerRegistry: 'AFD09'
    repository: 'azure-for-developers'
    command: 'buildAndPush'
    Dockerfile: '**/Dockerfile'
```

The preceding code snippet uses a single task, `Docker@2`, which is a generic task for interacting with container registries. This performs both `build` and `push` commands using the Docker CLI. It implicitly chooses the container registry defined when creating a service connection. If needed, we could split the operation into two separate tasks:

```
- task: Docker@2
  inputs:
    containerRegistry: 'AFD09'
    repository: 'azure-for-developers'
    command: 'build'
    Dockerfile: '**/Dockerfile'
- task: Docker@2
  inputs:
    containerRegistry: 'AFD09'
    repository: 'azure-for-developers'
    command: 'push'
```

There are a number of use cases for splitting the commands into two separate steps. One of them is running tests after an image is built. The native Docker commands have one limitation though – they don't allow you to pass additional parameters, which are useful in some scenarios. One of those scenarios is a multi-stage build, often used not only to build smaller images but also to extract results of tests while building a final image. In order to overcome that limitation, we'd need to run commands manually:

```
- task: Bash@3
  inputs:
    targetType: 'inline'
    script: |
      docker login -u $(Username) -p $(Password) mycr.azurecr.io
      docker build --target build -t azure-for-developers:09 .
- task: Docker@2
  inputs:
    containerRegistry: 'AFD09'
    repository: 'azure-for-developers'
    command: 'push'
    tags: '09'
```

With such a setup, we could introduce additional steps between building and pushing an image to create an interim container, run it, and extract the results of tests. Then, if the tests are successful, we could proceed with pushing an image to a container registry.

> **Note**
>
> Multi-stage builds for container images are a common pattern that can be used in any CI/CD tool allowing you to run Docker commands.

Let's see how we could achieve the same results in GitHub Actions.

Integrating Azure Container Registry with GitHub Actions

GitHub Actions offers a similar model for integrating with Azure Container Registry as Azure DevOps, but the main difference is the lack of service connections. Instead, we need to manually provide the necessary information for the actions used in our pipeline. One of the possibilities to connect with Azure Container Registry is using the Azure/docker-login@v1 action:

```
- name: Azure Container Registry Login
  uses: Azure/docker-login@v1
  with:
    username: ${{ secrets.Username }}
    password: ${{ secrets.Password }}
    login-server: myserver.azurecr.io
```

The issue with that action, though, is the fact that it currently may be considered deprecated. Instead, it's advised to use the following actions:

```
- name: Login to Docker Hub
  uses: docker/login-action@v3
  with:
    username: ${{ secrets.Username }}
    password: ${{ secrets.Password }}
    registry:  myserver.azurecr.io
- name: Build and push
  uses: docker/build-push-action@v6
  with:
    push: true
    tags: azure-for-developers:09
```

These two actions work in a very similar way to tasks used in Azure DevOps. You use a separate action for connecting with a selected container registry and then build and push an image in the next action. Note that docker/build-push-action allows you to decide whether you want to perform push or not – it's possible to just build an image by setting the push parameter to false.

Let's talk about one more thing related to CI/CD and containers, which is caching.

Using caching in CI/CD pipelines

Container images are useful when sharing applications or services and running them without worrying about installing dependencies or ensuring compatibility. They have one disadvantage though – they tend to grow quite big in lots of scenarios, and this requires significant network bandwidth if you need to download them often. In low-scale scenarios, the size of a container image can be ignored – most likely, it won't impact your network devices and connection. However, when building highly scalable solutions or hosting tens or even hundreds of containers, the ability to shorten between downloading an image and creating a container will have a significant impact on your ability to provide a reliable solution.

To understand the impact of an image download on your infrastructure and application, first, we need to understand how container engines operate. Let's consider the following scenario – we have a small cluster of three separate virtual machines (*Figure 9.6*). Each of those machines will run containers based on the same image.

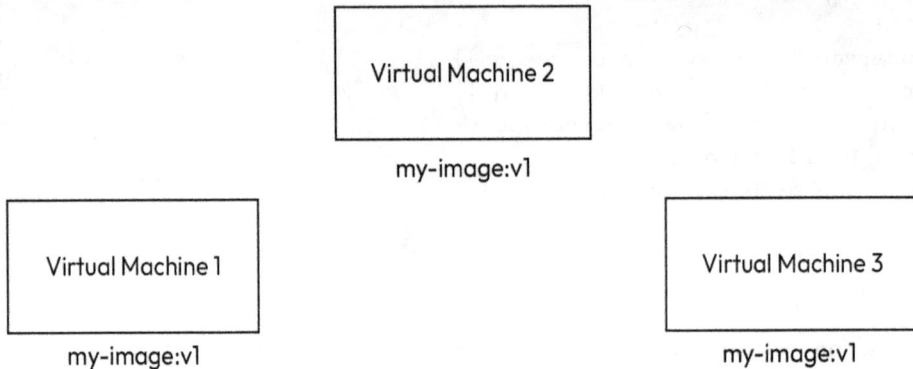

```
           ┌────────────────────────┐
           │                        │
           │    Virtual Machine 2   │
           │                        │
           └────────────────────────┘
                  my-image:v1

┌──────────────────────┐      ┌──────────────────────┐
│                      │      │                      │
│  Virtual Machine 1   │      │  Virtual Machine 3   │
│                      │      │                      │
└──────────────────────┘      └──────────────────────┘
     my-image:v1                   my-image:v1
```

Figure 9.6 – Small cluster of virtual machines running the same container

The way container engines work in such a scenario can be described by the following process:

1. The client asks to run the container based on the `my-image:v1` container image.

2. Engine checks whether an image is available on the host machine.

3. If an image isn't available, proceed to download it; otherwise, jump to the next step.

4. Create a container based on an image and run it.

This is, of course, a simplified process, but it will do the trick of explaining why we need to look at image sizes at some point in time. If the container engine requires an image to be available on the host machine, it means the image needs to be downloaded. If there's no caching mechanism available for an engine, an image will be downloaded each time we request a container based on any image. Most of the popular container engines will automatically cache an image the first time it's downloaded. This will happen every time a new image is selected (or you request a new image tag).

> **Note**
> Container images are layered, which allows the sharing of certain parts of an image between different images. This also means that requesting a new image may not necessarily imply that you need to download everything it defines – in many cases, only a subset of layers is downloaded, which improves performance and allows the container engine to save disk space.

In CI/CD, it's important to make a distinction between managed and self-hosted build agents. If you're using self-hosted ones, the caching of container images will be mostly done by the container engine. Such agents are persistent, meaning you don't lose data after your pipeline runs. This may simplify operational overhead but can also cause some issues with disk space, especially if you run workloads running completely different containers.

For managed agents, which are considered ephemeral, running containers may be challenging as they exist only for the time a pipeline runs. This means that everything downloaded by your pipeline will disappear shortly after it is completed. To overcome that issue, some CI/CD tools implement a caching mechanism that you can leverage to improve the performance of your CI/CD pipelines.

An example of such a mechanism is the cache in Azure DevOps, which is implemented with the following task:

```
- task: Cache@2
    inputs:
      key: 'docker | "$(Agent.OS)" | cache'
      path: $(Pipeline.Workspace)/docker
      cacheHitVar: CACHE_RESTORED
```

This allows you to define three important parameters:

- key – A unique key identifying a specific cache.
- path – The path where the cache is restored.
- cacheHitVar – A variable that is set if a cache is found for the given key.

Note that the value of the key parameter is custom and can be set to any value depending on your needs. In our example, we use only a single variable based on the operating system running our agent. It could include other information such as an agent version, the version of your application, or some pipeline-specific value. It's important to define a key that can be used for cache restoration – if you use a dynamic value (such as the current time), you may never hit a cache as the key will be different each time a cache is restored.

When using a cache for Docker, we also need to save and load cached data so our container engine can leverage cached data. In order to do that, we could use these two commands:

- docker save
- docker load

It's important to use them with a condition based on the variable set by the `cacheHitVar` parameter:

```
- script: |
      docker load -i $(Pipeline.Workspace)/docker/cache.tar
  displayName: Docker restore
  condition: and(not(canceled()), eq(variables.CACHE_RESTORED,
  'true'))
```

This allows you to save the cache only if it hasn't been hit and load it if the cache is available for your pipeline.

You can read more about this feature in the Azure DevOps documentation here: `https://learn.microsoft.com/en-us/azure/devops/pipelines/release/caching?view=azure-devops`. I strongly recommend you go through all the explanations as caching in general is quite a difficult topic, and requires implementing additional mechanisms to monitor the cache and revoke it if needed. You also need to consider data retention and the actual benefits of implementing that mechanism. As caching in Azure DevOps is a managed feature, you won't have full control over how data is stored and where. In some scenarios, implementing a cache may even worsen the pipeline's performance. As with everything, make sure you measure the performance before and after implementing a cache to see whether there are any improvements.

Let's talk now about one of the newer additions to Azure Container Registry, which is support for cache and multi-arch images.

Using cache and multi-arch images

Azure Container Registry is a live Azure service that gets new features and improvements constantly. Some of the most interesting functionalities added recently are artifact cache and multi-arch images. We'll discuss them in this section in detail as they can be easily incorporated into many applications and are easy to implement.

Leveraging artifact cache in Azure Container Registry

Before we start discussing how artifact cache works in Azure Container Registry, let's understand why one would need to use a registry as a cache. In the most basic scenario, when you want to run a container, your container engine checks whether a container image is available locally. If it's not, it will try to download it first. The process is visualized in *Figure 9.7*:

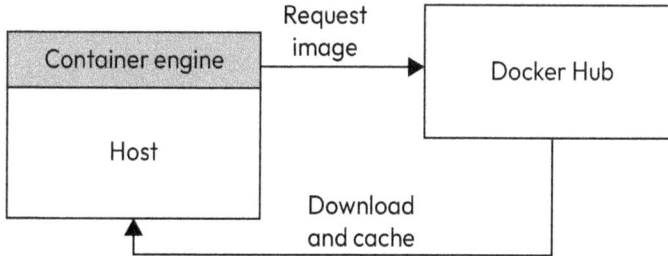

Figure 9.7 – The process of downloading and caching a container locally by using a public registry (Docker Hub)

This approach has some serious issues that need to be addressed in real systems:

- The selected public registry may not be available.

- We have no SLA for bandwidth, connection performance, and stability.

Even though, in such a scenario, the cache is represented by our host, it cannot be considered a shared cache that we could reuse across the whole platform. This is why a much better solution is using a proxy cache, which will take care of caching the images and downloading them if needed. Such a process is presented in *Figure 9.8*:

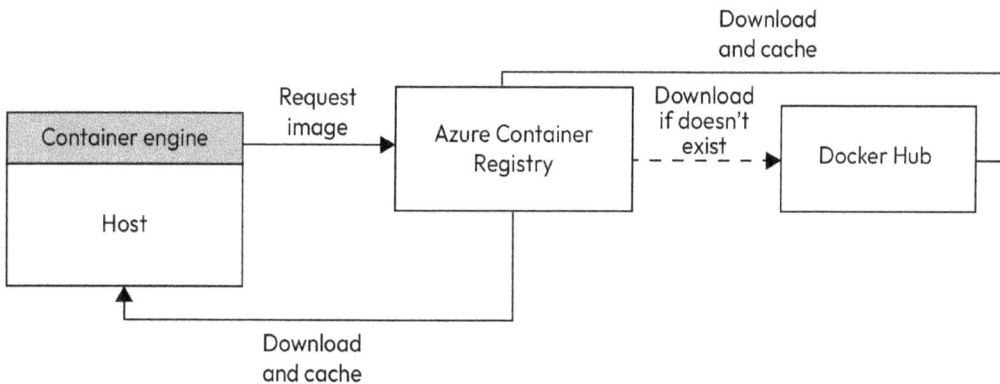

Figure 9.8 – Using Azure Container Registry as a proxy cache

In the process with a proxy cache, we simply change the way we reference container images. Let's say that you want to pull an image of nginx. To do that, you'd use the following command:

```
docker pull nginx:latest
```

By design, such a command will try to download the image from a public registry (in that case, Docker Hub). However, if you want to avoid add, you could reference the same image but this time using your registry name as the prefix:

```
docker pull <registry-name>.azurecr.io/nginx:latest
```

This will tell your container engine to fetch the image from the specific registry instead of the one defined implicitly. However, normally, images from other registries are not available in your private registry. To make them available, we need to introduce some kind of mapping. This is exactly what artifact cache does in Azure Container Registry – it allows you to define cache rules, which will be triggered and will cause image download whenever needed. Once the image is downloaded, any subsequent calls for the same container image won't require accessing the public registry and will be handled by Azure Container Registry instead.

An example of such a cache rule is presented as follows:

```
<registry-name>.azurecr.io/* => mcr.microsoft.com/*
```

If you add such a rule to your registry, all image calls will be considered to reference `mcr.microsoft.com` instead of your registry (technically, the calls will be performed against your own registry). As this rule uses wildcards, it may be too "greedy" in most scenarios (though it can be useful if you deploy a proxy cache registry for Microsoft images only). This is why you could make it more specific:

```
<registry-name>.azurecr.io/azure/* => mcr.microsoft.com/azure/*
<registry-name>.azurecr.io/dotnet/* => mcr.microsoft.com/dotnet/*
```

As you can see, we could introduce a repository-level rule, which is much easier to handle and can be utilized with no issues even if you want to use the same registry to store.

To learn more about the artifact cache feature, take a look at the detailed tutorial in the documentation, which covers how it can be implemented using the Azure portal: `https://learn.microsoft.com/en-us/azure/container-registry/container-registry-artifact-cache`.

Now, we're going to cover the last topic planned for this chapter, which is multi-arch images in Azure Container Registry.

Working with multi-arch images in Azure Container Registry

When containers were initially introduced, there was not much of a focus on providing multiple versions of the same image for different processor architectures. Nowadays, the situation is different – ARM processors are gaining in popularity, especially in the cloud area. Images produced for the standard x86 architecture cannot be used on machines running ARM CPUs, so there are two possible solutions for the problem:

- We need to prepare separate images for different architectures.
- We use the same image but make it support multiple architectures.

For operational simplicity and less complicated processes, the favored way of working is leveraging multi-arch images. To understand how a container image supports multiple architectures, we could use one of the publicly available images. Use the following command to download the image locally:

```
docker pull mcr.microsoft.com/mcr/hello-world:latest
```

Then, we can utilize the docker manifest inspect command to check the manifest of the image:

```
docker manifest inspect mcr.microsoft.com/mcr/hello-world:latest
```

In response, you will get the following JSON object (I removed parts that aren't important right now):

```
{
    "schemaVersion": 2,
    "mediaType": "application/vnd.docker.distribution.manifest.list.
v2+json",
    "manifests": [
      {
        "platform": {
          "architecture": "amd64",
          "os": "linux"
        }
      },
      {
        "platform": {
          "architecture": "arm64",
          "os": "linux"
        }
      },
      {
        "platform": {
          "architecture": "amd64",
          "os": "windows",
        }
      }
    ]
}
```

What is important for us now is the platform section. As you can see, it defines which processor architecture and operating system an image is intended for. Any image can be created for single or multiple platforms – it's up to the author to decide and express the intent.

> **Note**
>
> Some tools, such as Docker for Windows, can run images even if they aren't originally intended for a specific platform. For hosting scenarios, however, any kind of emulation is often discouraged, so an image that fully supports a processor architecture or operating system is advised.

When it comes to working with Azure Container Registry and multi-arch images, there's not much of a difference when compared to working with images intended for a single platform. The majority of work is performed when working with your container engine. For instance, if you want to prepare your image for different processor architectures using the Docker CLI, you'd need to use the following command:

```
docker buildx build --platform linux/amd64,linux/arm64 .
```

In the preceding example, we're building an image for two separate platforms (Linux as the operating system, and amd64 and arm64 as the architecture). However, for Azure Container Registry to fully support the multi-arch build, it's better to take a slightly different approach. Build your container image for multiple architectures separately and then use the following commands to push them to the registry:

```
docker tag <my-image>:amd64 <registry-name>.azurecr.io/<my-
image>:amd64
docker tag <my-image>:arm64 <registry-name>.azurecr.io/<my-
image>:arm64
docker push <registry-name>.azurecr.io/<my-image>:amd64
docker push <registry-name>.azurecr.io/<my-image>:arm64
```

Those commands will push the images to the registry but we still need to provide a manifest that links them. To do that, run the following commands:

```
docker manifest create <registry-name>.azurecr.io/<my-image>:multi-
arch \
<registry-name>.azurecr.io/<my-image>:arm64 \
<registry-name>.azurecr.io/<my-image>:amd64
docker manifest push <registry-name>.azurecr.io/<my-image>:multi-arch
```

Once you complete all the steps, any client that supports multi-arch images will be able to fetch the correct version of the image based on the manifest and run it on the desired platform.

We're slowly approaching the end of *Chapter 9*. For the final input, let's talk about use cases for Azure Container Registry.

Learning about use cases

Azure Container Registry is a great service if you want to quickly deploy a private container registry. With just a few clicks, you can deploy your very own host for container images, which is fully integrated with Microsoft Azure. As it's one of the simpler Azure services, you can also be sure that it doesn't have a steep learning curve to really utilize its potential.

It's also worth remembering that you can host generic OCI artifacts with all instances of Azure Container Registry. If you are looking for a place where you can store artifacts of your CI/CD pipelines or Bicep modules, Azure Container Registry seems like a good choice. Of course, it doesn't provide as many features as typical artifact registries such as Artifactory or Nexus but is a great choice for simpler architectures or if you just don't want to deploy a third-party component.

Azure Container Registry offers one additional feature we haven't discussed: tasks. These can be used to automate some operations such as updating a base image for your container images or rebuilding an image based on code changes. Most of the time, they're used for a number of operational activities. If you're interested in the topic, I recommend taking a look at the documentation at `https://learn.microsoft.com/en-us/azure/container-registry/container-registry-tasks-overview`.

That's all I have for you in this chapter. Let's summarize all the lessons and see what awaits in the next chapter.

Summary

In this chapter, we discussed Azure Container Registry, which is a managed Azure offering for a private container registry. We talked about deployment methods and how we can integrate with the service to push and pull container images. We also saw what the authentication methods are and how one can limit access to repositories in a registry. It's also worth mentioning that the knowledge from this chapter will become useful in the next chapters as some Azure services, such as Azure Web Apps and Azure Container Apps, integrate with Azure Container Registry and require prior knowledge of this service.

We also went through CI/CD integration for Azure Container Registry, which should be helpful if you're planning on automating the process of building and deploying your application.

In the next chapter, we'll take another step into containerized applications in Microsoft Azure by discussing Azure Container Instances, used for running ad hoc jobs and processes using containers.

10

Building Ad Hoc Workloads Using Azure Container Instances

Up to now, we've been focusing on using services such as Azure App Service or Azure Functions, which allow you to host your application's code in a similar way to hosting it on a server. They are suited for deploying either typical applications (**customer relationship management systems (CRMs)**, landing pages, blogs, **content management systems (CMSs)**) or event-driven functions and jobs. Sometimes, though, you need a simple service that allows you to run a piece of code for a moment and then discard obsolete infrastructure.

An example of such a service is **Azure Container Instances**. It's a fully managed cloud product with minimal configuration and small operational overhead. Thanks to that simplicity, you can quickly learn how to use and utilize it when needed.

In this chapter, we're going to cover the following main topics:

- Integrating Azure Container Instances with a web application
- Using Azure Container Instances for batch jobs
- Designing an application using Azure Container Instances
- Learning about use cases

Technical requirements

To perform the exercises from this chapter, you'll need the following:

- Azure CLI

- IDE of your choice (recommended – Visual Studio Code)

- Docker CLI and container runtime available on your computer (Docker, Colima, or similar)

The source code for this chapter is available at `https://github.com/PacktPublishing/Azure-for-Developers-Third-Edition/tree/main/ch10`.

Integrating Azure Container Instances with a web application

Before we get started with Azure Container Instances, let's try to understand how one can run a container. As you remember, containerized applications are built with two main steps:

1. Building a container image

2. Creating an instance of a container based on a selected container image

Depending on your needs, you may need a different tool to run such applications in a controlled manner. For typical applications (a single instance that can be scaled out when needed), you could use Azure App Service with containers (we will be discussing that in *Chapter 12*). For complex systems that require running tens or hundreds of containers, platforms such as Kubernetes are a much better choice. There are also options other than Azure App Service and Kubernetes that are designed to host multiple containers with minimal operational effort, such as Azure Container Apps (discussed in *Chapter 11*). They all have one thing in common – they are persistent. This means that once you deploy the service and run your application there, you'll be charged for it until you remove the deployed instance.

> **Note**
> Azure Container Apps may not fully fit the definition of a persistent service as Container Apps instances can be priced based on consumption. However, they're still meant to host persistent workloads most of the time and are too complex to be used for ad hoc deployments or jobs.

Azure Container Instances, on the contrary, is a unique service. Container instances require minimal configuration to get started and can be quickly set up to run a provided container. They're also very easy to manage as it's up to Azure to find the appropriate host where your container could run. Let's get started with a simple example to have a better understanding of the required steps.

Deploying your first container with Azure Container Instances

To deploy an instance of a container in Azure Container Instances, we need two things – a resource group and an instance of Azure Container Instances. We can create them with just two commands:

```
az group create \
-n <resource-group-name> \
-l <location>

az container create \
--g <resource-group-name> \
--n <container-instances-name> \
--image mcr.microsoft.com/azuredocs/aci-helloworld \
--dns-name-label <dns-label> \
--ports 8080
--cpu 1 \
--memory 2
```

While I think the first command is self-explanatory, let's focus on the second one. We're creating an instance of Azure Container Instances, which will run one of the publicly available container images. We will attach a custom DNS name to it, which will then be part of the URL used to access our application. We're also opening port 8080 to make the application available (the exact port to open depends on the container image). The last two parameters are there to determine how many CPUs (--cpu) and how much memory (--memory) will be provisioned. In our example, we're going to get 1 vCPU and 2 GB of memory.

> **Note**
> Remember that the selected DNS label needs to be unique for the whole region where your instance of Azure Container Instances will be deployed.

Once the command completes execution, let's try to obtain the URL of our application with the following command:

```
az container show \
-n <container-instances-name> \
-g <resource-group-name> \
--query ipAddress.fqdn
```

The value returned by the command will look like the following:

```
"afd10.westeurope.azurecontainer.io"
```

As your application could be available over HTTP or HTTPS, we need to prepend it with a proper HTTP protocol. Depending on the configuration of Azure Container Instances that you deployed, it could be HTTP or HTTPS. As we didn't configure a secure endpoint for our application, HTTPS can't be used. Instead, use HTTP to access it using the full URL (**fully qualified domain name (FQDN) with HTTP**). Use the full URL in your browser to access the application – you should see a web page similar to the one presented in *Figure 10.1*.

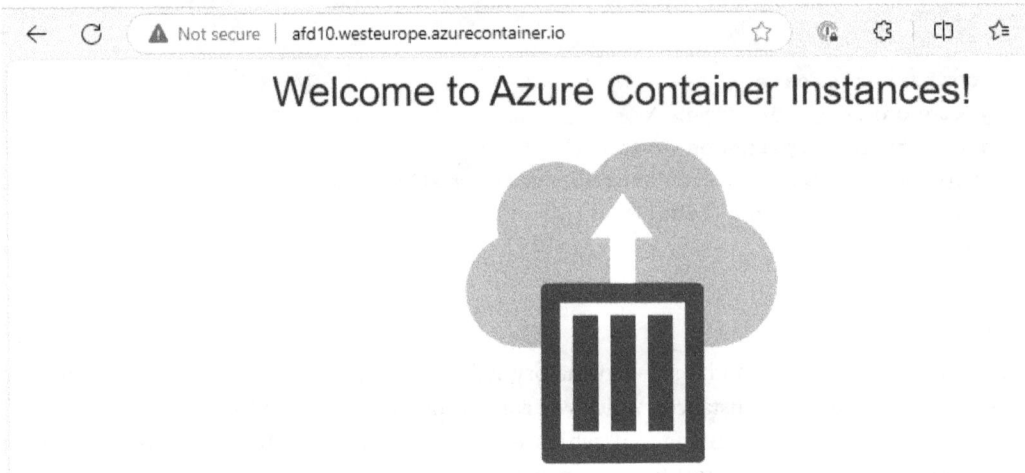

Figure 10.1 – Azure Container Instances running a standard web application

In this example, we used a boilerplate image prepared by Microsoft, which confirmed that our application was running. While it's not yet the target scenario I'd like to discuss, we can already highlight the following key takeaways:

- By deploying the example container, we didn't need to worry about underlying infrastructure. In fact, we didn't even specify what kind of hardware is needed.

- The configuration of our instance of Azure Container Instances can be kept to a minimum while still providing a working deployment.

- The application is automatically available publicly, and we don't need to manage ingress as the integral element of the application's infrastructure.

Let's now try to build an example application that can run a job in the background by preparing a container image, pushing it to our instance of Azure Container Registry, and running it using Azure Container Instances.

Building a custom image and running it using Azure Container Instances

In this exercise, we will prepare the following components:

- A Docker image
- Azure Container Registry
- An instance of Azure Container Instances running our Docker image

Let's get started with the exercise:

1. We will start by writing a Dockerfile executing a couple of commands, which will emulate a job running on a machine. Here's an example of what it could look like:

   ```
   FROM ubuntu:latest

   RUN mkdir /job
   WORKDIR /job

   # Create a new file with a unique name each 30 seconds
   CMD while true; do date +%s > $(date +%s).txt; sleep 30; done
   ```

2. Now, build the image and run it locally to test it. For `<image-tag>`, you could use any value – for instance, `my-application:v1`:

   ```
   docker build -t <image-tag> .
   docker run -d <image-tag>
   ```

3. As a result, you'll get a full identifier for a container running on your computer. Use it to gain access to its filesystem (here, I'm using the identifier returned for my computer; in your case, it will be a different value). In the following example, we're using the `docker exec` command, which allows you to run a command inside a running container (you can read more about it here: `https://docs.docker.com/reference/cli/docker/container/exec/`):

   ```
   docker exec -it
   4f7dcf5128a5c828ed3527f478285a9ad332efe1932e132f80848b839438769b
   /bin/bash
   root@4f7dcf5128a5:/job# ls -la
   total 28
   drwxr-xr-x 1 root root 4096 Oct 19 15:16 .
   drwxr-xr-x 1 root root 4096 Oct 19 15:14 ..
   -rw-r--r-- 1 root root   11 Oct 19 15:14 1729350867.txt
   -rw-r--r-- 1 root root   11 Oct 19 15:14 1729350897.txt
   -rw-r--r-- 1 root root   11 Oct 19 15:15 1729350927.txt
   ```

```
-rw-r--r-- 1 root root    11 Oct 19 15:15 1729350957.txt
-rw-r--r-- 1 root root    11 Oct 19 15:16 1729350987.txt
```

4. As you can see, files are being created twice per minute, and the overall process seems to be working as intended. We can now create an instance of Azure Container Registry and push the image there. To do that, use the following commands:

```
az acr create \
-g <resource-group-name> \
-n <container-registry-name> \
--sku Basic \
--admin-enabled
docker tag <image-tag> <container-registry-name>.azurecr.
io/<image-tag>:latest
az acr login -n <container-registry-name>
docker push <container-registry-name>.azurecr.io/<image-
tag>:latest
```

5. After a moment, you should see your image available in the Azure Container Registry instance you created. The last step left for us is using the created container image as the source for a container run using Azure Container Instances. Let's try to execute it:

```
az container create \
-g <resource-group-name> \
-n <container-instances-name> \
--image <container-registry-name>.azurecr.io/<image-tag>:latest
```

After a moment, the CLI should ask you for credentials to authenticate to Azure Container Registry. This is one of the use cases for admin credentials in Azure Container Registry, though it's also possible to use a managed identity to leverage **role-based access control** (**RBAC**) authorization instead. Once you provide both username and password, the deployment will start, and you should be able to see an instance of Azure Container Instances created for you.

> **Note**
> To use admin credentials, your Azure Container Registry instance must have that feature enabled. If you're uncertain how to work with an admin user in Azure Container Registry, reference *Chapter 9*, where we discussed it.

6. Once deployments finish, our container should start and begin performing the commands, which we incorporated into the container image. You can simply check that by running `ls -la` inside the running container. Here's an example for my instance of Azure Container Instances:

```
az container exec -g afd-rg -n afd1002 --exec-command "ls -la"
total 36
drwxr-xr-x 1 root root 4096 Oct 26 17:26 .
```

```
drwxr-xr-x 1 root root 4096 Oct 26 17:23 ..
-rw-r--r-- 1 root root   11 Oct 26 17:23 1729963424.txt
-rw-r--r-- 1 root root   11 Oct 26 17:24 1729963454.txt
-rw-r--r-- 1 root root   11 Oct 26 17:24 1729963484.txt
-rw-r--r-- 1 root root   11 Oct 26 17:25 1729963514.txt
-rw-r--r-- 1 root root   11 Oct 26 17:25 1729963544.txt
-rw-r--r-- 1 root root   11 Oct 26 17:26 1729963574.txt
-rw-r--r-- 1 root root   11 Oct 26 17:26 1729963604.txt
```

I used the `az container exec` command to run the `ls -la` command inside the running container (deployed inside the `afd-rg` resource group and named `afd1002`). As you can see, the result of running that command is what we expected – files are being created constantly until the container is stopped or crashes.

We'll dive into the topic of such containers later in the chapter when we discuss batch jobs. Let's see now what we could do in a real-case scenario to integrate Azure Container Instances with a web application.

Using Azure Container Instances with web applications

As you've seen, Azure Container Instances can be easily used to run both one-time jobs and continuous processes if needed. This makes Azure a great choice for offloading some work from your main web application, as you don't need to worry about scaling or performance. Let's consider the following scenario – you want to generate a PDF file for a record in your database, but as the process takes several seconds to complete, you don't want to do it in your main application. One possible solution is to deploy a dedicated service, which will be decoupled from the main application thanks to a queue (*Figure 10.2*):

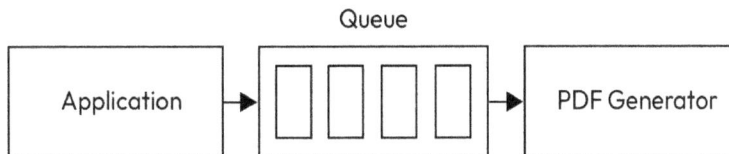

Figure 10.2 – An application offloading a heavy process to a dedicated component with a queue

The downside of such a solution could be the additional cost of infrastructure and operations related to the second service. If the dedicated service is simply another application that is hosted on a web server and runs all the time, we have fixed one issue, but we're still far from the optimal solution.

We could replace the dedicated service with a simple orchestrator that spins up an instance of Azure Container Instances each time a new PDF needs to be generated (*Figure 10.3*):

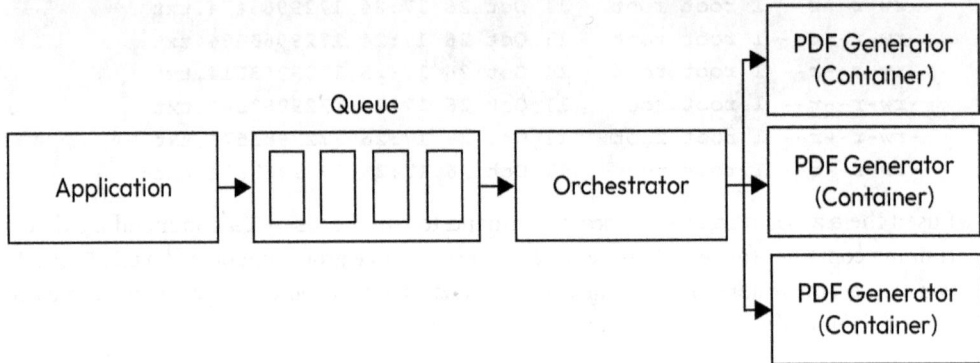

Figure 10.3 – Offloading a process to an orchestrator running containers

Such a process looks similar to platforms such as Kubernetes but, of course, is much, much simpler. The general idea remains, though – you run a dedicated process as an isolated container, which is alive only until it is complete. Once the job is done, the container is removed, and you can reclaim used resources. With Azure Container Instances, implementation of such an architecture is really simple – all you need is to find a proper way to provision containers. Let's see how we can implement that mechanism.

Deploying Azure Container Instances using Azure Bicep

If we want to deploy infrastructure from our code using Azure Bicep, we will need to install an SDK allowing us to perform such an operation. The whole concept will consist of the following two elements:

- A Bicep template we can parametrize
- A piece of code triggering the deployment by calling the correct SDK functions

To get started, we can prepare the following Bicep template:

```
param parLocation string = resourceGroup().location
param parTimestamp string = utcNow()
param parCustomerId string

resource aci 'Microsoft.ContainerInstance/containerGroups@2021-03-01'
= {
  name: 'aci-${parTimestamp}'
  location: parLocation
  properties: {
    containers: [
      {
```

```
    name: 'myjob'
    properties: {
      image: '<acr-name>.azurecr.io/<image-name>:latest'
      environmentVariables: [
        {
          name: 'customerId'
          value: parCustomerId
        }
      ]
      resources: {
        requests: {
          cpu: 1
          memoryInGB: 3
        }
      }
    }
  }
]
restartPolicy: 'Always'
osType: 'Linux'
  }
}
```

Let's discuss the template to have a better understanding of what it does. As you can see, it consists of three parameters:

- ParLocation: Used to define the deployment location of the resources.

- ParTimestamp: Used to provide a unique name for each instance of the resource.

- ParCustomerId: Custom value passed down to the starting container.

Once deployed, this template would create a new instance of Azure Container Instances and start a new container using the provided image definition. We could also pass a custom value (customerId) to allow the container to fetch correct data (for instance, use it to query a database). That custom value will be available later as an environment variable for the application running inside the container. This is useful in various scenarios as this functionality allows you to pass a dynamic value and inject it into a container.

> **Note**
> Remember that each instance of Azure Container Instances can run multiple containers.

Now, if we want to deploy such a template, we will need to install the correct package. The package we need is Azure SDK, which is available for several different programming languages:

- .NET – `https://learn.microsoft.com/en-us/dotnet/azure/sdk/azure-sdk-for-dotnet`

- Java – `https://learn.microsoft.com/en-us/azure/developer/java/sdk/`

- Go – `https://learn.microsoft.com/en-us/azure/developer/go/overview`

- Python – `https://learn.microsoft.com/en-us/azure/developer/python/sdk/azure-sdk-overview`

All those SDKs will provide a method to deploy a template, though we need to remember that **Azure Resource Manager** (**ARM**) is working with ARM templates rather than Bicep files. This is why we will need to compile the template first and use the result as our deployment artifact.

> **Tip**
>
> While the process of transforming a Bicep file into an ARM template may look cumbersome, it shouldn't be much of a problem in most cases. You could implement a task run locally each time the Bicep file is saved so that Azure CLI starts in the background and transforms the file. You could also leverage a **continuous integration/continuous deployment** (**CI/CD**) pipeline and just transform the file each time the application is built.

The method we need to use is named `BeginCreateOrUpdate()` and is available as part of an object named `DeploymentClient`. Here's how you can perform deployment using Python code:

```python
import os
import json
from azure.identity import AzureCliCredential
from azure.mgmt.resource import ResourceManagementClient
from azure.mgmt.resource.resources.models import DeploymentMode

credential = AzureCliCredential()
subscription_id = os.environ["AZURE_SUBSCRIPTION_ID"]

resource_client = ResourceManagementClient(credential, subscription_
id)

with open("aci.json", "r") as template_file:
    template_body = json.load(template_file)

rg_deployment_result = resource_client.deployments.begin_create_or_
update(
    "<resource_group_name>",
```

```
      "<deployment_name>",
      {
          "properties": {
              "template": template_body,
              "parameters": {
                  "parCustomerId": {
                      "value": "18363875"
                  },
              },
              "mode": DeploymentMode.incremental
          }
      }
  )
```

The same could be achieved using, for instance, Go. Here's a code snippet of the same operation we performed for Python but written in Go (reference `https://github.com/PacktPublishing/Azure-for-Developers-Third-Edition/tree/main/ch10` for the full code needed to perform the deployment):

```
deploy, err := deploymentsClient.BeginCreateOrUpdate(
    ctx,
    resourceGroupName,
    deploymentName,
    armresources.Deployment{
        Properties: &armresources.DeploymentProperties{
            Template: template,
            Parameters: "{\"parCustomerId\":
                {\"value\": \"18363875\"}}",
            Mode: to.Ptr(armresources.DeploymentModeIncremental),
        },
    },
    nil,
)
```

As you can see, for both Python and Go, we're using the very same method for deployment; in fact, the same is true for .NET and Java. For all the languages, what you need to remember is how the code will be executed:

- The application needs to authenticate to Azure and have the necessary permissions to deploy resources (the Contributor role on a resource group level will be more than enough).

- You need to use an ARM template instead of a Bicep file.

- When creating a deployment, remember to pass all the required parameters if the template doesn't provide default values.

An alternative approach for deploying Azure Container Instances would be to use a dedicated SDK published by Microsoft. Those SDKs (called Management SDKs) allow you to execute operations against ARM, so you can create or update a service, change its properties, or even delete it programmatically.

Interacting with Azure Container Instances using a dedicated SDK

If you decide to use a dedicated SDK to deploy Azure Container Instances, you need to understand what scope of operations is available there. As with the SDK for interacting with ARM, the SDK for Azure Container Instances can be found for all major programming languages:

- Java: `https://search.maven.org/artifact/com.azure.resourcemanager/azure-resourcemanager-containerinstance/2.44.0/jar/`

- .NET: `https://www.nuget.org/packages/Azure.ResourceManager.ContainerInstance/1.2.1`

- Python: `https://pypi.org/project/azure-mgmt-containerinstance/10.1.0`

- Go: `https://github.com/Azure/azure-sdk-for-go/tree/sdk/resourcemanager/containerinstance/armcontainerinstance/v2.4.0/sdk/resourcemanager/containerinstance/armcontainerinstance/`

Each version of the SDK allows you to perform the following operations:

- Attach to a container

- Execute a command

- Get container logs

- Start/stop a container

- Update the container definition

Those operations open several different possibilities when it comes to building an application. We can use them not only to monitor a background process but also to extract generated results or even open a WebSockets connection and start reading the output stream from a running container.

> **Note**
> The SDK allows you to perform even more operations, but most of them are related to the Azure resources themselves (add a tag; delete a resource) so aren't that useful when discussing web application integration.

One possible way to leverage the dedicated SDK would be to combine the deployment of Azure Container Instances on demand using the previously discussed SDK and then use the dedicated SDK to read the results generated by a container. Let's consider the following example (*Figure 10.4*):

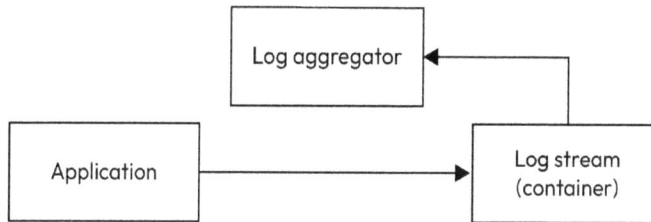

Figure 10.4 – An application fetching logs from a running container

The example from *Figure 10.4* includes the following components:

- **Application**: A generic service that provisions a new instance of Azure Container Instances to perform some background work.

- **Log stream (container)**: An instance of Azure Container Instances that performs background work and reports the progress by sending the data to the standard output.

- **Log aggregator**: An aggregating or streaming service (for instance, Prometheus exporter) that can read the data streamed by our container.

This example would involve the following operations provided by SDKs:

- Create/update Azure container instance.

- Start a container.

- Attach to a container and fetch logs.

You may wonder what's the trick in here. To understand that, let's look at what happens under the hood when you attach to a container run by Azure Container Instances using an SDK. All SDKs are an overlay for the REST API provided by the Azure service. In the case of attaching to a running container, it will use the following HTTP call:

```
POST https://management.azure.com/subscriptions/<subscription-
id>/resourceGroups/<resource-group-name>/providers/Microsoft.
ContainerInstance/containerGroups/<container-instances-name>/
containers/<container-name>/attach?api-version=2023-05-01
```

Note that the API version used in the request may change depending on the actual requirement (you can use any version that supports the "attach" operation).

What's important here is that in response, you will get the following JSON:

```
{
    "webSocketUri": "wss://web-socket-uri",
    "password": "password"
}
```

This JSON contains a URI to a WebSocket endpoint, which you could use to stream logs from both standard output and standard error provided by the running container.

An alternative approach would require reading logs on demand by executing a command inside a running container – for instance, the following:

```
tail -n 100 <log-file>
```

The easiest option would be to just use the `tail` command and execute it with the SDK. In the previous example, we would read the last 100 lines of the log file created inside the running container.

Another idea for the integration would be to fetch the results of a running background task scheduled as a container. The idea is presented in *Figure 10.5*:

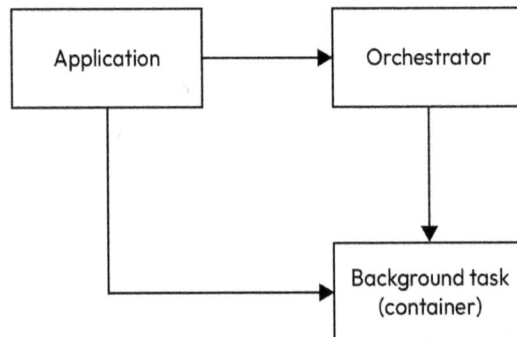

Figure 10.5 – An application scheduling work via an orchestrator
and fetching results from a running container

With such an approach, we could utilize our ability to run a command inside a running container. Let's consider the following algorithm:

```
var fileExist = container.Execute('-e /result.txt')
if fileExist == 0:
    var results = container.Execute('cat /result.txt')
else:
    // Check again in 5 minutes
```

The preceding pseudocode presents an idea where you check for the existence of a file that is supposed to be generated by a running container. If a file isn't available, we just proceed and check again in 5 minutes. All operations could be performed by simply executing two different commands inside the running container. This is, of course, a very simple example that may not always be connected with a real business scenario. Instead of checking if a file exists, we could simply change the flow of such an application by using a queue. Check *Figure 10.6* for a reference.

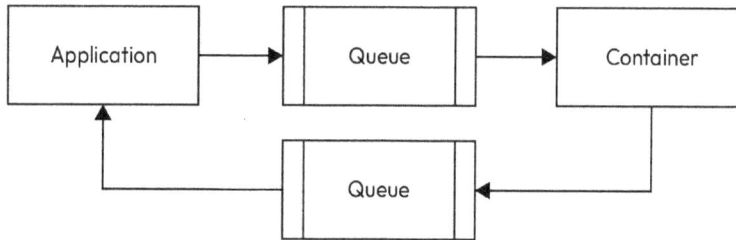

Figure 10.6 – Using a queue to orchestrate communication between an
application and a container running inside Azure Container Instances

In the concept presented in *Figure 10.6*, you can see that we're using two queues. The first queue is used to publish a message from an application and consume it inside a container. The second queue is used to notify an application about a process that finished. If the process includes a file being created, we would just wait inside a container until the file is ready and then send a message to an application. In the end, we could use the message to either pass the content of the file or (if it's too big) send just the metadata and allow the application to call the container and fetch the content by itself (as presented in *Figure 10.7*).

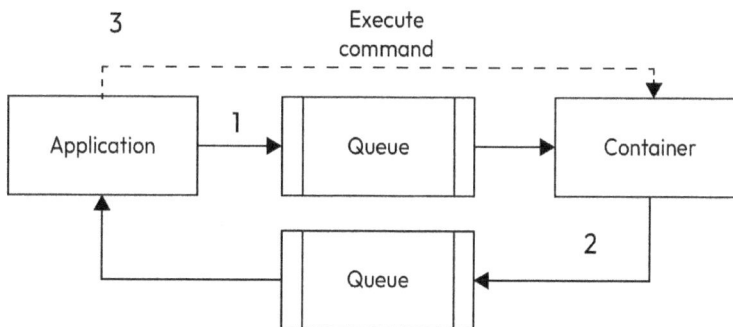

Figure 10.7 – Executing a command inside a container from an application once it is notified about a file

Let's now discuss how we could use Azure Container Instances for batch jobs.

Using Azure Container Instances for batch jobs

Batch jobs are basically a set of similar tasks that can be scheduled and executed together. They're often performed in the background and may require hours or days to complete. Most of the time, batch jobs are scheduled to interact with a database or generate files based on the provided data. Depending on the expected artifact type (local file; dataset in a database), we can either run a job and discard it or find a way to persist the result.

Azure Container Instances allows you to run any batch job of your choice, but you will need to understand how to collect its results. If the artifacts are going to be persisted to a database, the implementation will be fairly simple – all you need is to connect to a database and save the results. If you need, for instance, to export files and save them to a file share, the complexity of the process will depend on how difficult it is to connect to the share (a public share in Azure will be much easier to connect to than a share hosted inside your corporate network on-premises).

An interesting feature of Azure Container Instances is volumes, which work in a similar way to the volumes used when working, for example, with Docker. To work with them, you will need two additional components:

- Azure storage account
- File share created with File Service

Those two components can be easily created with just two Azure CLI commands:

```
az storage account create \
--resource-group <resource-group-name> \
--name <storage-account-name> \
--location <location> \

az storage share create \
--name <file-share-name> \
--account-name <storage-account-name>
```

Once both the account and file share are created, you could create a new instance of Azure Container Instances:

```
az container create \
--resource-group <resource-group-name> \
--name <container-instances-name> \
--image <image-name-and-tag> \
--azure-file-volume-account-name <storage-account-name> \
--azure-file-volume-account-key <storage-account-key> \
--azure-file-volume-share-name <file-share-name> \
--azure-file-volume-mount-path <mount-path>
```

> **Note**
> If you'd like to mount a share to a container that exposes a web application, remember to add `--port` and `--dns-label` parameters to the command.

Once a new instance of the service is created, it will make the file share mounted at the `<mount-path>` parameter value. There are certain limitations to that approach, however:

- As we're mounting a **Server Message Block** (**SMB**) share, we're unable to use a managed identity to authenticate to Azure Storage.
- Mounts don't work for Windows containers.
- The container must run as root.

Even though using an Azure Files share as a mount target won't work in all scenarios, it's an interesting approach if you don't want to export the results of your batch jobs as part of the script or application's code.

It's also worth remembering that Azure Container Instances can be made more or less reliable depending on the *restart policy*. When using Azure CLI or Azure Bicep, you can set the value of the parameter responsible for determining what Azure Container Instances should do at the end. Let's consider the following command:

```
Az container create \
-g <resource-group-name> \
-n <container-instances-name> \
--restart-policy <Always|Never|OnFailure>
```

As you can see, the `--restart-policy` parameter takes one of three different values (`Always`, `Never`, and `OnFailure`). For batch jobs, you need to decide which value reflects the actual use case:

- Use `Always` if you want to restart the job no matter if it succeeded or failed. It will work best if it's up to the external process to decide what to do and how to handle overlapping requests. In such a scenario, your container works only as a trigger for another component.
- Use `Never` if your container runs a process that requires external interaction if it fails and is also a one-time job. An example of such a process would be a container interacting with dynamic data and capturing its state at a particular moment in time.
- Use `OnFailure` for all jobs that are idempotent. They can be restarted at any time as they're self-healing, but once completed, they shouldn't run again.

Setting the correct value for the restart policy is one of the most important things for running batch jobs in Azure Container Instances as it reflects their non-functional requirements and directly translates to the reliability of the process.

Let's now discuss the last topic planned for this chapter – designing an application using Azure Container Instances.

Designing an application using Azure Container Instances

By now, you should be quite familiar with all the capabilities of Azure Container Instances and major use cases for this particular service. If we recap the main features of Azure Container Instances we discussed, we could list the following things:

- Serverless platform allowing you to run a workload anytime and pay only for usage
- Runtime isolation, which enables you to make your workloads compliant with internal and external regulations
- Persistent storage thanks to File Service mounts hosted on Azure Storage
- Portability and platform-agnostic deployment model
- Co-scheduled container groups that give you the ability to deploy several containers as a single unit to share network, storage, and lifecycle

If you select Azure Container Instances as your hosting platform, you will need to remember similar things as with other container-based platforms. The most important thing when designing an application based on Azure Container Instances will be understanding if you need (and where) to persist your data. Many storage solutions could be used in that case – a file share, a database, an FTP server, or a data lake service. We already mentioned that Azure Container Instances can easily leverage volumes in tandem with Azure Storage. Such an approach is a great solution if your data needs to be ingested and processed further. The same is true for databases as well, but typical relational databases (when integrated with customer-facing applications) are rarely used in typical *data analysis/processing* scenarios. However, if your workloads are supposed to prepare data or move it between different storage solutions, Azure Container Instances could be just the right match.

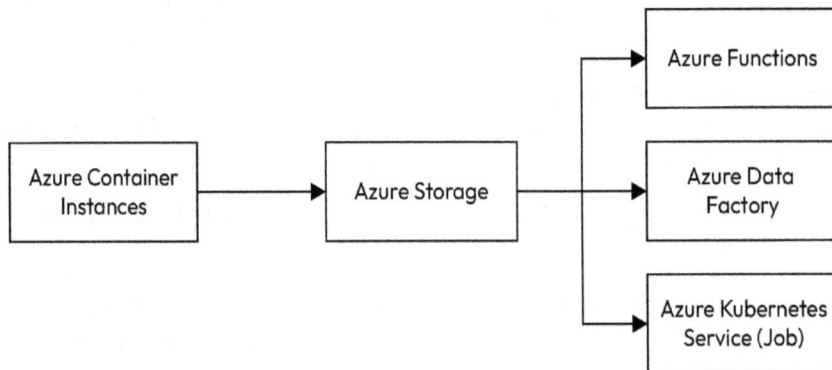

Figure 10.8 – Using Azure Container Instances to push data to Azure
Storage and ingesting it using three different Azure services

With Azure Container Instances, the approach for *storage integration* will depend on several factors:

- Type of data stored

- Storage placement (cloud/on-premises)

- The volume of data stored (file mounts may perform better in some scenarios when compared with various databases)

- Authentication method when connecting to the storage solution

For instance, if your intent is to store multiple small files, you may want to process them in batches instead of doing them one by one. If the process can be split into smaller ones, you could leverage container groups and just spin up multiple identical containers that will work on your data in an organized fashion.

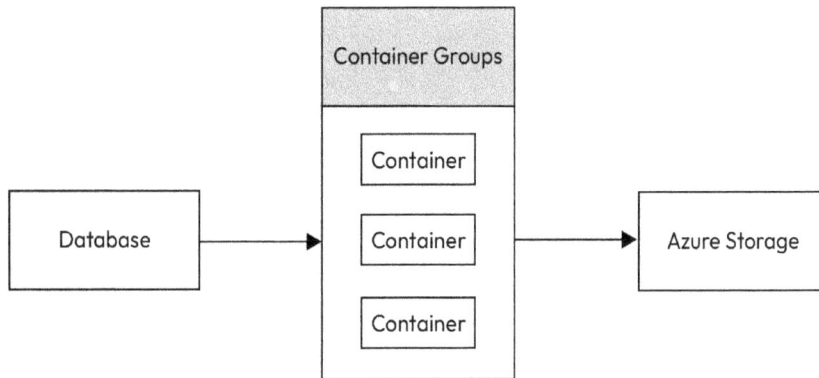

Figure 10.9 – A concept of spinning up multiple containers
querying a database and processing data in parallel

Storage placement will be important from the network perspective – fortunately, Azure Container Instances supports virtual networks in Azure, so it's possible to connect them to private networks as well.

> **Note**
> When considering networking for Azure Container Instances, you need to remember about limitations. One thing that isn't supported is placing Azure Load Balancer in front of your Azure Container Instances instance. You also won't be able to support global peering or expose containers integrated with a virtual network using a public IP FQDN.

When it comes to the volume of data stored, you need to consider the limitations of the selected storage solution. As your containers will most likely run your custom code, you will need to implement a proper mechanism for connecting to a storage and storing data. The downside of Azure container instances is how abstract they are when it comes to used infrastructure. As you don't control any of the typical aspects of the hosting environment (CPU, memory utilization, network interfaces), you may find Azure Container Instances quite cumbersome in scenarios that require careful optimization. If that's the case, you may find other services such as Azure Functions or Azure Container Apps better suited for your application.

One of the most important aspects of applications is *monitoring*. Azure Container Instances doesn't change much here – you can use the same mechanism for your application as you would use in any other cloud service. One thing to remember, though, is the dynamic nature of containers. If you spin up multiple instances of your service or job and those are short-living processes, you will need to implement a proper identifier to distinguish logs and metrics coming from different containers. Without that, it may be difficult to properly debug and troubleshoot your application.

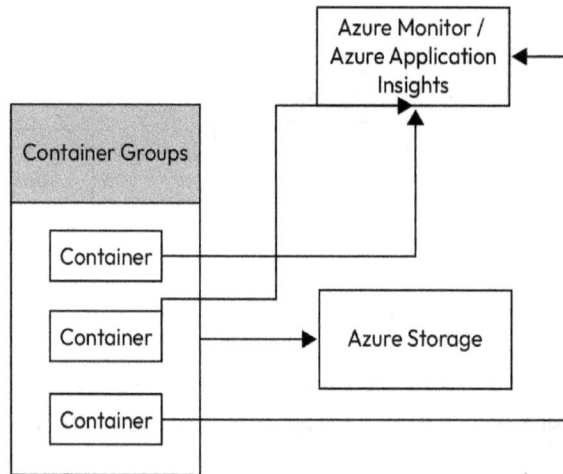

Figure 10.10 – Publishing logs and metrics from Azure Container
Instances to Azure Monitor or Azure Application Insights

The last thing to remember is how Azure container instances relate to *orchestrators* such as Kubernetes. You need to remember that Azure Container Instances doesn't provide typical mechanisms for the scalability or reliability of your services. Sure, you can use the proper restart policy, which we discussed in the previous section, but generally speaking, it's quite a simple and straightforward service. There's no such thing as node affinity, QoS of containers, service discovery, or load balancing. In some scenarios, running the same container on a **virtual machine** (**VM**) can be cheaper than doing the same using Azure Container Instances. This is why you should consider that Azure service for ephemeral and stateless workloads, which can be easily restarted or load-balanced by an external mechanism.

One of the most interesting use cases for Azure container instances is using them for virtual nodes in Azure Kubernetes Service. As Kubernetes takes care of properly load balancing containers and ensuring they meet availability criteria, even if a virtual node fails, it will spin up another to replace the broken one.

Learning about use cases

When it comes to use cases for Azure Container Instances, we need to keep in mind that it's quite a simple service that can be often overshadowed by other, more complex Azure products such as Azure Container Apps or Azure Functions. This is why it's important to understand where Azure Container Instances is useful and why you should use it instead of other services.

Personally, I always find Azure Container Instances extremely helpful if I need to quickly deploy and run a small job. Such a job could be a one-time action – by using Azure Container Instances, I save time by not forcing myself to configure additional infrastructure (such as Azure Functions requiring an Azure App Service plan and a proper deployment model). Being able to quickly spin up a running container could be also useful in scenarios where you need to quickly process some data. To fully utilize that approach, we'd need to use storage mounts and link them to the containers. This sounds like a much more complicated setup than it is – we talked in this chapter about the possibility of integrating Azure Storage with Azure Container Instances and how transparent and simple the configuration is.

Another use case for Azure Container Instances is running ephemeral workloads. Being able to quickly start a container and integrate it with an external service may be beneficial in many scenarios. For instance, you could utilize Azure Container Instances for CI/CD runners, especially having them integrated with your network. Such runners could be considered ephemeral, so even if they get restarted, the state can be safely created with no real impact on other workloads.

In theory, it would be also possible to run a web application with a web server using Azure Container Instances. While it's technically possible, I personally don't consider that a viable approach. Azure container instances lack several important features required for typical web applications, such as predictable scaling, stable performance, and isolated tiers, making them less useful.

That's all for *Chapter 10*! Let's summarize all the sections and see what we'll cover in the next chapter.

Summary

In this chapter, we took a look at Azure Container Instances – a serverless platform for running ad hoc jobs and simple services. We discussed how a container can be started using Azure Container Instances and what kind of operations are available when it's running. We also talked about batch jobs and how you could utilize Azure Container Instances in such a scenario. While those are quite simple scenarios, they should provide enough information for you to be able to start working with Azure Container Instances on your own.

One of the major topics in this chapter was related to using Azure Container Instances with web applications as an additional component or layer responsible for proceeding with data in an asynchronous way. Having that kind of understanding of how you're supposed to work with various cloud services will become handy when designing your own systems. While you could implement most functionalities using only a single service, incorporating additional services such as Azure Container Instances allows you to decentralize your application and offload some work to a dedicated component.

In the next chapter, we're going to explain Azure Container Apps – one of the newer services in Azure, which provides an easy-to-learn and robust platform for hosting even more complex, container-based applications.

11

Developing Microservices with Azure Container Apps

As of now, we've been discussing containers in Azure by either talking about infrastructure for container images (Azure Container Registry) or running simple workloads in a serverless fashion (Azure Container Instances). However, the services we're developing daily are different when it comes to their complexity and requirements for reliability and flexibility. For more microservice-oriented architectures, one of the most popular choices is platforms based on Kubernetes (such as Azure Kubernetes Service). They offer advanced configuration options and can be applied for several different use cases. Unfortunately, they have one major downside – they are difficult to maintain and, most of the time, require a dedicated team to administer clusters. Fortunately, Azure offers a solution, which sits in a sweet spot between Azure Container Instances and Azure Kubernetes Service – this solution is named Azure Container Apps.

Thanks to Azure Container Apps, you can build systems based on containers, which are not too complicated for developers to create and maintain while offering advanced features for more complex scenarios (including ingress service, service discovery, or built-in observability functionality). In the chapter, we'll discuss a subset of available features that are especially useful for developers of applications. This includes things such as revisions, deployments, and environment variables setup.

In this chapter, we're going to cover the following main topics:

- Understanding the differences between Azure App Service and Azure Container Apps
- Planning for hosting an application with Azure Container Apps
- Deploying an application using Azure Container Apps
- Learning about managing an application with Azure Container Apps
- Learning about use cases

Technical requirements

To perform exercises in this chapter, you will need the following:

- Azure CLI

- An IDE of your choice (preferably Visual Studio Code)

The source code for this chapter is available at `https://github.com/PacktPublishing/Azure-for-Developers-Third-Edition/tree/main/ch11`.

Understanding the differences between Azure App Service and Azure Container Apps

When we discussed Azure App Service, one of the major things to remember was how it is structured. As you remember, for typical web applications hosted using Azure App Service we need two separate components:

- Azure App Service plan – Our hardware providing compute (CPU, memory, disk space).

- Azure Web App/Azure Function App – A web server hosting our application and allowing us to interact with it thanks to the dedicated management layer for configuration management.

In Azure Container Apps, things work differently – we no longer need to provision the server ourselves – it's a serverless platform, which simplifies operations and deployment so developers can focus on building an application reflecting requirements given by the business.

As the name suggests, Azure Container Apps is also meant to host containers instead of running our application in-process. The deployment and hosting model looks similar to the one offered by Kubernetes, but it's aimed rather at giving developers as smooth a learning curve as possible. It's worth mentioning that Azure App Service can also host containers (as we will discuss in *Chapter 12*). The difference here comes from the approach you need to take when hosting the same application using either of those two services. In Azure App Service, when you want to host a container, you still need to utilize an Azure App Service plan. Also, the whole management layer stays as you'd host a typical application in-process. The only thing that changes is the source of the application – for containers, you need to integrate Azure App Service with either a public or private container registry. The rest of the setup stays as it was.

To help you better understand the similarities and differences, let's list them with a proper description. The things that are similar for both Azure App Service and Azure Container Apps are as follows:

- Both can be used for hosting web applications.

- Both allow you to use containers as a deployment method.

- Both can be used with an autoscaling feature.

- Both enable you to use an in-built authentication mechanism, so you can offload authentication to the platform instead of keeping it in your application.

- Both can be placed inside a virtual network for enhanced security and isolation.

As usual, when we compare those two services, we can find several significant differences:

- Azure App Service can be deployed as a fully isolated workload for predictable performance and increased security, while Azure Container Apps offers dedicated tiers, which will provide stable performance but not dedicated hardware.

- Azure Container Apps comes with a dedicated ingress object for handling incoming traffic; Azure App Service requires the deployment of an additional component (such as Azure Application Gateway or Azure Front Door) to achieve similar results.

- Azure Container Apps is billed using artificial units of vCPU-seconds and GiB-seconds, reflecting the utilization of the CPU and memory of the workloads they're hosting. In Azure App Service you pay a fixed monthly price, which can be increased or decreased depending on the number of running instances of your applications.

Before we jump to the next topic, let's emphasize one more key difference between Azure App Service and Azure Container Apps – the architecture you can build with them. Even though both services have similarities, Azure Container Apps will be much better suited for microservices when compared with Azure App Service. For single-tenant deployment scenarios, Azure Container Apps will be easier to utilize and maintain thanks to its lightweight deployment model and serverless nature. While Azure App Service can be used for such deployments, it works much better in multi-tenant scenarios, where you deploy a single application handling heavy load and scale it if needed.

Let's now see how we can plan a hosting and deployment strategy using Azure Container Apps.

Planning for hosting an application with Azure Container Apps

We have talked about differences and similarities between Azure App Service and Azure Container Apps that shed some light on proper planning for the deployment of an application based on one of those platforms. As we're focusing on Azure Container Apps now, we need to understand how to properly integrate our application with that service and what is needed to achieve expected reliability.

Let's start by discussing available deployment options to see how they can work with the services we're building.

Selecting the proper deployment option

Azure Container Apps is no different from other Azure services when it comes to deploying an application. As we discussed previously, the prerequisite is making our application available as a container image, which can be hosted on the selected platform. There are two elements we need to develop to deploy an application with Azure Container Apps:

- Manual or automated pipeline for the application
- Manual or automated pipeline for infrastructure

We are dividing deployment into two separate components as they are not strictly linked to each other. You can deploy your infrastructure separately from the application itself (though you need to remember, that infrastructure comes as the prerequisite for the first deployment of the application). We could design our CI/CD process as presented in *Figure 11.1*.

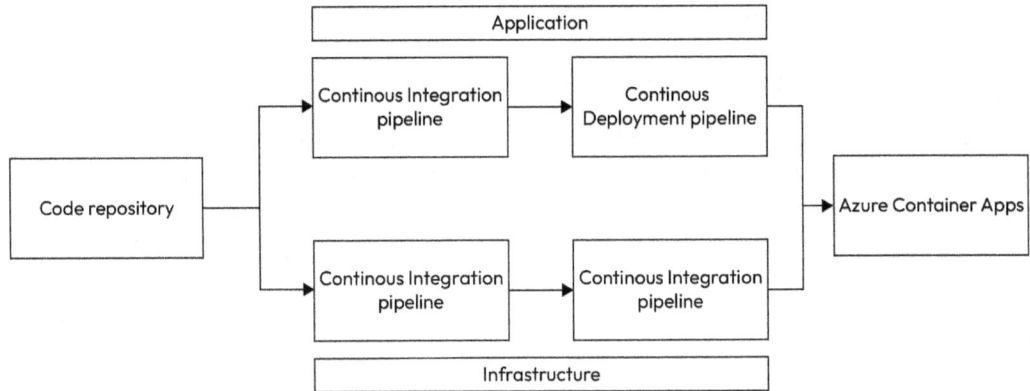

Figure 11.1 – High-level design of CI/CD pipeline for Azure Container Apps

If you take a close look at the diagram, you will see we're structuring the deployment process in two separate phases, which reuse the same conceptual steps. They both start with a code repository (it could be Git, SVN, Mercurial, or any other version control system) and end with an Azure Container Apps instance. For both application and infrastructure, we could follow the Continuous Integration approach (build and test the application, validate it, and prepare for deployment) and link it with Continuous Deployment (so all the changes are automatically pushed to the selected environment).

> **Note**
>
> We mentioned that pipelines could be manual or automated – the choice depends on the selected toolset, your skills, and actual requirements. Remember though, that the manual approach could work for limited use cases and will be difficult to manage and replicate. CI/CD pipelines, by definition, aim at full automation and benefit from all kinds of automated checks to relieve engineers from repeatable tasks.

As Azure Container Apps uses containers, any deployment will need to utilize a container registry. This is applicable if you want to have full control over the process. There's also a possibility to leverage the built-in feature of Azure Container Apps to build a container image. Internally, it uses CNCF Buildpacks (`https://buildpacks.io/`) to automatically detect the parameters of your application and generate a container.

Let's describe all the components involved in the process of building an application for Azure Container Apps:

- CI/CD pipeline
- CI/CD agent (managed or self-hosted)
- Container registry

The thing we need to fully understand is which components are mandatory, and which are optional. If we treat a CI/CD pipeline as something provided by our CI/CD software, then we will need to answer the following questions:

- Where do we want to build a container image?
- How do we want to build a container image?
- How will Azure Container Apps access and download our container image?

The advantage of platforms such as Azure is their ability to handle lots of different tasks that normally would be performed on your end. If we focus on the first question, which is *Where do we want to build a container image?*, we can think about various solutions. It could be our CI/CD agent, a dedicated virtual machine, or Azure Container Registry. It's true that we could utilize the same container registry we use to host container images to build our image. In Azure, it can be done with the following command:

```
az acr build --registry <registry-name> --image <image-name> .
```

When performing that command, it's important to remember that you need to execute it in the same place as you would do with similar commands such as `docker build`. Once the command starts, it will send the local context (files and configuration) to the selected Azure Container Registry and start building an image. This allows you to keep your host clean – you don't need to install Docker Engine or a similar tool to be able to build your container images.

> **Note**
>
> Building container images using Azure Container Registry isn't free. Each time you build an image, you execute a task in your registry. Tasks are priced per second – make sure you verify the price for your region if you plan to heavily utilize that feature.

It seems that one component of our deployment pipeline for Azure Container Apps could be offloaded to Azure if needed. It doesn't necessarily mean you should always utilize Azure Container Registry as your image builder. In some projects, you may not be able to use it that way due to regulations and compliance. For greenfield projects though, or in more agile companies (at least when compared with a typical enterprise company), it's an interesting alternative. You don't need to configure and host a container engine on your own, which means it cuts some operational costs.

The container registry part will be required for all deployments of services in Azure Container Apps that don't use public images as sources. It's also worth mentioning that Azure Container Apps may provision Azure Container Registry on its own if you don't provide one when deploying an application. This happens when using Azure CLI with a dedicated extension for Azure Container Apps. You can install it using the following command:

```
az extension add --name containerapp --upgrade
```

From now on, you will have access to `az containerapp` commands, which you can use both locally and in your CI/CD pipelines. The behavior of the commands will be the same in all environments, so you can easily test your idea before actually pushing it to your repository. Let's consider the following example:

```
az containerapp up \
 --name <container-app-name> \
 --source <path-to-application-source> \
 --ingress external
```

This command will create a new instance of Azure Container Apps with external ingress (meaning the application will be accessible from the public internet), a given name, and from the provided local path indicated by the `--source` parameter. As you can see, it performs lots of operations at once – if needed, you could use other commands to have more control over the process. The interesting thing, though, about that command is that it's able to look at your local files, build a container image, and push it to the container registry. If you wanted to split it into two separate steps, you could do something like this:

```
docker build -t <image-name> .
az containerapp up \
 --name <container-app-name> \
 --source <path-to-application-source> \
 --image <image-name> \
 --ingress external
```

Of course, you could also replace the preceding `docker build` command with `az acr build` to keep everything in the cloud. It doesn't really matter here how you build your container image – the point is that the process can be simplified by utilizing a single Azure CLI command.

> **Note**
>
> Keep in mind that the `az containerapp up` command can do all the heavy lifting by itself but may not be applicable in each scenario. If you require custom authentication against your repository or need to build a container image on a different CI/CD agent than the one deploying Azure Container Apps, you will still need to separate the commands.

As you can see, you can perform similar operations for Azure Container Apps with a completely different approach. The one advantage of that service over more advanced platforms such as Kubernetes is simplicity. To deploy both infrastructure and application, we don't need to implement additional tools besides Azure CLI. Of course, it's possible to incorporate additional elements in our pipelines that will validate and test deployments or check them against implemented policies. Conceptually, however, we're good to go with a minimal toolset.

When working with Azure CLI, you may find the following two commands confusing:

- `az containerapp up`
- `az containerapp create`

The first one is an additional layer atop, which performs various additional operations, as mentioned in this section. It will take care of creating an Azure Container App, building the application, and deploying it. The second one allows you to create an Azure Container App resource in Azure and configure it, but won't create Azure Container Registry and won't build the container image used for our service. In short, the former is more useful for developers who seek the ability to deploy an application quickly and without much of a hassle. If you opt for more control or just focus on individual infrastructure components, the latter will most likely be more useful.

You can read more about the `az containerapp create` command here: `https://learn. microsoft.com/en-us/cli/azure/containerapp?view=azure-cli-latest#az- containerapp-create`

Let's discuss now how we can manage multiple revisions (versions) of our application.

Managing revisions in Azure Container Apps

Each application deployed to its hosting environment has a defined lifetime. Applications are developed, tested, deployed, and maintained over the course of months or years. In the end, most, if not every, application is decommissioned and often replaced with a new version. In this section, we're interested in what happens between deploying and decommissioning an application.

Let's start with a simple visualization of the process presented in *Figure 11.2*:

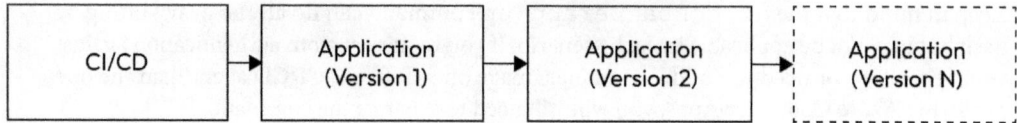

Figure 11.2 – High-level development and deployment process for an application

After deploying the first version of your application, you will most likely start working on the next one. The next version will be deployed after testing and may replace the currently working one. Such a process works if there are no integrations depending on the exact version of your application. Let's take a look at *Figure 11.3*:

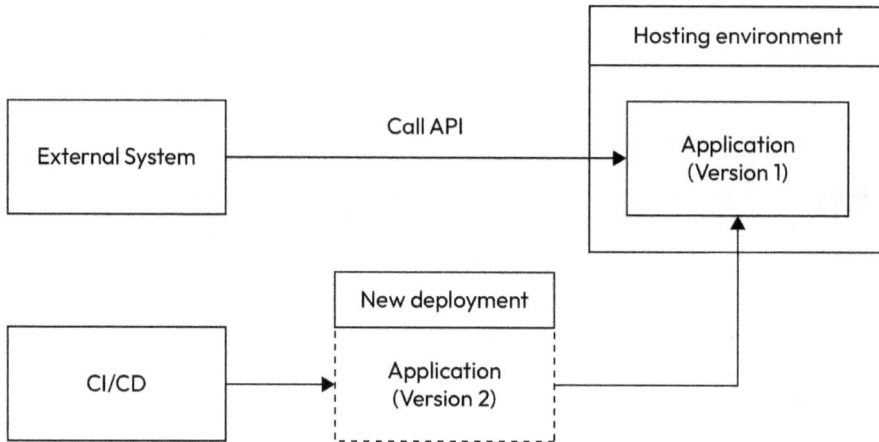

Figure 11.3 – Deploying a new version of an application with an existing integration

If we proceed with deployment of the new version (**Version 2**) of our application to replace the existing one (**Version 1**) we need to ensure any client (**External System**) calling the current version can safely use the new one. In other words, we need to ensure our application is backwards compatible. This can be achieved in a few ways:

- On the application level – Make sure it can handle requests for all the supported versions.

- On the infrastructure level – By deploying multiple versions of the application and properly routing the incoming traffic (this can be achieved by an API gateway and using a proper identifier for a version).

- On the process level – Make sure all the customers of your services switch to the new version.

For Azure Container Apps, we will focus on the second method of ensuring compatibility. There's a dedicated feature called **revisions**, which allows you to update your instance of Azure Container Apps and properly label each version. Thanks to that, you will be able to control how much traffic is sent to each revision.

We will talk more about revisions in the third section of this chapter, named *Deploying an application using Azure Container Apps*. Before we continue, however, let's discuss one more important topic related to properly planning a deployment – the scalability of Azure Container Apps.

Understanding the scalability of Azure Container Apps

When it comes to deploying an application, it's important to consider how it will scale in the future. While, for many applications, the initial deployment may consist of a single instance only, we need to have a clear plan for how and when the scale operation will happen. As Azure Container Apps is a service focused on hosting smaller services rather than monoliths, its approach to scalability will be different when compared with Azure App Service or Azure Virtual Machines (assuming you would consider using Azure Virtual Machines to host your application).

The interesting thing about Azure Container Apps is that you can scale it per revision. This is presented in *Figure 11.4*:

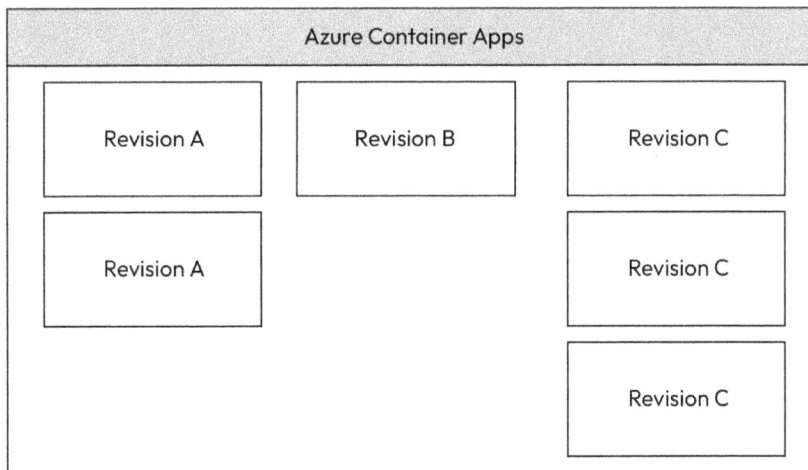

Figure 11.4 – Different number of instances (replicas) per revision

As each revision allows you to have a different number of replicas, it means you can scale them independently. This introduces a number of interesting possibilities:

- You can deploy pre-release versions of your application to a small subset of your customers without making it a full-blown deployment.

- You can gradually sunset old revisions the more customers are updating to the newer versions of your application.

- You can dynamically manage different versions of the application and scale them out/in depending on the current demand.

While the preceding scenarios are achievable with a custom implementation, it's also possible to utilize the in-built scaling mechanism of Azure Container Apps. We have three separate scaling rules to use:

- HTTP

- TCP

- Custom

The HTTP rule is based on the number of concurrent HTTP requests reaching a revision. The TCP rule does the same but for TCP connections. The custom rule is the most sophisticated one – conceptually, it's based on CPU and memory utilization, but it can use event-driven data sources as well. This includes services such as Azure Service Bus, Azure Event Hubs, Apache Kafka, and Redis. While the HTTP and TCP rules are easy to implement and use (you can configure them when deploying an Azure Container Apps instance), the custom rule requires the use of something that is called the KEDA scaler. We will not cover KEDA in this chapter, but if you're interested in the topic, take a look at the following page: `https://keda.sh/docs/2.16/scalers/`.

The interesting thing about the KEDA scaler is that it supports scaling based on authentication. What does that mean exactly? To understand the topic, we need to realize that this scaler uses Azure services to understand the current load of your application. In other words, it monitors the number of messages that are supposed to be handled by your service and makes scaling decisions based on their performance. It's a much better scaling mechanism than typical resource utilization monitoring, as in many scenarios, CPU and memory utilization starts to be visible too late. Let's consider the following example: Your application processes messages coming from various devices. Those messages are published in a queue for decoupling and asynchronous processing. The application may perform just fine most of the time and CPU and memory utilization will be stable. However, an increased number of messages may not directly translate to increased CPU or memory usage. If your application is unable to handle the increased load, the messages will just stay in a queue longer than usual without affecting resource utilization.

> **Note**
> Of course, the actual behavior of the application will depend on the implementation. If you process messages in the background and will be constantly fetching new messages from a queue, the increased CPU and memory utilization of the service will start to be noticeable as messages will be constantly processed instead of staying in a queue.

This is why the typical scaling based on CPU or memory won't work properly. To be able to handle such scenarios in a proper way and ensure a stable process, you will need to utilize a scaler mechanism, which understands the context of your application and its integration.

So how does Azure Container Apps support that mechanism? Thanks to the fact that you can base your scaling mechanism on services such as Azure Service Bus or Azure Event Hubs, you can make the whole platform aware of the current load affecting your application. The more messages that are coming, the more replicas of your service will be scheduled and hosted. It's a more service-oriented mechanism than traditional hosting of the whole platform (as we have with Azure App Service or Azure Virtual Machines). Conceptually, scaling in Azure Container Apps works similarly to Azure Functions, where scaling is also based on triggers of the functions. It allows for much more granular control over what and how is scaled and allows you to consider when designing your system.

Let's discuss now how we can deploy an application using Azure Container Apps.

Deploying an application using Azure Container Apps

Until now, we've been mostly focused on the introduction to Azure Container Apps and presenting its main features. In this section, we will try to deploy an application and see how we can utilize different capabilities of this Azure service.

To get started, we will prepare a simple containerized application that we can use for deployments.

Preparing a simple application

To be able to focus on Azure Container Apps, our application will be as simple as possible. To do that properly, we need to create a Dockerfile and push it to a registry. Let's start with the Dockerfile:

```
FROM nginx:latest
COPY index.html /usr/share/nginx/html/index.html
```

As you can see, we will use the latest available version of nginx to host a simple HTML page. The code for the HTML page will look like this:

```
<html>
<head>
    <title>Chapter 11</title>
</head>
<body>
    <h1>Hello!</h1>
</body>
</html>
```

Now, before we build and push the container image, we need a container registry. You can create it with the following command:

```
az group create \
-n <resource-group-name> \
-l <location>
az acr create \
-g <resource-group-name> \
-n <container-registry-name> \
--sku Basic
```

Once the registry is created, we can build the container image locally and push it there. Note that we're going to prepend our container registry name when tagging our image, so we don't need to retag it:

```
az acr login \
-n <container-registry-name> \
-g <resource-group-name>

docker build -t <container-registry-name>.azurecr.io/app .
docker push <container-registry-name>.azurecr.io/app
```

Once the image is pushed successfully, we can proceed to the next step of deploying our application to Azure Container Apps.

Deploying an application to Azure Container Apps

Deploying an application to an Azure Container Apps instance isn't a difficult task. All it takes is the following steps:

1. Before we deploy our application to Azure Container Apps, we need to ensure that the proper toolset is available on our machine. Use the following command to install extensions providing additional commands for working with that Azure service:

    ```
    az extension add --name containerapp --upgrade
    ```

2. Now, we need to create a dedicated environment for our Azure Container App. Environments are boundaries that allow you to group applications that are supposed to work together or that require the same level of isolation and security. You can create an environment with a single command:

    ```
    az containerapp env create \
    -n <environment-name> \
    -g <resource-group-name> \
    --location <location>
    ```

3. For the name of the environment, you can select any value. In many cases, it will include the name of a project and hosting environment (such as dev / test / prod). Also, as we're not providing additional details, Azure will create a Log Analytics workspace for us as it's part of each Azure Container Apps environment. If you want to create it on your own or point the environment to the existing workspace, use the following command:

```
az containerapp env create \
-n <environment-name> \
-g <resource-group-name> \
--location <location> \
--logs-workspace-id <workspace-id>
```

4. Once the environment is created, we can utilize it by creating an instance of Azure Container Apps pointing to it. This can be done with the following command:

```
az containerapp create \
--name <container-app-name> \
--resource-group <resource-group-name> \
--environment <environment-name> \
--image <container-registry-name>.azurecr.io/app \
--target-port 80 \
--ingress external
```

This command will create Azure Container App leveraging the environment we created and the image pushed to the container registry we created. It will also make it public as we're defining ingress as external. However, when you run the command, you will see the following error (or one similar to mine):

```
Failed to provision revision for container app 'afd11'.
Error details: The following field(s) are either invalid or
missing. Field 'template.containers.afd11.image' is invalid
with details: 'Invalid value: "afdch11cr.azurecr.io/app": GET
https:?scope=repository%3Aapp%3Apull&service=afdch11cr.azurecr.
io: UNAUTHORIZED: authentication required, visit https://aka.ms/
acr/authorization for more information.'
```

It seems that we cannot use the custom image that was pushed to the private registry as Azure Container Apps isn't authorized to access it. To fix it, first enable the admin user in Azure Container Registry (take a look at *Chapter 9*, where we discussed it).

5. With the admin user enabled, we can utilize its credentials and use them for our deployment:

```
az containerapp create \
--name <container-app-name> \
--resource-group <resource-group-name> \
--environment <environment-name> \
--image <container-registry-name>.azurecr.io/app \
--target-port 80 \
```

```
--ingress external \
--registry-username <admin-user-name> \
--registry-password <admin-user-password> \
--registry-name \
    <container-registry-name>.azurecr.io
```

6. After a moment, the deployment should be completed and Azure Container App ready to server requests. To check that, let's fetch its URL:

```
az containerapp show \
--name <container-app-name> \
-g <resource-group-name>   \
--query properties.configuration.ingress.fqdn
```

The result will be a unique URL you can use to access your application. In my case, it was the following:

```
"afd11.icymeadow-e19f2bcb.westeurope.azurecontainerapps.io"
```

7. You can now test your application – copy the URL and paste it into your browser's address bar.

You should be able to see the message we added to the HTML embedded within the container image (see *Figure 11.5*).

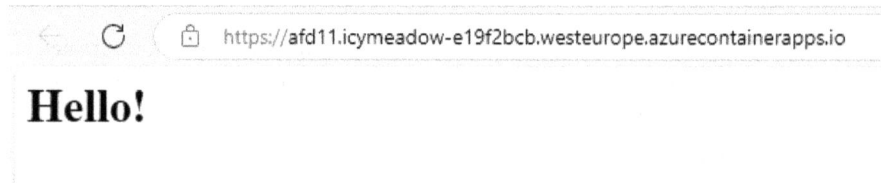

Figure 11.5 – Our simple application hosted by Azure Container Apps

Congratulations! You just deployed your first application using Azure Container Apps. Let's now see how we can update it and use revisions to support multiple versions.

Updating the application

To see the updated application, we first need to make some changes to the original code. Change the current HTML to the following:

```
<html>
<head>
    <title>Chapter 11</title>
</head>
<body>
    <h1>Hello!</h1>
```

```
    <h2>Azure Container Apps are the best!</h2>
</body>
</html>
```

Now, let's create a new image and push it to the registry:

```
docker build -t <container-registry-name>.azurecr.io/app:2.0 .
docker push <container-registry-name>.azurecr.io/app:2.0
```

The next step involves using the CLI to update our instance of Azure Container Apps. To complete the update operation, we need to use the following command:

```
az containerapp update \
-n <container-app-name> \
-g <resource-group-name>   \
--image <container-registry-name>.azurecr.io/app:2.0
```

As a result, you should be able to see the updated version of the application (*Figure 11.6*):

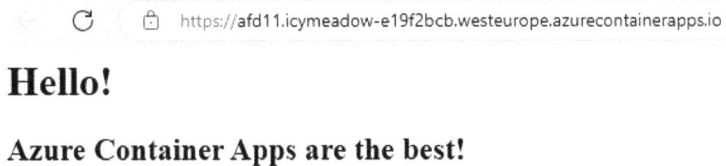

https://afd11.icymeadow-e19f2bcb.westeurope.azurecontainerapps.io

Hello!

Azure Container Apps are the best!

Figure 11.6 – Updated application with the newest content

We need to remember, however, that the update operation we performed replaced the previous version of the application with a new one. If we want to preserve the old version, we need to use revisions. We'll describe that in the next section. Before we proceed, we may need to clarify revision modes in Azure Container Apps. To have a better understanding, let's run the following command:

```
az containerapp revision list \
-n <container-app-name> \
-g <resource-group-name> \
-o table \
--all \
--query "[].{Name:name, Active:properties.active}"
```

As a result, you should see the following output:

```
Name            Active
-------------   --------
afd11--rd93y1x  False
afd11--af5hnd8  True
```

As you can see, we have two revisions already – one is active and the other one is inactive. It turns out that with each deployment to Azure Container Apps, a new revision gets created. Because the default revision mode is `Single`, in our application, only one revision is active, meaning we can't access the rest of them. If we want to be able to run multiple revisions, we will need to change the revision mode to `Multiple`. Check the next section for detailed instructions.

Updating the application using revisions

If you want to have your application deployed with multiple revisions in Azure Container Apps, you need to configure it to support them. You can do that with a single command:

```
az containerapp revision set-mode \
-n <container-app-name> \
-g <resource-group-name> \
--mode Multiple
```

Now, we can activate the previous revision, representing the very first version of our application:

```
az containerapp revision activate \
--revision "<revision-name>" \
--name <container-app-name> \
-g <resource-group-name>
```

Now our application will have two revisions up and running and available to the users. Each revision will be available under a different URL. In fact, with two active revisions, the application can be accessed using three different URLs (your URLs will be slightly different as both the name of the container app and revision will differ):

- `https://afd11.icymeadow-e19f2bcb.westeurope.azurecontainerapps.io/`: The main URL pointing to the most recent revision.
- `https://afd11--rd93y1x.icymeadow-e19f2bcb.westeurope.azurecontainerapps.io/`: The dedicated URL for the most recent revision.
- `https://afd11--rd93y1x.icymeadow-e19f2bcb.westeurope.azurecontainerapps.io/`: The dedicated URL for the older revision.

As revisions have their own URL, you can easily route users to the individual version of your application using various methods. This could be done using a dedicated gateway or a traffic manager and implementing routing by convention (such as a header or additional segment in the URL).

See *Figure 11.7* for details.

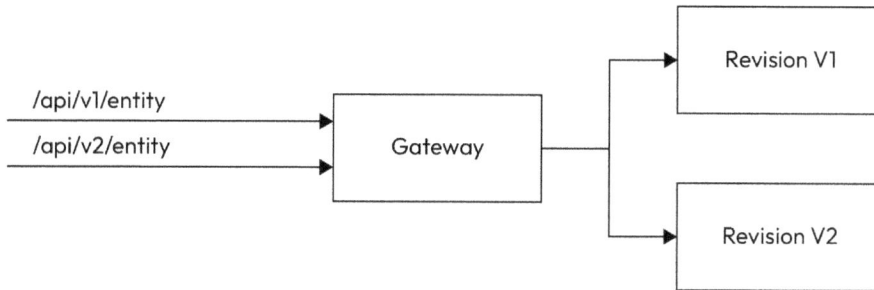

Figure 11.7 – Routing traffic to Azure Container Apps revisions using a gateway and URL segments

In the concept presented in *Figure 11.7*, the logic behind selecting the correct version is implemented within the gateway:

- If the URL contains **V1**, the request is forwarded to revision **V1**.

- If the URL contains **V2**, the request is forwarded to revision **V2**.

If you don't need to explicitly route the traffic to your revisions, you can change the traffic settings of each revision and decide how many requests are routed to a particular revision. For instance, if you want to split the traffic 50/50 for the two revisions, you could use the following command:

```
az containerapp ingress traffic set \
--revision-weight \
    <revision-1-name>=50 <revision-2-name>=50 \
--name <container-app-name> \
-g <resource-group-name>
```

Once the command is executed, go to the main URL of your container app and refresh your browser tab several times. You will see that, for the same URL, the revision you accessed is different from time to time.

> **Note**
>
> Splitting the traffic 50/50 doesn't give you a guarantee that traffic will be split equally with each request. In fact, this setting informs you about the probability of accessing a particular revision for a single user. At a higher scale, you're much more likely to see an even distribution than for a single user.

With the concepts described in this section, you could implement advanced deployment strategies such as **canary deployments** (*Figure 11.8* and *Figure 11.9*).

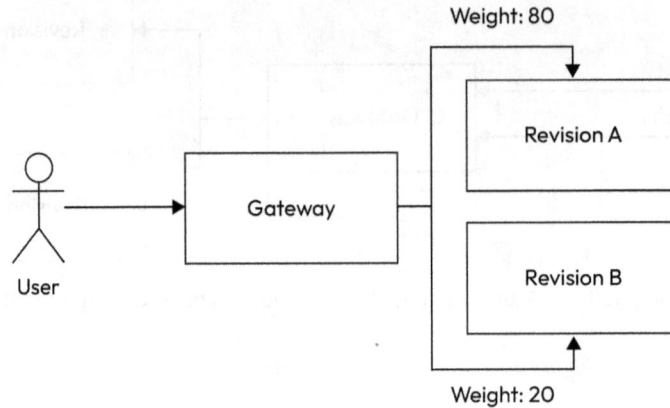

Figure 11.8 – Initial setup for weights when using canary deployment

In *Figure 11.8*, you can see the initial configuration for weights when deploying a new version of your application. You forward only 20% of the total traffic to the new revision in case there are any bugs or issues with the most recent release. Once you're ready, you can update the weights and route all the traffic to the new version (*Figure 11.9*).

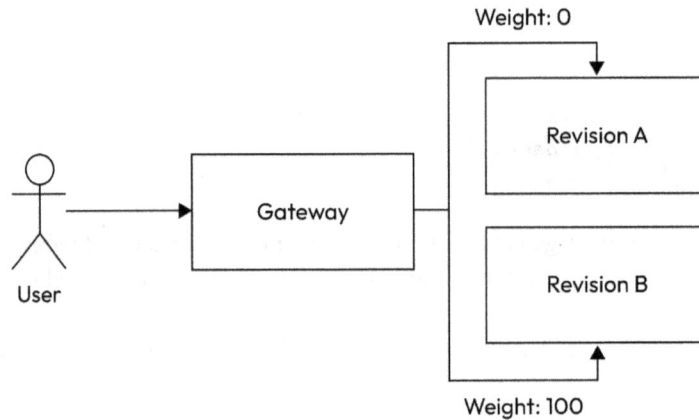

Figure 11.9 – Updated weights to route all the traffic to the new version (revision)

The same can be done as a blue/green deployment. In that case, you'd operate with the maximum and the minimum value for weight and switch between 0 and 100 only.

Azure Container Apps has many more features available to developers, which makes development easier. This includes add-ons, environment variables, and storage mounts. We will describe them in the next section of this chapter.

Learning about managing an application with Azure Container Apps

When it comes to management, Azure Container Apps consists of two main elements:

- Operations related to infrastructure (domains, certificates, network)
- App-related operations (secrets, storage mounts, session management, scaling)

In this section, we're going to cover the latter as those operations will allow you to better understand how to work with your applications hosted using Azure Container Apps as the hosting platform.

Managing environment variables

One of the most common scenarios for working with cloud services is configuring environment variables. When using container-based solutions, environment variables are the easiest way to customize the behavior of an application and inject custom values. In Azure Container Apps, using environment variables is also a standard pattern to provide dynamic parameters for an application.

You can provide environment variables using one of the commands we used previously to deploy a new version of our application:

```
az containerapp update \
-n <container-app-name> \
-g <resource-group-name> \
--set-env-vars <key>=<value>
```

If you want to set multi-environment variables with a single command, all you need is to provide `--set-env-vars` more than once:

```
az containerapp update \
-n <container-app-name> \
-g <resource-group-name> \
--set-env-vars <key>=<value> \
--set-env-vars <key2>=<value2>
```

When it comes to using variables in your application, it all depends on the technology stack you're using. Generally speaking, there's no additional layer needed to obtain environment variables for your applications when they're set on the Azure Container App level.

> **Note**
>
> Remember, that setting environment variables on a running instance of your container app will require restarting it to fetch new values. If you wanted to avoid that, you'd need to implement a custom mechanism for listening to changes and notifying your application.

It's also possible to reference secrets using environment variables in Azure Container Apps. The difference here is the syntax we use to reference it when setting the variable:

```
az containerapp update \
-n <container-app-name> \
-g <resource-group-name> \
--set-env-vars <key>=secretref:<secret-name>
```

The preceding example, however, will not be sufficient to properly access the secret as it's also required to have the secret configured on the Azure Container App level in order to reference it. We could do that when either creating or updating our instance of Azure Container Apps:

```
az containerapp create \
-n <container-app-name> \
-g <resource-group-name> \
--image <container-image> \
--environment <environment-name>\
--secrets DB_PASSWORD=<secret-value>
```

It's worth remembering that Azure Container Apps doesn't store secrets – instead, Azure Key Vault is used to store sensitive values, and you use only Key Vault references to securely retrieve secrets from the vault.

> **Note**
>
> When referencing secrets, you need to ensure they already exist. You can't both create and reference the same secret with a single Azure CLI command for creating/updating an instance of Azure Container Apps.

Let's check now how we can configure storage mounts for applications hosted on Azure Container Apps.

Configuring and managing storage mounts

The main use case for storage mounts is giving your application the ability to store and/or read files from a given location. It's useful when you want to either collect files from your customers or inject preprocessed information for an application for further use. Such a setup is a much better approach than forcing your application to actively handle all the data and manage the storage on its own.

In Azure Container Apps, there are three different kinds of mounts you can utilize:

- Container-scoped storage
- Replica-scoped storage
- Azure Files

It's quite important to understand the differences between them, so you can select the correct solution for your application. The most important thing about those mounts is whether they provide persistent storage or ephemeral. Both container-scoped and replica-scoped storage mounts are meant for ephemeral storage. For them, the difference lies in the actual scope of the mount. If you create container-scoped storage, its lifetime is tied to the container. For replica-scoped storage, the lifetime of a mount depends on the time the replica is active. See *Figure 11.8* for a better view of the topic.

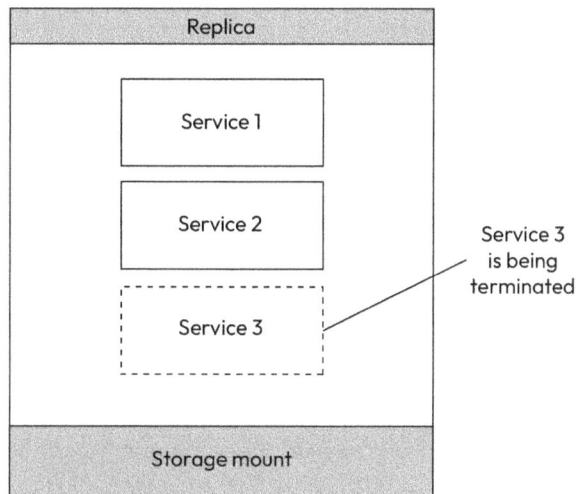

Figure 11.10 – A replica with a storage mount and multiple services accessing it

Figure 11.10 presents a situation where you have a single replica with multiple services running there. If a single service gets terminated, the storage mount is still available to the rest of the services (even if they're not utilizing it). Such a setup is useful if you don't fully control when the storage is accessed, or you don't need to isolate the mount from services. For container-based mounts, one of the most obvious use cases is cache. For replica-based mounts, it could be logs or building a data sink for further processing by an external service.

> **Note**
>
> It's worth noting that replica-based mounts allow you to persist files even if a container restarts. One of the possible use cases for them is also providing better reliability and data consistency for a single container. Still, you need to remember that such mounts are ephemeral, and you cannot fully rely on the availability of data stored there.

A different type of storage mount is Azure Files. It provides data persistence so you can use it to save data and have it replicated based on the replication settings of your share. The one thing common for Azure Files and replica-based mounts is that they both can be used multiple times for a single container. In other words, you can have multiple mounts of the same type for the same container.

When it comes to configuring storage mounts, the process depends on the storage mount type. For container-scoped mounts, you don't need to configure anything – the filesystem available for a container is managed automatically and gets erased once a container is destroyed. For replica-based and Azure Files mounts, you need to leverage the YAML definition of your Azure Container App to manage them. YAML definitions used by Azure Container Apps are like YAML files leveraged by Kubernetes – you can use them to manage your deployments and their configuration without using other methods such as the Azure portal or Azure CLI. To get the YAML for your container app, use the following command:

```
az containerapp show \
    -n <container-app-name> \
    -g <resource-group-name> \
    -o yaml
```

Once you get the result, note you're getting the typical output defining the configuration of our cloud service (you could use a similar command to get details of Azure App Service or Azure Container Registry). The reason we use YAML is, later, when we want to update our container app, we can use YAML as an input. In our case, we will be interested in the `template` object. For my instance, it looks like this:

```
template:
    containers:
    - image: afdch11cr.azurecr.io/app:2.0
      imageType: ContainerImage
      name: afd11
      resources:
        cpu: 0.5
        ephemeralStorage: 2Gi
        memory: 1Gi
    initContainers: null
    revisionSuffix: ''
    scale:
```

```
        maxReplicas: 10
        minReplicas: null
        rules: null
      serviceBinds: null
      terminationGracePeriodSeconds: null
      volumes: null
```

As you can see, the value of `volumes` is set to `null`. If we want to define any volume mount, we need to add two things:

- Volume mount – Defining which volume and where it will be mounted.

- Volume – Informing Azure Container Apps what kind of mount we'd like to use.

For replica-scoped mounts, we will use the following definition:

```
volumes:
  - name: <volume-name>
    storageType: EmptyDir
```

The important thing here is using `EmptyDir` for `storageType`. This informs Azure Container Apps that we want to use a replica-scoped mount instead of Azure Files. For an Azure Files mount, the definition will be similar – it requires one more field though:

```
volumes:
  - name: <volume-name>
    storageType: AzureFile
    storageName: <azure-storage-name>
```

The next step is defining a volume for your service. This step is the same for both replica-scoped mounts and Azure Files:

```
volumeMounts:
  - volumeName: <volume-name>
    mountPath: /<path>
```

Remember that `<path>` defines where a volume will be mounted. It's the location that will be accessed by your application so it's important to have it aligned with your code base. As a reference, look at the following YAML definition, which presents where volume mounts are defined:

```
template:
    containers:
    - image: afdch11cr.azurecr.io/app:2.0
      imageType: ContainerImage
      name: afd11
      volumeMounts:
```

```
        - volumeName: <volume-name>
          mountPath: /<path>
    volumes:
    - name: afd11
      storageType: EmptyDir
```

Once you have your mounts defined (remember, you can have more than a single mount configured), save the YAML on your computer and use the following command to update your container app:

```
az containerapp update \
--name <container-app-name> \
--resource-group <resource-group-name> \
--yaml <filename>.yaml
```

When the deployment is completed, the mount should be available for your application and visible as would any other file available inside the mounted filesystem.

> **Note**
>
> Adding a mount creates new revisions for your container app. If you have five active revisions and add a volume mount, you will see that they will become inactive, and Azure will create new revisions instead. This means that adding a volume mount isn't treated as deploying a new revision but rather reconfiguring all the existing ones.

Let's discuss one more topic related to the management of Azure Container Apps, which is session management.

Using session affinity in Azure Container Apps

Session affinity is a feature used in stateful applications, which allows you to ensure that a user is always routed to the exact same instance of your service. To understand the problem, let's take a look at the following diagram (*Figure 11.11*):

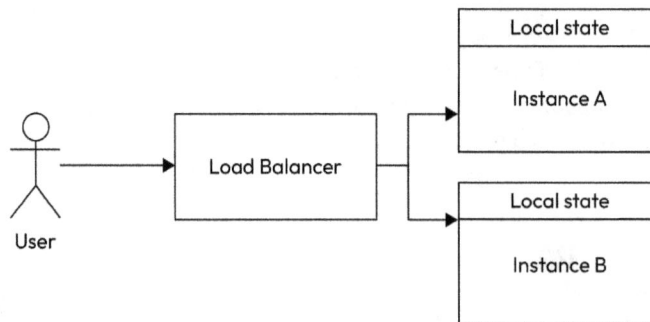

Figure 11.11 – User accessing multiple instances of the same service when local state exists

If each instance of your service has its own state, a user accessing different instances may experience issues when interacting with your application. For instance, let's say you're building an online shop and allow a user to stash multiple orders. If orders for a user are stored inside a local state (local cache), not being able to control which instance is accessed with each request would mean that one-time orders are visible and, with the next request, there are none. Session affinity solves that problem by routing a user to the same instance for the duration of the session (sometimes this feature is called sticky sessions).

> **Note**
>
> It's important to remember that session affinity is available only in single-revision deployments with HTTP ingress enabled. Unfortunately, you cannot use it if your service uses multiple revisions. If you're confused by that statement, remember that revisions aren't equal to replicas. Each revision represents a different version of your service, while a replica is another instance of the same revision.

To enable session affinity, use the following command:

```
az containerapp ingress sticky-sessions set \
    -n <container-app-name> \
    -g <resource-group-name> \
    --affinity sticky
```

Once enabled, Azure Container Apps will ensure that ingress handles all the requests in the context of a user. Using session affinity isn't a recommended approach as it limits the ability of Azure Container Apps to evenly distribute traffic. If you don't need it, try to avoid enabling it.

That's all for the management of Azure Container Apps. Let's now talk about use cases for this service.

Learning about use cases

As discussed at the beginning of this chapter, Azure Container Apps is a great service for building more complex systems without the complexity introduced by platforms such as Kubernetes. It abstracts away lots of difficult things such as cluster management, controllers, and resource management, and allows you to focus on application development. Of course, Azure Container Apps isn't as simple as Azure App Service. Having an additional layer to work with (containers) requires additional steps to be able to deploy an application. On the other hand, for most production systems, you still need to introduce additional layers and infrastructure components to follow the best practices. For instance, if you work with web applications and need to inject secrets into them, you will need to incorporate some kind of secrets store to work with them in a secure manner. Another example would be storage mounts – if you're unable to natively integrate with them using the API provided by your hosting platform, you will need to implement the whole logic on your own. This takes time and is error prone. Azure Container Apps provides that as part of its functionality.

When it comes to actual use cases and scenarios, Azure Container Apps is a great choice for the following applications:

- Microservices
- Modular applications that need to be hosted as separate services
- Event-driven applications (when integrating with KEDA)
- Jobs

One of the interesting topics is using Azure Container Apps as a hosting platform for microservices. While you can use that service without any additional layers and just start deploying multiple applications, there's also a possibility to integrate them with Dapr (`https://docs.dapr.io/concepts/overview/`). Dapr is a dedicated runtime for hosting distributed applications. It comes with a variety of useful features, such as the publish and subscribe mechanism, actors' pattern, workflows, jobs, and many more. I strongly recommend you take a look at the provided link to have the full picture of the capabilities of that platform. With Dapr, you can easily transform your instance of Azure Container Apps into a microservices platform. You can read more about integration here: `https://learn.microsoft.com/en-us/azure/container-apps/dapr-overview`.

In general, Azure Container Apps is quite a generic service. It allows you to host various applications sharing the same toolset without making many changes. This makes it quite an interesting choice for modern applications that focus on cloud integrations, need to be scaled individually and dynamically, and require portability thanks to containerization.

That's all for *Chapter 11*! Let's summarize all the lessons and see what awaits in the next chapter.

Summary

In this chapter, we talked about Azure Container Apps – a modern and flexible platform for hosting containerized applications. We discussed the differences between this and other Azure services and saw how our applications can be deployed to a container app. One of the most important topics was revision management, which allows you to have multiple versions of your application hosted in the same environment.

Another important topic was application management using Azure Container Apps features. Things such as volume mounts and session affinity are very often really important from the implementation perspective for proper state management and performance. With Azure Container Apps, having those things implemented is just a matter of a few changes to the configuration of a container app.

In the next chapter, we're going to cover the last topic related to containers in Azure, which is hosting containerized applications using Azure App Service.

Join the CloudPro Newsletter with 44000+ Subscribers

Want to know what's happening in cloud computing, DevOps, IT administration, networking, and more? Scan the QR code to subscribe to **CloudPro**, our weekly newsletter for 44,000+ tech professionals who want to stay informed and ahead of the curve.

https://packt.link/cloudpro

12

Hosting Containers with Azure App Service

In *Chapter 3*, we discussed how you can host your application using Azure App Service. To run our application there, we needed to deploy a package containing the binaries of our service, choose one of the deployment methods, and prepare the correct configuration. Such a hosting model works best if you don't need to worry about portability or vendor lock or just want to have an application up and running quickly. However, if you need to be prepared for changes such as a change of cloud vendor or hosting platform, it's best if you containerize your application first.

Fortunately, Azure App Service supports hosting containerized applications with minimal changes to the rest of the functionalities. If you have an existing application hosted as an Azure web app, you can migrate it to containers while keeping the rest of the infrastructure intact.

In this chapter, we're going to cover the following main topics:

- Integrating Azure App Service with container registries
- Deploying a containerized application to Azure App Service
- Solving common problems with containerized applications
- Learning about use cases

Technical requirements

To perform the exercises in this chapter, you will need the following tools:

- Azure CLI
- Container engine and CLI (such as Docker Desktop or Colima – you can also use Podman, but you will need to adjust the commands in the exercises)

Integrating Azure App Service with container registries

When working with containers in Azure App Service, the most important thing is integrating it with a container registry. It's possible to use both Azure Container Registry and an external registry if needed (or even a public one, for instance, Docker Hub). The choice depends on the use case or scenario, but for most of the typical business scenarios, you will select a private registry over a public one (due to security, compliance, or regulations).

In this section, we will configure Azure App Service with Azure Container Registry. In order to do that, we need both the container image and the infrastructure. Let's start with a containerized application and a container registry.

Preparing an application

To keep things simple, let's prepare an HTML-based application, which we will host using `nginx`. Here's the code for it, which will be displayed to a user when they access it:

```html
<html>
<head>
    <title>Chapter 12</title>
</head>
<body>
    <h1>Hello!</h1>
    <h2>
        This is containerized application for Azure App
        Service!
    </h2>
</body>
</html>
```

> **Note**
> Remember to save the HTML code as `index.html` in the same directory as the Dockerfile you will create in a moment.

Now, we need to prepare a Dockerfile, which we will use to build a container image. As we only need to select a base image and copy the HTML file, we will need only two lines to have a working application:

```
FROM nginx:latest
COPY index.html /usr/share/nginx/html/index.html
```

We have our application ready. Before we build the container image, let's prepare the container registry.

Creating a container registry

As we will use Azure Container Registry to host our container image and Azure App Service integration, all we need now is to run the following Azure CLI command. It will create a resource group and a registry:

```
az group create \
-n <resource-group-name> \
-l <location>

az acr create \
-g <resource-group-name> \
-n <container-registry-name> \
--sku Basic

az acr show \
-g <resource-group-name> \
-n <container-registry-name> \
--query loginServer
```

The last command will display a login server (which is basically the prefix needed for a container image, so it's pushed to the correct registry). It should be in the following format: `<container-registry-name>.azurecr.io`. Once the registry is created and you have the value of the login server, we can proceed to the next step, which is building a container image and pushing it to the registry.

Building and pushing a container image

To push a container image to Azure Container Registry, first, we need to build and name it. The most important thing here is naming the container image with a prefix (being the login server we got in the previous section), so that Docker (or any other container engine you have installed) knows where to push the image. Let's use the following commands to build and push the image:

```
docker build -t <login-server>/ch12/app:latest .
docker push <login-server>/ch12/app:latest
```

As the application is very simple, the whole process should only take a few seconds. Remember, though, that you may need to perform the login operation against the created container registry. If that's the case, use the `az acr login` command we described in *Chapter 9*.

Once the container image is available in the container registry, we can proceed with the next step, which is using the container image as the source for the application hosted in Azure App Service.

Deploying Azure App Service

To be able to host a containerized application in Azure, first, we need to deploy its infrastructure. We will start with the Azure App Service plan, as it's a prerequisite for deploying any Azure web app.

Let's use the following command to proceed with deployment:

```
az appservice plan create \
-g <resource-group-name> \
-n <app-service-plan-name> \
--sku F1 \
--is-linux
```

The command we're using will create a free Linux plan (as indicated by the `F1` value of the `sku` parameter and the `--is-linux` switch in the command). Once the plan is ready, we can proceed with creating the Azure web app. This is the command we will be using:

```
az webapp create \
-n <webapp-name> \
-g <resource-group-name>  \
-p <app-service-plan-name> \
--container-image-name <image-name> \
--container-registry-password <registry-password> \
--container-registry-user <registry-user>
```

As you can see, the command requires us to provide the username and password of a user with access to the registry. In the case of Azure Container Registry, we could obtain that once the admin user is enabled. You can do that using the following command:

```
az acr update -n <registry-name> --admin-enabled true
az acr credential show -n <registry-name>
```

As the result of running that command, you should get the following JSON result:

```
{
  "passwords": [
    {
      "name": "password",
      "value": "M9mq..."
    },
    {
      "name": "password2",
      "value": "85HPX..."
    }
  ],
```

```
  "username": "<registry-name>"
}
```

> **Note**
>
> Remember that, in your case, the values of secrets presented by the command will be different as they're unique for each container registry.

With both the username and passwords obtained, we can create an Azure web app, which will use the container image created in the previous step. Use the `az webapp create` command described previously and run the following one to get the URL:

```
az webapp show \
-n <webapp-name> \
-g <resource-group-name> \
--query defaultHostName
```

The result of running the `show` command should look like mine, which is the following:

```
afdch12.azurewebsites.net
```

Try to access the website using your browser. Once the application starts (it may take a while in the very beginning as Azure needs to spin up the whole runtime and download the container image), you should be able to see the following result:

← ⟳   ⚠ Not secure | afdch12.azurewebsites.net

Hello!

This is containerized application for Azure App Service!

Figure 12.1 – Working containerized application hosted using Azure App Service

As you can see, there's no additional configuration needed to be able to use containers to host a web application using Azure App Service. From now on, you can leverage the very same features (app settings, deployment slots, or even custom domains) as it was a traditional application hosted directly in the process.

One important thing here, though, is the fact that we used admin credentials for authenticating against Azure Container Registry. There's one more possibility to access the registry, which doesn't require providing credentials during deployment. We could use a managed identity and proper RBAC configuration, so no secrets are needed there. Let's see how we can configure that.

Deploying Azure App Service with a managed identity

Azure CLI has a dedicated parameter for deploying Azure web apps with proper access to Azure Container Registry. Here's the full command needed to create another web application with the same container image used previously:

```
az webapp create \
-n <webapp-name> \
-g <resource-group-name> \
-p <app-service-plan-name> \
--container-image-name \
    <registry-name>.azurecr.io/ch12/app:latest \
--acr-use-identity
```

Note that we're not using credentials for our registry here – instead, we're instructing Azure CLI to configure our Azure web app with a system identity and assign an `AcrPull` role to it on the correct scope (which is Azure Container Registry hosting the container image).

Alternatively, you could use the following command to configure and achieve the same result:

```
az webapp create \
-n <webapp-name> \
-g <resource-group-name> \
-p <app-service-plan-name> \
--container-image-name \
    <registry-name>.azurecr.io/ch12/app:latest \
--scope <container-registry-resource-id> \
--assign-identity [system] \
--role AcrPull
```

As you can see, we're explicitly instructing Azure CLI with the selected role and scope where it should be assigned. We're also providing `[system]` to indicate that we want to use the system-assigned identity here.

> **Note**
>
> If you want, you could use a user-assigned identity. Use `az webapp create -h` to see how to properly configure the command to use that kind of managed identity.

The benefit of using a managed identity instead of admin credentials comes from the fact that a managed identity offers a much easier deployment model, improved security, and simpler maintenance. Using admin credentials requires you to find a secure way to store and then pass them. While they may seem like the easiest way of integrating with Azure Container Registry, you should avoid them if you can use a managed identity, which simplifies the operations and improves security.

For other private registries though (which are hosted in other clouds or on-premises), you may not be able to use a managed identity. If that's the case, sticking with standard credentials will be a must.

Let's see now how containerized applications can be deployed and how to deploy multi-container applications using Azure web apps.

Deploying a containerized application to Azure App Service

In the previous section, we saw how we can deploy and host a containerized application using Azure App Service. While the process itself should now be self-explanatory, having the ability to host containers using that Azure service introduces some additional interesting capabilities. In this section, we're going to see how we can deploy a multi-container application using a single instance of Azure App Service. First, however, let's discuss what a multi-container application is and the benefits of using those.

Designing a multi-container application

When designing a web application, you need to consider its architecture. There are multiple possibilities:

- **Monoliths**: Software architecture where an application is deployed as a single unit, meaning you have a single package to manage but you're unable to granularly control how individual features are provisioned and scaled.

- **Modular monoliths**: An architecture similar to monoliths but providing more granular control over individual features of an application, thanks to placing them in separate packages. Even though modular monolith splits features into separate beings, the application as a whole is still mostly managed as a single unit.

- **Microservices**: A highly scalable and robust system architecture, which treats different modules of your application as separate services with dedicated deployment pipelines and their own infrastructure. It favors asynchronous communication using components such as queues instead of synchronous ones.

There are various reasons why you'd need to split your application into multiple services:

- Easier separations of concerns
- Isolated deployments, providing enhanced flexibility when releasing new versions
- Having multiple teams working on individual services
- Individual scaling out/scaling in of services

If you use containers, you can easily distribute your application across multiple environments. While containers themselves are not that useful in distributing monoliths (not because it's not possible, but rather because monoliths are rarely portable due to their size and the internal complexity they bring), you could leverage them in modular monoliths or microservices. In fact, dividing your application into smaller pieces and containerizing them brings us to the concept of a **multi-container application**. A multi-container application could be considered as one of the following two concepts:

- An application consisting of multiple containers hosted across multiple environments. Each container is a separate service, which can be deployed individually or as part of a bigger package. In that definition, containers aren't hosted within the same container environment.

- An application using multiple containers to isolate (separate) different concerns such as monitoring, logging, or routing requests.

When talking about separation, there's one more concept that is worth mentioning – **sidecars**. The best way to describe those is through a diagram (take a look at *Figure 12.2*).

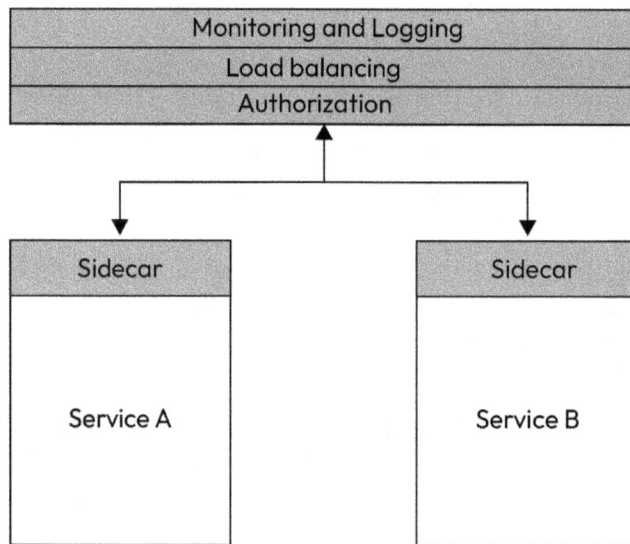

Figure 12.2 – Simple microservices architecture with sidecars

Sidecars allow you to offload common features such as monitoring, logging, load balancing, and authorization to a dedicated container. Such a container is tied to a container running your service and acts as a proxy for all incoming and outgoing communication.

> **Note**
>
> Sidecars are one of the main concepts of service meshes. Take a look at the following link to read more about one of the most popular service mesh products (Istio): `https://istio.io/latest/about/service-mesh/`.

Besides sidecars, container-based architectures have also a concept of an `init` container. Those containers are used most of the time to initialize the main container (service) and perform operations such as the following:

- Downloading files
- Migrating databases
- Bootstrapping an application

When it comes to Azure App Service, you can use sidecars when deploying your application. While it won't be a full-blown container orchestration such as Kubernetes (or even Azure Container Apps), being able to divide your application into multiple containers brings lots of flexibility and allows you to separate the main service containing business logic from the infrastructure.

Before we dive deeper into the topic, let's discuss how Azure App Service, Kubernetes, and Azure Container Apps differ and what one can do to select a proper service for their needs. First, let's discuss the operations required for deploying and managing an instance of a service. While Azure App Service and Azure Container Apps offer a simple deployment model that abstracts away lots of complexity related to routing, configuration, and scalability, in Kubernetes, you need to deeply understand both the network and software stack used for a cluster. The same applies to security – Azure App Service and Azure Container Apps are simple enough to avoid the most common misconfiguration issues. With Kubernetes, you control various levels of the software stack and can deploy various applications onto the same cluster. This means you need to consider both inter- and intra-service communication.

In fact, in many scenarios, having a Kubernetes cluster for a single application may be an overkill. A common approach is to have a single Kubernetes cluster to host several different applications. This simplifies and optimizes the deployment process but requires significant initial effort to set up everything from scratch.

If your goal is only to deploy a single application, you will most likely benefit from the simplest setup, which is Azure App Service. If you are looking for more advanced patterns such as event-driven systems and microservices, Azure Container Apps will be a good starting point. For full control over your system and infrastructure, consider using Kubernetes (especially the managed ones such as Azure Kubernetes Service).

Let's now prepare a simple application consisting of a main service and a sidecar and deploy it to Azure using Azure App Service.

Preparing a multi-container application

To prepare an application consisting of a main service and a sidecar, we will need two separate Dockerfiles. The first Dockerfile will be a modified version of our HTML web page and will look like this:

```html
<html>
<head>
    <title>Chapter 12</title>
</head>
<body>
    <h1>Hello!</h1>
    <h2>
        This is containerized application for Azure App
        Service!
    </h2>
</body>
<script>
    var response = fetch('http://localhost:3000');
    response.then(async _ => console.info(await _.text()));
</script>
</html>
```

This web page contains a small JavaScript script, which makes an HTTP GET request to http://localhost:3000. The reason why we're calling this specific endpoint will be clear in a moment.

To simulate a sidecar, let's use a simple API hosted as a separate container. To make it lightweight, we will use Express.js with Node.js as our web server:

```js
const express = require('express')
const app = express()
var cors = require('cors')
const port = 3000

app.use(cors())

app.get('/', (req, res) => {
  res.send('Hello World!')
})

app.listen(port, () => {
  console.log(`Example app listening on port ${port}`)
})
```

As you can see, we're defining a constant value, `const port = 3000`, which exposes our API using port `3000`. This is why the script from the HTML page is calling the localhost using this specific port – the sidecar is hosted within the same network, so all we need is to know which port it's using.

Now that we have the code for our application, we can build the container images. The easiest way to do that (and test the application) is using Docker Compose. To leverage it, we need to introduce additional configuration written in YAML:

```
services:
  main:
    build:
      context: .
      dockerfile: main.Dockerfile
    ports:
      - "8080:80"
  sidecar:
    build:
      context: .
      dockerfile: sidecar.Dockerfile
    ports:
      - "3000:3000"
```

The last step will be introducing two separate Dockerfiles. The one named `main.Dockerfile` is responsible for building our web page:

```
FROM nginx:latest
COPY index.html /usr/share/nginx/html/index.html
```

The second one builds our API:

```
FROM node:23

WORKDIR /usr/src/app
COPY package*.json ./
RUN npm install
COPY . .

EXPOSE 3000
CMD [ "node", "sidecar.js" ]
```

Note that you should name the HTML file as `index.html` and the API (sidecar) file as `sidecar.js`. While it's not required, making changes will force you to adjust Dockerfiles.

Once everything is ready, run the following command to start both containers:

```
docker compose up
```

After a moment, both container images should be ready and the containers up and running. To validate the setup, open your browser and open http://localhost:8080. As a result, you should see the web page we used previously in this chapter (*Figure 12.3*):

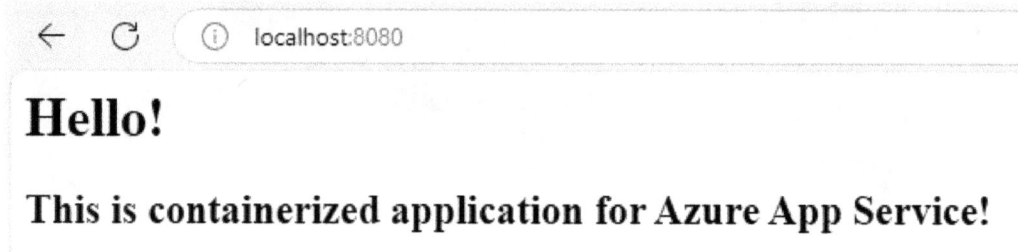

Figure 12.3 – Web page hosted inside a container locally

To confirm that our web page communicates with our sidecar, open **Developer Tools** (*F12* in most browsers) and check the console. If everything works, you should see a Hello World! message (*Figure 12.4*).

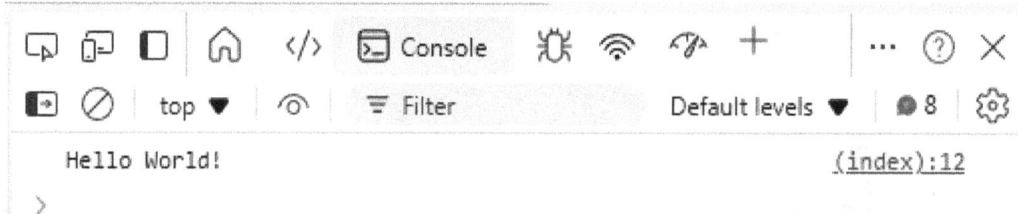

Figure 12.4 – Hello World! message returned from the sidecar

> **Note**
>
> If you don't see the message in the console, make sure you've set the proper message level. Messages returned from the sidecar are logged as information.

Great, it seems our multi-container application is running properly. Now we need to build and push container images to the container registry.

Pushing container images to a container registry

To use both images as sources for our application, we need to push them both to a container registry. To do that, simply run the `docker build` command twice:

```
docker build -f main.Dockerfile -t <registry-name>.azurecr.io/ch12/
main:latest .
docker build -f sidecar.Dockerfile -t <registry-name>.azurecr.io/ch12/
sidecar:latest .
```

Now, all you need is to run the `docker push` command to push the images to the registry. Once they're available in the registry, we can perform the last step, which is deploying Azure App Service using both container images.

Deploying multi-container application

Deployment of a multi-container application is similar to the deployments we performed previously in this chapter. The only difference is using additional parameters to indicate that we want to use additional configuration. Here's the command you could use to deploy the application:

```
az webapp create \
-n <webapp-name> \
-g <resource-group-name> \
-p <appservice-plan-name> \
--acr-use-identity \
--multicontainer-config-type COMPOSE \
--multicontainer-config-file docker-compose-deploy.yml
```

> **Note**
>
> The assumption here is that you will be using the same Azure App Service plan and Azure Container Registry as at the beginning of the chapter. If you're using different instances, make sure you're adjusting the commands and also that you created the resources.

Before we complete the deployment, though, we need to make adjustments to the Docker Compose file as currently it builds the images and doesn't reference them. To make the changes, create a new file, name it `docker-compose-deploy.yml`, and introduce the following amendments:

```
services:
  main:
    image: afdch12.azurecr.io/ch12/main:latest
    ports:
      - "8080:80"
  sidecar:
    image: afdch12.azurecr.io/ch12/sidecar:latest
```

```
ports:
  - "3000:3000"
```

Once the application is deployed, you can make the same verification of the correctness of the setup by entering the website URL. Note here that deployment to Azure didn't require making any changes to the code itself besides adjusting the Docker Compose file. From now on, a single Azure App Service instance will be hosting multiple containers, and you can leverage the fact that they will be using a single host (no need to handle DNS, routing, and other networking concepts). Let's discuss now the use cases for using multiple containers with a single Azure App Service instance.

Understanding use cases of multi-container deployments

When designing an application, you will be applying business requirements atop a technical solution you will choose. The requirements themselves will instruct you on the proper design and architecture of the whole system. The capability of Azure App Service to host multiple containers inside the same host allows you to implement a subset of design, which would normally require choosing other services such as Kubernetes, Azure Container Apps, or similar platforms.

You may wonder what's the actual difference between Azure App Service hosting multiple containers and other services mentioned. To visualize the difference, let's take a look at *Figure 12.5*.

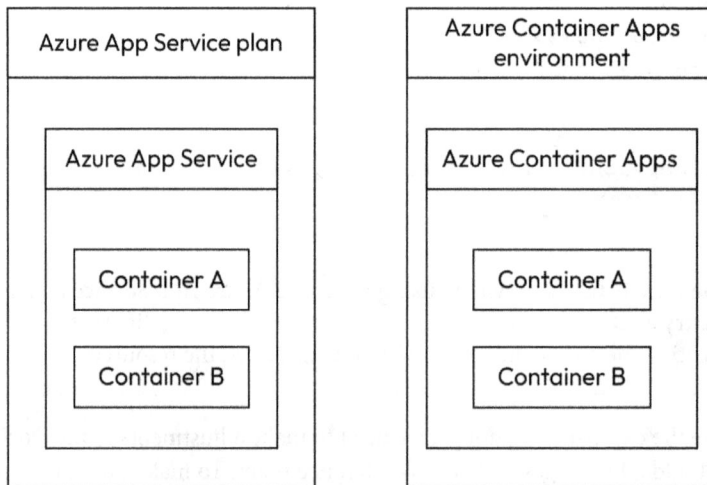

Figure 12.5 – High-level architecture of Azure App Service vs. Azure Container Apps

When comparing Azure App Service with Azure Container Apps, the high-level architecture will be the same. Both services require additional components (plan/environment) to provide infrastructure, and both act as specialized layers, which enable you to configure them without much effort. There's one key difference here, though – Azure App Service is a service focused more on typical web applications without a need to provide additional features such as load balancing, granular access to various features of an application, or sophisticated integrations with a modern stack including logging and monitoring. It is also much more common to use Azure App Service to host one big application when compared to Azure Container Apps, which was designed as a platform to handle workloads designed as microservices.

> **Note**
>
> It's worth mentioning that lots of advanced features for load balancing, API integrations, and security for Azure App Services are delivered by additional Azure services such as Azure Traffic Manager, Azure Front Door, Azure Application Gateway, Azure Key Vault, Azure App Configuration, and Azure API Management. While they can also be integrated with Azure Container Apps, they were originally quite a standard services stack when working with web applications in Azure.

We can find a much bigger difference when comparing Azure App Service to Kubernetes (see *Figure 12.6*).

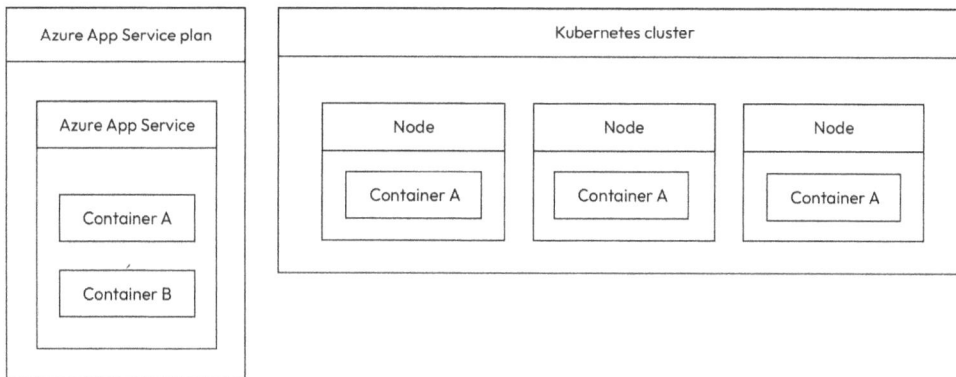

Figure 12.6 – High-level architecture of Azure App Service compared with Kubernetes

As you can see, when using Kubernetes, we will have many more infrastructure-related concepts as we need to consider and configure load balancing between multiple nodes and decide how our services will be replicated and what happens if they crash. Kubernetes is also much more challenging when deploying services as there are multiple deployment strategies that you may need to take into account.

The question now is whether multi-container (or even single-container deployments) are actually valid solutions when hosting an application in Azure. To better understand them, let's separate those into two isolated scenarios.

Single-container deployments

Containerizing an application is always a good solution if you want to keep your application portable. By packing it as a container image, you can easily switch hosts and environments as long as there are no external dependencies, which also need to be configured. When an application is available as a container image, you can perform your first deployment using Azure App Service and then, when you refine the architecture and design, it will be possible to switch to another service without making many changes to the application itself (apart from extracting certain features as separate services).

Multi-container deployments

Deploying your application using Azure Container Apps or Kubernetes seems like a very modern solution that applies to all greenfield projects. This is only partially true as many applications struggle with leveraging all the features available thanks to those platforms (service discovery, advanced deployment strategies, automated rollbacks, and many more). To be able to fully utilize the features, you need to design your application to use them, which is not always possible.

Using multi-container deployments in Azure App Service is a great idea if you want to gradually migrate from one big application to multiple services. Start with a single container, extract a part of business logic as a separate service, and simply deploy it as another container. As such a deployment doesn't introduce much complexity (you don't need to worry about DNS and service discovery, no network rules are in place and connectivity stays as your services would work on the same machine), making such a change should be swift. Then, if you're satisfied with the results, you can think about introducing more changes and, finally, switching to another service.

Personally, I also like multi-container deployments in Azure App Service for using the same tool that many developers already use to run an application locally, which is Docker Compose. This provides the benefit of keeping the same DevEx for both development and deployments. Even though you need to keep and maintain one more Compose file as the source for Azure App Service, it's still a much simpler approach than YAML files used for Kubernetes-based deployments.

For additional visualization of the concept of refining an application and moving from Azure App Service to other services, take a look at *Figure 12.7*.

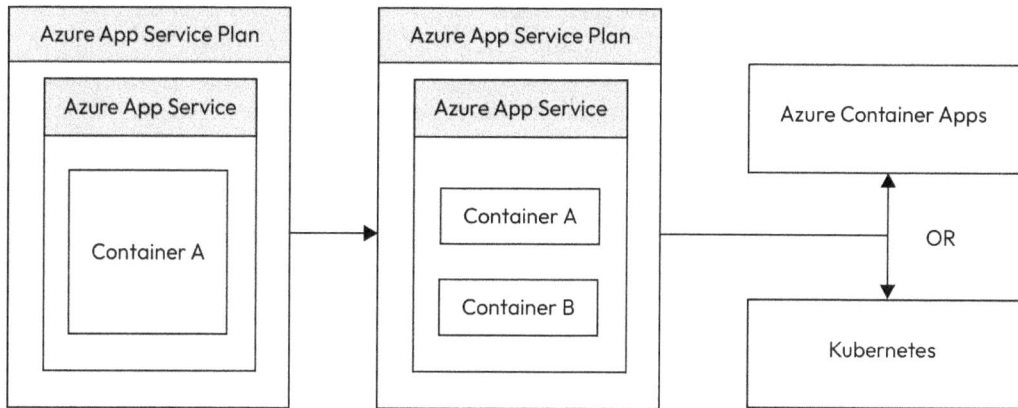

Figure 12.7 – Evolution of architecture when using containers with Azure App Service

Let's discuss now how to solve common problems with containerized applications when using Azure App Service.

Solving common problems with containerized applications

When you containerize an application, you need to remember that you are adding one more layer atop your code. This means that you may face additional challenges when running and hosting it. In this section, we will discuss common issues and problems that may arise when an application becomes containerized and how to solve them using Azure App Service.

Let's start with local environment preparations.

Preparing and unifying a local environment

If your application is containerized, it means it has become portable enough to run on any host that has a container engine installed. The truth here is that we're exchanging one problem (installing all the dependencies in the same way across hosts) with another (ensuring the container engine is installed and developers are familiar with it). Personally, I see two problems now when it comes to containerization:

- Unifying a container engine and CLI
- Providing a unified way to run a containerized application locally with all its dependencies

Some time ago, the golden standard for running containers locally was Docker Desktop. Unfortunately, as it requires a paid license after meeting certain criteria when it comes to the company's headcount and revenue, many people started to look for alternatives. In macOS systems, one of the best tools to run containers is Colima (`https://github.com/abiosoft/colima`). For Windows-based computers, you may be interested in Podman (`https://podman-desktop.io/docs/intro`). The main issue here is the difference in interfaces between Colima and Podman – for local development though, it may be acceptable.

For running an application with all the dependencies, the best choice is still to use Docker Compose. It's part of Docker installations and can be also installed separately if needed to be used with Colima and Podman.

> **Note**
>
> Podman requires you to install Docker Compose as an executable available on your computer. As Compose has become part of Docker installation, you may find it difficult to find proper instructions. Personally, I find it quite easy to satisfy that requirement by downloading the executable from `https://github.com/docker/compose/releases`.

When working with Azure App Service, the tool used locally for starting a container won't matter much. The most important thing is the tool used for local orchestration. Docker Compose seems like a great match, so it's really worth it to try to integrate it with the toolset you're using for your project.

Let's now discuss another challenge with containerized applications, which is integration with logging and monitoring tools.

Logging and monitoring of a containerized application

When working with containerized applications, it's important to find a tool that allows you to easily log and monitor the behavior of your application. In the context of Azure App Service, learning how to check the logs will be even more important as you don't have the same access level as you'd have when working with platforms such as Kubernetes or when hosting an application using IaaS (Azure Virtual Machine, for instance). Azure App Service offers limited features when it comes to accessing container logs (but it's still possible). When talking about logging and monitoring in general, the easiest platform to implement and integrate with will be Azure Monitor (in most cases, via Azure Application Insights).

Container logs for Azure App Service are easily accessible in the Azure portal. If you go to the deployed application, you will find the **Deployment Center** page in the menu on the left (see *Figure 12.8*).

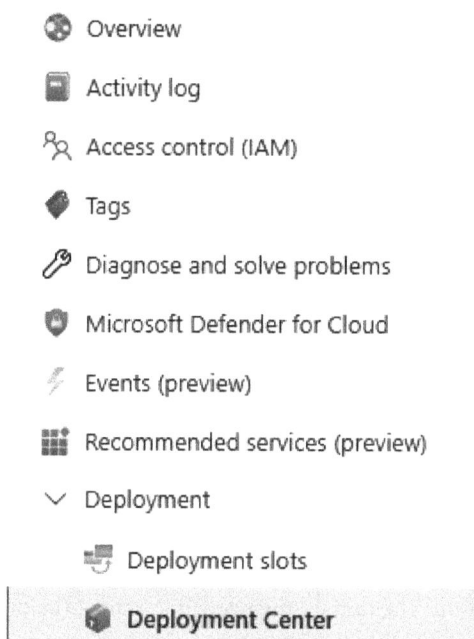

Figure 12.8 – Deployment Center in the Azure App Service menu

When you go there, there's a tab named **Logs** (*Figure 12.9*). Here, you will find all the information related to the application running inside the container.

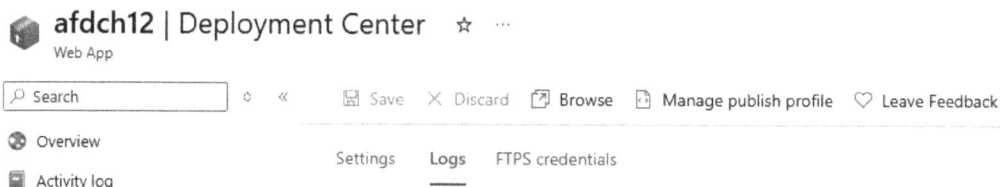

Figure 12.9 – The Logs tab in Deployment Center

It's important to remember that the logs presented here are related only to the provisioning phase of an application. It means that if your application sends logs in runtime, those won't be presented there.

> **Note**
>
> Logs presented in **Deployment Center** are useful in troubleshooting issues when the application starts. Many times, invalid configuration causes the whole container to crash when starting. This makes debugging difficult as, even if you have Azure Application Insights or a similar tool implemented, it may not start before a container crashes.

For most scenarios, though, the best approach for logging and monitoring is using a dedicated service. In the case of containerized applications, the fact that you're using containers shouldn't affect the technology stack that much. You can safely use Azure Application Insights as it offers quite a sophisticated set of features, simple configuration, and a cloud-native approach. The downside of that approach is that it may be difficult to extract logs from Azure Monitor and ingest them somewhere else (for instance, because you're using other cloud vendors and built a generic platform for logs collection).

When working with containers locally, you should be able to pretty easily collect and read all the logs as you have full access to the container engine running on your computer.

Let's now discuss the problem of cold starts in containerized applications.

Working with cold starts in containerized applications

As containerized applications introduce additional layers of abstraction over typical runtime, it becomes obvious that starting an application will be a longer process. Generally speaking, if performance is the key to your application, you should consider using containers unless you're able to spin them up really quickly. In Azure App Service, running a containerized application introduces a significant delay when starting an application. The initial time needed to start it (before warming up) is called a **cold start**. Cold starts happen in both on-premises and cloud environments. The difference here is the frequency. As cloud providers want to optimize how much they spend on the infrastructure, they will try to deallocate your resources as often as possible. This means that you need some kind of health check to keep your application up and running.

In Azure App Service you can leverage the **Always On** feature to have your application available, but you need to consider what happens when you deploy a new version. Deployments mean that your application needs to be restarted. If your application is containerized, it will cause a significant delay when the application restarts. This can be mitigated by deploying new versions outside of the core hours of your business, but it's not always possible. In such a case, you could leverage deployment slots, which allow you to swap new versions without affecting users (or at least limiting the effect of new deployment on users who are currently active).

> **Note**
> Remember that the **Always On** feature is available only for paid tiers of the Azure App Service plan. You cannot use it when using the Free (F1) tier.

Working with deployment slots and containers is technically the same as you would host your application in-process. You don't need to make any changes to the deployment approach (besides deploying container image instead of code package) and the configuration, and your CI/CD pipelines will stay the same.

In the last section of this chapter, let's talk about use cases for using containers with Azure App Service.

Learning about use cases

In this chapter, we talked a lot about multiple scenarios where running containers with Azure App Service is an applicable use case. In this section, we will summarize all the findings and try to gather all the information in a single place for better reference. To get started, let's remind you why one may want to containerize an application. Before containers became popular, the majority of systems were hosted *in-process* meaning they were tied to a specific platform. This approach, while it may seem old-fashioned and rather inflexible, brings several advantages:

- An application is designed for a dedicated environment, so the challenges are predictable and it's easier to debug an issue.

- It's almost guaranteed that you can move an application between environments sharing the same configuration without affecting the application's performance and behavior.

- When an application is hosted in-process, most of the time, it offers a better performance when compared to a containerized application.

- There's no need to install and maintain additional tools and platforms – you can run an application using its basic stack (web server and runtime).

As you can see, those are quite serious and important aspects that everyone needs to consider when designing and building an application. So, the question now is why you would need containers for your application. Let's find out.

Modern applications are expected to work in dynamic environments, which may change quite frequently (automated updates, load balancing, serverless platforms, and so on). If that's the case, it means an application needs to offer a way to quickly move it between hosts. If you need to move an application between hosts, you also need to find a way to quickly install and configure it. Of course, it's achievable using in-process hosting, but the downside of that approach is that you will often need an additional tool to configure the host. Each application requires a certain set of dependencies that need to be installed prior to deployment. You may prepare your own installation scripts, but most of the time, such operations are offloaded to a dedicated tool such as Ansible, Chef, or Puppet. Containers, on the other hand, encapsulate most of such actions as part of a container image definition. When a developer works on an application that is then containerized, they can manage the majority of the software needed for it to work properly. This aligns with the "shift left" approach, where lots of operations (installing and managing dependencies, customization, and bootstrapping) related to an application are shifted toward developers. Such an approach enables much more robust development of an application as developers know an application the best. When an application is containerized, a developer can prepare a definition (Dockerfile) that describes all that's needed for an application to start. Then, when a container image is built and pushed to a registry, any other engineer can pull such an image and host it anywhere where containers can be hosted.

> **Note**
>
> It's important to remember that not all dependencies can be containerized or included as part of a container image. Databases, message brokers, and external services often need to be configured separately, and it doesn't matter whether we're using in-process hosting or containers.

Now, let's talk about Azure App Service and containers. The first thing to discuss is how the in-process hosting model and containers are linked with each other. I'd like to emphasize that containers shouldn't be treated as the natural evolution of every application. There are still business cases that shouldn't be resolved using containers (this includes all the scenarios where platform performance is a priority). Containers are also challenging when you need to run them on a different operating system from Linux-based. For example, people working with .NET are often tasked with building an application that will work with Windows-based tasks only. Running containers on Windows is rather challenging and isn't considered the best practice. Migrating your application working in-process to containers in such a case will be difficult to justify unless there's a specific feature of containers you need to utilize.

When it comes to Azure App Service as a cloud service itself, you need to consider the scale and architecture of your application to see whether it's the best choice as a hosting platform. We mentioned that there are alternatives such as Azure Container Apps or Kubernetes (such as Azure Kubernetes Service). Azure App Service will serve the best when your application is a monolith or a modular monolith. The reason why is quite simple to explain – Azure App Service doesn't offer additional features for containers such as load balancing, quotas and limits for CPU and memory, RBAC, or advanced deployment strategies. Some of those features can be implemented using additional services and resources, and some can be implemented as part of your application. The advantage of native platforms is that they offer those features as their inbuilt functionalities. This means you don't need to implement and manage them on your own.

The advantage of hosting containerized applications using Azure App Service is the flexibility of such an approach. Once the application is containerized, you will have a subset of features needed for the alternative platforms as well. This simplifies the potential migration in the future and shortens the time needed to make the switch. While it may not be applicable to all the applications, the theoretical possibility for further evolution is important from both a business and architecture point of view.

We've now reached the end of *Chapter 12*. Let's summarize all the lessons and prepare for the next chapter.

Summary

In this chapter, we covered the concept of running containers using Azure App Service. You learned how to prepare your application to use that feature and the potential pros and cons when using that approach. We also discussed the possibility of running a multi-container deployment and its benefits.

We also discussed the differences between Azure App Service, Azure Container Apps, and Kubernetes when it comes to building and deploying an application. We saw that the service we should select will depend on our application's architecture. In the last part of the chapter, we talked about possible challenges with containerized applications and how to overcome those when using Azure App Service as your hosting environment.

In the next chapter, we're going to talk about how to use Azure Storage as your service for hosting data. It also marks the beginning of the next part of the book, which is titled *Storage, Messaging, and Monitoring*.

Part 4: Storage, Messaging, and Monitoring

In this part, you will explore essential Azure services for storing data, managing messaging between components, and monitoring application health. You'll learn how to work with both structured and unstructured data using Azure Storage and relational databases. The part also covers implementing message queues to enable reliable communication between services and adding observability using Azure Application Insights.

By the end of this part, you will be equipped to build applications that are not only data-driven but also maintainable, scalable, and performance-aware.

This part contains the following chapters:

- *Chapter 13, Storing Data with Azure Storage*
- *Chapter 14, Using Queues in Microsoft Azure*
- *Chapter 15, Using Relational Databases in Microsoft Azure*
- *Chapter 16, Adding Monitoring to Your Application*

13

Storing Data with Azure Storage

Almost every application built requires some kind of storage solution. In many cases, it can be a relational database or a file share mounted to the filesystem exposed to your application. The nature of data handled by an application dictates what kind of database or storage will be used; so, it's important to understand and know the available options when designing an application.

Until now, we've been mostly focused on Azure services, which allow you to host and run your application. This time, we're going to talk more about one of the most popular storage solutions available for Azure, which is Azure Storage. It's one of the oldest services implemented for that cloud platform – it's the backbone of many business applications and Azure itself.

In this chapter, we're going to cover the following main topics:

- Using Table Storage as a database for an application
- Using Blob Storage as a generic storage solution
- Understanding design patterns when using Azure Storage
- Learning about use cases

Technical requirements

To perform the exercises from this chapter, you will need the following:

- Azure CLI
- Azurite (`https://learn.microsoft.com/en-us/azure/storage/common/storage-use-azurite`)
- Azure Storage Explorer (`https://azure.microsoft.com/en-us/products/storage/storage-explorer`)

Using Table Storage as a database for an application

Azure Storage is a storage service in Azure, which consists of the following subservices:

- **Table Storage**
- **Blob Storage**
- **File Service (Storage)**
- **Queue Storage**
- **Data Lake Storage**

They are all part of the same service (Azure Storage) and can be deployed as a single unit. Historically, there was a possibility to deploy Azure Storage without some of those. Today, it's rather a matter of choosing which of the sub-services you will focus on the most. The choice won't affect the capabilities of Azure Storage but will rather give you some suggestions and insights on how to use the service in the most efficient way.

Our journey with Azure Storage will begin with using Table Storage. Table Storage is a simple **non-relational database**, which allows you to store and access your data quickly and efficiently. The most important features of Table Storage are as follows:

- Indexing based on two columns (which are named `Partition Key` and `Row Key` – we'll talk about them later in the chapter)
- Lack of fixed schema (you can store records with various schema using the same table)
- In-built concurrency handling (**optimistic concurrency**)
- Scales well even with millions of records assuming proper structure of data is implemented
- Doesn't support advanced filtering and queries

> **Note**
> It's worth mentioning that Table Storage does support the filtering and querying of data to some extent. Due to the nature of the indexing mechanism for that service, I tend to describe it as limited to Primary and Row Keys. We'll describe that in detail later in the chapter.

Table Storage can be easily used to handle data in scenarios where you don't need relations between records, the schema is not known or can be dynamic, and you can easily predict partitioning for data. While there are techniques that would allow you to create relations between records in Table Storage, they aren't implemented on the service level. This means you need to implement and manage them on your own.

Let's see how one can use Table Storage as the storage solution for an application.

Using Table Storage in an application

In this section, we will discuss two topics:

- How to find a use case for Table Storage

- How to implement a connection with Table Storage and how to query the service

Let's start with the former, as it will allow us to understand some additional concepts needed to be able to properly use the service.

Designing an application to use Table Storage

As mentioned before, Table Storage is a non-relational database, which automatically indexes your data based on two columns (`Primary Key` and `Row Key`). That information is very important from the design point of view – if you happen to start querying your data stored in Table Storage using any other column, it will heavily impact the performance of both your application and the service. Let's take a look at *Figure 13.1* to see the three in-built columns that are available in every table:

Primary Key	Row Key	Timestamp

Figure 13.1 – The three columns in every Table Storage table

Every table in Table Storage will have at least three columns:

- `Primary Key` is (as the name implies) the primary column used for indexing. You can consider it a way to group your records.

- `Row Key` allows you to identify records within a group indicated by `Primary Key`.

- `Timestamp` is an automatically managed column, which tells the service when a record was created and then updated.

> **Note**
>
> `Row Key` values must be unique within a partition (`Partition Key`). You can have records with the same `Row Key` value, but they must belong to different partitions.

Each table in Table Storage can have a number of custom columns. See *Figure 13.2* for visualization.

Table 1				
Primary Key	Row Key	Timestamp	Column 1	Column 2

Table 2			
Primary Key	Row Key	Timestamp	Column 3

Table 3				
Primary Key	Row Key	Timestamp	Column 4	Column 1

Figure 13.2 – Table Storage with three separate tables with different schema

It's important to remember that various tables can share the same column. You can even have tables with exactly the same schema – this approach is used in some designs to simplify the management of data. One of those designs targets data deletion – as deleting records from tables in Table Storage sometimes requires thousands of operations to be performed (which can be both slow and expensive); it's easier to just remove a table. Removing a table is a single operation, which is both cost-efficient and quick. We will discuss those designs and tricks later in the book.

The next important thing to discuss is how Table Storage handles data within the same table. Let's take a look at *Figure 13.3* and *Figure 13.4* to see the concept.

Table 1					
Primary Key	Row Key	Timestamp	Type	Color	Price
cars	1	12/15/2024 00:00:00	SUV	NULL	50000
cars	2	12/15/2024 00:00:00	Coupe	NULL	NULL
cars	3	12/15/2024 00:00:00	Sedan	Black	28000

Figure 13.3 – Three different records kept in the same table

Figure 13.4 presents a slightly different scenario when compared to *Figure 13.3*:

Table						
Primary Key	Row Key	Timestamp	Type	Address	Color	Brand
car	1	27.03.2025 00:00	NULL	NULL	Black	BMW
building	7s6asdkj7	28.03.2025 00:00	House	23 Street	NULL	NULL
car	2	29.03.2025 00:00	NULL	NULL	Red	Audi

Figure 13.4 – Records with different schema kept in the same table

If you take a closer look at the data presented in *Figure 13.3* and *Figure 13.4*, you will see that Table Storage supports both nullable columns and records with a completely different schema. Theoretically, every record could have a completely different schema. Practically, it's not achievable as Table Storage doesn't support more than 255 columns for each table. Still, you could have records that used only one additional column and records that used all 255 columns – all in the same table. This allows you to very easily introduce versioning of data to your application and simplify the management as no migrations are needed to handle schema changes.

> **Tip**
> If you want to keep data with changing schema in the same table, a good idea is to introduce a column that holds the information about the schema version. It then can be easily integrated with your application.

When a new column is introduced to a table in Table Storage, it gets automatically created, and all the records that don't have the value for that column will have a NULL value assigned instead. At any moment, you can update those records to use the new column with any custom value supported by it. The opposite happens when the last records using a custom column are removed – the column is no longer available in the table and needs to be re-inserted by using a record, which defines it once again.

As Table Storage may seem limited in some cases (as rows are indexed using only two columns – Partition Key and Row Key), it's worth understanding how to overcome those limitations by using well-defined patterns. Let's discuss them now to see how to implement certain scenarios for business applications.

Implementing design patterns for Table Storage

Table Storage offers extensive documentation explaining various design patterns for different scenarios. As that documentation is available publicly (at the following link: https://learn.microsoft.com/en-us/azure/storage/tables/table-storage-design-patterns), we're not going to explain them once again in this chapter. Instead, we will focus on understanding how to choose the ones that will suit your application and how to properly incorporate them into your code.

We already discussed that indexing in Table Storage happens only for two columns – `Partition Key` and `Row Key`. This forces you to plan the design of the database upfront as making changes in the future will be challenging. This is one of the major drawbacks when working with this service – while typical relational databases such as Microsoft SQL Server or PostgreSQL offer robust solutions for maintaining a database schema and automated migrations, Table Storage may look underdeveloped in that area. In fact, the difficulty of maintaining a dynamic schema for database tables is more or less the same for most NoSQL databases. This comes from a certain trade-off – you gain a much more flexible schema, which can be altered without hardcoded migrations, but also need to be much more careful when maintaining code, which interacts with such a schema. Let's consider the following scenario: you implemented a **database access layer** (**DAL**) in your application that adds a new row. This could be explained using the following pseudo-code:

```
var dal = new SomeTableDal();
var newRecord = new SomeRecord
{
    Id = 1,
    Name = "John",
    Surname = "Doe"
}
dal.Insert(newRecord);
```

The aforementioned example does the following things:

1. Creates a `dal` object to interact with a specific table
2. Defines a new record to be added with certain values
3. Adds the record using the `Insert` method

Now, let's imagine you want to add an additional field to the `SomeRecord` table. If you interact with a relational database, you will need to write a migration code (or use some kind of ORM, which will do that for you) and then implement a change in your code. If the new field is required, you will need to make sure that all instances of your application have a new code version deployed before you make new interactions with the database. Missing that step will result in errors returned from your application as it won't be able to add a new record due to a schema mismatch between a table and your code. For databases such as Table Storage, the only thing needed will be adding a field to the type in your code:

```
var newRecord = new SomeRecord
{
    Id = 1,
    Name = "John",
    Surname = "Doe",
    Phone = 100200300
}
```

The only thing to remember will be the fact that if there are any existing records in the table, they will have the Phone field set to a NULL value. This means that we'd need to consider what to do now:

- We can treat the new field as required, meaning we need to update the existing records to have the value provided or set to a default one.

- We can treat the new field as optional for old records and required for the new ones. This will make the implementation quite complex as we will need to understand which records are the old ones and which are the new ones (most likely, an additional field with a version number would be required).

- We can treat the new field as optional, which is the simplest scenario.

The final decision depends on the business requirements. Here, what we can see is that even though adding a record with altered fields may be quite easy when using Table Storage, maintaining such a code base with dynamic schema will become more and more challenging as time goes by. It's also worth mentioning that Table Storage offers three different methods to choose from when interacting with an entity stored in a table:

- `Insert`

- `Merge`

- `Replace`

They have completely different semantics so it's important to understand the difference between them, as described here:

- `Insert` adds a new entity to a table based on the `Partition Key` and `Row Key` values. If the combination of those columns would result in a duplicated record, an error will be thrown.

- `Merge` allows you to limit the amount of data sent to Table Storage by sending only the fields that you'd like to update. Those fields (or rather their values) will replace (or add new ones) the ones existing in an entity saved in the database.

- `Replace` allows you to replace an entity stored in Table Storage with the fields provided in a request. Note that fields that are not part of the request will be removed, so it's important to use that method with caution.

> **Note**
> Neither `Replace` nor `Merge` methods will work if an entity doesn't exist. The only method working with non-existing entities is `Insert`.

As you can see, even though Table Storage offers quite an easy interface for interacting with its data plane, there are lots of additional features available. This is why a proper upfront design will be important when using that service as your database.

Another example of using a proper design for an application is querying data. We discussed in this chapter the limitation of Table Storage, which is that it is unable to index data if it's not stored in the Primary Key or Row Key column. More traditional databases (especially relational ones) allow you to build a custom index using any column available for a table. Let's use the same example of a table as we did when discussing changes to the table schema. We will assume that our table looks like the one presented in *Figure 13.5*:

Table			
ID	Name	Surname	Phone

Figure 13.5 – A visualized structure of a table

In a relational database (such as Microsoft SQL), all those columns will be equal in the beginning. You can decide whether they have additional semantics by setting one of them as a primary key (most of the time, it would be the ID column), configure them with a unique index (so you'll get an error when adding a duplicate), or select one or several columns to create an index. Indexes allow you to optimize querying for data in a table by allowing a database engine to structure it in an optimal way. Let's assume you'd like to query data using both the Name and Surname columns. In a relational database, you'd build an index and save it to the database. Then, to utilize it, you'd just need to remember to use those columns in your queries:

```
SELECT
ID,
Name,
Surname,
Phone
FROM
[SomeRecord]
WHERE
Name = @Name
AND Surname = @Surname
```

The aforementioned example uses SQL syntax to build a query and expects two parameters: @Name and @Surname. You could provide any value for them if needed – what's important is that they are part of the WHERE clause and, based on our assumption of building an index containing those two fields, they would help us in getting a better performance from the query.

In Table Storage, things aren't that simple. If you're unable to make those columns part of the index (Primary Key and Row Key columns), then we'd need to find a better way to structure a table. Let's review our options:

- Name (Primary Key), Surname (Row Key): This won't work as people may have the same name and surname.

- `Surname` (`Primary Key`), `Name` (`Row Key`): This has the same issue as the previous option.

- `ID` (`Primary Key`), `Name_Surname` (`Row Key`): This will work just fine as long as we can always obtain a value for `ID` when querying for a record.

- `ID_Name` (`Primary Key`), `Surname` (`Row Key`): This is another working example that doesn't provide much of an improvement unless we need to reuse `ID` between the same names.

- `ID_Surname` (`Primary Key`), `Name` (`Row Key`): This is similar to the previous example.

- `Name_Surname` (`Primary Key`), `ID` (`Row Key`): This will work just fine but may result in imbalanced partitions due to various numbers of duplicated `Primary Key` values.

Based on the preceding examples, you can see that we may easily structure any table in various ways depending on our use case. Those patterns of providing different values for `Partition Key` and `Row Key` and merging some of the values are called **intra/inter-partition secondary index patterns**. Use them when you need to query your data using one of the value columns (columns that aren't either `Primary Key` or `Row Key`). One of the advised approaches for working with such designs is data duplication. If you need more than one secondary index, you may find it useful to create more than one record (one per index) in the table. This complicates the implementation and makes it prone to data drift. However, it allows you to keep the performance target and is a common practice when Table Storage is your actual storage.

> **Note**
>
> Designs and patterns used with Table Storage may look strange if you haven't got much experience working with NoSQL solutions. They are perfectly fine to be used in production scenarios and are well-tested even in heavily distributed and scaled-out services.

Using Table Storage will require some skill to be able to utilize its full potential so don't be discouraged by the number of different patterns and designs available for that service. For now, let's see how we can start using Table Storage in our application by leveraging its SDK.

Connecting with Table Storage from an application

When it comes to connecting to a Table Storage instance, you can use either its REST API directly or integrate with one of the available SDKs. Under the hood, the SDK will connect with the REST API as well, but the benefit of using it comes not from the connectivity point of view but, rather, from encapsulating all the implementation details such as authorization, concurrency, and reliability. In the following list, you can find all the available SDKs for different programming languages:

- **.NET**: `https://learn.microsoft.com/en-us/dotnet/api/overview/azure/data.tables-readme?view=azure-dotnet`

- **Java**: `https://mvnrepository.com/artifact/com.azure/azure-data-tables`
- **JavaScript**: `https://www.npmjs.com/package/@azure/data-tables`
- **Python**: `https://pypi.org/project/azure-data-tables/`
- **Go**: `https://pkg.go.dev/github.com/Azure/azure-sdk-for-go/sdk/data/aztables`

There are also additional SDKs available for PHP and Ruby, but as they offer only community support and aren't official SDKs, we're going to skip them in this chapter. The installation instructions for those packages can be found in the corresponding links. Once you have them installed, we can discuss how they're connected with the Table Storage instance.

The connection method will be the same for each SDK and those methods will be similar to the ones used to connect with other services such as Azure Container Registry, Azure Key Vault, or Azure App Configuration. When interacting with Table Storage, to authorize a connection, you can use the following:

- Access key
- **Shared Access Signature (SAS)** token
- Managed identity

The first two methods are native to Table Storage, meaning you can use them even if the entity connecting with your instance doesn't have an Azure account. The use of a managed identity will be preferred in most of the scenarios but will require providing Azure credentials (whether it's a service principal or a user). The use of an access key is very often discouraged as it doesn't allow you to control who accesses and how they access Table Storage. Let's discuss the possible use cases for different kinds of credentials mentioned before:

- Use an access key for admin-only access or quick prototypes that are created in sandbox environments and don't store real data.
- Use SAS tokens if you're unable to generate credentials for a customer connecting with your instance of Table Storage. Make sure they're short-lived and provide only the necessary permissions instead of all available.
- Consider a managed identity as the preferred way of connecting with Table Storage. Remember that you should follow the least privilege principle and avoid granting principals too broad roles (Azure Storage offers dedicated roles limited to either control or data plane only – you can check the documentation for a detailed overview: `https://learn.microsoft.com/en-us/azure/storage/tables/authorize-access-azure-active-directory`).

Depending on the selected authorization method, the implementation of connection in your application will be slightly different. Let's compare making the connection using a managed identity in three different programming languages, starting with C#:

```
var credential = new();
var client = new(
    endpoint: new Uri("<table-storage-endpoint>"),
    credential
);
```

The same can be done in Java with a similar syntax:

```
DefaultAzureCredential azureTokenCredential =
    new DefaultAzureCredentialBuilder()
        .build();
TableServiceAsyncClient client =
    new TableServiceClientBuilder()
        .endpoint("<table-storage-endpoint>")
        .credential(credential)
        .buildAsyncClient();
```

Let's also check the syntax for Python:

```
credential = DefaultAzureCredential()
client = TableServiceClient(
    endpoint="<table-storage-endpoint>",
    credential=credential
)
```

As you can see, the connection method using different SDKs will look the same no matter which programming language you're using. You can find more code examples in the repository for the chapter for a better overview of possible configuration values and syntax differences between various connection methods. Before we continue with code examples for interacting with Table Storage, let's briefly discuss SAS tokens, as they offer a slightly different experience when connecting to your data.

Using SAS tokens for connection

SAS tokens in Azure Storage are used to grant limited access to your data without using a managed identity. As mentioned previously, access keys are currently a deprecated way of connecting to Table Storage and similar services as you can't control who uses them and how they use them. SAS tokens, however, can be delegated to a particular service or a user and revoked when needed, so you have much better control over scope and security.

There are three different types of SAS tokens:

- **Account SAS** can give access to the whole storage account and multiple services
- **Service SAS** is dedicated to a single service (for instance, Table Storage)
- **User delegation SAS** is supported only for Blob and Data Lake Storage

The difference between user delegation SAS and the other SAS token types is the security method used to secure them – while account and service SAS tokens use a storage account key, user delegation SAS uses Microsoft Entra ID credentials. From the development point of view, you shouldn't see much of a difference when using those tokens. However, it's worth remembering that tokens secured by an account access key will be revoked each time the key is generated. This means that when you use them, you need to have a way to update them in a coordinated way, so users and services using them won't lose access to your data.

Generally speaking, an SAS token is a string containing a set of information, which can be used by Azure Storage to determine access. An example token may look like this:

```
"se=2025-01-30T20%3A00%3A00Z&sp=dac&sv=2022-11-02&ss=tb&srt=s&sig=oqYC
Is2Y%2Bwgd3lhy6KVeTf0qLd4dFnP7aCs2AHOxFno%3D"
```

To get a similar token, you'd need to use the following Azure CLI command:

```
az storage account generate-sas --account-name afd13 --services tb
--resource-types s --permissions acd --expiry 2025-01-30'T'20:00:00Z
```

It's also possible to generate such a token using the SDK or REST API – the examples can be found in the repository.

As you can see, a token looks like a query string, which you could attach to an HTTP request when interacting with the data plane of Azure Storage. It consists of a few parameters that provide information such as expiry date (`se`), permissions (`sp`), allowed services (`ss`), and signature (`sig`). To learn more about the structure of the token, take a look at the following page: `https://learn.microsoft.com/en-us/azure/storage/common/storage-sas-overview`.

Let's now discuss how SAS tokens can help you in properly designing an application. For the first example, let's consider providing an access key to multiple services. The concept is presented in *Figure 13.6*.

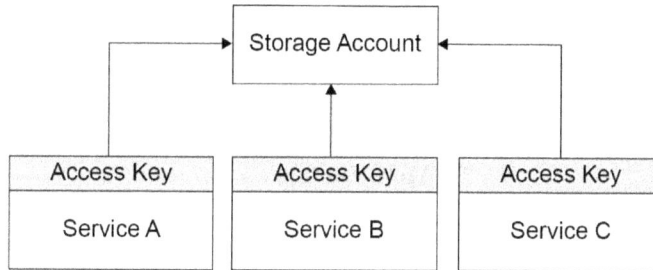

Figure 13.6 – Accessing a storage account using an access key

Figure 13.6 presents a simple scenario where we have three different services connecting to Azure Storage using the same access key. While such a configuration can be set up very quickly and with minimal operational overhead, let's see what happens if the access key is revoked (*Figure 13.7*).

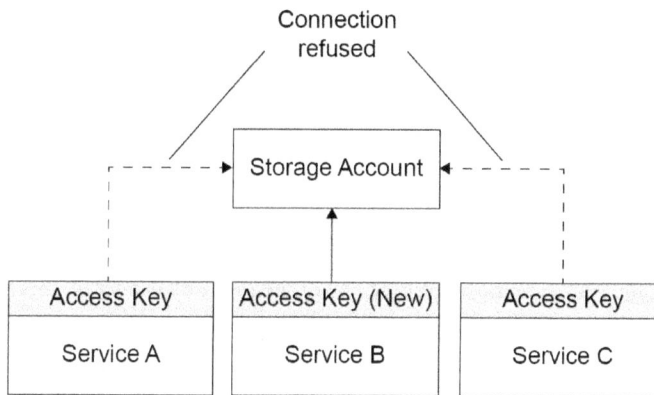

Figure 13.7 – Refused connection to Azure Storage for two services with an old access key

Figure 13.7 presents a scenario where one service was updated with a new access key while two others are still working with the old one. As you can see, they won't be able to communicate with Azure Storage unless they obtain the new access key. Another major thing visualized by those diagrams is the fact that you cannot differentiate the services based on the access key.

They all share the same access level, and as the access key isn't personalized, the only way to tell the difference when services are connecting would be by introducing a proxy between them and Azure Storage (see *Figure 13.8* for reference).

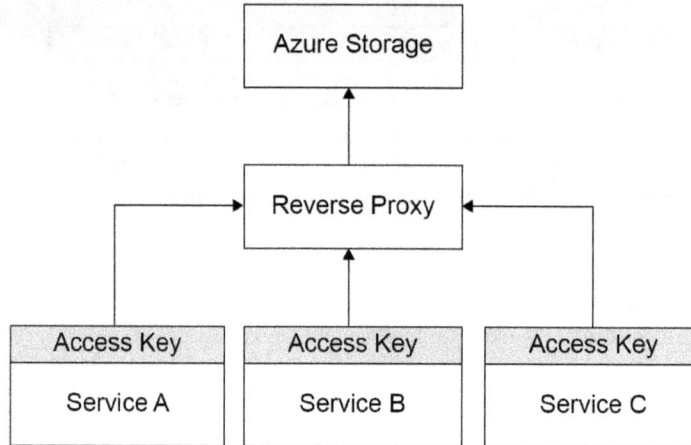

Figure 13.8 – A reverse proxy placed between services and Azure Storage to intercept requests

You may wonder why we'd place a reverse proxy in front of Azure Storage when an access key is used. This is actually one of the easiest methods to be able to detect what clients are connecting with your data (by investigating the source IP, hostname, or any of the request's headers). This method could be also used to centralize the use of the access key (see *Figure 13.9*).

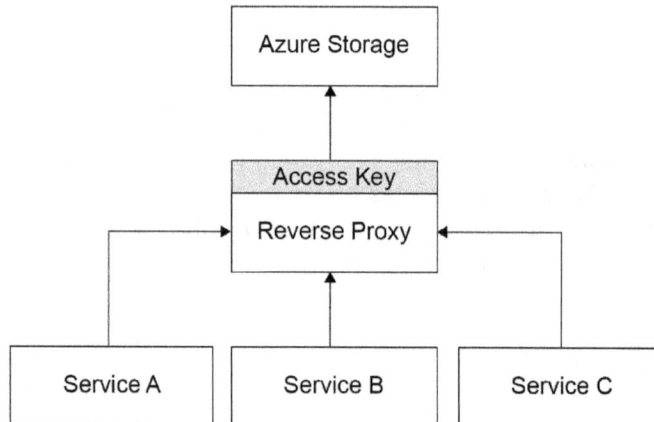

Figure 13.9 – Access key moved to the reverse proxy for easier management

Figure 13.9 presents you with a setup where an access key is used by a reverse proxy to authorize forwarded requests. While such a setup may not increase the security (as it means that every client connecting with the proxy will be able to communicate with Azure Storage), it definitely simplifies the management and revokes an access key.

> **Note**
>
> There are ways to have the access key moved to the proxy while still maintaining a certain level of security. You could have custom authentication implemented, so only a subset of clients could connect to the proxy. The services connecting with the proxy could also be considered safe by default thanks to network isolation. There are multiple possibilities and, as always, you need to consider all of them when designing your application.

Now, as we have discussed how a connection is authorized when an access key is used and what kind of problems and challenges it may generate, let's discuss how SAS tokens are helpful. We'll consider a similar scenario with three separate clients connecting to the same instance of Azure Storage (*Figure 13.10*).

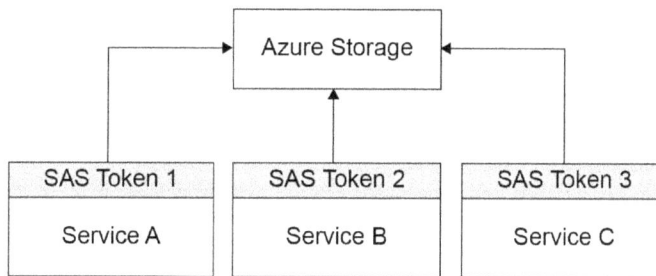

Figure 13.10 – Different services connecting to Azure Storage using different SAS tokens

In *Figure 13.10*, you can see how each service uses a different SAS token. Each token may provide a different set of permissions and have a different expiry date. A token could be also revoked individually (by using the stored access policy – you can read more about it here: `https://learn.microsoft.com/en-gb/rest/api/storageservices/define-stored-access-policy`), so you gain flexibility when compared with the approach using an access key. As SAS tokens are generated and granted for individual entities, you also don't need to introduce additional infrastructure components as a workaround for an access key limitation.

> **Note**
>
> While you could provide the same SAS token for different services, such a practice is considered a bad practice. You'd lose the flexibility of SAS tokens and gain nothing in return.

We can now discuss how to implement a proper access layer to a Table Storage instance in our application using the aforementioned SDKs and best practices for working with that service.

Interacting with Table Storage in an application

When integrating an application with Table Storage, you will most likely need an abstraction, which will help you with unit testing your code. An example setup is presented in *Figure 13.11* as a reference for further discussion.

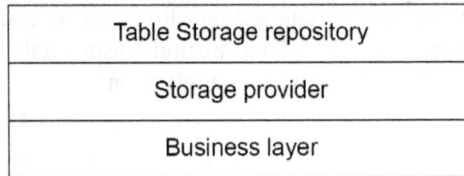

Table Storage repository
Storage provider
Business layer

Figure 13.11 – Simple visualization of the different layers in an application

Let's consider that the main code of our application resides within a business layer. If we want to connect with Table Storage, obviously, we could have direct references to the SDK within that layer. It will work in simpler scenarios and during initial iterations of development, but ultimately, we would rather seek more flexible and *clean* solutions. There are two possible paths:

- Add a single layer (such as a repository), which will encapsulate all the SDK-related code there and inject it into our business layer.

- If needed, add an intermediary layer (such as a storage provider), which can take care of choosing the storage our application needs to connect to. This setup works in scenarios where we may have multiple storage accounts available (or even multiple databases to choose from).

The next important thing is understanding the difference between a **Table service client** and a **Table client**. Those two separate concepts provided by the SDK allow you to either interact with the service itself (its control plane) to work with the tables or to interact with the data plane, so you can add, remove, and update data stored there. Take a look at the following example in .NET, which shows the difference between those two clients:

```
// Table service client
var serviceClient = new TableServiceClient(
    new Uri(storageUri),
    new TableSharedKeyCredential(
        accountName,
        storageAccountKey
    )
);
```

```
// Table client
var tableClient = new TableClient(
    new Uri(storageUri),
    "mytablename",
    new TableSharedKeyCredential(
        accountName,
        storageAccountKey
    )
);
```

You can find detailed examples with descriptions in the repository.

When working on your application with Table Storage, you will need to decide what kind of operations you need to perform against the tables. One of the crucial concepts is deciding who or what is responsible for creating the tables. You can have them created externally (manually or via some kind of automated script) or let your application do the work. If you decide that it's your application's responsibility, you need to consider when the tables will be created – most of the time, the best place to have that kind of code implemented is the initialization part of the application, which is executed only when an application starts. See *Figure 13.12* to see the visualized concept.

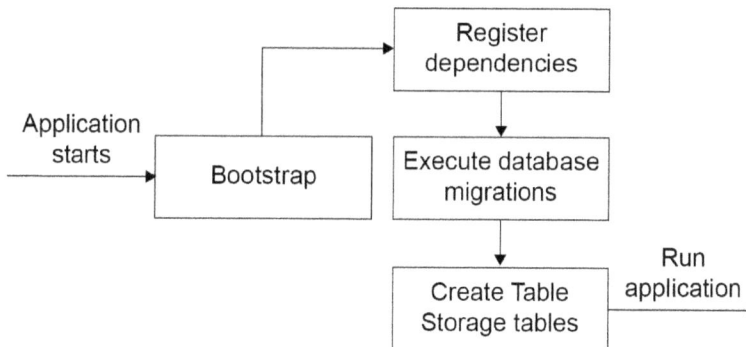

Figure 13.12 – Placing the code initializing the Table Storage tables in the application's bootstrap

The benefit of such an approach is a much lower impact on the application's performance when compared with creating a table as part of your data layer. For comparison, take a look at *Figure 13.13*, which explains a different concept:

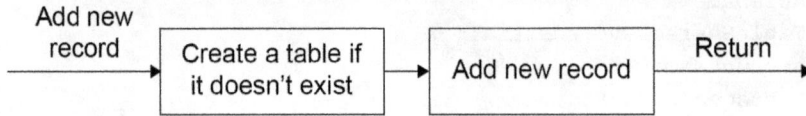

Figure 13.13 – Creating a table as part of a data layer

When you place the code responsible for creating a table as part of your data layer, you will need to make sure that a table doesn't exist already. Fortunately, the SDK already has those methods implemented so you don't need to do that on your own. The downside of that approach is that your application will always need to make another call to the Table service to ensure the request sent to the service doesn't conflict with the service's state. For individual calls, it won't be a problem; however, if you multiply those requests by thousands of calls, you may find it impacting the performance.

When interacting with Table Storage, it's also important to remember that the data is indexed only with two columns: PartitionKey and RowKey. When you want to query your data, you should only use those columns as part of your WHERE clause (SDKs allow you to provide a filter where you can place parameters). The clause (filter) may look like this:

```
PartitionKey eq 'cars' and RowKey eq '8556783'
```

In the aforementioned example, we created a filter that will look for a specific record in our table. As Table Storage doesn't provide an API for querying a single record only, even though the filter limits the returned data to a single entity, the result will still be a collection of entities (but obviously containing only a single entry). In fact, we could summarize the possible queries as follows:

- Use both PartitionKey and RowKey to query a single record. This is the most performant query.

- Use PartitionKey only to fetch data from a particular partition (such as displaying a list of stored records). Such a query won't be as performant as leveraging both PartitionKey and RowKey but still should provide decent performance.

- Use RowKey without PartitionKey if you want to look for records that share the same identifier, or you don't know the value of PartitionKey. This query will scan all the partitions, but as we're RowKey, it will be able to utilize some of the indexing capabilities of Table Storage.

The summary is also presented as a decision tree in *Figure 13.14.*

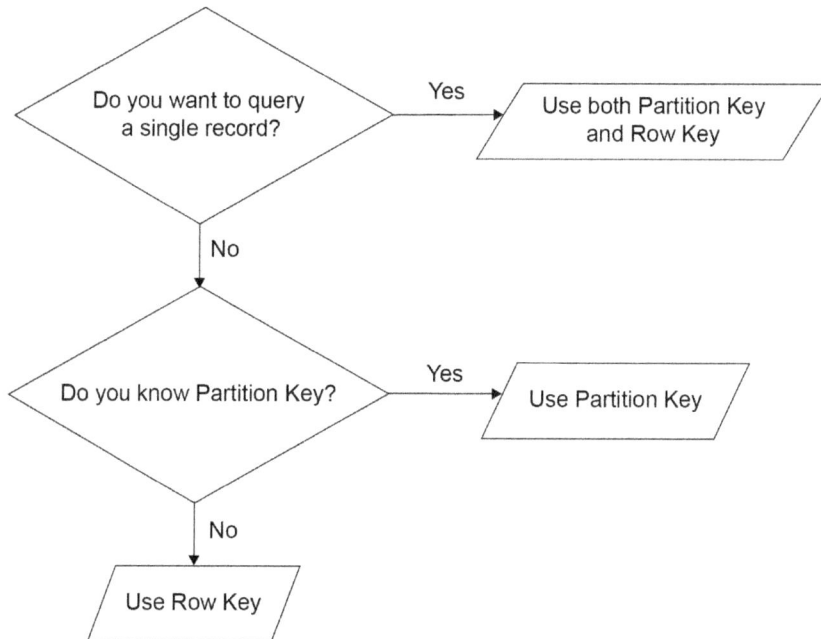

Figure 13.14 – A decision tree for selecting a proper identifier for a query

Not using either `PartitionKey` or `RowKey` generates a query that will cause all the records to be scanned. Avoid running such a query as they are not only very slow but can also be costly, especially if there's lots of data to scan.

> **Note**
> Table Storage is priced on the basis of two factors – data volume stored and data operations. Proper use of `PartitionKey` and `RowKey` limits the number of read operations performed when loading data. Hence, it allows you to keep the cost up to the minimum.

An interesting fact about Table Storage is that its API is fully compatible with the Table API offered by Azure Cosmos DB. This means you could start working on an application using a simpler and much cheaper service (Table Storage) and then switch to Azure Cosmos DB once your scalability demands and reliability expectations become stricter.

It's also worth mentioning here that switching to Azure Cosmos DB provides additional features that aren't available in Table Storage:

- You can create indexes using all the columns in a table – this simplifies database design and makes it much more flexible.

- You can create additional replicas of your database, so you can co-locate read/write locations with the locations of your customers.

- You can leverage the change feed offered by Azure Cosmos DB to distribute your data as a stream.

- You can use the backup and restore capabilities of Azure Cosmos DB to increase the reliability of your database and make it much more resistant to errors.

The downside of using the Table API instead of Table Storage is the huge pricing difference – Azure Cosmos DB is a much more expensive solution, which makes sense in bigger applications (spanned across multiple locations, with strict performance targets and low-latency requirements). If you don't need the advanced features offered by Azure Cosmos DB, I highly recommend giving Table Storage a try. It's a great service that is easy to learn, can be quickly implemented as the data layer of your applications, and is really cheap in the majority of business scenarios.

Let's discuss now another service offered by Azure Storage, which is Blob Storage – a generic solution for storing files and data.

Using Blob Storage as a generic storage solution

In the first part of this chapter, we talked about Table Storage, which could be used as a database for our application. While Table Storage is perfect for storing data in semi-structured format (rows inside a table but without struct schema), it can't help you in storing unstructured data or files. For those cases, we have Blob Storage – another service offered by Azure Storage, which you can use as a generic storage. However, what does *generic storage* mean? Let's try to explain the term here.

Most applications require some kind of storage. The nature of storage depends on the business requirements for those applications – those requirements shape the domain implemented by an application and tell architects and developers what technology will be suited the most to help with the implementation. If the data stored by an application has relations, a relational database will definitely be a good match. If data is semi-structured or loosely coupled, a non-relational database could work as well. Sometimes applications need to store unstructured data, though – those could be text or binary files or serialized data, which you don't want to store inside a database. For those cases, Blob Storage seems like a perfect fit. Let's quickly discuss the most important features of that service:

- It supports any file format.

- It allows you to organize files using a tree-like structure using containers (though it's important to remember that the structure is virtual – it doesn't work like a typical filesystem).

- It provides a way to tell which files should be available publicly and which ones are private.

- It supports authorization using access keys, SAS tokens, and Microsoft Entra ID (via RBAC).

- It supports various access tiers, so you can decide what the most important parameters are for you when integrating Blob Storage with your application (performance or price).

> **Note**
>
> Blob Storage offers a feature called **hierarchical namespaces**, which transforms the service from Blob Storage to Data Lake Storage. Data Lake Storage works in a similar way to Blob Storage but gives you more control over the structure of your files (it supports POSIX-like access control lists in addition to Azure RBAC) and targets working with high volumes of data (hundreds of gigabytes or more).

As the first topic in this section, let's discuss how access tiers affect your application.

Using the correct access tier for an application

As of now, Blob Storage offers four different access tiers:

- Hot

- Cool

- Cold

- Archive

Access tiers allow you to select the best approach for storing and accessing your data from an application. For instance, the **Hot** tier has the best cost ratio for frequently accessed data. On the other hand, if you access data less than once a week, you may find the **Cool** or **Cold** tiers much better suited for your needs. The last tier, **Archive**, is designed for storing data that is accessed only as the last resort (for instance, old backups or historical data stored out of compliance reasons).

The important feature of the Archive tier is the need to rehydrate (or resurface) data. It means that once a file is moved to that tier, you can't read it or write to it. See *Figure 13.15* for the explanation.

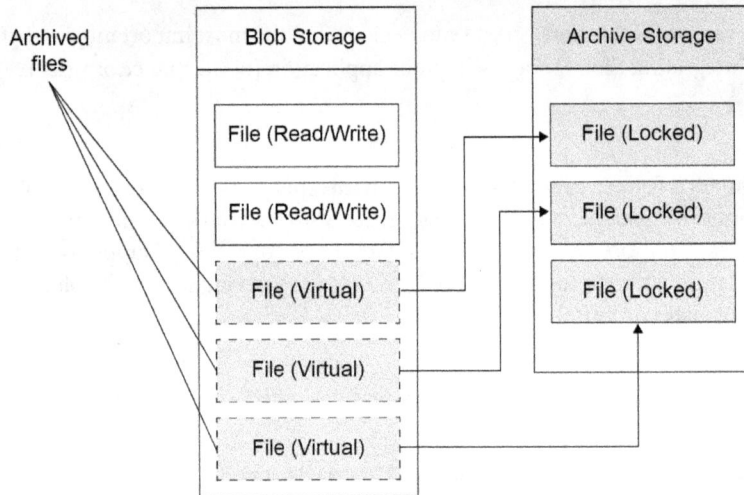

Figure 13.15 – Blob Storage with three archived files, which are moved to the archive storage and are locked. They exist only virtually within the standard structure of Blob Storage

The fact that data needs to be rehydrated before accessing it (and that process may take 15 hours) is why you need to carefully select which files are supposed to be archived. I'd also like to emphasize that, very often, spending too much time deciding which access tier is the best for your application isn't worth the money saved. It's difficult to tell the numbers (you need to make your own calculations), but most of the time, you need to store huge data volumes (hundreds of gigabytes) to see the difference between Hot and Cool/Cold tiers.

> **Note**
> You can find more information about access tiers here: `https://learn.microsoft.com/en-us/azure/storage/blobs/access-tiers-overview`.

From the system's point of view, it makes more sense to divide it into domains/modules, which are responsible for pushing and retrieving data and then finding a proper structure for the access layer. Take a look at *Figure 13.16* for a reference architecture, which we will discuss in a moment.

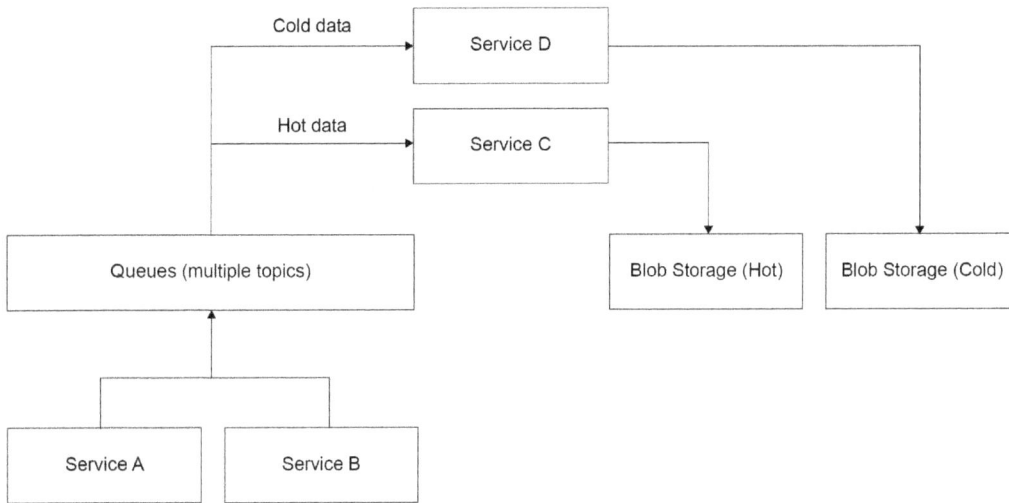

Figure 13.16 – A reference architecture with two services publishing data
to various topics. There are specific subscribers for those topics, which take
care of saving data to a Blob Storage with a proper access tier

Let's discuss how the architecture presented in *Figure 13.16* could help in the proper use of access tiers in Blob Storage. The fact that we're supposed to use a specific tier will often be linked with a set of non-functional requirements for all applications within our domain. For instance, you may need to log and save all the operations performed by a user when using your application. While those operations may not be presented to a user, you may still be obligated to store them because of compliance or regulations (even though they're not directly connected with the application itself). In such a scenario, it may be easier to delegate the responsibility of storing that data to an external service. As one of the possible solutions, you could use multiple topics:

- **Hot**: Topics used to transfer data directly connected to the functional requirements of your application.

- **Cold**: Logs, audit data, and regulatory data.

> **Note**
> If you're unfamiliar with the concept of a topic, take a look at the following documentation: `https://learn.microsoft.com/en-us/azure/service-bus-messaging/service-bus-queues-topics-subscriptions#topics-and-subscriptions`.

The use of topics allows you to implement a pub/sub pattern with multiple publishers and subscribers, who can select on their own what data to read. From the architecture point of view, the pattern presented in *Figure 13.16* decouples the business layer (applications publishing data to the topics) from the data access layer (the services that connect directly with Blob Storage). It also helps you in keeping user-facing applications decoupled from the underlying infrastructure. Most of the time, you don't want to wonder where data published by your application is supposed to be stored. All you need to know is the data that belongs to the Hot or Cold data processing path.

Let's talk now about the proper structure for folders and files when using Blob Storage.

Implementing data structure

We already mentioned that, by default, Blob Storage offers a rather flat structure for the data stored inside the service. When it comes to a high-level hierarchy of major objects, we can introduce the following concepts:

- Account (Azure Storage instance)
- Service (Blob Storage)
- Container
- Blob

When looking at the service itself, we can see that there are two major concepts we need to understand: a **container** and a **blob**. In Blob Storage, blobs cannot exist outside of containers; you always need to have at least one container to store data. Containers allow you to set basic access levels, which will impact how data will be accessed. You can have containers that allow for anonymous access [Container] (anybody with access to the internet can read them and list all the files they store), public [Blob] (available to anyone with a link but allowed to access only a specific blob only), and private (require proper authorization before you can access any of the files). A good practice is to have all the containers private by default – public ones only make sense as public repositories, for example, for new packages of your application.

> **Note**
>
> Access methods available for Blob Storage are the same as for Table Storage. You still can use an access key, SAS tokens, or Microsoft Entra ID tokens with Azure RBAC. The only difference is the access level for a container, which needs to work in tandem with the selected authorization method.

When designing a data structure for Blob Storage, you need to consider how you're planning to use the service. Depending on the purpose of the files stored, you may need a different approach:

- It's generally a good idea to separate Azure storage accounts storing your data if they require different access tiers.

- You may use a single account to store data coming from multiple applications, but as you don't pay for the service itself but rather for the data stored (and operations performed against the data), it's just easier to use multiple accounts.

- You shouldn't overcomplicate the data structure itself. For a hierarchical directory with several levels of nested folders, Data Lake Storage will be a much better fit.

- There are no performance benefits of having hierarchical storage over a flat structure of files. Creating multiple directories allows you to set different access levels for files and organize the structure, but Blob Storage isn't optimized for either of the possible designs.

A much more important topic when it comes to the data stored using Blob Storage is the type of blob itself. We'll describe that in the next section.

Using the correct blob type

In Blob Storage, you can use the following blob types when storing your files:

- Block
- Append
- Page

Each of the available types serves a different purpose and directly impacts how the files can be used, modified, and stored. For the majority of scenarios involving Blob Storage, you'll be interested in block blobs. Such blobs aren't optimized for any specific scenario. They allow you to store any file and modify it anytime. By default, there are no benefits of specific read patterns applied for those blobs, which makes them really easy to use, read, and update.

On the other hand, append blobs are specifically designed to be optimized for updates, which append data *at the end* of a file. By definition, it means that they're immutable unless you want to add something to a file. This makes them a great choice for scenarios such as storing logs or a history of conversation – in those cases, the data is often streamed as saved when it comes to the service storing it. Even if they're transformed, the transformation happens either before storing them or just in the time they're persisted in the underlying storage.

The concept is visualized in *Figure 13.17*.

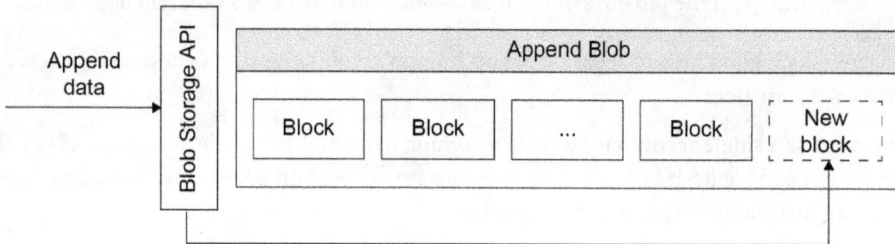

Figure 13.17 – Appending data to an Append blob

As append blobs are optimized for appending data, you shouldn't consider them a viable option if you need to modify a file rather than add something to it. For any scenario that requires modifying a file, consider a block blob to be a better option rather than an append blob.

> **Note**
>
> Append blobs can still be modified if needed. The difference here is that append blobs don't support modifying individual blocks, which are the base structure of all blobs in Blob Storage. This means that modifying an append blob requires rewriting the whole file. What's more, append blobs don't support tiering – you can change the access tier from Hot to Cold, Cool, or Archive when you decide to use that type of blob.

The last type of blob, page blob, is a specialized type that is optimized for random reads and writes. While, initially, they look like block blobs, the way you create and interact with them is completely different. When a page blob is created, you need to specify its maximum size. What's more, as page blobs are organized into pages of a specific size (512 bytes), all the write operations must align with a set of requirements. You can read more about those three types of blobs here: `https://learn.microsoft.com/en-us/rest/api/storageservices/understanding-block-blobs--append-blobs--and-page-blobs`.

From the application's perspective, selecting the incorrect blob type will have much more severe consequences than selecting the incorrect access tier. While an incorrect access tier will affect the pricing (which could be significant but requires reaching a certain scale), an incorrect blob type affects the implementation. Changing the implementation requires going through the whole release process for an application from the beginning, so focusing on choosing the right type from the beginning will save lots of effort later. The simple algorithm for choosing the correct blob type could look like this:

- Use a block blob as the default type unless you're not planning on modifying the data stored.
- Does the application store the data by appending new content to the already existing files? If so, an append blob may be useful if you can accept the trade-off (lack of tiering and immutability).

- Are you planning to store **virtual hard disks** (**VHDs**) or data that requires random reads or writes? If so, consider using page blobs, which are specifically for those scenarios.

Remember that once a blob is created, you can't change its type. If you realize the selected blob type isn't serving its purpose in your scenario, you will need to recreate a blob with a new blob type.

As the next topic, let's discuss the change feed in Blob Storage, which is one of the most useful features when building an application that integrates with that Azure service.

Using the change feed in Blob Storage

A change feed is a specific feature of a service that allows you to subscribe to a stream of events telling you what has changed within a specific time window. In other words, it's a stream of events that provide information about changes happening to files or data in general. You can use such a stream to react to changes by listening to those events in your application and implementing logic that can handle them. A high-level concept is presented in *Figure 13.18*.

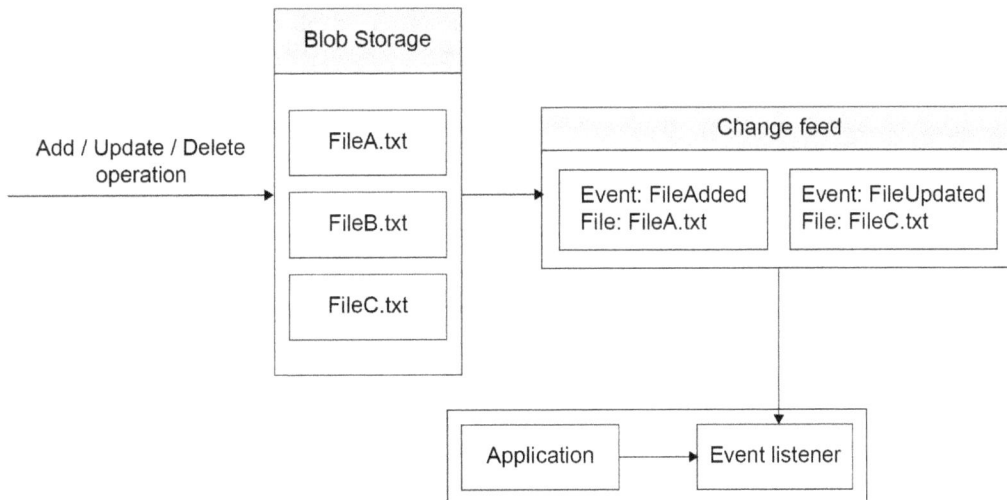

Figure 13.18 – A high-level concept of a change feed integrated with an application via an event listener

You may wonder what's the benefit of using a change feed over fetching both the metadata and files via standard APIs for Blob Storage. To understand that better, let's quickly discuss the possible options for interacting with external services:

- **Standard API calls** using the HTTP protocol without any specific pattern.

- **Short pooling** is an easy and quick-to-implement solution for simple APIs, which doesn't handle extensive web traffic. The concept here relies on repetitive calls made against a service to see whether there's data available.

- **Long pooling** allows you to keep the connection open until the data is available. This pattern introduces fewer calls to be made but, at the same time, tends to exhaust server resources quickly. It's a good solution if establishing a connection with a web server is a costly operation.

- **WebSockets** are a different protocol when compared with HTTP and allow for bi-directional communication (and even broadcasting messages to connected clients). They are used in communication-heavy applications such as chats or services requiring near-real-time updates.

Not all those patterns are available for Blob Storage (for instance, WebSockets aren't supported), but in general, you could interact with this Azure service using either generic HTTP requests, short pooling, or long pooling. The issue here is that applications handling lots of traffic (thus frequently interacting with Blob Storage) may require heavy optimizations to be able to handle the load within acceptable response times. As HTTP itself is quite a heavy protocol without state management, finding an alternative solution will be beneficial to keep the expected performance.

This is where a change feed comes in handy. While it's not a bi-directional communication as with WebSockets, it limits the unnecessary calls to Blob Storage and allows your application to save its resources for more important tasks rather than asking Blob Storage whether there is new or updated data available. By looking at *Figure 13.18*, you can see that there's a concept called an **event listener**. This part of your application (which could be an isolated service as well) acts as a bridge between the business logic implemented in your application and infrastructure (in our case, Blob Storage). Its responsibility is to listen to changes published by Blob Storage and process the incoming messages. You could think about change feed as a specific implementation of a publisher/subscriber pattern – Blob Storage is a publisher of changes happening within the data plane of the service and your application (which could consist of several different services) is the subscriber of the feed.

What's important is that change feed messages have a strict schema, meaning they are strongly typed and follow Apache Avro serialization specifications (see `https://avro.apache.org/` for more information). They are also saved as append blobs so, in fact, you have two possibilities to process them:

- Read them directly from the change feed in near-real time

- Load the serialized data from the append blobs

While the first approach is better suited for building applications that need to react to blob changes as quickly as possible, the second one may be beneficial if you're building data pipelines, which process data on their own and combine the results on their own. Both approaches are viable in business applications and it's up to specific requirements to choose the correct one. See *Figure 13.19* for a visualization of the second approach.

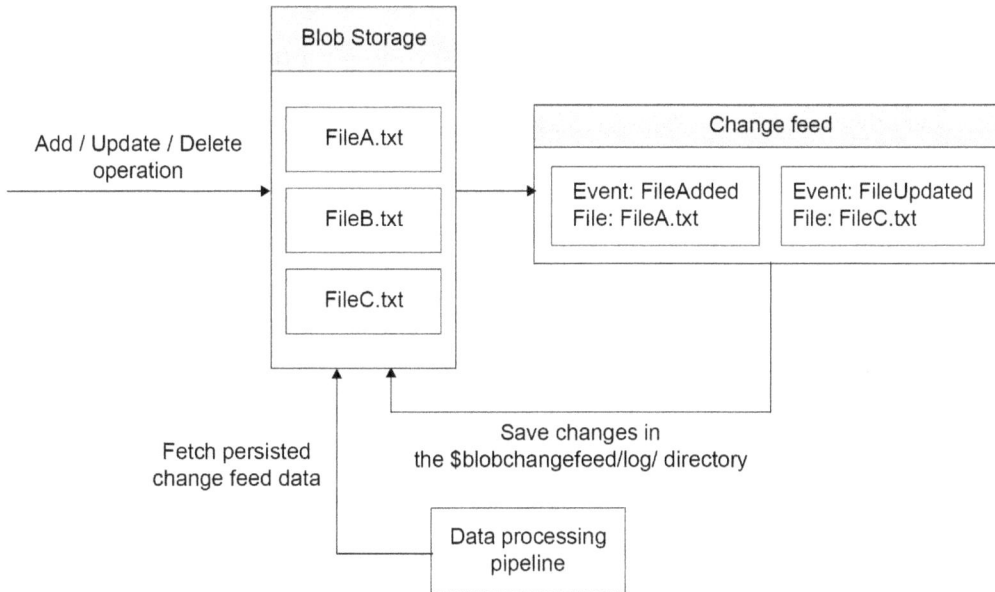

Figure 13.19 – Processing persisted change feed data

For more information about change feed and code examples, look at the following documentation page: `https://learn.microsoft.com/en-us/azure/storage/blobs/storage-blob-change-feed`.

As the last subtopic in this section, let's talk about the available emulators for Blob Storage, which are helpful in local development.

Using emulators for local development

Using cloud services is challenging when it comes to emulating the local environment on a daily basis. Most of the Azure services don't come with a viable emulation capability, forcing developers to either implement mocks or work with dedicated cloud environments. While having an isolated environment isn't bad (in fact, it's a great way to develop an application), many companies don't have the resources or money to implement and manage them. Fortunately, Azure Storage is one of the services that offer easy-to-install emulators, which are cross-platform and free to use.

Some time ago, the available solution for emulation for Azure Storage was Azure Storage Emulator. Unfortunately, it worked only with Microsoft Windows, greatly limiting development platforms available for Azure developers. As this emulator is currently deprecated, we're not going to discuss it further. However, if you'd like to learn about it (or you have a use case for it), feel free to read about it and install it with the help of the following documentation: `https://learn.microsoft.com/en-us/azure/storage/common/storage-use-emulator`.

The currently recommended emulator is called **Azurite**. It's an open source, free, and cross-platform service that you can install on the majority of machines. If you're using Visual Studio 2022 or higher, Azurite is already available to you. You can check its version by running the following command:

```
azurite -v
```

However, if the command isn't available, it may mean that Azurite is not yet installed. There are possibilities to install it with various tools:

- Using npm:

```
npm install -g azurite
```

- Using Docker:

```
docker pull mcr.microsoft.com/azure-storage/azurite
```

You could also build the emulator directly from the source code available here: `https://github.com/Azure/Azurite`. It's up to you to decide how you'd like to install and run it. While the emulator works out of the box after installation, you may find it useful to know how to change the ports it exposes for various services. The emulator emulates three separate services:

- Blob service
- Queue service
- Table service

Each of those services runs behind an individual port – `10000`, `10001`, and `10002`. If for any reason one of those ports is blocked (for instance, you're hosting an application locally), the service won't be able to start. To change the port, use this simple command:

```
azurite --blobPort / --queuePort / --tablePort 11111
```

After running the command, Azurite will restart the service and put it under a newly selected port.

> **Tip**
> Remember to make sure your application runs with an updated connection string after changing the port.

You can find more information about Azurite and connect to it in the Azure documentation: `https://learn.microsoft.com/en-us/azure/storage/common/storage-use-azurite`. I strongly recommend taking a look there to see what other options are available for Azurite and what's the best way to integrate it with your application.

Let's now switch our focus to the last topic in this chapter, which is design patterns for Azure Storage. While we have already discussed some of them, we'll summarize all the lessons and talk about the ones related to Blob Storage itself.

Understanding design patterns when using Azure Storage

As Azure Storage consists of multiple services (Table, Queue, Blob, and Files), design patterns applicable for one service may not be directly transferrable to another one. In this section, we'll discuss how to properly place them within the architecture of your application to make sure they're the best choice for it. To be even more specific, we'll focus on both Table and Blob services as they are the ones we discussed in this chapter.

Finding use cases for Table Storage

As mentioned previously in this chapter, Table Storage is a simple key-value storage, which is a great choice if you're challenged with storing semi-structured and structured data. It's basically a non-relational database, which limits its indexing capabilities to two in-built columns. To select Table Storage as a viable solution, first, you need to answer the following question: *Is your data relational or not?* If the data isn't relational, we could go to the next point directly. However, if data is relational, we may still discuss whether Table Storage should be discarded right away.

Using Table Storage for relational data

The fact that data processed by an application is relational may not be enough to discard Table Storage as your database. To find a proper solution here, we need to understand what advantages databases such as SQL Server or PostgreSQL have over Table Storage. The even more important thing here is understanding what advantages relational data possesses over non-relational data. The main advantage of having relations between records (or tables) in your database is the consistency of data. As relational databases allow you to create relations and enforce consistency by checking the defined constraints upon executing operations that mutate data, you can be sure that once the database schema is defined, no application or user will break the data contract. In non-relational databases, it's much more difficult to ensure consistency (though it's still possible to achieve).

If you want to use Table Storage for relational data, you will need to implement relations on your own. You will also need to provide your own mechanism to ensure that all constraints are respected and checked. While this is achievable within the application, you won't be able to ensure consistency on a database level. In other words, if you let somebody modify data outside of your application, you may find some records corrupted and no longer usable.

The reason you'd like to use Table Storage in such a scenario could be performance – no native relations mean fewer checks and a simpler database engine. Of course, this still could be a trade-off (as those checks would need to be implemented by your application), but as you control the whole process, you may decide when you want operations to be strict and when you want to make them more flexible.

Let's discuss another use case for Table Storage, which is storing logs.

Using Table Storage to store logs

Table Storage looks like a great choice for storing logs and integrating with various dashboards. As you control the partitioning of data, you could create partitions representing the expected time windows and query them to visualize data. This is a perfect example of how a proper database design may improve the overall performance of an application. With proper partitioning, you can leverage the indexes provided by Table Storage and implement a storage solution, which is not only very performant but also cheap (cheaper than typical relational databases).

Of course, you could store logs as append blobs and use Blob Storage for that. The downside of such an approach is forcing your application not only to download a file but also to parse and deserialize it. For integrations with visualization tools such as Grafana, I'd strongly recommend choosing Table Storage over Blob Storage.

Let's now talk about duplicating data in Table Storage the correct way.

Storing duplicated data in Table Storage

In relational databases, storing duplicated data is rarely a good idea (you have relations so most of the time you want to link records rather than duplicate them). In Table Storage, data duplication is actually one of the viable patterns for storing data and allowing your application to query it. Let's consider the previous example with logs; you may want to introduce three separate time windows for an application:

- Each hour
- 30 minutes
- 5 minutes

Now, to properly implement such a solution, there are two possibilities:

- Use a single partition for each hour and use it to query data. Then, if the client application wants to show only a subset of data, it will filter out some records on its own. The advantage of this solution is no data duplication. The downside is that you always return the full hour of data, even if the user wants to check for only 5 minutes.

- Duplicate the data and store each record in each partition separately. The downside here is data duplication. The advantage is that you can select the data with the expected granularity, lowering the cost of the infrastructure and most likely increasing performance.

The same reasoning can be applied to various other scenarios that require querying the same set of data using different parameters (consider revisiting inter and intra-partition design patterns for Table Storage for a detailed explanation of the concept). The important thing here is that you shouldn't worry about duplicating data with Table Storage – it's well suited for handling such an approach and it's actually an advised solution to improve the performance of your queries.

Let's now discuss the additional use cases and ideas for Blob Storage, as an alternative to Table Storage.

Finding use cases for Blob Storage

Blob Storage, which is well suited for storing unstructured data, offers some interesting capabilities that can be used in various applications. Most use cases for Blob Storage gravitate toward using it as simple file storage (remember, though, that Blob Storage isn't a file share; to implement file shares, you'd need to use File Service). As Blob Storage supports virtual directories, you can easily structure it in a way that limits access to various folders depending on the assigned role of a principal (user or application). As Blob Storage is simple to provision and set up, it's often tempting to just allow access to it by anyone with a link to a file. Let's see whether there's an alternative to that approach.

Generating URLs to files stored in Blob Storage

Let's consider the following scenario – you have an application that allows a user to upload a file. A user uploads it, and your backend service takes that file and places it in Blob Storage. Then, a user would like to share a file. The easiest option would be to get the download URL from the Blob service and just allow the user to use it. While such a solution may work in simple applications, in serious business applications, such an approach may cause some serious problems:

- You have no control over who accesses a file.
- You can't implement rate limiting for people accessing the files.
- You have no way of revoking access to a file.
- You can gather statistics about people and services accessing the file.

> **Note**
>
> In theory, you could implement all the preceding points by forcing a user to send a request through some kind of gateway (proxy). While it may be achievable in corporate scenarios, for public applications used by external users, it will be very difficult to achieve.

To overcome those challenges, a much better option would be to generate a URL to a file on your own and send it to a user. See *Figure 13.20* for an explanation.

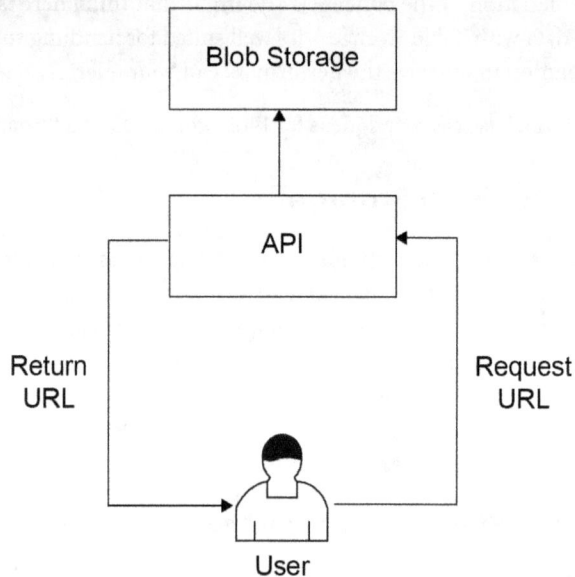

Figure 13.20 – Generating URL for a user to a file with an additional call to an API

Of course, those download URLs generated by an API could be generated beforehand (e.g., when a file is saved to Blob Storage). It's actually up to you to decide how you'd like to have it implemented. Once the URL is generated, a user will send a request that will go through your infrastructure (it could be routed through the API itself or an additional component if needed).

Choosing between change feed and Azure Event Grid events

When it comes to listening to changes happening in Blob Storage regarding stored data, there are two options available:

- Using the change feed described in this chapter
- Integrating with Azure Event Grid events

Both solutions allow you to avoid unnecessary pooling of Blob Storage itself and can improve the performance of your application. There's a slight difference though in the architecture they offer – while the change feed expects you to listen to it to get the changes, Azure Event Grid can be used to push events to the endpoints that are exposed by your application. While conceptually they may look alike, the implementation for those two solutions is quite different:

- Change feed doesn't require an additional Azure service to work.

- With change feed, all the changes are stored inside append blobs, which can be used by other data processing pipelines.

- Change feed has a bigger delay in data delivery when compared with Azure Event Grid, hence if your application expects to process messages as quickly as possible, the latter is a better choice.

- Azure Event Grid offers a simpler implementation when compared with change feed as it can work with typical HTTP endpoints. Change feed requires a separate service to be hosted with a listener reacting to the incoming messages.

- Azure Event Grid doesn't guarantee the order of the incoming events, meaning they may be out of order when they reach an endpoint. Change feed saves and delivers changes in order.

- Azure Event Grid incurs additional costs related to the service and event delivery process.

If you're interested in learning more, take a look at the following documentation explaining the topic in detail: `https://learn.microsoft.com/en-us/azure/storage/blobs/storage-blob-event-overview`.

Let's look at a few use cases now.

Learning about use cases

Azure Storage is a flexible service that is able to cover various use cases. Depending on the selected functionality, you could implement numerous different capabilities – all using a single Azure product. When deciding whether Azure Storage is the best match for your scenario, you will need to compare what this service offers with the available alternatives. Let's see how you could learn more about individual products offered by Azure Storage and what the additional resources are for improving your understanding of that service.

Using Table Storage as a database

Table Storage, as a non-relational database, has limited usability when used to handle relational data. However, with a proper design, it's possible to cover even such scenarios. The best place for learning more about that approach is by checking the Azure Storage documentation for the Table Storage service available here: `https://learn.microsoft.com/en-us/azure/storage/tables/table-storage-design-modeling`. That article explains in detail how one could model relationships and even implement inheritance. Also, make sure you understand how to properly query and modify data:

- `https://learn.microsoft.com/en-us/azure/storage/tables/table-storage-design-for-query`
- `https://learn.microsoft.com/en-us/azure/storage/tables/table-storage-design-for-modification`

Those additional resources should help you become proficient with Table Storage and use it with confidence.

Using Blob Storage as storage

Blob Storage is useful if you work with unstructured data. You could use it as either the final storage for your application (for instance, to store files uploaded by your customers or reports generated by your application) or an intermediary (staging) storage for data processing pipelines. It's a good idea to check the architecture best practices for that service, available here: `https://learn.microsoft.com/en-us/azure/well-architected/service-guides/azure-blob-storage`. Reading that article will improve your understanding of how various use cases apply when Blob Storage is used.

Using Queue Storage as a simple queue

Queue Storage offers quite a robust solution for implementing a queue for your service. Even though it has its limitations (as described in the chapter), it's still a viable choice for less critical workloads or communication between services where ordering isn't required. If in doubt, make sure you have gone through the following article: `https://learn.microsoft.com/en-us/azure/service-bus-messaging/service-bus-azure-and-service-bus-queues-compared-contrasted`. It will help you understand the differences between queues in Azure and make a better decision when choosing a queue solution for your application.

Summary

In this chapter, we discussed Azure Storage, which is a generic storage solution offered by Microsoft Azure. We focused on two components that are offered by this service: Table Storage and Blob Storage. They are very popular in application development and are widely used in many different scenarios.

We discussed how Table Storage differs from typical relational databases and how important proper data design is to get the most from the service itself. You learned how data is automatically indexed with `Primary Key` and `Row Key` columns and what patterns are useful in keeping the performance as high as possible.

When talking about Blob Storage, we considered its virtual directories as a logical way to separate and secure stored data. We mentioned various available blob types, which are selected depending on the use case. What's more, we considered the change feed as a great addition to implementing logic, which needs to react to changes happening to a blob.

In the next chapter, we will discuss queues available in Microsoft Azure, including Queue Storage, Azure Event Hub, and Azure Service Bus.

Summary

14

Using Queues in Microsoft Azure

When designing a system, you often need to decouple one service from another. Such an approach is useful if you want to secure endpoints from extensive loads, make sure incoming requests are not lost in case of an error, or control how they are processed. To implement such an architecture, you may use queues, which are a popular and well-known solution for asynchronous communication.

This chapter is dedicated to describing three separate Azure services that offer queue capabilities – **Queue Storage**, **Azure Event Hubs**, and **Azure Service Bus**. In this chapter, you will learn about various use cases, unique features, and limitations of each of those services. The knowledge provided will help you in implementing your own queue and processing messages in a reliable and performant way.

In this chapter, we're going to cover the following main topics:

- Using Queue Storage in Microsoft Azure
- Choosing Azure Event Hubs for queues with high load
- Implementing enterprise-grade queues with Azure Service Bus
- Learning about use cases

Technical requirements

To perform the exercises in this chapter, you will need the following:

- The Azure CLI
- An IDE (preferably Visual Studio Code)

Using Queue Storage in Microsoft Azure

In the previous chapter (*Chapter 13*), we started discussing Azure Storage and two of its services – Table Storage and Blob Storage. In this chapter, we will discuss the third service – Queue Storage. As mentioned in *Chapter 13*, if you want to use any of the available Azure Storage services, you just deploy a storage account (an instance of Azure Storage) and start integrating it from your application. With Queue Storage, nothing changes – you'd still need an instance of Azure Storage to start working with queues. For a reference on how to create your storage account, take a look at the information provided in *Chapter 13*.

Before we start discussing the technicalities of Queue Storage, let's describe its capabilities and limitations:

- It is part of Azure Storage.
- Its pricing is based on the amount of data sent and processed using Queue Storage queues.
- It supports the same authentication mechanism as the rest of Azure Storage services (access keys, SAS tokens, and managed identity).
- It supports messages with a size up to 64 KiB.
- A single queue cannot exceed 500 TiB.
- A single queue has a maximum throughput of 2,000 messages per second (assuming the size of a message does not exceed 1 KiB).
- A single storage account performance cap is 20,000 messages per second.
- It doesn't support more advanced messaging patterns, such as topics, various receive modes, transactions, or deduplication. If you're not familiar with those patterns, you'll find descriptions later in the book when we discuss Azure Service Bus.
- Replication of data stored inside queues follows the same patterns as the Azure Storage service itself, meaning messages could be replicated globally if such replication is selected.
- Messages can be configured so they never expire, though the default expiration time is seven days.
- It doesn't have **First-In, First-Out** (**FIFO**) guarantees, though most of the time messages are processed in order.

As you can see, Queue Storage follows the general concept of Azure Storage, being a rather simple but specialized service. It has its limitations, which may have quite an impact in some applications (for instance, the maximum size of a message), but often those limitations can be mitigated with a proper design. Let's now discuss the structure of Queue Storage to learn about the most important concepts.

Learning about the structure of Queue Storage

The structure of Queue Storage consists of two major concepts:

- A **queue**

- A **message**, which is placed inside a queue

The concepts are visualized in *Figure 14.1* for a better understanding.

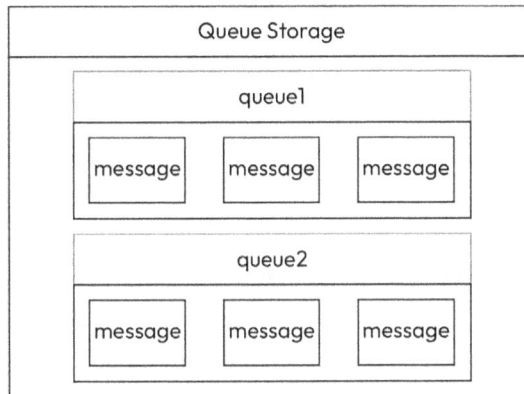

Figure 14.1 – General structure of Queue Storage

When creating queues, the important thing to remember is naming limitations – each queue name must be in lowercase and can consist of alphanumerical characters only. A name must be between 3 and 63 characters long. A queue can be created using the Azure portal, the Azure CLI, Azure PowerShell, or management SDKs. You could also use an infrastructure-as-code approach using Terraform.

> **Note**
>
> As queues are part of the data plane of Azure Storage, you can't use ARM templates or Azure Bicep to create them. Terraform, however (when using the AzureRM provider), uses a different API to interact with this service. Hence, it can create blobs and queues while interacting with the infrastructure of Azure Storage.

Let's now discuss what useful commands and packages are to work with Queue Storage using either the command line or the application's code.

Interacting with Queue Storage using the CLI and SDK

While it's possible to work with Queue Storage using the Azure portal, for automation and actual integration, you will need to use either a CLI or SDK. When it comes to an SDK, you will need to choose one that is supported by your programming language:

- **.NET**: `https://learn.microsoft.com/en-us/dotnet/api/overview/azure/storage?view=azure-dotnet`
- **Java**: `https://learn.microsoft.com/en-us/java/api/overview/azure/storage?view=azure-java-stable`
- **Python**: `https://learn.microsoft.com/en-us/python/api/overview/azure/storage?view=azure-python`
- **JavaScript**: `https://learn.microsoft.com/en-us/javascript/api/overview/azure/storage?view=azure-node-latest`

The packages listed in the aforementioned list give you access to the data plane of Queue Storage. If you'd like to manage the service itself, there are separate libraries offered by Microsoft:

- **.NET**: `https://learn.microsoft.com/en-us/dotnet/api/overview/azure/resourcemanager.storage-readme?view=azure-dotnet`
- **Java**: `https://learn.microsoft.com/en-us/java/api/overview/azure/storage/management?view=azure-java-archive`
- **Python**: `https://learn.microsoft.com/en-us/python/api/overview/azure/storage?view=azure-python#management`
- **JavaScript**: `https://learn.microsoft.com/en-us/javascript/api/overview/azure/storage?view=azure-node-latest#management`

If you want to use a different language to interact with Queue Storage, it will still be possible using the REST API offered by the service:

- **Data plane**: `https://learn.microsoft.com/en-us/rest/api/storageservices/queue-service-rest-api`
- **Control plane**: `https://learn.microsoft.com/en-us/rest/api/storagerp/`

As you can see, there are multiple possibilities depending on your use case and technology stack. When using those libraries, remember that they will require different access levels depending on the operation you're performing. If you authenticate using your Azure credentials (whether it's your personal account or managed identity), you will need to configure a different set of permissions depending on the context of the operations (control versus data plane).

You can read more about available in-built roles and assigning them in the documentation: `https://learn.microsoft.com/en-us/azure/storage/queues/assign-azure-role-data-access`. Examples that present interacting with Queue Storage are available in the repository, in the folder dedicated to *Chapter 14*.

Let's now talk about the messages themselves when transferring them over Queue Storage.

Sending messages with Queue Storage

As mentioned at the beginning of this chapter, each queue in Queue Storage supports messages up to 64 KiB in size. The question of whether it is enough depends on the business case you'd like to cover. For small payloads consisting of only a few fields, 64 KiB will be more than enough. For complex messages or binary formats, 64 KiB will definitely be too small. Another limitation is the content of the message itself. Queue Storage requires that all messages be included in XML requests with UTF-8 encoding. If that's not possible, the encoding of a message must be set to Base64 to make it compliant with this requirement.

Unfortunately, whether we use Base64 or not, it doesn't solve the issue of the message size being limited to 64 KiB. If we don't want to change Queue Storage to another service (which is a reasonable reason considering the simplicity and affordable pricing of Azure Storage), we need to find a way to make a message smaller in size. To do that, you could use one of the data compression algorithms (discussing them in more detail is, unfortunately, beyond the scope of this book). Some notable examples include the following:

- **Run-Length Encoding (RLE)**
- **Burrows-Wheeler Transform (BWT)**
- Combination of RLE and BWT

> **Note**
> Any text-to-text compression would work to overcome the limitation of Queue Storage. The algorithms listed here are not the only viable possibilities.

Another idea to overcome the limitation is combining Queue Storage with another Azure Storage service, such as Table Storage or Blob Storage. See *Figure 14.2* for a visualization.

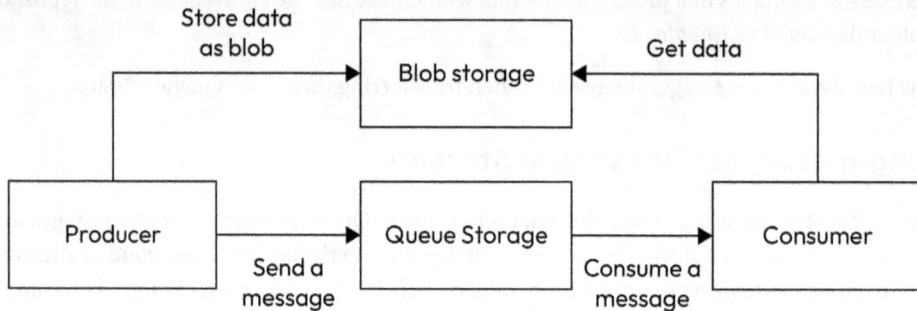

Figure 14.2 – Overcoming the message size limitation in Queue Storage using Blob Storage

The process presented in *Figure 14.2* could be explained as follows:

1. A producer saves the actual data in Blob Storage and obtains a handle (identifier) for a file.
2. Then, the producer sends a message with a file handle using Queue Storage.
3. A consumer consumes the message and obtains the file handle.
4. Using the file handle, the consumer can get the data, which would normally exceed 64 KiB.

While the explained approach may look complicated, it has its use cases in many scenarios, especially where an alternative solution requires implementing new architecture or deploying much more expensive queue services. It could be applied to both Blob Storage and Table Storage depending on your needs. It also allows for batching messages, as explained in the next section.

Sending batches with Queue Storage

By design, Queue Storage doesn't support sending and receiving batches of messages. Sure, you can tell Queue Storage how many messages you'd like to receive at once, but this approach is limited to a maximum of 32 messages received within a single operation. If you aim at much higher throughput, you need to find a way to overcome another limitation.

The idea presented in the previous section will come in handy when trying to send and receive more than 32 messages at once. If you save your data inside Table Storage or Blob Storage (or any other service that allows you to do so – it could even be a SQL database), you could send only handles/identifiers as a single message and then parse them on the consumer's side.

The concept is presented in *Figure 14.3*.

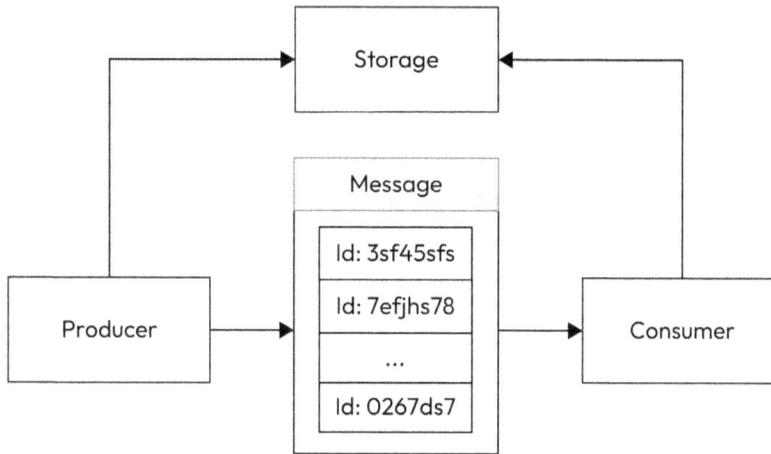

Figure 14.3 – Processing a batch of messages with a single message

The concept here is quite simple:

1. A producer saves data first using the selected storage solution and collects handles/identifiers, which can be used by a consumer when a queue message is consumed.

2. The handles/identifiers are placed inside a message – the number of those items depends on the requirements and the expected throughput for both the producer and consumer.

3. The consumer consumes a message and parses it so it can get the actual data from the storage solution selected for the process.

Using the approach described, you could start processing batches of hundreds of messages. While technically you'd process a single Queue Storage message at a time, in reality, the message would link to a huge volume of data to be processed further by a consumer.

Let's discuss now how to ensure that data is processed in the correct order when using Queue Storage.

Ensuring the proper order of messages

We mentioned at the beginning of this chapter that Queue Storage doesn't have guarantees for the order of messages sent through the queue implemented with that service. While not all applications require ordering guarantees (if that is the case, you can just start using the service), some need to ensure that messages are processed in the order they were sent (FIFO). Under normal circumstances, messages delivered by Queue Storage should be delivered in the order they appeared in a queue. However, there are some rare cases (such as a consumer's process crashing, which causes a message to reappear on a queue), where a message can be placed on a queue out of order. If you need to secure your application from such a situation, there are three ideas that may be helpful:

- Check the `DequeueCount` property of a message. If it's greater than `1`, you may assume a message is out of order because previous processing failed.

- Store the state of consumed messages and compare it upon receiving a new message – this solution may be quite complex as it requires not only storing the state but also providing a performant way to query it. In-memory cache such as Redis may be helpful but it could also be quite expensive if the state needs to be persisted and replicated.

- Each message comes with a concept called a **pop receipt**. Pop receipts allow a consumer to delete a message once it is processed. If a pop receipt no longer works, it means the message was processed by another consumer. Note that this method only works if two consumers process the same message concurrently – it won't work in a scenario where message processing fails.

If none of the solutions satisfies you, you may need to consider using Azure Service Bus instead of Queue Storage.

Understanding how messages are processed with Queue Storage

Message processing with Queue Storage is quite easy when compared with other queue solutions, such as Azure Service Bus. In general, it looks like this:

1. A producer sends a message.
2. The message is placed on the queue and replicated locally/globally.
3. A message is received by a consumer – it becomes hidden until a consumer confirms it was processed correctly.
4. If the consumer fails to process a message, it's enqueued once again and available for reprocessing.

As Queue Storage is a typical queue, it doesn't allow multiple consumers to read the same message at the same time. Different consumers could consume the same message only if they fail to process it once it's consumed. It's also worth mentioning that it's up to the consumer to delete a message from a queue once it's done processing it. This is done using a pop receipt, which is generated individually each time a message is dequeued. What's interesting is that the pop receipt must be used within a timeframe called the **visibility timeout**, which can be individually set for each message. If a consumer fails to delete a message before it becomes visible again, it may not be able to delete it using the original pop receipt. This happens if the message processing takes too long, so it becomes visible and gets consumed by another consumer. In that case, another consumer may be able to delete it using its own pop receipt.

As we have learned lots of concepts related to Queue Storage, let's now switch our focus to another queue solution, which is Azure Event Hubs.

Choosing Azure Event Hubs for queues with high load

In the previous section, we discussed the usage of Queue Storage in various queue-based scenarios. We talked about the limitations of that service, especially when it comes to the architecture of the possible solutions and the size of a message. If you find Queue Storage too limited for your scenario, you may consider an Azure service named Azure Event Hubs. Conceptually, Azure Event Hubs is another queue that can be integrated with your application. It's designed, however, to handle a much higher load, making it a great choice for applications that require streaming data rather than queueing it.

To get started, let's talk about the available features and limitations of Azure Event Hubs:

- It supports HTTP(S) and AMQP and is compatible with the Kafka protocol.

- It offers Schema Registry, which is useful for making sure messages sent through Azure Event Hubs queues are compatible with the schema used by your applications.

- It integrates with Azure Stream Analytics for real-time data processing and analytics.

- It has an in-built scaling mechanism (**Auto inflate**), which helps in properly scaling out the service when more messages come into the system.

- It offers a feature called **Capture**, which helps in data retention and further data processing (you can implement both hot and cold paths using only native features of the service).

- It allows you to host multiple consumers; hence, the same message can be processed in parallel.

- Azure Event Hubs comes with an emulator, which can be used in local development, so you don't have to deploy an instance of the service in Azure.

- It can be deployed using different tiers offering different capabilities and quotas with a message size varying from 256 KB to 1 MB and data retention from 1 day to 90 days.

As you can see, Azure Event Hubs offers a much broader set of features and capabilities. The fact that there are multiple tiers available makes this service a little bit more complicated to properly implement when compared with Queue Storage. Let's dive deeper into those tiers to understand when they should be selected and what the best use of them is.

Understanding the tiers of Azure Event Hubs

Azure Event Hubs can be deployed using one of the following tiers:

- Basic

- Standard

- Premium

- Dedicated

The main differences between these tiers are as follows:

- For the Basic tier, the maximum size of a message is 256 KB. For the rest, you can send messages up to 1 MB.

- The Basic tier allows for only a single consumer group. As consumer groups are used to process data in parallel, it means that by using that tier, you cannot implement multiple subscribers. We'll talk more about consumer groups later in the chapter.

- Data retention for the Basic tier is set to 1 day, for the Standard tier it's 7 days, and for the rest of the tiers, it's 90 days.

- Capture isn't available when using the Basic tier.

- Throughput is calculated differently depending on the tier – for the Basic and Standard tiers, it's provided via **Throughput Units (TUs)**; for the Premium tier, Event Hubs will use **Processing Units (PUs)**, while for the Dedicated tier, it uses **Capacity Units (CUs)**.

- Some additional features, such as IP firewall, geo-disaster, and virtual network integration, are available only for tiers above Basic.

When using Azure Event Hubs as a service to be integrated with your application, you will need to take into account all those differences. As the Basic tier is the most limited one, it's rarely usable in real-world scenarios (mostly because you can't make it secure enough). The most typical tier for production-ready applications is the Standard one. The more expensive tiers (Premium and Dedicated) are reserved for applications with higher performance demands.

> **Note**
> Higher tiers of Azure Event Hubs are also much more expensive. The Basic tier costs ~$11 per month, while the Premium one costs $912. The Dedicated tier is even more expensive – it costs $5,068 per month. All those prices were calculated for a single unit (TU/PU/CU) and for the Central US region. When working with Azure Event Hubs, choose the tier carefully to avoid spending too much on infrastructure capabilities you don't need.

Let's now talk about the basic architecture of Azure Event Hubs to understand how it can be integrated with an application.

Understanding the architecture of Azure Event Hubs

When it comes to using Azure Event Hubs, the main components used by it are the following:

- Namespace
- Hub
- Partition
- Message
- Consumer group

Those concepts are visualized in *Figure 14.4*.

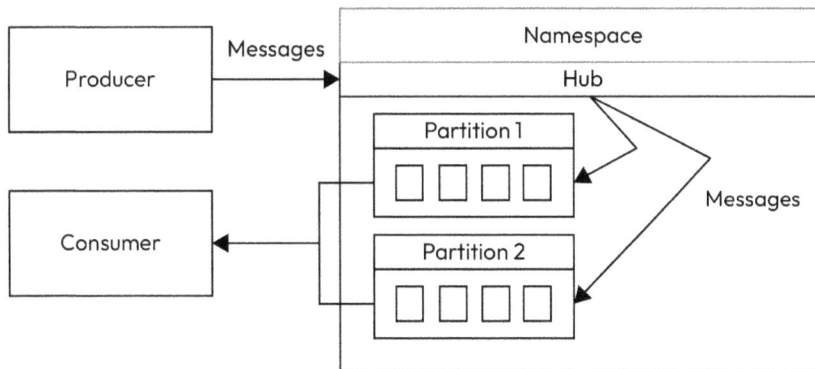

Figure 14.4 – High-level overview of the data processing process in Azure Event Hubs

The process described in *Figure 14.4* can be described as follows:

1. A consumer produces messages that are sent to a specific hub inside the Azure Event Hubs namespace.

2. A hub consists of multiple partitions (the upper limit of partitions depends on the tier of the Azure Event Hubs instance), which allows for an even distribution of messages.

3. A hub can have single or multiple consumers. Consumers may use the same or different consumer groups – the latter allows them to consume the same message multiple times.

Let's for a moment focus on the concept of **partitions**. As explained previously, each hub inside a namespace can have a specific number of partitions (32 for the Basic and Standard tiers, 100 for the Premium one, and 1,024 for the Dedicated one). Partitions are defined when a hub is created and cannot be changed later. The purpose of partitions is not only to have an even distribution of messages but also to enable connecting multiple consumers from the same consumer group. Let's look at *Figure 14.5* to understand the concept.

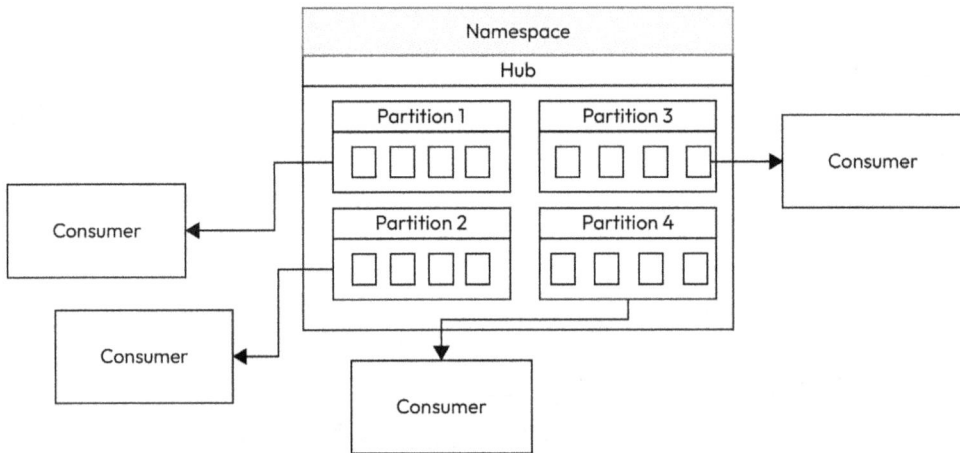

Figure 14.5 – Azure Event Hubs with four partitions and four consumers

As presented in *Figure 14.5*, you can see that we have a single hub with four partitions. Each partition is consumed by a separate consumer. Now, let's see what happens when a message is produced and placed in Azure Event Hubs:

1. A producer creates a message and sends it to Azure Event Hubs.

2. Azure Event Hubs decides on its own in which partition a message should be placed.

3. The message is enqueued on a queue represented by a partition.

4. A consumer connected to a partition consumes the message.

You may wonder what would happen if we removed one of the consumers (for instance, it crashed and hasn't reconnected again). The situation is visualized in *Figure 14.6*.

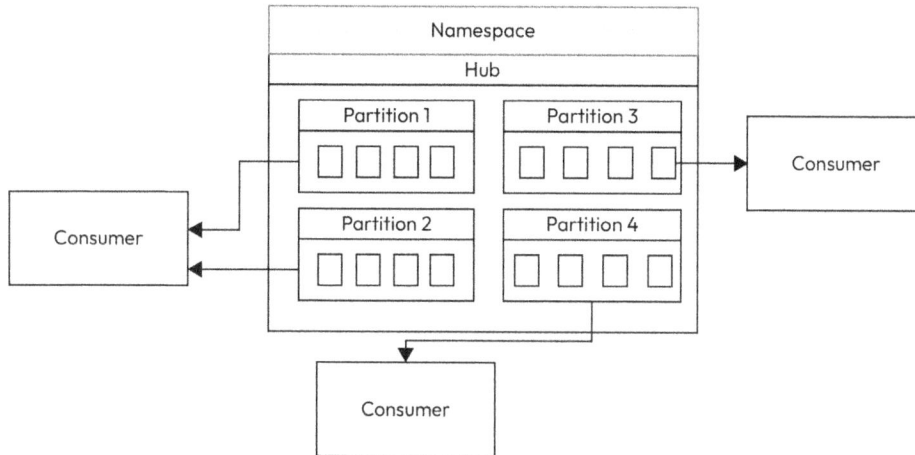

Figure 14.6 – A single consumer processing more than a single partition in Azure Event Hubs

If partitions don't have a corresponding number of consumers, the consumers start to consume partitions that are not yet connected to a consumer. Here we need to describe one more concept, which is called **partition leasing**. When a consumer begins to start consuming messages from Azure Event Hubs, it tries to create a lease for one of the available partitions. Once a partition has a lease created, it won't be assigned to another consumer unless a consumer crashes or you create new consumers, who attempt to take over the lease.

> **Note**
>
> You should avoid creating more consumers than partitions for a hub. While most of the time the SDK for Azure Event Hubs can handle those situations pretty well, many times, consumers start to compete with each other and your application will lose time on consumers switching between partitions.

The number of consumers can be adjusted dynamically – you can start with a lower number and increase it when needed. Each consumer consumes resources; hence, in lower environments (such as development or testing), which are meant to validate a solution, you should keep a smaller number of consumers to preserve resources unless you can afford to keep as many consumers as partitions.

> **Tip**
>
> Remember that lower environments may be deployed with Azure Event Hubs having fewer partitions than your production environment. While partitions are free no matter which tier is used, you may find it easier to manage if the number of partitions is kept to a minimum.

Note that from the producer's side, you may place a message on a particular partition. This approach is rarely used as it may cause the partitions to be overloaded; hence it may affect the consumer as well. However, as the order of messages is guaranteed only if they're placed on the same partition, you may find it useful to control the placement of the messages.

As the next step to better understand Azure Event Hubs, let's talk about consumer groups.

Using consumer groups in Azure Event Hubs

We mentioned at the beginning of the section describing Azure Event Hub that it's possible to process the same message multiple times using that service. To do that, we need to leverage the feature called **consumer groups**. Consumer groups may be described as *hubs inside hubs* – they allow consumers to be separated from each other so they don't affect the delivery of a message. See *Figure 14.7* for a graphical representation of the process.

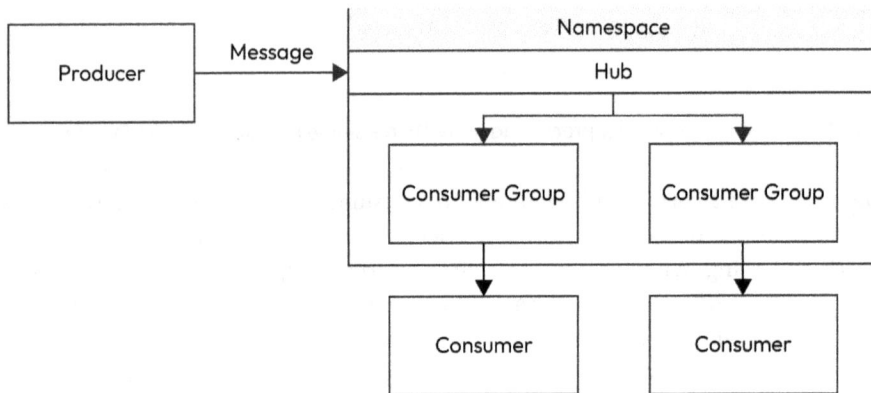

Figure 14.7 – Consumers using different consumer groups

The process of message delivery when multiple consumer groups are used looks like this:

1. A producer sends a message to Azure Event Hubs.

2. The message is multiplicated internally by Azure Event Hubs and delivered to all the consumer groups.

3. Consumers using different consumer groups get the same message delivered and can consume it without affecting other consumers.

> **Note**
>
> Using multiple consumer groups doesn't affect the placement of messages in regard to partitions.

The important drawback of using consumer groups is how they affect the throughput of your instance of Azure Event Hubs. Let's say you're using the Standard tier with 1 TU. It means that you can send up to 1,000 messages or 1 MB of data per second (whichever comes first). This calculation, however, is true only for a scenario with a single consumer group. If you're using two consumer groups, each consumer group will get up to half of the available throughput. The more consumer groups you have, the worse the throughput will be per consumer group. To achieve the same performance, you need to get X more TUs where X is the number of consumer groups configured for Azure Event Hubs.

> **Note**
>
> The way TUs are affected by the number of consumer groups is true only for the Basic and Standard tiers. As the Premium and Dedicated tiers use different units (PUs and CUs), which have no throughput quota, you can work with consumer groups without worrying about the overall performance.

A consumer group is selected by a consumer upon connecting to an instance of Azure Event Hubs. Look at the examples in the repository for *Chapter 14* to see the code in action.

As the next topic, let's talk about the feature called **Event Hubs Capture**.

Using the Event Hubs Capture feature in an application

If you want to persist messages sent through any queue, most of the time you need to consume it and save it using a storage solution of your choice. While this approach may look simple, it will affect the performance of your application (as you need to perform additional operations). Even if you find a way to delegate that additional operation to an additional process or service, you still need to make your solution more complex just to save the data. Fortunately, Azure Event Hubs comes with a specialized feature called Capture to do that work for you. Take a look at *Figure 14.8* for a visual explanation of the concept.

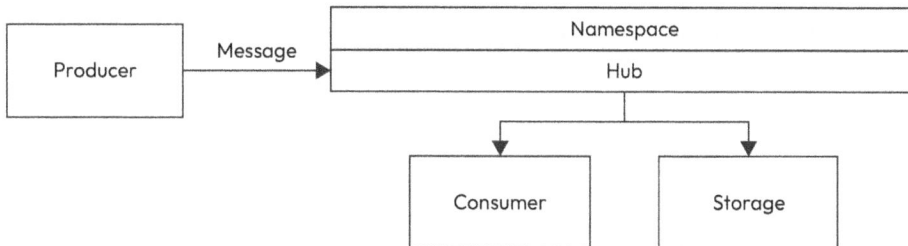

Figure 14.8 – A message delivered to a consumer with Capture enabled

What you can see in *Figure 14.8* is the following process:

1. A producer sends a message to Azure Event Hubs.

2. The message is delivered to a consumer.

3. At the same moment, Azure Event Hubs saves the message to the integrated store.

When it comes to the storage type used by Azure Event Hubs, there's not much of a choice. Once Capture is enabled, the service will integrate with Azure Storage and save messages inside blobs. Depending on whether hierarchical namespaces are enabled or not, data will be saved to either Blob Storage or Data Lake Storage.

> **Note**
> The steps needed to use Event Hubs Capture are the same for both Blob Storage and Data Lake Storage.

When data is captured, it's saved with the following convention:

```
{Namespace}/{EventHub}/{PartitionId}/{Year}/{Month}/{Day}/{Hour}/
{Minute}/{Second}
```

As you can see, the path where files are stored consists of lots of useful information – starting with the metadata of Azure Event Hubs itself. It also contains a time frame pointing to a specific point in time when a message was created. The path (or rather the format used to save data) can be adjusted depending on your needs. In the repository for this chapter, you'll find a Bicep file presenting how the format could be modified upon the creation of the service.

What's even more important, captured data is saved using the Apache Avro format. This means it's not only strongly typed but can be also integrated with lots of tools meant for big data processing without a need to implement your very own workarounds or interim services to translate it. The schema itself cannot be controlled by you, though – Event Hubs Capture comes with a predefined structure of data, so you will need to adjust to it. The schema and tools to decode it are described here: `https://learn.microsoft.com/en-us/azure/event-hubs/explore-captured-avro-files`. Look at the documentation to learn more about the feature itself and other cases for it.

As the next step, let's talk about sending batches using Azure Event Hubs, so you can increase the throughput of the data processing process.

Sending batches with Azure Event Hubs

Unlike Queue Storage, Azure Event Hubs comes with a native solution to send batches of messages. That operation is represented by a REST operation available on the service level:

```
POST \
    https://{eventBusNamespace}.servicebus.windows.net/\
    {eventHubPath}/messages
```

In fact, all data plane operations performed against Azure Event Hubs may be performed as typical HTTP requests (unless you opt in for the use of **Advanced Message Queueing Protocol (AMQP)**). A batch of messages may look like this:

```
[{"Body":"Message1"},{"Body":"Message2"},{"Body":"Message3"}]
```

For a better understanding, let's compare it with an operation sending a single message:

```
POST \
    https://{eventBusNamespace}.servicebus.windows.net/\
    {eventHubPath}/messages
{
    "Type": "Car",
    "Color": "Red"
}
```

As you can see, both operations use the same endpoint – the difference is in the payload schema used (an array of objects versus an object). There will also be a difference in the `Content-Type` header value:

- For a single message: `Content-Type: application/atom+xml;type=entry;charset=utf-8`

- For a batch of messages: `Content-Type: application/vnd.microsoft.servicebus.json`

Setting the correct `Content-Type` value will be important so Azure Event Hubs understands the data and acts accordingly.

> **Note**
>
> When using an SDK, you don't need to worry about setting the correct headers, as it's the responsibility of the SDK itself to configure them. The SDK will also select the protocol (HTTP/AMQP) depending on the connection string or endpoint you use when configuring the SDK client.

When talking about sending batches, we may revisit the solution we discussed for Queue Storage to send multiple messages at once. When using Azure Event Hubs, you need to remember that depending on the tier and configured throughput, you may hit some quotas. For instance, if you configure your hub to have 1 TU, you won't be able to send more than 1,000 messages at once. This applies also if you choose to use batches instead of individual messages. To overcome that limit, you need to choose an alternative approach:

- Compress all messages as a single message in a similar way as we did for Queue Storage.

- Use the `SendMessage` method instead of `SendBatchEvents`.

- Decompress the message once consumed by a consumer and process all the data accordingly.

The advantage of Azure Event Hubs over Queue Storage is the size of a message – even when using the Basic tier of Azure Event Hubs, we can send four times more data when compared with Queue Storage. Text compression may still be beneficial, but we could select less strict or easier-to-implement algorithms. Note that even if you choose to send a batch of messages, it's not guaranteed that those messages will be consumed at the same moment. It's because Azure Event Hubs behaves differently for input and output (it looks more like a data sink for the input and a structured log for the output).

Finding more information about Azure Event Hubs

As Azure Event Hubs offers even more features, I strongly recommend you take a look at the official documentation, which explains them in detail and suggests additional resources to improve your skills:

- Using application groups to logically group applications and services connected to the same Azure Event Hubs instance for simplified management and access control: `https://learn.microsoft.com/en-us/azure/event-hubs/resource-governance-overview`

- Implementing Schema Registry for Azure Event Hubs: `https://learn.microsoft.com/en-us/azure/event-hubs/schema-registry-concepts`

- Multi-site and multi-region federations of data processing: `https://learn.microsoft.com/en-us/azure/event-hubs/event-hubs-federation-overview`

- Geo-replication: `https://learn.microsoft.com/en-us/azure/event-hubs/geo-replication`

These links should help you understand the advanced features of Azure Event Hubs, which are useful in scenarios that require increased availability, durability of data, or simplified management. While you can use Azure Event Hubs without using any of those advanced capabilities, they will be helpful in enterprise-grade scenarios, where you work with much greater scale.

Let's now start learning about the next Azure service with queue capabilities, which is **Azure Service Bus**.

Implementing enterprise-grade queues with Azure Service Bus

Up to now, we have discussed two separate Azure services that are based on queues – Queue Storage and Azure Event Hubs. Both of these services can be used to implement messaging patterns that are useful in various applications, and while they offer various features and different limits, conceptually, they are pretty similar. The third service to be described in this chapter is Azure Service Bus. It's a service that internally shares lots of infrastructure with Azure Event Hubs (if you look at the URL of the Azure Event Hubs endpoint, you will see it contains the .servicebus suffix). From a use case perspective and the features offered, however, Azure Service Bus is quite a different service when compared with Azure Event Hubs and Queue Storage:

- It can be used to implement both queues and topics, meaning you can explicitly configure it to allow a specific messaging pattern.

- It allows for transactions, which are atomic operations consisting of multiple actions performed by consumers.

- It implements a dead-letter queue to handle problematic messages that can't be properly consumed.

- It supports scheduled delivery and message deferral to handle advanced scenarios where you want to wait until a specific point in time to deliver a message or set it aside because of existing circumstances.

- It provides a mechanism for the deduplication of messages, so identical messages are discarded. This saves processing time as consumers don't need to worry about processing the same message twice.

- By default, a queue or topic has a maximum size of 5 GB. If partitioning is enabled, the maximum size is set to 80 GB.

- Depending on the selected tier, the maximum size of a message is either 256 KB (Standard tier) or 1 MB (Premium tier).

As you can see, the number of additional and useful features in Azure Service Bus is astounding. This service is designed to help you in implementing queues, which need to support advanced and complex scenarios. The native capabilities of Azure Service Bus simplify implementation as you don't need to implement various features, such as scheduled delivery or transactions, on your own.

Let's now discuss queues and topics.

Understanding the differences between queues and topics

The easiest way to differentiate a queue and a topic is by checking whether multiple consumers can read the same message. If they do, then you're working with a topic. Topics are used to implement a publisher/subscriber pattern where a producer publishes a message and multiple subscribers consume it. Note that consumers don't always need to process the same message – in the case of Azure Service Bus, you may use **filters**, which allow you to define which messages are supposed to be delivered by which topic. We'll talk more about filters later in this section.

To understand topics better, take a look at *Figure 14.9* for a visualization.

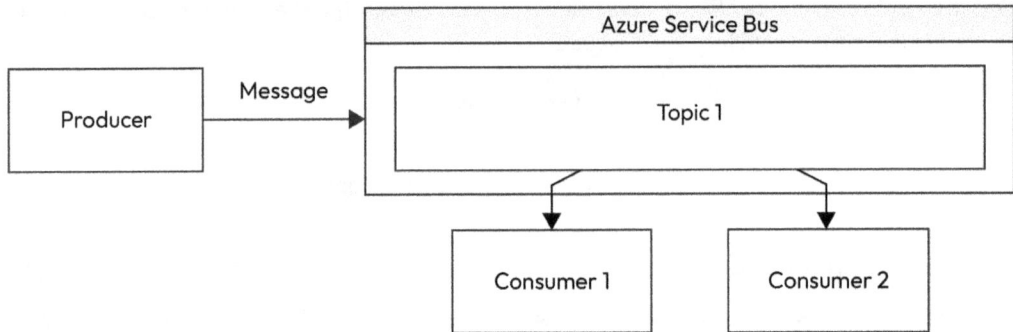

Figure 14.9 – Visualization of topics in Azure Service Bus

As presented in *Figure 14.9*, you can see each consumer is connected to the same topic. While those consumers could be connected to a single queue as well, they wouldn't be able to consume the same message at the same moment.

> **Note**
> You can think of topics as queues that multiply messages for connected consumers.

Topics in Azure Service Bus work in a different way when compared with consumer groups used in Azure Event Hub. While consumer groups used TUs defined for a hub (so you needed to increase them to keep the performance on the same level), topics don't affect the throughput of Azure Service Bus. What's more, topics support filters, which you can use to limit messages coming to a consumer. There are three types of filters available:

- SQL filter
- Boolean filter
- Correlation filter

SQL filters have their own syntax, which you can find here: `https://learn.microsoft.com/en-us/azure/service-bus-messaging/service-bus-messaging-sql-filter`. Whether you use a SQL filter, Boolean filter, or correlation filter, you need to remember two traits:

- To make filters work, you need to evaluate the message properties. Unfortunately, you can't use them to select messages based on their body.

- The more complex a filter is, the more compute power it will use to work. In other words, advanced filters will lower the overall throughput of the Azure Service Bus service.

The filters can be created using the management SDK directly from your application. Check the repository for this chapter for examples and a further explanation of the concept.

Let's talk now about the different receive modes available for Azure Service Bus.

Choosing the correct receive mode

Unlike Queue Storage and Azure Event Hub, Azure Service Bus allows you to select a receive mode to consume a message:

- Receive and delete
- Peek lock

Being able to choose a receive mode gives you flexibility when it comes to implementing a process that consumes messages. The first mode (receive and delete) is the simpler mode, which works as follows:

1. When a message is received by a consumer, it is marked as consumed.
2. If the message processing fails, it won't be consumed again.

Receive and delete mode reflects the at-most-once processing approach. It's suited for applications and services that can tolerate a message that is not fully consumed. Of course, you could reschedule a message on your own when using receive and delete mode. In that case, the processing approach would be at least once, but it's not something natively supported by this receive mode. Some examples of applications suited for using this receive mode are logs processing or services that monitor by themselves whether a message has been processed (and if not, they will just enqueue it once again).

The second receive mode, peek lock, is a little bit more complicated:

1. Each message consumption process starts with locking it so other consumers are unable to receive it.
2. Once the message is properly processed, an application notifies Azure Service Bus and asks to mark a message as consumed.

3. If an application is unable to consume a message, it has two possibilities:

- Let Azure Service Bus know to abandon a message, which makes it available for further processing by other consumers.

- Do nothing and wait until the timeout associated with a lock expires, so the message is unlocked and available to be processed again.

With peek lock mode, you can implement the at-least-once messaging pattern or, if you enable duplicate detection, you can achieve even the exactly once messaging pattern.

> **Note**
>
> Peek lock receive mode is like the way Queue Storage processes messages.

Receive mode is configured upon creating a consumer for a message or topic in your application. You can find an example of how it's done in the code examples presented in the repository for this chapter.

Remember that you should select a receive mode suited to your application. While going for a default may be tempting, receive modes have quite a significant impact on the implementation of your service. The most important question when building a queue-based system is how many times a message can be delivered. If you answer *exactly once*, then you need to use peek lock mode with duplicate detection. If your system can handle duplicates, then both modes will work (but receive and delete will require additional code to implement that pattern). Applications that can handle duplicates often integrate with a database or some other kind of storage, which allows them to see whether a message is a duplicate or not. The process is described here:

1. A consumer receives a message and decodes it.

2. Based on the properties provided by a message, a consumer checks the database for a record that represents a message (the most common approach is using a unique identifier).

3. If a record in the database is found, the message is a duplicate, hence it can be discarded.

4. If a record isn't found, a consumer creates it, starts processing a message, and notifies Azure Service Bus that processing is complete.

The aforementioned process, however, explains only the optimistic path. Let's see what happens if we add a new record but fail to process a message, hence it is processed once again. In that case, upon processing the message once again, the consumer would find the message ID in the database and discard it. The problem here is that the message was never processed correctly, and thus we may lose data because of that.

To solve that issue, you would need to implement a transaction that covers the following operations:

1. Adding a record to the database
2. Processing a message
3. Completing the message with Azure Service Bus

While it looks easy on paper, it's much more difficult to implement in a real-world scenario. Depending on the complexity of the message processing implemented in your application, reverting changes made during that process may be really difficult to do. Let's consider the following scenario – your application got a message that a customer created a new order for some products. The application is supposed to integrate with various external systems, such as a CRM, ERP, or something similar, to put an order there. Now, if message processing fails between various integrations, you have two options:

- Catch each error individually and try to revert it when an error happens.
- Complete a message even if an error happens and place a new message on a queue with the reverted outcome.

For instance, let's say that a new order integrates with a CRM to create a new customer and then fails when interacting with the ERP system. Instead of trying to delete a customer directly in your application (because we were unable to place an order and we don't want to have a customer in a CRM who has no orders), we could use another queue where we would place a message to delete a customer and mark our original message as completed from an Azure Service Bus perspective (so it doesn't get delivered again) but incomplete from our process perspective (for instance, by updating the order in the database as failed).

Messaging patterns and proper implementation of the business process with a queue get really complicated when you need to secure your application from various errors and inconsistencies. While the aforementioned example explains some of them, there's still room for improvement.

Let's talk now about how you may ensure FIFO delivery using Azure Service Bus.

Implementing FIFO with Azure Service Bus

When we discussed Azure Event Hubs, we were wondering what the solution to implementing order guarantees using that service is. While in Azure Event Hubs, we needed to point messages to the same partition so FIFO is preserved, with Azure Service Bus, we will use a different approach. To implement FIFO in Azure Service Bus, we need to use a feature called a **session**. Sessions are built in a way that ensures that multiple receivers may be connected to the same queue but still get messages in order. The concept is visualized in *Figure 14.10*.

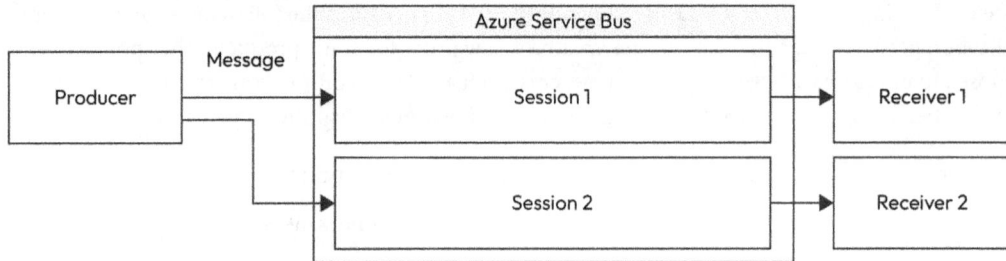

Figure 14.10 – A producer sending a message using two separate sessions used by two separate receivers

When receiving a message from a session, a receiver has two options:

- Use the session ID to point to a specific session.
- Do not use the explicit session ID so it gets assigned the first available session.

Those two options have their use cases. While not specifying a session ID may not look like a good option, if you have only one session and one receiver, you can get a FIFO guarantee with no additional code. However, as it's up to a sender to point a message to a session, you could implement separate receivers with different behavior – one consuming messages as they come and one connected to a specific session, so it consumes messages in order.

> **Note**
>
> To send a message using a session, a sender only needs to specify a session ID. There's no dedicated method or endpoint used there. A receiver, however, needs to explicitly state its intentions. A code example of the concept is presented in the repository for this chapter.

As sessions allow a producer and a consumer to communicate *directly* (by using the session ID), one more possibility opens up. In queue-based applications, you sometimes need to deliver the result of message processing to the sender. As queues decouple senders from receivers, implementing such a concept is quite cumbersome. There are various solutions to that problem (such as pooling a specific endpoint or registering webhooks).

In Azure Service Bus, you can leverage sessions to implement a pattern called **request-reply**. The pattern is visualized in *Figure 14.11*.

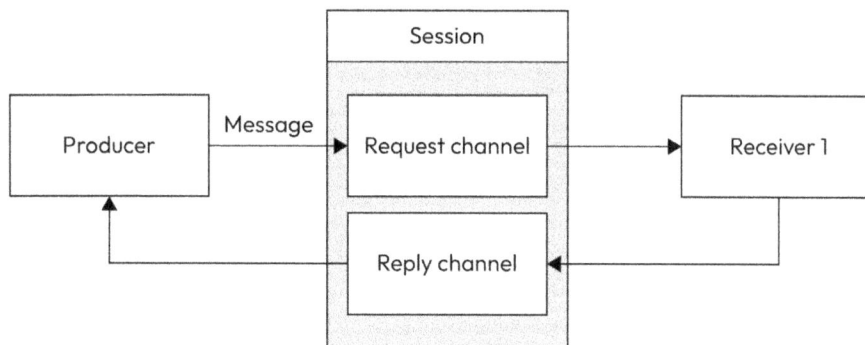

Figure 14.11 – A request-reply pattern visualized using an Azure Service Bus session

In *Figure 14.11*, you can see how both a producer and receiver communicate over two separate channels included within a single session. With this pattern, you can allow a producer to obtain a response from a receiver without implementing additional mechanisms to let them communicate. Communication here is based on using a unique session ID, which is used to listen to responses (so, in fact, what you use here is a bi-directional communication mechanism). Take a look at the repository for a code example presenting how this communication can be implemented.

In the next section, let's discuss duplicate detection in Azure Service Bus.

Implementing duplicate detection

In queue-based systems, applications sometimes fail to process a message. Depending on the messaging pattern (at least once, at most once, or exactly once), you may be challenged with duplicates coming your way. While the at-most-once and exactly-once patterns aren't bothered by duplicates, the most popular pattern, which is at-least-once, forces you to find a way to mitigate incoming duplicated messages. A **duplicated message** is a message that was placed in a queue and processed but not completed correctly. Depending on the place where processing was terminated, a duplicate may be more or less severe:

- If message processing is terminated before any action is taken, you can handle a duplicate without an additional mechanism as it can be safely retried.

- If message processing is terminated after it was partially processed, you need to take care of handling a duplicate, so the state isn't corrupted.

> **Note**
>
> A pattern that is helpful in handling duplicates is sagas: `https://learn.microsoft.com/en-us/azure/architecture/patterns/saga`. Also, durable functions are the ideal solution for handling such a scenario as their activities are executed only once per orchestration, so you could process the same message multiple times without worrying that the state will be corrupted.

Azure Service Bus comes with built-in duplicate detection, which you may find helpful if you don't want to worry about duplicates or you don't want to make your architecture more complex than necessary. It is based on checking the unique identifier of each message and is handled internally, which means that it's Azure Service Bus' responsibility to detect a duplicate. The most important thing here is managing the identifier of a message. When you publish a message, you can set its identifier to any value. While it can be any unique value, you may find it a much better fit to use something that is connected to the business process. Consider the following examples:

- `ID: 1`
- `ID: 7as6d-sd8976f-asd867sah-3234-sad12`
- `ID: customer-123/order-5623`

The first identifier is just an integer, the second one is a UUID-like string, and the third one is an identifier that combines other identifiers and matches them with business objects. While the first two may be easier to generate, without context, they provide little to no value. For duplicate detection, it's better to utilize the third identifier as it clearly states the intentions of a publisher. Semantically, it's also easier to understand the duplicate if its identifier isn't some random value.

From a technical perspective, when duplicate detection is enabled, the process looks as follows:

1. A producer sends a message with an identifier set to X.
2. The message is accepted and processed by the queue.
3. A consumer fetches the message and completes it.
4. In the meantime, a producer sends another message with the same identifier set to X.
5. Azure Service Bus accepts the message, but as the message was sent to the queue previously, it's never delivered again.

Duplicate detection works within a time window, which can be set from 20 seconds to a maximum of 7 days. Note that having a bigger window lowers the overall throughput of the queue as the more messages are stored internally for duplicate detection, the more time it takes to detect duplicates and update the state.

The feature can be enabled only when a queue or a topic is created, so it's important to validate how useful it is for you as soon as possible.

Let's talk now about the **dead-letter queue**, which is natively available for Azure Service Bus.

Handling dead-letter queues

A dead-letter queue is a subqueue that is used to store messages that the system couldn't deliver or process. There are a few scenarios in which a message is put on a dead-letter queue:

- A message reached its **Time to Live** (**TTL**).

- A message exceeded the maximum delivery count.

- An exception during processing a filter for a topic or sending a message to a topic with no subscribers.

- An explicit operation made by an application.

In Azure Service Bus, a dead-letter queue must be enabled (so it's an opt-in feature). Unlike duplicate detection, it can be enabled even when a queue or a topic is already created. To explicitly put a message on a dead-letter queue, you need to use a dedicated method from the SDK (for instance, `ServiceBusReceiver.DeadLetterMessageAsync()` in .NET).

One important thing about dead-letter queues is what to do with messages that end up there. Some companies integrate those queues with systems such as help desks, so people can be aware of issues and have an input already provided (so they can finish processing a message manually). It's also a good idea to create a metric based on the size of the dead-letter queue. Such a metric can be presented to the IT operations teams – if it grows, it means something is going wrong in the system.

Learning more about advanced features of Azure Service Bus

As Azure Service Bus is quite an extensive topic itself, we won't be able to cover all the features and capabilities. As the next step, I strongly recommend you take a look at the following links:

- SQL filter syntax: `https://learn.microsoft.com/en-us/azure/service-bus-messaging/service-bus-messaging-sql-filter`

- Message deferral: `https://learn.microsoft.com/en-us/azure/service-bus-messaging/message-deferral`

- Message prefetch: `https://learn.microsoft.com/en-us/azure/service-bus-messaging/service-bus-prefetch`

- Chaining and auto-forwarding: `https://learn.microsoft.com/en-us/azure/service-bus-messaging/service-bus-auto-forwarding`

- Transactions: `https://learn.microsoft.com/en-us/azure/service-bus-messaging/service-bus-transactions`

- How to optimize performance: `https://learn.microsoft.com/en-us/azure/service-bus-messaging/service-bus-performance-improvements`

Those additional topics will help you in getting a full understanding of the capabilities of Azure Service Bus. As they are quite advanced, you may not always find a use case for them. However, general knowledge about this service is helpful when assessing which queue is the best in your case.

To complete the description of Azure Service Bus, let's discuss how you use Azure Service Bus Explorer to help you develop your application.

Using Azure Service Bus Explorer to develop applications

When building an application that uses a queue such as Azure Service Bus, you need a way to peek at what messages are in the queue. You will also need a way to test whether a receiver works without using the producer. To help you with those tasks, you can use Azure Service Bus Explorer. That's a native feature of the Azure Service Bus instance, which is available in the Azure portal. To learn more about it, take a look at the following documentation page: `https://learn.microsoft.com/en-us/azure/service-bus-messaging/explorer`.

An alternative product to Azure Service Bus Explorer is a project named Service Bus Explorer, available on GitHub: `https://github.com/paolosalvatori/ServiceBusExplorer`. The difference between those two solutions is significant: the former is a web-based management tool for a single instance of Azure Service Bus, while the latter is a desktop application that you can use to connect to multiple Azure Service Bus and Azure Event Hub namespaces.

In the last section of this chapter, let's talk about use cases for the queues we've discussed.

Learning about use cases

In this chapter, we talked about three separate services:

- Azure Queue Storage

- Azure Event Hubs

- Azure Service Bus

Each service is a queue, which means it can be used to decouple multiple services and introduce asynchronous communication patterns. Upon closer look, however, you can see that they're quite different from each other:

- Queue Storage doesn't provide a way to have multiple subscribers for the same queue.

- Receive mode can be configured only for Azure Service Bus.

- Queue Storage offers the smallest message size out of the three described services (64 KB versus at least 256 KB for Azure Event Hubs and Azure Service Bus).

- Azure Event Hubs is designed more like a data sink with high throughput for both ingress and egress.

- Only Azure Service Bus natively supports advanced features such as sessions, transactions, and dead lettering.

- Only Azure Event Hubs and Azure Service Bus allow you to enable or implement features that guarantee FIFO.

Because of those differences, use cases for the services mentioned will be different. When choosing the right service for your needs, you need to consider the following things:

- Is a message expected to be delivered at most once, at least once, or exactly once?

- Do you expect to send batches of messages?

- What's the maximum size of a message you'd like to send?

- Do you need a dead-letter queue?

- Do you need a producer to interact with a consumer?

- Do you need to defer delivering a message?

- How would you like to handle duplicates?

- Do messages need to be delivered in order?

These questions should be helpful in choosing the right solution for your needs. While batches are natively supported only by Azure Event Hubs, you may implement them with other services as well. Dead-letter queue is supported natively only for Azure Service Bus but can also be easily implemented for Queue Storage. If you require FIFO from your queue, the available options are Azure Event Hubs (when explicitly selecting a partition) or sessions in Azure Service Bus. Deferring message delivery is only available with Azure Service Bus. The same is true for producer-communication communication, which natively works only when you choose Azure Service Bus.

Use cases for those queues are as follows:

- **Queue Storage**: Less critical workloads with no hard requirements on message order. It's a cheap and simple service that can be used to quickly get started with your work. An example of such a service is log aggregation.

- **Azure Event Hubs**: Systems requiring high throughput and near-real-time processing. This service is often used in IoT or mobile scenarios where you have lots of clients connecting to a queue and producing semi-structured data.

- **Azure Service Bus**: Queues focused on durability and handling complex business cases. Azure Service Bus is useful in scenarios such as processing orders and documents or integrating external systems.

The golden rule here is to always assess a service before selecting it. Bear in mind that in scenarios that require network isolation, the cost of a service will be much higher as those networking features are rarely available in the lower tiers.

To help you better understand the use cases for these services, here are some architecture ideas you may find useful for more information about messaging in Azure:

- Stream processing with Azure Databricks: `https://learn.microsoft.com/en-us/azure/architecture/reference-architectures/data/stream-processing-databricks`

- Transactional Outbox pattern with Azure Cosmos DB: `https://learn.microsoft.com/en-us/azure/architecture/reference-architectures/data/stream-processing-databricks`

- Pipes and filters pattern: `https://learn.microsoft.com/en-us/azure/architecture/patterns/pipes-and-filters`

Now, let's summarize what we have learned and see what's going to be discussed in the next chapter.

Summary

In this chapter, we discussed three separate services – Queue Storage, Azure Event Hubs, and Azure Service Bus. We talked about the overall approach to implementing queue-based applications and the challenges they may pose. We compared these services to see what scenarios they're applicable to.

We saw how you can implement sending batches using Queue Storage and Azure Event Hubs. When discussing advanced scenarios, we used Azure Service Bus to provide a native way to ensure the ordering of messages, bi-directional communication, and duplicate detection. The knowledge from this chapter will be helpful in choosing the right queue for your application and asking the right questions during implementation. Remember that queue-based systems are much more demanding in terms of design while also less forgiving. Take your time when working with them to avoid mistakes.

In the next chapter, we're going to see what the options for relational databases in Azure are. We'll focus on describing Azure SQL and managed PostgreSQL and see whether they change from the versions hosted on-premises.

15

Using Relational Databases in Microsoft Azure

Almost every application requires storage to store its state. While, of course, there are applications that can work without a database, for the majority of business-oriented services, you will need storage to store data. In this chapter, we will focus on relational databases offered as managed services in Azure. This will help in understanding the differences between databases provisioned on-premises and their cloud versions, so you can decide which option suits you best.

Understanding how relational databases work in cloud environments is important from both a design and implementation perspective. As you will see, there are some major differences present, so it's important to have a solution for potential challenges and limitations.

In this chapter, we're going to cover the following main topics:

- Using relational databases in Microsoft Azure
- Using alternatives to Azure SQL for a relational database
- Backing up databases
- Understanding integration options for databases in Azure
- Learning about use cases

Technical requirements

To carry out the exercises in this chapter, you will need the following:

- The Azure CLI
- An IDE of your choice (preferably Visual Studio Code)

Using relational databases in Azure

Before we get started with describing the relational databases available in Azure, let's revisit the concept of a relational database. In general, there are two types of databases:

- **Relational**
- **Non-relational**

Relational databases are designed to reflect connections and dependencies between different entities. They allow you to design a schema that reflects both physical and virtual relations between various business concepts using foreign keys. What's even more important is that once a schema is defined and implemented, a relational database will prevent breaking the data contract by rejecting changes that would not be compatible with the database schema itself.

On the market, there are many different implementations of relational databases, including the following:

- **Microsoft SQL Server**
- **PostgreSQL**
- **MySQL**
- **SQLite**
- **MariaDB**

While the features they offer may be different in detail, they are all full-blown relational databases, which can be used in both simple and advanced scenarios. When it comes to Azure, you can host any relational database by using an Azure virtual machine. As some databases can also run inside a container, you could leverage services such as Azure Container Apps or Azure Kubernetes Service to host them.

> **Note**
>
> Remember that running a database inside a container requires additional effort to not only persist its state but also make it stateful and reliable. You should approach this kind of hosting option with care that as an unstable database will heavily impact any application connecting to it.

However, in this chapter, we're going to focus on two major installations of a relational database offered as managed services:

- Azure SQL
- Azure Database for PostgreSQL

Azure also offers two additional managed database options – Azure Database for MySQL and Azure Database for MariaDB. Unfortunately, the latter is scheduled for retirement by September 2025, meaning it won't be possible to create new instances after that date and the service will drop support for existing instances.

When it comes to using a relational database in Azure, there are not many differences when compared with versions installed on-premises. Of course, there are some licensing challenges (whether you can migrate an existing license to Azure or not), but from an implementation perspective, a relational database hosted in Azure is the same as one hosted on-premises. The noticeable differences come from the hosting options and performance of the provisioned database servers. For instance, there are three different types of Azure SQL offering:

- SQL Server on Azure Virtual Machines
- Azure SQL Managed Instance
- Azure SQL Database

The first option is fully compatible with SQL Server installed on-premises. It's basically a virtual machine with SQL Server installed, meaning you can log in to the machine and manage the database server as if it were a machine within your infrastructure. Azure SQL Managed Instance is an option that abstracts away most of the infrastructure but still ensures compatibility with SQL Server. Azure SQL Database is a fully managed database server, which removes the complexity of infrastructure and provides a management layer for the whole database server so you can treat your database as you would any other managed service in Azure.

> **Note**
>
> The different options of Azure SQL are also tied to different cloud models – SQL Server on Azure Virtual Machines is considered IaaS, Azure SQL Managed Instance is PaaS, and Azure SQL Database could be defined as **Database-as-a-Service (DBaaS)**.

You may wonder how to properly select the proper Azure SQL hosting model for your application. While the answer to that question isn't simple, we could narrow down the possible scenarios so the choice becomes simpler. To get started, take a look at the following article in the documentation: `https://learn.microsoft.com/en-us/azure/azure-sql/database/features-comparison?view=azuresql`. It describes the differences between different flavors of Azure SQL, including both server-related and infrastructure-related discrepancies. Microsoft recommends using Azure SQL Database for greenfield applications, which don't have specific database requirements. That's a good choice for typical business applications – it allows you to ramp up development efforts and focus on implementing business value instead of setting up infrastructure for a database server. However, sometimes even those typical business applications require more control over the database. For instance, in Azure SQL Database, you can't initiate a backup operation on your own. If you require 100% control over that process, you may need to consider using Azure SQL Managed Instance instead.

Another big difference is cross-database queries/transactions. Those are also not available in Azure SQL Database. While the need for such a feature may depend on the architecture of your system (such transactions are often implemented in monolithic applications and are rarely applied in microservices), understanding the differences will help you make the right choice to avoid reimplementing database integration in the future.

Let's also look at the difference when creating a database using the CLI. Here's an example of how Azure SQL Database is created using the Azure CLI:

```
az sql server create \
--name <server-name> \
--resource-group <resource-group-name> \
--location <location> \
--admin-user <login> \
--admin-password <password>
az sql db create \
--resource-group <resource-group-name> \
--server <server-name> \
--name <database-name> \
--edition GeneralPurpose \
--family Gen5 \
--capacity 2
```

In this example, we will create an Azure SQL Database instance using the General Purpose tier with two vCores. For comparison, let's take a look at how an Azure SQL Managed Instance instance is created:

```
az sql mi create \
--admin-password <password> \
--admin-user <login> \
--name <instance-name> \
--resource-group <resource-group-name> \
--subnet <subnet> \
--vnet-name <virtual-network> \
--location <location>
az sql midb create \
-g <resource-group-name> \
--mi <instance-name> \
-n <database-name>
```

Note how for Managed Instance, you need to provide a virtual network with a subnet. That version of Azure SQL is much more focused on infrastructure when compared with Azure SQL Database, which makes its management more complicated. While it's not as difficult as when using a virtual machine, an additional layer of complexity should be considered when selecting it for your application.

> **Note**
>
> It's worth mentioning that Azure SQL Managed Instance offers much better performance, but it's also a much pricier option. If you opt for that type of Azure SQL database, make sure you're utilizing its capabilities.

Even though multiple flavors of Azure SQL exist and need to be evaluated when designing an application, once the choice is made, it will make no difference to your application (at least based on the code needed to integrate with a database). The same is applicable to other products representing a relational database – it shouldn't be noticeable on most applications if they are connected to a cloud version of a database instead of one run on-premises. So, what's the actual difference when using relational databases hosted in Azure? Let's discuss this in the next section.

Adjusting an application to work with a managed relational database

Even though many applications wouldn't be affected by changing a database from one hosted on-premises to a managed one, you should understand the possible issues if the databases aren't compatible. The first possible problem is the difference in performance between databases. For example, Azure SQL Database offers two different purchasing tiers:

- **DTU-based**
- **vCore-based**

A **Database Transaction Unit** (**DTU**) is an artificial metric used to indicate how much CPU and memory will be available for a database. The metric isn't fixed – the actual performance provided depends on the service tier selected:

- 1-4 IOPS per DTU for Basic and Standard tiers
- >25 IOPS per DTU for the Premium tier

This difference may cause issues when deploying a database with a different tier depending on the environment. For instance, you may select the Basic tier for non-production scenarios and Premium for the production instance. The same workload might work fine in the Premium tier but fail for the Basic or Standard one. An even trickier scenario is when there's no stable performance provided as the same amount of DTUs may provide different performance:

- 100 DTUs is equal to 400 IOPS
- 100 DTUs is equal to 100 IOPS

This means that your application may experience performance issues from time to time as the available performance occasionally decreases. To deal with that issue, you'd need to either increase the tier (so you get more IOPS than required for your applications) or change the purchasing model to vCore.

The vCore-based purchasing model is much closer to a typical on-premises SQL database as it allows you to select how many vCores (and memory) you need. It also comes with different tiers (General Purpose, Business Critical, and Hyperscale), which all provide different performance:

- 320 IOPS per vCore in General Purpose

- 4,000 IOPS per vCore in Business Critical

- Up to 327,680 IOPS for Hyperscale, which will depend on the workload

Because of these differences, it may be difficult to migrate a legacy application to Azure SQL Database as it will be challenging to select a proper tier. It's possible (with proper testing), but generally speaking, it's much easier to choose a tier for a greenfield application rather than finding the correct value for something that previously worked with on-premises SQL Server.

> **Note**
> You can read more about a benchmark used to determine a value for a DTU here: `https://learn.microsoft.com/en-us/azure/azure-sql/database/dtu-benchmark?view=azuresql`.

The second challenge when moving from an on-premises version of a SQL database to Azure is when your application depends on certain features available only for standalone Microsoft SQL Server. As the list of these features is quite lengthy, we're not going to include it in this chapter. For a reference, check out the following link: `https://learn.microsoft.com/en-us/azure/azure-sql/database/transact-sql-tsql-differences-sql-server?view=azuresql#t-sql-syntax-not-supported-in-azure-sql-database`.

However, remember that Azure SQL Database is just one of three different options available for a SQL database in Azure. If you need features that are not supported for that Azure service, you still have Azure SQL Managed Instance or SQL Server on Azure Virtual Machines. Choosing those options will pose other challenges (such as managing the infrastructure or the database), but regarding the database migration, you won't need to rewrite your application.

Let's talk now about one more feature of Azure SQL that may impact your application – **serverless compute**.

Using serverless compute in Azure SQL

The serverless compute option for Azure SQL Database is available only if you select the vCore purchasing model. Each SQL database in that model is divided into two components:

- Compute

- Storage

The general concept for a serverless database is as follows – the compute part is deallocated after a certain time if a database isn't used. The storage part is safely persisted, so the data stored there isn't lost. The benefit of a serverless SQL database is that it could potentially provide some cost savings. How much money would be saved depends on the utilization of the database. The problem with a serverless database, however, comes from the fact that the database needs to be re-allocated when you need it again. Even though the process doesn't take much time (it could be a few or more seconds), the database isn't available during that process. Look at *Figure 15.1* for a visualization.

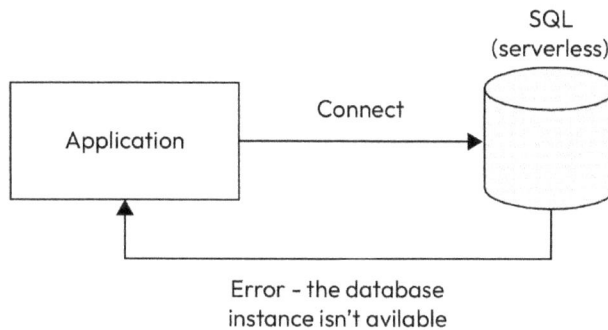

Figure 15.1 – Error when connecting to a serverless instance of Azure SQL that has deallocated

As the database is just starting (because we made a connection), we need to handle that within an application, so it's treated as a transient error. *Figure 15.2* depicts the concept visually.

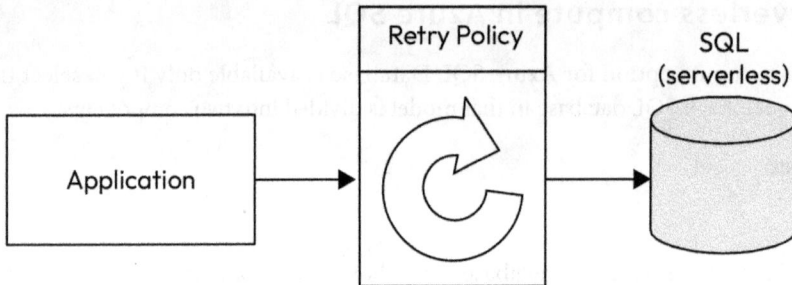

Figure 15.2 – Connecting to a serverless instance of Azure SQL Database with a retry policy

The retry policy presented in *Figure 15.2* will take care of retrying the connection when the serverless instance starts. From the user's/application's perspective, the first call will take much longer (as the database is not yet ready) and then, once the database is available, the rest of the operations will happen as usual.

The time needed for a database to go idle can be configured when an instance is created or on an existing instance:

```
az sql db create \
-g <resource-group-name> \
-s <server-name> \
-n <database-name> \
-e GeneralPurpose \
--compute-model Serverless \
-f Gen5 \
--min-capacity 0.5 \
-c 2 \
--auto-pause-delay 60
```

The aforementioned command would create a serverless Azure SQL Database with two cores (the -c parameter), a minimum capacity of 0.5 vCores (how many cores are allocated from the beginning of the database isn't paused), and an auto-pause delay of 60 minutes.

When working with a serverless option for the SQL database, you need to consider the usage patterns for it. While your application may rarely connect with the database, you could have additional features, such as database jobs or data processes, which constantly pool it. This would mean that even though you selected the serverless tier, you're unable to use and utilize it.

> **Note**
> Choosing the right value for an auto-pause delay heavily depends on your use case and the behavior of your system. Like with DTUs, it's best to properly test the application and the database to get the right result.

One more important topic to discuss here is scaling out and scaling up databases. Let's take a look.

Performing scaling operations with Azure databases

Databases such as Azure SQL, Azure Database for PostgreSQL, and Azure Database for MySQL offer a standard feature of scaling out or in and scaling up or down to allow a user to adjust a database's performance depending on the actual utilization. Depending on your service of choice and its tier, you may have different options available when it comes to performing that operation. We will start with Azure SQL as it offers the most sophisticated scaling model.

Scaling Azure SQL

We mentioned that Azure SQL offers two separate purchasing models – DTU-based and vCore-based. The choice of a specific purchasing model not only affects the performance offered and the cost of a database; it also changes the way a database can be scaled and what happens once the scaling operation is finished. It's important to remember that scaling up or down will always cause a brief disruption in connection with a database. This happens because that operation requires changing the underlying virtual machine and configuring it with more (or less) CPU and memory. If you plan to perform such an operation, you should always plan for it, so users of your application aren't affected. If you're unable to perform the operation outside of the core hours applicable to your application, you should ensure the application can handle a brief disconnection from the database. This can be achieved with several patterns, such as the following:

- Proper retry policy, which treats disconnection as a transient error and just retries the operations

- Circuit breaker, which terminates any attempts to connect to a database until it's disabled

- Maintenance window, which prevents users from using the application

Potentially, you could also leverage multiple replicas of a database. If your database is replicated, you could just switch your application from one instance to another, perform a scale-up or scale-down operation, and then restore the normal configuration of the application.

Note that Azure SQL doesn't support a typical scale-out or scale-in operation. Changing the number of resources allocated to an instance of a database is considered a scale-up or scale-down operation, with all the risks described previously.

> **Note**
> It's worth mentioning that performing the scale operation in Azure SQL is done in a safe way; that is, once you initiate the operation, Azure attempts to set up a different instance for you, and only once it's ready will the connections be initiated against it. If the operation fails, the original instance is unaffected.

Some alternatives to a typical scaling up or down operation include the following:

- **Read scale-out**: `https://learn.microsoft.com/en-us/azure/azure-sql/database/read-scale-out?view=azuresql`

- **Sharding**: `https://learn.microsoft.com/en-us/azure/azure-sql/database/elastic-scale-introduction?view=azuresql`

Take a look at those links for additional details. As the next step, we will discuss how a scaling operation can be performed in Azure Database for MySQL and Azure Database for PostgreSQL.

Scaling Azure Database for PostgreSQL and Azure Database for MySQL

Both Azure Database for PostgreSQL and Azure Database for MySQL follow the same pattern for scaling up and down. As a DTU-based purchasing model isn't available for them, you can change the performance of those databases by changing the number of vCores available or the compute tier (General Purpose, Business Critical, or Memory Optimized). Both services are affected by the scaling operation in the same way as Azure SQL, meaning you need to apply the same safeguard for an application, which uses them as data storage.

Azure Database for PostgreSQL offers one additional feature that may be useful in scenarios where your database gets bigger and bigger and you find it difficult to manage its size. The feature is called **autogrow** and can be enabled for both new and existing servers. Conceptually, it automatically resizes your database when it reaches at least 90% of its maximum capacity (or the available space is less than 64 GB) for databases bigger than 1 TB and at 80% of its maximum capacity (or less than 64GB). You can read more about it here: `https://learn.microsoft.com/en-us/azure/postgresql/flexible-server/how-to-auto-grow-storage`.

Let's now talk about the alternative options to Azure SQL, which are available as managed databases in Azure.

Using alternatives to Azure SQL for a relational database

As mentioned at the beginning of this chapter, Azure offers four different managed relational databases:

- Azure SQL
- Azure Database for PostgreSQL

- Azure Database for MySQL

- Azure Database for MariaDB

If you're not satisfied with those options, you could also install any relational database on a virtual machine hosted in Azure and use it with your application. The important thing here is that other databases than Azure SQL offer much fewer features in general (as Azure SQL is considered a first-class citizen in the Azure environment). Still, they're a viable option if you don't need SQL Server to be hosted for your application.

Let's briefly describe how those managed services behave in Azure and what unique value they bring when selected for your project.

Using Azure Database for PostgreSQL

In Azure, there are two options available for hosting a managed version of a PostgreSQL database:

- Single server

- Flexible server

As the former option is on the retirement path, the only viable version of managed PostgreSQL is the one with more granular configuration and better management. Before we describe the differences between those two options, let's discuss how the managed version of the described database differs from the self-hosted one. Generally speaking, when going for the self-hosted option, you could either host an Azure virtual machine and install PostgreSQL there or run it on-premises. Of course, you could even use another cloud provider, or a managed service offering provided by one of your vendors. Still, those are either a managed or self-hosted version. The benefit of using managed PostgreSQL is not managing the installation by yourself. In detail, the following things won't be in your scope:

- OS patching and configuration

- High-availability setup

- Backup and restore configuration

- Monitoring

- Security hardening

For many applications (especially at the early stage of development), focusing on solving actual business problems instead of pumping money into infrastructure operations is a preferred way to move forward. This doesn't mean though that being in control of all infrastructure aspects is a bad thing. It heavily depends on the type of service, the maturity of IT operations in a company, and many other things. If you have a team that specializes in provisioning infrastructure and managing it, having a self-hosted version of PostgreSQL will make lots of sense. For smaller companies and companies that have just started with their product development (such as start-ups), the managed version will be something they will most likely go for.

A detailed comparison can be found in the documentation: `https://learn.microsoft.com/en-us/azure/postgresql/flexible-server/overview-postgres-choose-server-options`.

The main differences between the single server and flexible server options are as follows:

- Single server supports versions 10 and 11 of PostgreSQL databases, while flexible server supports versions 11, 12, 13, 14, 15, and 16.

- Flexible server uses Linux as the OS.

- PgBouncer (connection pooler) can be used only with flexible server.

- Flexible server has many more connections available (5,000 versus 1,982 for single server).

- With flexible server, you can stop the database.

For the full list of differences, visit the following documentation page: `https://learn.microsoft.com/en-us/azure/postgresql/flexible-server/concepts-compare-single-server-flexible-server`.

Conceptually, Azure Database for PostgreSQL doesn't differ much from the Azure SQL Database with vCore purchasing type. Once the database is deployed, there's very little to do when it comes to management and configuration. It depends on your application's requirements whether using PostgreSQL (both self-hosted and managed) is the right choice.

Let's now describe Azure Database for MySQL.

Using Azure Database for MySQL

Azure Database for MySQL previously offered a similar situation as Azure Database for PostgreSQL – it had two options available (single server and flexible server). As the single server option was retired on September 16, 2024, now only the flexible server can be deployed for MySQL. The service itself is a standard MySQL database hosted using Azure infrastructure, which is managed by Microsoft. As of the time of writing, Azure supports the following versions:

- `5.7.44`

- `8.0.40`

- `8.4.2` (preview)

- `9.1.0` (preview)

> **Note**
>
> The interesting thing here is that Microsoft still supports MySQL 5.7 (as requested by some customers). That version will be retired in September 2025, and customers who won't migrate to a newer version of MySQL by then will be in the paid extended support program.

Azure Database for MySQL is structured in the same way as Azure Database for PostgreSQL. This means that when it comes to selecting a tier of the service, you have three options available:

- **Burstable**
- **General Purpose**
- **Business Critical**

An interesting option is the Burstable tier. It is backed by Azure virtual machines with burstable storage, meaning it can support applications with irregular demand for resources. It's a great choice if your application has higher demand within specific hours. If you seek predictable and stable performance, though, it's better to choose the General Purpose tier over the Burstable one.

> **Note**
>
> The Burstable tier (for both MySQL and PostgreSQL) has some additional limitations when compared with the rest of the tiers. For instance, it's impossible to deploy that tier using a multi-availability zone setup. Check the differences in the documentation before making the choice: `https://learn.microsoft.com/en-us/azure/mysql/flexible-server/concepts-limitations`.

Let's now see what is planned for Azure Database for MariaDB in 2025 and whether it's still a viable choice for a managed database in Azure.

Using Azure Database for MariaDB

As of the time of writing, Azure Database for MariaDB is scheduled for retirement in September 2025. This means that beyond that date, this service will no longer be supported, and the existing instances will be deleted. In the end, if you keep your databases running under MariaDB, you will lose all the data as Microsoft has no plans to keep the instances running on customer workloads. The advised migration plan includes migrating from Azure Database for MariaDB to Azure Database for MySQL. There's a dedicated guide explaining how to do that: `https://techcommunity.microsoft.com/blog/adformysql/migrating-from-azure-database-for-mariadb-to-azure-database-for-mysql/3838455`.

Currently, it's not even possible to create a new instance of a managed MariaDB database. Still, if you want, you can install a self-hosted version and support it on your own. This is a viable option if you don't consider changing the database engine as the right solution for your workload. Having a self-hosted database also protects you from being forced to change a database because the provider isn't interested in keeping it.

Making a choice about an alternative database engine in Azure

When discussing the alternatives to Azure SQL Database, we mentioned that the available database engines share similar infrastructure and configuration options. They allow you to select the same tiers (meaning the underlying infrastructure is mostly the same), they all have an in-built backup and restore mechanism, and they share the same monitoring options (Azure Monitor). This means that there are two main choices to make when selecting a database:

- Which engine you'd like to support

- Whether you want to install the database on your own and manage the infrastructure or would prefer a managed service

The solution to the first point depends on your application. If you want to use SQL Server, you will select Azure SQL. If you want a database that doesn't require a license, you will most likely select PostgreSQL or MySQL. The managed databases offered by Azure differ mostly when we compare deployment options, availability guarantees, and overall management. From an application perspective, there are rarely features that would impact the selection of the database itself.

For the second point, the solution is a little bit more complicated. Once the database engine is selected, we need to verify whether the managed version will work with our application. As mentioned at the beginning, when we discussed Azure SQL, there may be certain features that aren't available for the managed version of databases. What's even more important, when the managed version is selected, you don't have control over the update policy for the database, security fixes, and the availability of new features. This may be important for applications that heavily depend on database access in terms of optimizations – sometimes, to optimize a query, you need to perform a series of low-level operations, very often at the OS level. Those operations wouldn't be available for the managed version of the databases.

On the other hand, managing a database is a complex process that requires people with expertise in the field. Some activities required to make the process work include the following:

- Managing the storage

- Performing and storing backups

- Implementing a process to restore a database

- Monitoring (setting up metrics, storing logs, or setting up alerts)

- Updating the database and underlying software

- Scaling up and out

- Networking

For production systems, those activities require somebody working full-time to manage all the operations. As databases are the critical component for almost all applications, you would need more than a single person (as proper support needs to be provided 24/7). One thing that would simplify those operations would be hosting a database using Azure virtual machines. This would cover at least some of the activities (such as OS updates, monitoring, authentication, and backup) and help in keeping the setup cloud-oriented.

Let's talk now about one of the most important features of any database – performing a backup and restoring a database from it.

Backing up a database

Backing up a database is one of the most important topics when working with data. Frequent and reliable backups secure an application in case of an outage or a disaster and allow for a smooth recovery from those unpleasant events. In this section, we will focus on understanding how backups are executed for managed databases in Azure and how you can use them for application development.

Selecting a type of backup

In general, we could divide backups into two categories:

- **Automated backup**: They are performed with no human interaction using a fixed schedule, which is configured upfront and adjusted whenever needed. Automated backups are the most common type of backup as they require little to no supervision.

- **On-demand backup**: They require an action performed by an administrator or a service, and most of the time are performed only when necessary (without a schedule). These are helpful if you need to save a state of a database between automated backups (for instance, you're planning to deploy a set of breaking changes to the database schema and want to restore it to the latest possible state in case things go wrong).

In the context of Azure databases, all three services (Azure SQL, Azure Database for PostgreSQL, and Azure Database for MySQL) support both types of backups.

Here are some useful resources you could use to perform a manual backup for your databases:

- **Azure SQL**: `https://learn.microsoft.com/en-us/azure/azure-sql/database/database-export?view=azuresql&source=docs`

- **Azure Database for PostgreSQL**: `https://learn.microsoft.com/en-us/azure/backup/backup-postgresql-cli#run-an-on-demand-backup`

- **Azure Database for MySQL**: `https://learn.microsoft.com/en-us/azure/mysql/flexible-server/concepts-backup-restore#on-demand-backup`

> **Note**
>
> In Azure, the preferred way for backing up databases is using automated backups. While you can run backup operations manually, it may require setting up additional resources (such as Recovery Vault), which are not covered in this book.

If you're interested in how you could configure automated backups for databases, use the following links:

- **Azure SQL**: `https://learn.microsoft.com/en-us/azure/azure-sql/database/automated-backups-overview?view=azuresql`

- **Azure Database for PostgreSQL**: `https://learn.microsoft.com/en-us/azure/backup/backup-azure-database-postgresql`

- **Azure Database for MySQL**: `https://learn.microsoft.com/en-us/azure/mysql/flexible-server/concepts-backup-restore#automated-backup`

Let's talk now about backup retention and places where backups may be stored.

Storing database backups and choosing a retention policy

The most common place to store backups for Azure databases is Azure Storage. With the use of that service, you can not only store backup files but also leverage its capability to replicate data locally and geographically. As backups are a critical part of application data (as they allow you to perform a recovery operation), they should be highly available and reliable. When choosing how backup files are replicated, you may opt for the following approach:

- Use LRS/ZRS replication for non-production environments.
- Use GRS, RA-GRS, GZRS, or RA-GZRS for the production environment.

The reason for having such a distinction is cost optimization and simplification of operations. If you have many databases used in non-production, you won't need to worry about data synchronization between paired regions (Azure Storage geo-replication supports eventual consistency only, so data may not be fully replicated once the database goes down).

> **Note**
>
> The fact that Azure Storage replicates data to the paired region may be significant if you need to design your application against certain regulations, which could prevent you from storing data in some regions. Always double-check whether the paired region is compliant with your legal requirements. If it's not, make sure you disable automated replication or select LRS replication mode for backups.

The problem of eventual consistency for backups is something that needs to be taken care of when designing an application. To understand how critical it could be for a system, let's define the **Recovery Point Objective (RPO)** metric. RPO, once defined for an application, defines how much data may be lost. The amount of data potentially lost is expressed as a time window (e.g., 10 minutes, 30 seconds, 1 hour, etc.). As Azure Storage doesn't provide a guarantee of how much time it could take to replicate data, fulfilling the RPO with that service may be difficult. To solve that issue, you would need to implement the following pattern.

The last synchronization time for Azure Storage can be found with the following Azure CLI command:

```
az storage account show \
--name <storage-account-name> \
--resource-group <resource-group-name> \
--expand geoReplicationStats \
--query geoReplicationStats.lastSyncTime
```

Once you have the value, you can calculate what the difference is between now and the timestamp provided by the command. This can be explained with the following formula:

$$time\_diff = (now - last\_sync\_time)$$

If *time_diff > RPO value*, you could potentially lose more data than is allowed for your system. To avoid such a problem, you need to constantly monitor the `lastSyncTime` property and synchronize backups manually if needed.

> **Note**
>
> If you use automated backups with Azure SQL, the storage account used to store backups isn't visible and you don't have access to it, meaning you can't control the consistency of the backups replicated geographically.

The question now is what to do if the system is unable to meet the provided RPO. In that case, you may need to handle backups manually. It's the only solution that gives you full control over the replication process and can be adjusted to specific RPO requirements.

You can read more about disaster recovery scenarios with the following links:

- `https://learn.microsoft.com/en-us/azure/azure-sql/database/disaster-recovery-guidance?view=azuresql`

- `https://learn.microsoft.com/en-us/azure/postgresql/flexible-server/concepts-backup-restore`

- `https://learn.microsoft.com/en-us/azure/mysql/flexible-server/concepts-business-continuity`

There's also one more topic related to backups, which is the **retention policy**. A retention policy is a configuration, which defines how long backups are supposed to be stored. It also implies what the potential cost of storing backups is as the longer backups are stored and the bigger they are, the more expensive they will be.

In general, we could divide backups into two additional categories:

- Point in time
- Long term

Point-in-time backups are mostly used for differential backups and backing up a transaction log of a database, though it's also possible to use them for full backups. **Long-term backups** are meant for full database backups. The typical storage duration for those backups differs from several days for point-in-time backups to years for long-term ones. Both additional categories allow you to take a different approach to a database restore operation:

- With **Point-in-Time Restore** (**PITR**), you can return a database to any point in time in the past. This is useful if you made an accidental mistake during migration, somebody broke the state of the database on purpose, or you'd like to compare what has changed since a specific point in time.

- **Long-Term Retention** (**LTR**) backups are mostly used to satisfy various legal requirements. In some cases, you need to keep backups of data for more than a year (sometimes up to 10 years). In that case, you need to create full backups, which are ideally stored in cold storage, so you can optimize storage costs.

> **Note**
> The Archive tier in Azure Storage is the ideal option for storing long-term backups of databases. The cost of storing data is low and it's highly unlikely you will need to go back to any of those backups on short notice.

Let's talk now about how backups may be used for development purposes and how to build a proper structure to store and access them.

Using backups in development scenarios

Backups are not just important when it comes to restoring your application from a potential outage or a disaster. They are also useful when you want to set up a development environment. There are two possibilities that we could consider:

- Setting up a dedicated development instance of a database in Azure
- Exporting a database and using it locally

Utilizing a dedicated instance of a database, which is hosted in Azure, is a simple and quick way to organize a proper development environment. Such a database doesn't require maintenance and can be easily created and deleted if needed. What's more, the process of creating them could be easily automated. The downside of that approach is the additional cost incurred by running instances. Some companies also gravitate toward an approach where a single database is provided for a team. If possible, try to avoid such a solution as it makes development difficult due to developers sharing the same database instance. In such a scenario, changes introduced by a single developer will impact the whole team. See *Figure 15.3* for a reference.

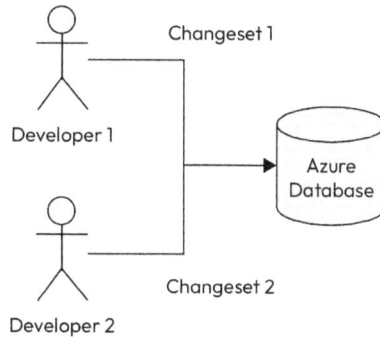

Figure 15.3 – Two developers working on two separate change sets using the same database

If you look at *Figure 15.3*, you will see that there are two developers who introduce two separate change sets to the instance of a database. If those change sets aren't compatible (for instance, one adds a non-nullable column while the second one adds some data and is unaware of the new required column), one of the developers may need to wait for another one to complete their work. A similar situation may arise if change sets are compatible but not yet merged with the main branch shared by the team. In that case, until the changes are reviewed and merged, the team may struggle with having a stable development environment. The solution to that problem is to have a dedicated database for each developer (as presented in *Figure 15.4*).

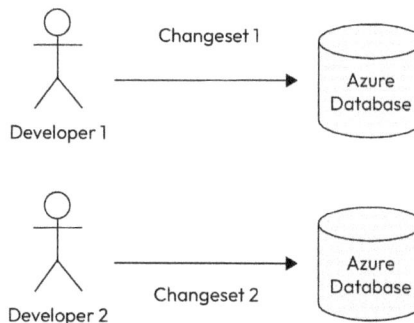

Figure 15.4 – A dedicated database per developer

Another option, as mentioned at the beginning of this section, is exporting a database and sharing it with the development team. For instance, you could use the `SqlPackage` tool to export an Azure SQL database as a BACPAC file:

```
SqlPackage /Action:Export /TargetFile:"<local-path>\<file-name>
.bacpac" \ /SourceConnectionString:"Server=tcp:{yourserver}
.database.windows.net,1433;Initial Catalog=<database-name>;
Persist Security Info=False;User ID=<username>;Password=
<password>;MultipleActiveResultSets=False;Encrypt=True;
TrustServerCertificate=False;Connection Timeout=30;"
```

This tool can be used with any SQL database and allows you to provide a connection string, which is then used to connect with the database and export it. You can read more about it here: `https://learn.microsoft.com/en-us/sql/tools/sqlpackage/sqlpackage?view=sql-server-ver16`.

Another useful resource for exporting a database is the following documentation page: `https://learn.microsoft.com/en-us/azure/azure-sql/database/database-export?view=azuresql`. It explains how to use other tools, such as the Azure portal, PowerShell, or SQL Server Management Studio, to perform the export operation. Similar instructions can be found for MySQL (`https://learn.microsoft.com/en-us/azure/mysql/flexible-server/concepts-migrate-import-export`) and PostgreSQL (`https://learn.microsoft.com/en-us/azure/postgresql/migrate/how-to-migrate-using-dump-and-restore?tabs=psql`).

The challenge of using exported databases locally is ensuring their consistency and removing sensitive data. For consistency, you could use a migration tool for the database schema and data, so all the changes are part of the code base. Removing sensitive data is a little bit trickier, though. While the team could use non-production data for their work, sometimes following that approach makes things more complicated, as artificial data is unable to represent the connections created by the live data coming from the production environment. In that case, companies often implement a concept called **anonymization**. Its purpose is to strip the data of any personal information, to which developers aren't supposed to have access. Unfortunately, Azure doesn't provide any native tools that could be helpful to perform that operation. Sure, Azure SQL has a feature called dynamic data masking, but it's meant to limit access to some columns when an unauthorized user queries a database table. You can read more about dynamic data masking here: `https://learn.microsoft.com/en-us/azure/azure-sql/database/dynamic-data-masking-overview?view=azuresql`.

Let's talk now about integration options when working with databases in Azure.

Understanding integration options for databases in Azure

Up to now, we've discussed how databases in Azure work and what their major features are. Besides the native features of those databases (provided by their engines), managed databases in Azure also offer a set of integration options that can be useful in a number of scenarios. Let's describe some of them case by case.

Using Microsoft Entra ID authentication

Azure SQL allows you to use Microsoft Entra ID as the identity provider for users using your database. This is useful if you want to provide a unified user experience for human users and also allow service principals to use their credentials to connect with a database. To use that feature, you need to first set a database admin with one of the following commands:

```
az sql server ad-admin create // For Azure SQL Database
az sql mi ad-admin create // For Azure SQL Managed Instance
```

Note that the preceding operations (setting up a database admin with Microsoft Entra ID) can also be performed with infrastructure as code, Azure PowerShell, the Azure portal, or even the REST API. Check out the following link for reference: https://learn.microsoft.com/en-us/azure/azure-sql/database/authentication-aad-configure.

Besides a database admin, you can also use Microsoft Entra ID to set up database users. To do that, you need to run a SQL query against the database for which you'd like to have a user created:

```
CREATE USER [<Microsoft_Entra_principal_name>] FROM EXTERNAL PROVIDER;
```

When running that command, you can provide a Microsoft Entra ID group, service principal, or user. Once the command runs successfully, the selected principal will be able to connect with the database using their credentials.

> **Note**
>
> Remember that adding a user in Azure SQL Database may not be enough for a principal to connect with the database. You may need to ensure that the principal either uses a whitelisted IP address or calls the database from within your network, so the connection is accepted.

Integration with Microsoft Entra ID is also available for Azure Database for PostgreSQL (https://learn.microsoft.com/en-us/azure/postgresql/flexible-server/concepts-azure-ad-authentication) and Azure Database for MySQL (https://learn.microsoft.com/en-us/azure/mysql/flexible-server/concepts-azure-ad-authentication).

Let's talk now about integrating databases with Azure Data Factory.

Using Azure Data Factory with Azure databases

Azure Data Factory is an orchestration service that can be used to implement data pipelines that load, transform, and process data. It natively supports connectors for all three database services we're discussing in this chapter:

- **Azure SQL**: `https://learn.microsoft.com/en-us/azure/data-factory/connector-azure-sql-database?tabs=data-factory`

- **Azure Database for PostgreSQL**: `https://learn.microsoft.com/en-us/azure/data-factory/connector-azure-database-for-postgresql?tabs=data-factory`

- **Azure Database for MySQL**: `https://learn.microsoft.com/en-us/azure/data-factory/connector-azure-database-for-mysql?tabs=data-factory`

Thanks to those connectors, you can easily start configuring a process that will connect with your database, query it for data, and process it further. It's an alternative to implementing data pipelines in code.

Integrating Azure databases with Office 365

To integrate Azure SQL with Office 365, there are a number of different options you could leverage. There are third-party tools such as CData Sync or Layer2 that allow you to connect with your database and integrate with platforms such as Office 365. While they are commercial products, they offer quite an extensive set of features, which you may find useful if you look for an out-of-the-box solution ready to work with your datasets.

> **Note**
>
> What's interesting is that both CData Sync and Layer2 support not only SQL Server (Azure SQL) but also MySQL and PostgreSQL, meaning you can use them to process data from all three database engines.

Of course, if you look for a native approach, Azure still has things to offer. You could use Azure Data Factory, which will connect with both your Azure database and Office 365. In that case, you could use Microsoft 365 connectors (`https://learn.microsoft.com/en-us/azure/data-factory/connector-office-365?tabs=data-factory`) to get the data from Office 365 and copy it into a database. However, for now, there's one quite significant limitation – the connector can only ingest data into Azure Blob Storage or Azure Data Lake Storage. If you want to ingest it into a database such as Azure SQL or similar, you need to chain the activities (steps in your data pipeline that process the data), so the source JSON data will be transformed into something that can be integrated with a database. Take a look at the connector documentation page for more information.

Setting up firewall settings for Azure databases

The important thing about databases in Azure is that they are private by default. This means that in order to allow other services to connect with them, you need to configure the firewall in a way that enables connectivity. Depending on whether your database has a public endpoint or not, the procedure to whitelist connectivity will be slightly different.

IP whitelisting

IP whitelisting is the simplest method of securing network access to your database. It's basically a simple firewall that validates the IP address of the incoming requests and validates it against the table of allowed IP addresses. This method works if you have a database that is available publicly. If you want to allow a service to connect with it, you need to obtain its IP address and add it to the list of accepted IP addresses. This can be done using the Azure portal, Azure PowerShell, the Azure CLI, or even Azure Bicep and Terraform. For instance, here's how you can whitelist an IP address for Azure Database for PostgreSQL:

```
az postgres flexible-server firewall-rule create \
--resource-group <resource-group-name> \
--server-name <server-name> \
--name <rule-name> \
--start-ip-address <start-ipP \
--end-ip-address <end-ip>
```

In the preceding command, you need to provide a name for a rule (a custom value that describes what a rule is for) and a range of IP addresses. If you want to whitelist only a single IP address, you need to provide the same value for both the start IP address and the end IP address.

You can find more information about the feature with the following links:

- https://learn.microsoft.com/en-us/azure/azure-sql/database/firewall-configure?view=azuresql

- https://learn.microsoft.com/en-us/azure/postgresql/flexible-server/concepts-firewall-rules

- https://learn.microsoft.com/en-us/azure/mysql/flexible-server/concepts-networking-public

There's also an option to whitelist connections coming from within the Azure environment without the need to provide a list of IP addresses. Let's check it out.

Allowing connection from within the Azure environment

Some services (including Azure databases) have a special feature that allows you to enable connectivity from within the Azure environment without the need to define ranges of IP addresses. This feature has lots of drawbacks, including the following:

- Enabling connections from other subscriptions, even the ones you don't manage
- Lack of proper control over whitelisted ranges of IP addresses
- Obscuring issues with network configuration, which leads to providing much broader network access than needed

It has its use cases. Sometimes it may be impossible to integrate Azure services without enabling that feature as you don't know the actual IP ranges or they're so dynamic, which makes it impossible to manage them in a live system. You can read more about this particular functionality here: `https://learn.microsoft.com/en-us/azure/azure-sql/database/network-access-controls-overview?view=azuresql#allow-azure-services`.

Securing Azure databases with Azure private endpoints

An Azure private endpoint (with the Azure Private Link service) is a dedicated service to make your PaaS service, such as an Azure database, available only via its private IP address. With Azure private endpoints, you may disable the public endpoint of your database, so the only way to connect with it will be from within a virtual network. Take a look at *Figure 15.5* for a reference.

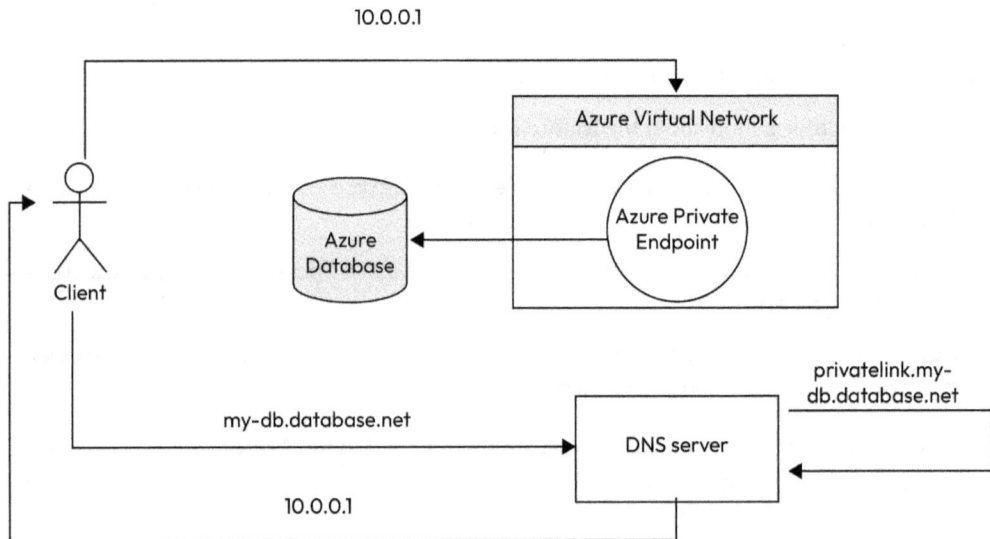

Figure 15.5 – Connection diagram presenting communication with an
Azure database with Azure private endpoint enabled

In *Figure 15.5*, you can see how a connection is processed when Azure private endpoint is enabled. The process can be explained as follows:

1. A client uses an FQDN to connect with a database server.

2. To connect using an FQDN, a client needs to communicate with the DNS server, which will respond with a proper IP address to use for communication.

3. As the FQDN used by the client is the public one, the DNS server translates the original query into another one, which is mapped to a private FQDN of the server.

4. In response, the DNS server returns a private IP address to the client.

5. The client uses the private IP address to connect to a database; however, the private IP address isn't assigned to the server itself, but rather to an Azure private endpoint, which acts as a network interface for the server.

With Azure private endpoints, you can make your database truly private. Nobody outside of a virtual network will be able to connect (which means that you also need to be inside the network to connect). Using private databases may pose some challenges during development. In that case, it's worth considering setting up a point-to-site VPN or using dedicated instances in the cloud, which don't have strict requirements for network isolation.

Let's now summarize some of our discussions from this chapter by talking about use cases for Azure databases.

Learning about use cases

Databases offered by Azure have one single purpose – they allow you to set up a database service without worrying about the whole infrastructure. Sure, you could leverage the IaaS-based option for Azure SQL with a virtual machine and SQL Server installed there, but the rest of the services (Azure SQL Database, Azure SQL Managed Instance, Azure Database for PostgreSQL, and Azure Database for MySQL) are designed toward typical benefits offered by PaaS services. Consider using an Azure database in the following cases:

- You don't have the expertise needed to host and maintain your own database server.

- You need to prototype an application and don't want to spend money and time on infrastructure.

- Your application doesn't need a database of all the types and you could consider using the serverless tier of Azure SQL Database to optimize costs.

- Your system is cloud-based, and you want to avoid transferring data from/to on-premises.

- You want to use Microsoft Entra ID as the identity provider for your database.

Azure-based databases are also a great option when starting a new project that will be hosted in the cloud. To migrate older applications to the cloud, viable options include Azure SQL Managed Instance or SQL Server on Azure Virtual Machines – consider them in lift-and-shift scenarios to avoid expensive database migration.

That's all for this chapter! Let's summarize what we have learned and see what is going to be discussed in the next chapter.

Summary

In this chapter, we focused on managed databases offered by Azure – Azure SQL, Azure Database for PostgreSQL, and Azure Database for MySQL. We talked about things those services have in common (simplified deployment model, automated maintenance, and native replication capabilities), different purchasing models (DTU-based and vCore-based), and integration options, including integration with Microsoft Entra ID for authentication. We also mentioned how Azure SQL can support lift-and-shift scenarios using managed instances or Azure virtual machines.

The knowledge from this chapter should help you better understand how to integrate your application with the selected Azure database. Remember that some applications may find Azure databases incompatible after migration – it's important to make the initial assessment and validation before you start to move your workloads to the cloud. Note that lots of topics related to Azure databases are focused on operations and administration, hence they have not been included in this book.

In the next chapter, we will discuss how to implement monitoring for an application hosted in Azure using Azure Monitor and Azure Application Insights.

Join the CloudPro Newsletter with 44000+ Subscribers

Want to know what's happening in cloud computing, DevOps, IT administration, networking, and more? Scan the QR code to subscribe to **CloudPro**, our weekly newsletter for 44,000+ tech professionals who want to stay informed and ahead of the curve.

https://packt.link/cloudpro

16

Adding Monitoring to Your Application

Applications running in the cloud (whether they are web applications, services, or jobs) need to have proper monitoring implemented, so you're able to tell what's happening inside of them. With an application hosted in the cloud, you're free to choose whether you'd like to leverage one of the solutions available in on-premises or native cloud services that take care of logging and monitoring configuration and infrastructure provisioning.

This chapter is going to focus on the latter – native Azure services such as Azure Monitor, Azure Log Analytics, and Azure Application Insights. We'll talk about things such as alerts, metrics, and events and see how those services can be integrated with your application. Knowledge from this chapter will help you start exploring different methods for implementing logging and monitoring for applications hosted in Azure using native Azure services. As monitoring of cloud applications differs when compared with monitoring on-premises applications, it's good to understand the differences, so you can adjust the implementation and avoid common errors.

In this chapter, we're going to cover the following main topics:

- Integrating Azure Application Insights with your application
- Reading logs, events, and traces
- Changing the configuration of Azure Application Insights
- Learning about alternatives to Azure Application Insights
- Learning about use cases

Technical requirements

To perform exercises from this chapter, you will need the following:

- Azure CLI

- An IDE of your choice (preferably Visual Studio Code)

Integrating Azure Application Insights with your application

Let's start this chapter by describing how monitoring can be implemented for an application hosted in the cloud. When it comes to monitoring, an application needs to publish some **metrics**, which can then be ingested, aggregated, and displayed. The metrics describe various dimensions important to you, as somebody who maintains an application. Examples of metrics include the following:

- CPU utilization

- Memory utilization

- Free disk space

- Number of processes running

- Number of messages waiting in a queue

As you can see, a metric may describe a concept, which makes sense from a monitoring point of view – it can be used to understand how the state of your application changes within a time range. For instance, if the average utilization of the CPU for the last 15 minutes exceeds 90%, you may expect your application to experience some difficulties in proper functioning as the CPU is working at almost full capacity. Metrics are useful for implementing alerts and dashboards but don't provide useful information when it comes to debugging if something isn't working right. This is where **logs** come in handy. A log is a stream of messages, often with a corresponding timestamp, which tells you exactly what action was executed by an application. Some examples of logs include the following:

- [2025-04-12 12:00:00] An order 1234 for user ABCD was sent to the processing queue.

- [1238627354] Authentication for user ABCD failed due to an invalid password.

- Service A, instance B is processing incoming request `https://some-domain.com/product/1`

The difference between a metric and a log is quite simple. Logs don't provide any specific value, as opposed to metrics. You can't build an alert based on a stream of logs (though you could potentially raise an alert if a specific message is reported to the log), but a stream of logs could help you understand why a specific metric is reported with a given value. Logs also require much more storage to keep them persisting for a longer period (this is why some applications implement a rolling window for logs, so they're kept only for a defined time). While cloud solutions may offer unlimited storage, you need to remember that data storage itself is cheap in the cloud – what's expensive are operations performed against a storage solution. If you have a big application that logs thousands of messages each minute, the cost of having them persist will be significant.

Back in the days when I was working on a system based on Azure Service Fabric, we implemented a logging solution that was constantly reporting the state of our nodes and operations performed against them. After a month, we realized that the monthly bill for infrastructure consisted mostly of costs related to our storage (Azure Storage), which kept our logs. Having logs being a major part of your cloud bill rarely makes sense. Hence, we needed to rewrite the solution to be much less greedy with saving log messages.

Depending on the hosting environment (Azure virtual machine, Azure Kubernetes Service, Azure App Service), you may find it easier or more difficult to use typical logging and monitoring solutions. For Azure virtual machines, solutions implemented on-premises will still work with some minor tweaks. Those solutions include the following:

- **C#**: Serilog, NLog, log4net
- **Java**: log4j2, Logback, SLF4J
- **Go**: Slog, Zap, Zerolog
- **Python**: Loguru, Structlog
- **JavaScript**: Winston

For the monitoring part, we have tools such as New Relic, Datadog, and Dynatrace. The common pattern for implementing logging using the aforementioned tools is presented in *Figure 16.1*.

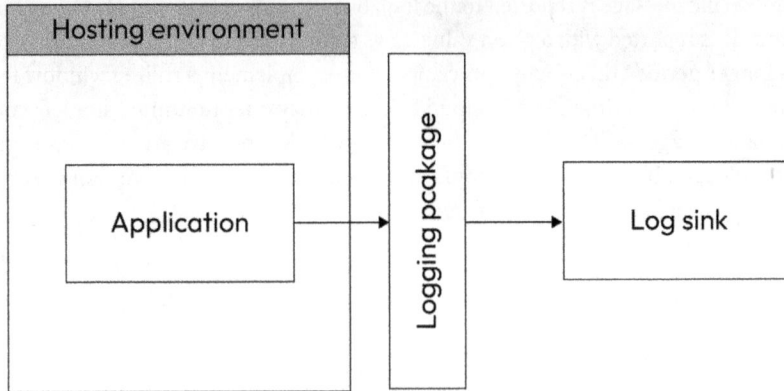

Figure 16.1 – Using a logging package in an application

In *Figure 16.1*, we have an application, which is hosted within a hosting environment (most of the time, a virtual machine), using a logging package to log messages. The logging package takes care of saving the log to a **log sink** (which could be a file on a separate disk, cloud storage, a database, or even some kind of in-memory structure). The important thing about logging packages is that they abstract the concept of logging from an application. Once the logs are saved, they could be ingested into a monitoring or reporting service, as presented in *Figure 16.2*.

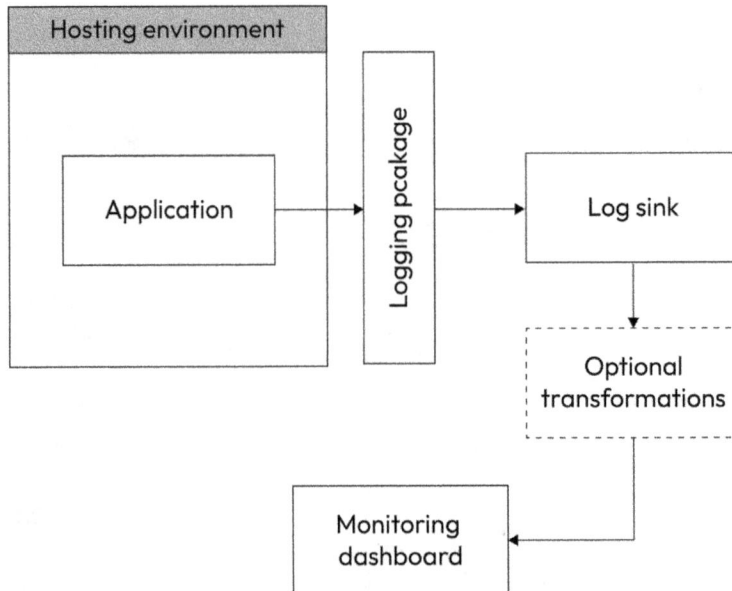

Figure 16.2 – Ingesting logs into a monitoring solution with an optional transformation step

In *Figure 16.2*, you can see how the logs saved to the log sink get ingested into a monitoring dashboard. What's interesting there is that you may need to implement an additional transformation step, which will adjust the schema of your log and make it presentable in the dashboard. You may wonder what the use of that optional step would be like. Well, remember that you don't always control how applications log data. The log stream may be presented in various formats, such as CSV, JSON, or a custom one. If the monitoring solution doesn't support them, you need to transform the log data from one format to another, so it can be both ingested and visualized.

> **Note**
>
> Transforming log data is out of the scope of this chapter as it focuses on using Azure Application Insights, which has the capability to transform the data. However, if you're looking for a custom solution, you could use a service such as Azure Data Factory, which allows you to build a data pipeline with transformations and then save it to a location that is integrated with your monitoring solution. Take a look at the following links for more information:
>
> - `https://learn.microsoft.com/en-us/azure/data-factory/connector-azure-blob-storage?tabs=data-factory`
> - `https://learn.microsoft.com/en-us/azure/data-factory/format-xml`
> - `https://learn.microsoft.com/en-us/azure/data-factory/connector-file-system?tabs=data-factory`

One of the most interesting capabilities of Application Insights is its ability to generate alerts for your application depending on the metrics selected as the alert rule. The process of creating an alert looks as follows:

1. (Optional) Publish a custom metric from your application.
2. Select a scope (for instance, Azure Web App or Azure Storage).
3. Select a signal and define alert logic (which could be your custom metric).
4. Provide an action, such as calling Azure Functions, a webhook, or Azure Logic Apps.

Once defined, alerts are automatically triggered when the alert rule evaluates to `true`. Look at *Figure 16.3* for a reference.

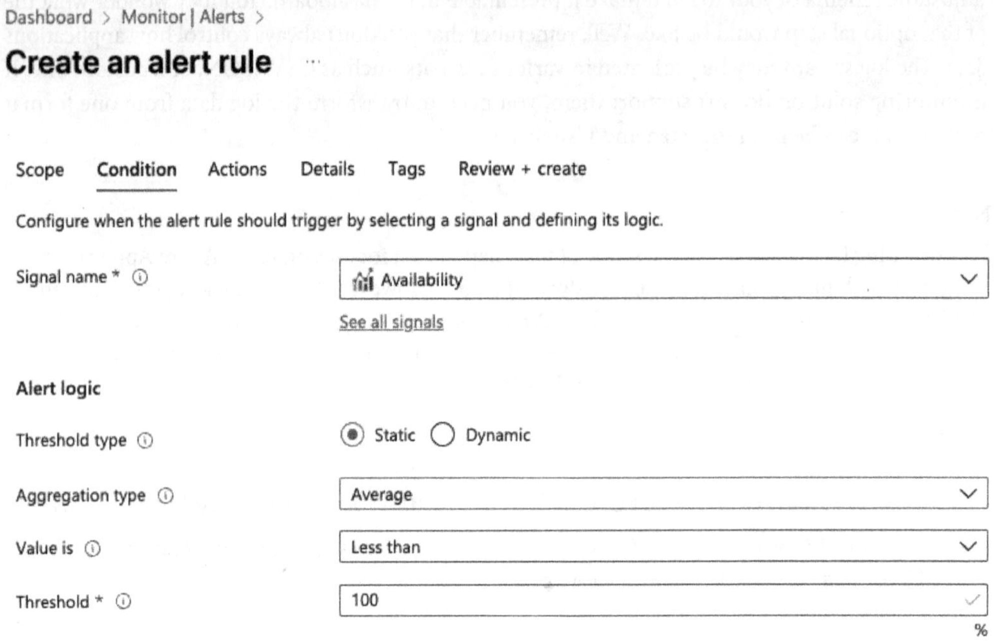

Dashboard > Monitor | Alerts >

Create an alert rule   ⋯

| Scope | **Condition** | Actions | Details | Tags | Review + create |

Configure when the alert rule should trigger by selecting a signal and defining its logic.

Signal name * ⓘ

▥ Availability   ⌄

See all signals

Alert logic

Threshold type ⓘ   ◉ Static   ○ Dynamic

Aggregation type ⓘ   Average   ⌄

Value is ⓘ   Less than   ⌄

Threshold * ⓘ   100   ✓
                                                                        %

Figure 16.3 – An example of an alert rule that triggers if the availability of Azure Storage is less than 100%

As there are many different types of alerts, I strongly recommend you look at the following documentation page: `https://learn.microsoft.com/en-us/azure/azure-monitor/alerts/alerts-create-metric-alert-rule`. It will not only provide additional details on different types of alerts but also explain how exactly you could define an alert for your application. I especially advise you to check the tutorial on how you could define an alert based on a log search: `https://learn.microsoft.com/en-us/azure/azure-monitor/alerts/alerts-create-log-alert-rule`. Those alerts may be useful if you're unable to publish a useful metric or are just looking for a specific string in logs.

> **Note**
> Remember that more complex rules for alerts may be quite expensive. Always check the cost estimate for a log displayed in the Azure portal before you create a rule to avoid unexpected charges.

Now, let's check how Azure Application Insights is able to provide you with both logging and monitoring solutions without a need to worry about transformations, ingestion, and sampling logs.

Implementing Azure Application Insights in an application

Before we get started, it's important to let you know that, currently, Microsoft offers two different ways to integrate logging and monitoring with your application using Application Insights. There's a classic API and the new one is called Azure Monitor OpenTelemetry. We're going to describe both as they are not fully compatible.

To integrate Azure Application Insights with your application, you will need an SDK. Instructions on how to install and configure such an SDK can be found at the following links:

- **JavaScript**: `https://learn.microsoft.com/en-us/azure/azure-monitor/app/javascript-sdk?tabs=javascriptwebsdkloaderscript`

- **Node.js**: `https://learn.microsoft.com/en-us/azure/azure-monitor/app/asp-net-core`

- **.NET (ASP.NET and console applications)**: `https://learn.microsoft.com/en-us/azure/azure-monitor/app/asp-net-core`

- **Go**: `https://github.com/microsoft/ApplicationInsights-Go`

- **Java**: `https://github.com/microsoft/ApplicationInsights-Java`

- **Python**: `https://learn.microsoft.com/en-us/python/api/overview/azure/mgmt-applicationinsights-readme?view=azure-python`

If you'd like to use Azure Monitor OpenTelemetry, there's a single instruction for all the supported languages: `https://learn.microsoft.com/en-us/azure/azure-monitor/app/opentelemetry-enable`.

The concept of integrating an application with Application Insights used to be related to the use of an **instrumentation key**. The instrumentation key was a secret value that you could use as a *password* for the selected instance of Application Insights. However, by the time you're reading this, instrumentation keys will be deprecated, and Microsoft advises to start using a **connection string** instead. To use connection strings, you also need to use one of the newer versions of SDKS:

- **.NET v2.12.0**

- **JavaScript v2.3.0**

- **Node.js v1.5.0**

- **Python v1.0.0**

The full instructions on how to pass a connection string can be found here: `https://learn.microsoft.com/en-us/azure/azure-monitor/app/connection-strings#set-a-connection-string`. A connection string for Application Insights looks like this:

```
InstrumentationKey=00000000-0000-0000-0000-
000000000000;EndpointSuffix=ai.contoso.com;
```

It could also include an explicit region:

```
InstrumentationKey=00000000-0000-0000-0000-000000000000;IngestionEndpo
int=https://southcentralus.in.applicationinsights.azure.com/
```

In the second example, you'd explicitly provide an ingestion endpoint for all the data sent by the SDK. This feature is useful if your application needs to satisfy certain regulations and needs to ensure that data won't leave a certain location. Both instrumentation keys and connection strings are considered to be of *sensitive value* – if somebody learns their value, they might be able to send their own logs and metrics or try to exfiltrate the data. To secure the ingestion endpoints, some systems implement **Azure Private Endpoints for Azure Monitor** (**AMPLS**), described here: `https://learn.microsoft.com/en-us/azure/azure-monitor/logs/private-link-security`. This approach provides an additional security layer as only services with network connectivity are able to communicate with Application Insights.

> **Note**
> Whether you use the Classic API or the new Azure Monitor OpenTelemetry, you will need to use a connection string to connect.

As the values we're discussing are considered sensitive, when hosting an application in Azure, you should consider storing them in Azure Key Vault and ingesting them securely either by using Azure App Configuration with the Azure Key Vault SDK or (if you're using Azure App Service) with app settings referencing them from Azure Key Vault. This is visualized in *Figure 16.4*.

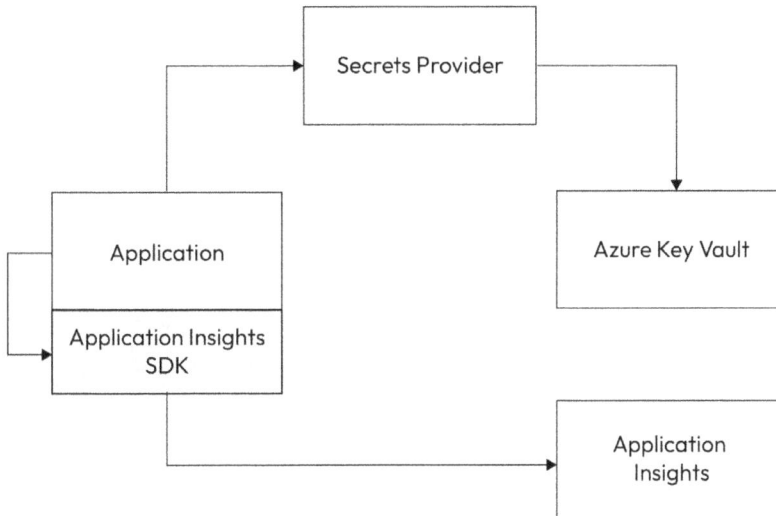

Figure 16.4 – A visualization where an application uses Azure Key Vault to store an instrumentation key/connection string for Application Insights

In *Figure 16.4*, you can see how an application uses a secrets provider (which will be different depending on the hosting environment) to fetch a secret from Azure Key Vault and use it to initiate the Application Insights SDK. Consider that a standard approach where the key used to initialize the SDK is considered the same secret as a database connection string or API key to an external service.

Let's now talk about environment separation when using Application Insights.

Separating environments with Application Insights

When integrating an application with Application Insights, you will start wondering how many instances you may need for your application. There are three different approaches available:

- One instance per environment.
- One instance for non-production environments and one for production environments.
- One instance for all environments.

If needed, you could also divide Application Insights into more groups:

- **Type of service**: frontend, backend
- **Region**
- **Type of data**: public, business use, sensitive

There's no single answer to the question of how many instances you may need. It all depends on the support model of your applications, the scale of the whole system, and the overall approach in your company.

> **Note**
>
> Some time ago, Application Insights (or rather Log Analytics, which is a service used to store logs) offered a free tier of 5 GB of data ingested for free monthly. This free tier was applicable to a Log Analytics workspace, meaning you could create multiple workspaces (and instances of Application Insights) and have that free tier applied to each of them. This was useful in a non-production environment, to keep the cost of Application Insights to a minimum. Unfortunately, it was changed some time ago and now the free tier is applied to a billing account (which is, most of the time, a subscription).

Committing to a specific model of hosting Application Insights isn't something that can't be changed later. Remember that a connection between an application and the selected instance of this cloud service is made with the use of a connection string. If you start with a single instance of Application Insights and then decide to make the split, all you need is to change the value of the connection string. Sure, you may not have a full picture of logs and metrics for some time, but as long as the previous instance isn't deleted, you're still able to query data there.

Let's now talk about dependency monitoring, which is available in Application Insights as an additional feature.

Using dependency monitoring (tracking) in Application Insights

Dependency monitoring is a feature that allows you to track dependencies such as calls to external services, databases, and Azure services used by your application. With dependency monitoring, you gain additional insights about the following metrics:

- The type of dependency (Azure service, API, database, other)
- How much time the application spent making a call to a dependency
- What kind of data was sent

This feature provides extremely useful information when hosting an application that needs to communicate with other services to operate.

Let's consider the following example: Your application makes calls to a database. Without dependency monitoring, you will need to rely on tools provided by your database server to understand what kind of queries are performed and how long they take. Ingesting and monitoring those metrics may be difficult sometimes, and if you use managed services in the cloud, it may even be impossible to fetch them easily.

With dependency monitoring, you can not only verify how long it takes to execute a query but with some additional code, you could even report what kind of SQL query (or any other query) was used.

> **Note**
>
> This feature may be especially helpful when using ORMs in your code that generate SQL queries on the fly so it's difficult to debug them in live environments.

When dependency monitoring is enabled, the following dependencies are tracked automatically:

- HTTP(S), WCF, and SQL calls
- Azure Storage calls (without Files Service)
- Azure Event Hubs and Azure Service Bus
- Azure Cosmos DB

Still, you can implement a custom tracking module, which will be able to track any dependency you want. This concept is well explained in the documentation, which you can find here: `https://learn.microsoft.com/en-us/azure/azure-monitor/app/api-custom-events-metrics#trackdependency`. The thing to remember is that you will need to use the TrackDependency API manually – call the `TrackDependency()` method yourself every time you'd like to report it to Application Insights.

> **Tip**
>
> Calling the mentioned method manually may be cumbersome if you need to always remember to add it. It's a good thing to think about implementing an interceptor pattern and putting the call to the TrackDependency API there. Most of the popular ORMs already have that pattern implemented – reference their documentation for more details.

Let's now talk about optimizing best practices when working with Application Insights.

Implementing best practices for Application Insights

Like all services, Application Insights also has its own set of best practices that you should follow if you want to get the best out of the service. The first thing we'll discuss is sampling.

How sampling works in Application Insights

Sampling is a method of taking only a subset of data logged by your application and sending it to the service. It allows you to minimize the volume of data ingested by Application Insights. Hence, it can also be considered cost optimization (pricing for Application Insights is based on GB of data sent to the ingestion endpoints and analyzed).

> **Note**
>
> For the OpenTelemetry API, sampling is configured differently: `https://learn.microsoft.com/en-us/azure/azure-monitor/app/opentelemetry-configuration?tabs=aspnetcore#enable-sampling`.

There are three types of sampling available:

- **Adaptive sampling**: This is a sampling data process that adapts to the rate of log messages, their structure, and their volume. It is also aware of the behavior of the ingestion endpoint, so it can adjust sending data depending on the ingestion endpoint capabilities.

- **Fixed-rate sampling**: This is the simplest method of sampling, which uses fixed values to sample data (for instance, sending a batch of data every 30 seconds).

- **Ingestion sampling**: This is a sampling method that is applied on the ingestion endpoint level; you can read more about it later.

All recent SDK versions for Application Insights support all three kinds of sampling, but if you use an older version of the SDK, you may find that it lacks one of the listed types. When it comes to configuration, you can configure only adaptive and fixed-rate sampling. Ingestion sampling, as happens at the ingestion endpoint, can only be adjusted, meaning you can set how much data will be discarded after arriving at the endpoint. The main difference between the types of sampling is exactly that – whether the limiting happens at the application level (so the application will send less data) or at the endpoint level (so the data is sent but may not be ingested into the Application Insights service). See *Figure 16.5* for a visual explanation.

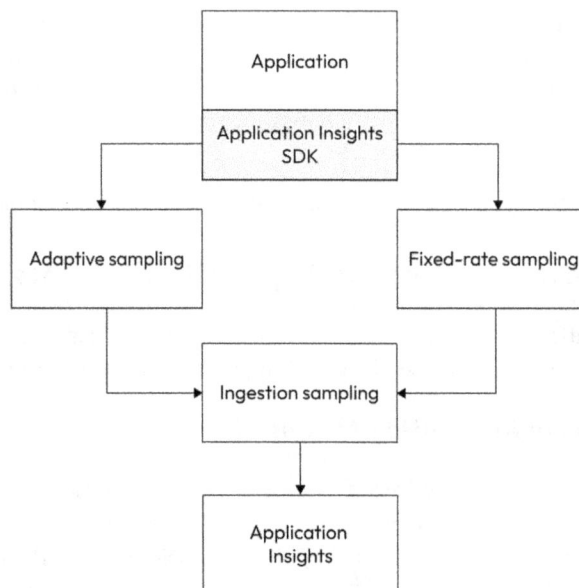

Figure 16.5 – All three types of sampling

The main use cases for sampling are as follows:

- If you want to limit the data sent by your application to Application Insights

- If you're using quota in Application Insights and want to be able to collect as much data as possible

- If you're being throttled by the Application Insights service, which is unable to process the amount of data sent to it

While sampling, by definition, means that some data may be lost, Application Insights renormalizes the dataset when data is presented to you. Of course, the renormalization process isn't 100% accurate, but as logging and monitoring are mostly based on statistics, the process is good enough to be considered transparent. You can read more about sampling here: `https://learn.microsoft.com/en-us/previous-versions/azure/azure-monitor/app/sampling-classic-api`.

Let's now talk about flushing the buffer in the Application Insights SDK.

Flushing the buffer

When data is collected using the Application Insights SDK, it's stored internally in a buffer. The buffer is periodically flushed, so the data is sent to the cloud service. The purpose of the buffer is as follows:

- To avoid an application being throttled by the Application Insights service

- To improve the performance of data collection

However, sometimes you may find it useful to flush the buffer manually. An excellent (although short) article describing the purpose, mechanism, and best practice for using the `Flush()` method is available here: `https://devblogs.microsoft.com/premier-developer/application-insights-use-case-for-telemetryclient-flush-calls/`. For a more detailed explanation, you can check the docs of the service: `https://learn.microsoft.com/en-gb/azure/azure-monitor/app/api-custom-events-metrics#flushing-data`.

Remember that you should avoid flushing data too often. Performing that operation may impact your instance of Application Insights, which may try to throttle your application if it detects that you communicate with it too much.

We will continue the discussion about best practices for Application Insights in the next section, where we will discuss events and metrics in detail.

Reading logs, events, and traces

Besides standard logs, Application Insights allows you to log the following types of messages:

- **Events**

- **Metrics**

- **Dependencies**

- **Page views**

- **Traces**

- **Requests**

- **Exceptions**

All those types of logs can be logged with the appropriate `Track..()` method, such as `TrackEvent()`, `TrackMetric()`, `TrackDependency()`, and so on. Each of the types has its own semantics, which we will describe as follows:

- **Events** in Application Insights are special metrics that can describe a point in time when something meaningful happened. It could be something related to the application (for example, configuration reloaded) or a user (order completed). Events can be tracked and visualized in Application Insights as individual occurrences, so you can better understand the behavior of the application.

- **Metrics** are just some generic dimensions you can use to build alerts and dashboards. The important thing about metrics is that they should be pre-aggregated, meaning your application should avoid reporting individual values but rather collect them (for instance, for 30 seconds or 5 minutes) and only then send them to Application Insights.

- **Dependencies** are metrics related to external services, which we described previously in this chapter.

- **Page views** are metrics, which are used in frontend applications and generated when a web page is viewed or loaded. It may be useful if you track the popularity of a particular page in your application. Those metrics are sent with user sessions and data, so you can build user flows out of them to understand how users use your application.

- **Traces** are useful to send additional data to Application Insights, which could help in debugging an error or understanding a strange behavior of your application. They allow posting bigger chunks of data such as the full content of a form sent to one of the application's endpoints. Traces should be used along with other metrics but provide the unique feature of including lots of useful information with them.

- **Requests** are metrics that automatically register and send information about HTTP requests. They are rather high-level metrics, though they can be useful if you want to get an overall overview of an operation performed against an application.

- **Exceptions** are metrics that contain an error or an exception. They are one of the most useful and important metrics, as they may indicate a problem with the application. Exceptions can include additional information such as stack trace or custom error messages.

When using the Application Insights SDK, you need to remember that it's up to you to use those various APIs. Some frameworks may natively integrate with the SDK, so they will automatically call some of the methods, but for more sophisticated ones such as traces or events, you need to build your own plan for implementing them. You will also find a detailed description of every metric here: `https://learn.microsoft.com/en-us/azure/azure-monitor/app/api-custom-events-metrics`.

Let's now check how the metrics can be read and displayed.

Reading and visualizing data from Application Insights

As mentioned before, data collected by Application Insights can be queried and visualized. Even though the Application Insights service doesn't store the data itself (it uses Log Analytics for that), the language for querying the data is unified across the whole Azure Monitor environment. There are four different options to visualize data collected by Application Insights using the native solutions offered by Azure:

- **Dashboards**: `https://learn.microsoft.com/en-us/azure/azure-monitor/visualize/tutorial-logs-dashboards`

- **Power BI**: `https://learn.microsoft.com/en-us/azure/azure-monitor/logs/log-powerbi`

- **Grafana**: `https://learn.microsoft.com/en-us/azure/azure-monitor/visualize/grafana-plugin`

- **Workbooks**: `https://learn.microsoft.com/en-us/azure/azure-monitor/visualize/workbooks-overview`

> **Note**
>
> For Grafana, you could use either the managed Grafana service available in Azure or have your own instance hosted in either an Azure Virtual Machine or in a completely different environment.

All logs collected by Application Insights can be queried using a language called **Kusto Query Language (KQL)**. KQL allows you to perform read operations only and was designed to give you tools to quickly analyze and process structured, semi-structured, and unstructured data. An example of a Kusto query is presented here:

```
OrderEvents
| where StartTime between (datetime(2025-04-01) ..
datetime(2025-04-30))
| where ProductId == "1234"
| count
```

This query would give you the number of orders placed in the system in April 2025 for a product with an ID set to 1234. Before we move on, let's discuss what OrderEvents is here because that part is most likely misleading.

Kusto operates on similar structures as SQL databases – databases, tables, and columns. OrderEvents, which you see in the preceding query, is a table that stores events. Tables are part of Log Analytics workspaces and can be created whenever you need them. With Application Insights, you don't need to worry about creating tables – they are created for you. For instance, if you use the TrackEvent API to collect events, they will all be stored in the customEvents table, which you could query as follows:

```
customEvents
| where eventType == "ORDER_COMPLETED"
| where orderId == '1234'
| project orderedBy, price
```

This query would look at the events table and look for one that satisfied the filter criteria. It would also give us only the name of the person who placed the order and its price (thanks to the project operator). Note that columns used in that query (orderedBy, price) are so-called custom properties – they are uniquely assigned to an event when it's created. It's up to you to structure the events (and other metrics) according to your expectations by providing as many custom properties as you need.

It's also worth mentioning that you may use Kusto queries for most Azure services when accessing the **Logs** blade in the Azure portal (see *Figure 16.6* for reference). The availability of data in Log Analytics tables will depend on the diagnostic settings you may enable for all deployed instances of Azure services. Learn more about them here: https://learn.microsoft.com/en-us/azure/azure-monitor/platform/diagnostic-settings.

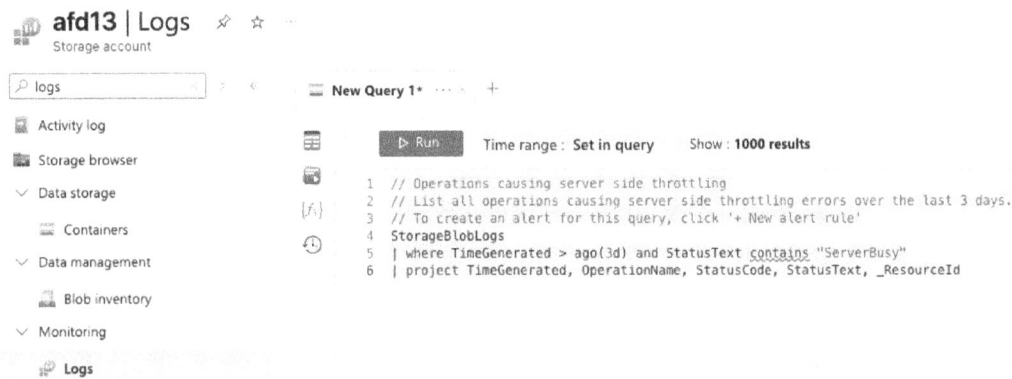

Figure 16.6 – The Logs blade in the Azure portal, accessed from a storage account

The data model for Application Insights is described here:

`https://learn.microsoft.com/en-us/azure/azure-monitor/app/data-model-complete`

Read more about Kusto here:

`https://learn.microsoft.com/en-us/kusto/query`

As the next step, let's talk about changing the configuration of Application Insights, so it works according to what's required for your application.

Changing the configuration of Azure Application Insights

When it comes to the configuration of Application Insights, there aren't many things that are related to the infrastructure itself as it's a managed service. However, as with many cloud services, it offers some options that may be customized or adjusted, so it works exactly as you need. There are the following key areas, which we will discuss in this section:

- Handling connection information
- Configuring telemetry modules and features
- Configuring workspace-based settings
- Advanced features such as IP masking and RBAC

As we have already discussed how to handle connection information (which is instrumentation keys/connection strings) using Azure Key Vault in the previous sections, let's focus on configuring telemetry modules and features.

Configuring telemetry modules and features

When you configure the Application Insights SDK in your application, you can choose what modules and features will be enabled, and what configuration is passed to them. The modules you may use include the following:

- **Sampling**: `https://learn.microsoft.com/en-us/previous-versions/azure/azure-monitor/app/sampling-classic-api`

- **Performance counters for legacy .NET applications**: `https://learn.microsoft.com/en-us/azure/azure-monitor/app/asp-net-counters?tabs=performancecounters`

- **Live metrics**: `https://learn.microsoft.com/en-us/azure/azure-monitor/app/live-stream?tabs=otel`

- **Filtering and telemetry initializers and processors**: `https://learn.microsoft.com/en-us/azure/azure-monitor/app/api-filtering-sampling`

All those features can be enabled when you initialize an instance of the `TelemetryClient`. Some modules are enabled by default, while others need to be enabled manually. Reference documentation for the most recent information about which module and feature is enabled for the current version of Application Insights SDK. Remember, that all features of Application Insights may be enabled or disabled by the configuration of your application. For instance, you may register a specific telemetry processor only for a non-production environment to collect specific information. Or, you could register a specific telemetry initializer to annotate collected data with custom information:

```
public class MyTelemetryInitializer : ITelemetryInitializer
{
    public void Initialize(ITelemetry telemetry)
    {
        var requestTelemetry = telemetry as RequestTelemetry;
        if (requestTelemetry == null) return;

        requestTelemetry.Properties["VersionNumber"] =
            "1.0.0-beta-js76asd";
    }
}
```

This code snippet will check whether a metric reported via the SDK is a request. If it is, it will add a custom property with a version number of the application to each such metric, so you can know for which released version of your application it was reported.

Configuring workspace-based settings

Application Insights allows you to configure some features at the workspace level, so you can adjust things such as data retention, daily cap (how much data can be ingested daily), or even change the pricing plan of the whole workspace. From the application point of view, the most important features you can configure are data retention and daily cap.

Data retention setting is important if you need to make sure that data is stored in Application Insights for a certain number of days. As this is a workspace-level feature, it is actually configured for Log Analytics, which is used under the hood. The process is explained at the following link: `https://learn.microsoft.com/en-us/azure/azure-monitor/logs/data-retention-configure`.

As data in workspaces isn't stored for more than 90 days, you may wonder how you could make it available for longer. To achieve that, you will need to implement data export from a workspace and store the data using another storage service such as Azure Storage. In that scenario, you could leverage the archive tier to cut down the storage cost as it's highly unlikely you will need to read that data in the future.

> **Note**
> Some time ago, the advised approach for exporting data from Application Insights was using the continuous export feature. This is, however, considered deprecated and, instead, you should use diagnostic settings to export the same data from workspace-based instances of Application Insights. The process is described here: `https://learn.microsoft.com/en-us/previous-versions/azure/azure-monitor/app/export-telemetry#diagnostic-settings-based-export`.

A **daily cap** is another important feature of Application Insights as it allows you to keep the cost of the service under control. When enabling logging with Application Insights, it's very easy to lose track of how much data is ingested by the service and how much it will cost. As the cost of this service is based on GBs of ingested data, you need to understand how to estimate how much data will be sent by your application. Unfortunately, this task may be very difficult to perform correctly as various metrics are generated dynamically and it's difficult to make the estimation based only on the code.

One of the possible solutions would be sending outbound requests to Application Insights via a proxy, which would calculate the daily payload to the Application Insights service, and based on that provide an insight into how much data is generated daily. If you don't have that possibility, you could try to assume an average size of each type of metric generated by your application and calculate them for each request of action performed by it. As, under the hood, all metrics are represented as JSON, you could just serialize all the values passed to tracking APIs (`TrackEvent`, `TrackDependency`, and so on) and use that for your estimation.

The process of setting up the daily cap is described here: `https://learn.microsoft.com/en-us/azure/azure-monitor/logs/daily-cap`. Note that this is an operation performed on the control plan of the service, meaning you need to have appropriate permission to perform it. When a daily cap is hit, Application Insights will stop ingesting data from all the applications connecting to it. This behavior is meant for non-production environments only, as not having metrics and logs ingested in the production environment may not only be problematic for debugging scenarios and root cause analysis but may have legal implications if you're obliged to collect and store them.

Let's now talk about advanced features of Application Insights.

Advanced features of Application Insights

Application Insights offers additional features that allow you to provide an additional security layer on top of the ones already discussed and help in making the service compliant with some regulations. These features include the following:

- **IP masking**
- **RBAC authorization**

By default, IP addresses are collected by Application Insights, but they are not stored. This means they are used only to populate some fields that provide an approximated location of the origin of a request:

- `client_City`
- `client_StateOrProvince`
- `client_CountryOrRegion`

The reason IP addresses aren't collected by default is to avoid collecting personal information, which could be problematic in some areas, such as Europe.

> **Note**
>
> Remember that, even if the IP address isn't masked, you may not be able to learn the true IP address of the requestor. This happens if a requestor is behind a proxy or VPN, which would provide the VPN's IP address instead of the original one.

If needed, IP masking can be disabled with the following methods:

- For PowerShell, use the following command:

```
Update-AzApplicationInsights -Name "<application-insights-
resource-name>" -ResourceGroupName "<resource-group-name>"
-DisableIPMasking:$true
```

- For the REST API call, use the following command:

```
PATCH https://management.azure.com/
subscriptions/<subscription-id>/resourceGroups/<resource-group-
name>/providers/microsoft.insights/components/<application-
insights-resource-name>?api-version=2018-05-01-preview HTTP/1.1
Host: management.azure.com
Authorization: Bearer <access-token>
Content-Type: application/json


{
    "location": "<region-name>",
    "kind": "web",
    "properties": {
        "Application_Type": "web",
        "DisableIpMasking": true
    }
}
```

- For Bicep, use the following code:

```
resource ai'microsoft.insights/components@2020-02-02' = {
    name: '<resource-name>'
    location: '<region-name>'
    kind: 'web'
    properties: {
        Application_Type: 'web'
        DisableIpMasking: true
    }
}
```

As you can see, all those methods have one thing in common – they use the `DisableIpMasking` property and set it to `true`.

The second advanced feature we'll discuss is RBAC authorization for Application Insights. By default, to be able to send telemetry to the service, you need the connection string. Additionally, if AMPLS is used, you may need to be in the same network to connect with the ingestion endpoint. In some applications though, the mentioned methods aren't enough. If you want to use Microsoft Entra ID for authentication, it's possible to force the service to accept only authenticated requests by disabling local authentication, as described here: `https://learn.microsoft.com/en-us/azure/azure-monitor/app/azure-ad-authentication?tabs=aspnetcore#disable-local-authentication`.

Once local authentication is disabled, all clients of the affected Application Insights instance will need to use Microsoft Entra ID to obtain an access token and use it when communicating with the service.

> **Note**
> The best way to authenticate from an application to Application Insights is using Managed Identity. While it's possible to use a service principal, that approach isn't recommended.

To use the credentials obtained from Microsoft Entra ID, you will need to configure them, then the Application Insights SDK is configured. Here's an example of how you could do that for a .NET application:

```
services.Configure<TelemetryConfiguration>(config =>
{
    var credential = new DefaultAzureCredential();
    config.SetAzureTokenCredential(credential);
});
services.AddApplicationInsightsTelemetry(new
ApplicationInsightsServiceOptions
{
    ConnectionString = "<connection-string>"
});
```

A similar setup could be done for JavaScript:

```
const appInsights = require("applicationinsights");
const { DefaultAzureCredential } = require("@azure/identity");
const credential = new DefaultAzureCredential(); appInsights.
setup("<connection-string>").start();
appInsights.defaultClient.config.aadTokenCredential = credential;
```

Take a look at the repository for this chapter for full examples (also for other programming languages).

Remember that setting up authentication won't be enough to connect to an instance of Application Insights. What's left is role assignment – in the case of Application Insights, you will need to use one of the built-in roles for Azure Monitor listed here: https://learn.microsoft.com/en-us/azure/role-based-access-control/built-in-roles/monitor - or use a custom one.

> **Note**
> Remember that to work with logs and metrics in Application Insights you need to find a role that provides permissions for the data plane of the service. One of the roles available is Monitoring Metrics Publisher, which is also advised by the Application Insights documentation.

You may also be interested in the following article, which describes the process of sending custom metrics to Application Insights using the REST API: `https://learn.microsoft.com/en-us/azure/azure-monitor/essentials/metrics-store-custom-rest-api?tabs=rest`. It provides additional details on how to use Microsoft Entra ID credentials to communicate with the service.

Let's now talk about alternatives to Application Insights.

Learning about alternatives to Azure Application Insights

When it comes to Azure, there are not many alternatives to Application Insights. Some services (such as Azure API Management and Azure Machine Learning) have native integrations with Application Insights, making it almost impossible to change the logging mechanism for them. Some notable alternatives include the following:

- New Relic
- Datadog
- Dynatrace
- AppDynamics
- Splunk
- Raygun

The aforementioned tools are third-party tools that can be hosted either in Azure or in your own environment and integrated with your applications. The downside of using them is the lack of integration options for cloud services. It would also be possible to consider Grafana and Prometheus together as an alternative to Azure Application Insights (especially now that we have managed Grafana in Azure). Note that it's perfectly fine to use a logging and monitoring solution other than Application Insights with Azure Monitor. What you would need is to evaluate how much money and time it will cost to have a third-party solution installed, configured, and managed by your team or your company. With Application Insights, you need to worry only about the cost (which can be managed with a daily cap and sampling), which makes it quite a serious option when comparing it with other tools.

As we're coming to the end of this chapter, let's now talk about use cases for choosing Application Insights over other logging and monitoring tools.

Learning about use cases

Azure Application Insights as a managed service offers the following set of functionalities:

- Performance monitoring

- Error detection and diagnosis

- User behavior analysis

- Distributed application tracing

- DevOps integration

- Monitoring across platforms

While the functionalities themselves look promising, we need to evaluate all aspects of Application Insights to understand how helpful they can be and why we would select this service over other tools. One of the most important things is how simple the setup is for the service. Once deployed, all you need is to install the SDK and integrate it with your application. This is all that is needed for the basic installation – no infrastructure is needed and no storage or replication for high availability. Besides the setup, Application Insights is also quite easy to configure and manage. If you want to keep the storage utilization up to a certain point, all you need is to set a daily cap. If the daily cap isn't enough (or the application still spends too much data), you can configure sampling and call it a day.

Application Insights also natively integrates with Azure Monitor, meaning you get not only an ingestion layer for logs and metrics but also the ability to configure and send alerts (you can find the overview of the feature here: `https://learn.microsoft.com/en-us/azure/azure-monitor/alerts/alerts-overview`).

One more thing worth considering is what the end goal for your monitoring solution is. If you are looking for a tool that will allow you to monitor your infrastructure, Application Insights won't be a good match as this service is purely application-centric. While third-party tools often offer a similar set of features, the key differentiator in that case will be native integration with Azure and cost-effective pricing.

Application Insights itself is a great service for monitoring your application in Azure but may require additional configuration to utilize 100% of the offered capabilities. I strongly recommend that you check the use of telemetry processors and initializers. They allow you to implement lots of interesting concepts, including enriching incoming requests with common data (such as some domain identifier – for instance, user ID or organization ID) or logging more information for debugging (as an opt-in feature, which can be enabled on demand to log additional information).

That's all that was planned for this chapter! Let's summarize all the lessons and check what will be discussed in the next chapter.

Summary

In this chapter, we talked about Application Insights and the capabilities of the service to implement logging and monitoring applications. We talked about basic features such as sending logs, customizing and configuring metrics, and best practices for implementing the service. We also discussed what language is used to query data ingested by Application Insights and how to implement additional features such as IP masking, Microsoft Entra ID authentication, and sampling.

If you're building an application that will be hosted in Azure, it's worth considering Application Insights as your solution for logging and monitoring (especially now, as it gets more and more attention, thanks to the Azure Monitor OpenTelemetry package).

In the next chapter, we're going to discuss how you could leverage Azure OpenAI Service to enrich your application with some AI functionalities.

Part 5:
AI, ML, and DevOps

This final part focuses on using modern Azure services to enhance your applications with artificial intelligence, machine learning, and DevOps practices. You will learn how to integrate AI capabilities using Azure OpenAI Service, streamline machine learning workflows with Azure Machine Learning, and adopt continuous integration and delivery using GitHub Actions. The part also covers how to develop, test, and deploy Azure Logic Apps in a structured and repeatable manner.

By the end of this part, you will be able to build intelligent, automated, and production-ready solutions using cutting-edge Azure technologies.

This part will have the following chapters:

- *Chapter 17, Integrating an Application with Azure OpenAI Service*
- *Chapter 18, Leveraging Azure Machine Learning to Automate Machine Learning Tasks*
- *Chapter 19, Using GitHub Actions to Build and Deploy Applications to Azure*
- *Chapter 20, Developing, Testing, and Deploying Azure Logic Apps*

17

Integrating an Application with Azure OpenAI Service

In recent years, the rise of AI has revolutionized the way businesses operate. The ability to leverage AI in real-time applications has become a game-changer for developers. As the demand for smarter applications continues to grow, Microsoft Azure offers a comprehensive suite of tools and services that empower developers to build intelligent solutions. Among the most exciting of these offerings is Azure OpenAI Service, a cloud-based platform that brings cutting-edge AI models from OpenAI to developers directly within the Azure ecosystem.

In this chapter, we will explore how Azure OpenAI Service works, what it enables, and how it can be seamlessly integrated into our applications. We'll delve into the key components that make up the service, including its core models, and discuss how they can be harnessed to solve complex problems in natural language processing, machine learning, and even code generation. By the end of this chapter, you will have a clear understanding of how to get started with Azure OpenAI, including best practices for integrating these AI models into your development workflow, and how to unlock the potential of AI to improve your applications and deliver richer, more intelligent user experiences.

In this chapter, we're going to cover the following main topics:

- Understanding how Azure OpenAI Service works

- Integrating an application with Azure OpenAI Service

- Learning about use cases for Azure OpenAI Service

Technical requirements

To perform the exercises in this chapter, you will need the following:

- The Azure CLI

- An IDE of your choice (preferably Visual Studio Code)

Understanding how Azure OpenAI Service works

Azure OpenAI Service is a product offered by Microsoft as part of Microsoft Azure, which provides access to powerful OpenAI models by abstracting away the challenging process of hosting the infrastructure required by those models and exposing their interfaces as a set of REST APIs. Those APIs can be integrated with your application thanks to various SDKs available on the market; they support programming languages such as C#, Python, Java, and Go. The list of available OpenAI models is dynamic and the status of which model is supported can be found here: `https://learn.microsoft.com/en-us/azure/ai-services/openai/concepts/models`. You may also wonder what the difference between Azure OpenAI Service and OpenAI is. The major difference here is the additional layer of features built on top of OpenAI models, which provide private networking, AI content filtering, and infrastructure automation.

To get started, let's define the fundamental concepts when working with Azure OpenAI Service.

Defining the fundamental concepts of the service

As with all Azure services, Azure OpenAI Service provides a set of unique features and functionalities, which are used by a user of that service to configure and use it. Some of the concepts should be familiar to you if you already have experience working with AI models.

What are prompts?

A **prompt** is a sentence that is written by a user (or generated automatically by a service), which is sent to the AI model and processed by it to generate a response. As writing a correct prompt is crucial for obtaining a valuable and precise response, there's a whole technique called **prompt engineering**, which explains how prompts should be written and how to adjust them to get the best results.

> **Note**
>
> It's worth remembering that the same prompt may work differently for different models (or different versions of the same model). If you plan on using any AI model, it's always a good idea to verify how it behaves depending on the prompt provided and its deviations. It will give you more information about the stability of the AI model and possibly allow you to select the one that answers the business need of the functionality you're building.

Let's consider the following prompt:

```
Generate a summary of AI models.
```

Do you think this prompt is good enough to provide useful information? Let's compare it with a second example:

```
You're an architect working for an FMCG company who evaluates the
available AI models for a new product that will be built within a
year. Create a summary of available AI models, containing a model
name, a link to its documentation, and valid use cases. Limit the
response to just LLMs as we don't model models that specialize in
media other than text.
```

As you can see, there's quite a difference between those prompts when we compare the level of detail provided to the AI model. The problem with the first prompt is how generic it is. Sure, once you send it to an AI model, you'll get an answer. But as you're not specifying details, the generated answer will also be generic. The second prompt not only gives much more context for the AI model but also limits the response and expects a certain format of the response. You can read more about prompt engineering here: `https://learn.microsoft.com/en-us/azure/ai-services/openai/concepts/prompt-engineering?tabs=chat`.

> **Tip**
>
> You can try those prompts using one of the publicly available LLMs, such as ChatGPT: `https://chatgpt.com/`.

As the next topic, let's discuss tokens in AI models.

Understanding tokens in AI models

When working with prompts, AI models need to process the input message and split it into chunks, which can be used to generate a response. Those chunks are called **tokens** and the process of processing the message into chunks is called **tokenization**. As not all models are meant to work with text (some are trained to work with images, video, or sound), the token definition will depend on the type of input. Different models may tokenize input in different ways, but a generic approach would look like this. Let's say you have provided the following prompt:

```
Generate a summary of AI models.
```

To understand the message, the AI model will split all the words into smaller parts and will also consider all the white characters. The tokenization process could, for instance, provide the following tokens for the model:

```
[Generate] [ a] [ summary] [ of] [ AI] [ models] [.]
```

With different tokenization algorithms, a model could also consider the following tokenization result:

```
[Ge] [ne] [rate ] [a ] [summary ] [of ] [AI ] [mo] [dels] [.]
```

No matter how the tokenization process happens, you need to have an overall understanding of the impact on both the model and (what's more important) the pricing of the service. As AI services such as Azure OpenAI Service base their pricing on the number of tokens processed, you may want to minimize the number of tokens sent to the service or optimize the prompts, so they require fewer tokens for processing. To understand this better, let's consider another example:

```
This is a number!
```

Depending on the tokenization algorithm, the preceding sentence could be split into various sets of tokens:

```
[This][ is][ a][ number!]
[This][ ][is][ ][a][ ][number!]
[This ][is ][a ][number][!]
```

Based on this example, we can see we have four tokens, then for the same sentence we could have seven tokens and we could also possibly have five tokens. The same sentence provides three different results. While the example may look a little simple, it greatly visualizes why choosing the proper prompt and AI model (plus its tokenization algorithm) is important.

> **Note**
>
> Of course, for binary data such as images, the tokenization process will look different and will be much more sophisticated. The concept is the same, though – some models may work better with JPEG; some may prefer PNG; and some will work best if provided with uncompressed data. As always, test thoroughly to get the best results.

You may wonder how to test the number of tokens generated without running tests against a real model. The good thing is that there are tools that can help you with this task:

- OpenAI Tokenizer online tool: `https://platform.openai.com/tokenizer`

- `https://github.com/openai/tiktoken`

- `https://www.npmjs.com/package/tiktoken`

- `https://token-calculator.net/`

These are just examples. There are various tools available, both online and offline, that you could embed into your application or use to develop a dedicated tool for your team working with prompts.

Let's now talk about deployments, which are a major part of hosting a model using Azure OpenAI Service.

Using deployments in Azure OpenAI Service

A **deployment**, in the context of Azure OpenAI Service, is a way to provision a selected model and make it available via your instance of Azure OpenAI Service. Deployments are created by a user (administrator) of the service and contain the basic information about the model that will be used for a deployment. Here's an example of how a deployment is defined using Azure Bicep:

```
resource deployment 'Microsoft.CognitiveServices/accounts/
deployments@2024-06-01-preview'= {
parent: aiServices
name: 'gpt-4o-mini-deployment'
sku : {
capacity: 50
name: 'GlobalStandard'
}
properties: {
model: {
name: 'gpt-4o-mini'
format: 'OpenAI'
version: '2024-07-18'
}
}
}
```

In the preceding example, we're deploying an instance of the GPT-4o mini model using a capacity of 50 and the `GlobalStandard` SKU name. The important thing here is selecting the proper SKU for your deployment. The available values for that field are the following:

- `GlobalStandard`
- `GlobalProvisioned`
- `GlobalBatch`
- `DataZoneStandard`
- `DataZoneProvisionedManaged`
- `DataZoneBatch`
- `Standard`
- `ProvisionedManaged`

They're all described in detail here: `https://learn.microsoft.com/en-us/azure/ai-services/openai/how-to/deployment-types`. The reason we're discussing them is that there's a huge difference in the initial price of the service if you decide to select the provisioned SKUs. By default, Azure OpenAI Service is billed per token usage as described on the pricing page: `https://azure.microsoft.com/en-us/pricing/details/cognitive-services/openai-service`. However, the downside of using the standard pricing is that it is unpredictable and difficult to estimate. The alternative is using provisioned throughput, but using it means that you're going to be charged no matter whether you're using the deployed model or not. Provisioned throughput defines how performant your instance of the service will be via the number of deployed **provisioned throughput units** (**PTUs**). The number of those units can be calculated using the calculator available here: `https://oai.azure.com/portal/calculator`.

> **Note**
>
> The prices for provisioned throughput vary greatly depending on the selected model. When this chapter was written, the prices varied between 700 USD and 1,500 USD for a month. The price can greatly decrease if you decide to reserve the capacity as described here: `https://learn.microsoft.com/en-us/azure/cost-management-billing/reservations/azure-openai#buy-a-microsoft-azure-openai-service-reservation`.

The full examples and process of creating an Azure OpenAI Service deployment are described in the following documentation article: `https://learn.microsoft.com/en-us/azure/ai-services/openai/how-to/create-resource?pivots=web-portal`. Use it as a reference if you'd like to deploy the service on your own.

Let's now talk about integrating an application with Azure OpenAI Service using the available SDKs and utilizing the features provided by the service.

Integrating an application with Azure OpenAI Service

To be able to integrate an application with Azure OpenAI Service, we will need to deploy it and install the selected SDK. The process of deploying the service is described in the Azure documentation, which is accessible through the link provided at the end of the previous subchapter. Once you have the service deployed, you will need to reference the SDK, which is available for the following programming languages:

- **C#**: `https://www.nuget.org/packages/Azure.AI.OpenAI`
- **Java**: `https://central.sonatype.com/artifact/com.azure/azure-ai-openai/1.0.0-beta.12`
- **Go**: `https://pkg.go.dev/github.com/Azure/azure-sdk-for-go/sdk/ai/azopenai`

- **Python**: `https://pypi.org/project/openai?azure-portal=true`

- **JavaScript**: `https://www.npmjs.com/package/openai`

Due to the various SDKs available, in this chapter, we'll be referencing only parts of the important code snippets. The full examples can be found in the repository dedicated to this chapter. As the first step, once the SDK is installed, you will need to authenticate to the service. Here's an example of how this can be done in C#:

```
var openAIClient = new(
    new Uri("https://your-azure-openai-resource.com"),
    new DefaultAzureCredential());
Var chatClient = openAIClient.GetChatClient("<deployment-name>");
```

To compare SDKs, let's also check how the same operation is performed for Python:

```
import os from openai
import AzureOpenAI from azure.identity
import DefaultAzureCredential, get_bearer_token_provider
token_provider = get_bearer_token_provider(DefaultAzureCredential(),
"https://cognitiveservices.azure.com/.default")
client = AzureOpenAI(
azure_endpoint = os.getenv("AZURE_OPENAI_ENDPOINT"), azure_ad_token_
provider = token_provider, api_version="2024-10-21")
```

As you can see, for both C# and Python, we can use the `DefaultAzureCredential()` object, which comes from the `Azure.Identity` package available for the supported programming languages. It allows us to leverage one of the available authentication mechanisms, such as the Azure CLI, managed identity, or environment variables. By using that method of authenticating the SDK, you can provide a unified authentication experience for the application no matter where it's hosted. Under the hood, the authentication process is processed with Microsoft Entra ID, so you can use either your personal account or a service principal.

An alternative method of authenticating to Azure OpenAI Service is using the API key as shown:

```
var apiKey = Environment.GetEnvironmentVariable("AZURE_OPENAI_API_
KEY");
var openAIClient = new(
new Uri("https://your-azure-openai-resource.com"),
new ApiKeyCredential(keyFromEnvironment));
var chatClient = openAIClient.GetChatClient("<deployment-name>");
```

In the preceding example, you can see that when creating the OpenAI client with an SDK, you can use the `ApiKeyCredential` object instead of `DefaultAzureCredential`. The difference here is that you will need to find a way to pass the API key in a secure manner. The example uses an environment variable for that as that's the most common pattern, but you could use any solution available to you.

> **Note**
>
> Remember that the API key is considered a sensitive value. You should treat it like other secrets such as passwords, private keys, or certificates. The best option to pass it securely to your application is using Azure Key Vault, as discussed in previous chapters.

Once your OpenAI client is authenticated, you can proceed by creating one of the specialized clients allowing you to interact with specific features of Azure OpenAI Service.

Creating a specialized client

The Azure OpenAI Service SDK supports creating dedicated clients, which you can use to interact with various capabilities of the service. Those clients include the following:

- Audio client for transcription and text to speech

- Chat client

- Embeddings client

- Fine-tuning (although it's not available for all programming languages)

- Images client

- Batch client (also not available for all programming languages)

- Completions client (currently considered legacy)

In the next part of this section, we will describe how to use each of these clients and how to integrate them with an application.

Using the chat client

We'll start with the **chat client** as it's the most intuitive one. This client can be used to implement applications such as chatbots, which leverage the features of LLMs to generate responses. Such services can be fine-tuned with specialized data, so they can be individual assistants with knowledge about specific areas.

Currently, Azure OpenAI Service supports two different APIs for implementing chats:

- Completions API
- Response API

The first one is considered the legacy approach as it's not supported by newer models such as GPT-4o, GPT-4o mini, and GPT-4 Turbo. Of course, there is nothing stopping you from using that API to implement your solution.

> **Note**
>
> At the time of writing this chapter, the Response API is still in preview, meaning it isn't suited for production scenarios.

The simplest possible example for implementing a chat with the Completions API is using the following snippet (this snippet is presented in C# but the repository for this chapter includes examples in other languages as well):

```
var chatClient = openAIClient.GetChatClient("<deployment-name>");
var completion = chatClient.CompleteChat(
[
new SystemChatMessage("You are a helpful assistant that talks like a
pirate."),
new UserChatMessage("Hi, can you help me?"),
new AssistantChatMessage("Arrr! Of course, me hearty! What can I do
for ye?"),
new UserChatMessage("What's the best way to train a parrot?"),
]);

Console.WriteLine($"{completion.Role}:{completion.Content[0].Text}");
```

Let's describe the example for a better understanding. Once the Azure OpenAI Service SDK client is created, we need to create a chat client. This client provides methods to interact with the underlying AI like we had a chat with it. There are three different types of messages available there:

- **System message**: Often described as a system prompt, it defines the behavior of the model, so it uses specific sentences, words, or language
- **User message**: A message sent by a user
- **Assistant message**: A message generated by our AI model

What you see in the preceding example is in fact a conversation history. The `CompleteChat()` method accepts an array of messages, which will be unique to each conversation initiated by a user. There's one challenge, though, when it comes to implementing such a chat: we need to persist the history of messages. This can be done with either in-memory storage (if you don't need to worry about losing the history) or, after serialization, by saving the message to a database or a storage service such as Blob Storage. There are also dedicated frameworks, such as Bot Framework (`https://dev.botframework.com/`), that come with native integration with Azure storage solutions such as databases or Azure Storage to persist the conversation state. Whether you need to have the state persisted or not depends on the business requirements – some applications, after restarting a conversation, need to load the previous messages, while others can just start from the very beginning. If you'd like to see an example of saving the conversation using Bot Framework, take a look at the following link: `https://github.com/microsoft/BotBuilder-Samples/tree/main/samples/csharp_dotnetcore/45.state-management`.

The second available API is the Response API, which is quite a new feature that is still in the development phase. Regarding SDK availability, at the time of writing this chapter, only the Python SDK is available. An example of generating a response using that API looks like this:

```
client = AzureOpenAI(
azure_endpoint = os.getenv("AZURE_OPENAI_ENDPOINT"), azure_ad_token_
provider=token_provider, api_version="2025-03-01-preview")
response = client.responses.create(
model="gpt-4o",
input="This is a test.")
```

The `response` variable will contain the response generated by the model used to create it. If you'd like to test the API but don't want to use the Python SDK, you can still implement a functionality using the REST API provided by the service available here: `https://learn.microsoft.com/en-us/azure/ai-services/openai/reference-preview#responses-api---create`. By learning about this API, you will see that to replicate the functionality presented by the preceding code snippet, you could use the following API endpoint:

```
POST https://{endpoint}/openai/responses?api-version=2025-03-01-
preview
```

The endpoint accepts the same parameters as the SDK method exposed by the Python library. What's interesting is that it supports two different response types:

- `Application/json`
- `Text/event-stream`

The reason you may use the second response type is related to the way that responses are generated. If the response is only a few sentences long, waiting for the whole response to be generated is acceptable most of the time. However, for very long responses, waiting for the whole response from the API will be challenging for the end user. This is why you could use streaming, which will provide chunks of responses on the fly, so you can dynamically present them to the user. Streaming can be enabled by setting the `stream` property to `true`. Full examples of the Response API with additional details, including a list of regions and models supporting it, can be found here: `https://learn.microsoft.com/en-us/azure/ai-services/openai/how-to/responses`.

Let's now talk about using the client to process audio input.

Using the audio client

Processing audio input is slightly different than processing text as it requires not only a different way to handle input (as it's a binary format) but also using an AI model that is suited for that type of data. LLMs can work with audio files, hence you should use GPT-4o audio or Whisper models. An example of using Whisper is presented with the following code snippet:

```
var client = openAIClient.GetAudioClient("whisper");
string audioFilePath = "<path-to-file>"; AudioTranscriptionOptions
options = new()
{
ResponseFormat = AudioTranscriptionFormat.Verbose,
TimestampGranularities = AudioTimestampGranularities.Word |
AudioTimestampGranularities.Segment
};
var transcription = client.TranscribeAudio(audioFilePath, options);
```

Let's describe this snippet:

1. First, we create an audio client by providing the name of a model we selected (in this case, Whisper).

2. We define additional options describing the response format and the granularity of timestamps (as we're going to get a transcription of the speech included in the audio file).

3. The last step is running the transcription with the defined client.

As you can see, with only a few lines of code, you could get a transcription of any audio file for any purpose. Of course, the result of using an AI model for transcribing audio may not be ideal because of the quality of the input data or the model itself may not fully understand what was said. While those factors can be adjusted, we also need to figure out how the audio files should be passed to the model and how the result should be stored and returned to the user or an application. Let's consider the idea presented in *Figure 17.1* for reference.

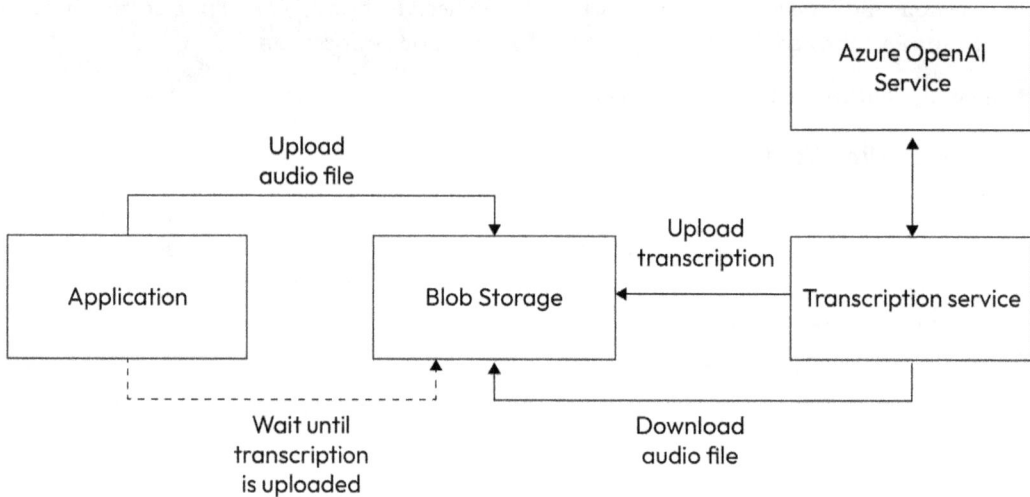

Figure 17.1 – Simple architecture of processing an audio file into a transcription

In *Figure 17.1*, we have an application that is integrated with Blob Storage to store audio files. To process those files, we'd have a separate service that will listen to blob uploads (this could be done, for instance, with Azure Functions and `BlobTrigger` or `EventGridTrigger`), and once a new audio file is available, it will call Azure OpenAI Service to process it with the audio client. Once the file is processed, the transcription can be uploaded back to Blob Storage and returned to the application. The setup may look trivial, but it allows you to implement quite a powerful feature with only a few steps.

Let's see now how one more type of data can be used and analyzed with Azure OpenAI Service – images.

Using an image client

The third data type that we could process using Azure OpenAI Service is images. Like audio files, images require dedicated AI models to get proper results as LLMs aren't suited to process them. In Azure OpenAI Service, you have the following models, which are useful when working with images:

- GPT-4.5
- GPT-4o

- GPT-4o mini

- GPT-4o Turbo

- DALL-E

Note that processing an image can be approached from two different perspectives – generating an image from text and analyzing an image to receive information such as image classification, description, or more advanced tasks including **optical character recognition** (**OCR**), document analysis, or **visual question answering** (**VQA**). The actual capabilities that can be leveraged depend heavily on the model used. For instance, if you want to generate an image based on the text input (prompt), you could use DALL-E. Here's an example of how it could be implemented using Azure OpenAI Service and the C# SDK:

```
var client = openAIClient.GetImageClient("dall-e-3"); /
var prompt = "A diverse group of people reading a book about Microsofy
Azure.";
ImageGenerationOptions options = new()
{
Quality = GeneratedImageQuality.High,
Size = GeneratedImageSize.W1792xH1024,
Style = GeneratedImageStyle.Vivid,
ResponseFormat = GeneratedImageFormat.Bytes
};
var image = client.GenerateImage(prompt, options);
```

Let's briefly describe the example. To work with images, we need to create an instance of an image client by providing the name of the deployment to use (remember that in Azure OpenAI Service, an AI model is selected when creating a deployment). Then, we're providing a prompt, which will be used to generate an image. If needed, we can provide additional details such as the quality of an image, its size, and its style. Once everything is up and ready, we can call a method that will generate an image that we could save locally or remotely.

Note

Remember that full examples are included in the repository for this chapter.

To use that feature in an application, we could come up with a simple architecture as presented in *Figure 17.2*.

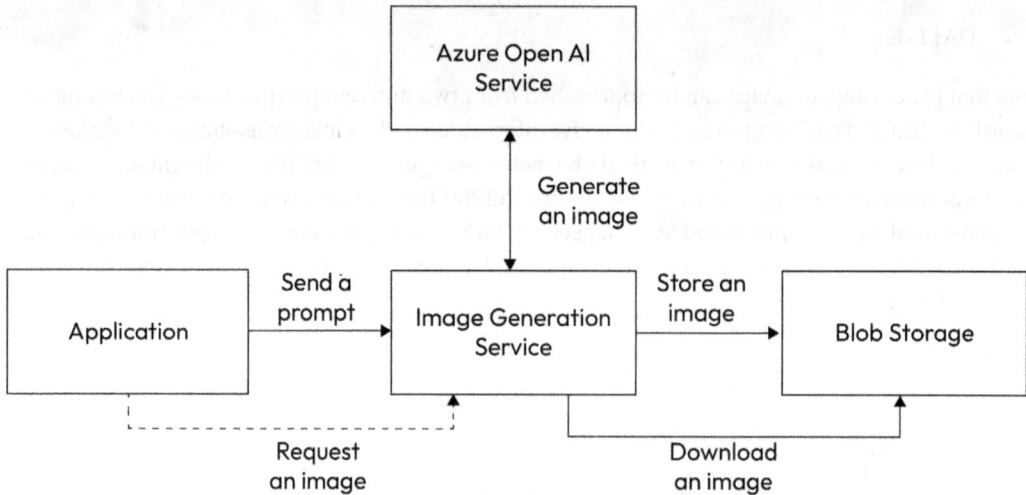

Figure 17.2 – Generating an image based on a prompt using Azure Open Service

In *Figure 17.2*, you can see how we have two separate applications – one providing an interface for a user to send a prompt and a second one that accepts and validates the prompt and connects with Azure OpenAI Service to generate an image. In this example, we're using Blob Storage to store the generated file and download it once requested from the user application. You may wonder why we're sending two separate requests to the image generation service instead of sending one and awaiting the result. We need to remember that generating an image may take time, especially if the prompt is very complex. The Azure OpenAI Service instance could also not be available. We could refine the architecture by adding a queue, which would ensure that no request is lost, as presented in *Figure 17.3*.

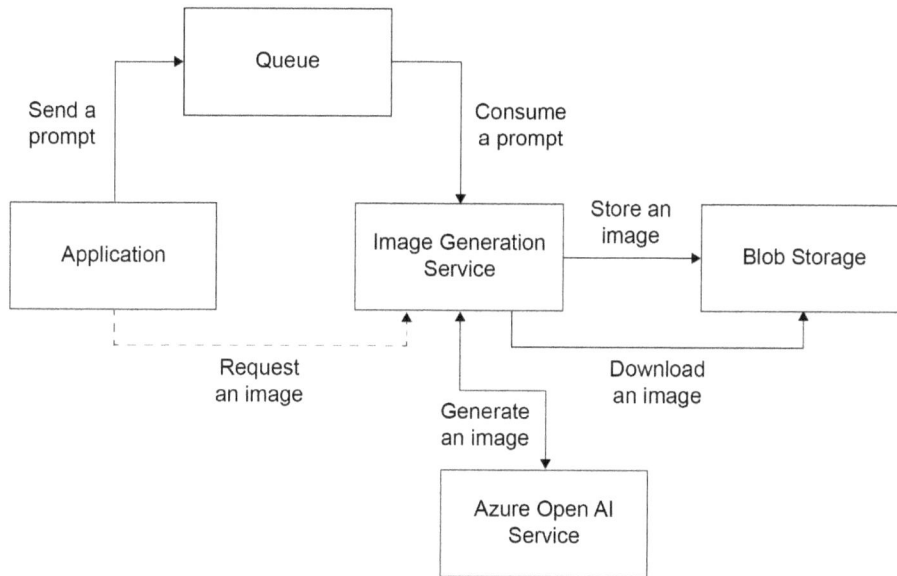

Figure 17.3 – Generating an image with a queue for increased reliability of the application

In *Figure 17.3*, you can see how we added a queue, which stores prompts, so the image generation service can process them in an asynchronous way. This setup increases the reliability of the whole architecture as it ensures that if Azure OpenAI Service isn't available or experiences difficulties, user prompts have persisted and can be consumed when the AI service is available again. Of course, this may not be suited for your application if you expect synchronous communication between the application and the service. As always, do not complicate a solution unless you're covering a specific requirement.

Let's talk about one more useful thing in some applications, which is embeddings.

Using an embeddings client

Before we see how we can use an embeddings client, let's characterize what **embeddings** actually are. The simplest description of embeddings is that they are a mathematical representation of data (whether it's text, audio, or video). In short, the provided input is transformed into vectors consisting of floating points. For a better explanation, let's consider the following two vectors:

- `Cat [0.2, -0.4, 0.7]`
- `Dog [0.6, 0.1, 0.5]`

Let's also visualize those vectors to see how close they are to each other (*Figure 17.4*). For simplicity, we'll ignore the third dimension.

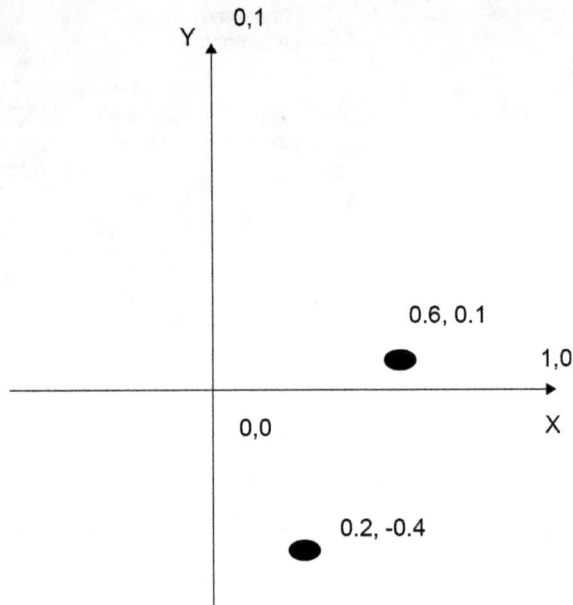

Figure 17.4 – Visual representation of embeddings based on two words (Cat and Dog)

For a comparison, let's consider the following words:

- Happy [-0.5, 0.9, 0.2]
- Sad [0.4, -0.7, -0.5]

Let's also visualize them so we can see how *close* they are to each other (*Figure 17.5*).

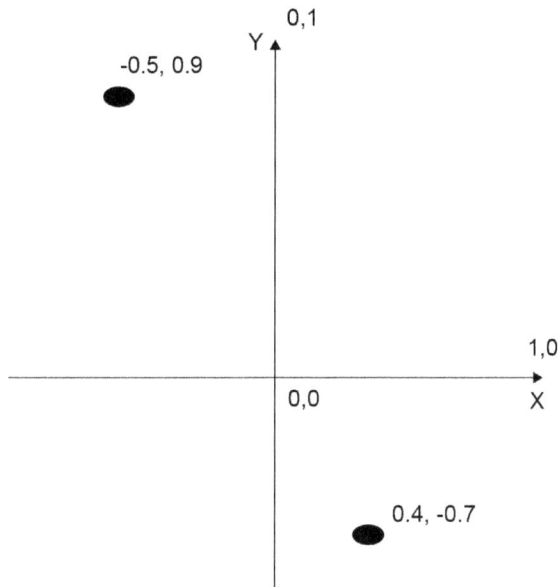

Figure 17.5 – Visual representation of embeddings for another
two words (Happy and Sad), which are opposites

Based on *Figure 17.4* and *Figure 17.5*, you can see how words, depending on their meaning, are represented differently with their vectors. What's even more interesting is that opposite words, such as *happy* and *sad*, are also presented on the opposite sides of the axis. Words that are similar (*cat* and *dog* – both are domestic animals) appear much closer to each other. This is exactly what embeddings are about – they give you information on how *close* the input data is to each other. With Azure OpenAI Service, you could get the embeddings by using a dedicated client from the SDK:

```
var client = openAIClient.GetEmbeddingClient("<deployment-name>");
var description = "This is a test embedding";
var embedding = client.GenerateEmbedding(description);
ReadOnlyMemory<float> vector = embedding.ToFloats();
```

The preceding code snippet works in a very similar way to the other code snippets presented for other SDK clients. Once you create a deployment with the selected AI model, you can use it to create the embeddings client and then generate embeddings based on the provided input.

You may wonder what the use case of the vectors returned by the embeddings client is. While the values collected for a single phrase won't provide much value, if you start collecting them for various data, you will be able to find interesting applications for them, including the following:

- Natural language processing
- Recommendation systems
- Image and video analysis
- Graph analysis
- Search engines

Let's discuss the two use cases that are the most common, which are **recommendation systems** and **search engines**. As embeddings give you a value that, when compared with another one, can tell how similar two things are, you could use them to recommend a certain feature or product to an end user. The only thing needed would be processing the description of something and saving it in the database. Then, you could use the embeddings to find things that are similar. Of course, that would require a little bit of mathematics as we'd need to compare vectors. An example of such a comparison would be using a concept called **cosine similarity**. To use it, you'd need to leverage its formula, which looks like this:

$$\cos(\theta) = \frac{A \cdot B}{\|A\| \, \|B\|}$$

Figure 17.6 – The formula for cosine similarity

As the formula uses cosine, it'll give you a value from -1 to 1, where -1 means that two vectors are completely opposite and 1 means that two vectors are the same. A simple example of calculating cosine similarity in Python could look like this:

```
import numpy as np

def cosine_similarity(x, y):
dot_product = np.dot(x, y)
magnitude_x = np.sqrt(np.sum(x**2))
magnitude_y = np.sqrt(np.sum(y**2))

return dot_product / (magnitude_x * magnitude_y)

dog = np.array([0.2, -0.4, 0.7])
cat = np.array([0.6, 0.1, 0.5])

similarity = cosine_similarity(dog, cat)
print(f"Cosine similarity between dog and cat: {similarity:.2f}")
```

For the preceding two vectors, the result will be 0.66. If you change the values to the Happy and Sad vectors, you'll get 0.33, which is low. I strongly encourage you to play a little bit with different values to see how the similarity changes depending on the vectors, so you understand how to use the values in a business application.

> **Tip**
>
> The method described where we calculate cosine similarity is useful if you want to compare values in code. It's also worth mentioning there are databases that natively support embeddings. Those databases are called vector databases, and their engines are built specifically to work with vectors. Examples of such databases include MongoDB Atlas, pgvector, Chroma, and Milvus.

Let's talk now about a slightly different topic than SDK clients. We'll see how we can fine-tune pre-trained models in Azure OpenAI Service to teach them more about our domain or feed them more domain-specific data.

Fine-tuning models in Azure OpenAI Service

Before you decide whether you should fine-tune your model, you need to understand whether it's the only method to improve the quality of responses received from it. Sometimes the issue isn't with a model but rather with the prompts used to interact with it. Another possibility to make things better is using **Retrieval Augmented Generation** (**RAG**) to include external sources and data automatically in the prompts. If those methods aren't changing anything, fine-tuning may be the solution you need. The process of fine-tuning Azure OpenAI Service models is described in detail on the following documentation page: https://learn.microsoft.com/en-us/azure/ai-services/openai/how-to/fine-tuning. Hence, we won't be rephrasing what's already available for you. Instead, we'll focus on incorporating the fine-tuning process into your application.

> **Note**
>
> Remember that not all models allow fine-tuning. Always reference documentation before you make efforts to implement a fine-tuning process for your application.

Conceptually, a **fine-tuning** process is a procedure that is supposed to increase the quality of responses from AI models and make them specialized in certain tasks. It's an alternative approach to training a model from scratch – a process that takes lots of time, money, and compute power to complete successfully. By fine-tuning a model, you tweak it rather than re-implement it, which limits the risk of having an overtrained or badly trained model. There is, however, one advantage of training from scratch: if you have a massive dataset that you'd like to incorporate into an AI model, fine-tuning may not be the best solution as it will require a tremendous amount of time to prepare that data for the fine-tuning process.

Fine-tuning, most of the time, consists of the following steps:

1. Selecting a pre-trained model
2. Preparing task-specific data
3. Modifying the model architecture
4. Training with adjusted parameters
5. Evaluating and optimizing

Some of those steps may be unclear, so let's explain them:

1. Selecting a pre-trained model: We need to select a model that not only is available for fine-tuning in Azure OpenAI Service but also reflects our business needs. There's no value in fine-tuning a model that isn't suited for the work we're doing.

2. Preparing task-specific data: We should prepare a curated dataset that is tightly coupled with the tasks we'd like to give the model in the future. This dataset should be also split into smaller datasets (training, validation, and test) and cleaned so there are no duplicates or invalid entries.

3. Modifying model architecture: This step is automatically performed by Azure OpenAI Service (or rather, Azure OpenAI Service doesn't allow you to modify the architecture of models) but is generally quite important when fine-tuning a model you host directly. It's about preserving the general features of a model by just adjusting the final layers, so they become task-specific.

4. Training with adjusted parameters: This step is focused mostly on training with stages, so you can ensure the stability of a model (i.e., see whether your efforts are improving the quality of responses or, on the contrary, they lower the ability of a model to reason properly).

5. Evaluating and optimizing: The last step is about verifying the result of fine-tuning by approaching the model with additional tasks such as testing using data never presented to a model (so you can be sure it's able to understand the context). This step includes additional iterations until a model achieves the expected accuracy.

Let's now check how fine-tuning can be approached in Azure OpenAI Service.

Incorporating fine-tuning into your application

In Azure OpenAI Service, when you want to fine-tune a model, you need to prepare training data in a specific format called **JSON Lines** (**JSONL**). Each line consists of a JSON object containing the system prompt, the user's prompt, and the response:

```
{
"messages": [
{
"role": "system",
"content": "You are a highly professional consultant who always
answers questions by providing at least one source you used to provide
an answer."
},
{
"role": "user",
"content": "Which Azure database service is considered the best?"
},
{
"role": "assistant",
"content": "It's difficult to definitively say which Azure database
service is the best, as it largely depends on the specific use case
and requirements of the application. However, some of the most popular
Azure database services include:\n\n1. **Azure SQL Database**: A
fully managed relational database service that is highly scalable and
offers built-in intelligence.\n2. **Azure Cosmos DB**: A globally
distributed, multi-model database service that supports various data
models including document, key-value, graph, and column-family.\
n3. **Azure Database for PostgreSQL**: A managed PostgreSQL database
service that provides high availability and security features.\
n4. **Azure Database for MySQL**: A managed MySQL database service
that offers scalability and flexibility.\n\nEach of these services
has its own strengths and is suited for different scenarios. For
example, if you need a globally distributed database with low latency,
Azure Cosmos DB might be the best choice. If you are looking for a
relational database with strong transactional support, Azure SQL
Database could be ideal.\n\nFor more information on Azure database
services, you can refer to the official documentation: [Azure Database
Services](https://azure.microsoft.com/en-us/services/)."
}
]
}
```

In the example, you can see how the system prompt and the answer instruct the model to answer according to our expectations. Of course, a single JSON line won't change how a model behaves – you'll need much more data generated to make fine-tuning worth trying. The amount of data needed to fine-tune the model will depend on your use case, that is, how specialized you'd like your model to become, how much detail is required in the answers, and how good the training data is. That's also why doing that in iterations is that important. Instead of preparing one big batch and then evaluating the results, you could do it round by round, so if needed you could adjust the data or discard the process and start from scratch.

The high-level concept of how you could continuously fine-tune your model is presented in *Figure 17.7*.

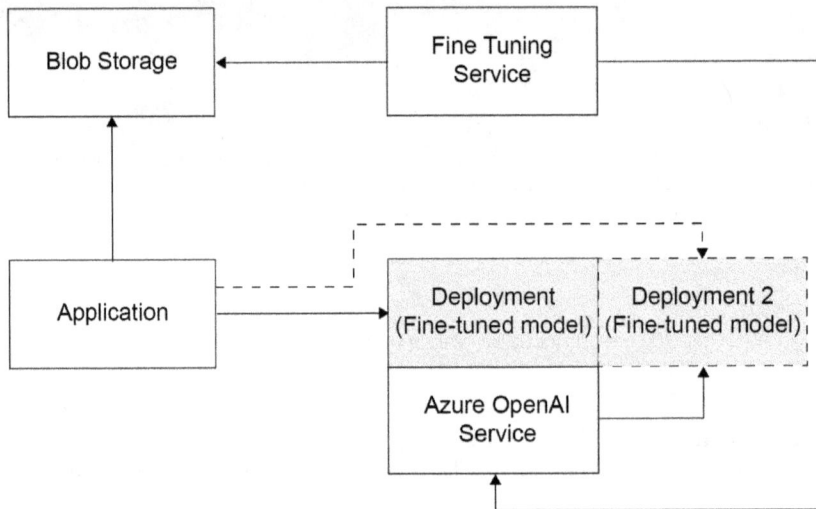

Figure 17.7 – A high-level architecture where an application uses a continuously fine-tuned AI model

In *Figure 17.7*, you can see how an application uses a deployed AI model from Azure OpenAI Service but also integrates with Blob Storage. Blob Storage can be used to store JSON objects used for fine-tuning after applying the following process:

1. The application sends a prompt to an AI model and collects a response.

2. The full training set (system prompt + user prompt + response) is then saved in Blob Storage using an append blob (as we need to have data prepared as JSONL).

3. JSONL files can be then refined by somebody with domain knowledge, so original responses from the AI model are adjusted so they reflect how the model should behave.

Once the training data is prepared, we could have a separate service (fine-tuning service) that is responsible for taking the training data and using it to fine-tune the model we're using. To achieve that, you'd need to call two API endpoints exposed by Azure OpenAI Service:

- **Import file**: https://learn.microsoft.com/en-us/rest/api/azureopenai/ files/import?view=rest-azureopenai-2024-10-21&tabs=HTTP

- **Create fine-tune job**: https://learn.microsoft.com/en-us/rest/api/ azureopenai/fine-tuning/create?view=rest-azureopenai-2024-10-21&tabs=HTTP

The reason you need to use two endpoints is that the second endpoint (the one that creates a fine-tuning job) requires a training file as input. The problem here is that the training file (its content) can't be passed as an input. You need to upload a training file first and then reference it when a job is created. When the fine-tuned model is ready, you will need to perform one more action – change the configuration of your application so it uses a new deployment name instead of the old one. This concept is presented in *Figure 17.8*.

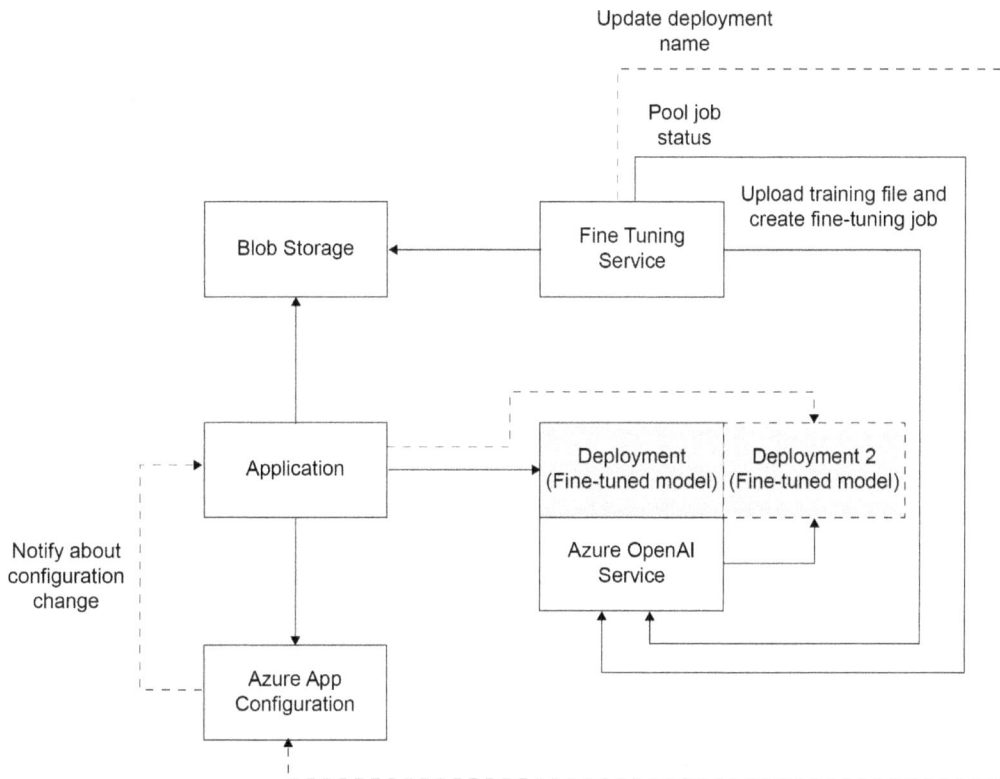

Figure 17.8 – Leveraging Azure App Configuration to update the
configuration of an application so it used another model

In *Figure 17.8*, you can see how we added one additional component – Azure App Configuration. We're then using it to notify an application if there's a change in the configuration. The change (in our case, new AI model deployment) happens when the fine-tuning service gets the information from Azure OpenAI Service that the fine-tuning job has been completed.

> **Note**
>
> To get the status of a fine-tuning job, you can use another API endpoint: `https://learn.microsoft.com/en-us/rest/api/azureopenai/fine-tuning/get?view=rest-azureopenai-2024-10-21&tabs=HTTP`.

With the approach described, you could implement a continuous fine-tuning process with only a few services. The benefit of using Azure OpenAI Service here is that it does all the hard work, such as hosting a model and running a fine-tuning job. Note that in this section, we discussed fine-tuning that is focused mostly on text data. If you'd like to fine-tune a model meant for images, check out the following link: `https://learn.microsoft.com/en-us/azure/ai-services/openai/how-to/fine-tuning-vision`.

For the last topic related to integrating an application with Azure OpenAI Service, let's talk about content filtering.

Understanding content filters

When using AI models, you need to be prepared for users who would like to exploit its limitations or get answers that are morally questionable. As AI models such as LLMs don't really think, they always try to provide an answer that is as correct as possible. This can lead to damage to your company's image, especially if the generated response is controversial even though the user's prompt looked correct (this may happen if a model isn't generalized, meaning it treats some prompts as completely different even though they have the same meaning). To avoid such a situation, you could use content filters.

> **Note**
>
> It's true that you could properly fine-tune a model so it doesn't respond to certain questions or doesn't generate images or audio that could be harmful. You need to remember, though, that covering all possible cases with Gen AI is a challenging task; it's easier to catch some inappropriate content with a filter rather than trying to find all the possible harmful prompts.

You can find a detailed description of how to implement a content filter using Azure OpenAI Service at the following link: `https://learn.microsoft.com/en-us/azure/ai-services/openai/how-to/content-filters`. For this section, though, let's focus on how content filters affect the way you integrate with Azure OpenAI Service to design your application in general.

The way content filters work is that they're applied to the prompt you're sending and verify whether the response should be blocked or not. If a content filter isn't applied, this is how a question and response will be handled. Let's say you're sending the following question:

```
{
"prompt":"A question about a harmful topic."
}
```

If the content filter isn't enabled, the AI model will respond as for any other topic:

```
{
"id": "example-id",
"object": "text_completion",
"created": 1743862259,
"model": "gpt-4o",
"choices": [
{
"text": "Even though the question is about a harmful action, the model
responds with a neutral statement. It does not endorse or promote any
harmful behavior, but rather provides a factual answer to the question
asked.",
"index": 0,
"finish_reason": "stop",
"logprobs": null
}
]
}
```

Let's now check what happens for the same prompt if a content filter is enabled:

```
{
"error": {
"message": "The response was filtered",
"type": null,
"param": "prompt",
"code": "content_filter",
"status": 400
}
}
```

As you can see, instead of giving us the standard HTTP 200 response, Azure OpenAI Service returns HTTP 400, meaning the request is considered invalid and should be fixed (in our case, the prompt should be changed to one that doesn't talk about a harmful or controversial topic). Technically, it's important to prepare our application for such situations, that is, catching the error returned from the service because the content filter blocked a response. For reference, let's assume we have the following code written in JavaScript:

```javascript
const client = new OpenAIClient(
endpoint,
new AzureKeyCredential(azureApiKey));

const deploymentId = "<deployment-name>";
const events = await client.listChatCompletions(
deploymentId, messages, { maxTokens: 128 });
```

Once Azure OpenAI Service returns a response, it will be assigned to the constant named events. Now, the response may contain either a normal answer or the one blocked by the content filter. This is why we'd need to perform a check for each answer and categorize it:

```javascript
for await (const event of events) {
for (const choice of event.choices) {console.log(choice.message);
if (!choice.contentFilterResults) {console.log("No content filter is
found"); return;
}
if (choice.contentFilterResults.error) {console.log( `Content filter
ran into the error ${choice.contentFilterResults.error.code}:
${choice.contentFilterResults.error.message}` );
} else {
const { hate, sexual, selfHarm, violence } = choice.
contentFilterResults;
console.log(`Hate category is filtered: ${hate?.filtered} with
${hate?.severity} severity` );
console.log(`Sexual category is filtered: ${sexual?.filtered} with
${sexual?.severity} severity`);
console.log(`Self-harm category is filtered: ${selfHarm?.filtered}
with ${selfHarm?.severity} severity`);
console.log(`Violence category is filtered: ${violence?.filtered} with
${violence?.severity} severity`);
}
}
}
```

This example presents a way to detect why a prompt was blocked based on the filter category (hate, sexual, self-harm, violence). When using content filters and integrating Azure OpenAI Service with an application, it's important to collect information about blocked prompts for further analysis. For some prompts, it may appear they're blocked because of an error (those would be false positives). However, if somebody or something is constantly sending harmful prompts, it may be an attempt to exploit your application.

That was the last topic about integrating an application with Azure OpenAI Service. Let's now talk about the use cases for using that service.

Learning about use cases for Azure OpenAI Service

Azure OpenAI Service itself is a generic service that can be used to host supported OpenAI models. As could also be seen in this chapter, it offers additional features, such as a managed fine-tuning process and content filtering, that can be incorporated into any application to enhance its capabilities. Azure OpenAI Service also comes with an SDK supporting various programming languages, so it's not limited to a single programming stack. Thanks to all those traits, it can support a number of different use cases. Let's characterize them.

Using Azure OpenAI Service for content creation

The most common feature (or the most popular one) when using AI models is content creation. Whether it's text, image, or audio, all you need to do is select the correct AI model, deploy it within the service, and create a dedicated client using the SDK. With Azure OpenAI Service, you can create descriptions of products based on provided input, prepare transcriptions of recordings, and generate images.

Using Azure OpenAI Service for automation

Another option for using Azure OpenAI Service is leveraging its capabilities to automate processes. For instance, you could use AI models to migrate the legacy code base to a new framework. While such a process requires human interaction to verify the result and instruct the model to provide correct results, with some effort required to automate that process, the only thing you'd need is to find a way to send the code base to the model and collect the results in a meaningful way.

The second idea for automation would be automating internal processes such as collecting documents and validating them. With a proper AI model, you could create an agent that will monitor different APIs and provide insights on what's missing to complete the onboarding process of a new employee.

Using Azure OpenAI Service for chatbots and assistants

Quite a common use case for using AI models is building chatbots and assistants. In this chapter, we mentioned Bot Framework, which seamlessly integrates with Azure OpenAI Service and allows you to easily incorporate an LLM into a conversation with a user. The benefit of such an approach over the legacy one, where all the conversation was static, is the ability to build a dynamic process, where the assistant may not only react to what a user is saying but also generate responses on the fly. With the addition of RAG, you could also enhance the given prompts to provide more accurate answers.

Using Azure OpenAI Service for product innovation

Let's consider the following use case – you own an e-commerce shop and sell clothing or shoes. With AI models, you could introduce lots of innovation to the user experience by generating videos or images of people wearing clothes or shoes you're selling. All you would need is to generate proper prompts, generate the content, and include it on your website. Of course, it requires lots of work to find the proper prompts and refine them later. This is, however, a creative process that allows you to get the exact results in no time.

Using Azure OpenAI Service for semantic search

In this chapter, we discussed the concept of embeddings and how they could be used when searching for data. This is an excellent example of how AI models can be utilized to improve the performance of your application or increase the accuracy of search results. To fully leverage that use case, remember that it'd be best if you had a vector database that could store embeddings and use them in queries.

Using Azure OpenAI Service for data labeling

One more use case worth mentioning for AI models is data labeling. If you need to attach labels to the data you stored, you could assign a team of people and let them do the work. This is, however, quite a tiresome task that makes most sense if the team is AI-assisted. Thanks to Azure OpenAI Service, you could deploy a model that will be used by the team to perform the initial labeling and then use the result to create a repository of initially labeled data. That repository can be then used to say whether the labels are right or wrong. While no AI-based result will be 100% correct, having this initial assessment made by an AI model speeds things up and lets you focus on more important tasks.

Utilizing open-sourced libraries for OpenAI

If you're interested in using Azure OpenAI in your projects, you may be interested in learning about the available libraries that can be used to integrate with OpenAI models:

- `https://github.com/openai/openai-python`

- `https://github.com/openai/openai-node`

- `https://github.com/openai/openai-dotnet`

They offer a seamless integration with hosted OpenAI models and are constantly updated whenever a new API is available.

That's all for this chapter! Let's summarize what we have learned.

Summary

In this chapter, we talked about Azure OpenAI Service – a managed service offered by Microsoft that allows you to host a selected AI model and integrate it with your application. We discussed the way an application can use Azure OpenAI Service using an SDK and what is needed to authenticate the service. We also saw multiple SDK clients that you could use to work with text, audio, images, or video.

We also saw in detail how embeddings work and how they could be used in an application. While a full understanding of the concept requires reading more about specific machine learning and mathematics concepts, the introduction presented in this chapter should be enough to get started with the topic and understand how it can help in providing business value out of the selected AI model.

There were also two additional topics that we described – fine-tuning and content filtering. Those two concepts are really important if you're thinking about making a real product based on AI models. Of course, without fine-tuning, your model will work just fine, but most companies don't look for a generic solution; they need specialized agents and assistants that are able to answer specific questions. Content filtering, though, is something every application should implement. Without those filters, users may accidentally receive unwanted responses, which will impact the image of your company. Content filters also prevent users from exploiting your service.

In the next chapter, we will talk about using Azure Machine Learning to automate machine learning tasks. If you liked this chapter, the next one is something you should check out.

18

Leveraging Azure Machine Learning to Automate Machine Learning Tasks

In the ever-evolving landscape of artificial intelligence and machine learning, automation has emerged as a cornerstone for driving efficiency, scalability, and innovation. Azure Machine Learning stands at the forefront of this transformation, offering developers, data scientists, and organizations a robust platform to simplify and accelerate their machine learning workflows. This chapter delves into how Azure Machine Learning's automated capabilities empower professionals to streamline the traditionally complex processes of model selection, training, deployment, and monitoring.

Azure Machine Learning provides a suite of tools designed to democratize machine learning. Its **automated machine learning** (**AutoML**) feature is particularly noteworthy for its ability to intelligently select algorithms with minimal human intervention. Whether you're tackling classification, regression, or forecasting tasks, AutoML reduces the barriers to entry for users with varying levels of expertise by delivering high-performing models tailored to your specific needs.

In this chapter, we're going to cover the following main topics:

- Understanding how AutoML works
- Implementing auto-training using AutoML
- Auto-training a forecasting model
- Integrating an ONNX model with an application
- Learning about use cases

Technical requirements

To perform the exercises in this chapter, you will need the following:

- Azure CLI
- IDE of your choice (preferably Visual Studio Code)

Understanding how AutoML works

Nowadays, more and more applications are expected to incorporate various advanced features to be able to compete with other services. Machine learning is one of those enhancements that allow your service to predict, assume, and discover without human interaction. The downside of the standard machine learning approach is that it is iterative and time-consuming. To overcome that challenge, one could implement an AutoML process, which allows people working with machine learning models to increase their velocity and shorten the time to market when delivering new versions of their solutions.

In short, AutoML consists of the following elements:

- Identifying the problem
- Choosing the coding environment (low-code or code-first)
- Specifying the sources of data
- Configuring the parameters of the automated process
- Running the training job and evaluating the results

We could also describe the process of AutoML by approaching the listed stages differently:

- **Data preparation**: AutoML tools automate preprocessing tasks such as handling missing values, scaling features, and encoding variables. This ensures the data is ready for modeling without requiring manual intervention.

- **Model selection**: AutoML automatically identifies the most suitable algorithms for a given problem based on the dataset and task type (e.g., classification or regression). It may also assemble ensemble models to improve predictive performance.

- **Hyperparameter tuning**: AutoML optimizes model parameters to enhance accuracy and prevent underfitting or overfitting. This process is automated and often results in better-performing models compared to manual tuning.

- **Deployment**: AutoML simplifies model deployment by wrapping models as REST API endpoints or integrating them into cloud platforms for scalability.

The overall process is described as presented in *Figure 18.1*.

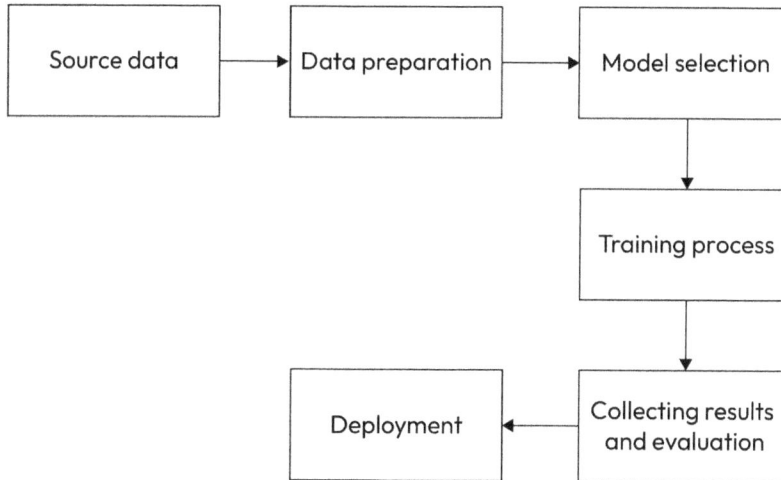

Figure 18.1 – High-level overview of the AutoML process

During the training process, you could evaluate various machine learning models to see which fits the data the most. It's also important to remember that, depending on the expected result, you should select a different category of models:

- Use a **classification model** for predicting a categorical variable from the given dataset
- For predicting continuous values, a **regression model** will be the best
- To reduce the number of features in a dataset you could try to use a **dimensionality reduction model**
- If you want to generate new data, use **generative models**
- For grouping similar data, **clustering models** sound like a good match

> **Note**
>
> If you aren't familiar with the whole process of selecting and training machine learning models, feel free to try the following web page, which explains in detail the overall process and provides lots of guidance for people who are getting started with the topic: `https://www.projectpro.io/article/model-selection-in-machine-learning/824`.

In applications that are expected to quickly react to the changes to the initial dataset or to implement new features based on the new data, AutoML is the only reasonable approach to consider. There are multiple benefits of automating the machine learning process, including the following:

- **Accessibility for non-experts**: It allows non-experts to work and train machine learning models without prior knowledge about the topic

- **Increased productivity**: Instead of losing time on repetitive tasks, people working with AutoML can focus on finding solutions to the real problem and spend more time refining the models or data

- **Optimized model performance**: AutoML often delivers high-performing models through techniques such as automated hyperparameter optimization and ensemble modeling, ensuring better accuracy and robustness

- **Efficiency**: Automation reduces the time required to build and deploy machine learning models, enabling rapid prototyping and faster time to insight for organizations

- **Handling data quality issues**: AutoML tools are equipped to manage missing values or noisy data, which improves model reliability in real-world scenarios

- **Scalability**: AutoML platforms integrate seamlessly with cloud services such as Azure Machine Learning, allowing models to scale efficiently across large datasets or applications

- **Improved interpretability**: Some AutoML frameworks provide tools for understanding model predictions through feature importance rankings or explainability reports, which are critical in regulated industries such as finance or healthcare

What's interesting about AutoML in Azure Machine Learning is that you can use both the Python SDK and Azure CLI to run your experiments. Let's check how it works.

Choosing between the Python SDK and Azure CLI

Both the Python SDK and Azure CLI can be a viable development environment for developing machine learning experiments using the Azure Machine Learning service. You may wonder how Azure CLI could be used here – all in all, it's just a command-line interface used for running various commands. With Azure Machine Learning, Azure CLI can be used as an orchestrator – using a dedicated schema, you can describe what (and how) you want to do and then use Azure CLI to run your code. The command used for running the experiments looks like this:

```
az ml job create \
--file <path-to-experiment-file> \
-w <ml-workspace> \
-g <resource-group-name> \
--subscription <subscription>
```

> **Note**
> Of course, running an experiment using Azure Machine Learning requires an instance of the service deployed first. You can read about creating an instance of this service here: `https://learn.microsoft.com/en-us/azure/machine-learning/quickstart-create-resources`.

In the preceding command, you need to provide four different parameters:

- `--file`: Path to the file that contains YAML describing an experiment.
- `-w`: Name of Azure Machine Learning workspace created by you (or for you).
- `-g`: Resource group name where the workspace is created.
- `--subscription`: Name of the subscription where the workspace is created. This parameter is optional; you may skip it if you are running the command being logged in to the same subscription where the workspace can be found.

The most important part of the command is the YAML file. The schema for the file is well defined here: `https://azuremlschemas.azureedge.net/latest/MLTable.schema.json`. We'll discuss various examples in the next part of this chapter.

The benefit of using Azure CLI over the Python SDK is a slightly easier setup, as you may skip some common operations such as authentication. When using the Python SDK, you always need to authenticate in Azure before using the actual SDK methods. While Azure CLI doesn't give you the ability to skip the authentication, the step is incorporated into the tool and just requires selecting the right command instead of installing an external package and configuring it.

> **Note**
> If you choose to run experiments using CI/CD pipelines, you will still be able to use Azure CLI to complete the process. The only thing needed will be to provide credentials for an agent running the command. If your CI/CD agents are installed on Azure VMs, you could leverage a managed identity. The alternative solution would include creating a service principal and injecting the credentials into your CI/CD pipelines.

If you want to authenticate to Azure in Python, you could use the `azure.identity` package, as follows:

```
from azure.identity import DefaultAzureCredential
credential = DefaultAzureCredential()
```

We'll use that code snippet more in the next part of this chapter, where we'll be building some functionalities based on Azure Machine Learning capabilities. To better understand how Azure CLI and the Python SDK are different in the context of Azure Machine Learning, let's do a quick comparison:

- Azure CLI works well in automation and scripted workflows as it offers seamless integration with CI/CD pipelines.

- The Python SDK excels in more sophisticated tasks, which require granular control and better control over the experiment run with Azure Machine Learning. It also integrates with Jupyter notebooks and various IDEs.

- Azure CLI may be limited in some areas, including experiment tracking, hyperparameter tuning, and model registration.

- Debugging may be difficult when using Azure CLI.

Before we discuss the auto-training mechanism for AutoML, let's focus for a moment on the scalability of machine learning models and how they can be autoscaled to meet the changing demand.

Autoscaling deployed models

When you complete training and deploy your machine learning model, you may realize that a single endpoint for that model isn't enough for the real demand. Also, as your application grows bigger and is available to new customers, you may need to scale out your models, so you don't have a single point of failure. Fortunately, Azure Machine Learning offers seamless integration with Azure Monitor, which enables us to configure the autoscaling mechanism based on the selected metric. You can find the concept of that functionality in *Figure 18.2*.

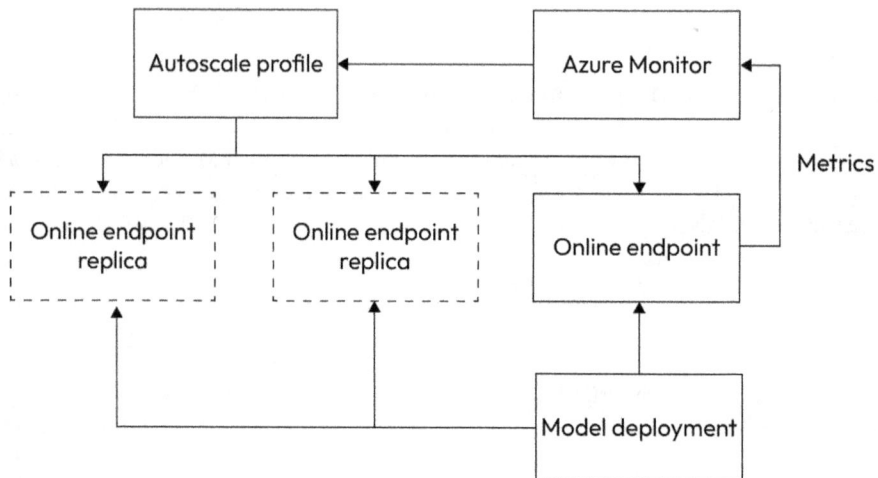

Figure 18.2 – Autoscaling concept with the use of the autoscale profile from Azure Monitor

In *Figure 18.2*, you can see how we're utilizing metrics published by our online endpoint to see whether we need to scale out the available endpoints. The whole functionality is based on the autoscale profile added to Azure Monitor. The whole operation can be performed with Azure CLI using the following commands:

```
DEPLOYMENT_RESOURCE_ID=$(az ml online-deployment show -e <endpoint-
name> -n <deployment-name> -o tsv --query "id")
az monitor autoscale create \
--name <autoscale-settings-name> \
--resource $DEPLOYMENT_RESOURCE_ID \
--min-count 1
--max-count 3
--count 2
az monitor autoscale rule create \
--autoscale-name <autoscale-settings-name> \
--condition "CpuUtilizationPercentage > 80 avg 5m" \
--scale out 1
```

With the preceding rule defined, Azure Monitor would trigger the deployment of a new endpoint each time the average utilization of CPU for the last 5 minutes exceeds 80%. If you want to learn more about the syntax of those commands, check the Azure CLI reference: `https://learn.microsoft.com/en-us/cli/azure/monitor/autoscale?view=azure-cli-latest`.

Now we have explained the initial concept of what AutoML is and how it can be used in an application, let's see how we can implement it using the Azure Machine Learning service.

Implementing auto-training using AutoML

As mentioned at the beginning of this chapter, AutoML is basically an approach where you improve the overall process of machine learning implemented for your service by leveraging automation. In this section, we will discuss various scenarios where such an approach may be beneficial, starting with processing tabular data.

Working with tabular data

Before we get started with describing how to implement AutoML for **tabular data**, let's describe what tabular data actually is. You can describe tabular data as data that is structured/organized using rows and columns. In some ways, tabular data resembles a table. One of the most common tabular data formats is **comma-separated values** (**CSV**). A simple example of such a format would look like this:

```
Johh,Doe,25,Warsaw,500600700
```

In some cases, CSV files may include the **header row** – a row that includes the names of columns for easier parsing:

```
Name,surname,age,home_city,phone_number
Johh,Doe,25,Warsaw,500600700
```

CSV files are also easily parsed by common tools, including typical office software such as Microsoft Excel. To work with such data in Azure Machine Learning, we need to complete a few steps, which will be described in the following pages. The first step is getting started with authentication and MLClient (needed for Python). An example code snippet for that operation would look like this:

```
from azure.identity import DefaultAzureCredential
from azure.ai.ml import MLClient
credential = DefaultAzureCredential()
ml_client = None
try:
ml_client = MLClient(
credential,
"<subscription-id>",
"<resource-group-name>",
"<workspace-name>")
except Exception as ex:
print(ex)
```

As you can see, we're using the `azure-ai-ml` package to create an `MLClient` object. To install the package (and the one used for authenticating to Azure), you could use the following command:

```
pip install azure-ai-ml azure-identity
```

The prerequisite for that is using the `azure.identity` package to create an instance of the `DefaultAzureCredential` object, so we get access to the credentials chain used to obtain the access token for Azure. If you want to use Azure CLI instead, the only thing needed will be this single command:

```
az login
```

Once we're logged in, the next step when working with tabular data would be specifying the data source and format. In the Python SDK, the concept used here is called MLTable. Creating MLTable is very simple – you just need a single method available in the SDK:

```
import mltable
paths = [
{'file': '<path-to-file>.csv'}
]
train_table = mltable.from_delimited_files(paths) train_table.
save('<training-data-path>')
```

Note the following things when analyzing this code snippet:

- MLTable can be created from multiple files
- Once MLTable is created, it can be saved locally to the selected directory

> **Note**
> Remember that the SDK must be able to access files to create MLTable from them. This is especially important if you're running the script remotely.

When using MLTable, you also need to take into account that it requires the predicted value (target column) to be presented in the dataset. Let's consider the following CSV file:

```
Name,surname,age,home_city,phone_number
Johh,Doe,25,Warsaw,500600700
```

It's just a fixed dataset that could be used for training, but there's no column to predict. This is why we'd need to change it to something like this:

```
Name,surname,age,home_city,phone_number,customer_classification
Johh,Doe,25,Warsaw,500600700,
```

In this example, we added the `customer_classification` column with a blank value. Now, we could use it when running the experiment, as in this example:

```
from azure.ai.ml.constants import AssetTypes
from azure.ai.ml import automl, Input
my_training_data_input = Input(
type=AssetTypes.MLTABLE,
path="<training-data-path>")
classification_job = automl.classification(compute=my_compute_name,
experiment_name=my_exp_name, training_data=my_training_data_input,
target_column_name="customer_classification",
primary_metric="accuracy",
n_cross_validations=5, enable_model_explainability=True)
```

This example presents how we could create a classification job that would try to predict the value of the `customer_classification` column. Note also how training data is being passed – we're using MLTable, which would be created in the previous step by providing the `<training-data-path>` parameter.

We could achieve the same result by using Azure CLI and the YAML file with the following structure:

```
$schema: https://azuremlschemas.azureedge.net/latest/MLTable.schema.
json
paths:
file: <path-to-file>.csv
transformations:
read_delimited:
delimiter: ','
encoding: 'ascii'
```

In the code snippet for Azure CLI, you can see how we're doing the same operation we did for the Python SDK – we read local files and transform them into a dataset used for training. To implement the classification job as we did for the Python SDK, we'd need to use a slightly different schema:

```
$schema: https://azuremlsdk2.blob.core.windows.net/preview/0.0.1/
autoMLJob.schema.json
type: automl
experiment_name: <name-of-the-experiment>
training_data: path: "./train_data"
type: mltable
compute: azureml:<my_compute_name>
primary_metric: accuracy
target_column_name: customer_classification
n_cross_validations: 5
enable_model_explainability: True
```

The MLTable object used in those examples can also work with other file formats/sources, such as the following:

- Parquet
- Delta Lake
- JSONL

Now, to configure the experiment, we'd need to use the following code in Python:

```
classification_job.set_training(blocked_training_
algorithms=["<algorithm>"], enable_onnx_compatible_models=True )
```

As the experiment considered in this section involves processing tabular data, the algorithms available are as follows:

- Classification
- Regression
- Forecasting

The last step involves running the experiment using the Azure Machine Learning service. This step is rather straightforward as it requires using `MLClient` to start the training job:

```
job = ml_client.jobs.create_or_update( classification_job ) endpoint =
job.services["Studio"].endpoint
```

The same can be achieved using the `az ml job create` command, as described in the previous section.

So far, we have created a training dataset, created a training job, and ran it with Azure Machine Learning. You may wonder where the actual AutoML approach is in here. In order to make it fully automated, we'd need to find a way to run the whole process without human supervision. Depending on the method (Python or Azure CLI), we'll need a slightly different approach. Let's discuss it in the next section.

Running the experiments automatically

Running experiments automatically using Azure Machine Learning will depend on the method we selected (Python SDK or Azure CLI). For Python, we have a number of different options available, but they will all have a common denominator – containerizing our Python application. Once the application is containerized, you could use the following Azure service to run the application:

- Azure Functions
- Azure Container Apps
- Azure Container Instances
- Azure Kubernetes Service

An example Dockerfile to create a container image could look like this:

```
FROM python:3.9-slim
ENV PYTHONDONTWRITEBYTECODE=1
ENV PYTHONUNBUFFERED=1
WORKDIR /app
COPY . /app
RUN apt-get update && apt-get install -y --no-install-recommends
build-essential libssl-dev libffi-dev python3-dev && apt-get clean &&
rm -rf /var/lib/apt/lists/*
RUN pip install --upgrade pip && pip install azureml-sdk[automl] &&
pip install -r requirements.txt
EXPOSE 5000
CMD ["python", "main.py"]
```

Once the Dockerfile is built and pushed to a container registry (such as Azure Container Registry), you can run it in the selected environment. The overall process is presented in *Figure 18.3*.

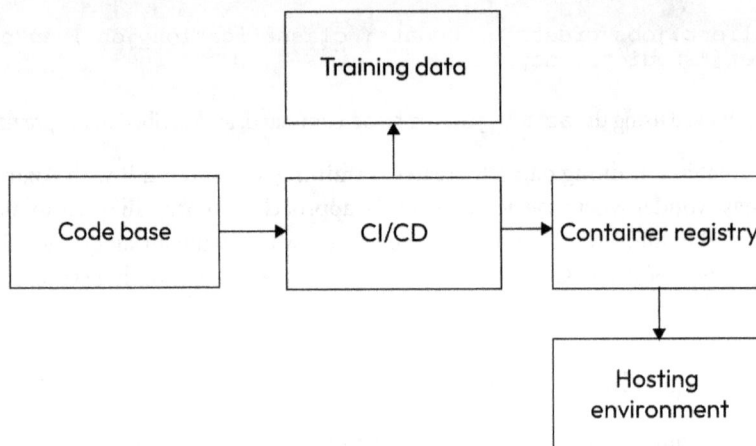

Figure 18.3 – Running automated experiments using CI/CD and containerized application

In *Figure 18.3*, you can see how our application is continuously built with CI/CD, and the training data is loaded whenever it's needed. The trick here is to update the dataset used for training and trigger the pipeline whenever new data is available. Each time a new container image is created, it can be deployed to the selected hosting environment, where it can run and return the endpoint, which we can use to interact with the trained model.

> **Note**
>
> The preceding example Dockerfile assumes that the training data would be downloaded onto the CI/CD agent and copied into an image. For large datasets, that approach may be cumbersome or generate large images. For alternative solutions, check out the idea presented later in this section.

If your training data is quite large (for instance, gigabytes in size), it may be better to either download it when the code used for training runs or is mounted via volume into a container. For the former, downloading it can be done in many different ways. For example, if the data is stored using Azure Blob Storage, you could use the following code:

```
from azure.storage.blob import BlobServiceClient
connection_string = "your_connection_string"
container_name = "your_container_name"
blob_name = "your_blob_name"
download_file_path = "path_to_save_downloaded_file"
blob_service_client = BlobServiceClient.from_connection_
string(connection_string)
```

```
blob_client = blob_service_client.get_blob_client(container=container_
name, blob=blob_name)
with open(download_file_path, "wb") as download_file: download_file.
write(blob_client.download_blob().readall())
```

Once downloaded, the training data could be read by one of the Python SDK methods we
discussed previously.

> **Note**
>
> To improve the overall security and simplify the code, you could use the `azure.identity`
> package in Python to leverage a managed identity. This would allow you to skip providing
> secrets such as the connection string for Azure Storage.

Another option listed previously was using volume. Depending on the selected hosting environment,
a different method for attaching a volume would be selected. Check the following pages for detailed
instructions on how to implement such a functionality:

- `https://learn.microsoft.com/en-us/azure/container-instances/container-instances-volume-azure-files`

- `https://learn.microsoft.com/en-us/azure/container-apps/storage-mounts`

- `https://learn.microsoft.com/en-us/azure/aks/concepts-storage`

We also discussed that Azure Functions could be used to implement the AutoML concept. This is a
very interesting idea as Azure Functions offer two important features that greatly simplify the setup:

- **Timer trigger**, which allows us to set up a schedule for running the experiment and constantly
  improve the model

- **Input bindings**, which can be used to dynamically mount the training data

The general structure for such a function could look like this:

```
import logging
import os
from azure.storage.blob import BlobServiceClient
from azureml.core import Workspace, Experiment, ScriptRunConfig,
Environment

def main(mytimer: func.TimerRequest, inputBlob: func.InputStream) ->
None:
```

In this code snippet, we're defining an Azure function that uses a timer trigger and Blob Storage binding to provide a reference for the data used for training. We could then get the data and connect to Azure Machine Learning with the following code:

```
training_data_path = "/tmp/training_data.csv" # Temporary file path
with open(training_data_path, "wb") as file:
file.write(inputBlob.read())
ws = Workspace.from_config()
```

The last step would be running the experiment:

```
experiment_name = "my-ml-experiment"
environment_name = "my-environment"
compute_name = "my-compute"
experiment = Experiment(workspace=ws, name=experiment_name)
env = Environment.get(workspace=ws, name=environment_name) script_
config = ScriptRunConfig(
source_directory="./",
script="train.py",
arguments=["--data", training_data_path],
compute_target=compute_name,
environment=env
)
run = experiment.submit(config=script_config)
```

As the function presented here presents a slightly different SDK than we discussed previously (it uses the Azure Machine Learning package for Python, which allows you to work with the service using the control plane), we could modify it to leverage the Python SDK for Azure Machine Learning:

```
# Connect to Azure ML Workspace using MLClient
credential = DefaultAzureCredential()
ml_client = MLClient(
credential=credential,
subscription_id="your_subscription_id", resource_group_name="your_
resource_group", workspace_name="your_workspace_name")
job = CommandJob(
code="./",
command="python train.py --data ${{inputs.training_data}}",
inputs={
"training_data": training_data_path
},
environment=environment_name,
compute=compute_name)
submitted_job = ml_client.jobs.create_or_update(job)
```

The benefit of using Azure Functions in such a scenario is simplicity – you don't need to configure volumes or make changes to the Dockerfile. In fact, you may not need to containerize your application at all – if all the files are shipped with your function, once it's deployed, it can be run by the Azure Functions host with no additional steps. This concept is presented in *Figure 18.4*.

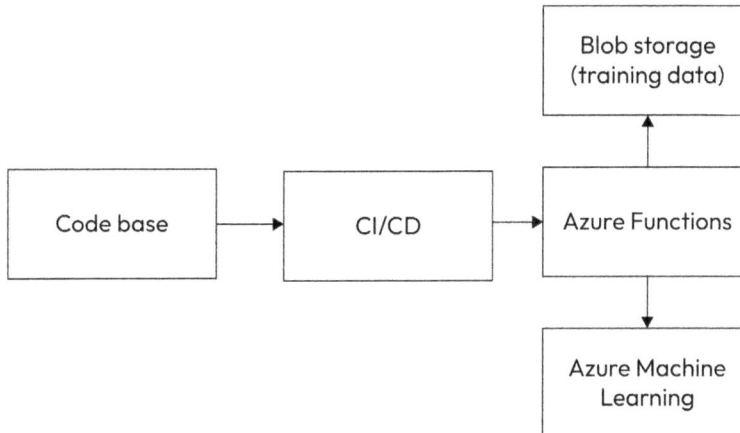

Figure 18.4 – Using Azure Functions to run experiments

In *Figure 18.4*, the presented concept involves CI/CD to continuously deploy your application and Azure Blob Storage to store the training data. Azure Functions uses the data and runs experiments with a fixed schedule thanks to the timer trigger. There's one thing that is left: obtaining the endpoint. To implement that functionality, you could use one of many options available:

- Checking the output of a function manually

- Saving the endpoint to a storage or a database

- Using Azure CLI to verify the state of an experiment and, once ready, get the endpoint

To check the state of an experiment, we will need to use the `az ml job show` command as presented here:

```
az ml job show \
--name <job-name> \
--query "{Name:name,Jobstatus:status}"  \
--resource-group <resource-group-name> \
--workspace-name <workspace-name>
```

As a result, we will get a response containing the status of the job running in the Azure Machine Learning service. Additionally, if we remove the `--query` parameter, we could get the whole response containing the job endpoint as well.

> **Note**
>
> You can check the response schema for the Azure CLI command by checking the REST API of the Azure Machine Learning service here: `https://learn.microsoft.com/en-us/rest/api/azureml/jobs/get?view=rest-azureml-2024-10-01&tabs=HTTP#get-automl-job`.

Let's now check how we could implement AutoML using Azure Machine Learning to train vision models.

Implementing AutoML for vision models

In the previous part of this chapter, we discussed how one could use AutoML to auto-train tabular data. As ML models may be trained on various sources and those sources may be in a different format than generic text, we need to understand how the same process could be implemented to implement experiments based on sources such as images, pictures, or audio. In this section, we will focus on vision models – models that can understand images and generate responses based on the binary format of input data.

Working with vision models is no different from working with tabular data when it comes to building pipelines and automation. Depending on the selected tool (Python SDK or Azure CLI), we need to specify the task that we're interested in. For Python, all we need is to create a job based on the type of task we'll be implementing. There are four tasks available as of now:

- Image classification
- Image classification multi-label
- Image object detection
- Image instance segmentation

The task is specified by choosing the right method from the SDK or by defining it in the YAML schema. For the Python SDK, all we would need is the following snippet (which defines image object detection as the task we're interested in):

```
from azure.ai.ml import automl
job = automl.image_object_detection()
```

For the YAML schema, we will need to use the following field:

```
task: image_object_detection
```

Any task used for machine learning in the Azure Machine Learning service will require input covering the training data and (in many cases) the dataset used for validating the output of our machine learning job. Those datasets could be prepared similarly to the ones we used in the previous exercises:

```
from azure.ai.ml import Input
from azure.ai.ml.constants import AssetTypes
training_mltable_path = "<local-path>"
validation_mltable_path = "<local-path>"
training_data = Input(type=AssetTypes.MLTABLE, path=training_mltable_
path)
validation_data= Input(type=AssetTypes.MLTABLE, path=validation_
mltable_path)
```

In our case, we'd need to define the local paths where both the training and validation data are present. As an alternative to the local paths, you could use remote paths, which look like this:

```
azureml://datastores/<datastore-name>/paths/<remote-path>"
```

In that case, what we'd need would be the datastore with data uploaded to it. A **datastore** in Azure Machine Learning is an additional feature that allows you to integrate one of the supported storage services with Azure Machine Learning, so it can manage them and authenticate without needing additional operations. Datastores can be created directly from your script (apart from creating them using the Azure portal or Azure CLI) using the following code:

```
from azure.ai.ml.entities import AzureBlobDatastore
from azure.ai.ml import MLClient
ml_client = MLClient.from_config()
store = AzureBlobDatastore(
name="<datastore-name>",
description="<description>",
account_name="<storage-account-name>",
container_name="<container-name>")
ml_client.create_or_update(store)
```

In this example, the created datastore would use Azure Blob Storage. The process of creating it would be authenticated using Microsoft Entra ID. There's an option to perform the same operation using a storage account key or SAS token. For more examples (including the ones using other storage services), take a look here: https://learn.microsoft.com/en-us/azure/machine-learning/how-to-datastore.

Once the datastore is created and available (and data is uploaded to it), you could use it similarly to the code presented as follows:

```
datastore_name = "workspaceblobstore"
remote_path = "path/to/your/images"
data_asset_name = "object_detection_dataset"
```

```
data = Data(path=f"azureml://datastores/{datastore_name}/paths/
{remote_path}",
type="uri_folder",
name=data_asset_name,
description="Dataset for object detection") registered_data = ml_
client.data.create_or_update(data)
image_object_detection_job = image_object_detection(compute="<compute-
name>",
experiment_name="<experiment-name>", training_data=registered_data.id,
target_column_name="<target-column>", primary_metric="mean_average_
precision", model_name="object-detection-model",
max_trials=5,
max_concurrent_trials=2)
```

The last step would be submitting the job to the Azure Machine Learning service with a single command:

```
submitted_job = ml_client.jobs.create_or_update(image_object_
detection_job)
```

> **Note**
>
> In the example, we used additional parameters such as `max_trials` and `max_concurrent_trials` when defining the job. They're optional but can help in running the experiment. You can read more about possible parameters and additional settings that can be specified for this particular job here: `https://learn.microsoft.com/en-us/python/api/azure-ai-ml/azure.ai.ml.automl.imageobjectdetectionjob?view=azure-python`.

The same approach as we did using the Python SDK could be implemented using Azure CLI:

```
$schema: https://azuremlschemas.azureedge.net/latest/commandJob.
schema.json
type: automl
name: <job-name>
description: "AutoML job for image object detection" experiment_name:
image-object-detection-experiment
compute: <compute-name>
task: image_object_detection
primary_metric: mean_average_precision
training_data:
data: azureml://datastores/<datastore-name>/paths/<remote-path>
type: uri_folder
target_column_name: label
outputs:
```

```
model: azureml://datastores/<datastore-name>/paths/<remote-path>
limits:
max_trials: 5
max_concurrent_trials: 2
model_settings:
model_name: object-detection-model
```

Now, to run the job with Azure CLI, we'd need to use the following commands:

```
az ml job create --file <file-path>.yml
```

For a better understanding of the fields we used in the YAML file, let's describe what they mean:

- `type`: Specifies the type of job (`automl` for AutoML tasks)
- `task`: Defines the task type (`image_object_detection` for object detection)
- `training_data`: Points to the dataset stored in the Azure ML datastore
- `target_column_name`: Specifies the column in the dataset that contains the object labels
- `primary_metric`: The metric to optimize (e.g., `mean_average_precision`)
- `limits`: Configures the maximum number of trials, concurrent trials, and timeout for the job
- `model_settings`: Specifies the name of the model to be trained
- `outputs`: Defines where the trained model will be saved

As the next step, let's check how we can use AutoML for a forecasting model.

Auto-training a forecasting model

A **forecasting model** is a model that uses well-known time series models to predict values. As the topic itself covers various areas and different methods that could serve the purpose, we're not going to include them in the book. Instead, before getting started, I recommend reading a short introduction available in the Azure documentation: `https://learn.microsoft.com/en-us/azure/machine-learning/concept-automl-forecasting-methods`.

The approach of creating an experiment for training a forecasting machine learning model in Azure Machine Learning is no different from the experiments we implemented for the previous tasks in this chapter. To get started, we will need to define the training data and create input. The following example uses local files to do it:

```
import mltable paths = [
{'file': './train_data/dataA.csv'},
{'file': './train_data/dataB.csv'}
]
```

```
train_table = mltable.from_delimited_files(paths)
train_table.save('./train_data')
```

Note how we're using CSV in the example, stating it's a tabular dataset (hence when creating the MLTable, we're using the `from_delimited_files()` method). The next step would involve creating and running the actual training job:

```
training_data = Input(
type=AssetTypes.MLTABLE,
path="./train_data")
forecasting_job = forecasting(
compute="<compute-name>",
experiment_name="stock-market-forecasting-experiment", training_
data=training_data, target_column_name="close", time_column_
name="date", primary_metric="normalized_root_mean_squared_error",
forecast_horizon=10,
frequency="D",
max_trials=5,
max_concurrent_trials=2)
```

In this example, we're using parameters that could be used when creating a forecasting model for a stock market price. To run the job, we'd use the standard method:

```
submitted_job = ml_client.jobs.create_or_update(forecasting_job)
```

To help you understand the steps involved in the whole process, let's describe the code line by line:

1. **(Optional) Install required SDKs**: Use `pip install azure-ai-ml azure-identity`.

2. **Prepare the dataset**:

    A. Ensure your stock market data is in a CSV file and uploaded to your Azure Blob Storage or datastore.

    B. The dataset should include at least the following:

        *   A `time` column (e.g., `date`)

        *   A `target` column (e.g., close for stock closing prices)

        *   Any additional features (e.g., `volume`, `open`, `high`, or `low`)

3. **Configure the forecasting job**:

    *   `forecast_horizon`: The number of time periods to forecast into the future

    *   `frequency`: The frequency of the data (e.g., `"D"` for daily, `"W"` for weekly)

4. Submit the job.

To read more about training such a model, take a look at the following documentation page: `https://learn.microsoft.com/en-us/azure/machine-learning/how-to-auto-train-forecast`. Before we continue our learning journey for Azure Machine Learning, let's describe one more concept, which was used in multiple exercises – compute targets. Each machine learning model, when trained, needs to run on a machine. In Azure Machine Learning, those machines are called **compute targets** – they are VMs that are selected for running experiments. As of now, Azure Machine Learning supports a variety of different compute targets, including the following:

- Compute clusters
- Serverless compute
- Compute instances
- Kubernetes
- Remote VMs
- Apache Spark
- Azure Databricks
- Azure Batch
- Azure HDInsight
- Azure Data Lake Analytics

For the whole reference, check the following page: `https://learn.microsoft.com/en-us/azure/machine-learning/concept-compute-target`. The interesting thing about compute targets is that they can be created on the fly when starting your experiment. You can find an example of how that operation is performed using the Python SDK as follows:

```
from azure.ai.ml.entities import AmlCompute
cpu_compute_target = "cpu-cluster"
ml_client.compute.get(cpu_compute_target)
compute = AmlCompute(
name=cpu_compute_target,
size="STANDARD_D2_V2",
min_instances=0,
max_instances=4)
ml_client.compute.begin_create_or_update(compute).result()
```

This script uses the `Standard_D2_V2` VM, which will be autoscaled depending on the need. You can adjust both the size of the machine and the number of instances by checking the following section in the documentation: `https://learn.microsoft.com/en-us/azure/machine-learning/concept-compute-target?view=azureml-api-2#supported-vm-series-and-sizes`.

Let's talk now about using an ONNX model in an application.

Integrating an ONNX model with an application

Open Neural Network Exchange (**ONNX**) is an open-sourced format for AI models, which is helpful when you want your models to be portable. In other words, models can be trained using a selected training framework, exported to the ONNX format, and consumed in a different tool. You can read more about it on its official web page: `https://onnx.ai/`.

In this section, we will discuss how we could consume the ONNX format and use it for implementing further actions. You can use one of the publicly available Jupyter notebooks to create and train a model, which you could use in the next exercises. It's available here: `https://github.com/Azure/azureml-examples/blob/main/sdk/python/jobs/automl-standalone-jobs/automl-classification-task-bankmarketing/automl-classification-task-bankmarketing-serverless.ipynb`.

There are a few steps needed to get started with ONNX models:

- Downloading the model
- Understanding inputs and outputs
- Preprocessing data
- Inferencing models

We will describe them in this part of the chapter, starting with the method to download a model.

Downloading the ONNX model

To download an ONNX model, it needs to be trained and available as an artifact. We will also need to use the MLflow package to interact with models and artifacts using the following commands:

```
pip install azureml-mlflow
pip install mlflow
```

Once installed, we could download the artifact (ONNX model) with the following command:

```
import mlflow
from mlflow.tracking.client import MlflowClient
job_name = ''
mlflow_parent_run = mlflow_client.get_run(job_name) best_child_run_id
= mlflow_parent_run.data.tags['automl_best_child_run_id']
best_run = mlflow_client.get_run(best_child_run_id)
onnx_model_path = mlflow_client.download_artifacts( best_run.info.run_
id, 'train_artifacts/model.onnx', local_dir )
```

In this example, you can see how we're using the MLflow client to get the best run out of all the experiment runs for the previously trained model and download it by referencing the name of an artifact. Note that `model.onnx` is only an example – it can differ depending on the name used when an artifact is created.

Now that we have the ONNX model, the next step is understanding what inputs and outputs are available, so we can use them to refine the model.

Understanding the inputs and outputs of the ONNX model

To load the model using the Python SDK and understand its inputs and outputs, we will need to use the ONNX runtime and run the inference session as follows:

```
import onnxruntime
session = onnxruntime.InferenceSession(onnx_model_path)
```

This code loads the model and uses the ONNX runtime to provide an interface we could use to interact with the model. We could then describe all the inputs and outputs with a simple loop:

```
inputs = session.get_inputs()
outputs = session.get_outputs()
for idx, input_ in enumerate(range(len(inputs))): input_name =
inputs[input_].name
input_shape = inputs[input_].shape
input_type = inputs[input_].type
for idx, output in enumerate(range(len(outputs))): output_name =
outputs[output].name
output_shape = outputs[output].shape
output_type = outputs[output].type
```

An alternative approach would involve using the `onnx` package instead of `onnxruntime` and downloading the model using `MLClient`:

```
model_name = "your_model_name"
model = ml_client.models.get(name=model_name, version=model_version)
model_path = model.download(target_dir="./models") onnx_model = onnx.
load(model_path)
print("Model Inputs:")
for input_tensor in onnx_model.graph.input:
print(f"Name: {input_tensor.name}, Type: {input_tensor.type}")
print("\nModel Outputs:")
for output_tensor in onnx_model.graph.output:
print(f"Name: {output_tensor.name}, Type: {output_tensor.type}")
```

Both methods, however, will generate the same result. The next step would involve preprocessing data so it can be run against the ONNX model we downloaded.

Preprocessing data for the ONNX model

Preprocessing data so it can be used to perform inferencing is a standard step needed when working with ONNX models. Depending on the type of data and your familiarity with various tools and frameworks, this step will look very different. For instance, let's assume we have tabular data that we'd like to preprocess. The following example shows the schema used and the initial steps used to prepare the data:

```python
import numpy as np
import pandas as pd
from sklearn.preprocessing import StandardScaler, OneHotEncoder
from sklearn.compose import ColumnTransformer
from sklearn.pipeline import Pipeline
data = {
"age": [25, 45, 35],
"income": [50000, 80000, 60000],
"gender": ["male", "female", "male"],
"purchased": [0, 1, 0] }
df = pd.DataFrame(data)
X = df.drop(columns=["purchased"])
y = df["purchased"]
```

Now, we can run the preprocessor and have data ready for inference with the ONNX model:

```python
numeric_features = ["age", "income"]
categorical_features = ["gender"]
numeric_transformer = StandardScaler()
categorical_transformer = OneHotEncoder(sparse=False, handle_
unknown="ignore")
preprocessor = ColumnTransformer(
transformers=[ ("num", numeric_transformer, numeric_features), ("cat",
categorical_transformer, categorical_features),])
pipeline = Pipeline(steps=[("preprocessor", preprocessor)])
X_preprocessed = pipeline.fit_transform(X)
X_numpy = np.array(X_preprocessed, dtype=np.float32)
```

As a result, we'll have a NumPy array consisting of float32 types, which are the requirements for inferencing with ONNX models. Let's check how we can do that.

Inferencing with the ONNX model

The last step needed in our example is inferencing with the ONNX model so it can make predictions. We prepared the data and introduced the necessary changes – to run the inference, we'll need the following code:

```
onnx_model_path = "path_to_your_model.onnx"
path session = ort.InferenceSession(onnx_model_path)
input_name = session.get_inputs()[0].name
output_name = session.get_outputs()[0].name
predictions = session.run([output_name], {input_name: X_numpy})
print("\nPredictions:") print(predictions)
```

An example result of running the inference could look like this:

```
Preprocessed Data (as NumPy Array):
[[-1.2247449  -1.06904497  1.          0.          ]
 [ 1.2247449   1.33630621  0.          1.          ]
 [ 0.         -0.26726124  1.          0.          ]]

Predictions:
[array([[0.1],
        [0.9],
        [0.2]], dtype=float32)]
```

Remember that, in our case, we're predicting the value of the purchased column from our initial dataset. Based on the result, we can see that we were close to the original values.

Let's talk now about how ONNX integrates into the AutoML topic we discussed in this chapter to have a full understanding of its capabilities.

Using ONNX in AutoML

ONNX itself is just an interface – it allows you to consume models using different tools and makes them portable across different environments. If we want to automate our setup, we need to understand how ONNX could be integrated with our pipelines. Let's take a look at *Figure 18.5*:

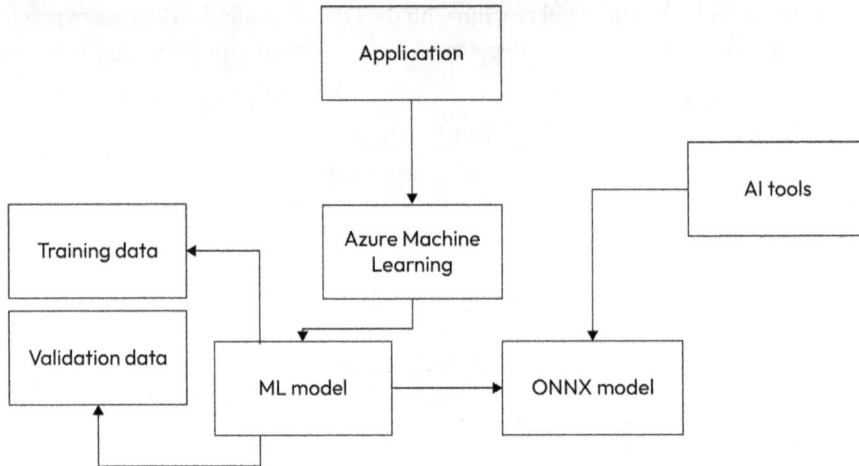

Figure 18.5 – High-level overview of using ONNX within machine learning processing pipelines

In *Figure 18.5*, you can see how an ONNX model is exported from a standard machine learning model and is used by other AI tools to provide additional value. The export can be implemented using the following approach:

```
torch.onnx.export(
    model, # model being run
    <input>,
    "<path-to-exported-model>.onnx",
    export_params=True,
    opset_version=11,
    do_constant_folding=True,
    input_names = ['input'],
    output_names = ['output'],
    dynamic_axes={
        'input':{0 : 'batch_size'}, 'output' : {0 : 'batch_size'}})
```

In this example, we're using the `torch.onnx.export()` function to export the model and save it to the desired location. To use that approach, you will need to install the following package:

```
pip install torch onnx
```

Once installed, you can use it in your script to generate the ONNX model and save it either locally or to the datastore in the Azure Machine Learning service.

Let's now talk about use cases for Azure Machine Learning and discuss how your applications may benefit from using that service.

Learning about use cases

In the context of machine learning in general, the Azure Machine Learning service has a variety of different use cases, which you may find beneficial when building an application. The most basic use case of that service is training and hosting models – each model trained in Azure Machine Learning can be hosted with an online endpoint, which can be consumed by other applications. To use that feature, you will need to create an endpoint for your model. It can be done with just a few lines of code:

```
timestamp = datetime.datetime.now().strftime("%Y%m%d%H%M%S") endpoint_
name = f"ml-endpoint-{timestamp}"
endpoint = ManagedOnlineEndpoint(
name=endpoint_name,
description="Online endpoint for serving the ML model",
auth_mode="key" # Use "key" for API key authentication or "aml_token"
for Azure ML token authentication )
deployment_name = "default"
model_name = "your_model_name"
model_version = "1"
deployment = ManagedOnlineDeployment(
name=deployment_name,
endpoint_name=endpoint_name,
model=f"{model_name}:{model_version}", instance_type="Standard_DS3_
v2", instance_count=1 )
deployment = ml_client.online_deployments.begin_create_or_
update(deployment).result() ml_client.online_endpoints.begin_
update(endpoint_name, traffic={"default": 100}).result()
```

In the preceding example, we create an online endpoint that is then linked to the specific deployment of a model. To consume that endpoint, we could use any technology and programming language. For instance, we could use the following Python script to test the model:

```
import requests
endpoint_url = "https://.azurewebsites.net/score"
api_key = "" # Provide API key
input_data = { "data": [ {"feature1": 1.0, "feature2": 2.0},
{"feature1": 3.0, "feature2": 4.0} ] }
headers = {"Authorization": f"Bearer {api_key}", "Content-Type":
"application/json"} response = requests.post(endpoint_url, json=input_
data, headers=headers)
```

To connect to the endpoints, you will need to use either API keys or Azure Machine Learning tokens. You can read more about them here: `https://learn.microsoft.com/en-us/azure/machine-learning/how-to-authenticate-web-service?view=azureml-api-1`.

Another use case for the Azure Machine Learning service is using it for implementing MLOps, thanks to its ability to version models, monitor them, and perform controlled rollouts. Thanks to its native capability to integrate with Azure, Azure Machine Learning is also one of the best choices when using Azure to build and train models. Use the following links to learn more about the various features this service has to offer:

- `https://learn.microsoft.com/en-us/azure/machine-learning/concept-model-management-and-deployment?view=azureml-api-1`
- `https://learn.microsoft.com/en-us/azure/machine-learning/concept-secure-network-traffic-flow?view=azureml-api-1`
- `https://learn.microsoft.com/en-us/azure/machine-learning/how-to-use-managed-identities?view=azureml-api-1&tabs=python`
- `https://learn.microsoft.com/en-us/azure/machine-learning/how-to-manage-workspace-cli`

That's all for *Chapter 18*! Let's summarize all the exercises and check what will be available in the next and final chapter.

Summary

In this chapter, we talked about the Azure Machine Learning service – a managed service allowing you to build, train, and host machine learning models without the need to manage infrastructure on your own. We saw how you can use both the Python SDK and Azure CLI to build the pipelines and run experiments. Remember that the choice of technology depends on your requirements – to address that, compare those approaches to see how different they are.

The major topic discussed was the overall AutoML approach and what can be achieved with the Azure Machine Learning service. We saw how, by using only the SDK, we can build the whole environment for training our models, including datastores and compute targets. We also checked how the ONNX project could be used to simplify the sharing of our machine learning models and provide additional value to our applications. Lessons from this chapter will help you organize your knowledge about Azure Machine Learning and key areas that are necessary to get started with the service.

In the next chapter, we will discuss GitHub Actions and best practices for deploying applications and services to Azure.

19

Using GitHub Actions to Build and Deploy Applications to Azure

Modern software development demands rapid iteration, reliable releases, and seamless integration between code repositories and cloud platforms. As organizations increasingly adopt DevOps practices, automation has become central to delivering high-quality applications efficiently. **GitHub Actions**, GitHub's native **continuous integration and continuous deployment (CI/CD)** solution, empowers developers to automate every aspect of their workflow – from building and testing code to deploying applications directly from their repositories.

This chapter explores how to harness GitHub Actions to build and deploy applications to Microsoft Azure, one of the leading cloud platforms for hosting scalable web applications and services. By integrating GitHub Actions with Azure, development teams can achieve true continuous delivery, ensuring that every code change is automatically validated and deployed to production or staging environments with minimal manual intervention.

In this chapter, we're going to cover the following main topics:

- Understanding the building blocks of GitHub Actions
- Integrating GitHub Actions with Microsoft Azure
- Using GitHub Actions to deploy applications to Microsoft Azure
- Integrating with Azure Key Vault
- Learning about use cases

Technical requirements

To perform the exercises in this chapter, you will need the following:

- Azure CLI
- IDE of your choice (preferably Visual Studio Code)
- GitHub account

Understanding the building blocks of GitHub Actions

If you're familiar with CI/CD platforms such as Jenkins, Azure DevOps, or TeamCity, you will find GitHub Actions quite easy to learn. It's a feature of GitHub that allows you to define your build and deploy pipelines using a specific schema. The main functionalities provided by that tool are as follows:

- Workflow automation
- Event-driven triggers
- Jobs and steps architecture
- Runners (hosted and self-hosted)
- Reusable actions and Marketplace
- Matrix builds
- Multi-container and Docker support
- Live logs and workflow visualization
- Secrets management

Throughout this chapter, we will go through most of those capabilities, so you can start building your own pipelines and start automating the building and releasing of your application to the selected environments. Let's start with the first topic – workflow automation.

Understanding workflows in GitHub Actions

A **workflow** in GitHub Actions is a configurable automated process defined by a YAML file stored in the `.github/workflows` directory of a repository. It consists of one or more jobs that run sequentially or in parallel on runner machines, and each job contains a series of steps that can execute scripts or reusable actions. A simple workflow file could look like this:

```
name: Basic Workflow
on:
  push:
    branches:
```

```
        - main
jobs:
  run-bash-command:
    runs-on: ubuntu-latest
    steps:
      - name: Run a Bash Command
        run: echo "Hello, GitHub Actions!"
```

In this example, you can see how we defined the following blocks:

- Name of a workflow (`name`)

- Trigger (`on`)

- Jobs (`jobs`)

The result of running that workflow would be a single workflow run, which runs a Bash command displaying the `"Hello, GitHub Actions!"` string.

Workflows are triggered by specific events, which can include the following:

- Events occurring within the repository, such as pushes, pull requests, or issue creation

- External events triggering a `repository_dispatch` event

- Scheduled times (`cron` jobs)

- Manual triggers initiated by users

This event-driven nature allows workflows to automate tasks such as building and testing code, deploying applications, or managing issues and labels. If we want to select multiple events that will trigger our pipeline, we need to define more than one trigger:

```
name: Basic Workflow
on:
  push:
    branches:
      - main
  workflow_dispatch: # Allows manual trigger of the workflow
  schedule: # Scheduled trigger
    - cron: "0 12 * * *" # Runs every day at 12:00 UTC
jobs:
  run-bash-command:
    runs-on: ubuntu-latest
    steps:
      - name: Run a Bash Command
        run: echo "Hello, GitHub Actions!"
```

This example would run the same job, but this time, there would be three events that would trigger the workflow:

- A push to a repository to the `main` branch

- Triggering the workflow manually

- CRON schedule

To change the schedule, we'd need to change the CRON expression. For instance, we could select different schedules depending on our needs:

- `"0 0 * * *"`: Runs daily at midnight UTC.

- `"0 0 * * 1"`: Runs every Monday at midnight UTC.

Schedules are useful in several scenarios common in application development, including the following:

- Nightly builds

- Running full test suites, which require significant time to complete

- Jobs

- Generators

A full list of events that can trigger a workflow can be found here: `https://docs.github.com/en/actions/writing-workflows/choosing-when-your-workflow-runs/events-that-trigger-workflows`.

Workflows can also trigger other workflows using the following events:

- `workflow_dispatch`

- `repository_dispatch`

- `workflow_call` (aka **reusable workflow**)

If you want to use the `workflow_dispatch` event, you could trigger a run of a workflow with the following methods:

- Using the GitHub REST API to create a workflow dispatch event

- Using existing GitHub Actions from the Marketplace

- Using a **personal access token** (**PAT**) or a GitHub App token for authentication

For example, let's say we want to use the API to run a workflow that is triggered using the `workflow_dispatch` event. The prerequisite for that is creating a GitHub token that can be used and passed to the script. The instructions on how to do that can be found here: `https://docs.github.com/en/authentication/keeping-your-account-and-data-secure/managing-your-personal-access-tokens`.

To trigger the `workflow_dispatch` event, we could use a simple Bash script:

```bash
#!/bin/bash
GITHUB_TOKEN="your_github_personal_access_token" # Replace with your
GitHub token
OWNER="your_github_username_or_org" # Replace with the repository
owner
REPO="your_repository_name" # Replace with your repository name
WORKFLOW_FILE="basic-workflow.yml" # Replace with your workflow file
name
REF="main" # Branch or tag to run the workflow on
curl -X POST
-H "Accept: application/vnd.github+json"
-H "Authorization: Bearer $GITHUB_TOKEN"
https://api.github.com/repos/$OWNER/$REPO/actions/workflows/$WORKFLOW_
FILE/dispatches
-d "{"ref":"$REF"}"
```

Note the use of the `$REF` variable, which defines for which branch the run would be triggered. This is important when you develop a new version of a workflow that you'd like to test first before committing to the `master` branch. The example uses the `main` branch, but you could change it to any value that represents an existing branch.

> **Note**
>
> Remember that both `master` and `main` branches are, most of the time, the same thing. Many tools, such as GitHub Actions, switched to using `main` as the default name for the default branch.

A similar approach could be applied if you want to use the `repository_dispatch` event, like so:

```bash
#!/bin/bash
GITHUB_TOKEN="your_github_personal_access_token" # Replace with your
GitHub token
OWNER="your_github_username_or_org" # Replace with the repository
owner
REPO="your_repository_name" # Replace with your repository name
EVENT_TYPE="custom-event" # Replace with your custom event type
curl -X POST
-H "Accept: application/vnd.github+json"
```

```
-H "Authorization: Bearer $GITHUB_TOKEN"
https://api.github.com/repos/$OWNER/$REPO/dispatches
-d "{"event_type":"$EVENT_TYPE"}"
```

> **Note**
>
> Remember that the token used in those requests must have the appropriate permissions so the operation is authorized.

As you can see, the `repository_dispatch` event is an event that is dispatched at the repository level (as opposed to `workflow_dispatch`, which is triggered at the workflow level). The result of both scripts will be the same – your workflow will start and will perform all the steps defined within the jobs.

As the next step, let's discuss the architecture of jobs and steps.

Using jobs and steps in workflows

A **job** is a collection of steps that will be performed in sequence. A **step** is an action that performs a specific operation, such as building an application, deploying it, or running a command. Steps in GitHub Actions can be published in GitHub Marketplace (`https://github.com/marketplace?type=actions`). For instance, let's say you want to check out your repository as the first step of your pipeline. To do that, you could use the following action:

```
jobs:
  checkout-code:
    runs-on: ubuntu-latest
    steps:
      - name: Check out the repository
        uses: actions/checkout@v4
```

The alternative to that would be checking out the repository with your own command:

```
jobs:
  checkout-code:
    runs-on: ubuntu-latest
    steps:
      - name: Set up Git
        run: |
        git config --global user.name "github-actions[bot]"
        git config --global user.email "github-actions[bot]@users.noreply.
        github.com"
```

```
- name: Clone the repository
  run: |
    git clone https://github.com/${{ github.repository }} repo
    cd repo
    git checkout ${{ github.ref_name }}
```

As you can see, it takes much more time to define the same operation if you're not using an action. Of course, not all operations have corresponding actions – in many scenarios, you will need to run your own command or even install a package that isn't available. Remember, though, that it's always a good practice to double-check whether an action you'd need already exists and use it if possible.

> **Note**
>
> All actions are versioned. If you reference an action like `actions/checkout@v4`, it means you're using version 4 of that action. Changing a version of an action should be performed with care, as new versions may introduce breaking changes.

In this example, you can also see that we're using GitHub variables:

- `github.repository`
- `github.ref_name`

Those are predefined variables available in all workflows. There's a dedicated documentation page explaining how variables can be used and which variables are always available. You can find it here: `https://docs.github.com/en/actions/writing-workflows/choosing-what-your-workflow-does/store-information-in-variables`.

In GitHub Actions, jobs group similar steps and can run in parallel if needed. To be able to run more than a single job at the same time, you need to have more than a single agent available. As we'll talk about agents in the next section, we're not going to dive into that detail now. Instead, let's see how we could make one job dependent on the second one so they run in sequence:

```
jobs:
  first-job:
    runs-on: ubuntu-latest
    steps:
      - name: Step 1 - Echo message
        run: echo "This is the first job."
  second-job:
    runs-on: ubuntu-latest
    needs: first-job # This job depends on the completion of 'first-
job'
    steps:
```

```
         - name: Step 2 - Echo message
           run: echo "This is the second job, which depends on the first
   job."
```

When we run this workflow, the second job will wait for the first job to complete instead of running in parallel. This is helpful if jobs rely on each other to provide artifacts or if you need to set up prerequisites before running the other parts of your pipeline.

Let's talk now about agents (runners) used in workflows to run your pipelines.

Understanding managed and self-hosted agents

A machine running your workflow is called an **agent** (although, in some places, you could also find the name **runner**). Most machines used in CI/CD pipelines are virtual machines hosted in the cloud or on-premises; still, it's perfectly fine to use any physical machine to run the agent software. Agents listed to the GitHub server waiting for events, which trigger workflow runs. You can specify which agents should be used when running your workflow by specifying the `runs-on` parameter:

```
jobs:
  linux-job:
    runs-on: ubuntu-latest
    steps:
      - name: Run on Linux
        run: |
          echo "Running on Linux"
          uname -a
  windows-job:
    runs-on: windows-latest
    steps:
      - name: Run on Windows
        run: |
          echo "Running on Windows"
          systeminfo
```

In this example, you can see how two jobs use two separate agents to run the defined steps. One agent is a Linux machine, while the second one is a Windows machine. You could also define the default agent for the whole workflow:

```
defaults:
  run:
    shell: bash
    runs-on: ubuntu-latest

jobs:
  linux-job:
```

```
    steps:
      - name: Run on Default Linux Agent
        run: |
          echo "Running on Linux (default agent)"
          uname -a
  windows-job:
    runs-on: windows-latest # Overwrite the default agent to use
Windows
    steps:
      - name: Run on Windows Agent
        run: |
          echo "Running on Windows (overwritten agent)"
          systeminfo
```

This time, we're using the `defaults` section to provide the information for GitHub Actions that we want to use the `ubuntu-latest` machine as the default one. This selection is overwritten by the second job (`windows-job`) that specifies that it needs to run on a Windows machine.

> **Note**
>
> The preceding example also specifies the default shell to be Bash. You can safely omit that parameter if you don't want to make any changes in your pipeline.

The agents specified in those examples are **managed agents** – agents provided and managed by GitHub. They are short-lived machines (they exist only to run your jobs, then they disappear) and are charged by the number of minutes utilized to run your workflows. The details of the pricing can be found here: `https://docs.github.com/en/billing/managing-billing-for-your-products/managing-billing-for-github-actions/about-billing-for-github-actions`. The advantages of managed agents are as follows:

- Simple configuration
- Simple pricing
- Various machine flavors available (Windows, Linux, and macOS)

There are also some serious limitations of the managed agents that we need to clarify:

- Managed agents can't connect with services hosted privately unless you whitelist the IP addresses of those agents.
- The pricing for those agents may be unpredictable if you have lots of different projects and workflows.
- Managed agents are ephemeral, meaning if you need to cache something or store a state, you need to use a remote solution instead of the local filesystem.

- You can't control the software installed on those agents. Sure, you could install tools and packages within your jobs, but those steps will need to be repeated each time a pipeline runs.

If you feel that those limitations affect your ability to build and deploy your application, you will need to host a self-hosted agent. A self-hosted agent is an agent you deploy, configure, and control. Depending on the type of self-hosted agent (virtual machine vs. physical machine), you will need to perform different steps to configure and connect it to your network infrastructure. Unfortunately, those steps are out of the scope of this book.

If you want to install and host your own agent, you will need to go through the documentation available here: `https://docs.github.com/en/actions/hosting-your-own-runners/managing-self-hosted-runners/about-self-hosted-runners`. Remember that you could deploy Azure Virtual Machine and use it to run an agent. In many scenarios, this may be the easiest solution if you want your agent to interact with your resources hosted privately.

Let's now talk about how we could integrate GitHub Actions with the Microsoft Azure environment.

Integrating GitHub Actions with Microsoft Azure

To integrate GitHub Actions with Microsoft Azure, you will need to decide which integration method suits you the most. Before we check the possible methods, let's understand how the integration actually works. In the previous section, we discussed how we can use both managed and self-hosted agents. Depending on the type of agent, we can use different authentication methods when connecting to Azure. The easiest method would be to use your personal credentials and allow an agent to log in. Even if it sounds like a quick and easy method, do not attempt to implement it. Not only may such a solution fail in various environments (as authenticating to Microsoft Entra ID may require MFA or be secured with conditional access) but it may also expose your credentials to other people. Instead, you should create a dedicated account for a GitHub runner that can be used in different workflows and has access scoped to only the required resources.

Authentication to Azure can be performed using a dedicated action named `azure/login`. This action looks like this:

```
jobs:
  azure-login:
    runs-on: ubuntu-latest
    steps:
      - name: Check out the repository
        uses: actions/checkout@v4
      - name: Log in to Azure
        uses: azure/login@v1
        with:
          creds: ${{ secrets.AZURE_CREDENTIALS }}
```

In this example, you can see how we're using the mentioned action as one of the steps of our job. This example also assumes that credentials to Azure will be introduced as a GitHub secret containing the following JSON object:

```
{
"clientSecret": "",
"subscriptionId": "",
"tenantId": "",
"clientId": "",
"clientSecret": ""
}
```

To use it properly, you'd need to populate the values by creating a service principal with a password. It could be done in the Azure portal, but you could also create it with the following Azure CLI command. The easiest way, however, to have that JSON object created is using the following operation:

```
az ad sp create-for-rbac \
--name "<principal-name>"
--role <role-name> \
    --scopes <scope> \
--sdk-auth
```

The benefit of that command is that it not only creates a service principal but also creates a role assignment with the selected role. For instance, if you want to create credentials for a service principal named github-actions and assign the contributor role for the selected subscription, you could use the following:

```
az ad sp create-for-rbac \
--name "github-actions" \
--role contributor \
    --scopes /subscriptions/<subscription-id> \
--sdk-auth
```

The downside of authenticating to Azure using that approach is that you need to create a service principal, rotate its password, and store it securely in GitHub. A better way would be to use a managed identity to achieve the same result. To do that, you'd need to use a self-hosted runner hosted in Azure. The reason for that is simple – only machines provisioned in Azure have access to the metadata endpoint used by the managed identity to obtain the token.

> **Note**
> If you use Azure Arc, you could use a managed identity even for machines that are managed by your organization outside of the Azure infrastructure.

Depending on the type of managed identity used (system- vs. user-assigned), you'd need to use a slightly different syntax of the `azure/login` action. For a system-assigned identity, the syntax looks as follows:

```
jobs:
  azure-login:
    runs-on: self-hosted
    steps:
      - name: Azure login
        uses: azure/login@v2
        with:
          auth-type: IDENTITY
          tenant-id: ${{ secrets.AZURE_TENANT_ID }}
          subscription-id: ${{ secrets.AZURE_SUBSCRIPTION_ID }}
```

For a user-assigned identity, you'd need to provide the client ID as well:

```
jobs:
  azure-login:
    runs-on: self-hosted
    steps:
      - name: Azure login
        uses: azure/login@v2
        with:
          auth-type: IDENTITY
          client-id: ${{ secrets.AZURE_CLIENT_ID }}
          tenant-id: ${{ secrets.AZURE_TENANT_ID }}
          subscription-id: ${{ secrets.AZURE_SUBSCRIPTION_ID }}
```

Note that, once again, we're using GitHub secrets to complete the setup. This time, however, the secrets aren't sensitive values such as keys or passwords. Instead, we're keeping the Azure identifiers as secrets to avoid exposing and reusing them by unauthorized persons.

> **Note**
>
> Azure identifiers aren't really secrets, and if somebody has access to them, they won't be able to immediately use them to authenticate. For a managed identity, you need to deploy a machine within a selected subscription and authorize the underlying principal to execute any action using Azure RBAC. Still, because those identifiers become part of your authentication mechanism, it's a good practice to keep them private.

The benefit of using that method of authentication is that it is much easier to set up and manage. You don't need to rotate credentials, the password doesn't need to be stored in GitHub secrets, and you need access to Microsoft Entra ID to complete the setup.

There's one more method of authenticating, which is considered the best practice as of now – it's called a **federated identity credential**. Let's see how one could use it.

At first glance, using federated identity credentials will look the same as using a managed identity. Here's an example of how you could incorporate them into your pipeline:

```
permissions:
  id-token: write
  contents: read
jobs:
  azure-login:
    runs-on: ubuntu-latest
    steps:
      - name: Azure login
        uses: azure/login@v2
        with:
          client-id: ${{ secrets.AZURE_CLIENT_ID }}
          tenant-id: ${{ secrets.AZURE_TENANT_ID }}
          subscription-id: ${{ secrets.AZURE_SUBSCRIPTION_ID }}
```

As you can see, the only difference is an additional section named `permissions` that is needed when federated identity credentials are used. In our example, we have two permissions:

- `id-token`: This permission says that the workflow will obtain an **OpenID Connect** (**OIDC**) token that can be used for authentication.

- `contents`: This is an additional permission that allows the GitHub token provided under the hood to read the contents of our repository.

You can read more about the permissions here: `https://docs.github.com/en/actions/ writing-workflows/choosing-what-your-workflow-does/controlling- permissions-for-github_token`.

However, specifying those fields in your workflow file won't be enough. You will need to configure those credentials in the selected user-assigned managed identity resource. Let's discuss the process as follows:

1. Create a user-assigned managed identity with the selected name:

    ```
    az identity create \
    --name GitHubActionsIdentity \
    --resource-group <resource-group> \
    --location <location>
    ```

2. Assign a role for the created managed identity resource (for instance, `Contributor`) on the selected scope. Take the value of the `client-id` parameter from the output of the previous column and remember to adjust the scope:

```
az role assignment create \
--assignee <client-id> \
--role Contributor \
--scope /subscriptions/<subscription-id>
```

3. Use one more command to configure the federated credentials. This command will be explained in detail in the following part:

```
az identity federated-credential create \
--name GitHubActionsFederatedCredential \
--identity-name GitHubActionsIdentity \
--resource-group <resource-group> \
--issuer "https://token.actions.githubusercontent.com" \
--subject "repo:<owner>/<repo>:ref:refs/heads/<branch>" \
--audiences "api://AzureADTokenExchange"
```

The command to create the federated credentials links the managed identity resource with your GitHub Actions repository. Note that we need to provide both the name of the owner (organization) and the repository name. For instance, if your repository is named `AzureInfrastructure` and you created it inside your personal account named `john-doe`, the value of the `--subject` parameter will be as follows:

```
"repo:john-doe/AzureInfrastructure:ref:refs/heads/<branch>"
```

4. The next step will be providing the name of the branch that is allowed to authenticate. Let's say we want to deploy to Azure from the `main` branch. In that case, the full value of the subject will be the following:

```
"repo:john-doe/AzureInfrastructure:ref:refs/heads/main"
```

There are other options that you could use instead of a branch:

- Environment
- Pull request
- Tag

The corresponding templates for those subjects will look like this:

- `repo:<owner>/<repo>:environment:<environment-name>`
- `repo:<owner>/<repo>:pull_request`
- `repo:<owner>/<repo>:ref:refs/tags/<tag-name>`

When running your workflows, you will need to ensure that they are triggered within the provided context linked with the subject (i.e., environment/pull request/specific tag). Failing to do so will result in not being able to authorize your operation when connecting to Azure.

> **Note**
>
> You can read more about GitHub environments in the documentation: `https://docs.github.com/en/actions/managing-workflow-runs-and-deployments/managing-deployments/managing-environments-for-deployment`.

The benefit of using federated identity credentials is that you can use them even if you don't have self-hosted agents. They work perfectly fine even with managed runners, improving the overall security of your setup.

For the next topic, let's discuss how you could deploy your code to Azure using GitHub Actions.

Using GitHub Actions to deploy applications to Microsoft Azure

We talked about the overall structure of GitHub Actions, workflows, and different ways of authenticating to Azure. In this section, we will see how workflows can be built and used to deploy both infrastructure and applications. To get started, let's prepare the initial structure of our workflow.

> **Note**
>
> The prerequisites for this part of the chapter will be having a user-assigned identity configured with federated credentials. You will also need to assign the `Contributor` role for the created managed identity resource on the subscription level.

Our initial structure will have a single task for now: to create a resource group. This can be done with the following code:

```
name: Azure Federated Login and Resource Group Creation
on:
  workflow_dispatch:
permissions:
  id-token: write
jobs:
  create-resource-group:
    runs-on: ubuntu-latest steps:
    - name: Check out the repository
      uses: actions/checkout@v4
    - name: Log in to Azure using Federated Credentials
```

```
    uses: azure/login@v1
    with:
      client-id: ${{ secrets.AZURE_CLIENT_ID }}
      tenant-id: ${{ secrets.AZURE_TENANT_ID }}
      subscription-id: ${{ secrets.AZURE_SUBSCRIPTION_ID }}
  - name: Create Azure Resource Group
    run: |
      az group create --name MyResourceGroup --location eastus
```

When you run that workflow, it should create a resource group with the provided name and used location (remember that you can customize the code whenever you want). As the next step, we could add another job, which will deploy an example resource – for simplicity, let's choose Azure Storage:

```
create-storage-account:
  runs-on: ubuntu-latest
  needs: create-resource-group
  steps:
    - name: Check out the repository
      uses: actions/checkout@v4
    - name: Log in to Azure using Federated Credentials
      uses: azure/login@v1
        with:
          client-id: ${{ secrets.AZURE_CLIENT_ID }}
          tenant-id: ${{ secrets.AZURE_TENANT_ID }}
          subscription-id: ${{ secrets.AZURE_SUBSCRIPTION_ID }}
    - name: Create Azure Storage Account
      run: |
        STORAGE_ACCOUNT_NAME="mystorageaccount$RANDOM"
        az storage account create \
          --name $STORAGE_ACCOUNT_NAME \
          --resource-group MyResourceGroup \
          --location eastus \
        --sku Standard_LRS
```

In this workflow, we're using Azure CLI to create a storage account with the provided parameters. Instead of doing that with an imperative approach, we could prepare an Azure Bicep file, add it to the repository, and use it to deploy the same configuration. Let's create a `storage-account.bicep` file and put the following code there:

```
@description('The name of the storage account. Must be globally unique.')
param storageAccountName string
@description('The location where the storage account will be created.')
param location string = resourceGroup().location
```

```
resource storageAccount 'Microsoft.Storage/storageAccounts@2022-09-01'
= {
  name: storageAccountName
  location: location
  sku: {
    name: 'Standard_LRS'
  }
  kind: 'StorageV2'
}
```

Now, let's add it to the repository and push it to the repository:

```
git add .
git commit -m "My first deployment"
git push
```

The next step would involve replacing the `create-storage-account` job with the following code:

```
- name: Deploy Storage Account using Bicep
  run: |
    az deployment group create \
    --resource-group MyResourceGroup \
    --template-file storage-account.bicep \
    --parameters storageAccountName=mystorageaccount$RANDOM
```

As you can see, that approach is a little bit simpler as it's easier to control all the parameters and configuration of the storage account using the Bicep script instead of incorporating it into a YAML workflow file. Let's quickly summarize what we have right now:

- The workflow was authenticated to use federated credentials.

- A resource group was created by GitHub Actions using Azure CLI.

- We created a storage account with Azure Bicep.

The next step will be building and deploying an application. Let's say we want to run a simple job that will upload a file to Blob Storage. This job should be containerized and run using Azure Container Instances. To complete this task, we will need the following changes to be introduced:

- We need to deploy Azure Container Registry and Azure Container Instances.

- The application needs to be built as a container and pushed to the registry.

- We also need to provide credentials for our container so it can connect with Blob Storage and upload a file.

As the first step for this, let's write some code for our application. In this exercise, I'll use .NET, but you could use any language you're familiar with. Let's also assume we will use a managed identity in the hosting environment, so we don't need to store and pass credentials. Here's a simple code that we could use to interact with Blob Storage and save a file there:

```
private static void Main(string[] args)
{
string blobServiceEndpoint = "https://<your-storage-account-name>.
blob.core.windows.net/";
string containerName = "<your-container-name>";
string blobName = "example.txt";
var clientId = "<your-user-assigned-client-id>"; // Replace with your
User Assigned Identity Client ID
var credential = new DefaultAzureCredential(new
DefaultAzureCredentialOptions { ManagedIdentityClientId = clientId });
var blobServiceClient = new BlobServiceClient(new
Uri(blobServiceEndpoint), credential);
var containerClient = blobServiceClient.
GetBlobContainerClient(containerName);
var blobClient = containerClient.GetBlobClient(blobName);
using (var stream = new MemoryStream(System.Text.Encoding.UTF8.
GetBytes("SomeContent")))
{
blobClient.Upload(stream, overwrite: true);
}
}
```

You will also need to install the missing NuGet packages:

```
dotnet add package Azure.Identity
dotnet add package Azure.Storage.Blobs
```

The next step will be creating a Dockerfile that will allow us to containerize the application:

```
FROM mcr.microsoft.com/dotnet/sdk:8.0 AS build
WORKDIR /app
COPY StorageClient.csproj ./
RUN dotnet restore
COPY . ./
RUN dotnet publish -c Release -o /out
FROM mcr.microsoft.com/dotnet/runtime:8.0
WORKDIR /app
COPY --from=build /out ./
ENTRYPOINT ["dotnet", "StorageClient.dll"]
```

Before we continue, please note the following line:

```
COPY StorageClient.csproj ./
```

If you create the application locally, you may use a different name from `StorageClient`. If that's the case, remember to also change it in the Dockerfile.

As our application will be containerized, we will also need Azure Container Registry. We could deploy it using Azure Bicep by creating the following `arc.bicep` file and adding it to our repository:

```
resource acr 'Microsoft.ContainerRegistry/registries@2023-01-01-
preview' = {
name: 'myContainerRegistry'
location: resourceGroup().location
sku: {
name: 'Basic'
}
properties: {
adminUserEnabled: true
}
}
```

In the preceding file, we're enabling the admin user for our registry. The reason for that is that we want to simplify authorization when our GitHub agent pushes the image. Of course, the alternative would be using Azure RBAC. In such a case, you'd need to create a role assignment for the user-assigned identity we used for our project and give it the `AcrPush` role. You could do that with the following command:

```
az role assignment create \
--assignee <managed-identity-client-id> \
--role "AcrPush" \
--scope /subscriptions/<subscription-id>/resourceGroups/<resource-
group-name>/providers/Microsoft.ContainerRegistry/registries/<acr-
name>
```

When you have this new Bicep file created, add it to your repository and push when ready. Now, it's time to modify our workflow file. Let's add one more job, which will deploy Azure Container Registry after deploying the storage account:

```
create-container-registry:
  runs-on: ubuntu-latest
  needs: create-resource-group
  steps:
    - name: Deploy ACR using Bicep
      run: |
        az deployment group create \
```

```
    --resource-group MyResourceGroup \
    --template-file acr.bicep
```

When you run your workflow, you should have the following components deployed:

- Resource group

- Storage account

- Azure Container Registry

We will also need one more thing deployed – the managed identity resource, which we could assign to Azure Container Instances so the application running there will have access to the storage account. Let's add the mi.bicep file locally with the following content and push it to the repository:

```
resource userAssignedIdentity 'Microsoft.ManagedIdentity/
userAssignedIdentities@2023-01-31' = {
name: 'myUserAssignedIdentity'
location: resourceGroup().location
}
```

We will deploy that file in the same way as we did for the Azure Container Registry and other Azure resources deployed by our workflow (you could add the following step to one of the existing jobs or just create a separate job for it and make it dependent on the one that creates a resource group):

```
- name: Deploy Managed Identity using Bicep
  run: |
    az deployment group create \
    --resource-group MyResourceGroup \
    --template-file mi.bicep
```

Great, we have all the prerequisites needed for our application ready. Let's start preparing a separate job for our workflow, which will be responsible for building and deploying our code to Azure Container Instances. To complete that step, we will need the following things implemented:

- Building the container image

- Pushing the container image to Azure Container Registry

- Deploying Azure Container Instances with our container image

To get started, let's build our container image using the Dockerfile we created. Here's the code needed to perform that action:

```
jobs:
  build:
    runs-on: ubuntu-latest
    steps:
```

```
      - name: Checkout code
        uses: actions/checkout@v3
      - name: Log in to Azure Container Registry
        uses: azure/docker-login@v1
        with:
          login-server: ${{ secrets.ACR_LOGIN_SERVER }}
          username: ${{ secrets.ACR_USERNAME }}
          password: ${{ secrets.ACR_PASSWORD }}
      - name: Build Docker image
        run: docker build -t ${{ secrets.ACR_LOGIN_SERVER }}/
storageclient:latest .
      - name: Push Docker image
        run: docker push ${{ secrets.ACR_LOGIN_SERVER }}/
storageclient:latest
```

In this code, we're using secrets containing three different values:

- ACR_LOGIN_SERVER

- ACR_USERNAME

- ACR_PASSWORD

To have that pipeline running successfully, you will need to populate those secrets in GitHub by yourself. To get the proper values, use the following commands:

```
az acr show \
--name <acr-name> \
--query "loginServer" \
--output tsv
az acr credential show \
--name <acr-name> \
--query "passwords[0].value" \
--output tsv
```

> **Note**
> Getting the credentials requires Azure Container Registry to have the admin user enabled.

In this example, we also used storageclient as the name of our image. If you want to choose a different name, feel free to do so, but remember to also use your customized name in the next examples.

We have our container image built and pushed to Azure Container Registry. The last step is deploying an Azure Container Instance, which will reference that image and use the managed identity we deployed. This can be done with a single step added to our workflow:

```
- name: Deploy Azure Container Instance
  uses: azure/CLI@v1
  with:
    inlineScript: |
      az container create \
      --resource-group MyResourceGroup \
      --name storageclient-container \
      --image ${{ secrets.ACR_LOGIN_SERVER }}/storageclient:latest \
      --registry-login-server ${{ secrets.ACR_LOGIN_SERVER }} \
      --registry-username ${{ secrets.ACR_USERNAME }} \
      --registry-password ${{ secrets.ACR_PASSWORD }} \
      --assign-identity ${{ secrets.MANAGED_IDENTITY_RESOURCE_ID }} \
      --cpu 1 \
      --memory 1.5 \
      --restart-policy Always
```

This step uses one more secret: MANAGED_IDENTITY_RESOURCE_ID. To obtain its value, you can use the following CLI command:

```
az identity show \
--name <managed-identity-name> \
--resource-group <resource-group-name> \
--query "id" --output tsv
```

Remember to provide the correct value for the name of your managed identity. If you followed the examples, the name we used was myUserAssignedIdentity.

To help you understand the whole setup, let's visualize both the workflow and deployed resources. First, let's look at *Figure 19.1*.

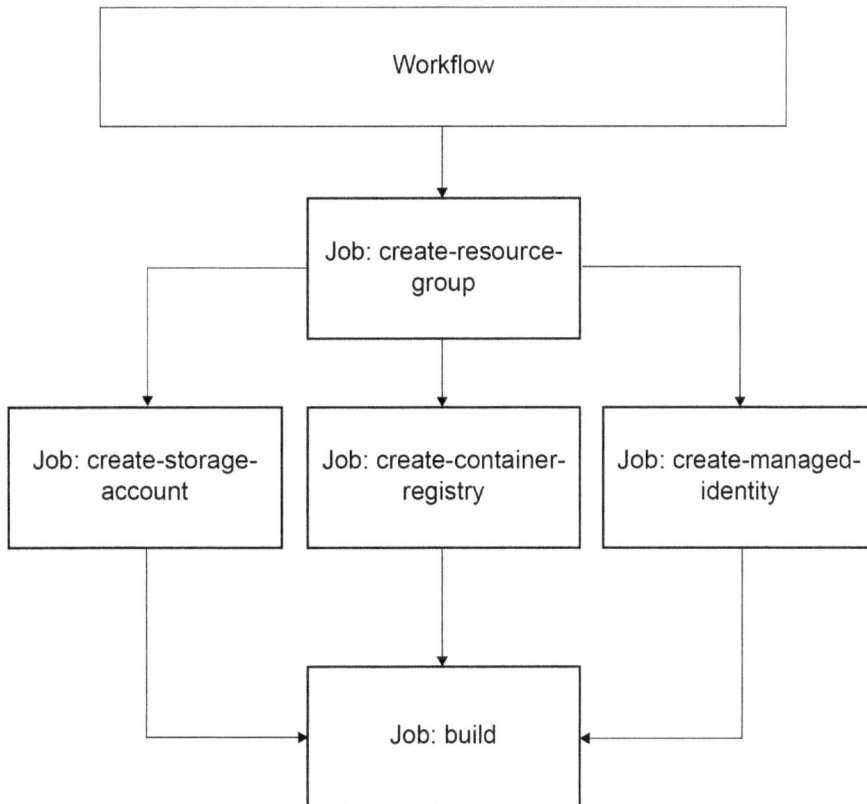

Figure 19.1 – Overview of the created workflow

In *Figure 19.1*, you can see how all the jobs are connected to each other. We create all our infrastructure before we deploy and build the application. Also note how the three jobs in the center may run in parallel if needed, as they are not related. Once the workflow is completed, you should be able to see resources as presented in *Figure 19.2*.

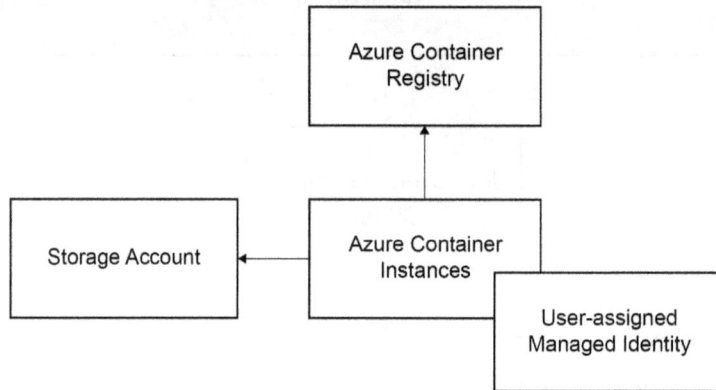

Figure 19.2 – Resources deployed using GitHub Actions

By implementing the whole workflow, you learned how to perform the following tasks using GitHub Actions:

- Deploy Azure infrastructure using both Azure Bicep and Azure CLI
- Authenticate to Azure using the selected authentication method (in our case, federated identity credentials)
- Build a container image and push it to a container registry
- Run the application using Azure Container Instances

Before we summarize this chapter, let's talk about one more important topic – managing secrets and integrating with Azure Key Vault.

Integrating with Azure Key Vault

Sooner or later, your workflow will need to use secrets. One of the options we already discussed was using GitHub secrets. That approach is a simple and robust solution as it allows you to store the sensitive values securely and share them between multiple workflows (or even repositories if you set the secrets on a GitHub organization level). In some scenarios, however, using GitHub secrets may not be enough. Some companies require you to fully control how and where sensitive values are stored. To satisfy that requirement, we could use Azure Key Vault.

Unfortunately, unlike Azure DevOps, GitHub Actions doesn't have a native integration with Azure Key Vault. This means we will need to use Azure CLI or a similar tool to do the job. Here's a simple example where we load the secrets inside a job:

```
jobs:
  load-secrets:
    runs-on: ubuntu-latest
    steps:
      - name: Checkout code
        uses: actions/checkout@v3
      - name: Authenticate to Azure
       uses: azure/login@v1
       with:
         client-id: ${{ secrets.AZURE_CLIENT_ID }}
         tenant-id: ${{ secrets.AZURE_TENANT_ID }}
         subscription-id: ${{ secrets.AZURE_SUBSCRIPTION_ID }}
      - name: Load secrets from Azure Key Vault
        uses: azure/CLI@v1
        with:
          inlineScript: |
             az keyvault secret show --vault-name ${{ secrets.AZURE_
KEYVAULT_NAME }} --name example-secret-1
             az keyvault secret show --vault-name ${{ secrets.AZURE_
KEYVAULT_NAME }} --name example-secret-2
```

While the workflow itself looks very similar to the ones we implemented previously in this chapter, there's one thing we need to do outside of it to make the workflow work. Azure Key Vault requires authorization, meaning the principal used by our runner needs to have the necessary permissions to access Azure Key Vault's data plane. With Azure Key Vault, we have two options available:

- Access policies

- Azure RBAC

For the former, we could use the following Azure CLI command:

```
az keyvault set-policy \
--name <keyvault-name> \
--object-id <managed-identity-object-id> \
--secret-permissions get
```

If Azure RBAC is the selected authorization method, we will need to assign proper permissions using one of the built-in or custom roles, as in this example:

```
az role assignment create \
--assignee <managed-identity-client-id> \
--role "Key Vault Secrets User" \
--scope /subscriptions/<subscription-id>/resourceGroups/<resource-
group-name>/providers/Microsoft.KeyVault/vaults/<keyvault-name>
```

Once the necessary permissions are provided, the workflow will be able to authorize Azure Key Vault and obtain the secrets.

There's also a possibility in which you'd prepare a workflow that uploads the secrets to Azure Key Vault so they can be fetched by other workflows. This concept is presented in *Figure 19.3*.

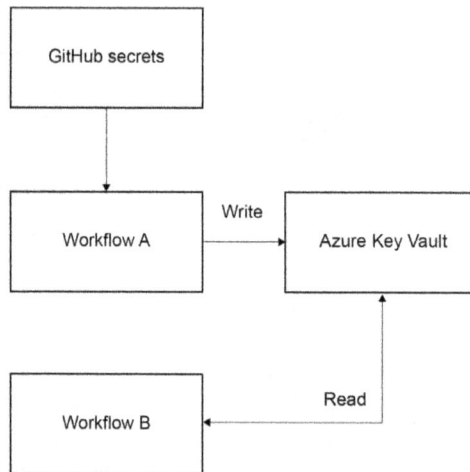

Figure 19.3 – Two separate workflows with a different set of permissions

The process behind the concept can be described as follows:

1.   Secrets are initially stored in GitHub secrets.

2.   Workflow A fetches the secrets from GitHub secrets and places them in Azure Key Vault.

3.   Workflow B loads the secrets from Azure Key Vault instead of GitHub secrets.

That approach may be beneficial if you want to use Azure Key Vault as your main store for secrets. The benefits of such an implementation include the following:

- The ability to version secrets

- Much more granular control over how we can do what with secrets

- Integration with Azure services

Of course, it would also be possible to insert the secrets into Azure Key Vault manually if needed. Having that automated may simplify management and unify the process so you don't need to grant permissions for people to make changes to your instance of Azure Key Vault. This improves security as well as making it easier to control interactions with Azure Key Vault if they're performed in a very strict way.

Let's talk now about use cases related to using GitHub Actions when building applications and deploying them to Azure.

Learning about use cases

GitHub Actions is a robust platform that allows you to build any application and deploy it to Azure with ease. By using this tool, you can easily set up your CI/CD pipelines and integrate them with your cloud environment. When it comes to use cases, GitHub Actions can not only work as your main mechanism for CI and releasing new versions of software but it's also possible to use it as an orchestration platform to perform several common activities, such as the following:

- Running jobs
- Generating documentation
- Running scanners
- Calling external services

Let's consider a workflow where you set up a schedule and run a few different activities, such as creating a container and collecting the results of such a run, or executing a Bash script that will query a database. You don't need Kubernetes, Azure Functions, or Azure Container Apps to perform such an operation – they could possibly run on your CI/CD agent if you look for a simple setup and don't need sophisticated functionalities. Consider the following example:

```
name: Generate Release Notes
on:
  workflow_dispatch:
    inputs:
      tag:
        description: 'Release tag (e.g., v1.0.0)'
        required: true
jobs:
  generate-release-notes:
    runs-on: ubuntu-latest

    steps:
      - name: Checkout code
        uses: actions/checkout@v3
```

```
   - name: Generate Release Notes
     id: release_notes
     run: |
        echo "Generating release notes for tag ${{ github.event.
inputs.tag }}"
        git log $(git describe --tags --abbrev=0)..HEAD
--pretty=format:"- %s" > release-notes.txt
        cat release-notes.txt
   - name: Upload Release Notes
     uses: actions/upload-artifact@v3
     with:
       name: release-notes
       path: release-notes.txt
```

This example presents how you can use GitHub Actions to generate release notes with each new tag pushed to your repository. It doesn't use any additional tool – the only thing required is the Git command line. If needed, you could change the trigger to a schedule so that release notes are generated on a fixed date.

Another example includes how we could run a dedicated script from our repository to call specific functionality and then save it to our repository. Before we discuss the YAML code, let's check how you could create a workflow using the GitHub UI. In each repository that has GitHub Actions enabled, you will have access to the **Actions** tab. From that tab, you will have the possibility to create a new workflow using the **New workflow** button (see *Figure 19.4* for reference).

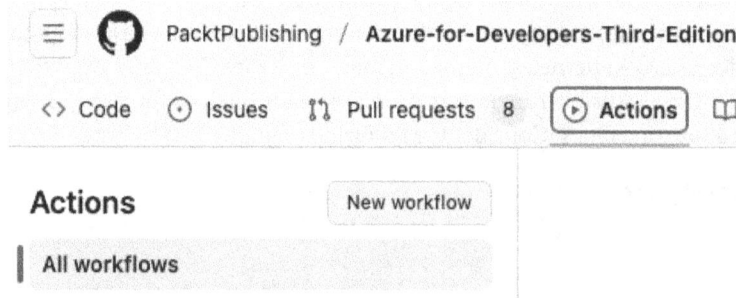

Figure 19.4 – GitHub Actions UI with the New workflow button

Clicking on the **New workflow** button displays a view where you can select a workflow template. Workflow templates are good if you're starting to learn the syntax of Actions and are looking for some inspiration. However, in this chapter, we're creating quite a custom workflow, so it's best to set up a workflow from scratch using the **set up a workflow yourself** link, as presented in *Figure 19.5*.

Choose a workflow

Build, test, and deploy your code. Make code reviews, branch management, and issue triaging work the way you want. Select a workflow to get started.

Skip this and set up a workflow yourself →

Figure 19.5 – Creating a workflow from scratch without a template

Let's start preparing our workflow now using the following YAML code:

```yaml
name: Call External Service
on:
  push:
   branches:
            - main
jobs:
  call-service:
    runs-on: ubuntu-latest
    steps:
      - name: Checkout repository
        uses: actions/checkout@v2
      - name: Set up Node.js
        uses: actions/setup-node@v2
        with:
          node-version: '21'
      - name: Install dependencies
        run: npm install
      - name: Call external service
        id: call_service
        run: |
          node -e "require('./src/service-caller').
          callExternalService()"
      - name: Save result to repository
        run: |
          echo "${{ steps.call_service.outputs.result }}" > result.txt
          git config --local user.email "action@github.com"
          git config --local user.name "GitHub Action"
          git add result.txt
```

```
        git commit -m "Add result from external service"
        git push origin main
      env:
        GITHUB_TOKEN: ${{ secrets.GITHUB_TOKEN }}
```

There are infinite opportunities available when working with GitHub Actions. Remember, though, that using this platform for orchestration requires proper evaluation of the possible options. If you feel that other services, such as Azure Functions or Kubernetes, provide more benefits and are better suited for the selected task, try to use them first before opting in to use GitHub Actions.

That's all that was planned for this chapter. Let's summarize the lessons and exercises.

Summary

In this chapter, we discussed GitHub Actions – a platform allowing you to implement CI/CD pipelines and automate deployments of new versions of your application. We went through the architecture of workflows and building blocks of the pipelines so you have the basics to start implementing your own jobs. We also compared managed and self-hosted agents so you can decide which option will cover the technical requirements of your application.

To better understand GitHub Actions, we implemented a full pipeline that builds and deploys a containerized application using Azure Container Instances. That exercise showed how the same result can be achieved using different methods, so you have a better understanding of alternative approaches and capabilities offered by the whole platform.

In the next and final chapter, we extend these automation principles by exploring how to develop, test, and deploy low-code solutions using Azure Logic Apps, helping you further streamline cloud application workflows.

20

Developing, Testing, and Deploying Azure Logic Apps

In *Chapter 7*, we discussed the initial concepts related to Azure Logic Apps, including building blocks of applications based on that service, basic structure, and deployment method for infrastructure. After the initial review of *Chapter 7*, it was clear that there are additional things worth mentioning about Azure Logic Apps. This chapter unfolds more detailed features, which will be helpful for anybody interested in using Azure Logic Apps as the building block for their system. It will act as a supplement for concepts introduced earlier in this book and will guide you through some development-oriented topics. Note that in this chapter, we'll focus on exploring new features using the JSON syntax of Azure Logic Apps. Still, all the examples are exercises that can be performed using the UI editor available in the Azure portal.

Having a deeper understanding of how to develop and test an application that is built with Azure Logic Apps will help you be more confident when comparing that service to more code-oriented Azure products, such as Azure Functions. Even though many developers refrain from using low-code solutions for building more complex systems, Azure Logic Apps still has its place when handling simpler business scenarios or offloading some work to less experienced teams.

In this chapter, we're going to cover the following main topics:

- Developing complex workflows in Azure Logic Apps
- Handling errors in Azure Logic Apps
- Writing unit tests for Azure Logic Apps
- Building automated deployments for Azure Logic Apps
- Learning about use cases

Technical requirements

To perform the exercises from this chapter, you will need the following:

- Azure CLI
- IDE of your choice (preferably Visual Studio Code)

Developing complex workflows in Azure Logic Apps

Workflows built with Azure Logic Apps allow you to incorporate various connectors, bindings, and logic into your Logic Apps code. In *Chapter 7*, you already saw how one can use simple conditional statements to decide which execution path should be selected. It turns out workflows can include much more advanced logic. Let's discuss that in this section, starting with working with variables.

Note that in this chapter, we'll be using the JSON syntax for workflows for portability. Full examples can be found in the repository for this chapter available here: `https://github.com/PacktPublishing/Azure-for-Developers-Third-Edition/tree/main/ch20`.

Creating and using variables

A variable in Azure Logic Apps is an object that holds a value, which can then be referenced by your workflow. It may be defined with a default value that can then be changed. The value of the variable can be modified anytime, meaning you can reference different values in different stages of your workflow. Let's consider the following example:

```
"Initialize_variable": {
  "type": "InitializeVariable",
  "inputs": {
    "variables": [
      {
        "name": "counter",
        "type": "int",
        "value": 0
      }
    ]
  },
  "runAfter": {}
}
```

In this code snippet, you can see how we define an action, `Initialize_variable`. The type of this action is set to `InitializeVariable`, meaning once executed, it will initialize a variable with the given name (in our case, `counter`). The variable has a default value of `0` and is a number (integer). When added to the Azure portal, you will see the following definition (*Figure 20.1*):

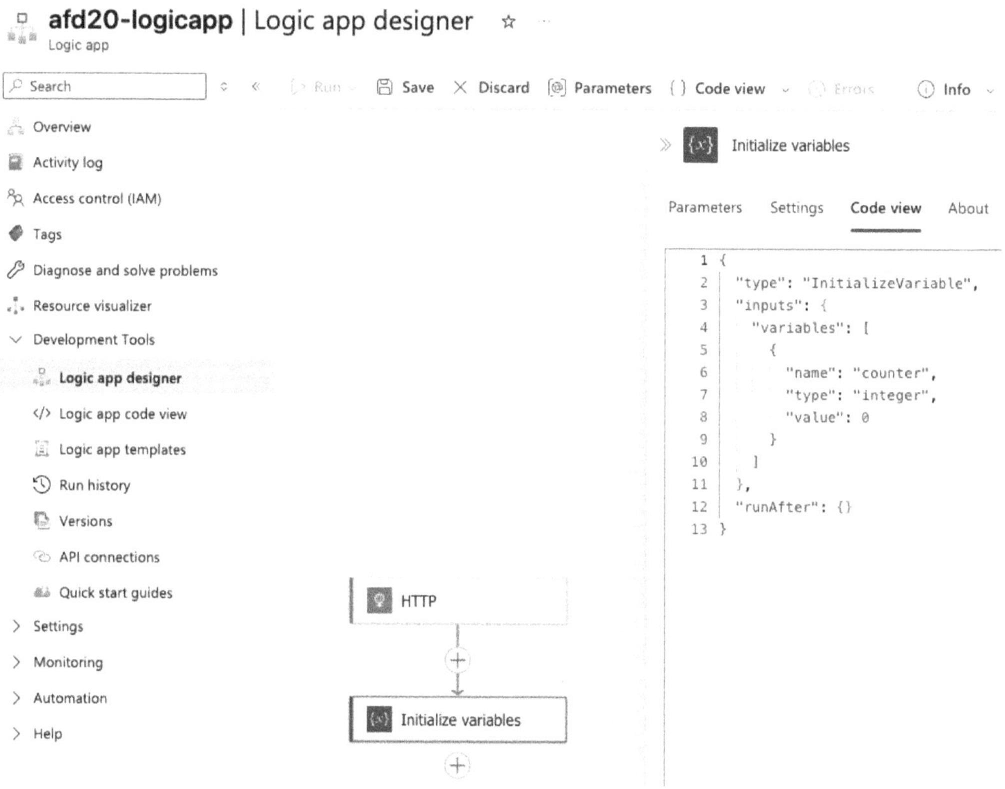

Figure 20.1 – Initializing a variable in the Azure portal

Now, we can increment its value by using another action:

```
"Increment_variable": {
  "type": "IncrementVariable",
  "inputs": {
    "name": "counter",
    "value": 1
  },
  "runAfter": {}
}
```

As you can see, we're using the `IncrementVariable` action, which increments the value of the given variable by one each time it's called. The change is also visible in *Figure 20.2*, where you can see how actions are now connected:

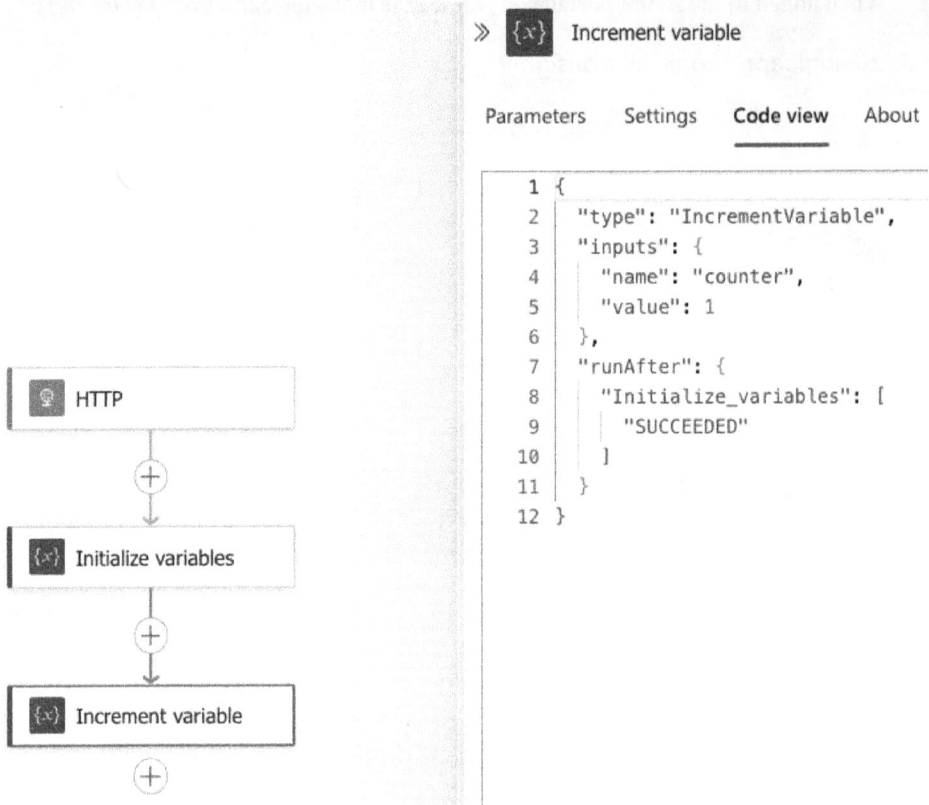

Figure 20.2 – Workflow with the Increment variable action added

We could then use the value of our value and perhaps make it part of the HTTP response (assuming our workflow is triggered by the HTTP request):

```
"Return_counter": {
  "type": "Response",
  "kind": "Http",
  "inputs": {
    "statusCode": 200,
    "body": {
      "message": "Counter value is @{variables('counter')}"
    }
  },
  "runAfter": {
```

```
    "Until": [
      "Succeeded"
    ]
  }
}
```

Here, you can see how we're using the special syntax `@{variables('counter')}` to reference our variable. Once executed, the reference will be replaced with the actual value of our variable. See also *Figure 20.3* for a reference of how the complete workflow looks from the designer's point of view:

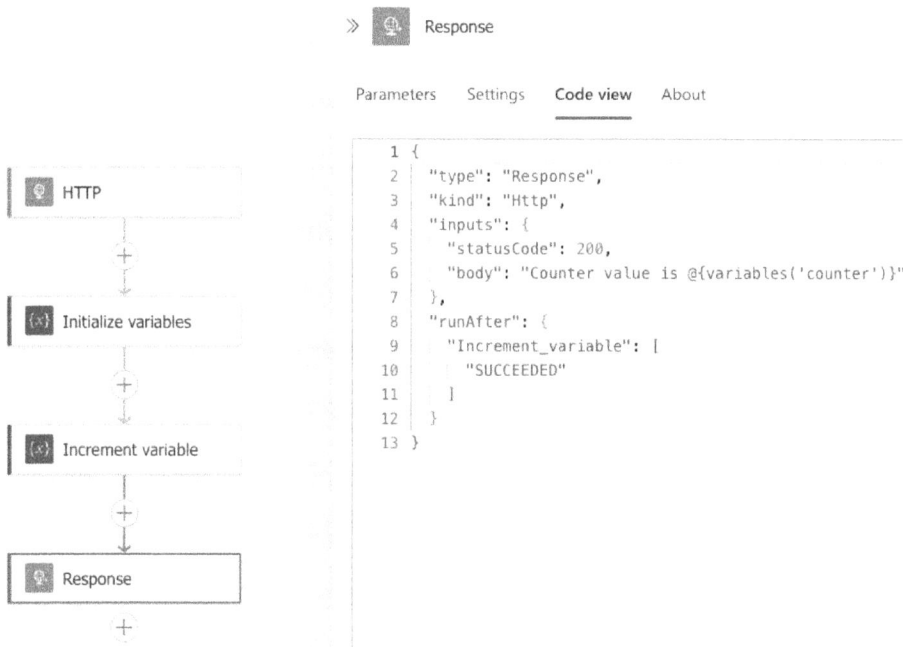

Figure 20.3 – Full workflow created in the Logic Apps designer

Let's now talk about composing variables into complex objects such as JSON, which can be utilized further in other ways.

Composing a complex object with variables

For composing a complex object, let's assume we have defined two variables:

- `name`
- `surname`

If we want to compose them into a complex object such as JSON, we could use the following action:

```
Compose_person": {
  "type": "Compose",
  "inputs": {
    "name": "@variables('name')",
    "surname": "@variables('surname')"
  },
  "runAfter": {
    "Initialize_surname": ["Succeeded"]
  }
}
```

Such a composed value can then be referenced by using the output of the action with @ `outputs('Compose_person')`.

In *Figure 20.4*, you can see the visualization of that workflow done by the Logic Apps designer. As you can see, we could set the variables in parallel and then just combine the results:

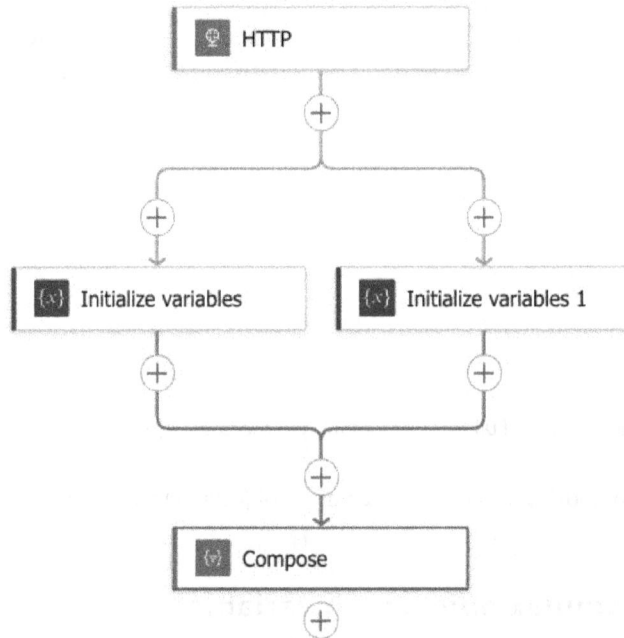

Figure 20.4 – Composing a JSON object in Azure Logic Apps

You may wonder how to achieve the dependency diagram seen in *Figure 20.4*. The trick here is to set the proper flow in the action's settings, as shown in *Figure 20.5*:

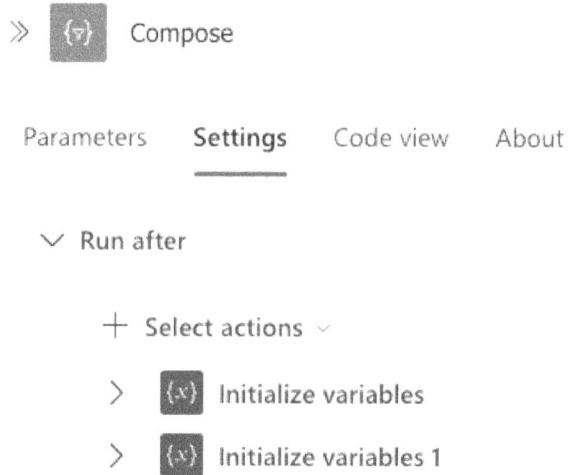

Figure 20.5 – Setting up two actions as parents for the next action

Akin to Compose, we could decompose a JSON object and use its values for our workflow. Consider the following example:

```
"Parse_JSON": {
  "type": "ParseJson",
  "inputs": {
    "content": "@triggerBody()",
    "schema": {
      "type": "object",
      "properties": {
        "name": { "type": "string" },
        "surname": { "type": "string" }
      },
      "required": ["name", "surname"]
    }
  },
  "runAfter": {}
}
```

The `Parse_JSON` action expects that the JSON sent as the body of our trigger will contain both name and surname fields. Then, they could be referenced with the following:

- `@{outputs('Parse_JSON')?['body/name']}`
- `@{outputs('Parse_JSON')?['body/surname']}`

You can find more examples of how to work with data in Logic Apps in the documentation here: `https://learn.microsoft.com/en-us/azure/logic-apps/logic-apps-perform-data-operations?tabs=consumption`.

Let's now check how we could call another workflow from our workflow.

Calling other workflows

To call another workflow, we need to use the following action:

```
"Call_Another_Workflow": {
  "type": "Workflow",
    "inputs": {
      "host": {
        "workflow": {
"id": "/subscriptions/<subscription-id>/resourceGroups/<resource-group>/providers/Microsoft.Logic/workflows/<workflow-name>"
        }
      },
  "method": "POST",
  "path": "/triggers/manual/paths/invoke",
  "body": {
    "name": "John",
    "surname": "Doe"
  }
},
"runAfter": {}
}
```

Note that we're referencing another workflow using its resource ID, which needs to match the full identifier of the target workflow.

> **Note**
>
> The body sent to the target workflow used in the example is just for reference. You will need to adjust it to the body expected by the target to make it work.

Remember that you could also call another workflow by using its HTTP(S) endpoint instead of using the action. That approach is useful for overcoming the limitation of the `Workflow` action, which requires that the target workflow be in the same logic app.

Let's discuss now how to correctly handle errors in our workflows. This will help you in making your workflows more reliable and avoid unnecessary stops in your business processes.

Handling errors in Azure Logic Apps

Handling errors in Azure Logic Apps includes two concepts:

- **Retry policies**: A way to avoid interruption of service by trying to call the dependency multiple times before failing.

- **Handling the workflow flow using the** `run after` **behavior**: A pattern specific to Azure Logic Apps, which allows you to control the flow of your logic app but configure when actions should be triggered.

As both methods to handle errors rely on the proper configuration of used actions, we describe them as one concept. Let's get started with retry policies. These apply to HTTP-based actions, which may need to retry their operations upon receiving a non-successful response, such as HTTP `429` or HTTP `5xx`. Here's an example of how that could be implemented:

```
"Http_with_Retry": {
"type": "Http",
"inputs": {
"method": "GET",
"uri": "https://example.com/api/resource"
},
"policy": {
"retryPolicy": {
"type": "exponential",
"interval": "PT5S",
"count": 4,
"minimumInterval": "PT5S",
"maximumInterval": "PT1M"
}
},
"runAfter": {}
}
```

In this example, you can see how we configured a retry policy that will retry the request every 5 seconds up to 4 times, each time increasing the interval between each call. You can also see the same as configured for an action in the Logic Apps designer, as presented in *Figure 20.6*:

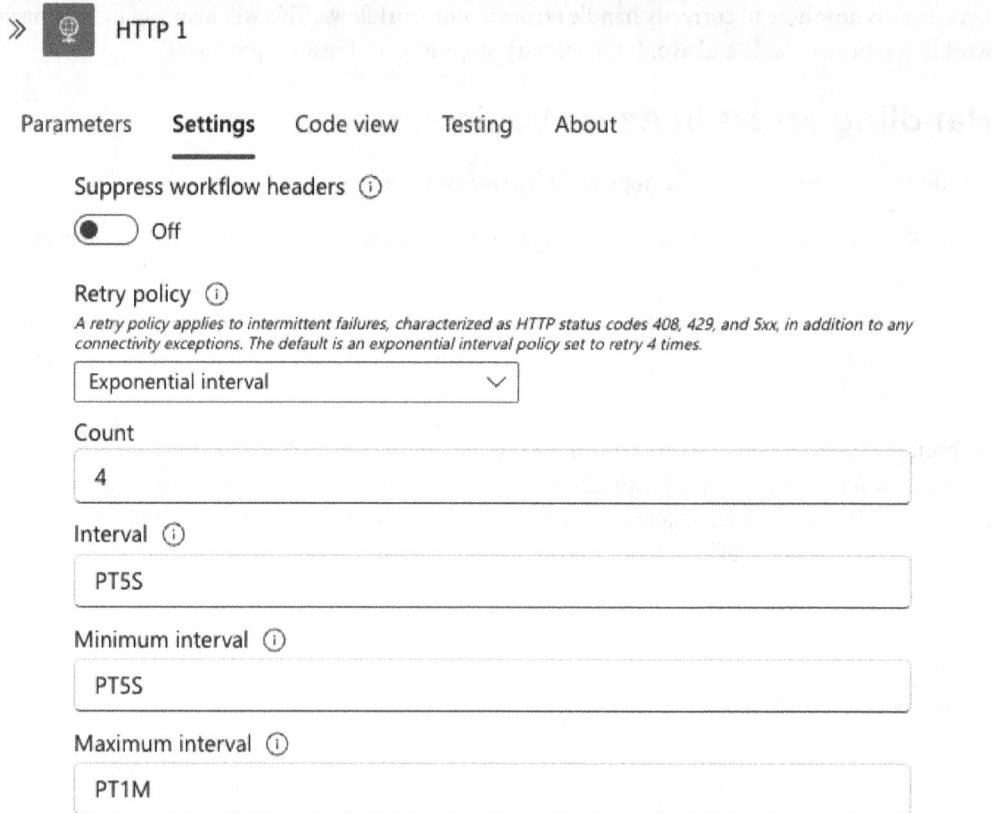

```
»  ⊕   HTTP 1
```

Parameters   **Settings**   Code view   Testing   About

Suppress workflow headers ⓘ

(●) Off

Retry policy ⓘ
A retry policy applies to intermittent failures, characterized as HTTP status codes 408, 429, and 5xx, in addition to any connectivity exceptions. The default is an exponential interval policy set to retry 4 times.

Exponential interval   ⌄

Count

4

Interval ⓘ

PT5S

Minimum interval ⓘ

PT5S

Maximum interval ⓘ

PT1M

Figure 20.6 – Configuring an exponential retry policy for an HTTP action

If that action fails anyway, we could intercept the error message and use it for logging or notifying a user about the issue:

```
"Return_error": {
"type": "Response",
"kind": "Http",
"inputs": {
"statusCode": 500,
"body": {
"message": "HTTP call failed after retries.",
"error": "@{outputs('Http_with_Retry')?['body']}"
}
```

```
    },
    "runAfter": {
    "Http_with_Retry": ["Failed"]
    }
    }
```

Note how we're using the `runAfter` property – in that case, the `Return_error` action runs only if `Http_with_Retry` fails. This encapsulates the error logic and allows us to control the behavior of the workflow. If you're working with Logic Apps using the designer, setting the `runAfter` behavior may be easy to miss. Check *Figure 20.7* for a reference:

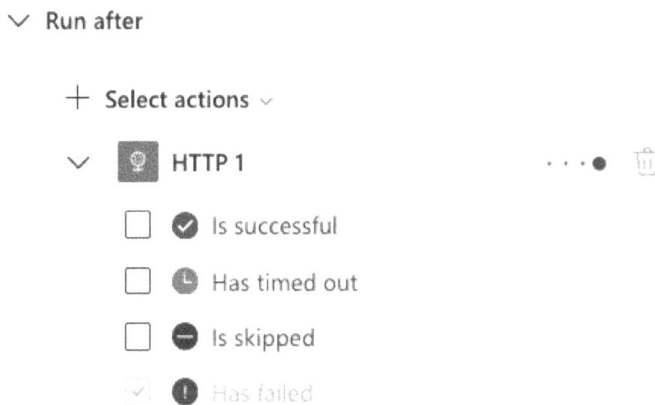

Figure 20.7 – Configuring the runAfter behavior on an action level

> **Note**
>
> Potentially, you could use your monitoring solution to collect logs and metrics generated by Azure Logic Apps by sending requests to the exposed endpoints. However, that approach may be difficult to implement using Azure Logic Apps and introduce unnecessary complexity while giving very little value in return.

Let's talk now about how we could write unit tests for Azure Logic Apps. This is quite an advanced topic if you're a beginner, but it's worth the time spent on learning various tools and concepts as logic apps, which are covered by tests, are easier to maintain and develop.

Writing unit tests for Azure Logic Apps

Testing workflows written using Azure Logic Apps is an important concept as it allows you to ensure your logic works correctly before publishing it to the production environment or end users. When it comes to testing, there are two concepts that you could consider:

- Testing using mocks

- The LogicAppUnit Testing Framework, available on GitHub: `https://github.com/LogicAppUnit/TestingFramework`

When implementing tests for Azure Logic Apps, you will need to remember that all testing frameworks have their limitations and flaws. Due to the serverless nature of Logic Apps workflows and the fact that they are heavily coupled with their connectors, it may be difficult to have a flawless test suite that never generates false positives (tests that are *green* but, when compared with end-to-end tests, provide a false sense of security).

When it comes to using mocks, you can start exploring the topic by reading about the **Testing** capability available in the Azure portal. The documentation of that feature is available here: `https://learn.microsoft.com/en-us/azure/logic-apps/testing-framework/test-logic-apps-mock-data-static-results?tabs=consumption`.

The alternative approach to mocks includes configuring your workflow in a way that enables you to run different logic depending on the input parameters. Let's consider the following example:

```
"actions": {
  "Initialize_environment": {
    "type": "InitializeVariable",
    "inputs": {
      "variables": [
      {
        "name": "environment",
        "type": "string",
        "value": "@{parameters('environment')}"
      }
      ]
    },
    "runAfter": {}
  }
}
```

In this code snippet, we're setting up a variable that allows us to enter the name of an environment. That value can then be used to create a condition in our workflow to make a choice between different execution paths. Take a look at the following definition:

```
"Condition_-_Check_environment": {
  "type": "If",
  "expression": {
    "equals": [
      "@variables('environment')",
      "test"
    ]
  },
  "actions": {
    "Mock_API_response": {
      "type": "Compose",
      "inputs": {
        "id": "mock-id-12345",
        "name": "Mock User",
        "email": "mock@example.com",
        "status": "active"
      },
    "runAfter": {}
    }
  }
}
```

As you can see, we're using an `if` statement to decide what action should be executed depending on the value of the `environment` variable. The alternative option to the mocked API response in our case would be calling the actual API endpoint, like so:

```
"else": {
  "actions": {
    "Call_real_API": {
      "type": "Http",
      "inputs": {
        "method": "GET",
        "uri": "https://api.example.com/users/1"
      },
    "runAfter": {}
    }
  }
}
```

A similar approach can be applied to any connector/action you'd consider to be used inside your workflow. This approach has the following pros:

- It doesn't require you to manually switch the testing mode for your workflow

- It can be automated and explicitly selected when introducing a new version of your workflow

- Each change to the workflow, including changes related to the mocked actions, can be reviewed and analyzed before applying the changes to the workflow with a deployment

Of course, that approach also has some disadvantages, including a more complex workflow, deploying mocked code to production (as you can't easily remove it without affecting the behavior of the whole workflow), and increasing the possibility of introducing bugs. From my perspective, though, the advantages outweigh the disadvantages when the alternative (the **Testing** feature from the Azure portal) is considered.

For the last topic in this chapter, let's discuss how automated deployments work for Azure Logic Apps.

Building automated deployments for Azure Logic Apps

As with most of the applications and services, Azure Logic Apps also offers a way to deploy changes and new features for the workflows in an automated way. When talking about automated deployments, we need to differentiate the deployment of infrastructure from the deployment of a workflow definition. For Azure Logic Apps, both components (infrastructure and workflow) can be deployed using a similar JSON definition – ARM template or using the Bicep language (look at the full definition here: https://learn.microsoft.com/en-us/azure/templates/microsoft.logic/workflows?pivots=deployment-language-bicep).

Due to the level of detail needed to be included in this chapter, the templates for deployment of both Azure Logic Apps infrastructure and workflows are included in the code repository. Conceptually, however, the steps needed to deploy such a template stay the same as they were for deploying infrastructure templates. For instance, the following Azure PowerShell and Azure CLI commands will generate the same results:

```
New-AzResourceGroupDeployment
 -ResourceGroupName <resource-group-name>
 -TemplateUri <path-or-link>
 az deployment group create \
 -g <resource-group-name> \
 --template-uri <path-or-link>
```

Note that when deploying a template and providing a path or a link to it as the command parameter, they need to be located either locally (if a path is provided) or publicly (when the link is provided). One of the common scenarios is storing a template in GitHub or inside Blob Storage. For both options, you will need to ensure that the template file can be accessed without credentials (or provide the credentials as part of the URL – for instance, you could leverage a short-lived SAS token for Blob Storage to avoid storing persistent credentials in your code).

When deploying our template, we could leverage additional automation and test our workflow by calling it and validating the results. Consider the following example:

```
- name: Deploy Logic App
  id: deploy
  run: |
    deployOutput=$(az deployment group create \
      --resource-group ${{ env.RESOURCE_GROUP }} \
      --template-file ./ch20/logic_app_deployment.bicep \
      --parameters \
        logicAppName=SimpleHttpLogicApp-${{ github.run_number }} \
      --output json)
    # Extract Logic App URL from deployment outputs
    logicAppUrl=$(
      echo $deployOutput |
      jq -r '.properties.outputs.logicAppUrl.value')
    echo "LOGIC_APP_URL=$logicAppUrl" >> $GITHUB_ENV
    echo "Logic App URL: $logicAppUrl"
```

Once executed, the URL of your Logic Apps workflow will be saved to an `environment` variable available within the current GitHub Actions workflow run. We can then use that URL as presented in the next code snippet.

The following example presents a step in a GitHub Actions workflow, which deploys our template and extracts the URL of the Logic Apps workflow for further use. That URL is saved to a variable, which will be available for the next steps inside the current job. We can then proceed with one more step:

```
- name: Test Logic App HTTP Trigger
  id: test
  run: |
    echo "Testing Logic App at ${{ env.LOGIC_APP_URL }}"
    response=$(curl -s -X POST "${{ env.LOGIC_APP_URL }}" \
    -H "Content-Type: application/json" \
    -d '{"test":"data"}')
    echo "Response from Logic App:"
    echo "$response"
    # Validate response
    message=$(echo $response | jq -r '.message')
```

```
if [ "$message" != "Hello from Logic App!" ]; then
  echo "Logic App response validation failed!"
  exit 1
else
  echo "Logic App response validation successful!"
fi
```

Those steps call the URL we fetched previously and validate whether the response is what we expected. That approach may not always be applicable, but different variations seem to be viable, so the same concept would stay the same, even though you'd need to check other triggers or responses. As always, the full example is available in the repository.

That's all that was planned for this chapter! Let's summarize the lessons and see what other topics may be useful to extend your knowledge.

Summary

In this chapter, we dove deeper into Azure Logic Apps. We talked more about more complex workflows, handling errors, and writing tests for workflows. While some of the concepts may look artificial in Azure Logic Apps, if you want to become proficient with that service, you will need to be familiar with them. Even though workflows in Azure Logic Apps aren't the same as typical applications written in programming languages, they offer enough flexibility to be able to handle even more complex business scenarios.

To start working with Azure Logic Apps seriously, you will need to start developing CI/CD pipelines for them. This is why we talked about how to write templates and deploy them in an automated way. If the topics from this chapter are interesting to you, don't forget to check the repository for this chapter. It includes full examples of workflows and CI/CD pipelines to serve as inspiration. You could also use them as initial pieces of your own code, so you don't need to create them from scratch.

This chapter was the last chapter of the book. I hope you found the topics presented interesting and insightful. Remember that additional examples and code snippets can be found in the repository linked to the book. They contain lots of comments, so you can try out different approaches and upskill yourself even more.

Stay Sharp in Cloud and DevOps – Join 44,000+ Subscribers of CloudPro

CloudPro is a weekly newsletter for cloud professionals who want to stay current on the fast-evolving world of cloud computing, DevOps, and infrastructure engineering.

Every issue delivers focused, high-signal content on topics like:

- AWS, GCP & multi-cloud architecture

- Containers, Kubernetes & orchestration

- **Infrastructure as Code (IaC)** with Terraform, Pulumi, etc.

- Platform engineering & automation workflows

- Observability, performance tuning, and reliability best practices

Whether you're a cloud engineer, SRE, DevOps practitioner, or platform lead, CloudPro helps you stay on top of what matters, without the noise.

Scan the QR code to join for free and get weekly insights straight to your inbox:

https://packt.link/cloudpro

Index

‹packt›

www.packtpub.com

Subscribe to our online digital library for full access to over 7,000 books and videos, as well as industry leading tools to help you plan your personal development and advance your career. For more information, please visit our website.

Why subscribe?

- Spend less time learning and more time coding with practical eBooks and Videos from over 4,000 industry professionals

- Improve your learning with Skill Plans built especially for you

- Get a free eBook or video every month

- Fully searchable for easy access to vital information

- Copy and paste, print, and bookmark content

Did you know that Packt offers eBook versions of every book published, with PDF and ePub files available? You can upgrade to the eBook version at packtpub.com and as a print book customer, you are entitled to a discount on the eBook copy. Get in touch with us at customercare@packtpub.com for more details.

At www.packtpub.com, you can also read a collection of free technical articles, sign up for a range of free newsletters, and receive exclusive discounts and offers on Packt books and eBooks.

Other Books You May Enjoy

If you enjoyed this book, you may be interested in these other books by Packt:

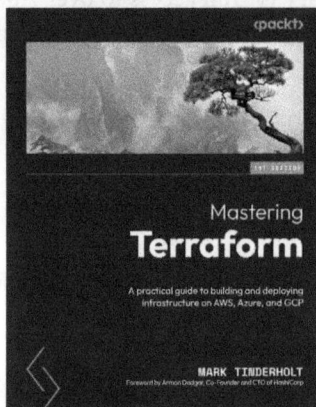

Mastering Terraform

Mark Tinderholt

ISBN: 978-1-83508-601-8

- Explore Terraform architecture and configurations in depth
- Integrate Packer with Terraform for VM-based solutions
- Containerize apps with Docker and Kubernetes
- Explore GitOps and CI/CD deployment patterns
- Transform existing applications into serverless architectures
- Migrate and modernize legacy apps for the cloud
- Implement Terraform on AWS, Azure, and GCP
- Use Terraform with teams of varying size and responsibility

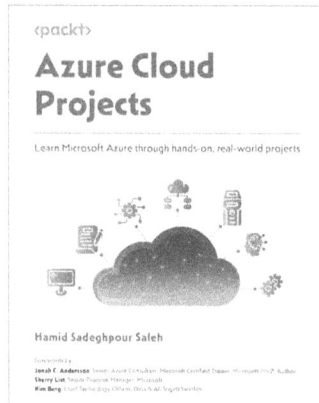

Azure Cloud Projects

Hamid Sadeghpour Saleh

ISBN: 978-1-83620-423-7

- Set up Azure and explore cloud fundamentals
- Implement Entra ID and hybrid identity solutions
- Build and secure storage with Azure Blob Storage
- Design virtual networks and configure VPN gateways
- Deploy your first web app using Azure App Service
- Automate workflows with Azure Functions
- Create CI/CD pipelines with Azure DevOps

Packt is searching for authors like you

If you're interested in becoming an author for Packt, please visit `authors.packtpub.com` and apply today. We have worked with thousands of developers and tech professionals, just like you, to help them share their insight with the global tech community. You can make a general application, apply for a specific hot topic that we are recruiting an author for, or submit your own idea.

Share Your Thoughts

Now you've finished *Azure for Developers, Third Edition,* we'd love to hear your thoughts! Scan the QR code below to go straight to the Amazon review page for this book and share your feedback or leave a review on the site that you purchased it from.

`https://packt.link/r/1-836-20351-9`

Your review is important to us and the tech community and will help us make sure we're delivering excellent quality content.

Download a free PDF copy of this book

Thanks for purchasing this book!

Do you like to read on the go but are unable to carry your print books everywhere?

Is your eBook purchase not compatible with the device of your choice?

Don't worry, now with every Packt book you get a DRM-free PDF version of that book at no cost.

Read anywhere, any place, on any device. Search, copy, and paste code from your favorite technical books directly into your application.

The perks don't stop there, you can get exclusive access to discounts, newsletters, and great free content in your inbox daily

Follow these simple steps to get the benefits:

1. Scan the QR code or visit the link below

https://packt.link/free-ebook/978-1-83620-351-3

2. Submit your proof of purchase
3. That's it! We'll send your free PDF and other benefits to your email directly

www.ingramcontent.com/pod-product-compliance
Lightning Source LLC
Chambersburg PA
CBHW072006230326
41598CB00082B/6776

9 781836 203513